CASEBOOK OF GENERAL MANAGEMENT IN ASIA PACIFIC

Edited by

Dominique Turpin and Xiaobai Shen

MACMILLAN
Business

First published 1999 by
MACMILLAN PRESS LTD
Houndmills, Basingstoke, Hampshire RG21 6XS
and London
Companies and representatives throughout the world

ISBN 0–333–71792–9 hardcover
ISBN 0–333–71791–0 paperback

A catalogue record for this book is available from the British Library.

This book is printed on paper suitable for recycling and made from fully managed and sustained forest sources.

10   9   8   7   6   5   4   3   2   1
08   07   06   05   04   03   02   01   00   99

Typeset in Great Britain by
Aarontype Ltd
Easton, Bristol

Printed in Great Britain by
Antony Rowe Ltd
Chippenham, Wiltshire

Contents

Preface

In recent years, demands from IMD's business partners and the sponsors of IMD management programmes, particularly those concerned with international business and Asian countries, have been increasing. In a survey we recently conducted, companies list *international* and *Asia* as high priority topics. During the last few years, IMD faculty members have produced a range of cases about businesses operating in the Asia-Pacific region or about Asian businesses expanding to the rest of the world.

The cases in this book do not cover international management topics or look at the Asia-Pacific nations exhaustively. They are not intended to be examples of 'best practices' (or of ineffective management). We selected them for their general interest and pedagogic value, the overall picture of doing business in Asia that they paint, and the specific issues on management across cultures and nations that they present. The business world has already shown a keen interest in these issues. We believe this interest will grow. The cases are based on our personal observations of companies and their operation in countries where the IMD faculty has done consulting or research.

This 'Asia casebook' is primarily designed for general management teaching purposes, particularly in the field of international management. We have used every case at IMD successfully with both MBA participants and executives. Taken together, they cover management subjects in human resources, corporate culture, strategy, cross-cultural marketing, marketing, manufacturing, alliances and partnership, information technologies, and strategy.

Almost all the cases in this book are comprehensive. They contain selected information about the companies, and the events and circumstances they operate in. This may include detailed characterizations of particular managers or accounts of their experiences. It may also include the region's history and broader descriptions of the global economic, political and social situation, always linked to the particular managerial circumstances and/or the particular company. Cases are especially designed for teaching – they highlight the issues important in developing a management framework by engaging participants in probing discussions.

Most important, this book features cross-cultural and cross-national issues. The cases furnish vital background materials on the economic, political and social environment in the Asia-Pacific countries, together with more detailed notes on industrial sectors, market segments, consumer behaviour, etc. In addition, the views of the managers and the experiences of the companies, different as they are from each other and from those of economists and scholars, are invaluable because they are based on experience in the field. After all, whether the managers or the companies in the cases have failed or succeeded, their first-hand experience is invaluable. One of the lessons is this: good management in Asia may not be much different from good management anywhere else!

DOMINIQUE TURPIN AND XIAOBAI SHEN

Acknowledgements

The editors would like to thank Professor Peter Lorange, President of IMD, Professor Phil Rosenzweig, Director of Research at IMD, Persita Egeli-Farmanfarma, IMD Case Administrator, Gordon Adler, IMD Senior Writer, Cheryl Petroski and Tessa Rowland for providing us with the resources necessary to put this book together. Our thanks also go to Professors Francis Bidault, Bob Collins, Jim Ellert, Pierre Goetschin, Song-Hyon Jang, Per Jenster, Vijay Jolly, Peter Killing, Jan Kubes, Nirmalya Kumar, Christopher Lovelock, Don Marchand, Phil Rosenzweig, Ser Toh Thian, George Taucher and Sandra Vandermerwe and Research Associates for contributing cases and teaching notes, and to the other IMD faculty members and research associates for their assistance and support. Last but not least, we would like to express our appreciation to our families: Minako, Hélène-Miyuki, Antoine-Akio, Léo-Yukio and Ben for their extended support in the completion of this project.

The editors and publisher would like to thank the following for permission to use copyright material: Business Times (Malaysia) for statistics from *Business Times*; Economic Information & Agency for statistics from the *China Statistical Yearbook*; The Economist Newspaper Limited for a chart from the article 'America's Empire Strikes Back', *The Economist*, 22 February 1992; Financial Times for the historical maps of Poland from *Financial Times*, 3 May 1991; InfoSource Management Services for statistics; *Official Journal of the European Communities*, L239, 26.8.1986, for statistics; Screen Digest for statistics from *Screen Digest*, March 1993; Sweet & Maxwell Asia for statistics from *The China Investment Guide*, 3rd edn.

Every effort has been made to trace copyright holders, but if any have been inadvertently overlooked the publisher will be pleased to make the necessary arrangement at the first opportunity.

List of Cases

Global Strategy

Marketing Strategy

Cross-cultural Management

Managing Information Technology

Organization and Human Resource Management

Alliances and Technology Transfer

Notes on the Editors

Dominique V. Turpin

Professor Turpin is a full-time faculty member of IMD (International Institute for Management Development) in Lausanne, Switzerland, and the Director of the IMD 'Master for Business Administration' (MBA) Programme. Dr Turpin is also director of several IMD executive programmes in Europe and Asia. He was previously director of another IMD executive programme entitled: 'Managing for Marketing Success' (1992–6). Dr Turpin has extensive experience in teaching, research and consultancy in the areas of marketing and international strategy in Europe, the Americas and Asia. Prior to joining IMD, he spent six years in Tokyo as representative of a French firm in Japan.

A French citizen, Dominique Turpin received his masters degree from ESSCA in France. He earned a doctoral degree in economics from Sophia University in Tokyo. His research has been widely published in more than fifty books, articles and case studies. Professor Turpin has been a regular contributor to *Nihon Sangyo Shimbun* (The Japan Industrial Journal), one of the leading business dailies in Japan. He is also the Continental Europe Editor for the *Long Range Planning Journal*, the international journal of strategic manage-

ment, and sits on the board of one of the largest Japanese firms.

Since 1990, Professor Turpin has been a Director of the Board of the 'Japan Strategic Management Society'. Dr Turpin is a partner in Strategic Management International, Tokyo and a member of the 'Who's Who in Asian Studies', Geneva. Since 1994, Professor Turpin has also served as the IMD representative on the Academic Council of the China–Europe International Business School in Shanghai (People's Republic of China).

Xiaobai Shen, Ph.D., M.Phil., B.Sc.

Xiaobai Shen is currently a consultant for China-related business in Edinburgh. She came to Britain in 1991 to take her doctoral programme in the University of Edinburgh, and worked as research fellow in IMD (the International Institute for Management Development) in Lausanne, Switzerland.

In her previous career in China, Xiaobai Shen spent five years working in manufacturing industry during the Cultural Revolution. Her interests in telecommunications technology date back to her undergraduate study and subsequent teaching experience in Telecommunications Engineering in

Shanghai Railway University. However, she became increasingly interested in the social and economic dimensions of technological change and the need to improve management methods for economic reform. Thus she was among those who actively introduced modern management methods to China and taught them to young managers in Shanghai industries. She then moved to Beijing to take an M.Phil. in Science & Technology Policy, at the Chinese Academy of Social Sciences, and worked for several years as a Research Fellow in the China Research Institute for Management Science.

Introduction: Why is Asia Pacific the Focus of Attention in the Business World Today?

Yesterday's Asian economic miracle, in popular view, has turned overnight into today's economic disaster, threatening serious consequences for the whole world economy. The clear lesson is that we must go beyond simplistic diagnoses, positive or negative, and give serious attention to what is happening in the Asia Pacific economies.

Asia Pacific Economies and Globalization

To many it was perhaps inconceivable that the recent financial crisis of Asia Pacific could have triggered such financial turmoil in the West, and dragged the whole world economy to the edge of a deep recession. The effects of the Asian Pacific crisis have spread out to Europe and the USA. Asia Pacific corporations have cancelled outward investment. Asian demands of imports have fallen sharply with their deteriorating ability to pay for their purchases from Western countries and have driven companies in the West to downsizing or even to bankruptcy. The consequent currency devaluation and fall in wage costs in Asia Pacific will put more pressure on competitiveness and jobs in the developed West.

These developments bring home the fact that globalization is not some abstract theory, but a hard fact of economic life today. Globalization has led to the structural transformation of the present world system, creating new linkages and interconnections between states and societies.[1] Firms and industries across the world have become more interdependent. Events, even decisions and activities, in one part of the world come to have significant consequences for some other actors in quite distant parts of the globe. In particular, the contemporary global financial system is one in which national markets throughout the world, though physically separate, interact together closely, often with dramatic consequences.[2] That is why a financial crisis emerging in Thailand has come to spread not only to the

[1] Dunning, Johne H. 'Globalisation and FDI in Asian Developing Countries', in the Proceedings of the Second Conference on Global Change – The impact of Asia in the 21st Century, 6 & 7 April 1998, Faculty of Management and Business, the Manchester Metropolitan University.
[2] Stopford, J. and Strange, S. (1991), *Rural States, Rural Firms*, Cambridge, Cambridge University Press.

entire Asia Pacific region, but further to the West and the world generally.

It is clear that in the past two decades many Asia Pacific countries have participated in the trend towards a globalizing world economy. They are at the forefront of the globalization process, both inwards, attracting foreign investment and stimulating demands for imports, and outwards, exporting goods to and investing overseas. Apart from the increasing number of enterprises in the region that have been able to build up their capabilities to compete in the world market, Asia Pacific has an enormous population with rapidly rising purchasing power and constitutes an indispensable market for the rest of the world. Countries across the region are experiencing dramatic change cutting across every aspect of society: in people's everyday lives, in the cultures of a society, and in the politics of nations, as well as just their economic systems. These changes are in turn, visibly or invisibly, influencing the rest of the world.

The shock experienced by Asia Pacific and the West alike indicates that we have perhaps not yet fully recognized the extent of change which the globalization has brought to the world. Governments in Asia Pacific countries have not realized the significant changes to their culture and traditions following their integration with the rest of the world, especially the West, and that the values adopted by the new generation may differ sharply from those held by their predecessors. Conversely, in the Western world the understanding of development in Asia Pacific countries has been inadequate in many respects. 'The Far East' was far removed not just in terms of physical remoteness, but also in the

levels of popular understanding and systematic academic enquiry. One example is the fact that the Asia-Pacific boom was still being called a 'miracle' when the region was on the very brink of collapse. As a result, policy makers in Western countries have not been properly equipped to deal with many essential issues arising in Asia Pacific countries. At the same time, firms from the West have been too ignorant of the operations of Asian Pacific economies and the changes that Asia business integration has brought about in the business world. Conversely, it is clear that firms in Asia Pacific have not sufficiently acquired the codes of business practice in the world, let alone their capabilities of technological innovation and productivity.

The Emergence and Boom of Asia Pacific Economies

Looking back over the past two decades or so, there is no doubting the important role of Asia Pacific countries in the development of the world economy. In a period when North America and West Europe were enduring prolonged economic stagnation, countries in the Asia-Pacific region began to boom. They showed surprisingly strong economic performance and became the driving force of the world economy in the process of recovering from recession. In the mid-90s, the region was regarded as the fastest-growing market of any size. Compared with the average GDP growth at 3.2% in North America and 2.6% in the European Union in 1995, in the Asia-Pacific region (excluding Japan), average GDP growth in 1995 was 7.3%.[3] The growth rate was far higher than in other developing regions, such as Latin America at 1.5%, the Middle East and North Africa at 1.6%, and Eastern Europe at 4.4% in 1995.

The Asian economic 'miracle' took place in three or four historical phases. Japan emerged first. Its GDP was one-eighth that of the US before its economy took off at the end of 1950s. It overtook the European economies during the 1960s, and even now is still ranked with America as one of the two most powerful economies in the world. Then began the rise of four newly industrialized countries (NICs): Hong Kong, Singapore, South Korea and Taiwan, known as the four 'Asian tigers'. According to *The World Competitiveness Yearbook 1998*, Singapore ranks second after the US, and Hong Kong third, with Taiwan and Korea at sixteenth and thirty-fifth respectively.[4] A larger group of countries, such as Malaysia, Thailand, Indonesia and the Philippines, have begun to follow step since the early 1970s. More recently China and Vietnam joined the tide. The Asia-Pacific was like an escalator, with Japan at the top, followed by the second-, third- and fourth-stage countries and the like growing like a snowball, involving about 110 million people at the beginning and now half of the world's population.

The Asian economy is a microcosm of the global economy, embracing the most advanced and the still relatively backward. From the richest country, Japan, with GDP per capita US$40,161, to the poorest countries in South Asia, with GDP per head of a couple of hundred US dollars, the gap is huge. But this allows richer countries like Japan and the NICs to push labour-intensive industries further into the countries which have lower labour cost. The NICs embarked upon the development process from low-cost economies based on labour-intensive manufacturing, to include high-technology industries in both manufacturing and services. In replacing the role of NICs, third-wave countries rapidly caught up in many areas. For example, Malaysia has become the world's largest producer of air-conditioners and a leading exporter of telephone appliances and televisions. The Pearl Delta in Guangdong province of China is today the biggest manufacturing centre in the world. Before the financial crisis, Asia possessed a considerable proportion of the world industry: 30% of the world steel production; 60% of consumer electronics; 30% of computer output; and 35% of the vehicle output.

With respect to financial resources, the concept of 'poor Asia' is no longer true. According to both the UN and the World Bank reports, both America and Europe are small investors in the Asian miracle compared with the Asians themselves.[5] Apart from affluent countries like Japan and NICs, a large number of the Asian Diaspora are sending their money back to the

---

[3] 'Global economic forecasts: World growth/inflation prospects are good', *Country Forecasts*, 12 January 1996.

[4] *The World Competitiveness Yearbook 1998*, IMD, Lausanne, Switzerland, 1998.

[5] 'Has Europe failed in Asia?', *The Economist*, 2 March 1996.

region. According to one report,[6] some 55 million entrepreneurial overseas Chinese had been the main force behind the rapidly growing economy in the Asia-Pacific region. Although precise figures are difficult to assess, Asian experts conservatively estimate them to control several trillion US$ in liquid assets. Also, the Asia-Pacific countries have higher domestic savings than the others. According to the 1996 *Business Asia* report, Singapore's gross domestic savings as a percentage of GDP were 48% and China's 40.5%, ranking second and third in the world, with Indonesia, Thailand, Malaysia, Korea, Hong Kong, Japan and Taiwan all in the top 15.[7] Despite the financial crisis, the region possesses a considerable reservoir of capital.

The Driving Forces

Inbound investment by foreign institutions and individuals in Asia Pacific was one of the powerful engines of growth driving the economic boom. Since the early 1980s there has been a huge increase in inbound investment into Asia Pacific countries. Most noticeably, foreign direct investment in China has increased significantly. The growth of foreign direct investment in the region mirrors the strength and vitality of the internal capital market. It is estimated that three-quarters of all direct investment in the developing countries of Asia Pacific between

1990 and 1995 originated from the region.[8]

The changing atmosphere in the world politics of economy was another element which promoted investment from Western industrialized countries. Australian and North American countries have been encouraging interest in the Pacific Rim through the formation of the Asia-Pacific Economic Co-operation forum (APEC). European countries' investment in this region began to grow rapidly in the late 1980s, and during the period 1988–1994 European trade with emerging Asia grew faster than its trade with Eastern Europe despite the opportunities arising from the collapse of the socialist block. This trend may have been pushed further by the grand summit of East and West in Bangkok in March 1996, where fifteen European leaders met with ten of their Asian counterparts.

In Asia-Pacific countries, the forceful yet market-friendly development strategies pursued by their governments have greatly increased incentives both in attracting inwards foreign direct investment and in promoting exports and outwards sourcing of technologies and markets. This inward investment at the same time perhaps sowed the seeds for the recent financial crisis because of the weak fiscal regulatory mechanisms in these emerging economies which were not able to effectively direct the investment, and instead nurtured speculative non-productive investment and concealed growing bad debts.

---

[6] 'The overseas Chinese', *Fortune* Vol. 130, No. 9, October 31, 1994.
[7] See note 3.

[8] UNVTAD (1997), *World Investment Report: Transnational Corporations, Market Structure and Competition Policy*, New York and Geneva, UN.

Many have seen the emergence of the Asia-Pacific region as essentially an economic phenomenon. However, it could be suggested that this has arisen because economic development has been given the top priority by cultures in the region. For example, while the former Soviet Union sought a highly ideological route out of communism, China has followed a more pragmatic path – in a way that has made possible spectacular economic progress. In China, many 'Tiananmen Kids' turned to economic activities after the 1989 clash in Tiananmen Square and put off for the foreseeable future the prospects of democratic social reform. There is, however, some debate about the role of democracy. We have seen that Japan and Korea may be democratic, but their political systems work in a different manner from those in the West. Equally, China has secured economic growth without political pluralism. What seems to have been critical, in the aftermath of the Asia-Pacific crisis, is the existence of mechanisms for proper regulation and scrutiny, and the consequent ability to combat corruption and financial mismanagement.

Culture was perhaps another important factor behind the economic growth in the region. It is interesting to note a recent study of the so-called 'East Asian Miracle' by the World Bank, which turned up no magic formula, no single set of government policies. Its experts concluded that the key to the development is culture: people in these economies have simply studied harder, worked harder, and saved more than people in other countries. This conclusion may not be a comprehensive summary of the reasons for East Asian success, but it had a good grasp of the important characteristics of this regional phenomenon. A similar conclusion is drawn by Professor Gordon Redding, Director of the University of Hong Kong Business School. After many years of study in this area, he firmly believes that there are three successful forms of capitalism in Asia Pacific: Japanese, South Korean and Overseas Chinese. Although they are different from each other – because each is grounded in a different societal culture, and each has had its own political and economic history – they have been seen as the most dynamic sources of capitalism in the world.[9]

A wealth of studies demonstrate that Asia Pacific is enormously diverse. Despite this, they broadly agree on some common points. They flag some common cultural themes: an emphasis on basic material satisfaction for life and the importance of self-help, a belief in the duties and obligations of individuals, a strong commitment to social cohesion, a commitment to the family, a pragmatic view of the state and religion, a powerful belief in the value of education, and an appraisal of wealth and high achievement through hard work. This list of characteristics, which is not exhaustive, might be assumed as the cultural inheritance of the region, and that is likely to endure and persist from generation to generation.

Putting aside for a moment these conclusions on cultural origins of the region, which may be controversial, the most resilient phenomenon is the struggle and competition to create and capture wealth either among peoples

[9] 'Overseas Chinese Networks: Understanding the Enigma', *Long Range Planning*, Vol. 28, No. 1, 1995, pp. 61–69.

in each country or among nations over the Asian-Pacific Rim. For over a century, the West has been overwhelmingly dominant in the world's economy, politics and culture. In this period, other civilizations, including notably the Asian-Pacific, have been overshadowed and have performed relatively poorly. Despite this, there has been a continued belief by people from across this region in what they can achieve, backed up by a strong sense of past successes and glories. The success of Japan and the four Asian tigers have enhanced their confidence. The investment pool formed in the mid '90s in the Asia Pacific has provided a great opportunity for all countries in the region. This has encouraged countries' and people's high hopes and enormous appetite for change.

However, the imprudent haste with which peoples, firms and governments of Asia-Pacific countries competed to jump on the bandwagon of economic boom and share in its spoils has contributed to the current economic crises. The crises will certainly slow down the globalization process of Asia-Pacific countries. Despite this, if these countries and the region as a whole can retain social stability and retain and restructure their economic base, recovery is likely to be rapid. Indeed, the immediate repercussions of the crisis will be to cool down the overheated atmosphere of economic expansion and force through the restructuring of hitherto weak financial management and regulatory systems. This, together with an economic context that will force players to concentrate on restructuring their activities and regaining world competitiveness, will put economic development on more solid ground. In the longer term, the Asia-Pacific region is likely to remain the most dynamic force in the global economy.

The Longer-Term Implications for the Business World

With half the world's population moving rapidly along the road to industrialization and prosperity, the consequences may be profound. In the longer term the economic revolution in Asia Pacific can be expected to transform global activity of all kinds – economic, political, cultural – and the environment. The pace of change in the world is accelerating. For instance, the industrialization which took Britain 150 years, for South Korea required a mere 30 years. *Globalization* has been reconstructing the world economy and politics. There has been a substantial relocation of manufacturing from the US and Europe to East Asia. The market for industrial goods which was once dominated by the West is moving East-wards. In the reverse direction, countries in the Asia-Pacific region have been dramatically increasing their scale of exports. In conjunction with this, an increasing number of companies are attempting to break into the US and European markets, following the lead of the Japanese. The recent economic crisis forces Asian firms to be even more competitive in their home and foreign markets.

The implications for the business world are at least threefold. First, as we have seen, under enormous pressure from the global reconstruction, more and more European companies are going abroad to search for markets and low costs of resources. At the same time, companies in the Asia-Pacific region have a need for capital, technologies and management skills. In relation to this, cross-cultural and cross-national management becomes more and more important. It is necessary for managers to change their mindset in order to fit the future trends.

Second, strategic management is crucial for companies in managing international business. Business strategies should be based on assessing internal strengths and weaknesses, understanding the external environment, and identifying potential opportunities and threats. As some future trends are foreseeable, whereas others are not, business strategy must be open to the performance of the entire business world. Business strategies therefore need to be adjusted over time to match the external and internal environment changes.

Third, it is necessary to improve general management skills in all aspects, in order to suit the business for an international dimension.

It is important to point out here that the rationale of today's business management is largely based on Western culture – Western values and the Western traditions of political and economic organization and legislative systems. Despite this, Western countries are still considered the appropriate models of doing business in the world, and Asian companies are copying them and significantly adapting their model in their own business environments. However, with the continuation of globalization, business models from Asia will grow, slowly but surely, and are likely to be increasingly influential.

Take Japan as an example. Japan has not intended to export its way of life. However, its impact on the Western world has been growing alongside its economic strength. This has been reflected in at least two ways: first, Japanese influence in the business world has grown through their new management and production systems (Just-In-Time, Total Quality Control and Lean Production) which are now *de rigueur* in many industries, especially in car manufacturing; and second, Japanese influence in people's lives is evident in a range of new consumer goods, especially electronic products such as computers and camcorders.

It is even possible that one day business contracts written in Chinese will be accepted by international business, just as readily as English-language contracts are today, as this is the language spoken by the largest population as a mother tongue. Where now young Asians are longing for *liuxue* (the Chinese expression for going to the West to study), perhaps young Europeans in the next generation will want to go to study in Asia Pacific. A knowledge of Asian cultures, Japanese or Mandarin, will be of growing importance.

Returning to practical issues today and in the very near future, the meaning of the Asia-Pacific transformation for business can be addressed to European and Asian companies in separate ways.

Western Companies

For Western companies, the most realistic and closely related question is, 'Can you afford to miss the market in Asia Pacific?' And if a company *is* seeking to be a player, no matter whether a strong or a marginal player in that market, then the next question is, 'How do you win that market?'

Can you afford to miss the market in Asia Pacific?

Given the size of their populations – China 1.2 billion, Japan 125 million, plus other countries amounting to a total across the region of 2.9 billion population – can you, can *any* company, ignore this market? One may argue that, taking China as an example, population size does not properly represent the market size: of 1.2 billion Chinese, over 70% are peasants and most inland provinces are still poor. But, with the affluent Chinese coastal population alone, which equals only a quarter of the population, the number is as large as about 300 million, which is the entire population of EU countries. For instance, even though in 1995 Chinese average income per head was very low, merely about US$ 450, nevertheless because of the huge size, its adjusted purchasing power parity (international $ at current prices and purchasing power parity) was US$ 3,053 billion,[10] ranked second after the US. Right now, this market can double the sales of a company of any kind, yours or your competitors'. If you decide to wait, your competitors may not – indeed, they may already be there.

Moreover, the population in Asia Pacific is growing, unlike some EU countries where the population today is shrinking. By the end of the decade, the population of the Asia-Pacific will rise from 2.9 billion to 3.2 billion.[11] If as forecast the adjusted purchasing power parity reaches US$ 10,000 billion, the Asia Pacific market is sufficiently big to create or break a multinational. When this market has developed its full size, it may well alter the consumption trends of the world, including the markets in the West. We have witnessed that where once Europe and America dominated the markets for industrial goods, increasingly it must share them with others. During the 1970s and 1980s, Europe had to adjust to Japanese competition in domestic markets. Before the financial crisis, Korean companies had made a determined push into European markets. In the longer run, a renewed Asia economy with sounder capabilities and resources might well encourage many other countries in the region to follow suit. The message is clear. Only a niche marketing player can safely get away with ignoring the Asia Pacific.

How do you win in that market?

Perhaps the better question is, 'How do you avoid losing in that market?', especially during this period of slowdown of the world economy. This is still an immature market, and market demands for different products vary

---

[10] *The World Competitiveness Yearbook 1996*, IMD, June 1996, Lausanne, Switzerland.

[11] 'Global economic forecasts: World growth/inflation prospects are good', *Country Forecasts*, 12 January 1996.

and change according to different phases of industrialization and the development of living standards and styles. If a company can sustain its operation platform in that market, even if does not gain very much in the short term, it will eventually profit one day.

In Asia-Pacific markets, the risks and rewards of involvement are both high. The relationships is between PRC, Taiwan and even Hong Kong remain uncertain. Tensions still exist between some countries, for example antipathy between South Korea and Japan. New wealth has brought domestic and new class tensions and exaggerated old ethnic anxieties inside countries. The increasing gap between the rich and the poor of individuals and regions has provoked concern in the central government in China. We have seen that the Indonesian government is increasingly vulnerable to the alienated urban poor. In addition, within the region long-term ethnic tensions have been refuelled by economic crisis (for example anti-Chinese sentiment in Southeast Asia, and especially Indonesia). The severe social unrest in Malaysia and Indonesia following their economic crises poses a serious obstacle to economic regeneration in their countries.

Asia-Pacific countries, in their economic system, legislative framework, market structures and value systems, are very different from the West. As we have mentioned above, business strategies are needed to win in this market, which should be built upon understanding of internal and external trends and accommodate short-term and long-term objectives. For European companies, there is an extra problem on top of these problems –

that is, to assess this changing environment, its opportunities and threats, and to anticipate the future.

Many Western companies, especially multinationals, have been doing business in the Asia-Pacific region for many years. They have studied this market pretty carefully and have had more or less successful experiences. However, many tend to look at the changing Asia-Pacific environment in terms of Western perspectives. Successful ones tend to simplify the complexities of operating in Asia-Pacific countries and anticipate the future development trends according to the patterns that the Western countries have been through, while less successful ones tend to emphasize the problems, the primitive business culture, the rudimentary economic system and so on.

For Europeans, it is natural to look at the world from Western perspectives. However, this may mislead companies in assessing the changing external environment. For instance, there is a tendency for European or Americans to speculate that the younger generation of business people in Asia Pacific will become completely westernized. This is not necessarily correct. The older Asia-Pacific civilizations, which had initially failed to recognize the challenge posed by the Western economies and were thus eclipsed for more than a century, have eventually learned to admire Western scientific, technological and business developments. And they have begun to learn from this experience. So it is not accidental that with their heads down Asians have studied more European contemporary history than Europeans have the contemporary history of Asia. Now it is Europe's turn to face a new challenge.

Asian Companies

For Asian companies, business today is no less tough than before. The current economic situation compels companies to rethink their future and position in the competitive world. Understanding the global reconstruction is also a big challenge. Companies who have benefited from the protectionism of local governments in the past are facing the challenge of a new business environment which is increasingly open to international competition. Therefore, competition in Asia-Pacific markets is intensifying. Apart from competing with companies from the West, companies in the Asia-Pacific region have to compete with a mushrooming number of local companies, as well as companies from other Asia-Pacific countries. Companies in less developed countries have to struggle very hard to overcome at least two key weaknesses: the lack of modern management skills, and low technologies.

countries is still rudimentary. In particular, companies in countries like China and Vietnam, for example, have very limited knowledge and practices of modern management because of their previous socialist, centrally planned systems.

The lack of professional managers and skilled engineers is a big headache for Asian companies. Old ways of managing business are not suitable for today's fast-changing business environment. Adopting modern management merely by copying Western general management methods involves other problems, particularly in human resource management, as this is related to the particular philosophies, such as the values, beliefs, commitments and aspirations, of employees. Now, many indigenous companies have found it difficult to compete with multinationals and companies with substantial resources to recruit and retain experienced managers and engineers.

Increasing competitiveness – to improve internal management

Competitiveness should be based on effective and sound general management. The low cost of local labour can be an advantage when competing in the international market for a short while, but it cannot sustain firms' competitiveness in the long term. Nor can low production costs make up for problems of other kinds stemming from poor product design, product quality, services, marketing, and the like. Usually, cheaper labour is associated with low skill and low technology, which certainly cannot meet fast-changing market demands. General management in many Asia-Pacific

Outsourcing – to learn from the West and the best

In today's business world, competitiveness is also based on technological competencies. In this regard, Asian companies, including many in NICs, especially in less developed countries, are at very low level compared with Western industrialized countries. There is very little room for Asian companies to accumulate technological competencies by following the US or the other advanced countries step by step. First, the technological gap between the Western industrialized countries and less developed Asian countries is huge; and second, it is not necessary, in technological terms, for late-comers to go through all the stages that the Western companies have been through. A late-comer can benefit from bypassing as many unnecessary stages as possible.

There are many options whereby Asian companies can obtain advanced technologies from the West and the best. While capital is pouring into the Asia-Pacific Region, together with multinationals and Western companies, the activity of pursuing technologies can be carried out by technology transfer from, alliances with or even acquisition of companies within the region, or by investing in the industrialized world to get inside the technology pool. Many Japanese companies have been successfully operating in such a way, followed now by South Korean and many other companies.

Conclusion

In history, opportunity comes and goes. Seizing it you are a winner, missing it you are a loser. In addition, it may be misleading to look at today and tomorrow in the terms of the past. In ancient times competitive advantage lasted for centuries, today we are talking about decades or even less. The globalization and engagement of an increasing number of Asia-Pacific countries are bringing about substantial changes in the business world. There are great challenges for both European companies and Asian companies, though in different respects.

We need to look to the future with open minds and imagination, building our competitiveness upon a sound business management.

About this book

Twenty-eight cases have been selected for this book: they are arranged in three parts. Part I, *Western Businesses in Asia Pacific,* covers subjects such as seeking new potential in Asia Pacific, entering new markets, competing there, and more specifically handling local market attributes, labour relations, crises and ethical problems, and strategic planning for future external environmental changes.

Part II, *Asian Businesses in Asia Pacific,* are the cases of Asian companies competing in either domestic markets or other Asia-Pacific countries. They are competing on the basis of their internal management strengths, technological advantages and marketing skills.

Part III, *Asian Businesses in Global Competition,* highlights the subject of Asian companies actively involving in global competition, particularly in Western markets. Asian companies have been engaging in the global market for a variety of different reasons, some to obtain resources which they lacked in home countries, and some to expand markets following their successes in their domestic market. Some cases responded to the demands of European companies.

PART ONE

Western Businesses in Asia Pacific

Introduction

The cases selected in this part highlight Western companies' operations in the Asia-Pacific region. Many companies have been operating in the Asia-Pacific region for years or decades and have had successful and/or frustrating experiences. Their experiences involve management strategy, human resources, marketing, ethical problems, external environment changes, building alliances and partnership, etc. The key to their success and failure has been mainly a matter of understanding between different nations and cultures.

However, we believe that it is wrong to over-stress the difficulties of Western companies operating in the region and overly emphasize the cultural differences. There may be differences in specific issues that relate to particular national and cultural settings. However, the basic principles and frameworks of general management theory, and in particular of international business management, still apply.

Instead of mapping all problems Western companies have encountered or will encounter, this part focuses on common themes in operating businesses in Asia-Pacific countries. Like other casebooks, the main purpose is to highlight key issues and to help put data, phenomena and information in all its complexity into the analysis. The approaches used or solutions suggested by these companies in the following cases are not uniquely the right ones. Other approaches, tried by other companies but not discussed in this book, can be explored by latecomers.

1. New Potential in Asia Pacific

It was very common in the past for Western companies to run their businesses in their own territory or within Western markets. The economic recession in the industrialized world has pushed them to look outwards. But whether Asia will be the next platform for many Western companies is still an open question. Invitations from Asian countries may make the prospect more tempting and drag Western companies into considering the possibility seriously. How should they decide if it is the right move to make? What alternatives should they take into account before making a decision? What strategies should they select? And finally, what steps should they begin with?

Potain S.A. presents the experience of Potain S.A., one of the two leaders worldwide in the tower crane market. It involves a very common challenge encountered by many

European and North American companies facing economic recession and business crisis at home when it received an invitation from the P.R. China. The case looks into the issues related to the transfer of technology, discusses the question of 'surrendering' technological advantage to a potential competitor and evaluates various technology pricing approaches.

Nestlé in ASEAN describes Nestlé's attempt to work out different synergies from the ASEAN markets and to plan a 'pan-Asian' strategy for better manufacturing efficiencies.

2. Competing in Deregulated Markets

Many companies find when they enter a new market that their competitors are also there. The most likely situation is that competitors are always competing with each other wherever they go. New markets can be a fresh chance for a company that has lost its battle to its rivals somewhere else. Different market elements in different systems will give some companies more opportunity than others, because each company has its own weaknesses and strengths. On the other hand, competition is like a game: win one, lose another. Pricing, advertising, distribution, product positioning and innovation of product design and after-sales services – all can be the key to success in a new market.

In *Philip Morris K.K.*, the Japanese subsidiary of Philip Morris Co. Inc. needs to react to R.J. Reynolds' introduction of a new product into the Japanese market. The case examines

the pricing issues in a highly competitive oligopolistic market, explores potential impacts of a broadened product line on overall competitive posture, and illustrates how competitive lessons learned in one part of the world can be applied in another.

3. Dealing with Cross-cultural Issues

Cultural issues are particularly important for marketing consumer products, for example food products, fashion and household items, and electronic appliances. In different societies, the pattern of consumer behaviour is different. The most important point for success in marketing is to know your customers: what and where they are, when and where they buy, and what they want. Markets are actually made up of many mini-markets, each with its own special needs. Only on the basis of good understanding of its customers can companies develop appropriate market strategies and plans. This section includes two cases, both involving Japanese consumer product markets.

Lestra Design illustrates and analyses alternative strategies for entry into a global market and highlights some of the cultural and business-practice-related obstacles that Western companies face in exporting to Japan. It looks at issues of trademark, pricing, distribution system, management's commitment to the local market, and specific requirements of local markets. It uses general marketing analysis to locate key problems for the company's unsuccessful operation and, in the meantime, explores the specificity of Japanese markets.

Delissa in Japan describes the experience of a European dairy company dealing with the Japanese market. It analyses general issues such as market entry strategies, product re-launch strategies, cultural differences and internationalization processes, managing a global business, and strategic alliances across cultural and national boundaries. Specifically, it gives an overview of the consumer products market in Japan.

4. Managing Labour Relations

Ace Electronics Korea Ltd. addresses the challenges for Western firms in dealing with labour issues in a non-Western context. Although a disguised case, 'Ace Electronics Korea Ltd.' describes the challenges of a Western firm dealing with real labour disruptions during the late 1980s and early 1990s in South Korea.

5. Managing Crisis and Ethical Problems

Many ethical crises can be avoided by appropriate management, for example setting the moral climate, and providing ethical guidelines and policies for business decisions. In spite of this, unexpected disruptions to normal business life can happen even though firms are very careful. Particularly, in managing business in different societies, it can be difficult to walk the fine line between publicly acceptable and unacceptable approaches. Often, in fact, what is ethical in one country can be improper or even illegal in another country. The most difficult thing is that some business approaches that are

conventional in some groups are not acceptable in others, sometimes even illegal. For example, in many Asian countries, 'corruption' and 'bribery', though officially illegal, are widely accepted in business and even social life. Sometimes, without these 'gifts', no business can be done. In such an environment, to handle ethical problems is a difficult undertaking, especially for Western managers. There are no fixed remedies in such a crisis. Managers need to handle individual situations on the basis of their own experience and wisdom.

In this section, there are two cases. They do not seek to specify how to manage particular situations, but rather highlight the general issues.

Lussman–Shizuka Corp. describes the challenges of an executive working for a European–Japanese joint venture and facing bribery charges. The case invites the students to sense possible problems in cross-cultural management in general and to learn how to locate the key factors and determine the best solutions.

Chen & Liew Ltd. looks at different dimensions of ethical issues in South-East Asia, together with implications for the firm, its managers and the community at large.

6. Strategic Planning for External Environment Changes

The external environment is composed of trends, events and forces that are beyond the direct control of a firm's management. Political, economic, social and technological changes in the external environment affect different businesses in various ways. Western companies can perceive managing business in some Asian countries as risky, where their political system, people's culture or religious sensitivity are different from those of Western countries.

In the past in some countries, unexpected disruptions have happened because of political or religious turmoil. For example, 1989's 'Tiananmen Square' in China frightened many Western companies that had established businesses there. Some did not know how they should react, apart from calling back all their expatriates. Companies that had prepared for this kind of external disruption were calmer. While letting their expatriates leave China and wait in Hong Kong, they began to plan their reactions in response to further development.

On the other hand, external environment changes are not always bad. They can bring opportunities for business as well. Therefore, if companies can identify new opportunities that may appear as developments unfold, then they can position themselves and exploit the opportunities presented by the external changes.

Obviously, it would be useful to define potential key factors that might change in the external environment and to monitor their development closely over time. But it is impossible to predict all of these and identify consequences. Strategic planning for

such possibilities would help companies to formulate their missions, organizational philosophy, management policies and business objectives in a longer term. Ciba in China (see case 6.1) has its own way of dealing with such uncertainty.

Ciba in China describes the successful operations of Ciba–Geigy in China. But how deeply, in terms of long-term business development, should the company commit to this market where political risks are high, according to experts? The case focuses on the issues linked to strategic planning for long-term business development of the company. Specially, it projects possible political and socio-economic changes in China, explores many alternative approaches in response to these changes, and assesses the advantages and weaknesses of each approach.

7. Implementing Global Strategies in Asia

Hilti Corporation describes how results in Hong Kong deteriorated after Hilti began enforcing their strict global strategy which does not allow sales through dealers. Should an exception be made? Just for Hong Kong, or for the region? The company has been very successful with its standardized approach elsewhere in the world.

1. New Potential in Asia Pacific

CASE 1.1 **POTAIN S.A.**

This case was based on teaching materials originally developed at the Lyon Graduate School of Business by Professors T. Atamer, Francis Bidault, Ham San Chap and Frank Zaeh. The English version of the case has been prepared by Research Associate Kimberly A. Bechler, under the supervision of Professor Francis Bidault, as a basis for class discussion rather than to illustrate either effective or ineffective handling of a business situation.

It was 8 January 1985 and Pierre Perrin, CEO of Potain S.A., had just received a letter from MACHIMPEX (China International Machinery Import–Export Company) requesting a proposal for a 5-year licensing contract on Potain's FO23B crane. The Chinese wanted total know-how and know-why for crane design and manufacturing (*refer to* **Exhibit 1**).

Perrin asked his secretary to send a copy of this letter to the Export director and to the SEREX manager ('Service Assistance Technique Export') immediately. An urgent meeting had to be arranged to discuss the Chinese opportunity before putting together an offer, and to select Potain's delegation that would go to Peking to negotiate the licensing contract.

What did technology transfer mean to Potain and how should Potain handle it? Should Potain provide the Chinese with all its technology? What should the price be and what conditions should be made?

Market Trends

In 1979, 16,000 tower cranes (including both top-slewing and bottom-slewing or self-erecting cranes) were sold worldwide. Since then, the world market had weakened and continued to decline. In 1983, world sales were just slightly over 9,000 units, and the first half of 1984 had led market followers to believe that the world market could fall below 7,000 units for the 1984–85 fiscal year (1 March–28 February). The forecast for the 1985–86 fiscal year offered little hope for improvement.

Potain's Situation

In one year, the number of employees at Potain S.A. had been reduced from 2,900 to 1,460. Heavily dependent on the crane market, Potain was near bankruptcy; a loss of FF94 million on a turnover of FF750 million had been estimated for the 1984–85 fiscal year (these figures included the expenses and necessary financial arrangements incurred by layoffs). There was even a question about whether Potain's 1984–85 forecasts for turnover would be achieved. In addition, the market decline was expected to continue for the next three years (*refer to* **Exhibits 2–5** for financial information).

Factory workers were worried about the rumours of bankruptcy, and some were already looking for other jobs. Perrin needed to take immediate action to put the company back on its feet, limiting the impact of a short-term problem on Potain's long-term future.

Competition

Potain's major competitors were: Liebherr and Peiner of Germany; and Edilgru, Alfa, and Cibin of Italy. The Dutch company Kroll was also a top challenger (*refer to Exhibit 6*). Even though Italian manufacturers had the largest volume worldwide, with 4,430 cranes per year, these were mainly bottom-slewing cranes.

Most competitors were either already licensing or moving in that direction, and it was clear that if Potain did not go into China, another company would be sure to claim that market.

History

Potain was founded in 1928 in the small town of La Clayette in France's Sâone and Loire region by Faustin Potain, an iron craftsman. In the beginning, Potain manufactured building equipment such as cement mixers, scaffolding parts and small cranes. At present, the Potain Group essentially manufactures tower cranes for buildings and public works projects. Potain has tried to diversify but has remained heavily concentrated in tower crane manufacturing.

In 1985, with its corporate headquarters in Ecully, near Lyon, the Potain Group consisted of Potain S.A. (holding company), BPR (a former competitor purchased in 1977), Sologat (a crane rental subsidiary), Sambron (a lift-truck manufacturer purchased in 1983), Simma (an Italian crane manufacturer that had been 51% controlled by Potain since 1972), Potain Iberica (a crane manufacturer and vendor in Spain) and sales subsidiaries in the US, West Germany and Switzerland.

Diversification Efforts

In the mid-1960s, the directors realized that Potain had become too specialized and started thinking about diversification. Potain formed an alliance with Poclain in 1968, creating Potain, Poclain Material (PPM) and targeting the mobile crane market. Mobile cranes were self-propelled cranes with a single telescopic arm, which were often used to erect top-slewing tower cranes. However, this alliance had the effect of limiting Potain's activity rather than providing a vehicle for expansion; Potain could not sell mobile cranes with a load capacity of greater than 1,600 lb (8 tons).

Potain had also tried to develop new products: tower cranes providing fast assembly and transport, mobile cranes travelling over any surface and lift-trucks. However, none of these products had a commercial success. Potain remained dependent on its original business of manufacturing tower cranes

In 1977, under the pressure of the French Ministry of Industry, Potain agreed to take over BPR, a company combining three of its competitors – Richier, Boilot and Pingon – this move marked an end to its diversification efforts, Potain remained a strong company. At the end of the 1970s, Potain completely dominated the French market and shared the world leadership position with Germany's Liebherr, both companies enjoying a 30% market share.

Finally, in 1980, after a long history of family control, Potain hired its first 'outsider' as CEO. Pierre Barrot believed that Potain's 'best diversification' was the tower crane and that further diversification should be limited in order to refocus the Group on its business and accelerate international growth. Owing to a disagreement with the board on the best way to manage the crisis, Barrot left Potain in June 1984. He was succeeded by Perrin, a long-serving senior executive who had held various positions, mainly in technology, engineering and business development.

Crane Developments

In early 1920s, the technology for cranes with liftable jibs was invented by the German firm Wolff. The trolley-jib was developed in the early 1930s. The jib (or arm) that had always been attached to the top of the mast was now laid horizontally across it. Underneath the jib was a trolley car running on tracks which served to distribute the load with more precision than the liftable jib alone. Trolley-jib cranes enabled the load to be moved at any height, distance or direction by using four movements – hoisting, slewing, trolleying and travelling or ground movement.

In 1935, Potain developed its first small crane with a liftable jib; gradually this technology was adopted by different manufacturers. Then in 1953, Potain introduced its first trolley-jib crane. Each of the crane movements could be controlled by the crane operator by remote control either from the cabin or from the ground. These 'firsts' were followed by: in 1956, the development of a telescoping system – enabling tower cranes to self-erect automatically; in 1961, the launch of electrical mechanisms with variable speeds – enabling better control of crane movements and at the same time better precision in the 'delivery' of loads; and in 1969, Potain held the world record for its '982' crane weighing 250 metric tons.

Cranes were defined according to six characteristics:

- height under the hook (vertical distance between the hook and the ground, the counterweights being at the extreme opposite end of the jib and the jib in its fully upright position);

- free-standing height (maximum height under the hook at which the crane could operate faced with bad weather conditions, without requiring auxiliary means for ensuring its stability);

- the reach (horizontal distance between the crane's point of rotation and the hook);

- serviceable load (weight of the load that could be suspended on the hook, this weight varying with the reach);

- maximum load (maximum serviceable load that the crane could lift); and

- load at the tip (serviceable load that the crane could lift at its maximum reach).

However, the most commonly used features to describe cranes were: free-standing height, maximum reach, maximum load and load at the tip (*refer to Exhibits 7–9*).

In addition to cranes used in the construction industry, there were other types of cranes. Each type of crane exemplified a different technology as the usage determined the required features. For example, harbour cranes required less precision in lifting and rotating than building cranes as port 'loads' were not as fragile as prefabricated boards. However, harbour cranes required greater durability for heavier loads and uninterrupted handling. Other examples were: forest cranes requiring shorter jibs and counter-jibs, and offshore cranes requiring special tempering and steel casings.

Potain manufactured and sold two types of cranes: construction cranes and travelling cranes (for industrial applications). In the construction crane segment (or tower cranes), Potain's product range spanned the two main categories: top-slewing and bottom-slewing (self-erecting tower cranes). Top-slewing tower cranes rotated at the *top*, had free standing heights of 108–328 feet, reaches spanning 131–262 feet, and load capacities from 2,200 lb at 131 feet to 44,000 lb at 262 feet. Site applications included small, low- and high-rise buildings, power plants, dams and bridges.

Potain's FO23B crane, for instance, was a top-slewing tower crane. Having a free-standing height of 202 feet, a reach of 164 feet, a maximum load of 20,000 lb and load at the tip of 4,600 lb, the FO23B was priced at FF1,400,000 (which included Potain's 20% margin on completed cranes). Adding the costs of transportation, customs and commissions, importing an FO23B would cost the Chinese FF2,100,000.

On the other hand, bottom-slewing or self-erecting tower cranes rotated at the *bottom*, had free-standing heights of 52–108 feet, reaches spanning 43–180 feet, and capacities from 1,000 lb at 40 feet to 4,400 lb at 180 feet. Site applications included small- to medium-sized buildings (10 floors), individual houses, condominiums, small bridges and as auxiliary cranes on large projects such as dams or bridges.

Manufacturing

Cranes were not mass produced but, rather, parts were specially made to meet the various crane and usage requirements. The entire crane was manufactured by Potain except for the electric motor, which was purchased from another company, Leroy-Somer.

Potain's crane manufacturing took place in four factories: La Clayette, Montbrison, Charlieu and Moulins. These factories had diverse responsibilities. La Clayette was dedicated to the more technologically sophisticated components (such as electrical parts); Montbrison subcontracted mechanics and/or soldering to Charlieu and Moulins. Moulins and Charlieu were each responsible for a particular range of crane models. The distribution of work between these two factories was often problematic as the market growth for the two main product lines was very different.

Marketing

Over the past years, Potain had experienced sustained growth, which placed it in the uncontested leadership position in the French market with a market share of 85%. On a worldwide basis, Potain's share of the crane market had increased to roughly 20% of the bottom-slewing crane market, and to 40% of the top-slewing crane market. Potain's market presence was expanded and enhanced through its subsidiaries and licensees. For example, Potain was present in Italy via its 51% ownership interest in Simma (since 1972), which had a 35–40% share of the Italian crane market.

Potain did not have much information about its customer base as it sold mainly to dealers and seldom to end users. However, Potain's market share had continued to increase because of Potain's reputation for quality, service and industrial dominance. Potain placed a high priority on service, including training and technical assistance, and after-sales service.

The Potain Crane Institute was based at La Clayette and employed about a dozen people. Training covered areas such as crane assembly, maintenance and repair (especially electrical and electronic) and crane handling. Potain's after-sales service included preventive maintenance, crane renovation and repair. A quarter of its after-sales activity was dedicated to the assembly and disassembly of top-slewing cranes – an activity which was not really profitable for Potain as there were many smaller firms offering this type of service at lower prices (FF90–95 versus Potain's FF120 per hour).

Internationalization

Export Sales and Subsidiaries

Potain 'internationalized' its business by emphasizing export sales, the development of subsidiaries and cultivation of licensees. Potain's International Business Organization was responsible for all of Potain's international operations: exports, subsidiaries and licences.

Export sales were divided into three zones: Asia, America and Europe–Africa. Potain had exported cranes since 1958 – first to Britain and the Commonwealth, then to Germany and Italy. In fact, exports were such a major portion of Potain's business that, in 1971, Potain received the 'Grand Prix de l'Oscar de l'Exportation'. For the 1983–84 fiscal year, 70% of Potain's crane sales had been made outside France.

Potain had five foreign subsidiaries, four of which were located in the largest tower crane markets: Germany, Switzerland, Italy and Spain. The fifth one was located in the US which, although a minor market, was considered strategically important as all the major competitors (especially Germany) were there.

Licensing
Licensing Policy

Potain's licensing policy was developed during the 1970s in reaction to the slowdown in the major European markets. Licensing was seen as a means to reach remote or protected markets where it was almost impossible to import finished products. Typically, Potain looked for a licensee that would locally manufacture the heaviest and bulkiest parts of the crane. The most sophisticated parts would be imported by Potain and then assembled by the licensee.

To support this licensing policy, Potain developed a group of principles and tools composed of: a coherent international development strategy, capable technical support, a flexible business policy and precautions to manage the risk of creating potential competitors.

Until the present time, the precautions taken by Potain to protect itself against a licensee turning into a competitor included:

- not selling its latest technology, while at the same time being careful not to sell the licence to products that were no longer part of its product line;

- requiring a minimum level of quality for products manufactured under licence in order not to compromise its brand image;

- establishing a minimum of five years for the contract – reserving the provision of components, especially of mechanical parts that would always be manufactured in France;

- not giving the licensee exclusivity in areas considered outside the licensee's national territory, and to establish Potain's own sales network in these areas;

- and, in the event of a major long-term strategic position, considering a 'joint venture' which would enable Potain to control the licensee's activity by linking it as a partner.

Integration of Technology

The integration of Potain's technology for production was done in phases. For the proposed China deal, integration of the technology for manufacturing the FO23B crane would have five phases, with one phase integrated per year. During Phase I, the technology for the whole mast and jib would be integrated; Phase II included the technology for the counter-jib and cat head (or 'A'-frame); Phase III comprised the technology for the crane chassis; Phase IV included telescoping accessories; and Phase V comprised the technology for the four mechanisms of hoisting, slewing, trolleying and travelling, plus the cabin with electrical switchboard, crane driver's post and control instruments. Phase V was usually not part of the 'technology transfer package'.

SEREX

Potain was experienced in technology transfer, signing its first licensing contract in 1972 with South Africa. Recognizing the need for the formalization of its know-how and technology, Potain created its SEREX ('Service Assistance Technique Export') department also in 1972. Within the Potain organization, SEREX reported to the Industrial Director, while functionally working with the Export Sales organization.

Initially, SEREX only served to provide licensees with technical documentation adapted to each country. But its general role had evolved to where SEREX was responsible for identifying potential licensing partners, and then for managing the transfer of technology and overseeing its local adaptation and implementation. Specifically, SEREX was: analysing potential licence candidates; defining the conditions for the integration of manufacturing by the licensee in coordination with the Export Sales organization; preparing the necessary documents and equipment for manufacturing; following up licensee orders for components, organizing training and technical assistance; and monitoring overseas licensee quality production.

Licensing Contracts

Potain's licensing contract with South Africa was followed by agreements with: Yugoslavia (1974), Iran (1974), Poland (1975), Venezuela (1976), Argentina (1976), South Korea (1978), Turkey (1979), Egypt (1980), Singapore (1980), Mexico (1981), Morocco (1981) and India (1983). These 13 licensing contracts were in various stages of activity, ranging in status from active to inactive.

Potain's partner in South Korea, for instance, was Hyundai, a company which produced two models of top-slewing cranes and one bottom-slewing crane. Until 1985, Hyundai had produced a total of 97 top-slewing and 11 bottom-slewing cranes; this licensing contract was slowly dying because of the incompatibility of the partners' objectives. In Singapore, as the market for new cranes had almost disappeared, Potain's licensing agreement was totally inactive. Therefore, the partner was moving towards Australia. The licensee, which had been a former agent in this marketplace, produced three different models of top-slewing cranes. Until 1985, this partner had produced a total of 80 cranes.

In contrast, Potain's licensing partnership in India was an example of a durable relationship. The licensee, a construction company, produced three models of top-slewing cranes and two models of bottom-slewing cranes. Up until 1985, 47 top-slewing and 59 bottom-slewing cranes had been produced.

China

The Marketplace

Potain had access to China through two channels: directly to China or indirectly via Hong Kong. Selling directly to China was Potain's weakest position; there were several sales agents with undefined territories and with little motivation to sell, and prices were not very competitive. However, Potain had a strong position in Hong Kong with almost 40% of the market.

In 1983, China's crane imports were FF32 million, while in Singapore they were FF79 million and in Hong Kong FF20.5 million. In 1984, China's crane imports were only FF12 million, where Hong Kong's were FF39 million. However, 50–70% of Hong Kong's imports were then sold to China. Over the next three years, total direct imports of completed cranes were estimated at FF50–100 million.

History of Potain in China

Since Deng Xiao Ping's arrival to power in 1978, the operational word in China was 'modernization'. To achieve this objective, Chinese leaders expressed their desire to introduce equipment, advanced technology and management experience from developed countries. The construction industry was China's priority for modernization.

With the agreement of the Chinese and French governments, a mission to China was organized by French construction companies in 1979. Pierre Perrin, then deputy operational director, accompanied by the director of international development, led this mission for Potain. They were received by the Vice-minister responsible for technology transfer. The mission turned into a symposium on materials, and equipment for building and public works projects. At the time of this trip, Perrin understood that China was not interested in importing products, merely product technology. Despite a letter expressing an intent to cooperate sent by Perrin to the Vice-minister, no activity or further communication had followed this visit.

Then in 1982, after three years of silence, MACHIMPEX sent a letter to Potain's International Business Organization requesting Potain to submit an offer for a licensing contract for the manufacture of construction cranes. MACHIMPEX invited Potain's technical experts to visit one of its factories in order to help it identify and define its technological needs. When two salesman arrived and were unable to answer MACHIMPEX's questions, the Chinese concluded that Potain was not serious about the proposition. Later, when one of Potain's engineers went to a construction site in Peking, he was invited to visit Peking's crane factory. As this engineer was able to answer all their technical questions, the Chinese had added Potain to their list of programmed visits for 1984 (which also included Liebherr and Peiner).

In January 1984, a Chinese delegation – composed of the Peking factory director and directors of research from the Institute of Technological Research for Mechanical and Electrical Construction – visited Potain; the delegation noted that Potain was well equipped to handle the transfer of its technology. However, the Chinese remained unsure about Potain's willingness to cooperate. Therefore, in March 1984, Perrin, Gendrault (Research Director), Liger (SEREX Manager) and a sales representative went to China. This visit lasted two weeks and ended with a two-day cross-examination, during which the Chinese engineers asked over 150 pointed technical questions to establish Potain's level of expertise.

The letter that Perrin had just received was the first news since that visit.

The China Deal

MACHIMPEX was demanding the whole technology – '100% integration' – Potain's FO23B top-slewing crane. This 'licensing opportunity' represented a new situation for Potain; the Chinese wanted to produce everything, including the mechanisms, and wanted the 'know-why' for crane design which was a determining competitive advantage in the industry. In the past, Potain had only agreed to license Phases I–IV. Perrin also considered the opportunity cost; Potain's margin per crane was FF280,000, but if Potain did not sell the technology, the market would be closed to Potain.

Looking at it from MACHIMPEX's perspective, Perrin thought about the costs incurred by China as a potential licensee. According to a SEREX study on China's production costs, China would save significantly on transportation and labour costs (direct production costs). Shipping and transportation costs for an FO23B crane would be FF350,000 before the transfer of technology process began. Over the proposed 5-year contract period, these costs would vary according to the number of completed products versus components imported by China.

SEREX produced a forecast of the full cost of a FO23B in China (*refer to Exhibits 10 and 11*). This forecast showed that the full cost of an FO23B would decrease from FF2,100,000 before the transfer of technology to FF383,000 when the licensee reached full integration. The final price to the end user would then be determined by a mark-up set by the Chinese Ministry of Industry. In similar industries, according to other Western companies that had done technology transfer in China, the mark-up was usually around 40% (i.e. a margin of 28%), leaving almost no profit to the factory. The price of the FO23B crane in China would thereby be fixed by the Ministry in terms of a 'cost+' basis (full cost+margin), keeping the retail price at a minimum in order to make the product affordable to local construction companies; profit in China did not seem to have the same meaning as it did in France.

In preparation for his meeting with his colleagues, Perrin consulted a memorandum he had received from Antoine Colas, Export Director (*refer to Exhibit 12*). Faced with an 'all or nothing' deal, Perrin thought about the complexity of the decision faced by Potain and the possible resulting long-term consequences.

Market Considerations in the Region

The world crane market basically included three zones: Europe (80%), the Far East and Asia (10–15%), and the Middle East (5–10%). The Far East and Asia, and the Middle East were the two markets expected to experience high growth in the future: the four 'dragons' – Japan, Korea, Singapore and Taiwan – were expected to exhaust their stock of cranes in 4–5 years; Indonesia, Malaysia and the Philippines were believed to be waiting to 'take off'; and Japan's construction companies were rapidly augmenting their technological expertise and developing a presence in foreign markets.

In addition, the Far East was potentially the second largest market after Europe for top-slewing cranes. With a potential market of 500 cranes, representing a turnover of roughly FF200 million, China would possibly be the fifth largest market after West Germany, Italy, USSR and France. China also had liberal technology transfer legislation (*refer to* **Exhibit 13**) as well as legislation providing cooperation and financial incentives for the development of 'Special Economic Zones' (*refer to* **Exhibit 14**).

However, it was uncertain how long Deng's policy of openness would last, and Potain did run the risk of the Chinese becoming competitors in the fast growing markets of the Far East.

The Meeting

It was 11 January, three days after Perrin had received the letter from MACHIMPEX. Pierre Perrin (CEO), Antoine Colas (Export Director), Bernard Liger (SEREX Manager), Philippe Gauguin (Director of Sales, Far East) and Paul André (Director of Operations) were assembled to discuss MACHIMPEX's letter and the implications for Potain. Perrin asked Liger to kick off the meeting by talking about SEREX's findings. The following discussion took place at the meeting.

Liger The FO23B top-slewing crane is the crane model that we believe would best meet the Chinese's needs. The integration of Potain's technology for manufacturing this model would be done in five phases, or one phase per year. During this 5-year period, the percentage of production costs per unit remaining with Potain would be:

Year 1	Year 2	Year 3	Year 4	Year 5
66	55	41	34	0

This would leave Potain with a significant amount of exports to China. In addition, the weighted average margin (%) on sales to the licensee for each phase would be:

Year 1	Year 2	Year 3	Year 4	Year 5
25	28	30	35	0

This illustrates that mark-up margins on components increase as the components become more sophisticated.

Perrin What if the Chinese decided to develop their own crane technology?

André If we look at R&D costs in China, the estimated development cost for a crane like the FO23B would be roughly FF2.6 million, including two elements, the crane structure at FF1,635,000 and the mechanisms and control units at FF1,050,000. But, this would take several years, four to five years at least.

Liger   Actually, R&D costs are not relevant since the Chinese have decided to buy technology from the 'outside' – either from Proton, Liebherr or Kroll (already producing in Hong Kong). The Chinese are in a hurry and they want the technology today! The idea would be to share the profits that would otherwise go into our competitors' pockets with our Chinese partners; that's the licence's appeal. Especially as China has decided to manufacture cranes, China will do it with others if not with us. China is a country where we sold one crane in 1983 and six in 1984.

Gauguin   Yes, but China has only been importing cranes for the past two or three years. In 1984, we sold six of the 20 cranes imported. In fact, 50% of the cranes imported by Hong Kong are then sent to China, where we represent 42.5% of the market.

André   We also need to consider what will happen three to five years from now. Where will we be? Potain will not be selling them anything and they will take the Asian markets away from us.

Perrin   It's true that we must consider the risks in the long term. The transfer of technology to China cannot be contemplated without considering our own strategy in the Asian zone. However, let's also review the facts of China's current situation. China's objective is to produce 1,000 cranes per year. There already exist seven factories in China producing tower cranes with jibs of less than 98 feet in length. They have manufactured a few jibs longer than that, but these are not appropriate; this is why they seek to acquire Western technology. For the moment, they want to manufacture jibs 131–196 feet long with reliable materials. For these modes, they have defined a need for 500 cranes per year, and they have estimated production at 500 cranes per year by the end of the third year of licensing. Looking at the construction activity in hotel and apartment complexes, it is my opinion that their needs will grow. In this type of situation, I believe, however, that the Chinese estimations will be cut in half; it would not be unrealistic to think that they will manufacture 25 cranes the first year, followed by 100 in the second, 150 in the third and then 250 in both the fourth and fifth years.

    In relation to our strategy in Asia and according to what I saw in China during our visit to their factories, I think it will be a long time before they will be able to export cranes. Their needs are great, and it would be difficult to imagine them producing at a level above their needs. Given their technological level, I would agree with André's evaluation that it would take them four to five years to integrate the production of mechanical parts. Furthermore, I believe that they will have to increase their imports of cranes having jibs longer than 196 feet to complement the local production of the FO23B which has a jib of only 164 feet. By the way, Mr Liger, what would be your best estimation of the transfer cost for the production of FO23B in the Chinese factory?

Liger   SEREX would need a budget of FF2.5 million (with 1.5 million being spent in the first six months) to cover the transfer costs including: training of Chinese staff in France; provision of technical assistance, preparation of the technical documentation; provision of the specifications for equipment and plant layout; preparation and negotiation of the contract; hiring of consultants (lawyer and interpreter); supervision of the transfer; and monitoring of the licence.

Perrin   And Mr. Colas, do you have any news about our competitors' bidding price?

Colas   In spite of Potain's intelligence effort, the export department has not been able to determine the price that the other crane manufacturers will be asking for a licence. But, let me say that, looking at the developing market in South-East Asia, I think we should also seriously consider proposing a joint venture with the Chinese, in addition to a licensing contract. A joint venture would enable us to sell on the Asian market with competitive prices; we could save on transportation and labour costs at least for the mast and jib. At the same time, we would establish a strong market position for the larger crane models.

Perrin   Yes, we should consider the possibility of a joint venture carefully. The 'Special Economic Zones' defined in South-East Asia have advantages which should not be overlooked. However, China's definition of these zones is a recent development. We should look at the operations already executed in formulating a conclusion. We will be better able to understand the movement of the South-East Asian markets after seeing the transparencies that Mr. Gauguin has prepared (*refer to* **Exhibit 15**).

Gauguin   Planned construction in South-East Asia includes two nuclear generating stations, and several other energy stations and hotel complexes. It would therefore not be surprising if China imports 50–100 more powerful cranes than those manufactured under licence. Of course, we must wait and see if China will have the money to finance these imports and whether its openness policy will continue.

I believe that we should see China as another opportunity for additional finished products sales. China has an immediate need for 25 model FO23B cranes, and I think that Potain would certainly be chosen as the supplier if it would show its 'good citizenship' by agreeing to transfer technology. In addition, this is an opportunity for the Chinese to become familiar with Potain's products, and we could expect Potain to be in a good position to provide specialized cranes (high-rise tower cranes and special cranes for complex construction sites) which would generate further revenue in the future. For me, the licence with China could enhance Potain's market position in the short term. Long term, if the Chinese do their own manufacturing, it is difficult to say what our position will be. However, a joint venture in a 'Special Economic Zone' could consolidate our position in the long term.

The group's consensus remained unclear; should Potain submit an offer for a licencing contract with MACHIMPEX? If yes, Perrin was still undecided about: the length of the contract; the use of Potain's brand name; export rights; what to include in the transfer of technology 'package' (old versus new technology); the price of the 'package'; and the degree and form of Potain's involvement.

EXHIBIT 1

Request for Submission of Offer

MACHIMPEX

POTAIN SA
18, rue Charbonnières
69130 ECULLY
FRANCE

Peking, 28 December 1984

SUBJECT: Request submission of an offer for the provision of know-how and know-why for the production of a top-slewing crane by the Peking construction machine factory.

Gentlemen,

Following our visit to your factories and your 1984 visit to Peking, we would like to request that you submit an offer for the provision of know-how and know-why for a top-slewing crane with a 20,000 lb maximum load and 164-foot jib, which could be manufactured at our Peking factory.

The offer should include a description of the know-how and know-why concerning: crane design and calculation, specifications of raw materials, manufacturing, quality control, testing, as well as crane installation, maintenance and utilization. The price for the know-how and know-why, and a proposed payment schedule, should be sent with the offer no later than 1 February 1985.

We would also like to invite you to come to Peking in April for final negotiations, after which MACHIMPEX and the PRC Ministry of Urban Construction and Environmental Protection will choose the technology transfer partner; our goal is to start production as quickly as possible and according to the most advanced techniques.

Thank you in advance for your timely handling of this matter.

EXHIBIT 2

Estimated Financial Position, 1984–85 (Fiscal Year: 1 March–28 February)

Potain: Estimated Profit and Loss Account for the 1984–85 Fiscal Year (in FF'000s)

TURNOVER	761 088
Other operating income	2 622
CONSUMPTION	500 150
ADDED VALUE	263 560
TAXES, DUTIES, COMPARABLE COSTS	−20 149
Payroll costs	−347 455
Operating subsidy received	106
TRADING PROFIT	−103 938
Operating appropriations	−21 755
Other charges	−7 168
Other income	64 989
TRADING ALLOWANCES	−67 872
NON-OPERATING REVENUES AND EXPENSES	−65 239
OPERATING RESULT BEFORE TAX	−133 111
EXTRAORDINARY ITEM	35 698
NET PROFIT	−94 413

Outline Estimated Balance Sheet for the 1984–85 Fiscal Year (in FF'000s)

FIXED ASSETS (1)	187 000	STOCKHOLDERS' EQUITY (2)	42 800
STOCK	241 000	RESERVE FOR	46 080
CLIENT	211 000	CONTINGENCIES	
RECEIVABLES		DEBTS (3)	604 000
OTHER RECEIVABLES	46 000		
AVAILABLE FUNDS	7 000		
TOTAL	692 000	TOTAL	692 000

(1) Including: Tangible assets		110 000
Financial assets		55 500
(2) Including: Revaluation differential		21 400
Reserves		63 100
Balance carried over		−105 278
Profit for the financial year		−94 419
Provisions required by law		51 500
(3) Including: DMLT		168 300
Suppliers		151 000

EXHIBIT 3

Comparison of Profit and Loss Accounts for Potain S.A. (in FF'000s)

	At 29/2/1984	At 28/2/1983	At 28/2/1982	At 28/2/1981
Operating loss	56 509			
Employees' profit share		2 029		
Losses from previous financial years	23 450	8 600	5 968	1 237
Extraordinary losses	3 995	9 192	4 761	9 923
Appropriations to reserves other than operating and extraordinary accounts	68 455	15 939	17 544	36 203
Provisions for Corporation Tax			16 670	6 033
Net profits		4 256	19 043	6 621
Total	152 409	40 016	63 886	60 017
Operating profits		2 121	28 662	14 375
Profits from previous financial years	17 366	3 910	3 248	1 778
Extraordinary profits	7 491	7 242	8 373	2 983
Provisions brought forward, excluding operating or extraordinary provisions	22 279	26 743	23 603	40 881
Net losses	105 272			
Total	152 409	40 016	63 886	60 017

EXHIBIT 4

Comparison of Operating Accounts for Potain S.A. (in FF'000s)

DEBIT	At 29/2/1984	At 28/2/1983	At 28/2/1982	At 28/2/1981
Stock at start of financial year	230 356	221 062	230 140	217 138
Depreciation	33 589	29 827	29 090	22 474
	196 767	191 235	201 050	194 664
Purchaser	490 699	449 243	415 529	447 714
Payroll costs	311 295	268 620	239 995	223 006
Taxes and duties	17 429	15 064	13 171	10 959
Work, supplies and services	134 839	141 622	135 449	117 087
Transportation and travel	44 416	47 503	43 261	34 488
Sundry management costs	21 942	24 576	18 728	16 743
Financial costs	43 522	39 318	37 432	35 160
Allocation to depreciation accounts	23 481	17 665	15 811	17 573
Allocation to contingency accounts	17 671	13 486	16 314	11 279
Share of joint venture companies	2			
Operating profit		2 121	28 663	14 375
Total	1 302 062	1 210 453	1 165 403	1 123 048

CREDIT	At 29/2/1984	At 28/2/1983	At 28/2/1982	At 28/2/1981
Stock at end of financial year	316 000	230 356	221 062	230 140
Depreciation	42 395	33 589	29 827	29 090
	273 606	196 767	191 235	201 050
Sales and income	925 008	951 687	927 391	876 544
Operating subsidies	283	27	56	47
Supplier rebates	964	3 678	1 858	2 452
Extra income	12 891	12 494	10 565	17 961
Financial income	17 261	21 446	17 169	13 010
Work done by the company for its own account	5 407	11 035	6 769	8 151
Share of results of holdings		40		
Operating loss	56 509			
Work and charges not attributable to trading of the financial year	10 205	13 279	10 360	3 833
Total	1 302 062	1 210 453	1 165 403	1 123 048

EXHIBIT 5

Comparative Balance Sheets for Potain S.A. (in FF'000s)

ASSETS	At 29/2/1984	At 28/2/1983	At 28/2/1982	At 28/2/1981
Capital assets				
Setting-up costs	69	94	184	137
Fixed assets	118 191	123 158	107 358	113 288
Other capital assets	115 854	97 382	100 207	105 328
Operating assets	273 605	196 767	191 235	201 050
Short-term realizable or disposable assets	262 686	277 444	253 907	211 397
Income (loss for the fiscal year)	105 272			
Total Assets	875 678	694 845	652 891	631 500

LIABILITIES	At 29/2/1984	At 28/2/1983	At 28/2/1982	At 28/2/1981
Shareholders' equity and reserves	214 632	214 570	200 414	189 806
Subsidy for equipment	12	19	25	31
Provision for losses and charges	70 457	24 254	30 631	37 190
Long- and medium-term debts	127 769	113 212	77 551	94 302
Short-term debts	462 808	338 534	325 227	303 550
Income (profit for the fiscal year)		4 256	19 043	6 621
Total	875 678	694 845	652 891	631 500

EXHIBIT 6

Crane Market 1984 (in units)

	POTAIN Bottom*	POTAIN Top*	BPR Bottom	BPR Top	SIMMA Bottom	SIMMA Top	LIEBHERR Bottom	LIEBHERR Top	PIENER Bottom	PIENER Top	EDILGRU ALFA Bottom	EDILGRU ALFA Top	CIBIN Bottom	KROLL Bottom	KROLL Top
Total Europe	467	148	95	49	76	115	718	125	94	40	192	42	500	69	10
E.E.C. Countries	358	102	87	18	76	115	567	87	77	33	150	42	500	36	4
COMECON		5													
Other Europe	109	41	8	31			151	38	17	7	42			33	6
Total Africa	91	31	35	9			25	19				3		1	15
Maghreb	80	10	26	3			12								15
Other Africa	11	21	9	6			13	19				3		1	
Middle East	23	11		4	1		5	18	1	5		2			
Far East	6	47		15			1	14	1	5		15		2	2
Total Asia	29	58		19	1		6	32	2			17		2	2
Oceania								1		40					
Total Americas	5	3	2	7				3		40					
North America	1	1		2				3							
Latin America	4	2	2	5											
World Total	592	240	132	84	77	115	749	180	96	120	192	62	500	87	27

* Bottom or top refers to whether the crane turns at the bottom (bottom-slewing) or top (top-slewing).

EXHIBIT 7

Topkit for FO23B

Local Fabrication

PHASE **I** – Mast and Jib
PHASE **II** – Counter-jib and Cat-head
PHASE **III** – Chassis
PHASE **IV** – Telescoping Accessories
PHASE **V** – Mechanisms, Cabin and
Electrical Switchboard,
Crane Driver's Post and
Control Instruments

Source: Potain Company Materials.

EXHIBIT 8

Tower Cranes – Top-slewing

Slewing axis

Jib tie

Slewing head

JIB

Cat-head

Counter-jib tie

Jib foot

Counter-jib

Jib sections

Jib nose

Mast
cabin

Counter-jib
ballast

Tower

Mast
sections

Climbing collar

Concrete
base

Source: Potain Company Materials.

EXHIBIT 9

Tower Cranes – Bottom-slewing and Self-erecting

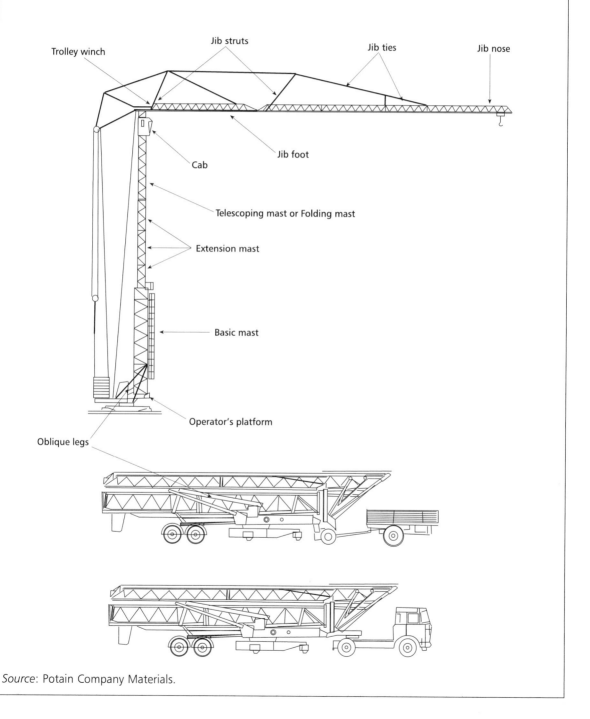

Source: Potain Company Materials.

EXHIBIT 10

Structure of Potain's Production Costs for FO23B

Raw materials (steel)	18%
Components (electrical devices etc.)	12%
Factory cost	35%
(labour + amortization = factory hourly rate)	
General & administrative	15%
Selling costs	20%
Full cost	100%
Margin = 20%	25%
(mark-up = 25%)	
Total	125%
Ex-Factory price of FO23B (before tax)	1 400 000
Shipping & forwarding	25%
Customs duties	25%

EXHIBIT 11

Breakdown of the Full Cost of FO23B in China (in 1000FF)

	Year 1	Year 2	Year 3	Year 4	Year 5	Before T.T.
	Phase I	Phase I–II	Phases I–III	Phases I–IV	Phases I–V	
1. Integration phase (operational)						
2. Cost of components and parts shipped by Potain to China	739.2	616.0	459.2	380.8	0.0	1120
3. Margin	246.4	239.5	196.8	205.0	0.0	280
4. Price including margin (ex-factory before tax) = 2 + 3	985.6	855.5	656.0	585.8	0.0	1400.0
Shipping and forwarding per unit						
5. As percentage	51%	38%	21%	15%	0%	100%
6. In 1000FF	178.5	133	73.5	52.5	0	350
7. Cost of imports per unit (before customs duties) = 4 + 6	1164.1	988.5	729.5	638.3	0	1750
Local costs of licensee (according to integration level)						
8. As percentage	34%	45%	59%	66%	0%	0%
9. In 1000FF	130.2	172.3	225.9	252.8	383	0
10. China costs before customs duties	1294.3	1160.8	955.4	891.1	383	1750
11. Customs duties rate	15%	15%	15%	15%	0	25%
12. Customs duties (1000FF)	147.8	128.3	98.4	87.9	0.0	350.0
13. Full cost per unit in China (before tax) = 10 + 12	1442.1	1289.1	1053.8	979.0	383.0	2100.0
14. Price per unit in China (fixed by Ministry of Industry)						

Source: SEREX (disguised data).

EXHIBIT 12

Memorandum

TO: Pierre Perrin
                        CEO, Potain SA

DATA: 9 January 1985

FROM: Antoine Colas
                        Export Director

SUBJECT: Organizational relationships of the key 'players' in the licensing negotiations

Mr Perrin,

This memo is in response to your fax of January 8th. I thought it would be helpful in planning Potain's strategy to know who we will be dealing with and their respective relationships. The schema is outlined below.

Antoine Colas

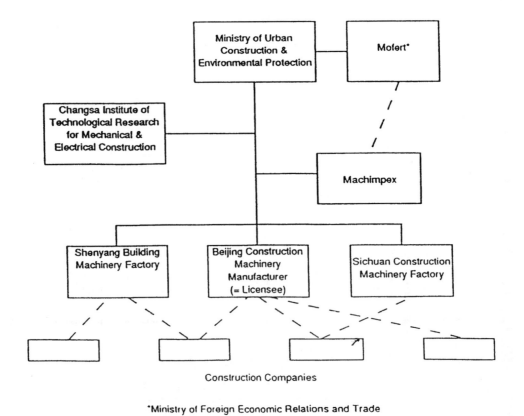

Construction Companies

*Ministry of Foreign Economic Relations and Trade

EXHIBIT 13

Chinese Legislation on Technology Transfer

Regulations of the People's Republic of China on the Administration of Technology Acquisition Contracts

Promulgated by the State Council on 24 May 1985

Article 1   These Regulations are formulated with a view to further expanding foreign economic and technical cooperation, upgrading the scientific and technical level of the country and promoting national economic growth.

Article 2   Importation of technology referred to in these Regulations means acquisition of technology through trade or economic and technical cooperation by any corporation, enterprise, organization or individual within the territory of the People's Republic of China (hereinafter referred to as 'the recipient') from any corporation, enterprise, organization, or individual outside the territory of the People's Republic of China (hereinafter referred to as 'the supplier'), including:
1. Assignment or licensing of patent or other industrial property rights;
2. Know-how provided in the form of drawings, technical data, technical specifications, etc., such as production processes, formulae, product designs, quality control and management skills;
3. Technical services.

Article 3   The technology to be imported must be advanced and appropriate and shall conform to at least one of the following requirements:
1. Capable of developing and producing new products;
2. Capable of improving quality and performance of products, reducing production cost and lowering consumption of energy or raw materials;
3. Favourable to the maximum utilization of local resources;
4. Capable of expanding product export and increasing earnings of foreign currencies;
5. Favourable to environmental protection;
6. Favourable to production safety;
7. Favourable to the improvement of management;
8. Contributing to the advancement of scientific and technical levels.

Article 4   The recipient and the supplier shall conclude in written form a technology import contract (hereinafter referred to as 'the contract'). An application for approval of the contract shall be submitted by the recipient, within thirty days from the date of conclusion, to the Ministry of Foreign Economic Relations and Trade of the People's Republic of China or any other agency authorized by the Ministry (hereinafter referred to as 'the approving authority'). The approving authority shall approve or reject the contract within sixty days from the date of receipt. Contracts approved shall come into effect on the date of approval. Contracts on which the approving authority does not make a decision within the specified period of time shall be regarded as approved and shall come into effect automatically.

Article 5   The conclusion of technology import contracts must conform to the relevant provisions of the 'Foreign Economic Contract Law' and other laws of the People's Republic of China. Both parties must specify in the contract the following items:
1. Contents, scope and essential description of the technology provided, and a list of patents and trademarks if they are involved;
2. Technical targets to be reached and time limit and measures for accomplishing the targets;
3. Remuneration, composition of remuneration and form of payment.

Article 6   The supplier shall ensure that it is the rightful owner of the technology provided and that technology provided is complete, correct, effective and capable of accomplishing the technical targets specified in the contract.

(continued)

Article 7	The recipient shall undertake the obligation to keep confidential, in accordance with the scope and duration agreed upon by both parties, the technical secrets contained in the technology provided by the supplier, which have not been made public.

Article 8 The duration of the contract shall conform to the time needed by the recipient to assimilate the technology provided and, unless specially approved by the approving authority, shall not exceed ten years.

Article 9 The supplier shall not oblige the recipient to accept requirements which are unreasonably restrictive. Unless specially approved by the approving authority, a contract shall not include any of the following restrictive provisions:

1. Requiring the recipient to accept additional conditions which are not related to the technology to be imported, such as requiring the recipient to purchase unnecessary technology, technical services, raw materials, equipment and products;
2. Restricting the freedom of choice of the recipient to obtain raw materials, parts and components or equipment from other sources;
3. Restricting the development and improvement by the recipient of the imported technology;
4. Restricting the acquisition by the recipient of similar or competing technology from other sources;
5. Non-reciprocal terms of exchange by both parties of improvements to the imported technology;
6. Restricting the quantity, variety and sales price of products to be manufactured by the recipient with the imported technology;
7. Unreasonably restricting the sales channels and export markers of the recipient;
8. Forbidding use by the recipient of the imported technology after expiration of the contract;
9. Requiring the recipient to pay for or to undertake obligations for patents which are unused or no longer effective.

Article 10 In applying for approval of contracts. applicants shall submit the following documents:

1. Written application for approval of the contract;
2. Copy of the contract concluded by both parties and its Chinese translation;
3. Documents evidencing the legal status of the contracting parties.

Article 11 Application and approval of any revision and renewal of the contract shall be made in accordance with the provisions stipulated in Article 4 and Article 10 of these Regulations.

Article 12 The authority to interpret these Regulations and to formulate detailed rules for implementing these Regulations resides in the Ministry of Foreign Economic Relations and Trade of the People's Repubilc of China.

Article 13 These Regulations shall enter into force on the date of promulgation.

24.9 Procedures for Examination and Approval of Technology Import Contracts

Approved by the State Council on 26 August 1985 and published by the Ministry of Foreign Economic Relations and Trade on 18 September 1985

Article 1 These procedures (hereinafter referred to as the 'Procedures') are formulated in accordance with the provisions of the 'Regulations of the People's Republic of China on the Administration of Technology Import Contracts'.

Article 2 Technology import contracts hereunder listed must be submitted for government examination and approval in accordance with these Procedures regardless of country of origin, source of funds and method of payment:

1. Contracts for transfer or licensing-in of industrial property rights and technical know-how;
2. Contracts for technical services, including that of feasibility studies or engineering designing entrusted to or in cooperation with foreign enterprises, that of provision of technical services through employing foreign geological exploration or engineering team(s), that of provision of services on technical renovation, technology or product design Improvement, quality control and enterprise management, etc. but exclusive of that for foreigners to be employed to work in Chinese enterprises;

3. Contracts for co-production which involves the transfer of industrial property rights and technical know-how or licensing, but exclusive of that for SKD or CKD operations, and processing with supplied materials or samples;

4. Contracts for the supply of complete sets of equipment such as plant, workshop or production lines, the aim of which Is to transfer or license-in industrial property rights and technical know-how as well as provision of technical services; and

5. Other contracts for the purchase of machinery, equipment or goods which involves the transfer of or licensing-in of industrial property rights and technical know-how as well as provision of technical services, but exclusive of those for the straightforward purchase or leasing of machinery and equipment, nor their after-sales provision of technical data, random operation manuals and maintenance instructions or maintenance service in general.

Article 3   For technical import contracts in which technology is acquired from foreign investors or other foreign parties in enterprises owned by foreign interests, and equity and contractual joint ventures that are established in the People's Republic of China, they must undergo the process of examination and approval according to these Procedures.

For contracts in which the industrial property rights or technical know-how concerned is entered as an equity share by foreign investors, they must undergo the process of examination and approval according to the provisions of the 'Regulations for the Implementation of the Law of the People's Republic of China on Joint Ventures Using Chinese and Foreign Investment' and other relevant laws and/or administrative regulations.

Article 4   Technology import contracts are examined and approved respectively in the light of the following conditions:

1. Given existing norm stipulations, the contract for an above-norm project, the feasibility study report or equivalent document(s) of which are approved by the State Planning Commission is to be examined and approved by the Ministry of Foreign Economic Relations and Trade;

2. Given existing norm stipulations, the contract for a below-norm project, the feasibility study report or equivalent document(s) of which are approved by the responsible ministry or administration directly under the jurisdiction of the State Council is to be examined and approved by the Ministry of Foreign Economic Relations and Trade or the above-mentioned responsible ministry or administration entrusted by the Ministry of Foreign Economic Relations and Trade, which, however, is invested with the overall responsibility to issue the 'Approval Certificate for the Technology Import Contract';

3. Given existing norm stipulations, the contract for a below-norm project for which the feasibility study report or the equivalent document(s) is approved by provincial, autonomous region or municipality government directly under the jurisdiction of the Central Government, special economic zones, coastal open cities and cities which come separately under national economic plans is to be examined and approved by the respective departments (commissions or bureaus) of the Ministry of Foreign Economic Relations and Trade. The contract or project for which the feasibility study report or equivalent document(s) is approved by city or county government Is to be examined and approved by the respective departments (commissions or bureaus) of the Ministry of Foreign Economic Relations and Trade of provinces, autonomous regions and municipalities where the organs of the above-said cities or countries are located; and

4. Except those stipulated in item 2 of Article 3 of these Procedures, a technology import contract signed by a foreign-owned enterprise, equity joint venture or contractual joint venture or other foreign parties is to be examined and approved by the departments (commissions or bureaus) of provinces, autonomous regions, municipalities directly under the jurisdiction of the Central Government, special economic zones, coastal open cities and cities which come separately under the national economic plans where the above-said enterprises are registered.

Article 5   Application for examination and approval for a technology import contract mentioned in Article 4 must be submitted by the contract recipient to the organs in charge within 30 days from the date of signature along with the documents as listed below:

1. Application;
2. Contract copy and its Chinese version; and
3. Certificate referring to the legal status of the contracting parties.

(continued)

If the organs in charge consider it necessary, the applicant may be asked to submit other documents/data needed for the examination and approval of the contract.

Article 6   After receiving the application, the organs in charge must pay attention to the following points:
1. Whether the contents of the contract conform to that of the feasibility study report or equivalent document(s) approved;
2. Whether the essential articles in the contract are as required;
3. Whether the property rights of the transferred technology and, where disputes arise over such property rights in the technology transfer, the obligations as well as the solutions thereof are explicitly and reasonably stipulated in the contract;
4. Whether there are reasonable stipulations in the contract for the technical level which should be achieved by the transferred technology, including the product quality guarantee, through the application of the said technology;
5. Whether the price and method of payment are reasonable;
6. Whether the stipulations in the contract for the contracting parties relating to their rights, responsibilities and obligations are definite, reciprocal and reasonable;
7. Whether any preferential taxation commitment is made in the contract without the consent of the Chinese Tax Authority;
8. Whether any provision is found in the contract violating the existing laws and regulations of China; and
9. Whether any provision is found in the contract that constitutes an encroachment of the sovereignty of China.

Article 7   The organ in charge must complete its contract examination and approval process within 60 days from the date of receipt of the application:
1. Once a contract is approved after examination, the organ in charge shall issue the 'Approval Certificate for Technology Import Contract' printed and numbered by the Ministry of Foreign Economic Relations and Trade; and
2. If a contract is not approved after examination, the organ in charge shall put forth as soon as possible the reason thereof and request the recipient signatory party to hold renegotiations with the supplier of the technology and then grant the approval provided that the contract is amended accordingly.
To facilitate approval for the contract, the recipient negotiator may consult the organs in charge for the main contents or certain articles in the contract before or during the renegotiations or requests for pre-examination.

Article 8   After approval of the technology import contract by the government authorities concerned, all organs in charge shall submit a copy of the 'Approval Certificate for Technology Import Contract' as well as the relevant data to the Ministry of Foreign Economic Relations and Trade.

Article 9   The 'Approval Certificate for Technology Import Contract' or a copy thereof must be presented when arranging for a bank guarantee, letter of credit, payment, settlement of exchange accounts, Customs clearance, payment of taxes or application for reduction or exemption of taxes or duties during the course of execution of the technology import contract; unless the said approval certificate is submitted, the bank, Customs and tax authorities are not entitled to process or handle the above request.

Article 10   Where substantive amendment or extension of the contract duration is made during the course of the execution of the technology import contract, re-application for examination and approval shall be made according to the relevant stipulations of these Procedures.

Article 11   The Ministry of Foreign Economic Relations and Trade shall be responsible for interpreting these Procedures.

Article 12   These procedures shall enter into force from the date of promulgation.

Source: *The China Investment Guide*, 3rd Edition, Hong Kong, 1983.

EXHIBIT 14

Note on Tax Issues

China places great importance on the introduction of new technology and foreign investment in China. Foreign companies not residing in China and receiving Chinese revenues (including interest, dividends, licensing fees and royalties) will be taxed at the source at a rate of 20%.

However, the French–Chinese Convention provides for 'tax sparing' so that a French company having done technology transfer in China can attribute a tax credit on its French revenues equal to 20% of the gross income earned.

Source: *Droit Chinois des Affaires*, Meyer, Verva and DuPont, September–October 1987.

EXHIBIT 15

Far-East: Market Trends & Potain Group's Market Position

Country	POTAIN SALES**				Market		Market Trends	
	1983 Units	1983 in 1000FF	1984 Units	1984 in 1000FF	1984 Units	1984 in 1000FF	Short-term 1986	Long-term 1989
Singapore	20	10912	30	16705	43	22670	–	=
South Korea	46	47380	21	8844	35	29444	–	=
Thailand	6	6200	5	3429	18	11424	–	=
Indonesia	0		2	2451	8	7561	–	+
Malaysia	7	10550	7	6277	16	10001	–	+
Philippines	0		0	0	0	0	–	–
China*	3	6500	6	2630	20*	11834	+	=
Taiwan	2		2	2099	5	11983	=	=
Hong Kong	10	11864	17	21883	40	38843	=	+
Australia			0	0	1	261	–	–
New Zealand			0	0	1	1299	=	=
Japan	0		0	0	0	0	=	+
Total Far East	92	93406	90	64318	187	145320	=	+
World Market	1845	935851	1316	659739	6178	1906543	=	=
F.E./W.M.	5.0%	10.0%	6.8%	9.7%	3.0%	7.6%		

* Imports only.
** Includes sales from Potain, its subsidiaries and licensees.

NESTLÉ IN ASEAN

This case was prepared by Professors George Taucher and Toh Thian Ser, Technological University, Singapore, with contributions from Professors Jim Ellert and Jan Kubes. The case is intended as a basis for class discussion rather than to illustrate either effective or ineffective handling of a business situation.

After meeting in early 1990 with Mr Helmut Maucher, CEO of the Nestlé group, Rudolph (Rudi) Tschan, head of Zone 2 (Asia/Oceania) of Nestlé, was very excited about the challenge ahead of him. Rudi had proposed a target, for himself and his top management group, that meant doubling turnover by the year 2000. Given the maturity of the food and beverage markets in Europe and North America, this goal would be a tall order. Rudi, however, was delighted. He saw what a great opportunity this challenge could provide for his zone. The Asia-Pacific region had seen rapid growth in sales turnover (over 30% per annum for some countries), and he was convinced that investment in Zone 2 would be a key element of Nestlé's growth strategy.

As Rudi considered his options, he noted that several of the plants in the ASEAN region were seeking approval to have their capital budgets raised so that they could expand their plants. Each proposal, on its own, was relatively small in relation to the Nestlé Group's overall capital budget. Rudi recalled, however, that in the last decade or so, at seminars attended by Nestlé's key managers in the region, he had heard individuals suggesting that there should be an ASEAN-wide regional project. He wondered if perhaps now was the right time for Nestlé to consider the concept of an ASEAN regional market more seriously.

The Nestlé Group

In 1990, with sales of over SF47 billion, the Nestlé group was the world's largest food company. Expansion, largely through acquisitions, had been especially rapid over the previous 10 years. Under Helmut Maucher's leadership, this growth had also been proportionately profitable.

Although about half of the group's sales were in Europe, growth through acquisitions in North America had also raised sales there to around one-third of the total. In the 'developing world', sales were still only around 20% of the total, but very rapid growth – in contrast to the stagnation found in industrial countries – would increase this percentage over the coming years.

The company's product line – which had started in the 19th century with sweetened and condensed milk – had expanded into a wide range of branded food products. NESCAFE, developed by Nestlé in the 1930s, was the world's leading soluble coffee and a major world brand in its own right. The company was also a major producer of chocolate and confectionery products, and had more recently moved heavily into beverages, including bottled water and various milk and soya-based drinks.

Nestlé was one of the few truly large multinational companies. Although share ownership was mainly in Swiss hands, sales in Switzerland represented only about 2% of total sales worldwide. Likewise, management was multi-national, with 6 nationalities represented among the 11 general managers.

Nestlé was organized in a matrix form, with heavy responsibility continuing to reside with market heads (country managers). Although these managers were responsible for developing Nestlé's traditional products such as NESCAFE, milk and chocolate, local managers were increasingly moving into new products to meet local tastes and demands. Notable examples included expansion into oriental noodles in Asia (also being introduced into Europe and elsewhere) and various soya-based products, mostly in Asia. Market managers were fully responsible for sales and profit development in their markets. The headquarters in Vevey, Switzerland, exercised tight control over financial results and quality, but marketing strategy and operations were largely delegated to carefully chosen market heads.

Although worldwide product managers had been in place for many years, their influence and power were not very strong. Product strategy had tended to be a sum of each of the markets. However, in recent years, global product management was being strengthened by the appointment of two 'strategic business group' general managers.

Market managers reported to regional (zone) managers (Europe, Middle East & Africa, North America, Latin America and Asia, including Australasia and Japan). These zone managers resided in Vevey but travelled a great deal, working with each of the market heads and their teams.

Traditional focus on market managers resulted in relatively little interchange between markets. The lines of communication all tended to point toward Vevey. In the ASEAN countries,[1] for example, the market heads rarely met and when they did meet, their agenda and interaction time were limited. Typically, an estimated 70% of sales in each of the ASEAN countries was locally sourced. Thus, production as well as marketing and sales tended to be local in nature. As a result, Nestlé had almost 200 factories in Europe with little cross-border activity. As European integration began to take hold, Nestlé had engaged in a massive reorganization of manufacturing and logistics, dramatically reducing the number of factories and increasing multi-market sourcing from the same factory. This change, still in process, clearly affected the traditional independence of the market heads. Outside Europe, this process was less well developed (cross-border restrictions and costs being less favourable than in Europe).

---

[1] For simplicity, Brunei's market, as it was very small, has not been discussed here. However, as a full-fledged member of ASEAN, Brunei's legal and financial role has been included.

ASEAN

ASEAN (Association of Southeast Asian Nations) was formed in 1967 and initially comprised Indonesia, Malaysia, the Philippines, Singapore and Thailand. It took 17 years before ASEAN's embrace was widened to include Brunei. ASEAN was conceived in a period when regional economic groupings were the vogue. It followed a trend which had seen a mushrooming of organizations aimed at boosting regional trade and growth. Well-known proponents included the European Community (EC), the Latin American Free Trade Association (LAFTA) and the Council for Mutual Economic Assistance (COMECON).

The key difference between ASEAN and these other groupings was that the ASEAN cooperation began in a low-key, consensus-seeking style. Rather than force the pace, ASEAN member nations avoided focusing on their differences in political or economic areas, and concentrated on developing the areas where they had common ground. ASEAN's strength was its ability to build relationships among its members so that differences could be aired privately while areas of similarity were openly discussed.

Given that the ASEAN nations had different administrative and legal frameworks, mainly because they had been influenced by different colonial administrations,[2] their varying levels of economic development and their differing policies toward foreign investment, it was difficult for them to work towards a customs union or a common market in the manner adopted by other regional groupings such as the European Community. Nor was this arrangement ever envisaged by ASEAN's political leaders.

This somewhat limited approach to cooperation allowed ASEAN to achieve success in such areas as tourism promotion and cultural exchange. More importantly, the ASEAN nations forged a common diplomatic front in areas such as Vietnam and Cambodia. They scored several successes at the United Nations General Assembly, which gave them the confidence to begin working more closely together in the area of economic cooperation.

The Bali Summit of 1976 heralded ASEAN's intention to step up the pace of economic cooperation. There was talk of setting up ASEAN-wide industrial projects, and the first steps in tariff reductions within ASEAN were announced. Despite the initial excitement, economic cooperation proceeded at a snail's pace. Both the ASEAN Industrial Complementation and the ASEAN Industrial Project schemes generated little interest, with only a handful of projects being implemented. Both schemes were based on the premise that production economies could be achieved in large, ASEAN-wide infrastructure projects which, at the national level, would not have been viable because of the limited market and capacity within each member nation. The projects were meant to be driven by the private sector, but the investment commitments were large and the gestation periods too long. Consequently, the ASEAN private sector preferred to leave this

---

[2] Thailand was never colonized, Indonesia was colonized by the Dutch, the Philippines by the Americans, Malaysia and Singapore by the British.

form of cooperation to the ASEAN public sector. The total value of production generated by these projects had no material impact on intra-ASEAN trade.

Even in the trade area, ASEAN had still seen little success by 1990. The Preferential Trading Arrangements (PTA) were put into effect as an ongoing exercise. ASEAN countries agreed to intra-ASEAN tariff reductions on many products. By 1990 more than 10,000 items were covered under the Preferential Tariff Arrangement. Yet there was little opportunity for improvement as trade in these items represented less than 1% of intra-ASEAN trade. An extreme example of a product category which was hardly traded but which came under the PTA was snowploughs, a product unlikely to enjoy much demand in the tropics!

In 1983, the private sector within ASEAN initiated a new basis for regional cooperation – the ASEAN Industrial Joint Venture (AIJV) Scheme. The ASEAN Chambers of Commerce and Industry (ASEAN-CCI) proposed a major simplifica-tion. An AIJV project could take off as long as two or more countries within ASEAN agreed to pursue it. This meant that the participating countries would extend tariff preferences to the products among themselves for a period of four years from the start of commercial production. The project would still have to be approved by the ASEAN Economic Ministers as a group, but this approval would not be withheld so long as two or more countries agreed to extend tariff preferences on a given set of products. After the four-year period had expired, however, the lower tariff applicable to the AIJV would be extended to other companies, both from the participating countries involved and other ASEAN member nations. During the four-year period, any country not party to the arrangement could join the AIJV participating nations by agreeing to give preferential tariffs to the set of products produced by the AIJV agreement.

For projects approved after 1990, there was a requirement that ASEAN equity ownership content be at least 40%[3] (51% previously). This change would be significant for a company like Nestlé which insisted on management control (*Exhibit 1* shows the process for approving an AIJV project).

Nestlé's Perspective in the ASEAN Marketplace

Nestlé had been operating in the ASEAN region for 85 years or so. In every location, it had at least a marketing office, if not one or several plants. In all the ASEAN markets, Nestlé was the market leader or was number two for the product category it was marketing. Nestlé could adapt quickly to the different government bureaucracies in ASEAN and had usually worked with senior host country nationals who, in addition to contributing to the understanding of the local market and customers, also helped Nestlé's top management maintain cordial relations with these governments.

Rudi Tschan was well aware of how rapidly markets were growing in ASEAN. For the several years before the Nestlé AIJV concept was born, turnover in several

---

[3] A further AIJV requirement was that each country that extended the tariff preference had to have a minimum 5% equity participation in the project.

ASEAN nations had grown at double-digit rates, with growth exceeding 30% per annum in some cases. He also realized that, although intra-ASEAN trade was low, at about 20% (or around 5% if Singapore was excluded), there was a potential market if ASEAN nations grew closer in economic terms.

By the late 1980s, there were 14 AIJV projects (the list in *Exhibit 2* also includes the five new Nestlé projects). There appeared to be limited interest in developing projects which would exploit the potential of the ASEAN market. In fact, no AIJV proposed before the Nestlé project had equity participation from all the ASEAN nations. The only exception was the project to print security notes, which had participation from all ASEAN nations at the time it was proposed. Most projects covered two or three ASEAN nations.

In part, the low level of interest sometimes reflected the tension felt by officials in ASEAN member nations, who had to face the dilemma of helping their homegrown industries while allowing the larger ASEAN market to be formed. This dilemma sometimes led to officials of some ASEAN countries discouraging companies which had put out informal 'feelers' on the likelihood of official support if they were to submit an AIJV proposal.

Rudi was convinced that, despite the general air of uncertainty over the AIJV concept, there was a role that Nestlé could play in the context of the ASEAN market. It was time for Nestlé to test ASEAN's true market potential.

Rudi contacted Johnny Santos, Market Head for the Philippines. Johnny was the ideal man for putting together an AIJV proposal, for he had led or worked in Singapore, Thailand and the Philippines, three of the five ASEAN nations where Nestlé had manufacturing plants. He therefore had a good feel for how these three market heads would respond. Coincidentally, the ASEAN committee responsible for approving AIJV projects, the Committee for Industry, Minerals and Energy (or COIME) had its administrative office in the Philippines. Ms Lilia Bautista, Head of COIME, was known to Johnny, and both were enthusiastic about the idea of Nestlé developing an ASEAN-wide AIJV proposal. They realized that such a proposal would amount to at least five projects, as all the ASEAN countries – with the exception of Brunei – had manufacturing potential.

Johnny set about talking to the market heads and learned that most of them felt it would be a long time before the project could take off. A couple were of the opinion that the AIJV scheme had not gone anywhere, although seven years had elapsed since the idea was first proposed.

Despite these doubts, the market heads were still willing to give the AIJV concept a try. Each could see the advantage of selling his products to the other markets in ASEAN at prices which were close to those of domestic manufacturers, because they would enjoy 90% tariff reductions. They saw two key advantages. On the one hand, domestic competitors were usually smaller local companies which did not enjoy the brand loyalty or recognition that Nestlé had in these markets. More competitive pricing could mean more demand. On the other hand, Nestlé's major competitors in the international market were exporters to the ASEAN markets and their products would attract full tariffs.

For some time, the market heads in Zone 2 had cooperated with each other on staff exchanges and occasionally rescheduling production to answer a call for assistance by another market which had to respond quickly to a competitor's new marketing initiative. To take this loose form of cooperation towards a more formal arrangement through the AIJV scheme did not appear to be too difficult.

The market heads realized that, while COIME could screen the projects to be accepted by the ASEAN Economic Ministers, the actual approval of manufacturing licences and preferential tariff applications would be made at the country level. Therefore, there needed to be a two-tiered approach to satisfy requirements at both the regional and the national levels. Their initial response was to hire an international consultancy firm to approach the various authorities involved. However, Nestlé was well established in the region, and the market heads and their senior local staff had developed strong contacts with senior officials at the national level. A consultancy firm might give the wrong impression, one that could hurt relationships. The decision was then made to use only Nestlé officers to approach both national and regional authorities.

A more complex issue that the market heads needed to settle was how the AIJV proposals could be put together. Which country would have which type of AIJV product? Johnny was well aware that the market heads would be moving beyond a loose form of cooperation to actually trading among themselves regarding the type of products each wanted located in his country of responsibility. It was agreed that marketing would remain autonomous. Also, although production decisions would have to take regional interests into account, each market head would retain substantial control over most of the production decisions in his country, since only a selection of their products would be truly regional in terms of production and preferential tariffs.

Although ASEAN was made up of six countries in 1990, the market heads agreed that there should be no production in Brunei – as its market was tiny compared with the others. To tie Brunei's interests into the AIJV proposals, it was agreed that Brunei's interests would be offered a stake in all five AIJV projects. It was also agreed that the basic principle for plant location would be the availability of local raw materials.

On this basis, it was decided that the five projects be allocated as follows (*refer to **Exhibit 3** for details*):

Country	Product	Major raw materials
Indonesia	Soya milk	Soya beans
Malaysia	'KIT KAT'/'SMARTIES' chocolate dragees Bouillon cubes	Cocoa
Philippines	Breakfast cereals	Corn, sugar
Singapore	Soya sauce powder	None
Thailand	'COFFEEMATE' non-dairy creamer	Tapioca, hydrogenated palm oil

The justification for the soya concentrate plant in Singapore was not based on raw material availability as Singapore did not grow any soya beans. In part, it was felt that Singapore should be given a role in the AIJV project because it was a hub for transportation and distribution in the region. The plant would be competitive in its own right as it could import soya beans from the world market, and manufacture and sell the soya concentrate at competitive rates. Its market included non-ASEAN countries such as Hong Kong, Taiwan and countries in Europe.

The size of most of the AIJV projects was based on initial projections by each market head of the demand for the product, based on the growth of the domestic market as well as ASEAN demand. In several instances where there was already local capacity, the proposed AIJV plant would more than double capacity. This projection was the result of the market heads being confident that they were facing healthy growth in both their home markets and in ASEAN.

The market heads also agreed that, as the requirements for equity ownership differed from the existing equity arrangements in their respective ASEAN nations, there would be a need for the AIJV project in each country to be owned by separate companies. In most cases, it was felt that the new manufacturing facilities could be kept close to existing plants to maximize cost-savings in such areas as plant maintenance and engineering.

However, fences and other devices were used to separate the physical facilities for the purposes of accounting and demonstrating to the respective governments that these were AIJV projects for the application of the Margin Of Preference (MOP).

One problem that raised considerable tension among the market heads was the proposal to close existing plants producing any of the products that came under the AIJV projects and to transfer the capacity to the new projects. Several market heads strongly believed that, as they were already profitably servicing their own domestic markets, it would be both risky and potentially disruptive if they had to shut down their plants and wait for the new plants to overcome their teething problems to produce for already-established markets.

Rudi and Johnny finally decided to let existing plants remain, with the exception of the breakfast cereals plant in Malaysia, which was needed for the Philippines production to begin. Otherwise, the AIJV projects would cater to new market demands. However, the market heads agreed not to expand the capacity of existing plants whose products came within the AIJV framework. Further details on each of the five markets are given in the next section (Appendix).

With the proposal in hand, each of the market heads and their senior local staff began approaching the industry ministry in the five ASEAN nations where plants would be set up. Johnny worked directly with COIME. Officials of the industry ministries would put out feelers – especially to those companies which enjoyed tariff protection and had significant market shares – to gauge their reaction to Nestlé's proposal. Most of the companies contacted had not heard much about the AIJV scheme. Few realized the implications of the Nestlé proposals, and the general feeling was that no one would be hurt. COIME asked for several presentations, and Nestlé officials flew to some of the conferences attended by senior officials of ASEAN as well as by Economic Ministers. They were on hand to answer questions and again the response was favourable. Overall approval was communicated to Nestlé in late 1991.

Johnny and the market heads now had four years to tap the potential of the ASEAN market for these products which would enjoy tariff reductions of 90% within ASEAN. The time had come to deliver the goods to Vevey, Nestlé's headquarters in Switzerland.

Appendix

Nestlé Malaysia Berhad

Nestlé's strong position in Malaysia in 1990 stemmed from both its long history in the country and a successful adaptation to the local situation. The former long-time managing director, Ernst Zulliger, was appointed Dato (roughly equivalent to a British knightship). This award was primarily based on Nestlé's huge contributions to school sports development in Malaysia. The fact that Nestlé heavily purchased Malaysia's agricultural products – such as cocoa, palm oil and coffee – also gave the company an important position in the country.

With 1990 sales of around Ringgit 700 million, five factories and 2,800 employees, Nestlé (Malaysia) Berhad (51% owned by Nestlé) was one of the more significant foreign companies. Conforming to Malaysian law, the remaining 49% was in public hands – with the bulk of the minority being held by institutions (the largest single shareholder after Nestlé was the Muslim Pilgrimage Fund). A small percentage of the shares was traded on the stock market. Nestlé's excellent performance was reflected in its share prices, to the gratification of its institutional investors. The Malaysian chairman in 1990 was a former top military personage; however, Nestlé's operation was fully controlled by the managing director, Mr Frits van Dijk (who was later also given a Datoship).

As a long-established and respected company, Nestlé had built up excellent relationships with the Bumiputra[4] dominated government. With a forward-looking personnel policy, the company had relatively cordial relations with local unions and the workforce in general.

Nestlé had successfully developed its business in the wide range of traditional products – coffee, milk, chocolate, etc. In addition, Nestlé (Malaysia) had been aggressive in developing local products, such as instant oriental noodles.

In considering the AIJV project, Mr van Dijk had to take into account the fact that he already had a small factory producing breakfast cereals (this was the only such factory in the ASEAN countries). The AIJV project called for the Philippines to produce this product; therefore, Nestlé Malaysia would have to shut down its plant. On the other hand, the high-technology and capital-intensive chocolate wafer and chocolate dragees operations[5] ('KIT KAT' and 'SMARTIES') could be introduced into Malaysia, and their production would be destined for the other ASEAN markets and possibly later for general export. Since the Philippines was already an important producer of cereal raw materials and Malaysia a major producer of cocoa, this seemed to make sense.

---

[4] Bumiputra means 'son of the soil'.
[5] This operation was in the hands of a separate 'minority' joint venture.

Bouillon would also be produced as an AIJV project, which would be predominantly exported to ASEAN countries.

Another AIJV product was non-dairy creamer. This product, largely used in coffee and tea, would be produced in Thailand. 'COFFEEMATE', the Nestlé brand, was commanding about 50% of the Malaysian market in 1990. The product was imported from the world market, mostly from the US (where Carnation, Nestlé's US subsidiary, was the major producer). Import duties were 25% at the time. Thai production was expected to match US costs and could, of course, be imported into Malaysia at the concessional duty of 2.5%. This would put pressure on the myriad of small local competitors who were buying the product on the world market (mostly from the USA) at dumping prices in the finished form or in bulk and then repackaging it in Malaysia, selling at prices around 30% below Nestlé.

Regarding Malaysia's production of chocolate wafer products (under the 'KIT KAT' brand) and 'SMARTIES' chocolate dragees for the ASEAN region, Mr van Dijk estimated that 80% would be exported. How would product differences, if any, be dealt with? How would packaging be handled? Would new products be introduced? These issues, previously not the market head's responsibility in the ASEAN region, would have to be resolved.

Brunei, the sixth member of ASEAN, was in 1990 a high GNP per capita country because of its oil revenues and small population. The AIJV project did not include any production in Brunei; with such a high income level and low population, it would be a difficult production site. The government of Brunei was not especially interested in industrial development, but the ASEAN rules required that each investment (i.e. the five factories included in the AIJV project) have a participation of 40% by local ASEAN interests. Brunei was assigned 5% of the total investment.

Because of the close relationship with Brunei, Mr van Dijk was made responsible for gaining the necessary investment from some organization in that country. Although Mr. van Dijk had contacts in the government, they were more focused on commercial and market activities than on finance.

Nestlé in the Philippines

The Nestlé operations in the Philippines had a long history as a joint venture with San Miguel Corporation. The joint venture was originally a 60/40 arrangement, with San Miguel having the larger stake but no voting rights. However, over time, San Miguel had become a very successful beer and beverages company, with some interests in food and packaging. The relationship with Nestlé continued to be an excellent one. By 1990, share ownership shifted to a 55% majority for Nestlé. As from the beginning, Nestlé continued to exercise operational control.

As one of the largest companies in the Philippines, San Miguel commanded important influence in the government. However, this influence was not free of controversy. The previous controlling owner, a close ally of deposed President

Marcos, had been expelled and the government 'took control of the company'. Who actually owned San Miguel was still not clear in 1990, although the government did not take a direct lead in the company's operations; in any case, it was being professionally managed.

Despite the unsettled state of the Philippines – notably the anti-Marcos coup and then the armed rebellion of parts of the armed forces, Nestlé Philippines performed well.

Nestlé was careful to maintain an open and correct relationship with the Philippines government. Although the company did not always enjoy ideal labour relations, its position with the government was good. The role played by Ms Lilia Bautista, a senior civil servant in the department of industry, was key to the liaison with the government. Ms Bautista knew the business operations of Nestlé Philippines, having dealt with them on a variety of issues concerning investments, technology transfer and intellectual property rights. She was particularly important to the AIJV project because she was the chairperson of COIME at the time, and thus would be directly involved in the project's administration.

Nestlé's success with its traditional products accounted for the company's five factories in the Philippines. None of them, however, related to the products proposed for the AIJV project. Therefore, the plan was to build a plant at Lipa, south of Manila, to produce breakfast cereals. It was foreseen that the raw materials for this plant would come from local production, largely from the southern islands. The Lipa location was also of interest to the Philippines government in that it would help justify the major port investment in Battangas, near the Lipa factory. It was estimated that 75–80% of the Lipa production would be exported within the AIJV scheme. Further expansion and exports to non-ASEAN markets in Asia were under active consideration.

As for the other AIJV products, soya products and bouillon cubes were already being imported and would therefore not have any impact on local production.

With chocolate, the problem was more acute. Nestlé's main competitor was a company called CFC Corporation owned by John Gokongwei. One of the 'six Taipans', this family company wielded considerable weight both politically and economically. Its very wide range of products touched Nestlé mainly in the chocolate area, where the company's 'me too' product sold for about two-thirds less than Nestlé chocolate. It was estimated to have around half the market. CFC Corporation imported its chocolate product, paying the 40% duty that the Philippines imposed. Thus, imported chocolate from Nestlé (Malaysia) would enjoy a 36% cost reduction over the competition.

Nestlé in Indonesia

Nestlé's Indonesian operations in 1990 were run from the head office in Jakarta, which handled marketing, financial reporting and coordination. Manufacturing plants were located in Kejayan and Waru, both in the environs of Surabaya in East Java, about an hour's flight from Jakarta.

While government approval for setting up the joint venture and getting the relevant tax incentives was going on in Jakarta, a parallel operating plan was being developed in Kejayan, the place where the factory for the Nestlé AIJV project[6] would be located.

The Kejayan site already had a track record, as the Nestlé factory there had been instrumental in working with the Indonesian government to introduce dairy farming concepts. The Nestlé agronomist in Kejayan at the time, Nick Meyer, was a Swiss national who had spent about 15 years in Indonesia, could speak the local language fluently, and was known as a tough but caring person among the farmers. He had built a strong team of local experts who were in a position to persuade the farmers, either individually or through their dairy cooperative, to adopt modern methods of dairy farm management. Dairy farming was a new activity for the farmers, the majority of whom had only small operations, i.e. around 0.25 hectares of land to farm.

Most grew rice and, during the 1980s, had taken up dairy farming with incentives provided by the government and technology transferred by Nestlé. Soya was not the crop of first choice, although several farmers had planted soya as an alternative crop to rice. They had seen the very low income typically earned by farmers improve after dairy farming was introduced, and by 1990 most farmers had the basic amenities, as well as refrigerators and television sets. However, the rural community was still far from modern – for example, both bullock carts and trucks were used to transport people and produce from village to city and port.

Nestlé was confident that, following the success of the dairy project, it could do more to develop a soya farming culture among farmers who were already cultivating soya on a small scale. The decision was taken by Zone 2 management based on the availability of soya beans in Indonesia. The key managers in Kejayan were told that they had been allocated the task of manufacturing soya milk powder.

Meanwhile, the Jakarta Office had applied to the relevant authorities for approval to set up the joint venture and to receive tax incentives, after it was informed in October 1991 that the ASEAN Economic Ministers had approved Nestlé's AIJV projects. By August 1992, the joint venture had a paid up capital of US$10 million and the following shareholders:

Nestlé S.A. (Switzerland)
The Development Bank of Singapore Limited (Singapore)
Lembaga Urusan dan Tabung Haji Pilgrims' Fund (Malaysia)
Rizal Commercial Banking Corporation (Philippines)
Perbadanan Tabung Amanah Islam Brunei (Brunei Darussalam)
Fred B. G. Tumbuan (Indonesia)

The approved project had a planned capacity of 10,000 tons of soya milk powder per annum, of which one-fifth would be consumed domestically and

---

[6] Eventually incorporated as P.T. Nestlé ASEAN Indonesia.

four-fifths exported. In addition, the joint venture would hire about 50 employees, including two expatriates and occupy about 20,000 square metres of land.

The administrators in Jakarta later had to contend with getting approvals for the MOP scheme (import duty concession) so that Nestlé could import the AIJV products made in other ASEAN countries at the concessional tariff rate of 10% of the duty. The other approvals required by Nestlé were granted by the Ministry of Industry, but the MOP approval for the AIJV products had to come from the Ministry of Finance. The Finance Minister, formerly the head of the inland revenue division, was reluctant to approve Nestlé's request. Only after Nestlé proved that the Philippines had given this concession, and the Minister of Industry wrote to the Finance Minister explaining that the products were approved by the ASEAN Economic Ministers, did Nestlé receive the MOP concession in Indonesia.

The soya milk powder manufacturing facility would be located in Kejayan, where there was a milk processing plant already in operation and enough unused land available. Constructing the plant was easily accomplished; it was already operating by December 1993, barely 15 months after approval for the project was obtained. The plant was equipped to de-husk and mill soya beans, and extract soya milk powder by an evaporation process.

At first, the Kejayan plant imported soya beans from Canada and China. The main objective was, however, ultimately to source soya beans locally, a more difficult goal than anticipated. Mr Meyer and his team found that the price of locally grown soya was higher than purchasing it in the international markets. Soya beans from Canada cost Rs875 per kg and from China Rs900 per kg, while the Indonesian variety – a smaller bean and generally a poorer grade – cost Rs1,100 per kg. One reason for the higher price for local soya was that the Indonesian farmers could sell their beans easily. Even low-grade soya beans, usually rejected by Nestlé for its Kejayan facility, could be sold to producers of tempeh, a popular Indonesian food item made from fermented soya. Also, soya beans were planted as an intermediate crop between rice harvests. Rice was sold to the government at controlled prices which were attractive to farmers. While the crops could be rotated in combinations such as soya/rice/soya, or soya/soya/rice or rice/rice/soya, most farmers preferred the cycle favouring rice.

It was assumed that persuading the dairy cooperative to work with Nestlé in soya farming would not be difficult. Mr Meyer and his team had worked with the cooperative for five years and had achieved a high level of cooperation with about 20,000 farmers supplying milk to the Kejayan facility. However, when the Nestlé team approached the dairy cooperative about a similar arrangement whereby the farmers would plant soya, it received a cool reception.

It discovered that, unlike dairy farming, farmers in the area had been planting soya for years and selling their crops to middlemen who were both dealers and financiers to the farmers. Many feared that working with Nestlé on an exclusive basis could hurt their relationships with the middlemen. This could be serious because, in a bad year, they depended on financial assistance from these middlemen to survive. The cooperative's leadership took the view that it should not work with Nestlé on the soya farming project given the sensitive relationship between farmers and the middlemen, and the fact that most of the farmers preferred to plant rice, for which the government paid a good price.

At this point, Mr Meyer and his team went outside the dairy cooperative and approached individual farmers who were closer to Nestlé. A couple of farmers were willing to take a more intensive interest in soya farming. They were given high-quality seeds (from Nestlé's R&D facility in Singapore), fertilizers and pesticides. They were encouraged to form small informal groups, with 6–30 farmers in each one. These groups were provided with the materials to erect simple storage facilities for the soya. Later, they would be loaned grading machines to sort out the higher quality beans for sale to Nestlé and the remainder would go to the open market. Nestlé understood that the farmers would also keep a small portion of the higher quality beans for the middlemen dealers, to maintain that relationship.

As soya was harvested in only three months, the team would be able to see the results quickly. Unfortunately, the first crop was a disaster, as heavy rains had caused low yields. Meanwhile, the farmers who had planted rice had excellent yields, since the wet weather benefited rice farming. Despite this setback, the team persisted and later crops produced much higher yields. The team also showed the farmers how to do line planting, instead of sowing by the broadcast method where seeds fell randomly on the ground. Line planting was more laborious, but it improved yields by a wide margin. Farmers working with Nestlé began achieving yields of 1.5–2 tons/hectare/year, which was 1 ton/hectare/year above the national average.

After a few crops, Nestlé had succeeded in persuading about half its soya farmers to switch to line planting. Despite some success, Mr Meyer's view was that it would take several years before Nestlé could depend entirely on local soya for its Kejayan factory. Thus, Nestlé was still committed to importing a large quantity of foreign soya from China and Canada. Despite this constraint, the factory was able to offer its product at competitive prices.

Its largest buyer was one of Nestlé's factories in the Philippines. Although the Philippines operation had its own source of soya prior to the AIJV project, the cost of production there was even higher than at Kejayan. Filipino farmers also enjoyed substantial protection and heavy duties were imposed on imported soya.

The price of milk was declining in 1990, which could have an impact on the demand for soya milk powder. China was also planning to have its own soya milk factory by 1996, but this was unlikely to be a problem as China was not a large buyer of the Kejayan product.

On the broader competitive front, Nestlé's brand competitors in Indonesia, particularly Kellogg's and Ralston Purina (imported by the indigenous Hero Supermarket chain), had become more aware of the competitive pricing of Nestlé's AIJV products, especially in the breakfast cereals market. They were beginning to lobby the authorities on the need to maintain import duties, but it appeared that they were too late. By 1992, Nestlé was making inroads with its AIJV products.

Nestlé in Singapore

Nestlé started local production in Singapore in 1968, three years after the country gained its independence. Between 1965 and 1984, the Singapore economy grew in real terms at 9% per annum on average. Then, turbulent conditions during the 1970s caused slower growth between 1974 and 1977. However, the country weathered the second oil shock and subsequent world recession without apparent difficulties.

Since the late 1960s, the country's rapid industrialization process meant that the demand for labour consistently exceeded supply. Singapore had a labour force of 1,305,400 at the end of 1989 (60.7% male), representing 48.6% of the population. By 1990, Nestlé operated two local companies, each with one factory, and employed over 360 people. The company continued to invest at a relatively high level, averaging around 12% of sales in 1989 and 1990. Nestlé's 1990 sales were around US$100 million.

Building on Singapore's 'soya culture', Nestlé Singapore was the first to introduce soya powder milk, supplied mainly by Indonesia and the Philippines. Since the Singapore market was relatively free, Nestlé Singapore faced considerable competition in all its major product lines. Singapore was one of the few countries where total trade (i.e. domestic exports and re-exports plus imports) was greater than total GDP. This situation reflected the continued importance of entrepôt trade, with Singapore acting as a regional processing and distribution centre as well as an international manufacturing base.

In 1990, Nestlé Singapore decided to set up a production facility for soya sauce powder. Although Singapore was an unlikely location for the new facility, there were some compelling arguments to go ahead with the project. First, the facility could be built next to the already existing Nestlé research facility. Second, it would be new and would be the only plant in ASEAN. Third, direct employment was low – about 20 people – thus the relatively high wage scale in Singapore was not a major concern. Finally, given the substantial ASEAN content, close to 90%, this would be a highly visible 'gesture' on Nestlé's part.

As the Singapore economy had nothing to lose and everything to gain from the venture, Nestlé counted on the government's support at home as well as in the region. Compared with the other ASEAN countries (Brunei excepted), in 1990 Singapore had:

- the smallest population – 2.6 million
- the highest per capita income – US$12,675
- the lowest inflation rate – 3.4%
- the lowest corporate tax – 27%
- the lowest personal income tax – 30%.

Nestlé in Thailand

Nestlé's non-dairy creamer operations in Thailand began when it bought the Carnation company in 1985. As early as 1979, Carnation had been distributing its

'COFFEEMATE' brand, ordering in bulk from the US and repackaging it for the Thai market. In 1982, the company decided to build a local non-dairy creamer plant, and by December 1983 the new facility came on-stream and production was underway. It had a capacity of 12,000 tons (the minimum efficient scale was 10,000 tons).

In Thailand, the AIJV project was to produce non-dairy creamer (i.e. 'COFFEEMATE') and other products using a non-dairy base. These products would be made from tapioca glucose syrup and hydrogenated palm kernel oil or HPKO. The tapioca glucose syrup could be locally produced, while the HPKO would be mainly imported from Malaysia and (through) Singapore. The final products which utilized the non-dairy creamer made by the AIJV project were:

Products	Brands
Non-dairy creamer	'COFFEEMATE' and 'KREMATOP'
Industrial products (for hotels, airlines and other industries)	'V-KREMA' (food ingredient specialities) and non-dairy creamer for coffee mix and UHT
Instant drinks	Nestlé Food Services' 'HOT COCOA MIX' chocolate drink and 'MILO' mix

The AIJV factory was to be located next to Nestlé's existing facility. Plans had already been made to increase capacity to 30,000 tons by building a new plant capable of producing 18,000 tons. Thus, the AIJV facility was really an expansion project that had already been planned. This arrangement was similar to the set-up in Kejayan, Indonesia.

The plan was that 70% of production would be for the local market and the other 30% for export to ASEAN. Although the domestic operation was officially independent of the AIJV project, it was assumed that after CMT ran out of capacity, it would devise a contract manufacturing agreement with the AIJV facility to ensure supplies to the domestic market. It was expected that by 1993 Nestlé would have 80% of the non-dairy creamer market in Thailand.

Although the required approvals were eventually obtained, Nestlé's AIJV products were being imported at full import duty, paid under protest owing to bureaucratic procedures which delayed implementation at operation level. It was anticipated that the excess duty paid would be refunded.

The AIJV agreement affected the Thai operation in several ways. For example, Thailand dismantled its lines for 'TWIN', a soya product, and sold it to China. As well, its bouillon production was sold to Sri Lanka. Nestlé's Thai operation also began importing more than 5 tons of soya sauce powder a month from the Singapore AIJV company. Among the challenges which the AIJV project encountered in producing for other ASEAN countries were differences in taste. For example, 'COFFEEMATE' and the other non-dairy products going to Taiwan had to be reformulated.

By 1993, sales of 'COFFEEMATE' had jumped 41% in Thailand. Despite competition from parallel imports (from the US), demand for Nestlé products remained strong, in part because Nestlé was prepared to counter the competition by introducing a wide range of packaging to meet different forms of demand and shelf-space opportunities at the supermarkets.

As well, the AIJV project was operating successfully. Demand in Singapore, Indonesia and the Philippines rose after the AIJV started selling its non-dairy creamer (in part, because these countries had to order in bulk from the US and their order sizes were small so that they were not well serviced; the AIJV was quick to meet their orders).

Nestlé reported the following production statistics for 1993:

	'CARNATION' Milk Thailand	AIJV (2 months' production)
Production volume (million tons)	11,433	1,504
Domestic sales	8,483	12
Exports	2,950	1,492

EXHIBIT 1

Institutional Procedures for Approval of AIJV

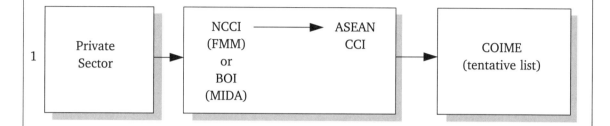

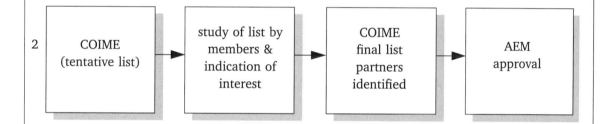

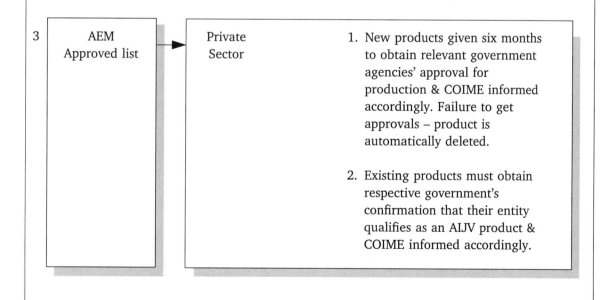

EXHIBIT 2

Final List of AIJV Projects

AIJV Products	Participating Countries
1. Complete assemblies (new) • Tie-rods • Tie-rod ends Parts of complete assemblies (new) • For the tie-rod assembly; housing; studs; bellows; bearings • For the tie-rod end/outer ball joints assembly; studs	Malaysia and Thailand AAE-TRW Components Sdn. Bhd.
2. Frit (new)	Malaysia and Thailand Asian Cerachem Manufacturing Co. Ltd.
3. Motorcycle electrical parts – main switch assembly; speedometer assembly; pilot lamps assembly; stop switch; head light assembly; horn; flasher; relay assembly; audio pilot assembly; wire harness; ignition coil assembly; fuel; gauge hose; rectifier regulator assembly; rectifier assembly and CDI unit assembly; line holder assembly; switch handle assembly (new)	Malaysia and Thailand Siam Electrical Parts Co. Ltd.
4. Slaughtered meat (existing)	Philippines and Thailand Thai Pacific Foods Ltd.
5. Security paper; banknotes; passports; cheques; postage stamps; postage/money orders; tax stamps; identity cards; lottery tickets; bonds/share certificates; land titles; driving licences; vehicle registration certificates; road tax discs; licences; immigration documents; institutional documents; insurance documents	Brunei Darussalam, Malaysia and Thailand ASEAN Security Paper Mills Sdn. Bhd.
6. Ball joints for motor vehicles (new)	Malaysia and Thailand AAE-TRW Components Sdn. Bhd.
7. Steering columns including shafts and linkages (columns include conventional, collapsible and adjustable columns) (new)	Malaysia and Thailand AAE-TRW Components Sdn. Bhd.
8. Ethoxylates, i.e. fatty alcohols, ethoxylates and nonyl phenol ethoxylates (new)	Indonesia, Singapore and Thailand Ethoxylates Manufacturing Pte. Ltd of Singapore
9. Multi-stage, high-powered centrifugal pumps (new)	Singapore and Indonesia Grundfors Pumps Pte. Ltd.
10. Titanium dioxide pigments	Malaysia and Indonesia c/o TAPL (Malaysia) Sdn. Bhd.

11. DAF steering columns/box, DAF steering pumps DAF fuel pumps	Thailand, Philippines and Malaysia H.J. Malal Maskhor
DAF rear axles	Thailand, Philippines, Brunei Darussalam and Malaysia DAF-Tan Chong Autoparts
DAF front axles	Thailand, Philippines, Brunei Darussalam and Malaysia Columbia Motor Corp.
DAF diesel engines 50–99 KWH-HP 115 WP 100–199 KWH-HP 135–272 >200 KWH-HP > 272	Thailand, Philippines, Brunei Darussalam and Malaysia Thai Rung Union Car
12. Enamel	Malaysia and Indonesia P.T. Ridjadson
13. Track-tyre tractors (bulldozers); wheel loaders; motor graders; hydraulic excavator diesel engines; gensets and components of these products	Malaysia and Indonesia P.T. Natra Raya
14. Aluminium hydroxide	Indonesia and Thailand P.T. Alhydro Bintan
15. Breakfast cereals	Indonesia, Malaysia, Philippines and Thailand NESTLE
16. Soya-based milk; soyex meat analogue	Indonesia, Malaysia, Philippines and Thailand NESTLE
17. Chocolate wafer; bouillon tablets	Indonesia, Malaysia, Philippines and Thailand NESTLE
18. Non-dairy coffee creamer	Indonesia, Malaysia, Philippines and Thailand NESTLE

Source: Extracted from COIME Report presented at the Executive Committee Meeting of the ASEAN-CCI Working Group on Industrial Cooperation (WGIC) on 26 July 1991 in Manila, Philippines.

EXHIBIT 3

Scope of Nestlé AIJV Projects

	Indonesia	Malaysia	Philippines	Singapore	Thailand
Project	Soya-based milk Soyex meat analogue	Kit Kat chocolate wafer Smarties Bouillon tablets	Breakfast cereals	Soya sauce powder	Non-dairy coffee creamer
Estimated investment	US$18 million soya-based milk US$2 million soyex	US$15 million Kit Kat US$6 million Smarties US$2 million Bouillon	US$35.5 million	US$12 million	US$15 million
Capacity	12 400 ktonnes soya-based milk (extended from 5400 ktonnes) 1500 ktonnes meat analogue (extended from 500 ktonnes)	2000 ktonnes Kit Kat 1000 ktonnes Smarties 3000 ktonnes Bouillon (extended from 1400 ktonnes)	5000 ktonnes	1000 ktonnes	18 000 ktonnes (extended from 9000 ktonnes)
Basic raw materials	Soya beans Vegetable fat Sugar	Cocoa beans Wheat flour Sugar Local meat/fat	Corn Sugar	Soya beans	Tapioca Vegetable fat
Asean content	90%	65%	70%	90%	90%
Direct/indirect employment	700	1300	500	50	500

Comments					
	Use of Nestlé's own technology developed over 20 years	ASEAN production of Kit Kat/Smarties will replace imports ex UK, Japan, Australia	Extensive use of indigenous corn	New technology	Incremental volume to replace imports from US
	Availability of soya-based milk will reduce ASEAN dependence on more expensive and imported milks	Only ASEAN plant for Kit Kat/Smarties	Use of new technology	Only ASEAN plant	Use local raw materials
	Promote development of soya cultivation: over 10 000 hectares	Extensive use of cocoa, thus higher added-value	Need to depend on Asean volume to justify investment	Will stimulate food production	Export potential outside ASEAN
	This is extension of facilities	Excellent export potential for Kit Kat, Smarties and bouillons	Extensive export potential	New project but now under construction	Extension of facilities
		New project for Kit Kat/Smarties	New project		

2. Competing in Deregulated Markets

PHILIP MORRIS K.K.

This case was prepared by Professor Dominique Turpin as a basis for class discussion rather than to illustrate either effective or ineffective handling of a business situation.

On 7 January 1988, Leonard D. Spelt, Marketing Manager of Philip Morris K.K. (PMKK), had gathered his marketing team at the PMKK headquarters in Tokyo to discuss the recent decision of competitor R.J. Reynolds to introduce a ¥200[1] cigarette brand in the Japanese market. After having reviewed and discussed all the options available, Leo Spelt had returned to his office to ponder the various alternatives which had surfaced during one of the most exhausting meetings he had had in Tokyo.

Philip Morris Companies Inc.

Based in New York City, Philip Morris Companies Inc. was the largest and most diversified tobacco, food and beverage company in the US and one of the three largest in the world. With an operating income of $4.2 billion out of operating revenues of $27.6 billion for fiscal year 1987 (*refer to* **Exhibit 1**), Philip Morris Companies Inc. was also ranked tenth in size among the US Fortune 500 industrials.

Since its early days in 1847, when Philip Morris, Esq. opened a tobacco shop in Bond Street, London, Philip Morris' core business had focused on the tobacco industry. In 1902, Philip Morris & Co. Ltd. was incorporated in the US (in New York) by Gustav Eckmeyer, Philip Morris' sole agent in the US for importing and selling the English-made cigarettes 1872. In 1919, a new firm owned by US shareholders acquired the US Philip Morris Company and incorporated it in Virginia under the name Philip Morris & Co. Ltd., Inc., which in turn became Philip Morris Incorporated in 1955.

The present organization had been set up in 1985 when the corporate framework of Philip Morris Incorporated was restructured to form Philip Morris Companies Inc., a holding company located in New York City. In 1988, Philip Morris Companies Inc. was still concentrating mainly on the tobacco industry. The two core companies, Philip Morris USA and Philip Morris International, were accounting for 27% and 25% respectively of Philip Morris Companies Inc.'s total operating revenues in 1987. In the 1980s, Philip Morris Companies Inc. also made major diversification moves into the food industry by acquiring Oscar Mayer in 1981 and then General Foods Corporation in November 1985. In 1970,

---

[1] Average exchange rate in 1987: ¥145 = $1.00.

Philip Morris Companies Inc. had also acquired the world's second largest brewer, the Miller Brewing Company, which currently accounted for 10% of total operating revenues. Financial services and real estate were the fourth major business activity of Philip Morris Companies Inc., representing 2% of total operating revenues.

Several of Philip Morris' cigarette brands, such as Marlboro, were among the most popular in the world. Originally introduced in 1924 as an unfiltered cigarette, Marlboro had rapidly become Philip Morris' flagship cigarette brand after being repositioned in 1955 as a full-flavoured cigarette for men. Supported by the first Marlboro cowboy advertising campaign, its red and white package soon became familiar. In 1987, despite a decline in the total consumption of cigarettes in the US market, Marlboro had gained market share in the US for the 23rd consecutive year to approach a 25% share of the US cigarette market. Worldwide, Marlboro has also continued to be the best-selling cigarette brand since 1971.

The success of leading full-priced brands, e.g. Benson & Hedges, Merit, Virginia Slims, Parliament, Lark, Chesterfield and Philip Morris, also reinforced Philip Morris' leading position in the world tobacco industry. Philip Morris International's products were sold in more than 160 countries around the world. In free competition[2] markets, Philip Morris International enjoyed leading market share. For example, in the European Economic Community, Philip Morris' aggregate market share for tobacco exceeded 20%.

Developing established brands and introducing new ones had traditionally been Philip Morris Companies Inc.'s strategy for increasing volume and market share worldwide. In particular, Philip Morris International had seen great potential in Asia, where lowered trade barriers in several markets had recently allowed Philip Morris' brands to compete more effectively with products marketed by local government monopolies. Since Philip Morris' share in most international cigarette markets was far below its US level, Philip Morris' executives felt that there was considerable room for future growth in this part of the world.

Philip Morris K.K.

Philip Morris had been present in Japan since the early 1950s, using Mitsui & Co., the trading company of the giant Mitsui Group, as the agent for importing its cigarettes into Japan. Its competitor, R.J. Reynolds, had designated Mitsubishi Corporation, the trading company of the Mitsubishi Group, as its import agent. In Japan, the products of Philip Morris' diversified businesses, like General Foods and Miller, were managed separately from PMKK through joint ventures with local companies.

As tobacco in Japan was a government monopoly until 1985, Mitsui & Co. was basically handling Philip Morris' cigarettes on behalf of the monopoly corporation.

---

[2] Markets without state monopolies.

In the late 1970s, Philip Morris entered into an association with Nissho Iwai, another large Japanese trading company, when Nissho Iwai acquired the distributor for Liggett & Myers Tobacco Co. in Japan. Liggett & Myers was an independent US tobacco company, producing several cigarette brands – Lark, L&M and Eve. In the early 1970s, Philip Morris had acquired the rights to produce and distribute Liggett & Myers' products outside the US. Following Nissho Iwai's acquisition of Liggett & Myers' distributor in Japan, Philip Morris K.K. (PMKK) renegotiated the distribution of all its tobacco products with Mitsui & Co. and Nissho Iwai. As a result of the new agreement, Mitsui & Co. became the exclusive distributor of all PMKK's brands in Eastern Japan, while Nissho Iwai became PMKK's sole distributor in the Western part of Japan. With the liberalization of the Japanese tobacco industry in 1985, Philip Morris K.K. was established as a wholly owned subsidiary of Philip Morris Companies Inc.

PMKK developed all Philip Morris' marketing activities in Japan. PMKK's tasks also included initiating and coordinating product development and production of cigarettes with the US. Jack Howard, Vice President of PMKK, expected to continue importing Philip Morris products so long as the parameters for the cigarette industry in Japan remained as they were at present. More than ever in 1988, production costs for the tobacco industry in Japan were higher than in the US. Moreover, since the manufacture of cigarettes in Japan was still the monopoly of Japan Tobacco Inc. (JTI), PMKK did not plan to consider manufacturing locally in the near future.

At this stage in its development, PMKK's objective was to grow as fast as possible by offering consumer products of the highest quality and by maintaining a good balance between market share and profitability. A major objective for PMKK was also to retain and expand its dominant share in the fast growing imported segment. In terms of product diversification, Jack Howard believed that: "this had to be put into context gradually. We want to build a good durable image for franchises which we can then expand over time. Therefore, we want to concentrate on a few good franchises that can be developed. Obviously, there will be new franchises coming on the market, and each of the existing franchises can also be expanded. Lark is a good example of franchise diversification. We now have this brand in various formats and sizes, which were introduced into the market over time."

The Tobacco Industry

In 1988, the world tobacco industry (90% cigarettes) included: free markets (such as West Germany, The Netherlands, the UK and some developing countries); state monopolies (such as Austria, Spain and most communist countries); and officially free markets, where customs or administrative regulations limited access to foreign products (such as the US, Canada, France, South Africa, etc.). The majority of cigarette consumption (60%) occurred in the free world, with the communist countries accounting for the other 40%. The world's leading four tobacco producers were: China (960 billion units); the US (682 billion units), the

USSR (380 billion units) and Japan (320 billion units). During the last 20 years, the world tobacco industry had doubled; the 1988 volume was estimated at 5.2 trillion units.

The international market had gradually become an oligopoly. Five major companies – Philip Morris, Brown & Williamson (an affiliate of British American Tobacco Co.), R.J. Reynolds, American Tobacco Co. and Rothmans International (also known as Tobacco Exporters International or TEI) – represented 80% of total free market sales volume (*refer to **Exhibit 2***). With more than a decade of external pressure from anti-smoking campaigns and internal pressure for growth, the six largest multinational companies had become increasingly diversified, moving into paper, food and beverages, cosmetics, packaging, financial services, real estate, etc.

The Japanese Tobacco Market

Japan was the second largest tobacco market in the non-communist world; in 1987, 308 billion cigarettes at a total retail value of ¥3 trillion were sold (a decline of 6% in volume and 20.5% in value over the previous fiscal year). Although smoking was declining among Japanese adult males,[3] the 62.5% rate of smokers was among the highest in the developed world. As S. Katayama, a PMKK Group Brand Manager, explained: "Japan offers great opportunities for inter-national tobacco companies. Not only will no one tell you to put out your cigarette at a bar or restaurant, but the practice of keeping a cigarette box and matching table lighter in the meeting rooms of many Japanese companies is a tradition still being maintained." Among females, only 12.5% claimed to be smokers. However, experts believed the figure was much higher, as many women smokers were reluctant to admit this fact to public researchers.

The Japanese cigarette market, just as in Europe or the US, was experiencing growth in flue-cured tobacco products and a decline in the dark tobacco sector. Flue-cured tobacco is a bright yellow tobacco to which flavouring ingredients are added to create distinctive aromas. Flue-cured tobaccos could be divided into several types; American blended and straight Virginia of the blend tobacco variety were the most common. Most cigarettes sold in the US and Europe were the American blended variety. However, in the UK and most Commonwealth countries, the straight Virginia tobacco products were overwhelmingly the most popular. The Japanese consumer's taste was somewhere between these two varieties. The really distinctive feature of the cigarettes in Japan, however, was the traditional charcoal filter imposed over time by the Japan Tobacco Inc. monopoly. These charcoal filters were made of tiny porous charcoal spheres that reduced the tar and nicotine while giving a smoother taste and aroma.

Until recently, international tobacco firms had traditionally commanded only a marginal share of the Japanese market. Despite a 1972 licensing agreement with Japan Tobacco and Salt Public Corporation (JTS) to manufacture Marlboro

---

[3] Over 20 years old.

cigarettes, Philip Morris had never achieved the significant size in Japan that it had typically enjoyed in free markets. High import duties (up to 350% in 1978) and the government monopoly had meant that Japan was practically a closed market for foreign tobacco manufacturers.

Before the market was liberalized in the early 1980s, PMKK had been confronted by a number of tariff and non-tariff barriers. Jack Howard had found that restricting the distribution of cigarette products to a given number of retailers had seriously limited the potential of PMKK's business. He also believed that the high duties imposed on imported cigarettes had forced PMKK to increase its prices to the point of being priced out of most of the market, as the Japanese consumer was not willing to buy a given product at any price.

Under pressure from the US since 1978 to accelerate the opening of its market, Japan had started in the early 1980s to progressively liberalize its tobacco industry. In April 1985, the JTS' monopoly was removed and, as a private company, became the Japan Tobacco Inc. (JTI). As part of the Japanese programme to liberalize the tobacco market, retailers were then allowed to handle tobacco imports and to receive the same 10% margin on imported as on domestically made cigarettes. Moreover, import duties had been eliminated by April 1987, and promotional activities including advertising were being permitted up to a limit of 6,300 GRPs[4] per brand family for television advertising. As a result, international tobacco firms saw their sales jump two and a half times – to 32 billion cigarettes in 1987 and their market share grow from 2.0% in 1984 to as high as 8.4% in a mere three years (*refer to* **Exhibit 3).**

The rapid success of international tobacco companies in Japan could be explained by their careful consideration of the Japanese market. Most salesmen used by the trading companies to distribute foreign tobacco products in Japan were being paid by the international tobacco companies. By listening to advice from their salesforce, foreign producers were able to develop products especially tailored to the Japanese market. For example, Winston and Camel brands did not have a charcoal filter in the US, but they did in Japan. The nicotine and tar contents of Kent Mild and Philip Morris Lights were kept at the same level as in Mild Seven Lights, the competing domestic brand. Another part of the foreign companies' strategy had been to keep the retail margin on foreign cigarettes higher than on Japanese cigarettes. Although retail margins were set at 10% of the retail price, the higher price of foreign cigarettes enabled retailers to receive a higher contribution. In S. Katayama's opinion, this was one reason that foreign cigarettes had become more competitive at the distribution stage. Moreover, S. Katayama believed that foreign cigarettes had a 'high-class' image among Japanese consumers. He felt that this image, coupled with good marketing and large advertising expenditures, were the key success factors which had helped foreign tobacco firms to rapidly gain their share of the Japanese market.

---

[4] GRP (Gross Rating Point) equalled the sum of all airings of a programme or spot announcements during a given time period. For example, a once-a-week programme constantly recording a 15% rating (15% of TV homes) received 60 GRPs for a 4-week period.

Japan Tobacco Inc.

After its privatization in April 1985, the presidency of JTI was assumed by Minoru Nagaoka, a former vice minister in the Ministry of Finance (the most powerful position in Japan's public administration). In December 1987, JTI's sales were predicted to drop by 2.3% compared with the previous term (ending 31 March 1987) to ¥2,875 trillion, while current profits were expected to dip sharply by 20% to ¥85 billion. "Japan Tobacco is following a rocky path," President Nagaoka stated.

In response to this situation, JTI had mobilized its 2,700 sales personnel in a desperate attempt to fight back. Japan Tobacco Inc. spent only 0.13% of sales on advertising compared with the 3% average outlayed by US companies. In 1986–87, JTI had also come out with 30 new products, compared with 27 during the preceding 5-year period. As a result, Japanese consumers were able to watch TV commercials which showed a female revue at the Crazy Horse in Paris where the dancers used their legs to spell out the letters LIBERA, one of the company's newest brands. Another commercial depicted happy US college students on campus, smoking JTI's Mild Seven FK cigarettes. JTI had also changed its marketing strategy by focusing less on traditional 'mom and pop' shops and more on large national retailers.

JTI's major handicap in competing with foreign brands was that it had to use a domestic tobacco leaf which cost three to five times more than an imported leaf. Japan Tobacco Inc. was required by law to purchase the entire domestic production of tobacco ¥200 billion in fiscal year 1986. Since the same amount of imported tobacco would cost only ¥70 billion, JTI was spending an extra ¥130 billion a year to abide by a political decision made by the Japanese government to protect domestic farmers. As a result, JTI was permitted to import only around one-third of its needs from abroad. This tobacco was subsequently blended with domestic tobacco.

Ever since the tobacco industry monopoly had been eliminated in Japan, JTI's share of the market had steadily declined. However, Mr Kazue Obata, special adviser in the marketing and planning section of Japan Tobacco Inc., had predicted in a recent press interview that Japan would not experience a serious penetration of foreign tobacco as had happened in France or Italy, where international tobacco firms had gained shares of 40% and 30% respectively. Mr Obata argued that Japanese employees were striving for higher sales and were not like the Italians and French who 'had no loyalty'. He also maintained that JTI's experience with Philip Morris' Marlboro brand had taught the company much about American blend tobacco. "We know the market intimately," he said.

In the meantime, Philip Morris had been able to maintain its share at around 60% of the total foreign tobacco market. At the end of 1987, JTI still commanded 91% of the cigarette market; PMKK was a distant second with a 5.2% share of market (refer to **Exhibit 4**). Although JTI's market share was still comfortably large, some industry analysts believed that JTI would be under pressure to close one of its 32 factories whenever it lost two points of market share to the competition. However, Leo Spelt felt that the relationship between the loss of market share and factories closing was much more complex than that.

Other Competitors

With JTI as the dominant manufacturer and distributor of cigarettes in Japan, competition in the imported markets clearly came from the other major international tobacco manufacturers: Brown & Williamson (B&W), R.J. Reynolds (RJR), American Tobacco Co. and Tobacco Exporters International (TEI). At the end of 1987, these four groups together with Philip Morris commanded 99% of the imported cigarette segment in Japan. In the imported brands market, PMKK commanded a 62% market share of this segment by the end of 1987, followed by B&W and RJR with a 25% and 9% market share respectively (*refer to Exhibit 3*). The three largest international competitors (Philip Morris, B&W and R.J. Reynolds) were competing mainly in the ¥220 or ¥250 segments with some of their traditional international brands: Kent, Lucky Strike and John Player Special (JPS) for B&W; Salem, Camel, Winston and More for R.J. Reynolds. JTI, on the other hand, had a broader product line with one brand in the ¥200 segment (Hi-Lite) and one in the ¥130 segment (Echo). (*Refer to Exhibits 5–7.*)

Distribution of Cigarettes in Japan

The distribution of cigarettes in Japan remained almost unchanged after the monopoly was lifted from the Japanese market. Unlike in the US, distributors were not easily chosen, and all shops selling tobacco had to be licensed. Moreover, supermarkets could not use tobacco as a speciality product for big sales, by offering a lower price than usual. Haiso, the company associated with JTI for distribution of tobacco in Japan, continued to distribute PMKK's products to the retailers through five regional operating companies. These wholesaling companies were in turn serving a total of 260,755 licensed retailers. Stores selling only tobacco, as well as liquor and grocery stores, each represented roughly 14% of the total cigarette retail sales in Japan.

A major characteristic of the Japanese tobacco market was the importance of vending machines in distributing cigarettes. In 1987, there were more than 1.6 million vending machines installed along Japanese streets (more than one machine for every 100 inhabitants) distributing almost everything from canned coffee, beer and whisky to batteries, newspapers and magazines, telephone cards, and even Bibles. The 428,000 vending machines installed in restaurants, bars, etc., as well as the ones along the streets, were used exclusively to distribute cigarettes. They accounted for 40% of all cigarettes sold in Japan. Typically, vending machines were owned by retailers (tobacco and/or liquor stores, restaurants, hotels, news-stands, etc.), although manufacturers would also lease or give away some machines. Each cigarette vending machine had 6–25 columns. Typically, retailers would arrange the cigarettes in the columns according to brand popularity. Generally, a retailer with a 12-column machine would place the 12 best-selling brands in the 12 columns. Since JTI dominated the cigarette market, distributors for foreign manufacturers had to convince retailers to allocate enough columns to them for their respective brands. Given the frequent difficulties in gaining adequate space, some distributors would buy columns by offering free products or financial incentives to major tobacco retailers.

In addition to importing, Mitsui & Co. and Nissho Iwai employed a sales merchandising force of slightly over 500 people whose function was to merchandise PMKK's products at the retail level. In other words, Haiso only acted as a distributor, while Nissho Iwai, Mitsui & Co. and PMKK acted as partners in marketing, advertising and merchandising. Competitors had a similar salesforce, ranging from 2,700 sales representatives for JTI to 200 salesmen each for B&W and R.J. Reynolds.

PMKK's Product Line

The Japanese cigarette market could be segmented in many different ways (sex, brands, imported versus domestic, cigarette lengths, etc.). However, PMKK relied primarily on two major dimensions: price and flavour (i.e. tar and nicotine contents). (See *Exhibits 8–10* for marketing information.)

In January 1988, Philip Morris K.K. was distributing three major brands. For many years, Lark had been PMKK's best-selling brand (*refer to Exhibit 11*). To meet smokers' changing tastes, PMKK had progressively extended the Lark line, adding Lark Milds KS (King Size), Lark Milds 100's and Lark Super Lights. Lark Milds KS was now the best-selling imported brand in Japan. At the end of 1987, the Lark family represented 56% of PMKK's cigarette sales in Japan, while PM, PMKK's second best-selling brand, accounted for another 24%. Parliament represented 11% of PMKK's share of sales volume. The Marlboro family was produced under licence by JTI, but it did not account for a significant share of the Japanese market (*refer to Exhibit 12*).

Despite PMKK's success with light and mild cigarettes in Japan, Philip Morris had never introduced any new product in the ¥200 segment (*refer to Exhibit 13*). Moreover, the 5% share of the Japanese market gained by Hi-Lite, the only brand in this price segment (launched by JTI), was declining (*refer to Exhibit 12*). In addition, given the time constraints with New Year approaching, there had been little time for the PMKK marketing team to investigate the overall implications of the new ¥200 segment.

The RJR Challenge

Through retailers, Philip Morris K.K. first heard rumours in the middle of November 1987 about a new brand introduction by R.J. Reynolds, but it was not until 15 December 1987 that Leo Spelt received confirmation of RJR's decision to introduce Islands Lights in Japan at ¥200 as of 1 February 1988. Immediately, PMKK's marketing department decided to evaluate possible alternatives to counter the RJR initiative. That same day, a project time schedule was made for potential development of a new product, including packaging, research and commercial production. PMKK executives were not familiar with RJR's Islands Lights brand, since this brand had never been introduced in the US or in any other market before. It seemed, therefore, that Islands Lights was either a code name for an existing RJR brand or a completely new brand tailored to the Japanese market.

Because of the word 'Lights', L. D. Spelt and PMKK brand managers assumed that Islands Lights would be positioned in Japan in the low-tar segment to compete with other light and mild cigarette brands. (Tobacco manufacturers were using either the adjective 'light' or 'mild' to label low-tar cigarettes, but no particular definition had been attached to either word.) In Japan, as in other industrialized markets, the low-tar segment had been growing more rapidly than other segments as smokers increasingly considered high-tar cigarettes less healthy.

In 1987, the low-tar segment accounted for 34% of the total cigarette market in Japan. By comparison, the full flavour (16 mg+) and the medium tar (11.1–16 mg) segments, representing respectively 15% and 51% of the market, were slowly declining by 1–2% a year. The ultra-low-tar segment (below 6 mg) was quite stable with 0.10% of the cigarette market in Japan (*refer to Exhibit 10*).

After the confirmation of RJR's decision to introduce Islands Lights in Japan, Leo Spelt and other marketing executives had tried to determine RJR's motivations and the objectives of its strategic move into the ¥200 segment. In Leo Spelt's view, R.J. Reynolds had been less successful than other international tobacco firms in the Japanese market. Its Camel brand, launched in 1983 by RJR Japan, had never achieved a significant market share in Japan. Moreover, in 1987, its Winston Lights brand had been ruined overnight by a report from Japanese authorities that Winston Lights cigarettes contained traces of a herbicide. This instant blow to R.J. Reynolds meant that Salem, a menthol cigarette, was that company's only successful brand in Japan.

Leo Spelt had almost no information on how much R.J. Reynolds would spend on advertising and promotion to launch Islands Lights, but judging from his own experience in Japan, he estimated that the launch would require around $20 million, with a potential payback period of two to three years (quite short by industry standards; over five years was typical).

The Alternatives

During the meeting with L.D. Spelt, the marketing team had outlined the various alternatives for PMKK:

1. Joining forces with JTI: Since RJR's launch of Islands Lights on 1 February 1988 had been confirmed, various options had been reviewed. George R. Austin, President of PMKK, had considered meeting with Mr K. Katsukawa from JTI to discuss the ¥200 issue as well as a possible import licensing agreement for Philip Morris' L&M Milds brand. This idea had been triggered by PMKK's reluctance to compete directly with R.J. Reynolds in a price

segment that meant smaller margins. Moreover, to distribute a new ¥200 segment in vending machines would mean convincing the owners either to grant Philip Morris one additional column in their machines or have Philip Morris lose a column containing a more expensive, higher contribution brand.

2. L&M Milds, which belonged to Philip Morris through its agreement with Liggett & Myers (an independent US tobacco manufacturer), was one brand being considered for licencing to JTI as part of PMKK's counter-move against the RJR initiative. Philip Morris International had introduced L&M in West Germany where it had achieved a market share of 1.3% in 1987. In the US, L&M's share under Liggett & Myers in this same year was 0.3%.

   Mr George R. Austin was not sure how JTI would respond to his proposal, since two obstacles had to be overcome. First, producing L&M Milds under licence would force JTI to import more American tobacco leaves, which would mean having to renegotiate its import policy with the Japanese authorities. Second, JTI management would also have to negotiate for the support of JTI labour union leaders, who had a strong voice in JTI. Mr Austin had proposed that JTI equally share the costs of launching this new brand by having PMKK handle all advertising and promotional costs. George Austin believed that this licensing agreement could benefit both JTI and PMKK, providing an estimated additional $1 million per month to JTI and a breakeven position for PMKK.

   If JTI were to decline Mr Austin's offer, PMKK could possibly launch L&M Mild or another new brand alone. However, this new product had to be imported from the US with the technical modifications necessary to meet the tastes of Japanese consumers.

3. L&M Milds in West Germany: Philip Morris had launched L&M in West Germany in 1982 following a competitive move in 1980 from Reemtsma, a local tobacco manufacturer. Until the end of the 1970s and early 1980s, Reemtsma had been the leader in the German cigarette industry. Then the company steadily began losing market share. One of its brands, Ernte, was seriously affected by competition from Marlboro. German discount chains, locked into heavy competition among themselves, had added generic brands of cigarettes to their product lines. These generics were being marketed about 25% below the prevailing price level for nationally advertised brands, which were retailing at DM3.80–4.00.[5] To counter this market trend, Reemtsma launched a new brand named 'West' in 1980. The advertising, packaging, etc. were clearly aimed at the market for Marlboro cigarettes. However, despite an expenditure of DM150 million, the West brand had captured only 0.4% share of the market by the end of 1982. After losing that battle, Reemtsma decided to cut the price of its West brand further – from DM3.80 to DM3.30. This time, West's market share grew rapidly, reaching 5% within a three-month period.

   Philip Morris Germany followed West's dramatic increase with concern, since it definitely affected Philip Morris' leading brands. The company chose L&M because all the other brands in the German market were either too small

---

[5] US$1 = DM1.8 in 1982.

or too narrow in appeal. At only DM3.00 for a pack of 19 cigarettes, L&M was the lowest priced national brand on the market. It was advertised as an international brand and supported with readily available media. In order to enhance the brand's image, only box packs were used. L&M was first introduced in the southern part of Germany where it rapidly achieved a 15% market share, thus becoming the second best-selling brand after Marlboro. L&M was later launched in the northern part of Germany.

By mid-1983, other major cigarette marketers had also reacted. L&M was no longer the only low-priced brand on the market. All major brands had lost market share to new low-priced competitors that had appeared everywhere. When one major competitor rolled back its prices from DM3.80 to DM3.50 for its leading brand, others including Philip Morris followed. L&M and other low-priced brands lost appeal and consumers switched back to national brands. In 1987, L&M had 1.3% of the German market, a 0.2% loss over the previous year. In 1987, leading brands, including Philip Morris' Marlboro, regained their dominant positions and price levels stabilized. At the end of the German cigarette war, Philip Morris had regained its former competitive position, albeit at a somewhat lower price level than before. The overall cost of launching L&M was $10 million.

While reflecting again on the German episode, Leo Spelt believed that the German price war and its successive price cuts had had major financial repercussions for Philip Morris in Germany. In Tokyo, Leo Spelt wanted to minimize the financial risk linked to a potential price war in Japan. Leo Spelt wondered whether the L&M advertising concept currently being used in Germany could work in Japan as well, if PMKK decided to introduce L&M in the Japanese market. However, in any case, PMKK could not use any TV commercial from Germany since tobacco advertising on television had been banned there. Moreover, Leo Spelt felt that L&M as a brand had two major weaknesses; first, L&M was difficult for Japanese consumers to pronounce, and second that name would not mean anything In Japan.

4. Cambridge: Because of these considerations, Cambridge, a Philip Morris brand of cigarettes made with a flue-cured tobacco, was also being considered as a launch possibility in the ¥200 segment. Cambridge could easily be pronounced by Japanese consumers, and the name had more potential for identification. However, Cambridge had not been successful in the US market. Sold as a generically-priced product, Cambridge had been positioned in the low-price segment with the help of discount coupons. In the US, the product was advertised in newspapers and magazines, but was not supported by image advertising. As a result, no advertising concept could be imported for use on Japanese television. Although Leo Burnett Kyodo Co. Ltd., one of the international advertising agencies under contract with PMKK, had its office in the same building as Philip Morris K.K., Akio Kobayashi, a PMKK brand manager, described getting approval for a new advertising campaign as a 'nightmare' and 'too risky'. Mr Kobayashi said: "Any new advertising concept must be approved by Philip Morris' Asian headquarters in Hong Kong and then by the head office in New York City. Developing an effective advertising and

promotional campaign in just three weeks is a big risk that PMKK should avoid. By rushing too fast, we could easily blow up the whole thing."

5. Philip Morris Superlights: During the meeting, A. Kobayashi suggested that PMKK reduce the price of either Philip Morris Lights or Philip Morris Superlights from ¥220 to ¥200. In Mr Kobayashi's view, repositioning one of these two brands was the quickest and safest way to respond to the Islands challenge. However, pricing issues on tobacco products had to be cleared first with the Japanese government, and it typically took 30–60 days to obtain government approval.

6. Other alternatives: Other options discussed during the meeting were the following: PMKK could choose to undercut R.J. Reynolds by launching L&M or Cambridge at ¥180 for a pack of 20 cigarettes. The exchange rate between the dollar and the yen during fiscal year 1987 had been favourable to imports into Japan, and a ¥180 price would still leave PMKK with a positive profit margin.

Another alternative was either to offer L&M or Cambridge at ¥200 for a pack of 22 cigarettes or ¥220 for 25. Although some retooling in the US manufacturing facilities would be required Philip Morris had ready production capacity to implement this option. 'Players' was the only brand sold in the US with 25 cigarettes in a pack, and its success had been limited. Larger packs would not be a problem for distribution in Japan, however, since Japanese vending machines could handle both the 22- and 25-pack sizes.

Leo Spelt's task now was to review all the alternatives discussed during one of the most animated meetings he had ever witnessed during his career at PMKK. It was also important that decisions regarding the marketing programme be resolved quickly. How should the company allocate the sales force, what advertising methods would be adequate, should soft or hard packs be used, etc.? The one point on which everyone had agreed was: it was essential that any new product launched by PMKK in Japan be a winner.

EXHIBIT 1

Financial Data
(in $million except per share amounts)

	1987	1986	1985
Operating revenues	$27,695	$25,409	$15,694
Net earnings	1,842	1,478	1,255
Earnings per share	7.75	6.20	5.24
Dividends per share	3.15	2.475	2.00
Funds from operations per share	11.73	9.28	7.41
Percentage increase over previous year			
Operating revenues	9.0%	59.2%	15.6%
Net earnings	24.7%	17.7%	41.3%
Earnings per share	25.0%	18.3%	44.6%
Dividends declared per share	27.3%	23.8%	17.6%
Operating revenues			
Philip Morris U.S.A.	$7,576	$7,053	$6,611
Philip Morris International Inc.	7,068	5,638	3,991
General Foods Corporation	9,946	9,664	1,632
Miller Brewing Company	3,105	3,054	2,914
Other*	–	–	–
Total operating revenues	$27,695	$25,409	$15,964
Income from operations			
Philip Morris U.S.A.	$2,683	$2,366	$2,047
Philip Morris International	631	492	413
General Foods Corporation	722	741	120
Miller Brewing Company	170	154	132
Philip Morris Credit Corporation**	51	55	23
Mission Viejo Realty Group Inc.**	21	18	12
Other*	19	(8)	45
	$4,297	$3,818	$2,792
Amortization of goodwill	104	111	32
Total income from operating companies**	$4,193	$3,707	$2,760
Compounded average annual growth rate	1987–82	1987–77	
Operating revenues	19.0%	18.2%	
New earnings	18.7%	18.6%	
Earnings per share	20.0%	18.7%	

* Income from operating companies is income before corporate expense and interest and other debt expense, net.
** Represents equity in net earnings of these unconsolidated subsidiaries.
*** Composed of The Seven-Up Company, of which substantially all the operations were sold in 1985.
General Foods Corporation was acquired in November 1985. Accordingly, consolidated results shown above include the operating results of General Foods Corporation after October 1985.

Source: Philip Morris Companies Inc., *Annual Report 1987*.

(continued)

EXHIBIT 1 (continued)

Selected Financial Data: 15-year Review

Summary of operations	1987	1986	1985
Operating revenues	$27,695	$25,409	$15,964
United States export sales	1,592	1,193	923
Cost of sales			
Cost of products sold	11,264	11,039	6,318
Federal excise taxes	2,085	2,075	2,049
Foreign excise taxes	3,331	2,653	1,766
Income from operating companies	4,193	3,707	2,760
Interest and other debt expense, net	685	770	308
Earnings before income taxes	3,348	2,811	2,329
Pre-tax profit margin	12.1%	11.1%	14.6%
Provision for income taxes	$1,506	$1,333	$1,074
Net earnings	1,842	1,478	1,255
Earnings per share	7.75	6.20	5.24
Dividends declared per share	3.15	2.475	2.00
Weighted average shares	238	239	240
Capital expenditures	$718	$678	$347
Annual depreciation	564	514	367
Property, plant and equipment (net)	6,582	6,237	5,684
Inventories	4,154	3,836	3,827
Working capital	1,396	1,432	1,926
Total assets	19,145	17,642	17,429
Long-term debt	5,222	5,945	7,331
Total debt	6,378	6,912	8,009
Deferred income taxes	1,288	994	872
Stockholders' equity	6,823	5,655	4,737
Funds from operations	2,789	2,214	1,775
Net earnings reinvested	1,093	888	776
Common dividends declared as % of net earnings	40.6%	39.9%	38.1
Book value per common share	$28.83	$23.77	$19.85
Market price of common share, high–low	$124\frac{1}{2}$–$72\frac{5}{8}$	78–$43\frac{7}{8}$	$47\frac{5}{8}$–31
Closing price year-end	$85\frac{3}{8}$	$71\frac{7}{8}$	$44\frac{1}{3}$
Price/earnings ratio year-end	11	11	8
Number of common shares outstanding at year-end	237	238	239
Number of employees	113,000	111,000	114,000

Note: Certain amounts appearing in the previous years' consolidated statements of earnings have been reclassified to conform with the current year's presentation.

Source: Philip Morris Companies Inc., *Annual Report 1987*.

EXHIBIT 2

Worldwide Cigarette Industry – Unit Volume Estimates (millions)

		1980	1981	1982	1983	1984	1985	1986	1987
Total world industry		4,474,400	4,571,000	4,583,800	4,563,700	4,700,000	4,850,000	4,975,000	5,118,000
US industry		620,500	638,100	614,000	597,000	599,700	594,700	583,500	571,000
World minus US		3,853,900	3,932,900	3,969,800	3,966,700	4,100,300	4,255,300	4,393,060	4,547,000
Philip Morris	Total	429,550	448,742	447,107	449,458	469,805	488,468	506,835	540,780
	USA	191,191	199,436	204,429	204,677	211,575	213,590	214,573	215,559
	Int'l	238,359	249,306	242,678	244,781	258,230	274,878	292,262	325,221
BAT	Total	548,900	563,200	550,000	522,500	522,000	543,000	554,000	542,000
	US	84,490	87,750	83,180	68,520	67,990	70,700	67,970	62,740
	Int'l	464,410	475,450	466,820	453,980	454,010	472,300	486,030	479,760
R.J. Reynolds	Total	283,710	295,280	289,390	271,620	274,440	274,900	278,020	284,290
	US	201,710	207,180	208,790	187,520	189,740	188,100	188,320	185,390
	Int'l	82,000	88,100	80,600	84,100	84,700	86,800	89,700	98,900
American Tob.	Total	106,005	95,515	87,265	85,455	81,295	79,500	77,000	79,500
	US	66,630	59,770	55,350	51,500	47,250	44,800	41,810	39,440
	Int'l	39,375	35,745	31,915	33,955	34,045	34,700	35,190	40,060
Rothmans	Total	162,011	158,866	154,183	151,400	145,700	138,500	133,000	134,400
	US	500	500	500	500	500	400	500	400
	Int'l	161,511	158,366	158,683	150,900	145,200	138,100	132,500	134,000
J.T.S.	Total	304,500	308,208	310,100	307,400	307,100	304,500	296,500	280,000
Liggett & Myers	US	14,350	15,450	17,900	28,600	34,000	29,200	22,730	20,280
Lorillard	US	60,200	57,560	54,360	55,000	48,900	48,100	47,440	46,970

EXHIBIT 3

Japan Market

	1983	1984	1985	1986	1987
(1) Total market					
Sales volume (billion sticks)					
Industry	311.7	312.5	310.5	309.2	307.6
Domestic	306.4	306.1	303.3	298.6	281.7
Import	5.4	6.4	7.3	10.6	25,9
SOM (%)					
Domestic	98.3	98.0	97.7	96.6	91.6
Import	1.7	2.0	2.3	3.4	8.4
(2) Import segment					
Sales volume for non-Japanese companies (million sticks)					
PMKK	4,241	4,766	5,391	7,945	16,077
B&W	316	335	430	829	6,203
RJR	584	827	951	1,171	2,364
Rothman (TEI)	101	160	282	330	369
AT	62	77	97	264	663
Share of market in the imported segment (%)					
PMKK	79.0	74.8	74.4	74.7	62.0
B&W	5.9	5.3	5.9	7.8	23.9
RJR	10.9	13.0	13.1	11.0	9.1
Rothman (TEI)	1.9	2.5	3.9	3.1	1.4
AT	1.1	1.2	1.3	2.5	2.6

PMKK: Philip Morris K.K.
B&W: Brown & Williamson (British American Tobacco/BAT).
RJR: R.J. Reynolds.
TEI: Tobacco Exporters International (Rothman International).
AT: American Tobacco.

Source: Philip Morris K.K., 1987.

EXHIBIT 4

Japan Pricing: 1987 SOM by Price Category and Manufacturer (%)

¥/Pack	JTI	PMKK	B&W	RJR	AT	TEI	Others	Total market
70	0.36	–	–	–	–	–	–	0.36
90	0.14	–	–	–	–	–	–	0.14
110	3.41	–	–	–	–	–	–	3.41
120	0.40	–	–	–	–	–	–	0.40
130	3.10	–	–	–	–	–	–	3.10
140	1.31	–	–	–	–	–	*	1.31
150	0.15	–	–	–	–	–	–	0.15
180	–	–	–	–	–	–	–	–
200	5.00	–	–	–	–	–	*	5.00
220	64.65	1.26	1.49	0.19	0.10	–	*	67.69
230	–	–	–	–	–	–	*	*
240	12.13	–	0.08	–	*	–	*	12.22
250	0.37	2.84	0.42	0.45	*	*	*	4.10
260	0.46	–	*	–	0.05	–	–	0.51
270	–	–	0.01	–	–	–	*	0.01
280	0.01	1.07	*	0.05	*	0.08	*	1.22
290	–	–	–	–	–	–	*	*
300	0.02	–	–	0.06	–	–	*	0.08
320	–	–	–	–	–	*	*	*
350	–	0.03	–	–	–	0.01	*	0.04
380	–	–	–	–	–	*	–	*
400	–	–	–	*	–	–	–	*
550	–	–	–	–	–	–	*	*
600	–	–	–	–	–	–	*	*
650	0.06	–	–	–	–	–	–	0.06
Total	91.52	5.21	2.00	0.75	0.21	0.11	0.09	99.87

* Denotes numbers which are too small to be significant.
– Denotes 'no participation'.

1. Sum of SOM by manufacturer in the above table does not add up to 100% owing to unknown volume by brands that are sold independently.
2. Sum of SOM by price category and by manufacturer is not necessarily equal to total figure, owing to rounding.
3. ¥110 and ¥120 brands for JTI are sold in 10s, while ¥650 is sold in 50s by JTI. Also, ¥70 brands are 'promotion packs'.

Source: Philip Morris K.K., 1987.

EXHIBIT 5

Competitive Profile in Japan, 1987

Philip Morris main brands	Price (¥)	Sales volume (bn)	Est. sales* revenues (¥ bn)	Share of volume (%)
Lark Milds KS	250	5.55	19.81	34.51
PM Super Lights*	220	1.63	4.72	10.14
Lark KS	250	2.11	7.53	13.12
Parliament 100's	280	1.81	7.67	11.26
PM Lights*	220	2.24	6.49	13.93
Lark Super Lights	250	0.86	3.07	5.35
VSL Menthol**	250	0.46	1.95	2.86
Lark Milds 100's	280	0.56	2.37	3.48
Others		0.86	3.07	5.35
Total		16.08	56.68	100.00

* PM: Philip Morris Super Lights.
** VSL: Virginia Slims Lights.
N.B.: Sales revenues = Retail price − taxes − distribution fee − retailer's margin.

Source: Philip Morris K.K., 1987.

EXHIBIT 6

PMKK Brand Mix Development in Japan

Philip Morris main brands	1982	1983	1984	1985	1986	1987
Lark Milds KS*	33.3	33.3	35.4	37.0	31.6	34.5
Lark KS	38.9	33.3	25.0	22.2	16.4	13.1
Lark Superlight KS	–	–	–	1.8	5.1	5.3
Lark Milds 100's	–	–	10.4	9.3	6.4	3.5
Lark Deluxe Mild 100's	–	–	–	1.8	1.3	0.6
Other Lark	8.3	9.5	8.3	5.7	3.8	2.5
Total Lark	80.5	76.1	79.1	77.8	64.6	59.5
PM Super Lights**	–	–	–	–	–	10.1
PM Lights	–	–	–	–	12.6	13.9
Total Philip Morris	–	–	–	–	12.6	24.0
Parliament 100's (soft)	8.3	11.9	16.7	18.6	16.4	11.3
Parliament KS	–	2.4	2.1	1.8	1.3	1.2
Total Parliament	8.3	14.3	18.8	20.4	17.7	12.5
VSL Menthol***	–	–	–	1.8	3.8	2.9
VSL Regular 20's	–	–	–	–	–	0.5
Total VSL	–	–	–	1.8	3.8	3.4
Other	11.2	9.6	2.1	–	1.3	0.6
Total PMKK (%)	100.0	100.0	100.0	100.0	100.0	100.0

* KS: King Size.
** PM: Philip Morris.
*** VSL: Virginia Slims Lights.

Source: Philip Morris K.K., 1987.

EXHIBIT 7

Competitors in Japan, 1987

Main brands	Price (¥)	Sales volume (bn)	Est. sales* revenues (¥ bn)	Share of volume (%)
R.J.Reynolds				
Salem Lights	250	0.91	3.20	38.56
Camel KS	250	0.13	0.45	5.51
Winston KS	220	0.18	0.51	7.63
More	250	0.14	0.49	5.93
Others		1.00	2.22	42.37
Total		2.36	6.87	100.00
JTI				
Mild Seven	220	80.51	259.89	28.59
Mild Seven Lights	220	41.41	133.67	14.70
Seven Stars	220	30.52	98.52	10.84
Caster	220	22.29	71.95	7.91
Cabin Milds	240	18.29	67.20	6.49
Hi-Lite	200	15.38	42.79	5.46
Hope 10's (10 sticks)	110	10.28	33.18	3.65
Echo	130	8.34	21.81	2.96
Libera Milds	220	2.71	8.75	0.96
Peace Lights	240	3.98	14.62	1.41
Marlboro Family	240	1.45	5.33	0.51
Others		46.49	150.07	16.52
Total		281.65	907.78	100.00
Brown & Williamson				
Kent Milds	220	3.80	10.93	61.29
Lucky Strike	250	1.29	4.58	20.81
JPS Charcoal	220	0.26	0.75	4.19
Kent 100's	250	0.11	0.46	1.77
Others		0.74	2.62	11.94
Total		6.20	19.34	100.00

* Sales revenues = Retail price − taxes − distribution fee − retailer's margins.

EXHIBIT 8

Japan Market Segmentation by Price, 1987 (units in millions)

¥ Price/Pack*	Jan '87	Feb '87	Mar '87	Apr '87	May '87	Jun '87	Jul '87
Premium (¥280 + above)	264.29	203.12	384.62	388.37	370.64	351.64	394.63
High (¥221–¥279)	3 519.31	3 568.15	4 416.16	4 641.09	4 549.77	4 347.39	4 639.58
Medium (¥220)	14 813.43	16 087.65	18 701.70	18 209.16	18 716.02	18 265.79	19 332.16
Low (below ¥220)	2 214.13	2 308.74	2 622.77	2 613.76	2 700.83	2 610.38	2 734.45
Unknown	0.00	0.00	0.00	0.00	0.00	0.00	0.00
Total	20 811.16	22 167.65	26 125.25	25 852.39	26 337.26	25 575.19	27 100.82

				(% SOM)			
¥ Price/Pack*	Jan '87	Feb '87	Mar '87	Apr '87	May '87	Jun '87	Jul '87
Premium (¥280 + above)	1.27%	0.92%	1.47%	1.50%	1.41%	1.37%	1.46%
High (¥221–¥279)	16.91%	16.10%	16.90%	17.95%	17.28%	17.00%	17.12%
Medium (¥220)	71.18%	72.57%	71.58%	70.44%	71.06%	71.42%	71.33%
Low (below ¥220)	10.64%	10.41%	10.04%	10.11%	10.25%	10.21%	10.09%
Unknown	0.00%	0.00%	0.00%	0.00%	0.00%	0.00%	0.00%
Total	100.00%	100.00%	100.00%	100.00%	100.00%	100.00%	100.00%

* All pack sizes other than 20s are treated as equivalent to 20s.

(continued)

EXHIBIT 8 (continued)

Aug '87	Sep '87	Oct '87	Nov '87	Dec '87	YTD '87	YTD '86	% VAR
384.71	373.08	387.75	357.35	467.87	4 328.06	3 338.04	29.66%
4 649.80	4 460.34	4 235.65	4 052.54	5 419.59	52 499.38	50 080.79	4.83%
19 122.07	19 624.55	17 767.73	16 964.25	22 247.71	219 852.21	221 314.02	−0.66%
2 749.51	2 608.20	2 474.06	2 353.26	2 932.41	30 922.51	34 471.85	−10.30%
0.00	0.43	0.37	0.17	0.24	1.22	0.00	100.00%
26 906.09	27 066.60	24 865.57	23 727.57	31 067.83	307 603.37	309 204.70	−0.52%

(% SOM)

Aug '87	Sep '87	Oct '87	Nov '87	Dec '87	YTD '87	YTD '86	% VAR
1.43%	1.38%	1.56%	1.51%	1.51%	1.41%	1.08%	0.33%
17.28%	16.48%	17.03%	17.08%	17.44%	17.07%	16.20%	0.87%
71.07%	72.50%	71.46%	71.50%	71.61%	71.47%	71.58%	−0.10%
10.22%	9.64%	9.95%	9.92%	9.44%	10.05%	11.15%	−1.10%
0.00%	0.00%	0.00%	0.00%	0.00%	0.00%	0.00%	0.00%
100.00%	100.00%	100.00%	100.00%	100.00%	100.00%	100.00%	

EXHIBIT 9

Japan Market: Imported Segment by Price, 1987 (units in millions)

¥ Price/Pack*	Jan '87	Feb '87	Mar '87	Apr '87	May '87	Jun '87	Jul '87
Premium (¥280 + above)	260.03	198.33	379.39	383.17	359.43	335.77	376.73
High (¥221–¥279)	505.07	417.54	773.15	1058.41	1156.77	1103.76	1219.39
Medium (¥220)	122.78	114.71	312.91	656.71	912.15	919.82	1057.80
Low (below ¥220)	0.00	0.00	0.00	0.00	0.00	0.00	1.73
Unknown	0.00	0.00	0.00	0.00	0.00	0.00	0.00
Total	887.88	730.58	1465.45	2098.29	2430.48	2359.35	2655.64

				(% SOIS)			
¥ Price/Pack*	Jan '87	Feb '87	Mar '87	Apr '87	May '87	Jun '87	Jul '87
Premium (¥280 + above)	29.29%	27.15%	25.89%	18.26%	14.79%	14.23%	14.19%
High (¥221–¥279)	56.89%	57.15%	52.76%	50.44%	47.59%	46.78%	45.92%
Medium (¥220)	13.83%	15.70%	21.35%	31.30%	37.53%	38.99%	39.83%
Low (below ¥220)	0.00%	0.00%	0.00%	0.00%	0.00%	0.00%	0.06%
Unknown	0.00%	0.00%	0.00%	0.00%	0.00%	0.00%	0.00%
Total	100.00%	100.00%	100.00%	100.00%	100.00%	100.00%	100.00%

*All pack sizes other than 20s are treated as equivalent to 20s.

Source: Philip Morris K.K., 1988.

(continued)

EXHIBIT 9 (continued)

Aug '87	Sep '87	Oct '87	Nov '87	Dec '87	YTD '87	YTD '86	% VAR
360.23	353.23	371.88	337.73	439.32	4 155.23	3305.97	25.69%
1195.12	1191.90	1202.98	1098.74	1421.95	12 344.78	6143.09	100.00%
1058.76	1101.78	1076.83	922.51	1167.32	9 424.09	1185.85	100.00%
1.54	2.49	2.49	6.29	7.33	24.00	0.00	NA
0.00	0.43	0.37	0.17	0.24	1.22	0.00	100.00%
2615.66	2649.83	2654.56	2365.44	3036.17	25 949.32	10 634.91	100.00%

			(% SOIS)				
Aug '87	Sep '87	Oct '87	Nov '87	Dec '87	YTD '87	YTD '86	% VAR
13.77%	13.33%	14.01%	14.28%	14.47%	16.01%	31.09%	−15.07%
45.69%	44.98%	45.32%	46.45%	46.83%	47.57%	57.76%	−10.19%
40.48%	41.58%	40.57%	39.00%	38.45%	36.32%	11.15%	−25.17%
0.06%	0.09%	0.09%	0.27%	0.24%	0.09%	0.00%	NA
0.00%	0.02%	0.01%	0.01%	0.01%	0.00%	0.00%	0.00%
100.00%	100.00%	100.00%	100.00%	100.00%	100.00%	100.00%	

EXHIBIT 10

Japan Market: Flavour Segmentation, 1987 (units in millions)

Flavour	Jan '87	Feb '87	Mar '87	Apr '87	May '87	Jun '87	Jul '87
Full flavour (16 mg+)	3 232.08	3 338.52	3 879.62	3 908.45	3 978.57	3 826.84	4 048.67
Medium (11.1–16)	11 084.96	11 771.90	13 821.82	13 567.31	13 828.22	13 281.11	13 935.83
Low (6–11)	6 462.58	7 032.87	8 376.85	8 329.25	8 485.31	8 424.68	9 068.54
Ultra low (below 6)	20.80	16.48	36.31	34.41	30.03	28.32	31.31
Unknown	10.74	7.87	10.65	12.97	15.13	14.23	16.48
Total	20 811.16	22 167.65	26 125.25	25 852.39	26 337.26	25 575.19	27 100.82

				(% SOM)			
Flavour	Jan '87	Feb '87	Mar '87	Apr '87	May '87	Jun '87	Jul '87
Full flavour (16 mg+)	15.53%	15.06%	14.85%	15.12%	15.11%	14.96%	14.94%
Medium (11.1–16)	53.26%	53.10%	52.91%	52.48%	52.50%	51.93%	51.42%
Low (6–11)	31.05%	31.73%	32.06%	32.22%	32.22%	32.94%	33.46%
Ultra low (below 6)	0.10%	0.07%	0.14%	0.13%	0.11%	0.11%	0.12%
Uknown	0.05%	0.04%	0.04%	0.05%	0.06%	0.06%	0.06%
Total	100.00%	100.00%	100.00%	100.00%	100.00%	100.00%	100.00%

Source: Philip Morris K.K., 1988.

(continued)

EXHIBIT 10 (continued)

Aug '87	Sep '87	Oct '87	Nov '87	Dec '87	YTD '87	YTD '86	% VAR
4 033.21	3 873.11	3 660.54	3 465.94	4 401.48	45 647.03	49 035.83	−6.91%
13 698.58	13 293.79	12 204.17	11 593.03	15 208.47	157 289.19	172 683.48	−8.91%
9 130.12	9 853.71	8 951.70	8 621.56	11 398.18	104 135.36	87 183.95	19.44%
29.44	30.08	29.29	25.32	32.73	344.52	239.94	43.59%
14.74	15.91	19.87	21.72	26.97	187.27	61.51	100.00%
26 906.09	27 066.60	24 865.57	23 727.57	31 067.83	307 603.37	309 204.70	−0.52%

				(% SOM)			
Aug '87	Sep '87	Oct '87	Nov '87	Dec '87	YTD '87	YTD '86	% VAR
14.99%	14.31%	14.72%	14.61%	14.17%	14.84%	15.86%	−1.02%
50.91%	49.12%	49.08%	48.86%	48.95%	51.13%	55.85%	−4.71%
33.93%	36.41%	36.00%	36.34%	36.69%	33.85%	28.20%	5.66%
0.11%	0.11%	0.12%	0.11%	0.11%	0.11%	0.08%	0.03%
0.05%	0.06%	0.08%	0.09%	0.09%	0.06%	0.02%	0.04%
100.00%	100.00%	100.00%	100.00%	100.00%	100.00%	100.00%	100.00%

EXHIBIT 11

Top 20 – Brand Family Evolution

	1981		1982		1983		1984		1985		1986		1987	
	Brand	SOM %	Brand	SOM %	Brand	SOM %	Brand	SOM %	Brand	SOM %	Brand	SOM %	Brand	SOM %
1.	M. Seven	37.54	M. Seven	41.47	M. Seven	43.99	M. Seven	44.20	M. Seven	44.41	M. Seven	45.92	M. Seven*	43.21
2.	S. Stars	17.07	S. Stars	15.64	S. Stars	13.83	S. Stars	12.93	S. Stars	12.06	S. Stars	11.53	S. Stars*	10.58
3.	Hi-Lite	10.96	Hi-Lite	9.52	Hi-Lite	8.04	Cabin	6.98	Caster	8.41	Caster	7.72	Caster*	7.73
4.	Hope	5.71	Hope	5.18	Cabin	5.04	Hi-Lite	6.95	Cabin	7.31	Cabin	7.33	Cabin*	6.85
5.	Echo	5.17	Cabin	5.09	Hope	4.81	Caster	6.87	Hi-Lite	6.07	Hi-Lite	5.56	Hi-Lite*	5.00
6.	Cabin	4.08	Echo	4.71	Caster	4.42	Hope	4.45	Hope	3.94	Peace	4.27	Peace*	3.87
7.	Peace	3.34	Peace	3.15	Echo	4.22	Echo	3.75	Echo	3.36	Hope	3.75	Hope*	3.44
8.	Cherry	3.28	Cherry	2.62	Peace	3.06	Peace	3.06	Peace	3.08	Echo	3.01	*Lark*	3.10
9.	Partner	2.89	Partner	2.56	Wakaba	2.03	Wakaba	1.78	Wakaba	1.58	*Lark*	1.67	Echo*	2.71
10.	Wakaba	2.42	Wakaba	2.23	Cherry	2.02	Cherry	1.58	*Lark*	1.31	Wakaba	1.42	Kent**	1.43
11.	*Lark*	0.95	*Lark*	1.01	Partner	1.72	*Lark*	1.24	Cosmos	1.30	Cherry	0.97	Wakaba*	1.30
12.	Mine	0.91	Tender	0.97	*Lark*	1.15	Partner	1.09	Cherry	1.24	Cosmos	0.83	P. Morris	1.26
13.	Shinsei	0.84	Mine	0.89	Tender	0.79	Mine	0.60	Partner	0.81	Sometime	0.65	Sometime	0.90
14.	Tender	0.67	Shinsei	0.72	Mine	0.73	Tender	0.56	Sometime	0.58	Partner	0.54	Limera*	0.88
15.	Just	0.63	Ministar	0.54	Shinsei	0.64	Shinsei	0.54	Mine	0.54	Mine	0.47	Cherry*	0.78
16.	Ministar	0.57	Just	0.50	Ministar	0.50	Sometime	0.52	Tender	0.49	*Parliament*	0.45	*Parliament*	0.67
17.	Current	0.48	Champagne	0.46	Sometime	0.46	Ministar	0.45	Shinsei	0.43	Tender	0.42	Cosmos*	0.66
18.	Mr. Slim	0.38	Sometime	0.44	Just	0.40	Mr. Slim	0.33	Ministar	0.42	Shinsei	0.42	*Marlboro*	0.49
19.	Sometime	0.33	Current	0.40	Mr. Slim	0.37	*Parliament*	0.32	*Parliament*	0.35	Ministar	0.38	L. Strike**	0.43
20.	Hitone	0.32	Mr. Slim	0.36	Hitone	0.26	Just	0.27	Mr. Slim	0.28	*P. Morris*	0.34	Tender	0.42

Italics = Philip Morris brands. Malboro family produced by JTI under licence from Philip Morris.
* JTI brands.
** B&W brands.

Source: PMKK Segmentation Analysis.

EXHIBIT 12

Japan Market Facts: Top 20 Brands

Family SOM (%)	1981	1982	1983	1984	1985	1986	1987
1. Mild Seven	37.54	41.17	43.99	44.20	44.41	45.92	43.21
2. Seven Stars	17.07	15.64	13.83	12.93	12.06	11.53	10.58
3. Caster	–	0.10	4.42	6.87	8.41	7.72	7.73
4. Cabin	4.08	5.09	5.04	6.98	7.31	7.33	6.85
5. Hi-Lite	10.96	9.52	8.04	6.95	6.07	5.56	5.00
6. Peace	3.34	3.15	3.06	3.06	3.08	4.27	3.87
7. Hope	5.71	5.18	4.81	4.45	4.07	3.75	3.44
8. *Lark*	0.95	1.01	1.15	1.24	1.31	1.67	3.10
9. Echo	5.17	4.71	4.22	3.75	3.36	3.01	2.71
10. Kent*	0.07	0.05	0.04	0.04	0.04	0.05	1.43
11. Wakaba	2.43	2.23	2.03	1.78	1.58	1.42	1.30
12. *Philip Morris*	–	–	–	–	0.01	0.34	1.26
13. Sometime	0.33	0.40	0.46	0.52	0.58	0.65	0.90
14. Libera	–	–	–	–	–	–	0.88
15. Cherry	3.28	2.62	2.02	1.58	1.24	0.97	0.78
16. *Parliament*	0.08	0.11	0.19	0.26	0.35	0.45	0.67
17. Cosmos	–	–	–	0.30	1.30	0.83	0.66
18. *Marlboro***	0.12	0.15	0.14	0.09	0.09	0.21	0.49
19. Lucky Strike*	*	*	*	*	0.04	0.12	0.43
20. Tender	0.67	0.97	0.79	0.56	0.49	0.42	0.42

Top 20 brand family ranking list is based on 1987 performance.
Italics denote PMKK's brand families.

*Kent and Lucky Strike belong to B&W's brand families.
**Marlboro belongs to Philip Morris, but is being produced and distributed in Japan by JTI under licence from Philip Morris.
All other names belong to JTI's brand families.

Source: Philip Morris K.K., 1987.

EXHIBIT 13

Sales Revenue per 1,000 sticks, 1987 (PMKK estimates)

Philip Morris	¥220	¥250	¥280	
	× 50	× 50	× 50	
	11,000	12,500	14,000	
Retail margin	1,000	1,250	1,400	
Excise tax	6,572	7,253	7,934	
Distribution	430	430	430	
	¥2,898	¥3,576	¥4,236	
B&W	¥220	¥250	¥280	
	× 50	× 50	× 50	
	11,000	12,500	14,000	
Retail margin	1,000	1,250	1,400	
Excise tax	6,572	7,253	7,934	
Distribution	450	450	450	
	¥2,878	¥3,547	¥4,216	
RJR	¥220	¥250	¥280	
	× 50	× 50	× 50	
	11,000	12,500	14,000	
Retail margin	1,100	1,250	1,400	
Excise tax	6,572	7,253	7,934	
Distribution	480	480	480	
	¥2,848	¥3,517	¥4,186	
JTI	¥130	¥200	¥220	¥240
	× 50	× 50	× 50	× 50
	6,500	10,000	11,000	12,000
Retail margin	650	1,000	1,100	1,200
Excise tax	3,135	6,118	6,572	7,026
Distribution	100	100	100	100
	¥2,615	¥2,782	¥3,228	¥3,674

Source: Philip Morris K.K., 1987

3. Dealing with Cross-cultural Issues

CASE 3.1 **LESTRA DESIGN**

This case was prepared by Professor Dominique Turpin as a basis for class discussion rather than to illustrate either effective or ineffective handling of a business situation.

Claude Leopold, President of Lestra Design, was wondering what action he should take. For several years, Lestra had been trying to enter the Japanese market for duvets and eiderdowns. The Japanese market for these products was certainly the largest in the world, but Lestra had faced a number of obstacles that had cooled Leopold's enthusiasm. Recently he had met with Daniel Legrand, a French consultant in Tokyo who had been supervising Lestra Design's activities in Japan for the last two years. Legrand had explained that despite the earlier difficulties, Lestra had several alternatives that could lead to success in Japan.

Lestra Design

Lestra Design was a subsidiary of Leopold & Fils, a family business in Amboise, a medium-sized town about 250 kilometres south-west of Paris. Claude Leopold's father had established the parent company in the early 1930s as a feather and down company. At first, the company traded mainly in down and feathers, but Leopold & Fils soon became a major French manufacturer of feather and down-filled cushions, pillows, bolsters and eiderdowns. When Claude Leopold took over the business from his father, he decided to establish two new companies: Lestra Design to produce and distribute feather and down duvets, and Lestra Sport to manufacture and distribute feather and down sleeping bags (*refer to Exhibits 1 and 2 in the plate section*). By using more aggressive sales management and the talents of his wife Josette, a renowned French fashion designer, Lestra Design rapidly became the leading duvet company in France.

Josette Leopold's creative ideas for using innovative fabric designs with attractive prints helped Lestra Design and Lestra Sports quickly establish an international reputation for high-class, fashionable products. Claude Leopold believed that the prospect of growth in international markets was extremely promising.

Sales over the past five years had experienced double digit growth, and exports to the UK, Germany and other European countries had recently started to boom, representing 20% of Lestra Design sales. Lestra Design had also placed an order in Japan through Kanematsu-Gosho Ltd., a 'sogo shosha' (large trading company) affiliated with the Bank of Tokyo and traditionally strong in textiles. However, the Japanese trading company had not reordered any product from Lestra Design for the last three years.

Lestra Design in Japan

Two years before, Georges Mekies, General Manager, and Leopold had met with Daniel Legrand, a French consultant in Tokyo. That same year, Legrand had conducted a market survey for Leopold that clearly highlighted a major growth opportunity in Japan. With close to 130 million inhabitants and half of the population using duvets, Japan was clearly the largest market for duvets in the world.

During the last five years, Leopold had been preoccupied with developing Lestra Design sales in Europe. As a result, he had not investigated the potential of the Japanese market for Lestra Design products. He had wanted first to provide the French and other European markets with good service, before addressing the US or Japanese markets. During an exhibition in Frankfurt, Germany, Leopold and Mekies were approached by a manager from Ogitani Corporation, a Japanese trading company based in Nagoya. Hiroshi Nakayama, the representative of Ogitani Corporation, wanted to import and distribute Lestra Design products in Japan. He especially liked the unique designs of Lestra Design's duvets and eiderdowns. He told Leopold and Mekies that the innovative designs and the French image – the 'Made in France' label – would be the two strongest selling points.

The Trademark Issue

Ogitani ordered 200 duvets to be delivered to Nagoya. However, after the goods were shipped, Mekies did not hear anything from his Japanese distributor. By chance, on a trip to Japan the following year, Mekies discovered that Ogitani had registered the two trademarks, Lestra Sport and Lestra Design, under the Ogitani name. Mekies decided to call Nakayama and request a meeting in Nagoya to discuss the trademark issue. Nakayama responded that he was too busy. Mekies then insisted that another executive from the trading company talk with him, but he was rebuffed.

That same day, a furious Mekies called Yves Gasqueres, the representative of the French Textile Manufacturers Association in Tokyo, for advice. Gasqueres, who also represented the well-known Lacoste shirts in Japan, explained that Lestra Design was not the only such case. The best advice he could give Mekies was to contact Koichi Sato, a Japanese lawyer who specialized in trademark disputes.

Mekies also saw Legrand, who confirmed Gasqueres' advice. Legrand said that, although trademark disputes were rapidly disappearing in Japan, there were still some recent disputes between Western and Japanese firms, especially with several big French fashion houses like Cartier, Chanel and Dior. Legrand also mentioned the example of Yoplait, a major French yogurt producer. A few years earlier, Yoplait had signed a licensing agreement with a major Japanese food company to manufacture and distribute yogurt in Japan. While negotiating the contract, executives at Yoplait discovered that the Yoplait name had been registered by another Japanese food company under various Japanese writing transcriptions.[1] Although the French company decided to fight the case in court, Yoplait finally decided to use another name ('Yopuleito' using the Katagana transcription) for its products in Japan.

Before going back to France, Mekies arranged for Legrand to supervise the trademark dispute with Ogitani. A few weeks later, Legrand learned from Nakayama at Ogitani that the Japanese firm had registered the Lestra Design and Lestra Sport brands under its own name only to prevent other Japanese competitors from doing so. Mekies was not fully convinced, however, that this was the truth. One month later, he learned from Legrand that the legal department of the French Embassy in Tokyo was going to intervene in Lestra Design's favour. Finally, a few months later, Legrand informed Leopold & Fils that Ogitani had agreed to give up the two trademarks in exchange for full reimbursement of the registration fees paid by Ogitani to the Tokyo Patent Office.

Looking for a New Distributor

During his short stay in Japan, Mekies was able to size up the many business possibilities offered by the Japanese market. Despite the bad experience with Ogitani, Leopold and Mekies felt that Lestra Design had a major opportunity for business development in Japan. The Lestra Design trademark was now fully protected by Japanese law. Leopold then commissioned Legrand to search for and select a new Japanese partner. To shorten the traditional distribution chain and reduce costs (*refer to **Exhibits 3** and **4***), Legrand decided to use his personal contacts at some of the major Japanese department stores. Department stores such as Mitsukoshi, Takashimaya and Seibu, which sold luxury products, enjoyed considerable prestige in Japan. Moreover, department stores had branches all over Japan, which would enable Lestra Design to cover the whole Japanese market. Most of these department stores were already carrying competitive duvets from Germany and France, including prestigious brands like Yves Saint Laurent and Pierre Cardin. Legrand thought that department stores would be the right outlet for Lestra Design to position its products in the upper segment of the Japanese duvet and eiderdown market.

Legrand also went to various Japanese companies in the bed and furniture industry as well as to several large trading companies such as Mitsui & Co., Mitsubishi Corporation and Itochu. He also visited Mr Inagawa, in charge of the Home and Interior Section of Kanematsu-Gosho, which had imported from Leopold & Fils. But Inagawa said that his company did not intend to import any more duvets from Lestra Design because its products were too expensive.

---

[1] The Japanese use three different types of transcription, together with the occasional use of the Roman alphabet. In addition to Chinese ideograms ('*Kanji*'), 'Katagana' is used for the exclusive transcription of foreign words and names. 'Hiragana' is used for all other words not written in 'Kanji'.

The general reaction from potential Japanese buyers was that Lestra Design's colours (red, green, white) were not appropriate for the Japanese market. However, most of these buyers agreed that, with some modifications to accommodate the Japanese market, the '*Made in France*' image was a great asset. Duvets and eiderdowns under names like Yves Saint Laurent, Courreges or Pierre Cardin were being manufactured in Japan under licence. They were selling successfully because Japanese distributors and potential customers viewed French interior textiles as another fashion product for which France was renowned.

To attract distributors, Legrand had advised Leopold & Fils to participate in the yearly Home Fashion Show held in Tokyo; however, Leopold and Mekies had not responded to this suggestion. Some potential distributors had already been identified, but most of them wanted to license the design and then manufacture in Japan rather than import the final products from France. Leopold clearly preferred to export directly from France and thus create more jobs for his own employees.

Akira Arai

One of the main prospects for distributing Lestra's products in Japan was Akira Arai, President of Trans-Ec Co. Ltd., Japan. Trans-Ec specialized in importing and exporting down and feathers.

Arai was enthusiastic about French duvets and quilts and Lestra Design products mainly because of the '*Made in France*' label and the prestige attached to French textiles. Like most of the potential distributors Legrand had talked to, Arai also perceived Lestra Design products as French fashion products similar to the duvets and quilts sold in Japan under prestigious names. Some French fashion designers almost unknown in France had built very strong reputations in Japan. Both Arai and Legrand felt that there was room in Japan for Lestra Design to achieve strong brand recognition.

Arai had had some experience working with other French firms. In the past, he had imported down and feathers from Topiol, a French company that was an indirect competitor of Leopold & Fils. Legrand thought that Arai, who had already heard about Lestra Design, could be a potential partner. Arai knew the down and feather industry thoroughly, and he had good connections in the complex distribution system of the Japanese duvet industry. Arai had also been highly recommended by Mrs Eiko Gunjima, who was in charge of fashion items at the Commercial Section of the French Embassy in Tokyo.

Meeting Japanese Tastes

Two weeks after their first meeting, Legrand and Arai met again in Roppongi, a fashionable district of Tokyo where Arai's office was located. Arai explained that it would be difficult to sell Lestra Design duvets in Japan as they appeared in the current Lestra Design catalogue. In his opinion, Lestra would have to adapt its products for the Japanese market. He proposed that Lestra Design send him a sample that would meet the market requirements (i.e. sizes, colours, fillings, etc.). In particular, he felt that the choice of colours was very important. Although Arai liked the innovative motifs and the colours of Lestra Design products, he told Legrand that Japanese customers would rarely buy a red, pink or black duvet. Most duvets sold in Japan were in soft colours with many flowers in the design. Legrand emphasized that Lestra Design was introducing something really new to the Japanese market, but Arai insisted that most Japanese customers preferred floral motifs. Indeed, Legrand had noticed that almost all the Japanese duvets in Tokyo stores had floral motifs.

Arai further recommended that Lestra Design duvets be smaller than French duvets and 'paving blocked' (quilted) to prevent the down from moving too freely inside. He provided all the technical details needed to manufacture the duvet. Arai's product was quite different from those manufactured by Lestra Design, but Legrand was confident that the French company was flexible enough to adapt its products to the Japanese market. Arai also requested that Lestra Design deliver the sample within a month. Legrand had trouble explaining that Lestra Design, like most French firms, would be closed during the whole month of August for its summer holidays. Arai joked about the French taking so many holidays in summer, but he agreed to wait until the beginning of September.

The Dust Problem

At the beginning of October, Legrand went to Arai's office with the sample that he had just received from France. With almost no hesitation, Mekies had agreed to completely redesign a duvet to meet the Japanese customers' expectations. The fabric was printed with floral motifs, paving blocked and exactly the requested size. Arai seemed pleased when he first saw the product. Then, as Legrand watched, Arai picked up the sample, carried it to the window, folded it under his arm and then slapped it vigorously with his hands. Both men were surprised to see a small cloud of white dust come from the duvet. Arai placed the sample on his desk, shook his head in disappointment and stated: "This is not a good product. If Lestra Design wants to compete against the big Japanese, German and other French brands, the product must be perfect."

Legrand immediately faxed Arai's reaction to Mekies. In Arai's opinion, the problem had to do with washing the duvet. Although Mekies was surprised by the result of Arai's test, he agreed to send a new sample very soon.

Just after New Year's Day, Legrand arrived at Arai's office with a new sample. Naoto Morimoto, who was in charge of the Bedding and Interior section of Katakura Kogyo,[3] a major textile trading company, had also been invited by Arai to examine the new sample. Morimoto was an old friend of Arai's as well as a

---

[3] In 1983, Katakura Kogyo had profits of US$5.5 million on sales of US$2.8 billion and employed 1,852 people.

potential customer for Lestra Design products. After the ritual exchange of business cards between Legrand and Morimoto, Arai proceeded with the same test. Again, some dust came out, although less than the first time. Arai and Morimoto decided to open the duvet and look inside for an explanation. In their opinion, the feathers had not been washed the same way as in Japan. Morimoto suspected that the chemicals used to wash the duvet were very different from those traditionally used in Japan. Moreover, Arai found that the duvet was filled with both grey and white down. He asked Legrand to recommend that Lestra Design use only new, white down and no feathers at all, even very small ones. In front of Legrand, Arai also demonstrated the same test with several Japanese and German duvets. No dust came out. As a result, Legrand and Arai decided to send Mekies samples of both a Japanese and a German duvet so that he could test the dust problem himself. With the two samples, Arai attached a note emphasizing that "to compete successfully in Japan, Lestra Design products must be perfect, especially since the Japanese customer generally believes that textiles and fashion products from France are of high quality."

At the end of March, a third sample arrived in Tokyo. Mekies had phoned Legrand beforehand, emphasizing that the utmost care had been given to this sample. But again this time, the sample failed Arai's test. Legrand immediately phoned Mekies to inform him of the situation. Arai was frustrated and, as he listened to Mekies' voice on the telephone, it sounded as if Leopold & Fils were about to give up on the Japanese market. Mekies could not fully understand Arai's problem, because in his whole career at Lestra design, he had not heard a single complaint about dust coming out of Lestra Design duvets.

Legrand thought that the only way to save the Japanese business would be for Mekies to visit Tokyo. Legrand emphasized again the considerable opportunities offered by the Japanese market and thus convinced Mekies and Jacques Papillault, Lestra Design's Technical Director, to board the next flight for Tokyo. Mekies said they would only be able to stay 48 hours in order to meet with Arai.

Mekies' Trip to Tokyo

A few days later, Mekies and Papillault were in Tokyo. Arai claimed that he was genuinely interested in selling Lestra Design products in Japan, but he explained that in order to compete with Japanese duvets, Lestra Design products had to meet the local standards of quality. Arai and Morimoto insisted that, since French textile products carried such a high image in Japan, they should be of the finest quality. Arai also stressed that only new white goose down should be used to fill the duvet.

In a side conversation with Legrand, Mekies asked if this requirement came directly from the final customer. Legrand replied that it did not seem to be the case. He himself had interviewed Japanese customers in down and duvet shops and had found that the average customer did not know about different qualities of down or even seem to care whether the down was grey or white. Mekies was therefore a bit surprised by Arai's requirement. In France, as in most

European countries, the customer was usually only concerned about price and design. Legrand explained that Arai meant to use 'new white goose down only' as a major selling point to market Lestra Design duvets as a high-quality product to the distributors and the retailers. From previous conversations with both wholesalers and retailers, Legrand explained that 'new white goose down only' was indeed a reasonable expectation, consistent with the upper positioning of European products in Japan as well as with the high quality associated with French fashion items.

According to the trade, the 'new white goose down only' argument would also justify the premium price charged by the retailers for Lestra Design products. Retail prices for Lestra Design products in Japan were expected to range from ¥60,000 to 110,000 and to be comparable with competitive, high-quality products imported from West Germany. However, prices varied greatly, from a retail price index of 100–300, depending on the quality of the down and feathers and their mixture inside the duvet. In fact, some stores, both in Japan and Europe, allowed customers to choose the filling for their duvets and eiderdowns, a policy that gave the customer a lot of pricing flexibility.

Retail prices for Lestra Design in Japan were more than twice as high as in France. Such a difference could be explained by the typically lengthy distribution system in Japan, which contributed to inflating the price of imported goods (*refer to **Exhibit 4***). For an ex-factory price index of 100, cost, insurance and freight would add 4%, and duties an additional 6%.

Arai would price the goods so that he could gain a 12% mark-up on his selling price to Morimoto, who would receive a 10% commission from the smaller wholesalers. In turn, the small wholesalers would put a 20% mark-up on their selling price to the retailers, who would finally sell Lestra Design products at a price which would allow them a 40–60% mark-up. On a retail price basis, Lestra Design products in Japan would be about 30–50% more expensive than most local products of similar quality. Cheap models (either made locally or imported from China) would sell for ¥40,000. On the other hand, Nishikawa, the market leader, offered many models in Lestra Design's price range as well as a few prestigious models over ¥1,000,000. In selling competitive products from West Germany in Japan, the German tradition in making duvets was strongly emphasized. Advertising for these products would often carry the German flag, feature the '*Made in Germany*' label and include a commercial slogan in German.

The Washing Formula

The conversation between Arai and Mekies then moved to the dust problem. Arai explained that, in his view, the problem lay with the composition of the chemical formula used to wash the down. Arai had already made arrangements to visit a Japanese duvet and eiderdown manufacturer in the afternoon. To get this Japanese company to open their doors, he had simply told the plant manager that a group of French importers was interested in buying the company's products. As a result, the Japanese manufacturer was quite willing to let the

French group visit the factory. Mekies and Legrand were impressed by the state-of-the-art equipment used by the Japanese firm. Papillault noticed that the Japanese were using microscopes and some very expensive machines that he had never seen in Europe to determine, for example, the greasiness of the down. Mekies was also amazed to observe three Japanese employees in white smocks separating down from small feathers with medical tweezers. According to Papillault, not a single Western manufacturer was as meticulous as this Japanese company. During the visit, Mekies also picked up some useful information about the chemical formula used by the Japanese manufacturer to wash the down and feathers.

The next day, Mekies and Papillault flew back to France fully aware that much remained to be done to crack the Japanese market. Before leaving, Mekies told Arai that this trip had been extremely useful, and that Leopold & Fils would work hard to make a new sample that would meet the Japanese quality standards. Arai also promised Mekies that he would try to get more information about the chemical formula used by the Japanese company they had visited.

New Challenges

Two weeks later, Arai sent Leopold & Fils some additional information on the chemical formula. Mekies then contacted a large French chemical company that immediately produced an identical formulation for Lestra Design. At the end of April, Arai told Legrand that Lestra Design should hurry with its new samples. Most wholesalers would be placing orders in May for late October delivery to the retail shops. Arai also indicated that Morimoto from Katakura Kogyo had already selected some designs and had basically agreed to order 200 duvets at the FOB (Freight on Board) price of FF1,200 each, provided that Lestra Design solved the dust problem.

In late May, three new duvet samples arrived in Japan. Arai found them much better than the previous ones. However, he still felt that the dust problem was not completely solved. Arai and Morimoto decided to have the fabric inspected in the laboratories of the Japanese Textile Association in Osaka. They both explained to Legrand that the fabric used by Lestra Design did not have the same density of threads per square inch as most Japanese duvet fabrics. Legrand reported this latest development to Mekies, who was obviously upset by this new complaint from the Japanese. Legrand was also worried that the time required to have the fabric inspected would further delay the manufacturing of the 200 duvets that Morimoto was planning to order. In the meantime, Lestra Design had been obliged to order the fabric with the printed design selected by Morimoto in order to get exclusivity from its French supplier.

'Gokai' (Misunderstandings)

At the end of June, Takeshi Kuroda, an executive from Katakura Kogyo who was on a business trip in the southern part of France, visited Mekies and Leopold in

Amboise. Mekies had trouble communicating with Kuroda because of the Japanese executive's limited ability in English. However, Mekies understood from Kuroda that Lestra Design had the green light to manufacture 200 duvets using Morimoto's selected fabric. Mekies communicated the good news to Legrand, who phoned Morimoto to thank him for the order. Morimoto was surprised by Legrand's call because he personally had not taken any steps to confirm the order. Morimoto had first wanted to have the results of the Osaka test. Finally, in early July, the report from the Japanese Textile Association brought bad news for Lestra Design. The Japanese laboratories found that the density of Lestra Design's fabric was far below that of most Japanese duvet fabrics.

The test results confirmed the fears of Arai and Morimoto that the fabric problem was a major obstacle for selling Lestra Design duvets in Japan. Although the test could not legally prevent Lestra Design from selling on the Japanese market, Arai and Morimoto insisted that the French products had to be perfect to be sold in Japan. Thus, Morimoto told Legrand that he would not be able to proceed with importing the 200 duvets into Japan. Legrand tried to counter with the argument that the test was merely a non-tariff barrier for Lestra Design products in Japan. However, Morimoto answered that Lestra Design had to meet the market requirements to succeed in Japan.

When Legrand phoned the Lestra Design office in Amboise, Mekies was very upset. As far as he knew, the Japanese were the only ones in the world to conduct this kind of investigation, which he believed was a non-tariff barrier to prevent non-Japanese products from entering the Japanese market. Mekies' exasperation grew because, following Kuroda's visit, the 200 duvets for Katakura Kogyo had already been manufactured. Because the duvets had been made to fit Japanese specifications, they could only be sold in Japan. Legrand replied that he would explain the situation to Morimoto and that he would try to convince him to do something about it. During the following days, Legrand tried hard to persuade Morimoto to accept the order. It seemed to him that Kuroda was directly responsible for the misunderstanding. But Morimoto remained inflexible and said that he could not buy products inferior in quality to those sold by Japanese competitors.

During the latter half of the year, little communication took place between the French and the Japanese. Leopold and Mekies were upset by the attitude of the Japanese. On the Japanese side, Arai and Morimoto said that it was too late to meet with the distributors as most of their orders had already been placed in late July for the winter season. However, Legrand and Arai had remained loosely in touch. Arai later confirmed that he was still interested in importing Lestra Design products. Both Legrand and Arai were also convinced that, despite all the setbacks, there was still hope for Lestra Design to grasp a share of the huge Japanese market for duvets. Legrand had learned that Lestra Design's major French competitor had faced similar problems in Japan and had decided to give up the Japanese market. On the other hand, he knew that several German competitors were operating successfully in Japan.

Legrand took advantage of a business trip to France to visit Leopold and Mekies in Amboise. He was aware that Lestra Design was making a successful start in the US. In fact, Leopold was just back from an exhibition in New York where a major order had been placed. Legrand emphasized again the great potential of the Japanese market and the need to take a long-term view of this market. Legrand recognized that, although Japan was a tough market to crack, persistence would eventually pay off. Leopold said that he had already tried hard and confessed that he was still quite disappointed by the Japanese market. However, at the end of the meeting, Leopold said that he would consider one last try.

The Alternatives

A few weeks later, Legrand met once again with Arai and Morimoto. Morimoto said he would be interested in buying the original designs from Josette Leopold and then have the duvets manufactured in Japan under licence. Claude Leopold was not keen about this idea. He knew that Yves Saint Laurent, Lanvin and Courreges duvets were manufactured this way in Japan. Leopold also knew that Lacoste shirts, although considered a universal product, had been completely adapted to suit the Japanese market. The colours, shape and even the cotton material of Lacoste shirts sold in Japan were different from the Lacoste products sold in the rest of the world. Bernard Lacoste, the son of the famous tennis player and a personal friend of Leopold, ran the Lacoste business around the world. A few months earlier, Leopold had heard from Lacoste himself that in the previous year, the Lacoste company had had trouble with its Japanese licensee. Gasqueres, the French consultant in Tokyo who was monitoring Lacoste's operations in Japan, had discovered that the licensee had at one point in time 'forgotten' to pay the full amount of royalties due to Lacoste in France. Leopold was therefore wondering if licensing would be the best solution.

Arai had also proposed that Lestra Design buy some Japanese fabric and manufacture the duvets in France. He argued that this would definitely solve the dust problem. That way, Lestra Design products could still carry the 'Made in France' label that was so appealing to Japanese customers.

Another alternative recommended to Mekies was buying fabric for the duvets from Germany, where textile standards were similar to the ones in Japan. Lestra Design could then print Josette Leopold's designs on the German cloth and make the duvets in France. Because the Japanese insisted on floral motives, Lestra Design could even buy fabric with floral prints in Germany. Arai had found that many Japanese companies like Nishikawa (the leading duvet manufacturer in Japan) were already buying a lot of German fabric for duvets. However, in order to be granted the design exclusivity, Mekies needed to buy a minimum amount of fabric, the equivalent of 300 duvets.

As he was reviewing these alternatives for Lestra Design, Leopold wondered if he should continue trying to gain a foothold in the Japanese market, or should he simply forget about Japan and focus more on Europe and the United States?

EXHIBIT 1

See Plate Section

EXHIBIT 2

See Plate Section

EXHIBIT 3

Comparative Distribution Channels for Duvets and Interior Textiles

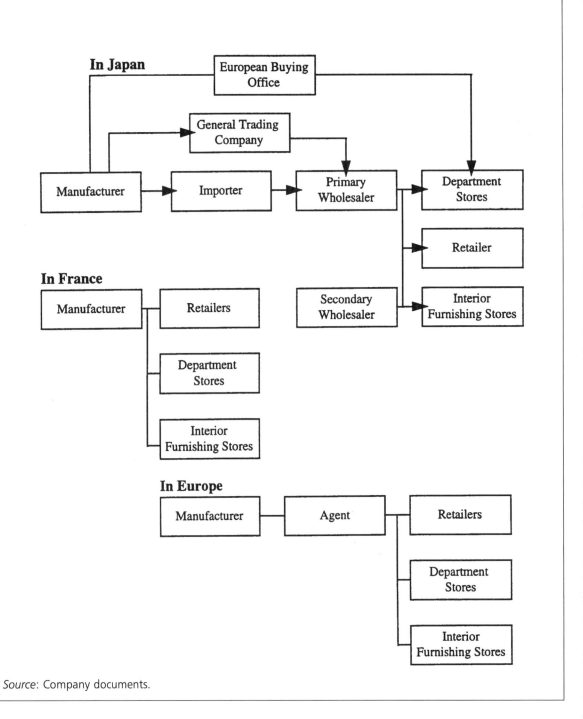

Source: Company documents.

EXHIBIT 4

Short Note on Distribution in Japan

According to Daniel Legrand, Japan's distribution system was still considered lengthy and complex when compared to US or European practices. Common criticisms were that:

- Distribution channels are long and complex;

- Some distribution channels are controlled by large manufacturers;

- Some import agents prefer high margins and low volume, leading to high prices for imported goods;

- Costs of setting up one's own distribution are high and time-consuming.

The Japanese Retail Market

By Western standards, the Japanese retail market remained very fragmented. Despite recent legal reforms from the Japanese Administration to ease the entry of foreign goods into the Japanese market, independent stores accounted for more than one third of retail sales in Japan compared with a few percentage points in the US and in the UK. Japan had twice as many as in most European countries.

According to a number of officials from the Japan External Trade Organization (JETRO),* reasons for the fragmentation of retailing were closely related to Japan's social, cultural and economic environment:

- Shopping patterns: The typical Japanese housewife usually shops once a day. This custom is directly related to the size of the average home in Japan, which cannot accommodate large quantities of food.

- Economics: The price of land in Japan precludes establishing Western-style supermarkets. Most retail sales in Japan are still handled by small independent retailers who own the land on which the store is located. These family stores do not have to consider return on investment as a supermarket setting up a large-scale operation on the same site would.

- Regulation: Opening a supermarket requires that a company make cumbersome applications for many separate approvals under several different laws.

- Service: Smaller stores are located near one's home and give housewives a place to socialize. Small retail stores also have longer business hours which make it easier to shop at night. Independent retailers will also deliver orders for their customers and extend credit. The neighbourhood shopping centre near a subway or train station is a firmly established institution in Japan.

The same JETRO officials argued that given the Japanese preference for more convenience and service, the retailing sector in Japan was not necessarily a backward and underdeveloped system.

Implications

The implications of greater fragmentation in retailing were that either the manufacturer or the wholesaler must provide the services for small stores which they cannot provide themselves. Some of the most important examples were: finance, collection of bills, inventory, risk absorption, marketing and merchandising, and marketing feedback.

Trade Practices

- Margins: For duvets, the margin for the primary wholesaler (as a percentage of retail price) is approximately 15% and that of the secondary wholesaler about 10%.

(continued)

EXHIBIT 4 (continued)

- Rebates: Payments from the manufacturer to the wholesaler and from the wholesaler to the retailer on such factors as sales performance are a common practice in Japan.

- Physical distribution: Construction of delivery centres has been encouraged to modernize physical distribution. When a distribution centre has been constructed, typically the merchandise flows directly from the manufacturer to the centre and then to retail outlets, even though orders and other information may pass through wholesaler intermediaries.

- Payment terms: Payment periods run from 60 to 180 days after delivery of goods.

- Consignment sales: Sales on consignment is the rule in most Japanese industries. Retailers and wholesalers can reserve the right to return unsold goods to the manufacturer.

- In-channel sales promotion: Wholesalers engage in sales promotion activities similar to those of manufacturers.

Planning for Distribution in Japan, Jetro Marketing Series, Tokyo.

DELISSA* IN JAPAN

'We Can Maintain Our Presence in Japan or We Can Pull Out...'

This case was prepared by Research Assistant Juliet Burdet-Taylor and Professor Dominique Turpin as a basis for class discussion rather than to illustrate either effective or ineffective handling of an administrative situation. All names and figures have been disguised.

In the autumn of 1997, Bjorn Robertson, who had recently been named Managing Director of Agria, Sweden's leading dairy products cooperative, met with his team to review the international side of the business. The four men sat around a table piled high with thick reports, Nielsen audits, film storyboards, yogurt cups and a mass of promotional material in Japanese. Agria's 'Delissa' line of fresh dairy products was sold all over the world through franchise agreements. Several of these agreements were up for review, but the most urgent one was the agreement with Nikko of Japan.

"In the light of these results, there are several things we can do in Japan. We can maintain our presence and stay with our present franchisee, we can change our franchisee, or we can pull out. But, let's look first at how badly we are really doing in Japan." Bjorn Robertson looked across the conference table at Peter Borg, Stefan Gustafsson and Lars Karlsson, each of whom had been involved with Agria's Japanese business over the past few years.

Robertson read aloud to the others a list of Agria's major foreign ventures featuring the Delissa yogurt brand: "USA launch date 1977, market share = 12.5%; Germany launch 1980, market share = 14%; UK launch 1982, market share = 13.8%; France launch 1983, market share = 9.5%; Japan launch 1987, market share today = 2–3%." Robertson circled the figure with his marker and turned to look around at his team. "Under 3% after 10 years in the market! What happened?" he asked.

History

Agria was founded in 1973 when a group of Swedish dairy cooperatives decided to create a united organization that would develop and sell a line of fresh dairy products. The principal engineers of the organization were Rolf Andersen and Bo Ekman who had established the group's headquarters in Uppsala, near Stockholm. In 1980, after the individual cooperatives had been persuaded to drop their own trademarks, the Delissa line was launched. This was one of the few 'national' lines of dairy products in Sweden. It comprised yogurts, desserts,

---

* Disguised name.

fresh cheese and fresh cream. In the two decades that followed, Agria's share rose from 3% to 25% of the Swedish fresh milk products market. Andersen's vision and the concerted efforts of 20,000 dairy farmer members of the cooperative had helped build Agria into a powerful national and international organization.

By 1997, more than 1.1 billion Delissa yogurts and desserts were being consumed per year worldwide. In fiscal year 1996, Delissa had sales of $2.1 billion and employed 4,400 people in and outside Sweden.

Industrial franchising was not very widespread in the 1980s, and few Swedish dairy products firms had invested money abroad. However, Ekman's idea of know-how transfer ventures, whereby a local licensee would manufacture yogurt using Swedish technology and then market and distribute the product using its own distribution network, had enabled Delissa to penetrate over 13 foreign markets with considerable success and with a minimal capital outlay. In contrast, Delissa's biggest competitor worldwide, Danone – a French food conglomerate marketing a yogurt line under the 'Danone' brand name – had gone into foreign markets, mainly by buying into or creating local companies, or by forming regular joint ventures.

By the time Bjorn Robertson took over as European marketing director in 1991, the Delissa trademark – with the white cow symbol so familiar in Sweden – was known in many different countries worldwide. Delissa was very active in sponsoring sports events, and Robertson – himself a keen cross-country skier and sailor – offered his personal support to Delissa's teams around the world.

When he reviewed the international business, Robertson had been surprised by the results of Agria's Japanese joint venture which did not compare to those achieved in most foreign markets. Before calling together the international marketing team for a discussion, Robertson requested the files on Japan and spent some time studying the history of the alliance. He read:

Proposal for Entry into the Japanese Market
In early 1985, the decision was made to enter the Japanese market. Market feasibility research and a search for a suitable franchisee is underway, with an Agria team currently in Japan.

Objectives
The total yogurt market in Japan for 1986 is estimated at approximately 600 million cups (100 million ml). The market for yogurt is expected to grow at an average of at least 8% per year in volume for the next 5 years. Our launch strategy would be based on an expected growth rate of 10% or 15% for the total market. We have set ourselves the goal of developing a high-quality range of yogurts in Japan, and of becoming well-known to the Japanese consumer. We aim to reach a 5% market share in the first year and a 10% share of the market within three years of launch. We plan to cover the three main metropolitan areas, Tokyo, Osaka and Nagoya, within a two-year period, and the rest of the country within the next three years.

Robertson circled the 10% with a red pen. He understood that management would have hesitated to set too high a goal for market share compared with other countries since some executives felt that Japan was a difficult market to enter. But, in 1993, the Japanese operation had not reached its target. In 1997, Delissa's share of the total yogurt market had fallen to 2%, without ever reaching 3%. Robertson wrote a note to the Uppsala-based manager responsible for Far Eastern business stating that he felt Agria's record in Japan in no way reflected the type of success it had had elsewhere with Delissa. He began to wonder why Japan was so different.

The report continued with a brief overview of the Japanese yogurt market:

Consumption

Per capita consumption of yogurt in Japan is low compared with Scandinavian countries. It is estimated at around 5.3 cups per person per year in Japan, versus 110 in Sweden and 120 in Finland. Sales of yogurt in Japan are seasonal, with a peak period from March to July. The highest sales have been recorded in June, so the most ideal launch date would be at the end of February.

Types of Yogurt Available in Japan in 1986

In Japan, yogurt sales may be loosely broken down into three major categories:

- Plain (39% of the market in volume)
  Called 'plain' in Japan because the colour is white, but it is really flavoured with vanilla. Generally sold in 500 ml pure pack cups. Sugared or sometimes with a sugar bag attached.

- Flavoured (45% of the market in volume)
  Differentiated from the above category by the presence of colouring and gelifiers. Not a wide range of varieties, mainly vanilla, strawberry, almond and citrus.

- Fruit (16% of the market in volume)
  Similar to the typical Swedish fruit yogurt but with more pulp than real fruit. Contains some colouring and flavouring.

Western-type yogurts also compete directly in the same price bracket with local desserts – such as puddings and jellies – produced by Japanese competitors.

Competition

Three major Japanese manufacturers account for about half of the total real yogurt market:

- Snow Brand Milk Products is the largest manufacturer of dairy products in Japan and produces drinking milk, cheeses, frozen foods, biochemicals and pharmaceuticals. Turnover in 1985 was 443.322 million yen ($1 = ¥234 in 1985).

- Meiji Milk Products, Japan's second largest producer of dairy foods, particularly dried milk for babies, ice cream and cheese. Its alliance with the Bulgarian government helped start the yogurt boom in Japan. Turnover in 1985 was 410,674 million yen.

- Morinaga Milk Industry, Japan's third largest milk products producer, processes drinking milk, ice cream and instant coffee. It has a joint venture with Kraft US for cheeses. Turnover in 1985 was 301,783 million yen.

The share of these three producers has remained stable for years and is approximately: Yukijirushi (Snow Brand) 25%; Meiji 19%; Morinaga 10%.

The Japanese also consume a yogurt drink called 'Yakult Honsha' which is often included in statistics on total yogurt consumption as it competes with normal yogurt. On a total market base for yogurts and yogurt drink, Yakult has 31%. Yakult drink is based on milk reconstituted from powder or fresh milk acidified with lactic acid and glucose. Yakult is not sold in shops, but through door-to-door sales and by groups of women who visit offices during the afternoon and sell the product directly to employees.

Along with some notes written in 1985 by Mr Ole Bobek, Agria's Director of International Operations, Robertson found a report on meetings held in Uppsala at which two members of Agria's negotiating team presented their findings to management.

Selecting a Franchisee

We have just returned from our third visit to Japan where we once again held discussions with the agricultural cooperative, Nikko. Nikko is the country's second largest association of agricultural cooperatives; it is the Japanese equivalent of Agria. Nikko is a significant political force in Japan but not as strong as Zennoh, the National Federation of Agricultural Cooperatives which is negotiating with Sodima, one of our French competitors. Nikko is the price leader for various food products in Japan (milk, fruit juice and rice) and is active in lobbying on behalf of agricultural producers. Nikko is divided into two parts: manufacturing and distribution. It processes and distributes milk and dairy products, and it also distributes raw rice and vegetables.

We have seen several other candidates, but Nikko is the first one that seems prepared to join us. We believe that Nikko is the most appropriate distributor for Agria in Japan. Nikko is big and its credentials seem perfect for Agria, particularly since its strong supermarket distribution system for milk in the three main metropolitan areas is also ideally suited for yogurt. In Japan, 80% of yogurt is sold through supermarkets. We are, however, frustrated that, after prolonged discussions and several trips to Japan, Nikko has not yet signed an agreement with Agria. We sense that the management does want to go ahead but that it wants to be absolutely sure before signing. We are anxious to get this project underway before Danone, Sodima or Chambourcy[1] enter Japan.

---

[1] Chambourcy was a brand name for yogurt produced and distributed by Nestlé in various countries. Nestlé, with sales of $52 billion in 1996, is the world's largest food company; its headquarters are in Vevey, Switzerland.

The same report also contained some general information on the Japanese consumer, which Robertson found of interest:

Some Background Information on the Japanese Consumer

Traditionally, Japan is not a dairy products consumer, although locally produced brands of yogurt are sold along with other milk-based items such as puddings and coffee cream.

Many aspects of life in Japan are miniaturized owing to lack of space: 60% of the total population of about 120 million is concentrated on 3% of the surface of the islands. The rest of the land mass is mountainous. In Japan, 85% of the population live in towns of which over one-third have more than half a million people. This urban density naturally affects lifestyle, tastes and habits. Restricted living space and lack of storage areas mean that most Japanese housewives must shop daily and consequently expect fresh milk products in the stores every day as they rarely purchase long-life foods or drinks. The country is fairly homogeneous as far as culture and the distribution of wealth is concerned. Disposable income is high. The Japanese spend over 30% of their total household budget on food, making it by far the greatest single item, with clothing in second place (10%).

The market is not comparable to Scandinavia or to the US as far as the consumption of dairy products is concerned. There are young housewives purchasing yogurt today whose mothers barely knew of its existence and whose grandmothers would not even have kept milk in the house. At one time it was believed that the Japanese did not have the enzymes to digest milk and, only a generation ago, when children were given milk, it was more likely to be goat's milk than cow's milk. However, with the market evolving rapidly towards 'Westernization', there is a general interest in US and European products, including yogurt.

Although consumption of yogurt per capita is still low in Japan at the moment, research shows that there is a high potential for growth. When we launch, correct positioning will be the key to Delissa's success as a new foreign brand. We will need to differentiate it from existing Japanese brands and go beyond the rather standardized 'freshness' advertising theme.

Distribution

Traditionally, Japanese distribution methods have been complex; the chain tends to be many-layered, making distribution costs high. Distribution of refrigerated products is slightly simpler than the distribution of dry goods because it is more direct.

The Japanese daily-purchase habit means that the delivery system adopted for Delissa must be fast and efficient. Our basic distribution goal would be to secure mass sales retailer distribution. Initially, items would be sold through existing sales outlets that sell Nikko's drinking milk, 'Nikkodo'. The milk-related products and dessert foods would be sold based on distribution to mass sales retailers. The objective would be to make efficient use of existing channels of distribution with daily delivery schedules and enjoy lower distribution costs for new products.

The Japanese Retail Market

The retail market is extremely fragmented with independent outlets accounting for 57% of sales (versus 3% in the US). With 1,350 shops for every 100,000 people, Japan has twice as many outlets per capita as most European countries. Tradition, economics, government regulations and service demands affect the retail system in Japan. Housewives shop once a day on average and most select the smaller local stores, which keep longer hours, deliver orders, offer credit and provide a meeting place for shoppers. Opening a Western-style supermarket is expensive and complicated, so most retailing remains in the hands of the small, independent or family businesses.

Japan has three major metropolitan areas: Tokyo, Osaka and Nogaya, with a respective population of 11, 3 and 2 million inhabitants. Nikko's Nikkodo, with a 15% share of total, is the market leader ahead of the many other suppliers. Nikko feels the distribution chain used for Nikkodo milk would be ideal for yogurt. Each metropolitan area has a separate distribution system, each one with several depots and branches. For instance, Kanto (Great Tokyo) – the largest area with over 40 million people – has five Nikko depots and five Nikko branches.

Most of the physical distribution (drivers and delivery vans) is carried out by a subsidiary of Nikko with support from the wholesalers. The refrigerated milk vans have to be fairly small (less than 2 tons) so that they can drive down the narrow streets. The same routes are used for milk delivery, puddings and juices. Our initial strategy would be to accept Nikko's current milk distribution system as the basic system and, at the same time, adopt shifting distribution routes. Japan's complicated street identification system, whereby only numbers and no names are shown, makes great demands on the distribution system and the drivers.

The Franchise Contract

Robertson opened another report written by Ole Bobek, who had headed up the Japan project right from the start and had been responsible for the early years of the joint venture. He left the company in 1990. This report contained all the details concerning the contract between Agria and Nikko. In 1985, Nikko and Agria had signed an industrial franchise agreement permitting Nikko to manufacture and distribute Delissa products under licence from Agria. The contract was Agria's standard Delissa franchisee agreement covering technology transfer associated with trademark exploitation. Agria was to provide manufacturing and product know-how, as well as marketing, technical, commercial and sales support. Agria would receive a royalty for every pot of yogurt sold. The Nikko cooperative would form a separate company for the distribution, marketing and promotion of Delissa products. During the pre-launch phase, Per Bergman, Senior Area Brand Manager, would train the sales and marketing team, and Agria's technicians would supply know-how to the Japanese.

By the end of 1986, a factory to produce Delissa yogurt, milk and dairy products had been constructed in Mijima, 60 miles north-west of Tokyo. Agria provided Nikko with advice on technology, machinery, tanks, fermentation processes, etc. Equipment from the US, Sweden, Germany and Japan was selected. A European-style Erka filling machine was installed which would fill two, four or six cups at a time, and was considered economical and fast.

Robertson opened another report by Bobek entitled *Delissa Japan – Pre-Launch Data*. The report covered the market, positioning, advertising and media plan, minutes of the meetings with Nikko executives and the SRT International Advertising Agency that would handle the launch, analysis of market research findings and competitive analysis. Robertson closed the file and thought about the Japanese market. During the planning phase before the launch, everything had looked so promising. In its usual methodical fashion, Agria had prepared its traditional launch campaign to ensure that the new Agria/Nikko venture guaranteed a successful entry into Japan for Delissa. "Why then," wondered Robertson, "were sales so low after nine years of business?" Robertson picked up the telephone and called Rolf Andersen, one of Agria's founders and former chairman of the company. Although retired, Andersen still took an active interest in the business he had created. The next day, Robertson and Andersen had lunch together.

The older man listened to the new managing director talking about his responsibilities, the Swedish headquarters, foreign licensees, new products in the pipeline, etc. Over coffee, Robertson broached the subject of the Japanese joint venture, expressing some surprise that Delissa was so slow in taking off. Andersen nodded his understanding and lit his pipe:

Yes, it has been disappointing. I remember those early meetings before we signed up with Nikko. Our team was very frustrated with the negotiations. Bobek made several trips, and had endless meetings with the Japanese, but things still dragged on. We had so much good foreign business by the time we decided to enter Japan, I guess we thought we could just walk in wherever we wanted. Our Taiwanese franchise business had really taken off, and I think we assumed that Japan would do likewise. Then, despite the fact that we knew the Japanese were different, Wisenborn – our international marketing manager – and Bobek still believed that they were doing something wrong. They had done a very conscientious job, yet they blamed themselves for the delays. I told them to be patient and to remember that Asians have different customs and are likely to need some time before making up their minds. Our guys went to enormous pains to collect data. I remember when they returned from a second or third trip to Japan with a mass of information, media costs, distribution data, socio-economic breakdowns, a detailed assessment of the competitive situation, positioning statements, etc. But no signed contract. [Andersen chuckled as he spoke.] Of course, Nikko finally signed, but we never were sure what they really thought about us, or what they really expected from the deal.

Robertson was listening intently, so Andersen continued:

The whole story was interesting. When you enter a market like Japan, you are on your own. If you don't speak the language, you can't find your way around. So you become totally dependent on the locals and your partner. I must say that, in this respect, the Japanese are extremely helpful. But, let's face it, the cultural gap is wide. Another fascinating aspect was the rite of passage. In Japan, as in most Asian countries, you feel you are observing a kind of ritual, their ritual. This can destabilize the solid Viking manager. Of course, they were probably thinking that we have our rituals, too. On top of that, the Nikko people were particularly reserved and, of course, few of them spoke anything but Japanese.

There was a lot of tension during those first months, partly because France's two major brands of yogurt, 'Yoplait' and 'Danone', were actually in the process of entering the Japanese market, confirming a fear that had been on Bobek's mind during most of the negotiation period.

Andersen tapped his pipe on the ashtray and smiled at Robertson,

If it's any consolation to you, Bjorn, the other two international brands are not doing any better than we are in Japan today.

What About These Other European Competitors?

The discussion with Andersen had been stimulating and Robertson, anxious to get to the bottom of the story, decided to speak to Peter Borg, a young Danish manager who had replaced Bergman and had been supervising Agria's business in Japan for several years. Robertson asked Borg for his opinion on why 'Danone' and 'Yoplait' were apparently not doing any better than Delissa in Japan. Borg replied:

I can explain how these two brands were handled in Japan, but I don't know whether this will throw any light on the matter as far as their performance is concerned. First, Sodima, the French dairy firm, whose Yoplait line is sold through franchise agreements all over the world, took a similar approach to ours. Yoplait is tied up with Zennoh, the National Federation of Agricultural Cooperative Associations, the equivalent of Sodima in Japan. Zennoh is huge and politically very powerful. Its total sales are double those of Nikko. Yoplait probably has about 3% of the total Japanese yogurt market, which is of course a lot less than their usual 15–20% share in foreign markets. However, Zennoh had no previous experience in marketing yogurt.

Danone took a different approach. The company signed an agreement with a Japanese partner, Ajinomoto. Their joint venture, Ajinomoto–Danone Co. Ltd., is run by a French expatriate together with several Japanese directors. A prominent French banker based in Tokyo is also on the board. As you know, Ajinomoto is the largest integrated food processor in Japan, with sales of about $3 billion. About 45% of the company's business is in amino acids, 20% in fats and 15% in oil. Ajinomoto has a very successful joint venture with General Foods for 'Maxwell House', the instant coffee. However, Ajinomoto had had no experience at all in dealing with fresh dairy products before entering this joint venture with Danone. So, for both of the Japanese partners – Ajinomoto and Zennoh – this business was completely new and was probably part of a diversification move. I heard that the Danone joint venture had a tough time at the beginning. They had to build their dairy products distribution network from scratch. By the way, I also heard from several sources that it was distribution problems that discouraged Nestlé from pursuing a plan to re-introduce its Chambourcy yogurt line in Japan. Japanese distribution costs are very high compared with those in Western countries. I suspect that the Danone–Ajinomoto joint venture probably only just managed to break even last year.

"Thanks Peter," Robertson said. "It's a fascinating story. By the way, I hear that you just got married to a Japanese girl. Congratulations, lucky chap!"

After his discussion with Borg, Robertson returned to his Delissa–Nikko files. Delissa's early Japanese history intrigued him.

Entry Strategy

The SRT International Advertising Agency helped develop Delissa's entry into what was called the 'new milk-related products' market. Agria and Nikko had approved a substantial advertising and sales promotion budget. The agency confirmed that, as Nikko was already big in the 'drinking milk' market, it was a good idea to move into the processed milk or 'eating milk' field, a rapidly growing segment where added value was high.

Bjorn Robertson studied the advertising agency's pre-launch rationale which emphasized the strategy suggested for Delissa. The campaign, which had been translated from Japanese into English, proposed:

Agria will saturate the market with the Delissa brand and establish it as distinct from competitive products. The concept 'natural dairy food is good to taste' is proposed as the basic message for product planning, distribution and advertising. Nikko needs to distinguish its products from those of early-entry dairy producers and other competitors by stressing that its yogurt is 'new and natural and quite different from any other yogurts'.

The core target group has been defined as families with babies. Housewives have been identified as the principal purchasers. However, the product will be consumed by a wider age bracket from young children to high school students.

The advertising and point-of-sale message will address housewives, particularly younger ones. In Japan, the tendency is for younger housewives to shop in convenience stores (small supermarkets), while the older women prefer traditional supermarkets. Housewives are becoming more and more insistent that all types of food be absolutely fresh, which means that Delissa should be perceived as coming directly from the manufacturer that very day.

We feel that the 'freshness' concept, which has been the main selling point of the whole Nikko line, will capture the consumers' interest as well as clearly differentiate Delissa from other brands. It is essential that the ads be attractive and stand out strikingly from the others, because Nikko is a newcomer in this competitive market. Delissa should be positioned as a luxurious mass communication product.

The SRT also proposed that, as Japanese housewives were becoming more diet conscious, it might be advisable to mention the dietary value of Delissa in the launch rationale. Agria preferred to stress the idea that Delissa was a Swedish product being made in Japan under licence from Agria Co., Uppsala. It thought that this idea would appeal to Japanese housewives, who associated Sweden with healthy food and 'sophisticated' taste. The primary messages to be conveyed would, therefore, be: 'healthy products direct from the farm' and 'sophisticated taste from Sweden'. Although it was agreed that being good for health and beauty could be another argument in Delissa's favour, this approach would not help differentiate Delissa from other brands, all of which project a similar image.

In order to reinforce the product's image and increase brand awareness, the SRT proposed that specific visual and verbal messages be used throughout the promotional campaign. A Swedish girl in typical folk costume would be shown with a dairy farm in the background. In the words of the agency: "We feel that using this scene as an eyecatcher will successfully create a warm-hearted image of naturalness, simplicity, friendliness and fanciful taste for the product coming from Sweden." This image would be accompanied by the text: 'Refreshing nature of Delissa Swedish yogurt; it's so fresh when it's made at the farm'.

The following was included in the SRT proposal:

Advertising
To maximize the advertising effort with the budget available, the campaign should be run intensively over a short period of time rather than successively throughout the year. TV ads will be used as they have an immediate impact and make a strong impression through frequent repetition. The TV message will then be reinforced in the press. The budget will be comparable to the one used for launching Delissa in the US.

Pricing
Pricing should follow the top brands (Yukijirushi, Meiji and Morinaga) so as to reflect a high-class image, yet the price should be affordable to the housewife. The price sensitivity analysis conducted last month showed that Delissa could be priced at 15% above competitive products.

Launch

In January 1987, Delissa's product line was presented to distributors prior to launch in Tokyo, Osaka and Nagoya. Three different types of yogurt were selected for simultaneous launch:

- plain (packs of 2 and 4);

- plain with sugar (packs of 2 and 4);

- flavoured with vanilla, strawberry and pineapple (packs of 2). (Fruit yogurt, Delissa's most successful offering at home and in other foreign markets, would be launched a year or two afterwards.)

All three types were to be sold in 120 ml cups. A major pre-launch promotional campaign was scheduled for the month before launch with strong TV, newspaper and magazine support, as well as street shows, in-store promotions, and test trials in and outside retail stores. On 1 March 1987, Delissa was launched in Tokyo, and on 1 May in Osaka and Nagoya.

1990: Delissa After Three Years in Japan

Three years after its launch, Delissa – with 2% of the Japanese yogurt market – was at a fraction of target. Concerned by the product's slow progress in Japan, Agria formed a special task force to investigate Delissa's situation and to continue monitoring the Japanese market on a regular basis. The results of the team's research now lay on Robertson's desk. The task force from Uppsala included Stefan Gustafsson (responsible for marketing questions), Per Bergman (sales and distribution) and Peter Borg (who was studying the whole operation as well as training the Nikko salesforce) The team spent long periods in Tokyo carrying out regular audits of the Delissa–Nikko operations, analysing and monitoring the Japanese market and generating lengthy reports as they did so, most of which Robertson was in the process of studying.

Borg, eager to excel on his new assignment, sent back his first report to headquarters:

Distribution/Ordering System
I feel that the distribution of Delissa is not satisfactory and should be improved. The ordering system seems overcomplicated and slow, and may very well be the cause of serious delivery bottlenecks. Whereas stores order milk and the juice by telephone, Delissa products are ordered on forms using the following procedure:

Day 1 a.m.: Each salesman sends an order to his depot.

Day 1 p.m.: Each depot's orders go to the Yokohama depot.

Day 2 a.m.: The Yokohama depot transmits the order to the factory.

Day 2 p.m.: Yogurt is produced at Nikko Milk Processing.

Day 3: Delivery to each depot.

Day 4: Delivery to stores.

Gustafsson agrees with me that the delivery procedure is too long for fresh food products, particularly as the date on the yogurt cup is so important to the Japanese customer. The way we operate now, the yogurt arrives in the sales outlet two or three days after production. Ideally, the time should be shortened to only one day. We realize that, traditionally, Japanese distribution is much more complex and multi-layered than in the West. In addition, Tokyo and Osaka, which are among the largest cities in the world, have no street names. So, a whole system of primary, secondary and sometimes tertiary wholesalers is used to serve supermarkets and retailers. And, since the smaller outlets have very little storage space, wholesalers often have to visit them more than once a day.

I wonder if Nikko is seriously behind Delissa. At present, there are 80 Nikko salesmen selling Delissa, but they only seem to devote about 5% of their time to the brand, preferring to push other products. Although this is apparently not an uncommon situation in many countries, in Japan it is typical – as the high costs there prohibit having a separate salesforce for each line.

Borg's report continued:

Advertising
Since we launched Delissa in 1987, the advertising has not been successful. I'm wondering how well we pre-tested our launch campaign and follow-up. The agency seems very keen on Delissa as a product, but I wonder if our advertising messages are not too cluttered. Results of recent consumer research surveys showed only 4% unaided awareness and only 16% of interviewees had any recall at all; 55% of respondents did not know what our TV commercials were trying to say.

A survey by the Oka Market Research Bureau on advertising effectiveness indicated that we should stress the fact that Delissa tastes good...delicious. Agria's position maintains that according to the Oka survey, the consumer believes that all brands taste good, which means the message will not differentiate Delissa. Research findings pointed out that Delissa has a strong 'fashionable' image. Perhaps this advantage could be stressed to differentiate Delissa from other yogurts in the next TV commercial.

Delissa in Japan: Situation In and Leading Up To 1997

In spite of all the careful pre-launch preparation, ten years after its launch in Japan, Delissa had only 3% of the total yogurt market in 1997. Although Agria executives knew the importance of taking a long-term view of their business in Japan, Agria's management in Sweden agreed that these results had been far below expectations.

A serious setback for Agria had been the discovery of Nikko's limited distribution network outside the major metropolitan areas. When Agria proposed to start selling Delissa in small cities, towns and rural areas, as had been agreed in the launch plan, it turned out that Nikko's coverage was very thin in many of these regions. In the heat of the planning for the regional launch, had there been a misunderstanding on Nikko's range?

Robertson continued to leaf through Agria's survey of Japanese business, reading extracts as he turned the pages. A despondent Borg had written:

1994: The Japanese market is very tough and competition very strong. Consumers' brand loyalty seems low. But the market is large with high potential – particularly among the younger population – if only we could reach it. Nikko has the size and manpower to meet the challenge and to increase its penetration substantially by 1996. However, Nikko's Delissa organization needs strengthening quickly. Lack of a real marketing function in Nikko is a great handicap in a market as competitive as Japan.

Distribution is one of our most serious problems. Distribution costs are extremely high in Japan, and Delissa's are excessive (27% of sales in 1994 versus 19% for the competition). Comparing distribution costs with production costs and with the average unit selling price to distributors of 54.86 yen, it is obvious that we cannot make money on the whole Delissa range in Japan. Clearly, these costs in Japan must be reduced while improving coverage of existing stores.

Distribution levels of about 40% are still too low, which is certainly one of the major contributing factors for Delissa's poor performance. Nikko's weak distribution network outside the metropolitan areas is causing us serious problems.

1995: Delissa's strategy in Japan is being redefined (once more). The Swedish image will be dropped from the advertising since a consumer survey has shown that some consumers believed that 'fresh from the farm' meant that the yogurt was directly imported from Sweden which certainly put its freshness into question! Ads will now show happy blond children eating yogurt . . .

Over time, the product line has grown significantly and a line of puddings has recently been added. Nikko asks us for new products every three months and blames their unsatisfactory results on our limited line.

By 1997, plain yogurt should represent almost half of Delissa's Japanese sales and account for about 43% of the total Japanese market. The plain segment has grown by almost 50% in the past three years. However, we feel that our real strength should be in the fruit yogurt segment, which has increased by about 25% since 1994 and should have about 23% of the market by next year. So far, Delissa's results in fruit yogurt have been disappointing. On the other hand, a new segment – yogurt with jelly – has been selling well: 1.2 million cups three months after introduction. Custard and chocolate pudding sales have been disappointing, while plain yogurt drink sales have been very good.

Robertson came across a more recent memo written by Stefan Gustafsson:

Mid-Year Results
Sales as of mid-year 1996 are below forecast, and we are unlikely to meet our objective of 55 million 120 ml cups for 1998. At the present rate of sales, we should reach just over 42 million cups by year-end.

Stores Covered

In 1997, Delissa yogurt was sold mainly in what Nielsen defined as large and super-large stores. Delissa products were sold in about 71% of the total stores selling Nikko dairy products. We think that about 7,000 stores are covered in the Greater Tokyo area, but we have found that Nikko has been somewhat unreliable on retailer information.

Product Returns

The number of Delissa products returned to us is very high compared with other countries. The average return rate from April 1996 to March 1997 was 5.06% versus almost 0% in Scandinavia and the international standard of 2–3%. The average shelf life of yogurt in Japan is 14 days. Does the high level of returns stem from the Japanese consumer's perception of when a product is too old to buy (i.e. 5–6 days)? The level of return varies greatly with the type of product: 'health mix' and fruit yogurt have the highest rate, while plain and yogurt with jelly have the lowest return rate.

Media Planning

Oka's latest results suggest that Delissa's primary target should be young people between 13 and 24, and its secondary target – children. Budget limitations demand that money be spent on advertising addressed to actual consumers (children), rather than in trying to reach the purchasers (mothers) as well.

However, during our recent visit to Japan, we found that Nikko and the agency were running TV spots – which were intended for young people and children – *from 11 : 15 to 12 : 15 at night*. We pointed out that far more consumers would be reached by showing the spots earlier in the evening. With our limited budget, careful media planning is essential. Nikko probably was trying to reach both the consumer and distributor with these late night spots. Why else would they run spots at midnight when the real target group is children? Another question is whether TV spots are really what we need.

Looking at some figures on TV advertising rates in Japan, Robertson found that the price of a 15-second spot in the Tokyo area was between 1,250,000 and 2,300,000 yen in 1997, depending on the time it was run, which seemed expensive compared with European rates ($1 = ¥121 in 1997).

Robertson continued to peruse the report prepared by Stefan Gustafsson:

Positioning

I'm seriously wondering whom we are trying to reach in Japan and with what product. The Nielsen and Oka research findings show that plain yogurt makes up the largest segment in Japan, with flavoured and fruit in second and third positions. It is therefore recommended that regular advertising should concentrate on plain yogurt, with periodic spots for the second two categories. However, according to Nikko, the company makes only a marginal profit on plain yogurt, thus they feel it would be preferable to advertise fruit yogurt.

In light of this particular situation and the results of the Oka studies, we suggest that plain yogurt be advertised using the existing 'brand image' commercial (building up the cow on the screen) and to develop a new commercial for fruit yogurt based on the 'fashion concept'. We also believe that, if plain yogurt is clearly differentiated through its advertising, sales will improve, production costs will drop and Nikko will start making money on the product.

Last year, to help us understand where we may have gone wrong with our positioning and promotional activities, which have certainly changed rather often, we requested the Oka agency to conduct a survey using in-home personal interviews with a structured questionnaire; 394 respondents in the Keihin (Tokyo–Yokohama) metropolitan area were interviewed between 11 April and 27 April 1997. Some of the key findings are as follows.

Brand Awareness

In terms of unaided brand awareness, Meiji Bulgaria yogurt had the highest level with 27% of all respondents recalling Bulgaria first and 47% mentioning the brand without any aid. Morinaga Bifidus was in second place. These two leading brands were followed by Yoplait and Danone with 4% unaided awareness and 14% and 16% recall at any time. For Delissa, the unaided awareness was 3% and 16% for recall. In a photo aided test, Delissa plain yogurt was recognized by 71% of all respondents with a score closer to Bulgaria. In the case of fruit yogurt, 78% recognized Delissa, which had the same level as Bulgaria. Awareness of Delissa was higher than Bifidus and Danone but lower than Yoplait. In the case of yogurt drink, 99% of all respondents were aware of Yakult Joy and 44% recognized Delissa (close to Bulgaria).

Interestingly, the brand image of Meiji Bulgaria was the highest of the plain yogurt brands in terms of all attributes except for 'fashionability'. At the lower end of the scale (after Bulgaria, Bifidus and Natulait), Delissa was close to Danone and Yoplait in brand image. Delissa was considered less desirable than the top three, especially as far as the following characteristics were concerned: taste, availability in stores for daily shoppers, frequency of price discounting, reliability of manufacturer, and good for health. Delissa's image was 'fashionable'. ["Is this good or bad?" Gustafsson had scribbled on the report. "Should this be our new platform? We've tried everything else!"]

Advertising Awareness

In the advertising awareness test, half of all respondents reported that they had not noticed advertising for any brand of yogurt during the past six months. Of those who had, top ranking went to Bifidus with 43%, Bulgaria 41% and Delissa in third place with 36%. Danone was fifth with 28% and Yoplait sixth with 26%. Respondents noticed ads for Delissa mainly on TV (94%), followed by in-store promotion (6%), newspapers (4%) and magazines (4%); 65% of the people who noticed Delissa ads could recall something about the contents of the current ads, and 9% recalled previous ads. However, when asked to describe the message of the Delissa ads, 55% of the respondents replied that they did not know what the company was trying to say.

Consumption

77% of all respondents had consumed plain yogurt within the past month: 28% Bulgaria, 15% Bifidus, 5% Yoplait, 4% Danone and 3% Delissa. The number of respondents who had at least tried Delissa was low (22%) versus 66% for Bulgaria, the best scoring brand. In the plain category, Delissa was third of the brands mainly consumed by respondents. Bulgaria was number 1 and Bifidus number 2. In the fruit segment (under yogurt consumed within the past month), Delissa was in third place (5%) after Yoplait (10%) and Bulgaria (8%). Danone was in fourth place with 3%. ["So where do we go from here?" Gustafsson had scrawled across the bottom of the page.]

Robertson closed the file on Gustafsson's question.

Where Do We Go From Here?

Robertson looked around the table at the other members of his team and asked: "What happened? We still haven't reached 3% after ten years in Japan!" Bjorn knew that Borg, Gustafsson and Karlsson all had different opinions as to why Delissa had performed badly, and each manager had his own ideas on what kind of action should be taken.

Gustafsson had spent months at Nikko, visiting retailers with members of the salesforce, instigating new market research surveys and supervising the whole Nikko–Delissa team. Language problems had made this experience a frustrating one for Gustafsson, who had felt cut off from the rest of the Nikko staff in the office. He had been given a small desk in a huge room along with over 100 people with whom he could barely communicate. The Japanese politeness grated on him after a while and, as no one spoke more than a few words of anything but Japanese, Gustafsson had felt lonely and isolated. He had come to believe that Nikko was not committed to the development of the Delissa brand in Japan. He also felt that the joint venture's market share expectations had been absurd and was convinced the franchisee misrepresented the situation to Agria. He felt that Nikko was using the Delissa brand name as a public relations gimmick to build itself an international image. When he spoke, Gustafsson's tone was almost aggressive:

> I don't know what to think, Bjorn. I know I don't understand our Japanese friends and I was never quite sure that I trusted them, either. They had a disconcerting way of taking control right from the start. It's that extreme politeness. You can't argue with them, and then suddenly they're in command. I remember when the Nikko managers visited us here in Sweden . . . a busload of them smiling and bowing their way around the plant, and we were bowing and smiling back. This is how they get their way and this is why we had such

mediocre results in Japan. Agria never controlled the business. Our distribution set-up is a perfect example. We could never really know what was going on out there because language problems forced us to count on them. The same with our positioning and our advertising: 'We're selling taste; no, we're selling health; no, we're selling fashion – babies, to grandmas, to mothers'. We thought we were in control but we weren't, and half the time we were doing the opposite of what we really wanted.

Bjorn, the Japanese will kill Delissa once they've mastered the Swedish technology. Then, they'll develop their own brand. Get out of the joint venture agreement with Nikko, Bjorn. I'd say, get out of Japan altogether.

Robertson next turned his attention toward Borg, who had a different view of the problem. He felt that the Nikko people, trained to sell the drinking milk line, lacked specific knowledge about the eating milk or yogurt business. Borg – who had also taken over sales training in Japan after replacing Bergman – had made several trips a year to train the Nikko people both in marketing the Delissa brand, and in improving distribution and sales. He had also trained a marketing manager. Borg had worked closely with the Japanese at the Tokyo headquarters.

Borg said: "I understand how Stefan feels…frustrated and let down, but have we given these people enough time?"

"Enough time!" said Gustafsson, laughing. "We've been there for over ten years and. if you look at our target, we have failed miserably. My question is 'have they given *us* enough support?'" Turning to Gustafsson, Borg continued:

I know how you feel, Stefan, but is 10 years *that* long? When the Japanese go into business abroad, they stay there until they get a hold on the market, however long it takes. They persevere. They seem to do things at their own speed and so much more calmly than we do. I agree on the question of autonomy. It's their very lack of Western aggressiveness that enables them to get the upper hand. Their apparent humility is disarming. But, Bjorn, should we really leave the joint venture now? When I first went to Japan and found fault with everything we were doing, I blamed the whole thing on Nikko. After nearly six years of visits, I think I have learned something. We cannot approach these people on our terms or judge them as we would judge ourselves. We cannot understand them any more than they can understand us. To me, the whole point is not to even *try* to understand them. We have to accept them and then to trust. If we can't, then perhaps we should leave. But, Bjorn, I don't think we should give up the Japanese market so easily. As Stefan says, they can be excruciatingly polite. In fact, I wonder – beneath that politeness – what they think of us.

Lars Karlsson, the product manager, had been looking after the Japanese market only a short time, having been recruited by Agria from Procter & Gamble 18 months earlier:

Bjorn, for me, perhaps the most serious defect in our Japanese operation has been the poor communication between the partners and a mass of conflicting data. I came into the project late and was amazed at the quantity of research and reporting that had taken place over the last ten years by everyone concerned. Many of the reports I saw were contradictory and confusing. As well, the frequent turnover of managers responsible for Japan has interrupted the continuity of the project. And, after all the research we did, has anyone really used the findings constructively? How much is our fault? And another thing, have we been putting enough resources into Japan?

There are so many paradoxes. The Japanese seem to be so keen on the idea of having things Western, yet the successful yogurts in Japan have been the ones with that distinctive Japanese flavour. Have we disregarded what this means? Agria people believe that we have a superior product and that the type of yoghurt made by our Japanese competitors does not really taste so good. How can this be true when we look at the market shares of the top Japanese producers? It obviously tastes good to the Japanese. Can we really change their preferences? Or should we perhaps look at our flavour?

It's interesting. Yoplait/Zennoh and Ajinomoto/Danone's joint ventures could be encountering similar problems to ours. Neither has more than 3% of the Japanese yogurt market and they have the same flavour that we do.

Robertson listened to the views and arguments of his team with interest. Soon, he would have to make a decision. Almost ten years after launching Delissa with Nikko, should Agria cancel its contract and find another distributor? Or should the company renew the arrangement with Nikko and continue trying to gain market share? Or should Agria admit defeat and withdraw from Japan completely? Or was it, in fact, defeat at all? Robertson was glad that he had gathered his team together to discuss Delissa's future, their thoughts had given him new insights on the Japanese venture.

4. Managing Labour Relations

CASE 4.1

ACE ELECTRONICS KOREA, LTD.

This case was prepared by S. H. Jang and Associates, Inc. and Research Associate Mark E. Brazas under the supervision of Professor Dominique Turpin as a basis for class discussion rather than to illustrate either effective or ineffective management. Although certain names and other references have been disguised, the general situation described in the case is based on actual labour disruptions during 1987–1990 in South Korea.

In May 1990, Robert Morgan was appointed president of Ace Electronics Korea, Ltd. ('Ace Korea'), the Korean subsidiary of Chicago-based Ace Electronics Corporation. Previously, Morgan has led Ace's Singapore subsidiary. In his early 40s, he was considered an intelligent, energetic and capable general manager by many of his colleagues.

At Morgan first executive meeting in June 1990, Hae Jin Song,[1] Ace Korea's Personnel Manager, reviewed labour relations at Ace Korea during the past three years. (A summary of Song's presentation is included later in this case.) Song warned Morgan that if this year resembled the last three, the 'spring labour offensive' would soon be underway. Song suggested that he and Morgan discuss what major issues might be raised by labour – and what management's position should be on each of these issues. Song also suggested that the two of them plan strategies to keep any negotiations moving forward, thus minimizing the risk of Ace Korea becoming involved in a serious labour disruption.

Company Overview

Established in September 1982, Ace Korea was organized in three divisions based on its major products: double-sided printed circuit boards (PCBs), multi-layer PCBs and flexible PCBs. In 1988, Ace recorded sales of 20.9 billion won,[2] 20% share of Korean PCB production value. Exports, mainly to the US, Europe and South-East Asia, provided over 80% of sales.

Ace's only plant was located in Inchon (the port of Seoul), with the head office in the Yoido district of Seoul. Ace employed 310 people in manufacturing, and 55 in administration and sales.

Ace Korea's unionization had begun in 1984, when 27 employees joined the Ace Electronics Korea Trade Union. Membership had grown, especially since the summer of 1987, when the South Korean government had liberalized restrictions on unionization and other labour activity. In June 1990, the union

---

[1] In Korea, the surname is customarily placed first, e.g. 'Song Hae Jin'. We have followed the Western practice of placing the surname last, e.g. 'Hae Jin Song'.

[2] US$1.00 = W823 (1987); W731 (1988); and W671 (1989). Average rate for year, from IMF.

ph2

ph3

ph4

ph5

ph6

represented some 80% of Ace Korea's workforce. From 1987 to 1989, labour disputes had cost Ace about W300 million.

The South Korean Labour Relations Environment

From 1971 to mid-1987, labour organizing had been tightly constrained by the South Korean government in the name of economic growth and national security. Government planners had implemented laws heavily favouring the *chaebol* – the large, closely-held industrial companies comprising the mainspring of the export-oriented Korean economy. Backed by the military, the government had virtually abolished the right to strike, banned industry-wide unions and allowed formation only of pro-management unions.

Korean workers and the general public had acquiesced in these suppressive policies (and tolerated an authoritarian government) because very strong economic growth was, in fact, delivered. From 1963 to 1988, real Korean GDP growth averaged 10% annually; the average Korean's income, which had only reached $100 in 1963, surpassed $4,000 in 1988. This performance was easily the best in the world and especially remarkable for its duration. Among the key factors in this 'Korean miracle' were an export-oriented growth strategy with a high degree of government direction and control, and the sheer hard work of the well-educated Korean labour force. Koreans worked longer hours than people in other countries, for nearly the lowest pay in the world.

Korean workers put self-interest on hold in the surge of national pride and prosperity which accompanied the remarkable spectacle of a poor agricultural country, devastated by war in 1950–53, rising to challenge the Western economies – and, especially, long-time rival Japan. Pride in Korea's new place on the world stage tended to mitigate, temporarily, discontent over unequal distribution of the country's newfound wealth.

The political crisis which shook South Korea in the summer of 1987 changed not only the rules of presidential succession and the South Korean constitutional framework, but the labour relations environment as well. Following the grant of amnesty and restoration of civil rights to some 2,335 political prisoners in July 1987, and other concessions by the ruling Democratic Justice Party, Korean workers waged long-subdued collective labour actions. Freed from government interference, new unions proliferated. By June 1989, there were 7,380 unions in the Republic of Korea, compared with 2,263 in December 1986; 3,749 labour disputes occurred in 1987, compared with 276 in 1986. Most of these disputes were settled quickly, but violent clashes – leading to one worker's death – took place between striking workers and police at Hyundai's shipyard in Ulsan. This dispute was finally settled by government intervention; the regime pushed both labour and management to the bargaining table, and continued to pressure both sides until a deal was reached.

Most strikes aimed to increase wages and improve working conditions. In recent years, however, workers' demands had expanded into managerial and personnel issues, such as performance evaluation and management perogatives.

Although Korean workers achieved major wage gains from 1983 to 1988, the benefits were diluted somewhat by general inflation[3] and particularly by the skyrocketing cost of housing, especially in Seoul, where one out of every four South Koreans lived. By 1990, labour unions increasingly pursued welfare programmes (such as interest-free housing loans), trying to avoid the confrontation and disorder which characterized industrial relations in 1987–89.

Overall, labour relations in 1990 appeared to have cooled. 462 disputes were reported from 1 January to 7 May, compared with 1,523 in the same period of 1989. The corresponding figures for wage increases were 8.4% and 16.7%, respectively. This change could be attributed largely to government action, ranging from its 'crackdown on illegal strikes to its arbitration of labour disputes at the Korea Broadcasting System (KBS) and at the Hyundai Heavy Industries Company.

However, these two labour disputes illustrated the widening scope of labour grievances and the increasingly militant tactics of some Korean labour unions. A major issue in the KBS dispute concerned union opposition to the appointment of K.W. Suh as company president; Suh was identified with the highly unpopular regime of former national president Doo Hwan Chun. The KBS trade union, as well as the unions for newspapers and the Munhwa Broadcasting Company, also tried to negotiate a union right to participate in editorial policy. Eventually, the KBS union head was indicted for illegal labour activities – while Mr Suh did not resign. Government announced that management prerogatives should not be challenged at the bargaining table and that strikes over such non-bargainable issues would henceforth be regarded as illegal. In the 1990 Hyundai disputes, seven labour activists waged a hunger strike which aroused substantial public sympathy and concern.

In 1990, the future labour relations climate in Korea was not clear, even in the short run. Political and student activist groups continued to agitate, in solidarity with radical labour groups and social activists in Korea's Christian (Protestant and Roman Catholic) religious communities. Tough collective bargaining sessions were anticipated for several key labour organizations, such as the Seoul subway conductors' union and the Seoul taxi drivers' unions, which had experienced severe disputes in the past.

On the bottom line, productivity loomed as an increasingly important issue for South Korean managers. In the 1982–88 time period, productivity growth (measured by real GDP per employee) had averaged 7.7% annually, the best performance in the world. Over the same period, however, real manufacturing wages in Korea had increased by 10.0% annually.

Ace's Collective Bargaining and Labour Disputes, 1987–89

1987

In the evening of 12 August, to the surprise of management, about 150 Ace Korea employees went on strike. The striking workers' demands included:

---

[3] Change in consumer price index, Republic of Korea: 1986 = 2.3%; 1987 = 5.0%; 1988 = 5.5%; 1989 = 4.0%.

- Increasing monthly wages (averaging W195,000) by W50,000 per month.

- Raising Ace's annual bonus from 550% to 700% of one month's pay.

- Introducing family supplemental wage allowances: W5,000 per month per family member, for up to four family members.

- Introducing a 'progressive' element to Ace's retirement allowance system. (Ace currently paid retiring workers a lump sum computed as monthly base salary at retirement multiplied by the number of service years. The workers demanded that the multiplier be raised to 1.5, rather than 1, for service years 11–20 and to 2 for service years in excess of 20.)

When the strike continued the following day, Ace Korea decided to enforce a temporary lockout from 8 a.m. until nightfall, which allowed the company's second shift to continue to operate. On the afternoon of 13 August, the government's regional Labour Office sent a supervisor to Ace Korea's Inchon plant. The officer advised the workers to elect representatives from the members of the labour union, executive committee and from those workers participating in the strike, so that the three parties – labour, management and the government – could meet. However, the workers refused to comply, believing that government intervention would only strengthen management's hand.

On the morning of 15 August, the striking workers, now 200 in number, demanded that Charles Hills, then President of Ace Korea, personally appear and apologise for the lockout, taking the position that no dialogue would occur in his absence. Following instructions issued by Mr Hills at the time of the lockout, Ace's executives, managers and administrative staff did not go to work on 15–16 August.

At 6 p.m. on 17 August, the striking workers received a written explanation of the lockout signed by President Hills. Rejecting this as insufficient, the workers threatened to occupy Ace's head office in Yoido, and demanded further explanation of the lockout. Ace's top management decided not to yield to this demand.

At 3 p.m. on 20 August, President Hills met with representatives of the striking workers and announced that he was delegating his authority to negotiate the dispute to Vice President Sei Won Park. When the negotiations began later the same day, management's representation comprised: Vice President Park; Ha Yon Choi, a Director; Hae Jin Song, Ace's Personnel Manager; and Hyunsoo Koo, the Production Manager. Labour's four elected representatives included: Tae Kun Noh, Head of the Ace Electronics Labour Union; Dae Jung Kwon, the union's Negotiation Officer; and Kyung Hwan Choo and Sam Jong Kim, the leaders of the Radical Socialist Labour Group (RSLG), a militant labour group.

On 21 August, labour and management reached agreement on four minor points,[4] but remained polarized on the major issues cited above. At the meeting,

---

[4] Increase paid holidays for Lunar New Year and Korean Thanksgiving from one day to two; provide better meals; increase commuter buses from 2 to 4; and provide summer uniforms.

management requested that labour end the strike immediately, but labour claimed it would persist until complete agreement had been reached on all disputed issues.

Resuming the following day, the meeting quickly broke off over the agenda. Management proposed that only the allowances issue be put on the table, while labour insisted that the day's business include *all* unresolved matters. The breakdown in negotiations prompted some 150 workers to prepare to leave for the Seoul head office and confront the police near the plant's main gate. Ace had reported to the police that some Ace workers were preparing to wage illegal labour activities outside the plant. The labour and management representatives reconvened, without result.

On 23 August, management introduced its counterproposal to the initial workers' demands:

- a wage increase of W10,000 per month;

- a bonus increase to 600%;

- introduction of family allowances; and

- introduction of the progressive retirement allowance system.

Labour did not accept the proposals, and the meeting was again broken off.

On 24 August, labour revised its proposal to specify a W40,000 wage increase, with other items unchanged. Management stated that it would not make any concession from its own proposals made on the previous day. At this point, the situation took a sharp turn for the worse. Several managers' cars were set on fire by workers. Additionally, a rumour spread that workers were planning to initiate a hunger strike while holding management representatives as hostages. At the head office, some 30 workers initiated a sit-in strike which had drawn the support of 30 additional workers by 6 p.m.

On 25 August, about 80 additional Ace employees infiltrated the police cordon to join the sit-down strikers at Ace's head office. The Ministry of Labour tried to arrange arbitration, but the workers refused. In the afternoon, the labour representatives proposed resuming negotiations, while management favoured moving the discussion off company grounds because of the threatening atmosphere in the plant and around the head office.

On the afternoon of 26 August, the labour–management council meeting resumed at the plant's main conference hall, but no agreement was reached. Three days later the meeting was reconvened, with management announcing its final offer:

- W20,000 wage increase per month;

- 600% bonus per year; and

- 46-hour working week.

When the workers' opinion of this management offer was solicited by the labour representatives, a majority indicated that the propositions were not satisfactory but were acceptable. On 31 August, labour and management agreed to terms:

- W20,000 wage increase per month;

- bonus to be raised from 500% to 600% per year;

- family allowance of W10,000; and

- long-service allowance of 0.5% of the basic wage for 10 years or more of service.

A final contract was not concluded at this time owing to disagreement on the timing of the wage increase. On 1 September, both parties finally signed an agreement covering 10 items including those from the tentative agreement, and also agreed to go back to normal operation on 3 September, ending the 50-day labour dispute.

1988

On 3 March 1988, Ace's first wage negotiation for 1988 began at the main conference hall of its Inchon plant. Six labour representatives and three employer representatives, including Vice President Park, participated. Labour demanded wage increases averaging 19.3%, with management offering 4.1%. No progress occurred in the first round of negotiations.

On 6 March a second meeting was convened, but each party stuck to its original position. A third meeting was scheduled for 12 March. In the evening of 6 March, however, 11 Executive Committee members of the union met and agreed that workers should refuse to work overtime. The workforce initiated this overtime refusal beginning 9 March, in line with the committee's decision.

At the third wage negotiation meeting on 12 March, management upped its wage increase proposal to 5.5%, while labour refused to move from its original 19.3% figure. Again, negotiations broke down. The union's Executive Committee decided that all union members would wear ribbons calling for a 19.3% wage increase, and formed a temporary Dispute Management Committee of 29 union members to lead the strike activity.

Of the 11 Executive Committee members, 8 belonged to the Radical Socialist Labour Group (RSLG), a regional organization whose name indicated its ideology. The RSLG enjoyed some support among 'progressive' Catholic priests. The 8 RSLG Executive Committee members attempted to remove the 3 non-RSLG members from the Committee, without success, and in a similar manner attempted to 'pack' the Dispute Management Committee with their candidates.

Alarmed by these developments, Ace management decided internally to fire those workers it had identified as hard-core RSLG agitators, if no progress were made in the next two negotiation meetings. Management's intentions 'leaked' to labour, as well as its decision to concede a 10% wage increase, but to enforce a lockout if labour would not accept this offer. Some members of management believed that any lockout would deepen the dispute and perhaps result in a strike.

The regional Labour Office, an agency of the Ministry of Labour, advised the union to stay within the law governing wage negotiations, and advised management to increase wages as much as possible.

The fourth labour–management negotiating session (17 March) ended with no result. The next meeting was scheduled for 23 March when Charles Hills, Ace's President, would be back from the US. The RSLG and non-RSLG factions on the union's Executive Committee agreed to patch up their differences and take a united course if the fifth negotiation session failed.

At this fifth meeting, both parties revised their proposals. Labour revised its bid downward to an 18% wage increase; management offered 9%. President Hills did not attend the meeting for personal reasons, but delegated negotiating authority to Vice President Park. Several union leaders began to distribute printed material calling for collective action of the workers.

As the situation deteriorated, the head of the Labour Office met with Vice President Park and other executives of the company. The Ace managers informed the Labour Office representative that Ace was prepared to increase wages by 10.4% and pay some amount of extra bonus by 31 March, when the current wage agreement would expire. The Labour Officer then contacted several labour leaders, informed them of the management plan, with the consent of management, and tried to persuade labour to make concessions at the next negotiation session.

No progress was made in the morning session of the 25 March negotiations. Late in the afternoon, the meeting resumed. Mr Jong Sam Hwang, the union head and a labour representative, made a tentative offer to settle at an average 11.5% wage increase. The negotiating delegates for labour convened a meeting of the union representatives for each production line to explain the tentative agreement. At this meeting, several hard-line RSLG members rejected the tentative agreement, perhaps because Hwang and two other key union officers were not RSLG members.

To see if he could get more support among the RSLG members, Hwang proposed that the union initiate a work refusal. But the RSLG representatives insisted on employing a prolonged-negotiation strategy, contending that a work refusal was less likely to produce real gains. They finally agreed that workers would not fill in the work slips which were used as attendance records as well.

On 27 March, around 10 RSLG labourers stuck bills on the walls of Ace's plant denouncing all of labour's current negotiation representatives – including those from the RSLG, suggesting that the RSLG itself was experiencing internal conflicts.

The next day, at the union's wage negotiation committee meeting, union head Hwang demanded that the committee delegate full negotiation authority to him. He assured the committee he would succeed in gaining a 12.5% wage increase. Without this authority, he said that he would quit the committee. After the Labour Office had spoken to several committee members, they were persuaded to agree to Hwang's proposal. The Labour Office also informed Ace management of the union's wage target.

On 1 April, union chief Hwang and Vice President Park held the eighth wage negotiation meeting, reaching a tentative agreement for a 12.5% wage increase. After the meeting, Hwang convened a wage negotiation committee meeting. Four of its members accepted the tentative agreement, with two members absent, officially ending the 1988 wage negotiations.

However, the negotiations were *not* over as far as some of labours more militant elements were concerned. On 2 April, 12 RSLG labellers hung posters around the Ace main office grounds arguing that the 1 April agreement was illegal because a majority of the board of representatives of the union and the executive committee had never ratified it. They insisted that the union organize a new negotiation committee. On the other side of the hill, management immediately planned to refer 16 'hard-core agitators', including the 12 RSLG members rejecting the 1 April agreement, to the Disciplinary Committee, a company committee with three company and two labour representatives.

For several days, the two sides tried to enlarge their support. The 12 RSLG dissidents distributed leaflets and gathered signatures for a petition to overthrow the 1 April agreement, while management tried to make its case to the workers through newspaper ads, spot radio announcements and a reprinted statement of President Hills.

On 3 April, the regional government's Labour Office organized a meeting to try to keep the conflict from escalating. This meeting included the mayor and city marshal of Yoido, the Labour Office chief, Vice President Park and Mr Hwang. The Labour Office strongly recommended that Ace's management abandon its plan to punish the 16 hard-core labour organizers.

On 4 April, over 100 workers, mostly RSLG members, held a convention which elected 5 new negotiation representatives and adopted a resolution stating that the 1 April agreement was invalid. Management indicated that it would not accept the new representatives – and imposed heavy punishment on 16 of the militants.

The Labour Office was concerned that these punishments would cause serious problems. A labour dispute could stir social unrest led by religious and anti-government groups. The Labour Office again tried to persuade Ace management to rescind the punishments, but the company refused.

On 7 April, Ace announced the punishment of 15 workers (the 16th had given management a written promise that he would not participate in any future labour activity). The 'RSLG 12' were dismissed, and the Ace plant was shut down for one day. The discharged workers were escorted to the plant's gate by 150 members of the Relief Force, or 'Koo-sa Dae', non-union workers who supported the management position.

The 12 discharged workers were met by about 170 other workers at the gate, where they initiated a protest demonstration. Father Lee, a Catholic priest and one of the top RSLG leaders, joined the group soon after, as did several other labour activists. The emotional tone of the protest quickly heated up, with much yelling, singing and drumming. The protesters kept reiterating their demands: withdrawal of the dismissals, and renegotiation of the wage increase. At midnight, about 40 college students joined the protest.

At 9 a.m. on 8 April, the police arrested nine of the protest's leaders. At 10 a.m., around 70 of the remaining protesters moved to Father Lee's church in nearby Pupyong. Vice President Park and two other management representatives met with five dismissed workers through the mediation of the chief commissioner of the Labour Relations Committee. At the meeting, the workers proposed that management:

- withdraw the dismissals;

- refer wage negotiations;

- allow workers to return to work, starting the next day.

After the meeting, management consulted Ace headquarters in Chicago by telephone and confirmed that it would not revoke the dismissals. Management then organized a Dispute Management Committee (separate from the labour–management standing committee of the same name). This new committee comprised 13 senior and junior managers, charged with blocking intervention by radical students or other social and religious groups and trying to keep previously uninvolved workers from joining the protesters.

On 10 April, Vice President Park and Ha Yon Choi, an Ace Director, met with three priests of the Pupyong church, but reached no solution in the dispute. At the meeting, the company offered several concessions, including:

- payment of full wages for the shutdown period; and

- payment of retirement allowances, plus W1 million, to dismissed workers who submitted resignations.

Management also announced that it would not withdraw the discharge decision, and would stick to the agreed-upon wage increase of 12.5%. At the meeting, both parties agreed that the plant would reopen as soon as possible.

On 11 April, the nine protest leaders who had been arrested by the police on 8 April were released; they immediately rejoined the group staying at the Pupyong church.

That same day, six laid-off workers, three management representatives and the chief official of the Labour Office met at the Inchon Labour Office. The workers demanded that the 12 discharged workers be reinstated, and that Vice President Park and Director Choi retire. Management responded that withdrawing the discharges was impossible and that the executives' retirement would not be considered. Management reiterated the offer of W1 million in severance pay plus retirement allowances to the discharged workers. The Labour Office official recommended that the workers ask the Labour Relations Committee, a government agency responsible for mediation and arbitration, to consider their complaint of unfair labour practices, and to stay within the law during the current dispute.

At this time, over 97% of the employees were reporting to work at the Inchon plant, which had reverted to normal operation. Considering the high attendance rate, management expected that collective actions would diminish.

Disputes occurred intermittently from mid-April to late August. During this period, union chief Hwang resigned from Ace, being replaced (as acting chief) by Roh Kyung Ryu, the union's secretary general, in mid-May. At the end of June, several social and labour activist groups, including radical college students, launched protests in support of the fired workers. Only 32 Ace workers were involved in these protests; the vast majority continued on their jobs.

On 24 July, the laid-off workers and 30 of their supporters signed agreements with Ace and with the union. The agreement with the company stated:

- Ace will not interfere with lawful union activities by its employees;
- Ace will recognize worker absences during dispute periods as personal vacation and will take no measures disadvantageous to workers involved in the disputes.

  The agreement with the labour union stated:

- the acting head of the union (Roh Kyung Ryu) accepts seven demands as the union's, to be negotiated with the company during the coming 1988 collective bargaining session;
- the union will initiate direct election of its leader by the membership

Vice President Park also promised that he would try to persuade President Hills to have the fired workers restored, but this intervention proved unsuccessful.

On 12 August, 30 workers initiated a new strike at the Inchon plant. They demanded:

- an additional wage increase;
- restoration of laid-off workers; and
- retirement of *sweetheart*, or 'ou-yong', labour union officers (sympathetic to management), including Mr Hwang.

The next day, more than 300 participants joined the dispute. Ace announced that its Inchon plant would be shut down indefinitely. President Hills planned to enforce a lockout if the disputes were not resolved at a general meeting of all Ace employees.

Conflicts within the union became evident when this general meeting was held on 18 August. At 10 : 30 a.m., some 250 of Ace's 350 workers were present for the start of the meeting. At 11 : 30 a.m., 100 workers supporting the acting union head, Roh Kyung Ryu, initiated a strike at Ace's main plant gate. Simultaneously, 40 dissidents, mostly RSLG members, began a strike inside the plant. Ace submitted a report on the strike to the Labour Relations Committee and other authorities.

On 20 August, a labour–management council meeting was held, attended by 25 people representing the two sides. Labour demanded an additional wage increase of W30,000 annually. Management suggested W10,000, and announced that it would revoke the lockout only if 50% of all employees voted for the agreement negotiated with union chief Hwang, which would then be signed by representatives of labour management.

On 22 August, the strikes were stopped inside and outside the Ace plant. The next day, a collective bargaining agreement was concluded between the labour union and Ace, on these terms:

Item	Old	New
Composition of the disciplinary committee	Labour 2 Management 3	Labour 3 Management 3
Paid holidays	11 days	14 days
Annual bonus	600%	650%
Long-term service allowances	0.5% of basic wage for 10 or more service years	W5,000–25,000

On 24 August, a majority vote ratified this agreement at a general meeting of all Ace employees. The hard-line group which had led the disputes also decided to accept the agreement. Ace reopened its plant.

On 14 September, the union held its general meeting and conducted elections for its officers, including the union head. Kung Hae Lee, an RSLG member and one of the protest leaders during the recent disputes, was elected union chief.

The next day, 7 more of the 12 discharged workers resigned, each receiving retirement allowances and W1 million in severance pay – joining 3 others who had previously resigned in May. On October 3, Ace rescinded its dismissals of the remaining 2 workers and allowed them to return to work on 2 November. Management also decided that wages for the layoff period would be paid according to the Labour Standards Act. The 1988 labour dispute at Ace Electronics Korea had ended.

1989

The first round of Ace's 1989 labour–management negotiations was held on 17 March. Labour's initial demands included:

- an average wage increase of 29%;

- abolition of the personnel evaluation system (based on the perception that the evaluation system was used as a tool to discourage workers from joining the union or becoming involved in collective labour actions);

- housing aid for workers;

- payment of all tuition fees for workers' children through high school;

- exclusion of Vice President Choi (Mr Park had resigned in December 1988) from all upcoming negotiations.

On 23 March, 11 members of the union's Executive Committee initiated a strike, demanding that President Hills personally participate in the negotiations.

At the second meeting on 24 March, President Hills announced that all management negotiating authority was delegated to Ha Yon Choi, who had been promoted from Director to Vice President, replacing Mr Park, early in 1989. A power of attorney letter to this effect was given to the labour representatives. Labour reiterated its previous proposals, while Ace offered a 5.7% wage increase. During and after this meeting, several union members who also belonged to the RSLG began taking signatures from workers in support of strikes or other militant action, such as work refusal.

The third negotiation meeting on 29 March broke down as labour launched new demands for increased annual bonuses and family allowances.

On 30 March, a group of radical labourers went on strike, and Ace operations were shut down. Management urged the strikers to stop the dispute and go back to the negotiation table, but they refused.

On 31 March, about 20 agitators seized the Ace head office, driving out most of the office staff but detaining several executives and managers including Vice President Choi and Tae Soo Min, Ace's Director of Human Resources and General Affairs. The agitators urged the detained managers to hold wage negotiations with them, but the detained managers refused. Ace submitted a report on the strike to the government's Labour Relations Committee. The next day, most workers occupying the head office went back to the plant, and in the evening, three of the detained Ace executives escaped through a window.

Labour disputes inside and outside the Ace facilities continued until 9 April. That day, the union's Executive Committee decided that three labour representatives would be given full authority to bargain. Through the active mediation of a labour relations official, Vice President Choi, Director Min and Personnel Manager Song met with the labour representatives, but reached no conclusion.

On 11 April, a labour–management meeting was held in the regional Labour Office. The labour and management proposals advanced were as follows:

Labour	Management
20% wage increase	12% wage increase
Withdraw personnel evaluation system	Unacceptable
Housing aid	Acceptable in principle, depending on specific terms
Tuition aid for employees' children	Conditionally acceptable, as with housing aid

The gap between the two sides could not be closed on the first two issues, and the meeting broke off.

On 12 April, six labour and six management representatives agreed that all negotiating authority be delegated to Vice President Choi and union chief Lee, and exchanged powers of attorney to this effect. This delegation apparently broke the negotiating logjam: on 16 April, Choi and Lee signed an agreement stipulating:

- 13.1% wage increase;
- revision of the personnel evaluation system, to be determined after further discussion;
- payment of housing aid after an evaluation and recommendation by the labour members of the labour management council;
- 70% of children's tuition fees to be paid by Ace; and
- no litigation related to the 1989 labour dispute.

This agreement was ratified at a general meeting of the union on the following day.

Conclusion

Following his presentation on Ace's recent experience in industrial relations, Personnel Manager Song indicated that there had recently been some signs of labour unrest among the more militant union activists at Ace. Some posters urging a strike had appeared around the Ace plant, and the RSLG was holding frequent meetings. Song also reported that the personnel department was making every effort to better prepare for future collective bargaining by monitoring the recent activities of the union and the RSLG group, analysing the government's guidelines on labour relations, observing industry trends in wage negotiations, etc.

Vice President Choi proposed to establish, as soon as possible, a comprehensive action plan for labour relations.

When the meeting finally ended, Robert Morgan found himself reflecting on what he had heard and turning different ideas over in his head as he looked out of his office window. It was reassuring to see the peaceful sight of the weeping willow trees trembling slightly in the breeze along the Han River in this 'Land of the Morning Calm'.

5. Managing Crisis and Ethical Problems

LUSSMAN–SHIZUKA* CORP.

This case was prepared by Dominique Turpin, with the assistance of Research Associate Joyce Miller, as a basis for class discussion rather than to illustrate either effective or ineffective handling of a business situation. Research for this case was made possible by a grant from Egon Zehnder. All names and data have been disguised.

It was 6.00 p.m. on 22 June 1991, and Rudolf Richter, President of Lussman–Shizuka Corp., could see several photographers and journalists representing Osaka's major newspapers gathered outside on the street 20 floors below. Richter sighed and glanced nervously at his secretary who was signalling him that yet another reporter was on the telephone wanting his view of the allegations recently made against the company. Four hours earlier, the Japanese authorities had arrested three of Richter's employees and accused them of bribing university professors to win orders of the company's products. In his entire 25-year career with Lussman Pharmaceuticals, Richter had never faced a more difficult situation.

Lussman in Japan

Located near Osaka, Lussman–Shizuka Corp. was a 50/50 joint venture between Lussman Pharmaceuticals based in Dusseldorf, Germany and Shizuka Corp., a Japanese chemical firm. Formed to produce and distribute anti-cancer drugs in Japan, the venture had operated since 1971 in what Richter called "one of the toughest, most competitive markets in the world." Richter had headed Lussman–Shizuka for the past six years and was the only foreigner working in the joint venture. Although he had begun learning Japanese, his ability to handle a business discussion was still limited. Consequently, most meetings were conducted in English. Two executives from Shizuka Corp., Hiroshi Shibuya and Yasumi Kato, served as vice presidents of Lussman–Shizuka and were involved in the daily operations of the joint venture. They both had a reasonably good command of English.

For many years, Japan had kept foreign products out of its national market with what Richter described as "high tariffs and complex production and import procedures." Through negotiations with the European Community, these trade barriers had gradually been dismantled, but importing goods into Japan was still cumbersome in Richter's view. Lussman Pharmaceuticals had entered the market by tying up with a leading Japanese company. The venture represented a rare success for a European company in Japan. Lussman–Shizuka sold quality products at competitive prices, serviced through a national distribution network. Technological leadership had given the venture its initial edge in the fight for

---

* Disguised name.

market share. Currently, the company manufactured 10% of its products in Japan and imported the remainder from a Lussman factory in Germany.

Over-the-counter drugs in Japan were primarily available through doctors rather than pharmacists. Japanese physicians typically charged low fees for clinic visits, relying on the sale of drugs for the bulk of their income. Doctors had a great deal of influence over their hospitals' buying decisions as well as the drug purchases of their former students now working in other medical institutions.

The Lussman–Shizuka Affair

Three weeks earlier, five doctors who worked at prominent university hospitals in Osaka had been arrested for accepting improper cash payments from Lussman–Shizuka. Two doctors, who had previously purchased Lussman products, had reportedly received $22,000 for entertainment expenses. Another was arrested for accepting $31,000 from Lussman–Shizuka for attending an academic conference in the United States. Two other professors in a major Japanese university were each accused of receiving $18,000 from Lussman–Shizuka, but prosecutors had not yet released their names. Shortly after this incident, the Ministry of Health, together with the Ministry of Education, advised all state university hospitals against purchasing drugs from Lussman–Shizuka for an unspecified period of time, a move that could have devastating consequences for Lussman's business in Japan.

Dr Yutaka Hayashida, an Osaka physician, observed: "Pharmaceutical companies commonly court doctors to buy their drugs because it is such a competitive market. Salesmen will do almost anything to get access to the most influential practitioners. They'll give them presents, buy drinks, pay for trips, even help their kids get into the best universities." Dr Hayashida added that he had made a personal decision to turn down all such offers, although there was no hospital requirement to do so. He continued: "Low-paid university professors and newly-established doctors are particularly vulnerable to such offers. The Lussman–Shizuka affair is just the tip of the iceberg. Most companies and most doctors do the same thing. In fact, much of the competitive bidding that does happen in hospitals is meaningless, because the doctors have decided in advance which drugs they want to buy and the specifications are set so that only those products will be accepted."

The Reaction from Shizuka Corp.

Yasumi Kato, a director in the Japanese parent company who was also a vice president in the joint venture, offered his view of the situation:

> The fact that Lussman–Shizuka is an outsider makes the company especially vulnerable to exposure. Furthermore, in Japan, stability is very important. We brought attention to ourselves by marketing aggressively. Within less than a decade of its founding, Lussman–Shizuka moved to the top ranks in the industry in its particular speciality. Our share of the market did not come cheap. Where most Western companies in Japan will seek a small position

and focus on maintaining high profits, Lussman–Shizuka wanted to be at the top in anti-cancer drugs and the company matched Japanese discounts blow for blow. Now we are paying the price.

Richter knew that the venture's quick climb had created a lot of tension among the competitors. In fact, his Japanese partners had warned him of the danger of disrupting the market with an aggressive sales policy. Industry leaders had frequently complained that prices had fallen too low. Now, the venture's Japanese staff speculated that a competitor had leaked inflammatory information to the press. Richter was aware that scandals typically broke in the Japanese press after reporters were fed information aimed at undercutting foreigners who were seen to be undermining the *status quo*.

Why was Lussman–Shizuka singled out? According to Richter: "In some respects, the company has been too honest. When investigators raided our office last week and demanded to see the company's accounts, we had only one set of books with a straightforward accounting of our activities. Many local companies have two sets of books or, at a minimum, they have couched the payments to doctors in vague terms, such as cooperative research. The reality in this industry in this country is that you are not a fully-fledged salesman until you have reached the point where a doctor will accept your gifts and agree to meet with you."

Hiroshi Shibuya, a vice president in the joint venture, felt that what had put the company into difficulty was its effort to woo university professors. Investigators had told the press that Lussman–Shizuka had compiled a list of influential doctors to be regularly targeted by its salesmen.

Where To Go Next

Richter had to decide how to proceed, and quickly. He could not help thinking that a scandal now would jeopardise his forthcoming retirement. His wife had already moved back to Bavaria, and Richter himself was scheduled to leave Japan permanently at the end of December. Now, the Japanese authorities had forbidden him to leave the country, and he could face a long trial if convicted.

While his Japanese partners tended to blame Richter openly for the consequences of aggressive selling, Richter felt they also shared some responsibility for the current situation. Although he knew that 'gift-giving' was a long-standing Japanese tradition and standard industry practice, Richter felt that the salespeople may have overdone it.

While Richter had been mulling over his alternatives, the crowd outside the office building had grown considerably. And, there were likely to be more waiting for him at his home, all with the same questions. Should he talk to the press and give his own version of the story, or should he try to avoid the media at all costs? Since Japanese doctors and the salespeople considered the alleged actions as acceptable industry practice, should he follow the advice of one of his managers to meet with the competition to work out some common actions? Should he also ask for assistance from his government, as one of his German business associates had suggested? Should he try to get help from his European headquarters?

CASE 5.2 # CHEN & LIEW LTD.

This case was prepared by Professor Pierre Goetschin and revised by Professor Dominique Turpin as a basis for class discussion. It is based on facts, but all names have been disguised.

Mr David Lee, product manager in Chen & Liew Ltd., a major Asian office equipment manufacturing company, learned, through hearsay, that two sales representatives working in a subsidiary had offered important 'gifts' to some civil servants in one of the municipal offices. They had also granted friends and members of their families better conditions than those accorded to normal clients. The result had been an increase in sales for the two sales representatives.

As a result of his own enquiry, Lee was able to confirm this state of affairs. The behaviour of the two representatives did not conform to the internal policies of the company – supposedly known to all – so he immediately terminated their contracts.

Several weeks later, one of the representatives, Mr Chiang, committed suicide. The second, Mr Wang, decided to attack the company in court for breach of contract, and demanded substantial financial compensation. In addition, having got wind of the affair, the municipality had launched its own enquiry. A delegation had spoken to several officials as well as to Mr Wang. The latter had declared that giving gifts to buyers was current practice, and that his company discreetly encouraged its representatives to adopt this custom when it enabled them to take orders of a certain magnitude.

Mr Wang and several members of the family of his deceased colleague openly implied that it would not be long before they informed the local press, which was known not to be particularly well disposed towards Chen & Liew Ltd.

Mr Lee informed Mr Harry Choo, General Manager of Chen & Liew, of the state of affairs. While maintaining that the decision to dismiss the representative was correct, the two men wondered what attitude to adopt in these circumstances. The company had never, to their knowledge, consciously approved any form of graft. But how could they prove it? How could such an incident be prevented in the future? Was it possible to avoid a legal battle and, above all, a possible press campaign, both of which would only tarnish the reputation of the company? Would it be advisable to propose an out-of-court financial settlement to the interested parties? What would be the cost? Should the company take the initiative by bringing a legal case against Mr Wang, or by calling a press conference? What should the charges be? And what should the journalists be told?

David Lee and Harry Choo decided to do nothing for the moment – to think out some possible courses of action and to choose one or several measures that would cause the least inconvenience for the company and themselves.

Questions

1. Define the ethical problems raised by the events described above.
2. Are the various problems of the same kind and of the same gravity? Can one differentiate between them? If 'yes' on the basis of what criteria?
3. Has the company itself made errors which laid it open to such incidents? If 'yes' who is to be blamed for these errors?
4. What decision would one expect the court to make?
5. What would you do if you were a journalist?
6. What would you do if you were Mr Wang or a member of Mr Chiang's family?
7. What moves should the company make in the immediate future? And how would you justify them?
8. What measures should the company take to prevent the recurrence of similar events?

6. Strategic Planning for External Environmental Changes

CIBA IN CHINA

This case was prepared by Professor Dominique Turpin as a basis for class discussion rather than to illustrate either effective or ineffective handling of a business situation.

In April 1996, Dr Jacques Barman, Member of the Executive Committee of Ciba–Geigy Limited in charge of Asia, and Guy Clayton, Chairman of Ciba–Geigy (China) Ltd., met in Basel, Switzerland to reflect on the different activities of the group in the People's Republic of China (P.R.C.). Both could be proud of the results achieved so far. Ciba's activities in Asia for the previous four years had grown by 24.2%. Excluding Japan, growth had reached an even higher figure of 31.2% (compared with a growth for the group of 8.3%, or 5.9% excluding Asia). Ciba had been one of the most successful multinational companies in China. Its growth in Asia had outpaced global competitors such as BASF of Germany and DuPont from the US. However, both Jacques Barman and Guy Clayton were aware of three major challenges ahead:

- Growth had slowed down in 1994 and 1995, and although business in the P.R.C. was moving ahead quickly, growth was much more pronounced in the industrial chemicals than in the pharmaceuticals and agrochemicals areas (two of three of the group's pillar businesses).

- Several Chinese partners showed considerable difficulties in living up to their contribution to the joint ventures; foremost, financing had become a major issue with some local companies. At the same time, the Chinese government was not looking favourably at foreign investors extending their ownership to ease the pressure on local partners.

- The 'rules of the game' were being modified. Some of the changes (such as the reduction on value-added tax refunds for exports, new taxes on equipment imports, changes in tax heavens, etc.) affecting pending projects were occurring at an accelerated rate.

Ciba–Geigy Limited

Ciba–Geigy Limited was the result of a merger in 1970 between the Geigy Chemical Company, founded in 1758 by Johann Rudolf Geigy, and Ciba, an organic chemical company founded in the middle of the 19th century. At the time of the merger, Ciba–Geigy was Switzerland's leading multinational company in drugs and pharmaceuticals. Although the company was officially renamed Ciba in 1992, the name Ciba–Geigy continued to be used extensively within the group. In 1996, Ciba was operating in three key business sectors: Healthcare, Agriculture and Industry. In 1996, the Healthcare sector represented about 40% of the group sales (and 57% of its operating income), while the Industry and Agriculture sectors contributed 39% (25%) and 21% (18%), respectively. Ciba's business portfolio comprised 14 divisions and 33 strategic business units (*refer to Exhibit 1*). With Headquarters in Basel (Switzerland), CIBA employed 83,900 people in more than 50 countries, and in 1995 had recorded a profit of US$1.4 billion out of sales of US$16.1 billion.

In 1990, Jacques Barman embarked on restructuring Ciba's activities in Asia. At the time, as Barman himself suggests, Ciba was "...aware that, in order to remain a global player, Asia would have to play a much more important role in Ciba's portfolio than up to this date." At a meeting of all group company presidents, the goals for Asia were formulated as follows:

- Achieve 20% of the group's turnover (or 5 billion Swiss Francs at the then prevailing exchange rates) by the end of the 1990s.

- Achieve market shares at least equal to the worldwide average in all important businesses.

- Do so profitably.

All group companies were asked to develop their own, individual growth strategies and targets. China, of course, was expected to play an important role in this 'Asia/Australia growth challenge'.

Ciba in China

Geigy's products had originally been sold in China since 1886, when Geigy distributed a range of dyestuffs through an agent in Shanghai. This trading activity increased in the following years as Geigy successfully carried out its sales activities through different trading companies. This continued until 1946, when Geigy set up its own branch office in Shanghai. Ciba, on the other hand, had become active in China in 1923 when the interests of the company were represented by a trading company in Hong Kong. In 1947, Ciba opened an office which was later relocated to Hong Kong in 1949.

After the merger in 1970, Ciba–Geigy (Hong Kong) was established, but business with China initially remained very small. It was not until 1979 that liaison offices were set up in hotel rooms in Beijing and Shanghai. A permanent corporate office was opened in 1986. In January 1987, Ciba–Geigy established 'Beijing Zhong-Rui Ciba Geigy Pharmaceutical Company Limited', its first joint venture in China. Between 1987 and 1996, a number of Ciba's Divisions were established in China – from minority stakes in joint ventures to wholly owned subsidiaries (*refer to Exhibit 2*). Ciba's sales of finished products to China had climbed from $90 million in 1993 to close to $140 million in 1995. By early 1996, Ciba already had 30 projects in China, and had made major investments in production plants for pharmaceutical and veterinary products. In 1996, these projects represented total investments of about $300 million and employed about 1,000 people.

Developing Ciba's Strategy for China

Ciba's top management had been preoccupied with China since the early 1980s, when Deng Xiao Ping launched China down the path of 'socialism with Chinese characteristics' and declared: 'Getting rich is glorious!'

Jacques Barman explained:

"Back in the late 1980s, we were confronted with a series of major questions and challenges:

- What should be our ambitions for China, both qualitatively and quantitatively?

- How should we approach China...by region, via licensing, through bricks and mortar, through joint ventures?

- What role should our operations in Hong Kong and Taiwan have in the perspective of a 'Greater China' strategy?

- Where could we find the necessary resources in terms of people and finance to grow in China?

- With 14 divisions used to having full responsibility for global businesses and a great deal of autonomy, how could we coordinate our different activities in China without losing the flexibility of our independent organization?

- Finally, what businesses should we push as priorities into China?

"On this last question, we quickly came to the conclusion that we would be in businesses where we could achieve a leading position in China. In our view, pharmaceutical specialities were not going to be one of those. Healthcare in China is driven by generics and one customer, the state, which buys at the lowest possible cost! Agrochemicals is a very different market from the rest of the world, with China being self-sufficient for fertilizers and technically outdated crop protection products that constitute a serious environmental liability. The need to feed a growing population on a diminishing acreage clearly called for the most advanced crop protection technologies for which China was still well behind world standards. Finally, the need to quickly build a modern infrastructure to support the ambitious expansion programme the government had embarked upon constituted a significant opportunity for speciality chemicals. The idea was therefore:

- to establish a presence in pharmaceuticals which would allow us to build a base for a branded generic business;

- to push vigorously into advanced crop protection markets; and

- to exploit the opportunities in the industrial chemicals sectors.

"The latter was a culture shock for some of our managers! Speciality chemicals' growth rate in Europe was something like −4% between 1989 and 1994, while it was growing by 40% in Asia!"

As Guy Clayton explained:

"In 1988, two questions had to be analysed and answered. First, whether the Chinese government's planned opening of the country to external trade would succeed, and second, what China's policy, towards Hong Kong would look like post-1997, when the British colony reverted to China. The analysis (*refer to Attachment 1.1*) was carried out by a working group from Ciba Hong Kong, composed mainly of middle managers with extensive experience of China. They developed three scenarios for the future of China: 'Dance with the Dragon' – optimistic; 'Chop Suey' – neutral; and 'Great Leap Backwards' – negative (*refer to Attachments 1.2 to 1.4*). The analyses were discussed by a wider public, and the prognosis tended to go in favour of the positive scenario, with the knowledge that there would be setbacks along the way. On the basis of this, a final policy under the 'Dance with the Dragon' scenario was laid down – a sort of snakes and ladders progression upwards (*refer to Attachment 1.5*).

"At that time, we could not believe that our thinking would be so severely tested so quickly. On June 1989, with the events of Tienanmen Square in Beijing, we witnessed a clear manifestation of the social risks of forcing economic development, overheated expectations and the resultant corrective measures by the government. We held our breath and waited for the 'Great Leap Backwards'. Our foreign employees were withdrawn from Beijing and Shanghai, and our representation was left in the hands of Professor Gus Liu, our legal advisor. Five weeks afterwards, a delegation from Ciba Hong Kong visited the city. It signalled back the 'all clear', even though things had not yet got back to normal. The scenario planning team confirmed the positive analysis. However, in Basel, the optimistic predictions about China were seen more cautiously.

"Those of us who were directly connected with business in China were supported in our optimism through our contacts, who reliably informed us that Deng Xiao Ping's 'open door' policy would return. This was confirmed later the same year by our joint venture partners when our foreign managers returned to China to a warm welcome. If we examine the internal economic policy of the Chinese government since the events of Tienanmen Square, it is clear that the government regards the achievement of private wealth by the Chinese population as a primary target. The government does not expect any recurrence of the events in 1989, and the even stronger tendency to openness since the famous journey to the south undertaken by Deng Xiao Ping in 1992 has created an extremely positive climate.

"Last year, gross domestic product in China grew by 12.8%. The outlook for our business in China is very good – our optimistic scenario for 1988 looks as if it will come true, and the 'Dance with the Dragon' can begin!"

The '13 Key Messages' and the Four 'C's' of Ciba

In 1990, after the discussion at the local level had led to the formulation of the three scenarios, Dr Barman approached first the executive committee of Ciba and later in the year the board of directors to obtain a basic agreement to shift resources from other parts of the world to Asia. Thirteen key messages were presented, which were used to formulate the 'Asia/Australia Growth Strategy' in the following year (*refer to* **Attachment 2**). Already at this time, the importance of strategic alliances and the critical aspects in selecting proper partners had been recognized (*refer to 'Key Messages' 10 and 13 in* **Attachment 2**).

For Dr Barman and Guy Clayton, joint ventures in China were viable alternatives, but only under certain special circumstances. "Ciba has always taken a cautious view on joint-venture alliances unless there are exceptional circumstances," explained J. Barman. "But in the P.R.C., we realized that aside from political needs, there was a clear need to team up with local partners because of lack of resources and insider knowledge."

The first experience seemed to confirm the sceptical view on joint ventures, and from these first experiences some rules were derived. "In all joint ventures, certain basic criteria had to be fulfilled," emphasized Dr Barman. "Our first principle is that alliances would only be successful between *competent* partners aiming at congruent targets sharing the same *commitment* to success. The last 'C' concerned *culture*. A mutual respect for cultural differences and the ability to understand them are also crucial."

In the meantime, Dr Barman had added a fifth 'C' as 'condition *sine qua non*' for a joint venture, namely '*capability*' which addresses the ability to deliver both in financial and other critical areas in line with agreed terms of responsibilities in a joint venture.

"Ciba's presence in China," continued Dr Barman, "reflects both this concept as well as the historic development of the opening of China. In a first phase, only joint ventures with Chinese management (Chairmen, General Managers) were allowed, hence our first projects (our Pharma Joint venture in Chong Ping and the Changzhou Toledo Scale Company) were conceived as joint ventures with Chinese management. In the case of our Mettler–Toledo business, this was very successful; in the case of pharmaceuticals, this proved to be a very cumbersome and difficult approach. So, as we gained experience, the Pharma venture was renegotiated. We acquired a majority ownership and full management rights. This taught us an important lesson, namely that the most crucial aspect when setting a strategic alliance is the selection of the proper partner. There is nothing very spectacular about this statement, but in China, the list of ventures which have failed because they ignored this basic requirement is long and all-encompassing. It is critical to make absolutely certain that a future partner:

- Sees in the joint venture a tool for achieving the same goals (congruent targets).

- Is committed to achieving these common targets.

- Has the competencies and capabilities to do so, including the financial resources (one reason why the first Additives JV negotiations dragged on without end was that our partner did not want to lose face by admitting that it would not be given the resources to finance its share).

- And finally, both partners must be willing to cope with cultural differences (such as management practices, accountability, labour efficiency and environmental responsibility) in a way which is acceptable to both. This requires a common base of trust which is not easily or quickly achieved (because of language, culture, political heritage, etc.).

"Hence in China – as in the rest of Asia – a significant investment into developing personal relations is a prerequisite to success. An aggressive 'down to the facts' approach, acceptable in Western culture, is not only considered rude, it is the basis for rejection and failure."

Strategy for Greater China

"Contrary to other companies," explained Dr Barman, "our approach to China has not been a central Group approach, nor have we built a regional management responsibility at the operational level as most other companies do. It is the Divisions which identify opportunities within their given franchises and develop the strategies best adapted to their individual markets and matched with key success factors. The Group's support – primarily through the Hong Kong Group Company and at headquarters – is focused on:

- Providing the necessary infrastructure to allow the Divisions, efficiently and without loss of time, to take advantage of the opportunities as they present themselves.

- Setting up government contacts to facilitate negotiations with the various government agencies, including the ministries responsible for a given area of the economy.

- Providing a base from which to exploit synergies between Divisions.

- Managing the financing of projects and ventures at a country level.

- Creating a 'pull-effect' via the local Division heads and at the Parent Company Divisions.

"At first, Guy Clayton had to convince me that we should follow a Greater China strategy," confessed Jacques Barman.

"Yes!" smiled Guy Clayton. "Jacques wanted to manage Taiwan separately from the P.R.C. market, but the synergies became obvious quickly. It did not make sense to replicate in the P.R.C. the dedicated plants we already had in Taiwan. Therefore, we decided to have complementary plants. For the Chinese authorities in Beijing, investing in Taiwan is simply investing in one of the P.R.C. provinces!

"Our people in Taiwan also are a critical source of support for the P.R.C. market. Divisions were allowed to decide whether to integrate Taiwan or not," highlighted G. Clayton. "Most of our competitors first looked at Taiwan as a separate market, but in the last 12 months, most of them have also adopted a 'Greater China' strategy mainly using Taiwan know-how to get into the P.R.C.

"The tendency by local management," added Clayton, "is to keep the best qualified people in the local organization. The strategy in centralized organizations, on the other hand, goes against the idea of building resources in each organization. How do we develop sufficient talents in different organizations at the rate these fast-growing markets need them? This still remains a challenge."

Western Competition

"I think that we've got many things right," said Guy Clayton. "Some of our competitors worked with the local people but did not worry about top government officials. They did not understand politics in China – regional versus central governments. At Ciba, we are very open with the central government about what we're doing in the provinces. American firms are more reluctant to use our 'amoeba' approach. I do not think that US–China politics has much impact on the success of our American competitors in China – the Chinese are too pragmatic for that. However, I wonder if the Americans are making the effort to become true insiders."

Japanese Competition

"Our Japanese competitors tend to play a different game in China from Western corporations," continued Jacques Barman. "Until recently, the Japanese have been very reluctant to transfer 'state-of-the-art' technology to China. They have been concentrating on trading and the build-up of infrastructure. However, we believe that whoever wants to build an industrial position in China must make a major commitment at the forefront of technology."

"To make money," added Guy Clayton, "we need to export from China, and for that we need the latest technology; we cannot repeat what we have done in the past in terms of technology transfer. The P.R.C. has its own requirements in terms of products and technologies. We need to adapt both to the local requirements!"

"Sure!" confirmed Jacques Barman. "The Japanese are trying to maintain their high profitability and advanced know-how in their domestic market. They tend to use China as an export market as well as a procurement base for local products. I believe that the Japanese chemical industry is not global yet. At best, it's a regional industry, and the Japanese have much to lose from a global competition developing in China."

China as a Learning Platform

"We, too, had to learn the lessons the hard way," admitted Jacques Barman. "The lesson from the failure of the first Crop Protection venture was that although dealing with a competent partner, the Division was reluctant to transfer advanced technologies to a country with no intellectual property rights protection. The partner refused old products and old technologies, and we lost 7 years in a country where every 5-year plan stressed the need for modern agrochemicals to secure food for one billion people. Some of our competitors, like DuPont and Rhône Poulenc, took the risk and built modern plants. As a consequence, they are among the first in this market segment.

"In the case of the Additives joint venture, we did not fall into the same trap. After two years of negotiation and the recognition that our ambitions were not congruent with those of our partner, in spite of obvious irritation of the ministries involved, we cancelled the letter of intent, started a new search for a more suitable partner, and found what looks like a promising new partnership for a project which will be based on our most advanced technologies."

New Approaches to China

"The Animal Health Division very cleverly entered into joint ventures with a number of partners," remarked Guy Clayton, "one having the infrastructure to build a plant, a second controlling the distribution of these types of products, plus the two key opinion leaders in the sector of animal husbandry. In addition, one of the key issues for every project in China, the generation of foreign exchange to pay for imports of equipment and/or active ingredients, was elegantly solved by substituting for a planned investment in Grimsby (United Kingdom). This allowed the exports of active ingredients produced in China to the Group to pay for imports of active ingredients needed by the joint venture in Shanghai.

"Our Industrial Divisions – with the exception of Additives – are following different approaches," commented Jacques Barman. "It would be quite unreasonable to go through a major asset reduction programme in Textile Dyes while adding new assets with a foreseeable long-term pay-back in China. Therefore, Textile Dyes have embarked on the selection of a partner which would contribute a sound manufacturing base, a good distribution system and knowledge of the market. We will contribute modern manufacturing, product, application and environment protection technologies which will give the venture a competitive base from which to supply the Chinese market.

"Given our experience in China, I feel I should stress the following lessons," said Jacques Barman:

"1. Identifying the proper partner is the most important prerequisite for success, in particular because the exit for failure of a joint venture is not easy in China!

2. Just as important is the delegation of qualified project managers who are prepared to accept and live the cultural challenge, which will always be part of such an assignment. That's a major challenge! We absolutely must, both at corporate and divisional level, develop a more sophisticated approach for selecting, developing, training and rewarding those key people who will make or break a project.

3. Any attempt to unload old technologies or products is doomed to failure. Competition will be fierce; if we do not compete at the forefront of technology, others certainly will. The issue cannot be to build projects on 'cheap labour' as a key success factor; rather, the issue is to use the appropriate technology to ascertain maximum productivity.

4. The generation of foreign exchange to pay for imports must be built into every project.

5. When selecting a partner, we must be very careful first to identify our weaknesses. Weaknesses must be compensated by the partner's strengths. This may require selecting different partners for each project on a different set of criteria.

6. When deciding on the place to locate a venture, there are still other issues to consider such as:

   • Accessibility (favouring the large coastal cities).

   • Bureaucracy (that is, the provincial government's attitudes towards foreign investments and its ability to stand up to central pressure).

   • Availability of qualified middle managers (an aspect which favours Beijing and Shanghai and some coastal provinces).

   • The question as to whether future expatriates and their families will be able and willing to live in a given town is also critical.

   • Availability of key raw materials which are usually distributed and allocated by the provinces, rather than by the central government, has proven a key factor. (Provinces aspire to maximize value added and will only 'export' surplus to other provinces.) Competitors have built plants only to find out that they are not able to procure the needed raw materials!"

Ciba China Company (CCC)

"Despite all its economic liberalization," commented Dr Barman, "China is still a country with many administrative challenges. There are many internal and external issues to address – for instance, recruitment of employees, management development, social packages and also the representation of Ciba's interest with the authorities, to name just a few."

"To form a unified holding company umbrella for all Ciba's activities in China under the Ciba China Company (CCC) to address these challenges was a good initiative" acknowledged Guy Clayton. "It was not easy to convince the authorities of a concept which was unknown and not foreseen in the law of the country, but we succeeded in convincing them of the mutual advantages of such a holding company."

"The choice of Beijing over Shanghai as the headquarters of the new company, given the nature of the contacts with the authorities in the P.R.C., was also well-founded," reinforced Dr Barman.

"The development of the organization and structure of the CCC will depend very heavily on the development of the economy and Ciba's activities in China," continued Dr Barman. "Basically, only those activities that cannot be carried out more efficiently by the divisions will be carried out centrally. We will also have to redefine the role of the five liaison offices we have in China, as soon as the CCC's charter has been agreed with the Chinese authorities."

Looking Ahead

"Ciba seems to be ready to address the challenges in China," concluded Jacques Barman. "We have remained consistent in our efforts. We started to be an insider well before our competitors did, and we defined the game to a certain extent. Consistency has been our strength in China. I also think that it is important that in every joint venture, we use our very best technology. I'm convinced that this is the way to go."

Both Jacques Barman and Guy Clayton agreed that despite the success of Ciba in China, a number of key challenges still lay ahead.

"Managing scarce human resources and financing are probably our two major challenges," highlighted Guy Clayton.

"With no local financial supply, all projects had to be financed and refinanced from outside the P.R.C. We need to recognize that change is faster in China than anywhere else in the world," added Dr Barman. "The rules of the game change every day. For example, when China decided to introduce a value-added tax, we had to adjust on the spot. When the Chinese authorities changed the import taxes on equipment procured from abroad for projects in construction, we had to redefine suppliers, etc."

"Indeed," confirmed Guy Clayton. "In China, one needs to cope with a high degree of uncertainty. As a result, we need to focus on our key competencies, remain flexible enough to act and react quickly to any kind of situation. We also need to develop a learning organization, not to reinvent the wheel every time; we must make the best use of our scarce resources and continue to invest in relationships. The investment we make in building relationships will be even more valuable in case of bad times for China!"

"Managing expectations is another key challenge for management involved in the P.R.C.," added J. Barman. "Whoever goes there for a quick return in our type of business will be disappointed. Even boards of directors sometimes grow impatient or frustrated by continuously changing external parameters... but then, the founders of our company took risks in internationalizing our company... today the challenge to globalize rests on us!"

EXHIBIT 1

CIBA's Business Portfolio (1996)

Pillar Businesses	Pharmaceuticals
	Specialities, generics
	Plant Protection
	Weed control, disease control, insect control,
	seed treatment
	Additives
	Additives for: plastics/elastometers/fibres, coat
	lubricants, PVC stabilization
Core Businesses	Textile Dyestuffs
	Reactive dyes, wool, polyamide and silk dyes
	Polyester, cellulose, polyacrilnitril
	Dyeing Auxiliaries
	Chemicals
	Chemtex, detergents and cosmetics, paper, leather fur
	Polymers
	Resins, formulated materials
	Pigments
	High-performance pigments, classical pigments,
	inorganic pigments, dispersions
	Mettler–Toledo
	Laboratory balances, industrial and retail weighing
	analytical and process systems
Growth Businesses	Self Medication
	Zyma, CCP/USA
	Diagnostics
	Composites
	US materials, Euro materials, structures & interiors
	Ciba Vision
	Lenses, lens care, ophthalmic pharmaceuticals
Development Businesses	Seeds
Niche Businesses	Animal Health

Source: Ciba.

EXHIBIT 2

Outlook of Ciba's Involvement in China (1996)

Venture	Products involved	Markets	Status
Jiangsu Ciba Agro Chemicals Ltd. – new facilities: • Kunshan • Jiangsu Province	Formulation, packaging and marketing of crop protection products	Crop protection market in China	Launch in 1996
Joint venture with Qingdao Pesticide Factory to Qingdao Ciba Agro	Two important products for cotton	Crop protection and insect control	Planned for beginning of 1996
Joint venture with Qingdao Dyestuffs Factory and Pigment Division	Production and marketing of organic pigments	Organic pigments	Operational in 1996
Joint venture agreement with Shanghai Ciba Gaoqiao Chemical Co. Ltd. and Additives Division. Partners: Gao Qiao Petrochemical of Sinopec, Nippon Alkyl Phenol, JV of Ciba with Mitsui Petrochemical	Irganox 1010/1076 and Irgafos 168	Anti-oxidants	Plant to be operational in 1997
Joint venture agreement with Qingdao Dyestuffs Factory and Chemicals Division	Manufacture and marketing of selected synthetic tanning agents	Leather	Agreement signed December 1994
Agreement with Institute of Microbiology and Epidemiology, Beijing Kunming Pharmaceutical Factory, CITIC Techno.	Development of a novel orally active, fixed combination anti-malarial drug	Anti-malaria	Agreement signed December 1994
Opening of new contact lens production facility in Shanghai to support Shanghai Ciba Vision Contact Lens Co. Ltd.	Production of both conventional and planned replacement lenses	Conventional and replacement lenses	Production facility opened in 1995
Agreement to join with Qingdao Dyestuffs in production at Qingdao in Shandong Province	Disperse dyes, broadening and deepening of the cooperation regarding licensing agreement for the production of POLAR dyes for wool dyeing	Polyester dyeing	Agreement signed February 1995
Joint venture agreement with Shilou Town Economic Development Co. Ltd. to establish a Guangdong Ciba Polymers Co. Ltd. in Guangdong Province	Manufacturing and marketing of ARALDITE	Epoxy/resins and other related products for electronics, electrical engineering and coating	Agreement signed July 1995

Source: Ciba.

ATTACHMENT 1.1

CIBA's China Scenario Plan to Year 2000

1. Need for a Scenario Plan

China has traditionally been an economy driven by State policies and administration rather than free market principles. In the past decades, economic development was slow and often interrupted by extreme political changes. Reliable business planning was difficult, and most foreign companies responded to the uncertain environment with short-term contingency planning.

In recent years, however, China has undergone significant changes that are expected to continue with increased momentum in the future. The present leadership has implemented more coherent policies to reach ambitious economic targets by the year 2000. Foreign companies are being encouraged to participate in the economic development of China through capital ventures and technology transfer agreements. The emergence of a new type of partnership role of foreign companies is opening up many new opportunities and highlights the need for mid- to long-term strategic planning.

The scenario planning method was chosen as the most suitable means to provide Ciba–Geigy's management with insight into the future possibilities and limitations of a rapidly changing China.

2. Methodology

The China Task Force (CTF) defined three basic scenarios dealing with China's future, namely:

1. Dance with the Dragon: an optimistic outlook.
2. Chop Suey: an in-between outlook.
3. Great Leap Backwards: a pessimistic scenario.

Scenario writing
The scenarios were based on an objective analysis of four core areas: politics, economy, science/technology and society, each of which dealt with specific parameters which were identified as being important to China's development.

Probability score
Each scenario was given an overall probability rating based on average individual scores given by the CTF members for each parameter (10 = very likely, 0 = unlikely).

Ciba HK scenario
Because of the closeness in ratings between the first two scenarios, the CTF critically reviewed the parameter statements in order to eliminate ambiguity and overlap of ideas.

Subsequently, a fourth scenario ('Growing in Harmony with China') was created, based on the most likely future development described in the first three scenarios.

Time scale
The scenario plan covers the period up to the year 2000, with regular monitoring and updating of the scenarios planned.

Source: Ciba.

ATTACHMENT 1.2

CIBA's China Scenario Plan to Year 2000

Scenario 1: Dance with the Dragon

Political world stability, economic resilience

All is well politically in a local and economic climate which enables China to pursue its political and social change objectives without such setbacks as world recession, uncontrollable inflation or social and ethnic unrest.

GNP growth: 3 × OECD

As a result of this, growth continues smoothly in the region of 8–10% GNP average per annum. China's full acceptance into the developed world is going smoothly. Western and Japanese commercial enterprises adopt a confident, open attitude in their dealings with China. The more contact, the better the understanding, and the less the risk of failure.

Greater China

Taiwan Accord

The earlier part of the scenario period (1988–95) sees the rapid development of Greater China as economic ties with Taiwan gather pace. There is a progressive easing of travel restrictions and direct contacts. 'One nation, two systems – SAR (Special Administrative Region)' seems an increasing likelihood for Taiwan and becomes an accepted agenda between Beijing and Taipei for the year 2000.

China adjusts to capitalism

Internally, China's establishment, its bureaucratic procedures and its physical and economic infrastructure quickly adjust to its new role. Hong Kong plays an appreciable part in those procedures and remains the centre for financial services and business consultancy at the same time as seeing a smooth change of administration in 1997.

Educational standards continue to improve rapidly, and China quickly makes up for the lack of skills inherited from the Cultural Revolution.

Potential competitor

China becomes an interesting market for Ciba–Geigy products, but also a potential competitor as it moves into the top five economies in the world.

Decentralization
Quality

Asia-Pacific common market

Decentralization occurs swiftly and efficiently down to the level of individual enterprises. Internal competition emerges, resulting in greatly improved quality and productivity. China, with Japan, becomes the dominant economic growth area of the Western Pacific basin, which, with the ASEAN countries and Australia, forms an increasingly self-sufficient Asia-Pacific common market block. Internal trading within the block becomes more important than bilateral trade with the US.

Chemical industry expansion

The expansion of the chemical sector is marked by increased pressure on Western and Japanese companies to offer 'state-of-the-art' technology. There will be rapid growth, but the ability of Chinese chemical enterprises to compete worldwide will be restricted by a lack of home-grown inventions and organizational (provincial) fragmentation. Only towards the year 2000 will we see restructuring and concentration of individual corporations of specific strength for which they have a critical mass market share. Areas where this would happen first are dyes, agrochemicals, fertilizers and wood glues. There will be a marked increase in R&D expenditures from 1995 onwards. Some former State chemical institutes will be wholly owned by foreign concerns.

Source: Ciba.

ATTACHMENT 1.3

CIBA's China Scenario Plan to Year 2000

Scenario 2: Chop Suey

'Stop goes' — Whatever the leadership's intentions may be, China cannot avoid 'stop goes'. These may be induced by China's inability to insulate itself from Western economic cycles or by the tendency to overheat the internal economy and the need to take corrective action sometimes. In spite of these hiatuses, there is, on the whole, steady economic progress with GDP averaging 5–7% but fluctuating between 0 and 15% for short periods.

Inconsistency — There is consequent inconsistency in the bureaucratic interference into affairs, which presents problems to foreign enterprises who perceive greater risk in their opportunistic decisions to become engaged in this market, with the result that many decide that China is too much trouble.

Nerve and commitment — For Ciba, the market is still a must, but with 'bad news' stories of others' failures, we will need nerve and long-term commitment. If we get it right, the pickings will be good.

Foresight needed in HK — For Hong Kong, there will be moments of ecstasy and moments of gloom; risk taking will abound, but the brain drain will stretch human resources and skills to the limit. Manpower planning will be an important success factor for China dealings.

Technology transfer patchy — Chemical industry development will be patchy. The problem of sophisticated technology transfer will be exacerbated by lack of trained Chinese. Japanese will continue to avoid 'state-of- the-art' technology transfer. Some Western

Some will succeed — companies are able to establish a 'most-favoured' relationship by a consistent approach and good top contacts. Dyes and agrochemicals offer best chances because of the strength/size of the end use markets. Joint ventures will be the most likely approach.

Source: Ciba.

ATTACHMENT 1.4

CIBA's China Scenario Plan to Year 2000

Scenario 3: Great Leap Backwards

Very negative	This totally negative scenario is more unthinkable to the Chinese than it is imaginable to the Western world.
Cultural Revolution dead	The misery of the Cultural Revolution is vivid and repugnant. The last ten years of the 'Deng Era' have, by contrast, helped ordinary Chinese realize that they have a way out through their own efforts and that they have the potential to become an economic entity.
Low likelihood	It is the opinion of the Hong Kong China Task Force that the likelihood of this scenario is very low indeed, and that further elaboration here is unnecessary because, faced with this eventuality, even our limited China engagement so far will be rendered useless.
HK disaster	For Hong Kong, the effects would be disastrous. No 'drain' will have sufficient capacity to cope with the 'brains' evacuating!
Heavy chemicals only *No chance for Ciba*	The chemical industry will only develop at the heavy end, albeit slowly and unprofitably. No place for specialization. A number of joint ventures will fail, and foreign investors will cut their losses and go home.

Source: Ciba.

ATTACHMENT 1.5

CIBA's China Scenario Plan to Year 2000

Scenario 4: Ciba–Geigy Growing in Harmony with China

Introduction

When it comes to rating the likelihood of each of these scenarios, the China Task Force overwhelmingly felt that 'Great Leap Backwards' was negligible. Although 'Chop Suey' was the most likely scenario, a surprisingly large percentage of likelihood was given to 'Dance with the Dragon'. Remembering that the Task Force was made of Ciba's most experienced 'Chinapreneurs', it was thought right to try to articulate one more scenario between 'Dance with the Dragon' and 'Chop Suey'. This scenario was called 'Ciba–Geigy Growing in Harmony with China'.

Reforms	Both the 13th China Communist Party Congress and the 7th National People Congress were marked by the retirement of many senior leaders, including Deng Xiao Ping, in order to give way to an emerging younger and better educated new leadership to carry on the political reforms for China to become one of the world's leading nations in the next century.
Power distribution	No major conflicts over the fundamentals – continuation of reforms, raising the living standards of the people, the new coastal area strategy, an increase in agricultural production, improvements in infrastructure and a cut in bureaucracy – are expected to come up between the reform-minded Party Chief Zhao Ziyang and the rather conservative Prime Minister Li Peng. However, differences will arise regarding the pace of reforms and especially the adoption of an appropriate formula to boost the economic development. Consequently, this scenario foresees the predominance of political stability with some manageable ups and down, as against the stops and goes experienced in China up to 1979.
Party role	The political reforms also aim at clearly defining the roles of the party, government and industry with regard to China's productive sector. Mr Zhao has pledged to boost productivity and spur efficiency by reducing party bureaucracy, particularly the traditional interference in daily enterprise management.
Greater China	Greater China links are tightening with Hong Kong's transformation into a Special Administrative Region under the P.R.C. government on 1 July 1997, and recent steps by the Taiwanese government towards a relaxation of Chinese–Taiwanese relations.

Source: Ciba.

ATTACHMENT 2

Dr Barman's 13 Key Messages

1. Without a strong position in Asia, Ciba cannot live up to the challenge of maintaining its global leadership position.
2. 'Asia' is a geographical term – the region contains countries at varying stages of development with very different market demands.
3. Growth in 'Asia' is fuelled to an increasing extent by 'internal' demand.
4. Japan is going to be the most challenging competitor to confront in Asia.
5. With few exceptions, most countries do not exhibit a net labour surplus; hence, costs for qualified labour will continue to increase rapidly in most countries.
6. The strength of Western companies is their technical expertise. This must be leveraged to the utmost.
7. Pay-back is even more critical for projects in a part of the world where industries shift rapidly. Alternatives to owning 'bricks and mortar' must be evaluated more aggressively.
8. Ciba's commitments to China must be seen as a long-term, strategic move. There will be ups and downs and set-backs that we must be prepared to accept and address.
9. China represents a large potential local market, exhibits a net labour surplus and its eagerness for new technologies in certain areas equals that of the world leaders.
10. Strategic alliances fail foremost because of poor partner selection (4C's).
11. China is not a dumping ground for old technologies or products. We can only compete successfully at the forefront of technology.
12. Foreign exchange is and will remain a major issue for any project considered.
13. Partners must be selected on the basis of their ability to compensate for our weaknesses.

7. Implementing Global Strategies in Asia

CASE 7.1 **HILTI CORPORATION**

This case was prepared by Professor Peter Killing as a basis for class discussion rather than to illustrate either effective or ineffective handling of a business situation.

In the summer of 1993, the new executive board of Hilti Corporation, led by Dr Pius Baschera, was meeting to discuss the less than satisfactory operations of the Hilti company in Hong Kong. Dr Baschera and the other three members of the board would not officially take up their new positions until January 1994, but to ensure a smooth transition, the group began functioning in mid-1993. Whatever decision they came to about Hong Kong would have to be agreed to by Michael Hilti, the current CEO, and other members of the outgoing executive board.

The way forward in Hong Kong was not clear. The country manager was proposing a course of action that was a marked deviation from Hilti's well-proven worldwide strategy of selling construction tools and fasteners directly to end users. Yet something had to be done. In a market that was growing at least 10% per year, it appeared that Hilti Hong Kong would have 1993 sales and profits 5–10% lower than those of 1992.

Hilti Corporation

The Hilti company was founded in 1941 by Martin and Eugen Hilti in the Principality of Liechtenstein, which is nestled between Austria and the eastern border of Switzerland. The Hilti brothers laid the foundations for the company when they obtained an order to manufacture threaded studs and nails for a pistol-like tool that was intended for fastening work in construction. Although not fully developed, this tool was recognized by the Hiltis as having great potential for the rebuilding of Europe. Patents were obtained, and a product line centred on high-velocity tools was created. (*Refer to **Exhibit 1** in the plate section* for a selection of products from Hilti's line of drills, anchoring systems and direct fastening systems.)

By 1960, Hilti had a major production facility in Liechtenstein and was well established in European markets. Martin Hilti's belief that 'market share is more important than factories' had led to a great emphasis on understanding and responding to customer needs. Recognizing that customers would value knowledgeable advice on how to best use Hilti tools, the company had established a direct sales force, rather than using distributors or dealers.

The 1960s and 1970s were years of strong growth for Hilti, as construction in the company's major markets of Europe and the United States was booming. Key to Hilti's success were the strong-willed entrepreneurs running each country operation who pushed their sales forces for ever better results. As sales and profits grew, production facilities were added throughout Europe, and a plant was built in the US.

In the early 1980s, however, Hilti was hard hit by a worldwide recession in the construction industry. Sales and profits slumped, and the managers in major markets like Germany, France and the US informed Hilti that little could be done in this adverse economic environment. Market shares were already high, so growth was not an option: they would just have to ride out the storm and wait for better times. One younger manager commented:

> When the markets turned down, we began to realize that these Hilti 'country kings' were not very complete managers. They successfully grew sales volumes in boom times, but they had failed to develop their organizations and their people.
>
> I have to give credit to Schaan (Hilti's head office), as they recognized the problem, and in the next few years replaced most of the country kings. They promoted or brought in from the outside younger managers, better educated, with broader skills.
>
> Of course simply changing the senior managers was not enough, as there were many others in the country organizations also used to doing things their own way. So we brought in McKinsey to perform an overhead value analysis, which resulted in changes in our processes and structures that gave us more flexibility. And we were not happy with central research and development – it seemed to be an empire unto itself – so we also brought in BCG (Boston Consulting Group), and created four divisions at head office that were responsible for developing, manufacturing and sourcing products that were then sold to the country units for resale to final customers.
>
> These changes went some way to curbing the power of the countries, and improving the innovation process in the company.

Strategy 2000 – the Beginning

In 1984, for the first time, a week-long meeting was held to bring together all senior Hilti managers from around the world. As the thirty or so country managers made presentations on their business, it became clear that, in the words of one of the attendees: "we had no vision, no strategy, no coherence. We were simply a collection of countries each doing its own thing, and the results were not nearly as good as they could have been."

A decision was made to begin a major strategy review, again with the help of BCG. The work began in the United States, where Hilti's performance had been suffering. The challenge was both to increase profitability and return to higher rates of growth. A close examination of Hilti customers and their needs made it clear that Hilti's policy of selling direct to end customers should be maintained. It was also decided that telephone-based customer service should be instituted. Thus, a customer could contact Hilti by phone, or by direct contact with the salesman.

Hilti USA was divided into three business units, each to serve a particular customer segment for the whole country. This was a sharp change from the previous area-based organization in which a salesman sold all Hilti products to all customers in his geographic region. A senior manager commented:

> A change like this is dramatic, because it means that many of our customers are now dealing with a new salesman, and they have to get to know each other. Remember that we are not just selling products; we are also giving advice and training – and it is those things and our product quality that allow us to price our products 20–30% above competitors like Bosch or Makita. So the salesman has to learn his product line in depth, and a market segmented approach encourages that. Once the salesman understands the applications of his product line in the trades he serves very well, he will begin to demand modifications and new products from our product development people.

With the US model in place by the late 1980s, attention turned to Europe. Pius Baschera, head of Hilti's operation in Germany at the time, recalled the situation:

> Germany was (and still is) Hilti's largest operation, and we were performing well. The country was divided into five geographic regions, and within each region the sales force was segmented by trade group – plumbers, electricians, and so on. So we could see the US rationale for dividing the sales force – although we thought they had the trades segmented incorrectly – but we could not see the rationale for creating whole business units for each trade. Our plan was to keep the sales force specialized by trade, but at the management levels above the sales force, we did not see the need for specialization.
>
> There was a lot of pressure on the German management team to make a quick transition to the US model, however. The president of Hilti Western Hemisphere was given the responsibility for the total core business worldwide, and as a member of the executive board, he worked with the new head of Germany (Baschera's successor) to push changes through. There was a lot of resistance: almost no one, for example, thought that the quick move to set up a central customer service function and closing all the regional sales offices was a good idea. Several key managers left the German company.

The Evolution of Strategy 2000

As the roll-out of Strategy 2000 continued in Europe, adjustments were made in a number of areas. Agreement was reached on the best way to segment the sales force, for example, which meant that the US adopted the trade segments used in Europe. The German drive for maintaining regional centres was not supported, however.

In the early 1990s, a diagram was created that captured the heart of the Hilti 2000 strategy on a single page. This chart, shown in *Exhibit 2*, became known in the company as the 'mother of all charts' and was widely displayed in company facilities all over the world. The creation of a common, simply communicated strategy was seen by employees at all levels as extremely valuable, and the items on the chart became a part of everyday communication.

As European countries gradually moved to implement Strategy 2000, the resistance in Germany continued. In the early 1990s, with East Germany opening up, Germany was growing at 20% per year. Instituting a programme of major change did not make sense to many people in the German operation. But by 1991, it was clear that the change would happen; by early 1993, it was largely complete.

A Challenge for New Management

In mid-1993, significant changes were taking place at the most senior levels of Hilti. Michael Hilti, the son of Martin, was to become Chairman of the Board, and Pius Baschera, aged 44, would be the first non-family member to take over the CEO role. At the same time, the other two members of the executive board would also change, as Hilti's mandatory age limit of 55 necessitated their retirement.

The Hong Kong situation was the first major issue addressed by the new management team. Pius Baschera commented:

> In 1991, dealer sales accounted for one-third of our total sales in Hong Kong. But in 1992, this figure fell to 19%, and is heading for zero in 1993 as strategy 2000 is fully implemented. To compensate, we have increased our direct sales force, but sales are not increasing yet. Without dealers, we find it difficult to access the small customers – and they are growing in number. We estimate that there were about 6,000 construction companies in Hong Kong in 1983, with an average of about 16 employees. Today, there are closer to 13,000 with an average of fewer than ten employees. So there are more and more small guys in this business, and at the moment, they account for at least 15–20% of the Hong Kong market. In the West, small operators play a less important role.
>
> What the Hong Kong general manager is proposing is that we use a controlled number of 'local sales elements' (the name he gave to dealers) to carry a limited number of our product lines most suitable for small customers. In this way, he argues, we can regain our lost ground, and participate fully in the growth of the market.
>
> Taking a broader perspective, we must remember that while approximately 60% of our two billion Swiss francs of annual revenue comes from Europe, and only about 12% from Asia, our greatest growth prospects are in Asia and Eastern Europe. And we are not currently meeting our targets of double digit growth in sales and profits – so we need to get our approach to Asian markets just right.

Another member of the new executive board added the following:

> We must bear in mind that there are good reasons for our direct sales approach. First, we are not just selling products. We add value by giving

advice and training. Our customers trust us. We can only create such relationships by selling direct. Second, by working with customers, we get valuable ideas for new products and applications. Third, if we have two competing channels, we hurt our sales force. And remember, of the 12,000 people in this company, 4,000 are salesmen! These people live on their commissions, and being an exclusive channel for Hilti products is very much part of their livelihood. We do not want to set up a conflict in the company.

The other risk of using dealers is that we lose control of pricing. We have international customers who can quite effectively take advantage of any global anomalies in our pricing policies. And of course, we lose some of our profit margin by selling to dealers.

And if we do this in Hong Kong, it will only be the beginning. I can name at least three other countries that are just implementing Strategy 2000 who will argue that they too should be allowed to use 'local sales elements'.

A third board member commented:

We will never survive if we just copy what other people are doing. Bosch uses dealers and is very good at it. They have drill bits packaged nicely to be displayed in dealer premises. They have point of purchase material, incentive programmes for dealers, and so on. We have none of this. It is not our way of doing business. We need to stick with our unique Hilti strengths and approach to doing business wherever we can.

Secondly, I must stress that while the roll-out of Strategy 2000 into Asia is extremely important, we *also* need to extend our Hilti culture to the Asian region. As our small country operations in Asia grow, we need to ensure that we manage our people there the same way as we do elsewhere. We must emphasize worldwide training programmes, for example, which will stress the Hilti values of self-responsibility, freedom to take risks, openness, commitment and freedom of choice.

As he sat at the board table with his new team, Pius Baschera reflected on the views of Michael Hilti and his executive team, the people to whom he had to make his new management group's recommendation:

Michael and his executive team have been working very hard to put Strategy 2000 in place. It has not always been easy, as the struggle in Germany shows, but they have been firm and persistent. If we come in as the new management team and as our first act encourage Hong Kong to walk away from Strategy 2000, I do not know how it will be received.

EXHIBIT 1

The HILTI Product Line

See Plate Section

EXHIBIT 2

Global Strategy

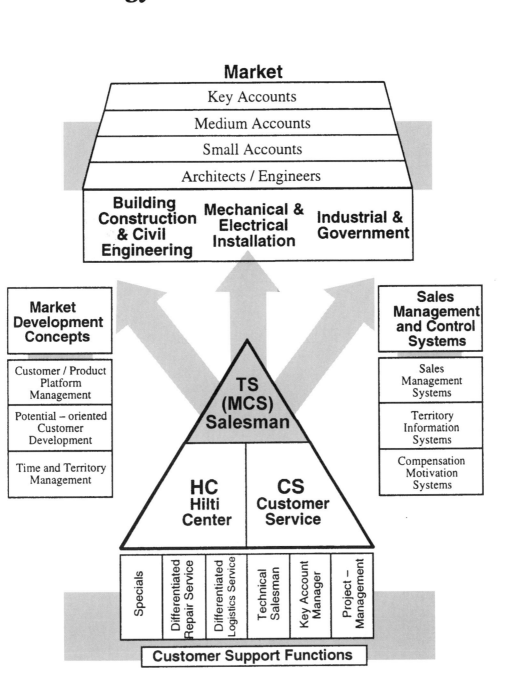

Source: Hilti Corporation Company Document.

PART TWO

Asian Businesses in Asia Pacific

Introduction

With Japan in the forefront, the 'four Asian tigers' – Singapore, Hong Kong, South Korea and Taiwan – have also been very dynamic markets in Asia. In the last ten to fifteen years, the economies in Malaysia, the Philippines and Thailand have also taken off. Large economies like China, which had been struggling for centuries in poverty, are quickly catching up.

In terms of business environment, there is a great diversity in the Asia-Pacific countries. For instance, management skills in Japan and the NICs are much more sophisticated than those in other countries of the region. However market competition in these countries is highly intensive. As mentioned in the introduction to the book, many companies in these countries have been expanding their businesses all over the region, seeking cheaper labour resources and new markets. At the same time, companies in Japan and the NICs are pursuing excellence in high-technology industries and services.

In this part, eight cases are included. Four of them are about Japanese companies. The other four are the cases of a Chinese Bank, a Philippine multinational company, the Malaysian airline and a review of Asian civil aviation business.

8. Domestic Competition in Japan

It would be controversial to suggest that Asian countries are following the Japanese model of development. Despite this, Japan has been at the leading edge of economic and technological development and of business management in the region. Companies' comprehension of business management is associated with the sophistication and competitiveness of the business environment.

Sanraku Inc. presents the case of the leading Japanese alcohol beverage company, facing a critical restructuring after having experienced a steady decline in profits over many years. It puts students into the position of the manager in charge of a turnaround situation and encourages them to analyse restructuring options in the Japanese context. It also lets participants determine the best strategy for the company in the long term. Particularly, the case provides insight into the Japanese business environment, with cultural and economic constraints.

Konica Corp. reviews the circumstances in the Japanese photographic film industry at a time when Konica was facing Kodak's challenges in its domestic market. It invites students to become familiar with the concepts and approaches for market segmentation, market analysis and customer behaviour.

Kirin Brewery Co., Ltd. – The Dry Beer War presents the challenges facing Kirin Brewery Co., Ltd, in its attempts to compete with other breweries in the Japanese domestic market. It looks into general marketing issues, such as how to create and introduce new products in a mature market, and how to assess a marketing strategy by going through possible alternatives and their advantages and risks. Meanwhile, it provides a particular picture of Japanese consumers' expectations. It invites students first to assess the strengths and weakness of the major brewers in Japan, and the performance of Kirin, and then to anticipate competitors' reactions.

9. Competing in the Asia-Pacific Region

Asia-Pacific countries are enormously diverse, in terms of culture, wealth, political and social systems. Nevertheless there are many advantages for Asian companies doing business in the other countries within the region. More or less, they have close links between each other, such as family links, some similarities in culture, and geographical proximity.

In recent years, competition in the Pacific region has been intensifying. Asian companies have to increase their competitiveness by improving internal management and information technology to enhance their customer services.

Hong Kong & Shenzhen Bank introduces the challenges for a bank to become more customer oriented. This dynamic case series (A) to (F) on the service industry presents the different phases of a customer service project led by a female executive in Hong Kong.

The Matsushita Group in Malaysia presents the successful experience of a Japanese company, Matsushita Group in Malaysia. Specifically it highlights the general pattern of internationalization followed by the company in terms of export and foreign investment (different from the so-called 'Western' pattern). It looks into the key elements, including aspects of the company's management philosophy, organizational structure and management policy, etc.

Malaysian Airline System – Flying into the Future describes how this Asian-based airline came up against rising operating costs at a time when the costs for financing its ambitious expansion programme were reaching their peak. At the same time, management had to begin laying down strategies to capitalize on the opportunities represented by the new international airport being constructed 80 km outside Kuala Lumpur, and due to open in 1997.

China's XFM project is a very appropriate vehicle for an exam or an end-of-module exercise for MBA students. The case looks at the introduction of a 'motorized bicycle' in the special context of the Chinese environment. The students must take into account potential customer segments and their different appeal for the product, competitors' products, tough distribution issues, costs and government regulations.

FoodWorld Supermarkets in India chronicles the development of the first chain of supermarkets in India targeted at the growing middle class and highlights the challenges of introducing a new format in an established marketplace populated with small 'mom and pop' retail stores. The case may be useful in exploring retailing in the context of an environment so different from those familiar to most Western students that many preconceptions about consumer behaviour market conditions can be questioned. It may also be used to ferret out some of the issues involved in cross-border retailing, a fundamental question being raised by many retail companies that are exploring international market opportunities. What indeed are the challenges and opportunities that may be encountered in entering new markets?

8. Domestic Competition in Japan

SANRAKU INC.

This case was prepared by Professor Dominique Turpin as a basis for class discussion rather than to illustrate either effective or ineffective handling of a business situation.

In October 1987, Tadao Suzuki, President of Sanraku Inc., and the 'RS Team' ('Restructure Sanraku') were reviewing a 7-month in-depth investigation of Sanraku's situation. Established in 1934, and listed on the First Section of the Tokyo Stock Exchange since 1949, Sanraku was a leading Japanese manufacturer and distributor of alcoholic beverages. In 1987, Sanraku had boasted the largest market shares in wine and 'shin-seishu' (a kind of 'sake'), and had held fourth place in whisky sales. Since 1984, Sanraku had also begun selling and distributing the de-luxe imported brandy, Rémy Martin. Despite this record of achievements, Sanraku had been facing a steady decline in profits and sales since 1984 (*refer to Exhibits 1 to 3*). At the end of fiscal year 1986 (April 1986–March 1987), net sales of Sanraku had declined from ¥70.4 billion in 1985 to ¥62.4 billion (US$445.9 million), and net income had dropped from ¥1.4 billion to ¥947 million (US$6.8 million) during the same period of time (in 1987, US$1 = ¥139). In April 1987, Sanraku's shareholders had appointed Tadao Suzuki as CEO of the company with the challenging task of turning the company around.

Sanraku

Founded in 1934 by Chuji Suzuki, grandfather of the present president, Sanraku was originally established as the 'Alcoholic Beverages Division' of Ajinomoto (Japan's largest food manufacturer) to produce 'sake' and 'shochu' (another popular Japanese white spirit). Since rice was too expensive to make 'sake' (Japan's traditional alcoholic beverage) at the beginning of this century, Ajinomoto's engineers invented a new way to produce 'sake' from the fermentation of wheat starch, a by-product made by Ajinomoto. As the 'Alcoholic Beverages Division' of Ajinomoto grew larger, Chuji Suzuki decided to spin it off and establish it as an independent company under the name Sanraku (literally 'three pleasures'). Over time, Japanese people associated the name Sanraku with 'shochu' and 'sake', and the company was soon recognized as one of the finest Japanese manufacturers, importers and distributors of wines and spirits.

The corporate philosophy that guided Sanraku's management over the following 50 years was to 'provide good quality liquors at affordable prices for the general public to enjoy'. During the 1960s and 1970s Sanraku had diversified into chemicals, pharmaceuticals and feedstuffs. As a result, in 1987, 'sake' and 'shochu' represented 31.2% of Sanraku's total revenues; wines and spirits: 48%; chemicals and pharmaceuticals: 10.8%; and feedstuffs: 9.8%.

Sanraku had a domestic network of 20 branches and plants, and one research facility, as well as five overseas affiliates and one branch office (*refer to Exhibits 4 and 5*). The company also enjoyed a cooperative relationship with the Ajinomoto Group in the areas of sales, distribution and information processing. In 1987, Sanraku had some 1,500 employees, with half of them in production. Sales and administration employed 350 and 250 people, respectively, while 120 people worked in research and development (*refer to Exhibit 6* for Sanraku's Organization Chart).

Tadao Suzuki

Before joining Sanraku Inc., Tadao Suzuki had spent his whole career with Ajinomoto Co. Inc., a company founded by his grandfather and his elder brother, which had become one of Japan's leading food and beverage manufacturers. After graduation from Keio University in Tokyo in 1951 with a B.A. degree in economics, he studied at the Graduate School of Northwestern University, Illinois, and received an M.A. in economics before returning to Japan. During the first decade of his career with Ajinomoto, Tadao Suzuki learned the various aspects of the Ajinomoto businesses by rotating as Section Manager through different departments such as Production Control, Accounting, Marketing, Planning, Domestic Sales and Product Development. From 1961 to 1962, Tadao Suzuki lived in Switzerland and became the first Japanese executive to study at IMEDE.[1] In 1963, T. Suzuki was appointed Department Manager, responsible for joint ventures with US corporations – including Kellogg, CPC International (Knorr products), etc. In 1971, he joined the Board of Directors of Ajinomoto. Two years later, T. Suzuki was elected Managing Director, responsible for International Operations, to plan and implement overseas projects in France, Brazil, etc. Also part of Tadao Suzuki's mandate was to coordinate various joint venture projects with General Foods Corporation and to establish Ajinomoto General Foods, Ltd., in Japan. In 1981, T. Suzuki was elected Executive Vice President of Ajinomoto and, in 1987, he became President of Sanraku Incorporated, and was appointed, concurrently, Executive Vice Chairman of Ajinomoto Co., Incorporated. Tadao Suzuki was one of the most respected and influential top executives in Japan's beverage industry, holding such positions as Chairman of the Japan Wineries Association, Executive Director of the Japan Federation of Employers' Association and Director of the Federation of Economic Organizations.

The Alcoholic Beverages Industry in Japan in 1987

When Tadao Suzuki took over his new position as President of the company, Sanraku was facing some rough times. 1986 had been a difficult year for many

[1] IMEDE, Lausanne, merged with IMI, Geneva, in 1990 to form IMD.

Japanese companies. The yen's continued strength had held down export earnings and put competitive pressure on the domestic market. Although retail sales of alcoholic beverages had been growing at an average annual rate of 2.5% between 1976 and 1986, growth rates varied widely by market segments (*refer to Exhibit 7*).

'Sake'

Although consumption of 'sake' varied by regions, sales of 'sake' had been steadily declining since 1976 at an average annual rate of −1.6% per annum. 'Sake' was a popular drink with the older generation of Japanese and with blue collar workers, and it still accounted for 18% of all alcoholic beverages drunk in Japan. However, the younger generation was gradually moving away from this traditional alcoholic beverage. As a result, total consumption of 'sake' in Japan had dropped from 1,491 million kl in 1982 to 1,380 million kl in 1986 (*Exhibit 7*).

'Shochu'

Sales of 'shochu', another popular drink, had soared during 1984 and 1985, thanks to the emergence of a new category: 'Chuhi' (a combination of 'shochu' and soda to which fruity flavours like plum or lemon were added). Retail sales of 'shochu' had grown from 289,737 kl in 1982 to 589,086 kl in 1986 (*Exhibit 4*). However, industry experts felt that the 'Chuhi boom' had reached a peak. The Japanese government was expected to increase taxes on the retail price of 'shochu', from ¥140 to ¥220 for a 1.8-litre bottle sold currently to the public at ¥1,000. A recent decrease in the sales of this major product for Sanraku resulted in depressed sales in this segment. In the 'shochu' market, Sanraku was ranked 4th with a 10% market share, behind Takara (35%), Godo (15%) and Kyowa (13%).

Whisky

The Japanese whisky industry was dominated by one major player: Suntory Ltd., with a 72% market share. Other competitors in this market were Nikka Whisky Distilling Co. Ltd. (18% market share) and Kirin–Seagram (a joint venture between Kirin, the giant beer company, and Seagram, a Canadian company) with 6%. In 1987, Sanraku ranked fourth in this industry with a 3% market share. Consumption of whisky accounted for 4% of all alcoholic beverages drunk in Japan. Although retail sales of whisky in Japan were down from 373,989 kl in 1982 to 301,322 kl in 1982, some sub-segments of the whisky market were still enjoying some growth (*Exhibit 7*).

Following political pressures, mainly from the European Economic Community (EEC), the Japanese government had recently decided to lower the rate of customs duties on imports of whiskies by 20% in 1986 and 30% again in 1987, and to increase taxes on domestic products, which resulted in a dramatic drop in market share for local brands. The recent 50% re-evaluation of the yen against the US dollar and other Western currencies had hurt all local producers of whiskies. As a result, sales of Sanraku's domestic whiskies (the 'Ocean' line) had fallen below the previous year's level. 'White Ocean', a second-grade whisky representing 80% of Sanraku's whisky business, was expected to see a price increase to ¥1,230 per bottle of 640 ml from ¥640, or almost double the current retail price.

Sanraku was determined to stay ahead of diversifying consumer tastes by releasing new products. One recent example was 'Thirty-Love', a light whisky for the youth market, released as an addition to the Ocean whisky series. 'Ocean Mild Blend', which had gone on sale in the spring of 1986, had been targeted at the growing market for quality blended whiskies. In spite of the many competitors that had appeared during the year, the product attracted attention as Japan's first 'brandy-flavoured' whisky. 'Ocean Mild Blend' featured a subtle brandy base, blended with malt and grain whisky, for the mildest taste and aroma ever in a Japanese blended whisky. In November 1986, Sanraku had unveiled four very special new products: the 'Karuizawa' aged, single-malt whiskies. In limited release and aged from 10 to 21 years, these whiskies had been well received by the market and had enhanced the perceived value of Sanraku's whiskies in the Japanese consumers' minds.

For fiscal year 1987, the new reduction of liquor import duties was expected to lead to stepped up competition, particularly from whisky distillers overseas. Little growth was anticipated in the domestic whisky market. Japan's new alcoholic beverage tax laws would have a major impact on the domestic whisky industry. Under the proposed system, the heretofore designated 'second-grade whisky' with low malt content would no longer be permitted to use the 'whisky' label. As one of Japan's leading whisky distillers, Sanraku had to position itself to maintain product credibility while adjusting to this change. A special inhouse committee was in the process of reviewing Sanraku's corporate strategy in the light of the new legislation.

Beers

Beer was the most popular alcoholic beverage in Japan, with a 65.9% share of all alcoholic drinks consumed in Japan. Sales of beer had grown from 4,674,773 kl in 1982 to 4,958,690 kl in 1986. The Japanese beer industry was characterized by an oligopoly of four brewers: Kirin (60% market share), Sapporo (25%), Asahi (12%) and Suntory (9%). The year 1987 had been marked by the formidable success of 'Asahi Super Dry', a new draught beer launched by Asahi Breweries Co., Ltd.[2] Some industry analysts were predicting that a 'dry war' between Kirin and Asahi was imminent.

Other Spirits and Liquors

As Japanese consumers were becoming more affluent during the 1980s, their consumption of expensive spirits and liquors had greatly increased over the

---

[2] For more information on the Japanese beer industry 'dry war', see *Case Study 8.3.*

Retail Sales of Alcoholic Beverages in Japan in Kilolitres (1976–86)

Type of Beverages	Retail Sales Share	Average Annual Growth Rate
Beer	65.9%	3.2%
Sake	18.4%	1.6%
Shochu	7.8%	11.6%
Whiskies	4.0%	1.1%
Wine	0.9%	5.3%

Source: National Tax Administration Agency, Tokyo (1987).

previous decade with an average annual growth rate of 15.5% and 16.9%, respectively. In 1984, Mercian had become the exclusive distributor of Rémy Martin fine cognac in Japan. However, sales of Rémy Martin cognac were significantly diluted by the appearance of parallel imports and new products introduced by the competition.

Wine

Sanraku had quickly recognized that the fast-growing wine segment offered major business opportunities for the company. The Japanese wine market in fiscal year 1986 was nearly 70,000 kl, equivalent to about ¥107 billion. In the 10-year period between fiscal year 1976 and 1986, sales had increased almost 230% above the fiscal 1976 level of about 30,000 kl, showing an average annual growth of 8.7%. According to data prepared by the Central Bureau for Distilled Liquors in the Netherlands, per capita wine consumption in 1986 in France, Italy, Portugal and Spain was 78.4 litres, 73.2 litres, 70.8 litres and 45.0 litres, respectively, while that of Japan was only 0.67 litres.

In 1987, Sanraku was the largest wine distributor of both domestic and imported wines in Japan with an estimated shipment volume of 11,100 kl in 1986 and a market share of 15.5%. Suntory Ltd. was a close second with 15.1% market share, and Manns Wines Co., Ltd. ranked third with 7%.

'Mercian', the domestic wine brand of Sanraku, was the best-selling wine brand in Japan. Sanraku owned the Mercian Katsunuma Winery in the Yamanashi Prefecture where Mercian wines were being produced and matured. In 1986, Mercian wines had won two more gold metals in international competitions, and Mercian wines had been served at the state reception for Prince Charles and Diana Princess of Wales, held in Tokyo in May 1986.

In the imported segment of the wine industry, Sanraku was a distant second with a 6.1% market share, behind Suntory and its 19.1% market share. Other competitors in this fast-growing segment included Asahi Breweries Ltd. (5.3%), Meidi-ya Co., Ltd. (4.9%), Kirin–Seagram (4.7%) and the Nikka Whisky Distilling Co., Ltd. (4.7). Suntory imported and distributed the 'Calvet' wines (No. 1 brand in volume imported into Japan), 'Valchemberg' (No. 2), 'Mateus' (No. 4) and other well-established brands. Sanraku represented European firms like G.A. Schmitt, Albert Bichot, Chéreau Carré, etc. In June 1986, Sanraku had entered into an agreement with the prestigious California vintner, Louis M. Martini Co., based in the Napa Valley.

Imports of bottled wines in 1987 had risen a steep 60.4% in value and 71.6% in quantity above the previous year, to reach 30,000 kl. Imports of bulk wines to be used as a basis for domestic wines amounted to a little less than 20,000 kl in 1987. These imports had reached a peak of 27,000 kl in 1983 and had been decreasing since then.

Among the countries exporting wines to Japan in 1987, France topped all other countries and accounted for 45.5% of Japan's total imports of bottled wines. Imports from West Germany ranked next (22.1%) and those of the US ranked third (15.7%). Imports from these countries were followed by those of Italy, Australia, Portugal and Spain.

In 1986, the Japanese wine market continued to suffer the repercussions of the 1985 diethylene glycol contamination incident in which traces of this chemical had been found in a number of domestic and imported wines. As a result, sales of imported bottled wine between 1985 and 1986 had dropped 15.8% in quantity and 20.6% in value. Naturally, all Sanraku wines had been tested at the time of the incident and found to be free of any contaminants. As Japan's largest wine maker, Sanraku had played a leading role in winning back consumer confidence in wine and had adopted stringent new labelling standards for all wine products. Despite the generally depressed state of the wine market, Sanraku's sales of domestically produced wines had shown healthy growth as a result of aggressive product development. A highlight of the year had been the international wine festival held in Yugoslavia in July 1987, where 'Sanraku Château Mercian 1981' (red) wine was awarded a grand gold medal and 'Mercian Aizu 1984' (white) wine, a gold medal. Held under the auspices of the 'Office International de la Vigne et du Vin', the competition had attracted over 1,100 wines from 20 countries. These prizes brought the total number of international awards won by Mercian wines to 10, placing Sanraku far ahead of other domestic winemakers.

Sanraku's Other Businesses

Chemicals and Pharmaceuticals

In the mid-1960s, two major antibiotics had been developed by Sanraku and the Institute of Microbiological–Chemical Research; these were followed by the introduction of anti-cancer drugs. Since then, no significant new product had been introduced. In 1986 and early 1987, the impact of the yen's appreciation had been strongly felt in the chemical markets. Demand for chemicals had been generally poor in recent years and heated competition had forced prices down. A recent downward revision of standard list prices of pharmaceutical products imposed by the Ministry of Health had caused a reduction of Sanraku's selling prices, with a substantial decrease in profits. As a result, Sanraku's sales in this sector had fallen 9.7% in 1986 to ¥7,359 million ($52.6 million). Sales of 'Josamycin', one of the first antibiotics developed by Sanraku, had grown in volume but price reductions had forced revenues down. Stagnant exports in 1986 had also contributed to a drop in sales of 'Kasugamycin', an antibiotic used in agrochemicals. These two antibiotics, introduced in the mid-1960s, had been milestones in the development of Sanraku's advanced fermentation technology and had played a significant role in the Chemical Division's swift progress.

Feedstuffs

Sanraku held a pioneering position in Japan's feedstuffs trade, having entered the industry in 1957 by becoming the first liquor manufacturer to make animal feed from alcohol by-products. The company's traditional experience in fermentation provided just the right technical skills for a successful move into feedstuffs.

Sanraku's leadership in the aquaculture feed market was another example of fast response to an emerging business opportunity. The importance of fish in the Japanese diet had created a thriving domestic aquaculture industry, and Sanraku was poised to serve this important market.

In fiscal year 1986, the strong yen had reduced already low prices for imported grain, and sales had suffered accordingly. Feedstuffs revenues, which had been a growth area prior to the yen's rise, had fallen by 15.7% to ¥6,801 million ($48.6 million) Despite lacklustre demand in the early part of 1987, Sanraku had made vigorous sales efforts in terms of bulky-type blended feedstuffs, an area which Sanraku had developed ahead of all the competition. Sanraku was also working hard on various aquaculture feedstuffs and 'Tairon', a mushroom nutrient created through application of Sanraku's own fermentation technology. In order to succeed in this project, Sanraku had stationed researchers exclusively responsible for its development at Sanraku Central Research Laboratories. Overall, Tadao Suzuki felt that Sanraku's feedstuffs business lacked stability owing to its cyclical nature.

New Consumer Trends

In Japan, the early 1980s had been characterized by significant changes in consumer habits. Tadao Suzuki believed that these new consumer trends were changing Sanraku's businesses. Thanks to a stronger yen, 6 million Japanese travelled abroad in 1986, and this figure was expected to double in 1992. As a result, more and more Japanese were exposed to the wines, spirits and liquors of the countries they visited (e.g. in Europe). Especially in the whisky market, Sanraku expected that a substantial part of domestic brands sales would be replaced with imports in the standard to premium category.

In the 1980s, Japanese consumers were also changing their dietary habits. The number of European restaurants had dramatically increased. For example, the *NTT Town Page Telephone Directory* (February 1987 issue) listed an impressive number of Western restaurants, of which more than 85% served French or Italian food. The leading force behind the surge in dining out were women in their 20s and 30s, the majority of whom were working outside the home. Housewives, restaurants and French-type 'pâtissieries' were also baking more Western cakes – including many that used Western liquors, which offered additional business opportunities for companies like Sanraku.

Turning Sanraku Around

Shortly after being appointed President of Sanraku, Tadao Suzuki spent a great deal of time meeting with managers, visiting plants, talking with employees, customers and distributors. He quickly became convinced that Sanraku was suffering from a lack of corporate business strategies both for the short and the long term. "Morale among employees was low," remembered T. Suzuki. "I found that the company was suffering from a lack of policy regarding allocation of management resources, and a lack of organizational capability to define and implement the requisites of functional strategies, if any." In June 1987, Tadao Suzuki decided to organize a team of experienced managers to serve as an advisory body. The special project team called the 'RS Team' ('Restructure Sanraku') consisted of:

Names	Position	Years with the Company
J. Takahashi*	Manager, Company Secretariat	30
A. Hori	Deputy Manager, Accounting Dept.	25
T. Morishima	Deputy Manager, Production Dept.	26
K. Shimizu	Deputy Manager, Sales Control Dept.	21
S. Goto	Deputy Manager, Development Dept.	27
F. Otani	Sales Section Manager, Tokyo Branch	16
C. Teramoto	Technician, Product Assurance Dept.	14
T. Kato	Administration Clerk, Personnel Dept.	8
M. Nakamura	Analyst, Sales Control Dept.	8
O. Fukuchi	Technician, Kawasaki Plant	7

* Team Leader.

The selected ten people, while remaining in their original positions (*refer to* **Exhibit 6**), focused time and energy on tackling the major issues faced by Sanraku.

Corporate Issues

After several months of investigation, interviews and meeting with customers, distributors, employees and managers, Tadao Suzuki and his team had come to the conclusion that Sanraku was facing a number of organizational issues. In particular, Tadao Suzuki had become convinced that the company lacked:

- a clear and definite corporate philosophy;

- specific corporate objectives to be achieved in 5 years, or 10 years, as well as specific guidelines to act upon;

- prescribed job responsibilities and authority;

- established business development procedures and skills (because jobs belonged to individuals rather than positions or systems);

- a mechanism in personnel management that would make the best use of an individual employee's capability and enable people to grow, as well as providing aggressive support;

- concern about the market and the customer.

Strategic Issues by Business Division

Tadao Suzuki and the RS Team had also determined a number of strategic issues that the business had to address.

Wine

- To develop/expand the business in imported products to make Sanraku No. 1 in the total Japanese retail wine market (both for domestic and imported products).

- To reshuffle the product portfolio to improve profitability through a better balance between costs and prices.

- To reinforce sales/promotion/publicity efforts for more effective trade penetration and consumer/trade education.

Whisky

- To change the way that Sanraku had traditionally been doing business in order to overcome the structural loss position, mainly caused by meagre brand power.

- To develop and launch new products to replace the domestic second-grade whisky (mainstream category), which would be seriously affected by the new tax reform.

- To adapt the second-grade whisky to reformed tax requirements in order to increase sales and make the business pay off.

'Sake' and 'Shochu'

- To re-evaluate the existing market and improve brand marketability so as to increase its share in a declining market.

- To reinforce Sanraku's position in areas where the company had a relatively high market share (for example, Sanraku had a 90% market share for 'shochu' in most parts of Kyushu, the major Japanese southern island, but only a 10% share in Hokkaido, the major northern island).

- To develop post 'Chuhi boom' products.

Other Liquors

- To discover products with a high potential in peripheral areas of the liquor business – such as low-alcohol beverages – in order to nurture new business.

Tadao Suzuki and the RS Team were also very much aware of the importance of the chemical and feedstuffs businesses for Sanraku. Both businesses were also facing critical issues, one being to invest more in R&D. In both its wine and chemical businesses, Sanraku had continually introduced many new products. However, the new management team believed that most of these innovations were coming from engineers and technicians, rather than from marketing.

With the exception of the wine business, Tadao Suzuki believed that, so far, the new products in other businesses were mostly 'me-too' products and that few were unique. "For too long, we sold what we made. Now we must be more sensitive to new customers' needs," explained Tadao Suzuki.

But, changing the company's approach was, in Tadao Suzuki's words, "easier to say than to do."

> Sure, we have to invest in new products, but where am I going to find the money? Despite having sizeable assets in securities, land, etc., borrowing already amounts to ¥25 billion, which means a tremendous amount of money must be paid in interest. As CEO of the company, I also have a major responsibility to my employees.[3] Sanraku practises the so called 'lifetime employment' philosophy. It is my duty to take good care of my employees. I also must make sure that Sanraku will be able to attract new talent. How can Sanraku convince new employees to join our company for the rest of their lives if our results do not improve? Today, our company is full of obedient, sincere individuals with good potential. However, due to the absence of proper intra- and inter-departmental communications, many Sanraku employees lack initiative and the spirit of challenge. Information is also a problem. Right now, no information vital to management is being provided in terms of effective systems at work. Though computerized information systems have been put in place to some degree in the area of accounting, in other areas such as sales, inventory, physical distribution and production, collecting and using information remains a major problem.

As Tadao Suzuki and the RS Team were preparing to review the list of issues faced by Sanraku, T. Suzuki felt that the major task of setting priorities had to be addressed first. "All right, gentlemen," Mr. Suzuki said, "where shall we start?"

---

[3] See Appendix: *Major Characteristics of Traditional Japanese Management.*

Appendix: Major Characteristics of Traditional Japanese Management

- Lifetime employment
- Seniority-based wages and promotion
- Enterprise-based Union
- Participative decision making ('Ringi seido')
- Group-oriented behaviour
- Low employee turnover
- Cooperative labour–management relations
- Long-term corporate orientation

EXHIBIT 1

Sanraku's Financial Summary*

	1986	1985	1984	1983
Net sales	62,420	70,380	71,695	59,903
Operating income	1,387	2,480	3,659	3,994
Net income	947	1,375	1,125	1,008
Additions to property, plant & equipment	3,430	3,376	1,420	1,433
Depreciation	1,700	1,473	1,333	1,374
Shareholders' equity	20,297	19,619	13,762	4,362
Total assets	60,286	61,800	58,303	50,067
Net income per share	8.54	13.08	11.72	11.56
Shareholders' equity per share	67.14	69.44	50.00	50.00
Cash dividends per share	5.00	5.00	5.00	5.00

* In millions of yen, except per share figure.

Source: Annual Report.

EXHIBIT 2

Sanraku's Non-Consolidated Balance Sheets

Assets	Millions of yen		Thousands of US dollars
	1985	1986	1986
Current assets			
Cash	¥3,308	¥3,636	$25,971
Time deposits	3,981	3,774	26,957
Marketable securities	3,080	4,580	32,714
Trade receivables			
Notes	7,308	7,269	51,921
Accounts	12,476	11,363	81,164
	19,784	18,632	133,085
Less allowance for doubtful accounts	167	156	1,114
	19,617	18,476	131,971
Inventories	14,924	11,757	83,979
Other current assets	1,200	803	5,736
Total current assets	46,110	43,026	307,328
Property, plant & equipment			
Land	1,294	1,316	9,400
Buildings	8,529	9,455	67,536
Machinery & equipment	17,342	19,338	138,128
Construction in progress	82	56	400
	27,247	30,165	215,464
Less accumulated depreciation	16,049	17,334	123,814
	11,198	12,831	91,650
Investments & other assets			
Investments in and advances to subsidiaries and affiliates	1,350	1,342	9,586
Investments in securities	826	835	5,964
Deferred charges	973	868	6,200
Other assets	1,343	1,384	9,886
	4,492	4,429	31,636
Total	¥61,800	¥60,286	$430,614

Source: Annual Report.

(continued)

EXHIBIT 2 (continued)

Liabilities & shareholders' equity	Millions of yen		Thousands of US dollars
	1985	1986	1986
Current liabilities			
Short-term bank loans	¥12,940	¥12,820	$91,571
Current portion of long-term debts	918	1,043	7,450
Notes & accounts payable:			
Subsidiaries & affiliates	2,982	2,319	16,564
Trade	6,108	4,856	34,686
Construction	926	1,288	9,200
Other	2,179	1,984	14,171
Accrued expenses	4,571	5,520	39,429
Accrued income taxes	864	619	4,422
Other current liabilities	2,711	3,029	21,636
Total current liabilities	34,199	33,478	239,129
Long-term liabilities			
Long-term debt	5,942	4,723	33,736
Retirement allowances	1,418	1,457	10,407
Other long-term liabilities	621	331	2,364
Total long-term liabilities	7,981	6,511	46,507
Shareholders' equity			
Common stock:			
Authorized – 200,000,000 shares			
Issued 50 yen per value:			
1985 – 105,127,223 shares	7,300	–	–
1986 – 110,926,380 shares	–	7,448	53,200
Additional paid-in capital	6,394	6,541	46,721
Legal reserve	960	1,015	7,250
Retained earnings	4,966	5,293	37,807
	19,620	20,297	144,978
Contingent liabilities			
Total	¥61,800	¥60,286	$430,614

Source: Annual Report.

EXHIBIT 3

Sanraku's Non-Consolidated Statements of Income

	Millions of yen			Thousands of US dollars
	1984	1985	1986	1986
Net sales	¥71,695	¥70,380	¥62,420	$445,857
Cost of sales	53,538	52,832	46,602	332,871
Gross profit	18,157	17,548	15,818	112,986
Selling, general & administrative expenses	14,498	15,068	14,431	103,079
Operating income	3,659	2,480	1,387	9,907
Other income (expenses):				
Interest & dividend income	738	759	637	4,550
Interest expense	(1,814)	(1,679)	(1,375)	(9,821)
Other – net	635	1,801	1,953	13,950
	(441)	881	1,215	8,679
Income before taxes	3,218	3,361	2,602	18,586
Income taxes	2,093	1,986	1,655	11,822
Net Income	¥1,125	1,375	¥947	$6,764
Net income per share	¥11.72	¥13.08	¥8.54	$0.061
Cash dividends per share	¥5.00	¥5.00	¥5.00	$0.036

Source: Annual Report.

EXHIBIT 4

Sanraku's Network

Head Office: Tokyo

Branch Offices: Sapporo, Sendai, Tokyo, Kanto, Yokohama, Nagoya, Osaka, Hiroshima, Fukuoka, Kumamoto

Factories: Sapporo, Tomakomai, Karuizawa (Distillery), Katsunuma (Winery), Nagareyama, Kawasaki, Fujisawa, Iwata, Kansai, Osaka, Tsukuda, Yatsuhiro

Sales & Technical Cooperations
Wines
* Champagne Pommery (France)
* Maison Albert Bichot S.A. (France)
* Sarrau S.A. (France)
* Chereau Carre S.A. (France)
* Administration Schloss Reinhartshausen (Germany)
* Gustav Adolf Schmitt'sches Weingut (Germany)
* Moselland EG (Germany)
* Lenz Moser Gesellschaft m.b.H. (Germany)
* Cantine Giacomo Montresor S.p.A. (Italy)
* Louis M. Martini Winery (U.S.A.)
* Monimpex Hungarian Foreign Trade (Hungary)
* Gonzales Byass S.A. (Spain)
* Codorniu S.A. (Spain)
* Slovin (Yugoslavia)
* Mildara Wines Limited (Australia)

Whiskies
* William Grant & Sons Ltd. (U.K.)
* Hiram Walker & Sons Ltd. (U.K.)
* Jim Beam Brands Co. (U.S.A.)

Cognac
* E. Rémy Martin & Co. (France)

Liqueur
* John de Kuyper & Zoon B.V. (The Netherlands)

Vodka
* V/O Sojuzplodoimport (USSR)

Chemical
* E.R. Squibb & Son, Inc. (U.S.A.)
* Laboratoire Roger Bellon (France)
* Hoechst AG (Germany)
* H. Lundbeck & Co. A/S (Denmark)
* Dong-A Pharmaceutical Co. Ltd. (Korea)

Source: Annual Report.

EXHIBIT 5

Sanraku's Domestic Network

EXHIBIT 6

Sanraku's Organization Chart (1986)

Board of Directors

President

Auditor

Secretarial Office

Auditing Dpt.

Business Control Dpt.

Accounting & Finance

Public Relations Dpt.

General Affairs Dpt.

Personnel Dpt.

Management Committee

Mr. T. Suzuki	President
Mr. N. Yanagata	Exec. V.P.
Mr. T. Ito	Exec. V.P.
Mr. T. Sakanaki	M. Director
Mr. T Inui	M. Director
Mr. Y. Suda	M. Director
Mr. M. Kawasaki	M. Director
Mr. T. Ishikura	M. Director
Mr. A. Watanabe	M. Director

Planning & Development

Sourcing & Purchasing

Distribution Systems

Sales Planning Dpt.

Special Aides to Director

New Products Devplt.

Production Dpt.

Western Style Liquors Dpt.

Japanese Style Liquors Dpt.

Alcohol Dpt.

Pharmaceuticals & Chemicals Dept.

Feedstuffs Dept.

SALES BRANCHES

Tokyo, Osaka, Nagoya, Sapporo, Sendai, Kanto, Yokohama, Hiroshima, Fukuoka, Kumamoto

PLANTS

Tomakomia, Fujisawa, Yatsushiro, Nagareyama, Iwata, Kawasaki, Kansai

OCEAN
Karuizawa Distillery

MERCIAN
Katsunuma Winery

Source: Sanraku Inc.

EXHIBIT 7

Retail Sales of Alcoholic Beverages in Japan (Fiscal Years 1976–86) (Unit: kl)

Category	1982	1983	1984	1985	1986	Annual increase rate (%) 1976–86
Sake						
Special	52,536	46,800	39,416	37,603	36,080	−8.1
1st Grade	782,562	739,683	640,126	621,584	619,627	−3.7
2nd Grade	656,137	658,673	644,625	675,688	724,906	1.4
Subtotal	1,491,245	1,445,158	1,324,181	1,334,864	1,380,634	−1.6
Shochu	289,737	376,279	545,750	593,347	589,086	11.6
Beer	4,674,773	4,784,490	4,574,089	4,724,846	4,958,690	3.2
Wine	78,944	83,972	87,585	79,909	86,675	5.3
Whiskies						
Special	201,233	198,438	162,486	150,059	155,133	1.2
1st Grade	56,506	58,056	48,980	41,934	39,917	−0.8
2nd Grade	116,251	120,552	106,239	100,989	106,272	1.9
Subtotal	373,989	377,063	317,716	292,998	301,322	1.1
Spirits	9,869	15,074	34,799	31,827	25,012	15.5
Liqueurs	19,516	23,632	74,558	80,422	76,769	16.9
Total:	6,938,073	7,105,668	6,958,678	7,138,213	7,418,188	2.5

Source: National Tax Administration Agency, 1987.

KONICA CORP.

This case was written by Professor Dominique Turpin as a basis for class discussion rather than to illustrate either effective or ineffective handling of a business situation. Some names have been disguised to respect confidentiality.

At the end of October 1987, Toshiyaki Iida, manager of the Photographic Film Division, was back in his Tokyo office after a series of meetings with several colleagues from Konica, the second largest photo film manufacturer in Japan. Mr Iida and his colleagues had shared their latest information about competitors in the (non-professional) photographic film market in Japan. Data suggested that throughout 1986, Fuji Photo Film, the leading domestic film manufacturer, had maintained its 67.5% market share for retail sales of photographic film in Japan. Also, Eastman Kodak had accelerated its Japan market offensive by increasing its market share from 10.1% to 11.2%, while Konica had lost one point of market share – moving from 22% to 21% during the same time period. At the end of the meeting, Mr Matsumura, General Manager of the Photographic Film Division, who was chairing the meeting, expressed concern about Kodak's dramatic performance and entrusted Mr Iida with the task of reviewing the segmentation of the photographic film industry in Japan.

Konica

Established in 1873, Konishiroku Photo Industry (which became Konica Corp.) got underway when Rokuemon Sugiura began selling photography and printing material in Tokyo. Since 1903, when Konica was the first to sell photographic print paper and cameras mass-produced in Japan, the company had steadily built up its resources in silver halide, optical and precision instrument technology, and brought out numerous well-known cameras. In 1934, it introduced the first X-ray film made in Japan and was first again in developing infra-red, 16 mm movie film and colour film of domestic make.

In 1987, Konica was the second largest producer of photosensitive materials in Japan and the third in the world after Eastman Kodak and Fuji Photo Film. For several generations of Japanese, Konica's products were better known to the general public under their Sakura and Konica brand names. Sakura had been the trademark for all film made and sold by the company, while Konica had been the brand name for the cameras manufactured and distributed by the company. In July 1987, the company had officially changed its name from Konishiroku Photo Industry Co. to Konica and had united all product lines under the Konica brand. According to Mr Ide, President of the company at that time, this change had been decided to "reflect both the company's continuing diversification throughout the information imaging industry and its increasingly international stature."

For the fiscal year ending 2 April 1987, Konishiroku Photo Industry (referred to hereafter as Konica) and its consolidated subsidiaries had registered a net profit of ¥5,128 million for sales of ¥298,893 million[1] (refer to **Exhibit 1**). In early 1987, the company and its consolidated subsidiaries comprised some 13,000 employees overseas and about 4,900 in Japan.

In recent years, a key policy of the company had been to expand its international marketing force with the establishment of direct sales agencies overseas both in North America and Europe. A coordinated policy for international marketing was also to locate production facilities within or near user markets. A subsidiary which would manufacture its U-Bix photocopiers was to begin operations in October 1987, and the construction of a plant to produce photographic paper had just started. Plans were also underway to build a plant in Maryland (US), which would produce consumables for photocopiers and computer terminal printers.

Konica's Product Line

In early 1987, Konica's chief product lines included: photographic film (26.9% of total sales); photographic paper (17.5%); photo-related industry equipment (14.2%); business machines (27.6%); cameras and optical products (9.5%); and magnetic products (4.3%).

Mr Iida had decided to review some of the recent trends in the film industry, and so there were several piles of data and reports on his desk waiting to be examined.

The World Film Industry for Amateurs

The photo market for amateurs could be divided into three major segments: film, photofinishing, and cameras and accessories.

The film industry in 1987 was expected to enjoy steady growth throughout the world. In 1986, there had been over 43 billion images shot worldwide, with more than 85% exposed on colour negative film. Worldwide, three companies dominated the market for photographic film. Eastman Kodak was the world's top photo film producer, with close to 65% of the world market. Right behind Kodak was Fuji Photo Film Co. with an 18% share, followed by Konica with 12%. A fourth company, Agfa–Gevaert from West Germany, was credited with less than 10% of the world market by Mr Iida. Each company had its own geographic strengths. Kodak and Fuji had an almost dominant position in their respective home markets, but Konica was clearly the leader in such countries as India, Saudi Arabia and Scandinavia – either under the Konica name or through private brands.

---

[1] Average exchange rate in 1987: US$=135 yen.

The Film Industry for Amateurs in Japan

With 7 billion images shot in 1986, Japan was the third largest market in the world for film for amateur photography, right after the US and Western Europe (*refer to Exhibits 2 and 3*). At the retail level, the value of the total amateur photography market in Japan was estimated at ¥814 billion in 1986 with photographic film representing nearly 20% of this market (*refer to Exhibit 4*).

Traditionally, the photography market was divided between two types of customers: professionals and amateurs. In number of units, amateurs accounted for 82% of the total film market in Japan. In terms of exposures, the Japanese amateur market had grown 3.6% in 1986. In Japan, the average number of exposures per capita in 1986 was 60.5 shots per person[2] (versus 61.5 in the US). This figure had doubled during the last 10 years. Colour film represented 76% of the total amount of photographic film sold to amateurs in Japan. Colour print film represented 73% of this total versus 3% for colour slide film. Mr Iida estimated that, on average, Japanese consumers were spending ¥12,257 a month on photographic material (twice the 1976 figure). Of this number, ¥6,210 was spent on cameras and accessories, ¥1,146 on film and ¥4,901 for photofinishing.

The Japanese Photofinishing Industry

Within the amateur photography industry, photofinishing represented almost half the total retail value. In 1986, the total value of the Japanese photofinishing industry was estimated at ¥28 billion (*refer to Exhibit 5*). Photofinishing was a synonym for 'developing and printing' pictures. After being bought at a store and then exposed, a film would be dropped off for processing and printing at a film counter. Although most pictures were taken by men on weekdays, film was usually returned for processing on Mondays, with 70% being dropped off by women.

The photofinishing industry could be divided into two sub-segments: the 'retail level' and the 'finishing level' (*refer to Exhibit 6*). The 'finishing level' referred to the wholesale or 'macro' labs where film was processed, developed and printed. The 'retail level' referred to the network of retailers that served as intermediaries between the customers and the 'macro' labs.

In 1987, camera shops accounted for 58% of all film purchases by amateurs and for 61% of the photofinishing market for data processing and colour printing. However, their market was being eroded by new competition which occurred with the recent development of convenience stores offering the same service.

The retail network for the film and the photofinishing industries comprised 214,000 outlets: 31,000 camera stores, 36,000 drug stores and 17,000 supermarkets and convenience stores (*refer to Exhibit 7*). Many retail stores were also affiliated with film manufacturers. Fuji Photo Film had four affiliated chains with

---

[2] In 1986, there were 121.67 million inhabitants in Japan.

a total of 12,500 stores. Konica and Kodak had 9,200 and 4,400 store members, respectively. Affiliated stores were either exclusive or selective distributors for one, two or three film manufacturers for both film sales and photofinishing.

Competition on the price of photofinishing was intense. Both the average price of developing the film and the average price of colour printing had been going down substantially during the last five years (*refer to Exhibit 8*). Mini-labs were also frequently being installed in camera stores and were charging comparable prices to those being charged by wholesale finishers ('macro' labs) – and even less in some cases. This price erosion had many Japanese wholesale finishers concerned about their future. In 1985, the number of 'macro' labs declined for the first time, and Mr Iida estimated that mini-labs would capture about 25% of the amateur photofinishing market by the end of 1989.

The Japanese Camera Industry

Since the late 1960s, the world camera industry had been clearly dominated by such Japanese manufacturers as Canon, Nikon, Minolta and Asahi Pentax. In 1986, Japanese still camera manufacturers had exported 70% of their production overseas. However, since 1981, total shipments of Japanese still cameras were slowly decreasing in volume (both in units and value). In value terms, total shipments were down from ¥490 billion in 1980 to ¥470 billion in 1986. In the domestic market, the trend was identical. The Japanese camera market was mature; the household penetration rate was 87% (versus 65% in France and 77% in Germany). From 1981 to 1986, total camera sales in Japan were down from ¥105 to ¥104 billion, although trends differ from one segment to another (*refer to Exhibit 9*). For example, sales of 35 mm SLR cameras were down from ¥44 billion in 1981 to ¥25 billion in 1986, while sales of 35 mm SL cameras were up from ¥46 to ¥72 billion during the same time period.

To revitalize the market, Japanese camera manufacturers were launching a range of new products targeted at teenagers, women and semi-professionals, respectively. In 1986, teenagers accounted for 23% of all camera purchases (a 3-point growth over three years). In 1986, 31.5% of all cameras sold in Japan were bought by women (*refer to Exhibit 10*) and, increasingly, women were shifting from pocket cameras to more expensive 'still' cameras. As a result, women in the 25 to 34-year-old bracket were also buying more film than males in the 16 to 24-year-old group (*refer to Exhibit 11*).

A Canon executive had explained the trend to Mr Iida in these words. "New cameras are getting much easier to use. In our view, new features such as auto-exposure, built-in motors for self-winding and rewinding systems, the quick-charging auto-flash, and multi-mode zoom lenses have been successful attempts by all Japanese manufacturers to make cameras more user-friendly. Moreover, introducing more sophisticated products through the use of new optico-electronics has also been a way to rejuvenate the market and gain market share." (*Refer to Exhibit 12*.)

Fuji Photo Film and Konica competed with each other in the lower end of the Japanese 35 mm camera market. Konica had only a 5.5% share while Fuji commanded 9% of this market. Konica had always been active in developing new products. In 1986 alone, the company launched three different versions of its Konica MT-11, a fully automatic motorized camera with close-up capacity to 45 cm with a 35 mm f/2.8 lens. Four new models, including the Konica Jump/ Manbow (a fashionable caseless, water-resistant 35 mm camera targeted at women), were scheduled to be launched in 1987. Moreover, Konica was also working on a filmless camera, the Konica Still Video Camera KC-400, to be introduced in the late part of 1987.

Recent Developments in the Camera Industry

Several Konica executives believed that a major threat to the traditional camera market was the growing sales of video cameras (also called camcorders). Mr Iida felt that sales of camcorders were contributing to an erosion of the camera market and could eventually emerge as the preferred way to capture memories of holidays and family events, particularly as camcorders were declining in price and households increasingly had a video recorder. Between 1983 and 1986, domestic sales of video cameras had grown from a few thousand to more than a million units by the end of 1986. In comparison, domestic sales of VCRs (videocassette recorders) in Japan had grown from 964,000 units in 1980 to 6.3 million in early 1987. The ownership ratio of VCRs in Japan was estimated in 1987 to be 53%, or 60.3 machines per 100 homes.

Consumer electronics firms like Sony Corporation, Toshiba and Matsushita Electric etc. had recently used their expertise in video equipment to introduce filmless cameras (also called electronic or floppy cameras). This new technology allowed up to 50 video stills to be recorded on a single reusable 2-inch floppy disk. Electronic cameras could be played back immediately on a standard TV with an adapter. Electronic pictures could also be printed by a special machine, but the cost of such a printer was much more expensive than a typical computer printer. Moreover, the quality of the printed electronic images was not as good as traditional colour prints.

Although traditional camera manufacturers (including Konica) had also been pioneering this new product, in order to compete with the consumer electronics firms, so far filmless cameras had had only a limited impact on the market for traditional cameras. Prices, however, were dropping quickly, and Konica was now working on an electronic camera to be introduced in early 1988, which would be sold to the end user for less than ¥100,000. Yet, Mr Iida considered that the average price of an electronic camera alone (excluding the price of both a TV adapter and a printer) was still too high (typically around ¥250,000) for most Japanese consumers. The most sophisticated systems in the market cost ¥1–10 million. As a result, sales of electronic camera systems were mainly restricted to professional users such as advertising or news agencies. Sales of filmless cameras were less than 20,000 units in 1986. However, industry experts estimated that the demand for electronic cameras would climb to 3.8 million units by 1995.

Another major recent development in the camera industry perceived by Mr Iida was the growing presence of Korean manufacturers in the Japanese market. Although Korean cameras still had only a small share of the camera market in Japan (less than 5%), they were attacking the lower end of this market, where most of Konica's cameras were positioned.

Disposable Cameras in Japan

During the past two years, the development of disposable cameras had been a novelty within the film industry. Disposable cameras were first launched in Japan in 1986. This product concept stemmed originally from Fuji Photo Film's awareness of an everyday situation – sometimes people wanted to take pictures, but had forgotten to bring a camera. A disposable camera was actually a film that had a lens and shutter in a compact 35 mm film package using regular colour negative film. When the pictures were taken, the package was dropped off for processing at a film counter. The film manufacturers (Fuji, Kodak and Konica) believed that this new product would generate increased picture-taking opportunities and make photography a more convenient pastime. Fuji was clearly the leader in Japan for this new type of film. In July 1987, Fuji Photo Film had launched a new disposable camera with lens/flash, which significantly boosted picture-taking possibilities. Konica, which had launched its first disposable cameras in September, was planning to launch another model with flash three months later.

During the previous two years, the disposable camera market had grown at a very rapid rate. More than 2 million disposable cameras had been sold in 1986. Mr Iida expected that this number would triple by the end of 1987 and projected a market of 30 million units by 1990 or 8–9% of total 35 mm colour film sold in Japan. In 1987, sales of disposable cameras represented less than 5% of total sales of film to amateurs in Japan, and Fuji had more than 70% of this market.

Competitors in the Japanese Film Industry

Three companies – Fuji, Konica and Kodak – with a respective market share of 67.5%, 21% and 11.2%, dominated the Japanese film market. Private brands accounted for the small remaining fraction of the market. Agfa–Gevaert, the German company, had pulled out of the Japanese colour film market for amateurs in 1976.

Fuji Photo Film

Established in 1934, Fuji Photo Film, the world's second largest producer of photographic film, was trying hard to catch up with Eastman Kodak in world markets. Fuji Photo Film boasted steady management with no bank borrowing. In fiscal year 1986. Fuji Photo Film recorded a net profit of ¥54 billion from net sales of ¥644 billion (*refer to* **Exhibit 13**). The company had 11,100 employees and was diversified into various non-silver salt products such as cameras, magnetic tapes and 8 mm video cameras. Consumer photography products sales (a category including film for both amateur and professional use, photographic paper, cameras, electronic imaging equipment and other related products) accounted for 49.4% of the company's total sales. The domestic market accounted for 66% of the company's total sales in 1986.

Kodak Japan Ltd.

Based in Rochester, New York, Eastman Kodak was the largest photography company in the world, with total sales of $11.5 billion in 1986, of which 57% came from amateur, professional and commercial imaging equipment and supplies. In 1986, Eastman Kodak had 124,400 employees worldwide. The US company had been present in Japan for nearly 100 years. In the early 1920s, Kodak had signed an exclusive distribution agreement with Nagase Sangyo, a local trading company which had been the exclusive importer and distributor of Eastman Kodak products in Japan. The impetus for Kodak's decision to increase its penetration of the Japanese market began in 1983 when Kodak underwent a major personnel reorganization, and Colby Chandler was appointed Chairman of the Corporation.

Until 1983, Japan had been part of a much larger geographic zone which included Asia, Africa and Australia, referred to by Kodak executives as the 'Triple A'. In 1984, Kodak decided to open a branch office in Tokyo (Kodak Japan Ltd.) through a 50/50 joint venture with Nagase Sangyo; its objective was to push Kodak into the number two position in Japan. Industry experts estimated that with the recent 30% re-evaluation of the yen against the US dollar, Kodak would gain a major price edge over its Japanese competitors.

Mr Iida believed that Kodak was now working on new product developments for the amateur market, partly in response to some criticism that its film tended to make Japanese look yellowish. Kodak was also working on increasing the number of its affiliated retail stores as well as the number of developing laboratories. In 1987, Fuji Photo Film had about 400 affiliated laboratories in Japan (versus 200 for Konica), which served a large number of retail store outlets. As one insider described Fuji's strength: "No matter where you go, even in the most remote areas of Japan, you see the green Fuji film name everywhere." In contrast, Kodak had established 28 developing laboratory companies to date. But, in the long term, Konica executives believed that boosting the number of its developing laboratory affiliates would be the key to Kodak's success in Japan. To achieve this goal, Eastman Kodak had established Kodak Imagika K.K. in 1987, through a joint venture with Imagika Corp., which had been processing Kodak film for years. Holding a 51% equity in the new company, Kodak was believed to be using this company as the basis for expanding its laboratory system.

Mr Iida also knew that another goal for Kodak was to develop its basic research in Japan. Besides a research centre in Rochester, Eastman Kodak had research centres in the UK and France. Kodak was now completing a four-storey 4,000 m² R&D building in Yokohama which could accommodate as many as 250 researchers.

During the past three years, Kodak had also improved its marketing mix. Until recently, Kodak had been selling film in US packaging that was printed only in English. In 1984, Kodak decided to use a new packaging with the date and instructions written in Japanese. Kodak also installed neon signs in Ginza and Shinjuku stations, two of the busiest places in Tokyo. Kodak had been focusing on sales promotions in major department stores in central Tokyo and had started to advertise aggressively on television. Since 1984, Kodak had also become active in sponsoring local events, and national sports events like sumo and judo tournaments, to become better known by the Japanese public.

Using a different management style, sales of film, copiers, chemicals and other Kodak products in Japan had more than doubled between 1984 and 1986. While Kodak had yet to announce its sales figures for fiscal year 1986, management did state its goals in early 1987: to quadruple sales from 1985 to 1988; and reach a sales target of $1 billion in Japan by 1989.

The New Konica Colour Film Line

For more than 50 years, Konishiroku Photo Industry had been selling colour film for amateurs under the Sakura name[3] with its red and orange packaging. However, to reflect the recent management decision to unify all product lines under the new Konica name, every Sakura product was being redesigned and given new packaging with the Konica name. The variety of colour photographic films offered by Fuji, Konica and Kodak was about the same. The three competitors offered about 20 different types of colour negative film, with a range of different sizes (from 35 mm to colour reversal sizes) and different sensitivities (from ISO 25 to ISO 1600).[4]

Colour 35 mm negative film was the size that accounted for 94% of all film sold in Japan. ISO 100 film was by far the most popular film speed and accounted for close to 90% of total film sales in Japan (*refer to Exhibit 14*). In July 1987, Konishiroku Photo Industry began marketing its new Konica series of colour print film, including a completely new ISO 3200 film speed for a segment in which Konica had a monopoly (*refer to Exhibit 15*).

January 1987, Konishiroku Photo Industry also introduced a new film for colour prints targeted at teenagers. The packaging of this new product featured Snoopy, the popular dog from the Peanuts cartoon (*refer to Exhibit 16*, *in the plate*

---

[3] 'Sakura' is the Japanese word for cherry blossoms.
[4] ISO is an international standard that defines the sensitivity of photographic film according to different light exposures.

section). At a retail price of ¥510 for 24 prints, sales of the Snoopy Colour Prints line were quite successful in Japan, contributing to an extra 13% increase in total units sold. However, because royalties had to be paid for using the Snoopy character, Konishiroku Photo Industry's profits on this product were only modest.

Retail prices of photographic film were fixed by the manufacturers[5] (*refer to Exhibit 17*). However, some retailers offered discounts (of up to 15%). Film manufacturers were also competing aggressively through their retailers, using promotions offering packs of two, three or more films. Film packs often were accompanied by some promotional present like a small picture frame, pens, tissues, etc.

Behaviour of Film Consumers in Japan

Mr Iida believed that, because of the desire of the Japanese for more leisure and the recent appreciation of the yen against the US dollar, tourism was by far the most common reason for taking pictures. In 1986, 48% of all colour prints were taken during a domestic (35%) or overseas trip (13%). Family pictures were the second most popular theme, followed by special events (19%), and then business pictures (16%). Reasons for taking photographs varied according to both age and sex (*refer to Exhibit 18*). Research commissioned by Mr Iida showed that 51.2% of women buying film and cameras were new mothers and grandmothers who wanted to take pictures of their first baby or grandchild from birth to 4 years.

Seasonality affected picture-taking occasions (*refer to Exhibit 19*). Also, indoor pictures were on the increase. In 1972, indoor pictures had represented only 19% of all colour pictures taken in Japan, but this figure had climbed to 38% by 1986. Family events represented 36% of all indoor pictures taken.

After having reviewed all the data he had in front of him, Mr Iida felt that re-segmenting the traditional photographic film industry could be a fruitful exercise. He knew that no magic formula existed. However, he believed that with all the information he had gathered and a bit of imagination, a new segmentation of the market could offer new business opportunities for Konica.

Also, he had to determine what actions should be taken as soon as he had the new segmentation on paper.

---

[5] Japanese legislation allowed retail price fixing for items under ¥1,000.

EXHIBIT 1

Konishiroku Photo Industry (Konica) Selected Data

	Sales	Operating profit	Current profit	Net profit	Earnings per share	Dividend per share	Equity per share
Income (¥ million)							
April 1984	258,077	11,654	16,593	10,282	¥41.1	¥9.0	¥462.4
April 1985	272,906	13,145	18,688	9,828	36.0	9.5	500.4
April 1986	313,612	16,988	15,909	7,102	23.0	10.0	499.4
April 1987	298,893	11,729	11,566	5,128	16.1	10.0	509.1

Financial data (¥ million)	April 1987
Total assets	449,953
Fixed assets	163,045
Current assets	277,472
Current liabilities	212,818
Working capital	64,654
Bank borrowing	98,532
Capital stock	25,599
Capital surplus	66,268
Shareholders' equity	150,287
Equity ratio (%)	33.4
Interest & dividend net	–

Sales breakdown (Oct. 1986, %)	
Photosensitive materials, cameras, copiers & others	64
Business machines	27
Optical goods	9

Prices

	High	Low
1983	¥676	¥560
1984	780	529
1985	755	601
1986	811	580

Export ratio	44%
Facility investment (¥ million)	16,100
R&D expenditures (¥ million)	16,900
Employees (age)	4,938 (35)

Source: Company Records, 1987.

EXHIBIT 2

World Amateur Photographic Exposures (Units in Billions)

	1987 (est.)	1986	1985	1984	1983
US					
Conventional	17.7	15.9	15.1	14.3	13.6
Instant	0.9	0.8	1.0	1.0	1.2
Combined	18.6	16.7	16.1	15.3	14.8
Europe					
Conventional	9.0	8.6	8.2	7.9	7.6
Instant	0.4	0.4	0.4	0.4	0.5
Combined	9.4	9.0	8.6	8.3	8.1
Japan					
Conventional	7.4	7.0	6.8	6.5	6.1
Instant	0.2	0.2	0.2	0.2	0.1
Combined	7.6	7.2	7.0	6.7	6.2
Others					
Conventional	9.0	8.7	8.2	7.8	7.5
Instant	0.3	0.3	0.4	0.4	0 5
Combined	9.3	9.0	8.6	8.2	8.0
Worldwide					
Conventional	43.1	40.2	38.3	36.5	34.8
Instant	1.8	1.7	2.0	2.0	2.4
Combined	44.9	41.9	40.3	38.5	37.2

EXHIBIT 3

Japanese Photography Exposures (Billion Shots)

Year	Total	Colour** Total	Negative	Slide	B&W
1987*	7.394	6.827 (92.3%)	87.4%	4.9%	0.567 (7.6%)
1986	7.030	6.399 (91.0%)	86.2%	4.8%	0.631 (9.0%)
1985	6.784	6.093 (89.8%)	85.2%	4.6%	0.691 (10.2%)
1984	6.531	5.784 (88.6%)	84.1%	4.5%	0.747 (11.4%)
1983	6.118	5.434 (88.8%)	84.1%	4.7%	0.684 (11.2%)
1982	5.444	4.937 (87.5%)	83.1%	4.4%	0.707 (12.5%)
1981	5.267	4.561 (86.6%)	82.2%	4.4%	0.706 (13.4%)

* Estimated.
** The colour exposures are shown as total, with share of overall exposures, and the breakdown of that share into colour negative and colour transparency.

Source: Konica, 1987.

EXHIBIT 4

Japanese Amateur Total Photographic Expenditures (¥100 million)

	1987 (est.)	1986	1985	1984	1983
Photofinishing					
Colour	4,045	3,812	3,642	3,490	3,323
B&W	187	201	223	237	250
Film					
Colour	1,544	1,442	1,390	1,350	1,216
B&W	62	69	77	84	79
Lenses & cameras	2,036	1,949	1,844	1,721	1,823
Accessories	663	675	679	676	665
Total	8,537	8,148	7,855	7,558	7,356

Source: Konica, 1987.

EXHIBIT 5

The World Photofinishing Industry (US$100 million)

	1983	1984	1985	1986
US				
Amateurs	32.95	35.50	38.10	41.40
Professionals	21.80	23.40	25.10	28.70
Total	54.75	58.90	63.20	70.10
Japan				
Amateurs	14.90	15.55	17.60	24.30
Professionals	2.25	2.40	2.75	3.80
Total	17.15	17.95	20.35	28.10
Europe				
Total	34.50	35.60	44.00	59.50
Others				
Total	24.25	25.05	26.05	28.45
World				
Total	130.65	137.50	153.60	186.15

Source: Konica, 1987.

EXHIBIT 6

Photofinishing Sales in Japan (¥ billions)

	1986	1985	1984	1983
Retail level				
Total	401.3	386.5	372.7	357.3
Colour	381.2	364.2	349.0	332.3
B&W	20.1	22.3	23.7	25.0
Finisher level				
Total	259.2	261.0	258.5	247.0
Colour printing	210.2	210.0	208.3	199.5
Film processing	49.0	51.0	50.2	47.5

EXHIBIT 7

Sales of Data Processing by Type of Outlet (% of Total Value)

Type of outlet	1986	1985	1984	1983	Total of outlets (1986)
Camera store	61%	62%	62%	64%	31,000
Supermarket & department store	17%	16%	17%	17%	9,000
Convenience store	4%	3%	2%	2%	13,000
Cooperative Association	2%	2%	3%	3%	10,500
Drugstore	5%	5%	5%	5%	36,000
Station stand	1%	1%	1%	1%	5,500
Other	10%	11%	10%	8%	85,000
Total					190,000

Source: Konica, 1987.

EXHIBIT 8

Photofinishing Prices in Japan (¥)

	1987 (est.)	1986	1985	1984	1983
Colour					
Developing (price for 24-E prints*)	1123.4	1155.8	1165.2	1188.6	1209.0
Average print	34.3	36.1	36.7	37.6	38.7
E-Size print*	29.1	30.7	31.3	32.4	33.5
B&W					
Developing	330.0	325.0	315.0	304.0	301.0
Average print	36.0	35.0	34.8	34.4	33.0

* E-print (82.5 × 117 mm) accounted for 76% of all regular picture sizes for photo printing in Japan.

Sources: Konica, 1987.

EXHIBIT 9

Sales of Still Cameras in Japan
(in Millions of Yen)

Types of camera	1986	1985	1984	1983	1982
Domestic 35 mm SLR	25,143	23,752	20,863	28,885	34,887
35 mm LS	72,190	68,045	65,880	55,776	48,549
35 mm imports	910	410	735	400	452
Cartridge	579	1,549	1,948	3,171	5,239
Import pocket	846	844	961	872	830
Import folding	1,202	486	514	659	935
Import 60 mm	897	2	3	3	3
Domestic others	579	1,310	1,932	2,035	1,667
Import others	2,016	2,387	2,236	2,873	5,808
Total: in value	104,362	98,785	95,072	94,674	98,370
in units	5,878,712	5,087,527	4,699,748	4,642,052	4,947,514

EXHIBIT 10

Sales of Cameras in Japan by Sex and
Age Group (%)

	Type of camera and year							
	35 mm SLR*		35 mm LS**		Pocket cameras		Total	
	1986	1985	1986	1985	1986	1985	1986	1985
Sex								
Male	94.1	94.5	64.7	67.3	37.7	41.5	68.5	70.1
Female	5.9	5.5	35.3	32.7	62.3	58.5	31.5	29.9
Age group								
Under 19	6%	10%	13%	12%	40%	40%	13%	12%
20–29	23	25	26	26	23	22	26	25
30–39	28	25	21	21	17	18	21	22
40–49	16	17	14	14	8	7	15	14
Over 49	26	23	26	27	12	13	25	27

* SLR: Single-lens reflex cameras.
** Lens shutter cameras.

Source: Konica, 1987.

EXHIBIT 11

Sales of Photographic Film in Japan by Sex and Age Group

Sex	Age group	Number of rolls used per year
Men	15 and under	2.9
	16–24	3.1
	25–34	4.4
	35–44	3.6
	45–54	3.5
	55 and over	3.5
Women	15 and under	1.2
	16–24	2.2
	25–34	3.2
	35–44	2.8
	45–54	2.7
	55 and over	2.6

Source: Konica, 1987.

EXHIBIT 12

Market Shares in the 35 mm SLR Camera Industry in Japan (1975–86)

1975		1980		1985		1986	
1. Nikon	26%	1. Canon	24%	1. Canon	41%	1. Minolta	25%
2. Asahi	22%	2. Nikon	22%	2. Nikon	25%	2. Canon	24%
3. Canon	18%	3. Asahi	21%	3. Asahi	13%	3. Nikon	16%
4. Minolta	14%	4. Minolta	8%	4. Minolta	4%	4. Asahi	10%
5. Others*	20%	5. Others	25%	5. Others	17%	5. Others	25%

*Others include: Olympus: 9.5%; Fuji: 9%; Konica: 5.5%; also Kyocera, Ricoh and Kowa.

Sources: *Nikkei Business*, 1987.

EXHIBIT 13
Fuji Photo Film Selected Data

	Sales	Operating profit	Current profit	Net profit	Earnings per share	Dividend per share	Equity per share
Income (¥ million)							
October 1984	566,396	92,325	95,774	45,057	¥122.0	¥11.5	¥875
October 1985	646,212	114,288	122,566	54,652	147.9	13.5	1,010
October 1986	644,957	102,172	113,907	54,836	147.8	13.5	1,149
October 1987*	700,000	105,000	128,000	56,000	150.0		

Financial data (¥ million)	*October 1986*
Total assets	686,542
Fixed assets	224,447
Current assets	462,095
Current liabilities	165,087
Working capital	297,008
Bank borrowing	0
Capital stock	20,437
Capital surplus	39,054
Shareholders' equity	426,677
Equity ratio (%)	62.1
Interest & dividend net	14,496

Sales breakdown (Oct. 1986, %)	
Cameras, film	46
Business/commercial use products	41
Magnetic products	12

Prices

	High	Low
1982	¥2130	¥60
1983	2490	1480
1984	2330	1440
1985	2210	1550
1986	3930	1720

Export ratio (1986)	34%
Facility investment (¥ million, 1986)	42,400
R&D expenditures (¥ million)	42,700
Employees (Av. age)	10,950 (39)

*Estimated.

Source: Company Records, 1987.

EXHIBIT 14

Sales of Colour Negative Film in Japan by Size, Sensitivity and Prints* (Film for Amateurs Only)

Sales by size

Colour negative 35 mm size	92.4%
Colour negative rolls	4.5%
Colour negatives 110	2.9%
Colour negatives 120	0.2%

Sales by size and sensitivity

	35 mm	110 mm
ISO 25	0.1%	–
ISO 100	84.8%	94.4%
ISO 160	–	–
ISO 200	3.7%	3.0%
ISO 400	9.1%	2.6%
ISO 1000	0.1%	–
ISO 1600	2.2%	–
ISO 3200	0.1%	–

Sales by size and no. of prints

	35 mm	110 mm
12 prints	19.0%	16.0%
24 prints	60.5%	84.0%
36 prints	20.5%	–

*N.B.: No significant differences between Fuji, Kodak and Konica.

Source: Photo Market, 1987.

EXHIBIT 15

Konishiroku Photo Industry Product Line for Colour Print Film (Film for Amateurs Only)

Colour films	ISO	Size & no. of exposures	Characteristics
Konica GX100	100	135 mm – 12, 24, 36 120 mm – 12 110 mm – 12, 24	Most popular speed, ultra-fine grain, especially effective for scenery
Konica GX100 'Snoopy'	100	135 mm – 24	Same characteristics as Konica GX100 but targeted at teenagers
Konica GX200 Professional	200	135 mm – 12, 24, 36 120 mm – 12	Extra-fine grain, especially effective for portraits
Konica GX400	400	135 mm – 12, 24, 36 120 mm – 12 110 mm – 24	High speed, especially effective for fast action
Konica GX3200	3200	135 mm – 24, 36 120 mm – 12	World's first colour print film in its speed class. Best suited for action or poor light conditions

Source: Konica, 1987.

EXHIBIT 16

Konishiroku Photo Industry Product Line for Colour Print Film (Film for Amateurs Only)

See Plate Section

EXHIBIT 17

Comparative Retail Prices for Colour Print Film in Japan 1987*

	12 prints	24 prints	36 prints
Konica ISO 100	¥400	¥510	¥700
Fuji Super HRII ISO 100	¥400	¥510	¥700
Kodak ISO 100	¥400	¥510	¥700
Fuji Super HR100 ISO 400	¥456	¥575	–

* Retail Prices at a Tokyo department store, 1987.

EXHIBIT 18

Photographic Subjects for Colour Prints by Sex and Age Groups

	Males						Females					
	Under 20	20–30	30–40	40–50	50–60	Over 60	Under 20	20–30	30–40	40–50	50–60	Over 60
Playtime	30%	44%	59%	38%	12%	17%	61%	53%	61%	25%	17%	12%
Driving	45	84	71	63	50	31	59	79	64	52	41	27%
Picnic	20	27	38	38	24	23	32	36	50	35	25	20
Camp	14	13	9	10	1	1	11	5	14	8	2	1
Sports	3	5	12	8	1	1	6	7	17	6	1	–
Seaside	35	52	50	35	15	9	42	43	49	22	8	9
Zoo-park	21	38	57	38	21	23	41	50	57	33	30	22
Exhibition	21	29	28	29	28	21	31	27	30	32	26	23
Travel												
Japan	23	44	55	55	65	67	54	40	53	50	65	60
Overseas	3	9	9	10	10	7	5	17	5	4	7	6
Photo as a hobby:	7%	13%	14%	13%	17%	18%	7%	10%	8%	4%	3%	5%

Source: Photo Market, 1987.

EXHIBIT 19

Photographic Subjects for Colour Prints by Season* (ISO 100, Colour Prints 1980–86)**

	Winter	Spring	Summer	Autumn
1980				
Domestic tourism	30%	43%	52%	41%
Overseas tourism	3	4	7	5
Family pictures	30	24	16	19
Event pictures	20	17	10	22
Business pictures	17	12	15	13
	100%	100%	100%	100%
1983				
Domestic tourism	30%	44%	48%	33%
Overseas tourism	8	4	7	5
Family pictures	24	19	17	15
Event pictures	20	19	13	29
Business pictures	18	14	15	18
	100%	100%	100%	100%
1986				
Domestic tourism	26%	38%	48%	40%
Overseas tourism	8	6	12	7
Family pictures	31	18	17	14
Event pictures	18	22	10	25
Business pictures	17	16	13	14
	100%	100%	100%	100%

*Winter: December to February; Spring: March to May; Summer: June to August; Autumn: September to November.
**Unit: % of total colour prints as processed by laboratories.

Source: Photo Market, 1987.

CASE 8.3

KIRIN BREWERY CO., LTD. – THE DRY BEER WAR

This case was prepared by Professor Dominique Turpin and revised with Professor Christopher Lovelock and Research Associate Joyce Miller as a basis for class discussion rather than to illustrate either effective or ineffective handling of an administrative situation. Some names have been disguised to respect confidentiality.

On 22 February 1988, Kirin Brewery decided to launch its own dry beer to compete with Asahi's Super Dry in the Japanese beer market. Kirin's decision to launch 'Kirin Dry' was backed by strong consumer pressure. In liquor stores, more and more regular Kirin consumers were asking for Kirin's dry beer, and disappointed customers were switching to Asahi's Super Dry. Kirin's executives had anticipated that both Suntory and Sapporo would jump at the new opportunities created by Asahi to attack Kirin and gain a larger share of the beer market by developing the dry niche. In fact, a few days after the introduction of Kirin Dry, both Sapporo and Suntory launched their own dry beers. By early autumn, the market for dry beer had expanded enormously, and Asahi was currently selling half of the dry beer produced in Japan.

In late September 1988, Kazuhisa Tani, who headed Kirin's Beer Division, organized a meeting with several managers from the Marketing and Corporate Planning departments. After reviewing Kirin's performance, Tani remarked:

> Kirin may have lost this summer's battle, but we are still fighting the war. Kirin must swallow its pride and commit itself to the dry beer competition, because the market is truly different now. It's all part of the game – even if dry beer triumphs enough to dislodge the old standbys, lager and draught. Campaigning for the 1989 sales year starts now. We have to be ready for the next round of the fight.

The Japanese Beer Industry

The beer industry in Japan was born in 1853 when a doctor 'test brewed' some beer at home using the description in a Dutch book. Although Shozaburo Shibuya was said to have been the first Japanese to brew and sell beer as a business in 1872, it was not until the Sino–Japanese War (1937–41), and then World War II, that millions of Japanese people, mostly soldiers, enjoyed their first taste of beer.

By 1987, beer was a popular beverage throughout Japan, representing 67% of all alcoholic beverages consumed. It was followed by Japanese sake, 17.7%; Shochu (a white spirit), 7%; and whisky and brandy, 4%. Per capita consumption of beer had doubled from 20.2 litres in 1965 to 43.8 litres, while total consumption of all alcoholic beverages had grown from 36.3 litres to 65.3 litres. Japan was the fourth largest beer market in the world, with an annual per capita consumption of just under 500 million kilolitres (kl). However, international comparative data ranked the Japanese as the 28th greatest consumers of beer in the world on a per capita basis, with a consumption less than half the US figure and under one-third that of Germany, Czechoslovakia, Denmark and New Zealand.

Production

The production and sale of beer were heavily influenced by seasonality, with 36% of sales made during the three months of June to August. Kirin's Production Manager estimated that the process of brewing beer was similar among competitors. But economies of scale could be significant.

The production of beer was controlled by the state through a licensing system, which made it difficult for newcomers to enter the market. According to Kenji Yamamoto, Deputy Manager in Kirin's Beer Division: "Investment in production is still dictated by market share, and today, one point market share is worth ¥5 billion in terms of marginal profits."[1] In 1987, Kirin had 14 brewing plants, while Sapporo, Asahi and Suntory had 10, 6 and 3 plants respectively. Yamamoto believed that its extensive network of production facilities gave Kirin a logistical cost advantage. Also, most of Kirin's breweries were built close to Japan's largest cities to ensure freshness, an element that had become a major selling point for many Japanese consumers. Yamamoto noted: "For beer lovers, the fresher, the better."

Each brewery had an average production capacity of 250,000 kl. Kirin executives estimated that in 1987, building a new brewery would represent a ¥50 billion investment (including the price of land). However around Tokyo, such a construction could require an investment of up to ¥80–90 billion.

Product Categories and Market Segmentation

The Japanese beer market was divided into two major categories: 'lager' and 'draught'. By international standards, lager was a beer with a long brewing process. However, in Japan, consumers regarded lager as a beer pasteurized by heat, while draught beer (also called 'nama' in Japan) was unpasteurized under strict microbiological control, a technique called microfiltration. While draught beer represented 9% of the total beer market in 1974 (versus 91% for lager), its share had grown to 20% in 1980. By 1987, draught accounted for 42%, lager for 51%, with the balance going to malts, dry, light and foreign beers. Kirin held over 90% of the lager category, while sales of draught were split among the four brewers (*refer to* **Exhibit 1**). Kirin's Lager was by far the best-selling beer in Japan, and the firm's position over the past 40 years had been built almost exclusively on this single product.

---

[1] In 1988: ¥1,000 = US$7.25 = SF10.44 = £4.30.

Foreign beer accounted for 3% of the total beer market. All the major Japanese brewers had tied up with large foreign brewers to distribute and brew their brands in Japan. Budweiser (from the US), brewed and distributed in Japan by Suntory, was the most popular foreign brand with the equivalent of 3.1 million cases[2] sold in 1987. Heineken (from the Netherlands) had a similar agreement with Kirin and was the second best-selling brand. Beer imports, primarily from the US, West Germany, France and Denmark, had doubled in volume between 1984 and 1987, reaching 22.4 million litres.

The total adult population (aged 20 years old and over) in Japan was increasing at an average annual rate of 1.2%. The population of males aged 40 and over (regarded by Japanese brewers as the 'heavy user' segment) had been growing more rapidly, at an average annual rate of 1.4%. 'Heavy users', Asahi's key target for Super Dry, were defined as consumers drinking more than the equivalent of 8 regular (633 ml) bottles of beer each week. They represented 15% of the beer drinking population and accounted for 50% of beer consumption. 'Middle users' (15% of beer drinkers) consumed the equivalent of 3 to 8 bottles of beer weekly. Finally, 'light users' (70% of beer drinkers) consumed fewer than 3 bottles each week. 'Middle and light users' each represented about 25% of the volume of beer consumed. In Japan, less than 10% of the total population never drank beer.

One notable trend was the growing number of female beer drinkers. Japanese women tended to be more health and weight conscious than men. To meet the needs of this segment, as well as to increase daytime consumption, Kirin had introduced Kirin Beer Light in 1980 and Kirin Palm Can in 1985. Kirin Beer Light had a lower alcohol content and attractive packaging that differentiated it from Kirin's other beer products. During the 1987 season, sales of light beer represented 0.3% of Kirin total beer revenues versus 83% for lager.

In Japan, 70% of the beer volume sold was consumed at home versus 30% in bars and restaurants. The Japanese associated no class connotation with beer, and it was quaffed with equal enthusiasm everywhere from four-stool diners to elite restaurants. However, consumption patterns were somewhat different from many Western countries. Most beer was consumed after 6:00 p.m., before dinner, after the traditional 'ofuro' (Japanese bath), or after sports. A Kirin executive explained:

> Drinking together after working hours is as much a part of Japanese business as coming to work on time. However, most Japanese feel guilty drinking beer during the day on workdays. Because we Japanese have a different enzymology (enzymes in the human body), we tend to blush very quickly after a drink or two. If employees have a beer during the day, their working colleagues would notice immediately, and this could be quite an embarrassing situation.

Japanese consumers considered beer to be a light casual drink, while wine was perceived as light but more formal. Kirin's consumer research showed that beer was seen as a healthy and natural drink because it was brewed with no

---

[2] One case contained 20 bottles of 633 ml each.

artificial additives. Shochu, another popular drink. was also considered casual, but it was a strong drink and was losing its popularity. The consumption of shochu, a distilled spirit, had experienced a major boom from 1982 to 1987. However, shochu was now seen by industry analysts as a fashion fad, and some predicted that the Super Dry boom could be the same.

Competition and Marketing Activities

The Japanese beer market was an oligopoly with four companies (Kirin, Asahi, Suntory and Sapporo) representing over 99% of the total sales volume. Two small brewers, Hokkaido Asahi and Orion, operated on a local basis only – on the northern island of Hokkaido and in Okinawa in the most southern part of Japan, respectively.

Kirin Brewery

Kirin was the top brewer in Japan and the fourth largest in the world after Anheuser–Busch and Miller of the US and Heineken of the Netherlands. Kirin's 1987 sales amounted to ¥1,300 billion with profits of ¥31,000 million. Kirin traced its origins back to 1870 when a US entrepreneur, W. Copeland, established Spring Valley, 40 kilometres south of Tokyo. The brewery was active until 1884. The organization was subsequently revamped, and operations resumed under the management of Japan Brewery Company, Ltd., which was taken over by Kirin Brewery Company, Ltd. in 1907. Building on its predecessor's philosophy, Kirin established the management tenets that still guided the company 80 years later: 'Quality First' and 'Sound Management'.

In 1954, Kirin captured top share in the beer industry from Sapporo Breweries. However, Asahi, Kirin and Sapporo remained close competitors with roughly one-third of the market each (*refer to Exhibit 2*). Since the 1950s, as far as the public was concerned: 'Beer meant Kirin'. In 1966, Kirin's market share passed 50%. But Kirin pushed its advantage even further, seizing a 63% share of the Japanese beer market in 1979. At this point, under the provision of the Japanese Anti-Monopoly Law, the Fair Trade Commission threatened legislation to break Kirin Brewery into two separate companies. In the end, the Kirin organization remained intact.

In 1971, Kirin began to diversify its operations. Through an agreement with the Canadian firm, J.E. Seagrams & Sons, Kirin began to import liquor produced overseas, including Chivas Regal. Five years later, a joint venture in Australia was established, and through a domestic venture, Kirin began to market Koiwai food products. In 1977, Kirin established KW Inc. to bottle and market Coca-Cola in the US, and later created Kirin USA, Inc. Kirin also planned to expand its presence in the US market using beer brewed in Canada by Molson Ltd. In addition, Kirin had tied up with Heineken N.V., Europe's largest beer brewer, and the company had set up several joint ventures in the United States in the field of biotechnology. In 1987, Kirin arranged to exchange information and technology with several organizations in Czechoslovakia.

Despite its diversification into soft drinks, dairy products, whisky and biotechnology, Kirin was still heavily dependent on beer. Kirin's President elaborated: "In 1987, beer represented 93% of our sales volume. This makes us vulnerable to Asahi's recent attack. We need to review the market situation and also to react adequately to Asahi's challenge."

Sapporo Breweries Ltd.

Sapporo had once been the dominant player in the market. However, it had gradually lost share to its three competitors. In 1987, it was the second largest brewer in Japan with a 20% share of the domestic market. Sapporo had a dominant position in the draught segment, holding a 40% share (*refer to Exhibit 1*). Although Sapporo had diversified into soft drinks, wine and imported liquors such as J&B whisky, beer still accounted for 94% of the company's total revenues.

Suntory Ltd.

Established in 1899 by Shinjiro Torii, the father of the firm's current president, Suntory was the major producer of whisky in Japan as well as a leading importer of Scotch whiskies, bourbons, whiskeys, cognacs, wines, liqueurs, beers, etc. In 1986, Suntory had total sales of ¥625,843 million and was credited with a 63% share of the Japanese whisky market. In comparison, Kirin–Seagram (the third largest whisky company) held a 7.6% share and Nikka Whisky (the second largest local whisky producer) had a 21% share.

Suntory was a privately-held company headed by Keizo Saji, who had a reputation for an aggressive management style. In 1960, Saji had turned his attention to beer-making, since Suntory had reached a virtual monopoly position in whisky. Most beers available in Japan at that time were German-style lager beers, so Suntory began searching for alternatives. After considerable research, Saji concluded that beer produced under strict microbiological control – similar to Danish-style beer – would have a 'cleaner and milder' flavour and be a better match for Japanese cuisine. Suntory's first beer went on the market in 1963. Four years later, the company began producing only unpasteurized bottled and canned draught beer. Suntory had gradually caught up with Asahi in terms of market share. By the end of the 1987 season, Suntory had captured 9.6% of the total beer market. The company focused on the draught segment and was the leading brand in the 'all malts' draught sub-segment (*refer to Exhibit 1*).

In addition to brewing its own beers. Suntory produced and marketed several foreign beers in Japan through licensing agreements with Anheuser–Busch Co., Inc. of the United States and Carlsberg, a Danish brewer. Since 1984, Suntory had also brewed beer in China. In fiscal year 1986, beer represented 27% of Suntory's total revenues.

Asahi Breweries Ltd.

Asahi was the third largest brewer in Japan in 1987. The company had gradually lost ground to Kirin, Sapporo and Suntory, falling below 10% market share in 1985. While sales had grown substantially between 1976 and 1986, net profits declined from ¥2,130 million in 1976 to ¥1,510 million in 1986, but climbed up again in 1987. An Asahi manager explained:

> In the 1970s, our company was the prisoner of a vicious circle. Sales were gradually slowing down, resulting in slower inventory turnovers and changing tastes, which affected our sales and our image. Also, since consumers did not have a high opinion of our products, retailers did not push our products, no matter how much effort our salesmen put in the trade. The salesmen blamed the engineers for not turning out good products, and the engineers blamed the salesmen for not being able to sell a product that they thought was as good as the competition.

To overcome Asahi's declining market share, management pushed to reduce the dependence on beer by expanding sales of soft drinks, foods and pharmaceuticals. Asahi had, in fact, become less dependent on beer than both Kirin and Sapporo. In 1987, soft drinks represented 25% of Asahi's total sales. On the basis of field research indicating that consumer preference was shifting from the bitter and richer taste of Kirin's Lager to a sharper draught taste, Asahi's Marketing Department proposed changing the taste of the company's draught beer. Launched in early 1986, the new Asahi Draught, 'koku-kire' (rich and sharp), got off to a smooth start. However, Asahi's share of the total beer market continued to drop, and the number of retailers carrying the Asahi brand was also declining.

Marketing Activities

Marketing expenditures by the four brewers had almost doubled from ¥65 billion in 1984 to ¥117 billion in 1987, partly as a result of Asahi's launch of Super Dry (*refer to* **Exhibit 3**). Typically, 80% of all marketing expenditures were made between January and May.

Advertising and Promotion

For Kuichi Matsui, the General Manager of Asahi's Marketing Department, advertising was crucial in Japan's highly competitive marketplace "where neon is king and gimmickry is commonplace." Matsui was referring to a 'packaging war' that occurred between 1984 and 1986 when various 'gadget products', such as the Suntory Penguins and the Kirin Beer Shuttle, had been used to attract consumer attention. By 1987, Matsui felt that consumers had become bored with such sales tactics.

Pricing

The National Tax Agency advised Japanese brewers on the appropriate prices for alcoholic beverages. In Japan, beer was the most heavily taxed alcoholic beverage, at a rate of 46.9% (versus 36.3% for whiskies and brandies and 17–20% for sakes and shochus). This meant that when a consumer paid ¥300 for a regular 633 ml bottle of beer, ¥140.7 was collected by the state. Kirin executives estimated that profits increased by ¥4 billion for each yen in price increase.

Distribution

The brewers sold beer to the consumer through a group of primary wholesalers. In turn, some of these sold to sub-wholesalers, who distributed products through a large number of retail outlets. Wholesalers and retailers were both licensed by the state, which strictly limited the issue of new licences. Most distributors in the Kanto (Greater Tokyo) dealt with all four brewers, while exclusive distributors had a stronger position in the Kansai region (Western Japan). The number of sub-wholesalers was declining, and developing personal relationships with the wholesalers was still a key success factor for the brewers. In 1987, more than 1,800 wholesalers distributed beer and other alcoholic beverages. Kirin worked with 800 of these and had exclusive agreements with 70% of them.

Distribution was said to be a major barrier of entry for new entrants. As the executive of a Danish brewery explained:

> It's pretty difficult to distribute beer in a country with more than one million bars, pubs and restaurants, and hundreds of thousands of stores in huge cities with virtually no street names. Tying up with a local player is almost a prerequisite. To establish our own distribution network through primary wholesalers, secondary wholesalers and sometimes tertiary wholesalers would probably take us at least 10 years.

Retailers were liquor store owners who sold to consumers as well as to neighbourhood bars and restaurants. Typically, retailers independently selected which beer to sell according to the popularity of each brand. However, each major brewer had a merchandising sales force to ensure that their company's products were effectively displayed in the stores.

Junichi Nakamura, a 54-year-old retailer in Shinagawa and one of the 130,000 liquor store owners in Japan, wondered how successful Asahi's Super Dry would be in the long run. He was used to seeing some 40 kinds of new beer packaging arrive on his shelves every year, then disappear after a few months because the brewers launched new products one after another and gave up quickly when a new product did not sell well. Nakamura also wondered if many consumers could really tell the difference between Asahi Dry and other regular beers.

Asahi Super Dry

In the spring of 1986, Hirotaro Higuchi took over the presidency of Asahi Breweries, replacing Tsutomu Mural, who was appointed as the company's

Chairman. Higuchi intended to pursue the objective set earlier by Mural; namely, to turn Asahi into a truly customer-oriented company. His ultimate objective was to restore Asahi's market share to the level the company had enjoyed right after World War II, when Asahi competed neck-and-neck with Sapporo and Kirin.

Higuchi felt that over the past 30 years, Asahi had developed a corporate culture where everyone blamed someone else for the annual loss of market share. His first step was to change the perception of Asahi Beer within the company. Higuichi's new corporate philosophy emphasized equality first, followed by customer orientation, respect for each other, labour–management conciliation, cooperation with the trade and social responsibility. A corporate booklet with 10 commandments was distributed to all employees as a guide to daily behaviour. These 'commandments' were also read aloud at work each morning so that every employee would understand Asahi's new direction.

To change Asahi's image, Higuchi decided to develop new packaging. All beers carrying the old-fashioned imperial flag were recalled from the retailers' shelves. Higuchi aimed to send the trade, the public and the competition a strong message that Asahi had changed significantly. As well, he implemented a 'Quality First' policy and instructed the Purchasing Department to use only the best raw materials, even if this meant higher costs. Finally, Higuchi decided that the company would increase its advertising and promotional expenditures, even at the risk of eating up all net profits.

When Higuchi discussed the 'dry' concept for the first time with 12 Asahi executives in the autumn of 1986, no one really supported the idea. Higuchi recalled that his Production Director went so far as to say: "We can't produce a dry beer, this is nonsense to me." The marketing people explained that the meaning of the word 'dry' was important: "Dry suggests something new, decisive and bold. We found out that a 'wet' person is very strongly attached to family, the company and friends, while a 'dry' type is more individualistic."

Higuchi felt that he should postpone the launch of Super Dry until the new Asahi draught had established a stronger position in the market. Yet, young managers in the Marketing, R&D and Production Departments were quite comfortable with the concept of Super Dry. As well, the production engineers indicated that 'dry beer' would not require a major breakthrough in production technology. A young marketing executive had told Higuchi: "I think that the 'dry' concept is viable, but I can't tell you how much we can expect to sell."

Launch of Super Dry

By early 1987, the R&D department had managed to develop a 'dry' beer. Meanwhile, the Marketing Department had gathered more data using 'hands-on' test markets to determine favourable consumer attitudes. It had developed a comprehensive marketing plan and set a first year sales target of 800,000 cases. On 17 March 1987, Asahi's 'Super Dry' beer was officially launched.

Super Dry was designed as a draught beer targeted at heavy drinkers. Made with less residual sugar, the beer was less sweet. It contained 0.5% more alcohol than the 4.5% regular draught beers, and had been defined as much sharper and softer than traditional draught beers (*refer to* **Exhibit 4**). Super Dry was made using the best hops from Czechoslovakia and Germany, and malts from the United States, Canada and Australia. Asahi's production engineers had shortened the time from production to consumption to an average of 20 days, while other brewers operated on a 23–25 day cycle. The Super Dry silver label with Asahi's new logo and modern lettering reinforced the image of a truly different product.

Asahi's marketing budget had been increased from ¥25.5 billion in 1986 to ¥38.1 billion (*refer to* **Exhibit 3**), and ¥4.2 billion was spent on advertising to promote Super Dry in 1987. Hakuhodo, Japan's second largest advertising company, designed a campaign featuring Nobuhiko Ochiai, a former US oilman who had become a respected, international journalist. To launch Super Dry, Asahi ran full-page advertisements in all five major dailies. The ads were spread across three weeks: a 'coming soon' preview, a 'debuts today' announcement, and a 'have you tried it yet?' follow-up ad. Television commercials were double the normal volume for a new product campaign. Asahi also distributed free samples to a million people throughout Japan. In addition to its 500 sales people (versus 520 for Kirin), Asahi had set up sales teams with 1,000 'field ladies' to promote and merchandise the new product at the retail level and collect additional marketing data from consumers regarding preference, purchase habits and so on.

In the autumn of 1987, while the beer market in Japan had grown by 7%, Asahi's total sales had soared by 34%, mainly thanks to Super Dry.

Kirin's Response to Asahi

Asahi's performance had had the effect of a small earthquake within the Kirin organization, and various teams were put to work to generate alternatives to meet the Asahi challenge. In late October 1987, Kirin's President, Hideyo Motoyama, called a special meeting of the Beer Division's executives to decide Kirin's strategy for the 1988 beer season. The outcome of this meeting included decisions to launch three new products – Kirin Dry, Kirin Fine Malt and Kirin Fine Draught – to relaunch Kirin Beer as Kirin Lager beer, and to make a price cut.

The objective in launching Kirin Dry was to respond to consumers' needs, fill the niche created by Asahi, and beat Asahi on its own turf with a superior product. The Kirin Dry concept was similar to Asahi's Super Dry. The new product had 5% more alcohol than regular beer, the same number of calories, and a drier, less sweet taste. Kirin's Dry (like the dry beers launched by Suntory and Sapporo) used the same silver packaging that Asahi had used for its Super Dry and contained the following message in English:

> Our superior fermentation technology and carefully selected hops have produced a beer with an exceptionally delicate taste, well-balanced with a dry finish. The connoisseur's beer 'KIRIN DRY', will add a new taste of pleasure to your day.

Kirin Dry was offered in 633 ml and 500 ml bottles and in 500 ml and 350 ml cans. Asahi's Super Dry was sold in 633 ml, 500 ml and 334 ml bottles, in 350 ml, 250 ml and 135 ml cans as well as in 2, 3 and 10-litre barrels for on-premises outlets.

On 20 April 1988, Kirin announced that it would cut the price of one of its mainline products, 500 ml cans, citing an increase in foreign exchange gains due to the appreciation of the yen as the reason. Kirin had indeed saved ¥3.4 billion over the past two years on imported hops and malt used in the brewing process. The result for the consumer was a reduction in the retail price of a 500 ml can of beer from ¥280 to ¥270. A Goldman Sachs & Co. analyst commented:

> The major reason for Kirin's action was to restore its market share under the impact of increased competition from Asahi's Super Dry. Kirin's price cut was immediately followed by Asahi and Sapporo. These cuts (all ¥10 per can) were the first changes in 26 years. The Kirin people believed that the impact of such a price cut would be minimal while Sapporo and Asahi would each suffer damage in the range of ¥300 million by following Kirin down in price.
>
> Real competition in dry beer is starting now. We believe that distribution capability and financial resources to back strong advertising campaigns will dictate that Kirin wins in view of its larger size.

Kirin's management decided to change the name as well as the packaging of Kirin's regular beer from Kirin Beer to Kirin LAGER Beer with a large red 'LAGER' printed on all labels. In mid-June 1988 just before the summer season, Kirin launched 'Kirin Fine Malt' and 'Kirin Fine Draught', both positioned as 'after-dry' products to reinforce Kirin's presence in the draught segment and to signal an end to the dry beer boom. 'Kirin Fine Malt' was first introduced in some local areas and launched nationally a few months later.

Reorganization at Kirin

In early 1988 Kirin's President appointed Kazuhisa Tani to head a task force to recommend and implement a new corporate strategy for Kirin's Beer Division. Tani had broad responsibilities for marketing and corporate planning and he reported directly to Motoyama.

Tani had joined Kirin Brewery in 1962 right after graduating from university. He had first worked as a controller in the Amagasaki brewery before joining headquarters in 1971 to work on Kirin's joint venture with Seagrams. From 1982 until early 1988 Tani had headed Kirin–Seagram apart for one year at the M.I.T. Sloan School of Management in the United States to earn an MBA degree. Kirin–Seagram was considered to be much more market-oriented than the conservative Kirin organization and Motoyama expected that Tani would be able to transfer some of the entrepreneurial spirit of the joint venture.

Tani recommended the development and the introduction of two new management control systems: MRS (Management Reporting System) and ME (Marketing Engineering). MRS was a system to evaluate each salesman's performance in relation to sales volumes and expenses. The ME system involved developing a marketing database for the brand managers. Under the new organization of the Beer Division, headquarters and the breweries were cost centres, and the only profit centres were the sales branches, with brand managers responsible for the profitability of their own operations.

In the spring of 1988, Tani recommended accelerating the plan to expand the sales network from 17 branches to 40 additional sales offices, and to increase the sales force from 550 to 800 by 1990. Tani also pressed to speed up the development of the KIC network (Kirin Intelligence & Communication), which would enable Kirin to monitor the market more closely. Information technology had been a central theme of Kirin's 1981 diversification plan. In May 1985, Kirin became the first Japanese brewer to offer a line of computers (the KN Line) to wholesalers and retailers throughout Japan. The KIC project aimed to install on-line computers in an additional 350 liquor wholesalers and 1,000 retail stores by 1990, providing them with a variety of speedy services, such as cash register, inventory control, sales data, invoicing, etc. The computer network would also provide Kirin's management with immediate feedback on the rotation of stocks and daily sales trends for all Kirin products as well as those of the competitors.

The Dry War

The simultaneous introduction of dry products by Kirin, Sapporo and Suntory triggered an immediate marketing war. None of these dry beers was clearly differentiated from Asahi's Super Dry in concept, taste or packaging, which led Asahi to request that its competitors modify both the packaging and the concept of their dry beers.

Asahi's rising voice against 'unfair competition' attracted the attention of the press, and the dry war suddenly became a national affair. While Asahi and its competitors were fighting through the intermediary of the press, an advertising war was also taking place. Asahi was massively advertising Super Dry using journalist Nobuhiko Ochiai as the central character of its campaign. Meanwhile, Kirin had signed up the Hollywood actor Gene Hackman for its Kirin Dry campaign around the theme: 'I'm so happy I could cry Dry, Dry!'. Suntory had developed an advertising campaign featuring Mike Tyson, the world boxing superchampion: 'Hi, I'm Mike Tyson. I like Suntory DRY'. A Suntory manager explained that Tyson had been chosen "to communicate the power and the punch of dry beer." Finally, Sapporo had signed up Japanese sports celebrities for its Sapporo Dry campaign.

Suntory and Sapporo had followed Kirin's strategy, advertising and aggressively pushing their traditional products: '100% Malt' for Suntory and 'Black Label' for Sapporo. The four brewers had increased their advertising budgets by an average of 20% over the previous year, exposing consumers to more beer advertising than they had probably seen in their entire lives. Although consumers had been somewhat confused at first by the dry war, they did realize that Asahi was the original inventor of the dry beer concept. A liquor store owner in Tokyo commented:

Japanese consumers are fascinated by this all-out marketing war. They enjoy reading about the battle for market share in their newspapers. They also like watching hired hands (Mike Tyson and Gene Hackman, for example) fight it out in a deluge of TV and print ads. Keeping up-to-date dominates the chats in my store. Employees also discuss the beer war with their colleagues. When I deliver beer to the neighbouring bars and restaurants, I can hear people expressing options on possible upcoming trends. People wonder what will happen next. It's a social phenomenon.

Situation in Autumn 1988

By summer's end, when beer consumption typically began to decline, Asahi had clearly won the dry beer sweepstakes. In the beer industry, where a hit product reached sales of 1 million cases in its first year, the 13.5 million cases achieved by 'Super Dry' were an amazing success. Asahi had reached three major milestones that would have been unthinkable a scant 16 months earlier. For the first time in two decades, Asahi's share of total beer sales in Japan had broken the 20% market share barrier. In August 1988, Asahi confirmed that after 23 years it had overtaken Sapporo as Japan's second largest brewery. Asahi was now selling half of the dry beer produced in Japan.

In July 1988, Kirin was actually producing more dry beer than Asahi, although Asahi's sales of the new product remained larger by a slim margin. At this time, total beer sales were 1% lower than the year before. The summer's relatively cool, rainy weather had been bad for beer sales, but ironically good for Asahi. A month later, dry beer accounted for a heady 34% of total beer sales, while lager had 38% and draught 25%. Yoshio Matsuda from the Brewers Association of Japan remarked:

> This is an amazing phenomenon. Just think – in the US it took 18 years for light beers to obtain a 25% share of the total beer market, and it took Asahi only 16 months to achieve a similar result in Japan. Only a year earlier, 51% of all beer sold in Japan was lager and 42% was draught. The good weather in August and September put a new kick in the beer industry and by early October 1988, the market had grown by 7.6%. Meanwhile, Asahi sales had shot up by 72%. I think that the rapid growth of the dry beer market was due to three factors. First, Super Dry was a unique concept and a well-accepted taste, based on extensive marketing research. Second, having the total participation of the four major breweries involved in an advertising war with massive budgets developed awareness and interest in the dry segment. Third, Japanese consumers are inclined to quickly follow fashion trends.

However, other factors had played an important part in Asahi's success. Sales activities had aimed at promoting fresh product rotation. Over the past year, Asahi increased its capital investment in plant and equipment by 50%. By 1988, its production capacity was 2.5 times the level it was in 1986.

The dry war had social consequences as well. Since August, many liquor store owners had placed apologetic signs on their doors saying they were out of Super

Dry beer. The press had also reported that Asahi's President had asked his employees not to buy Super Dry because every precious drop had to be reserved for its customers. An Asahi manager acknowledged that the company's success was also an issue:

> This summer, we had a major problem with capacity. We were planning to sell 13.5 million cases in 1988, but we are only at the end of September and we have already sold more than 83 million! Right now, we have 3 plants producing beer only and 5 plants producing both beer and juice. To meet the demand during the summer, we had to stop producing juice and turn all these plants into breweries. Asahi is now devoting nearly all of its brewing capacity to Super Dry. Despite these efforts, we could cope with only 70% of the demand for dry beer. Moreover, we don't have enough capacity to brew Coors locally, as originally agreed under Asahi's 5-year 1987 licensing pact with Adolph Coors. Last June, our capacity crunch was so severe that we arranged to import the Coors we couldn't brew in Japan. To meet the bare minimum of our licensing agreement, Asahi – at a cost of $2.3 million – chartered 15 Boeing 747 jumbo jet freighters to transport 141,450 cases of Coors and Coors Light in 12-oz. cans and bottles from Golden, Colorado, over a period of three months. We now have to decide whether to invest in building one or two new breweries, since we expect industry sales to grow at around 7% annually over the next three years.

The dry war that had been taking place in Japan had also attracted the attention of the large foreign brewers. The Miller Brewing Company, for instance, had recently begun conducting market research on dry products in the United States.

New Competitive Moves in Japan

In the autumn of 1988, the future of the dry boom remained uncertain. Asahi had recently published the results of a marketing survey called 'The Asahi Super Dry Era', concluding that Super Dry was here to stay. However, Asahi's competitors were more divided about the future of the dry segment. In 1988, each major brewer was strong in a different type of beer. Kirin's best-seller was lager, Asahi had dry, and Sapporo had draught. Looking at Asahi's success, Kazuo Arakawa, Sapporo's Executive Vice President, said: "Asahi helped Sapporo by jolting Kirin. Dry beer has gotten people talking about beer, has widened the range of products available, and generally invigorated the market."

Taking advantage of the turbulent environment created by the dry war, all brewers were launching new products to prepare for what Sapporo executives called the 'after-dry era'. Japanese consumers now had a wide choice of beers available, varying from 4.5 to 9% in alcohol content. Sapporo had recently launched its 'On-the-Rocks Beer', a high alcohol (9%) beer that was meant to be sipped over ice like whisky. Sapporo had also announced its 'Winter's Tale' beer to be sold only from November to February. Suntory had launched '5.5', a dry beer with a higher alcohol content (5.5% versus 5% for regular dry beers).

Ken Takanashi, a Suntory manager, believed that Suntory's 'malts' could be a particular threat to Asahi Super Dry. He explained: "Malts were a hit last year until being eclipsed by the dry war along with lager and draught, but as of August they seem to be bubbling again." To counter an expansion of the malt sub–segment, Kirin had introduced Kirin Fine Malt (a 100% malt beer) in June 1988, initially on a regional basis, then nationally in the autumn of 1988. Kirin Fine Malt was positioned as a new draught beer.

Defining Kirin's New Product Line Strategy

In late September 1988, Kazuhisa Tani met with several managers from the Marketing and Corporate Planning Departments. After reviewing Kirin's performance relative to the competition in each of the major categories of beer (*refer to **Exhibits 1 and 5***), he asked his product managers to put forward their proposals for new products.

Messrs. Fukuyama and Makita, respectively in charge of R&D and Marketing for the Beer Division, presented two new products. *Malt Dry* was a 100% malt draught beer with a 5% alcohol content, which would occupy a unique position on the market. In Makita's opinion, Malt Dry was a new concept serving the two fastest growing segments of the market: dry and all malt. *Kirin Cool* was an extra smooth beer with a 4.5% alcohol content and a softer taste, targeted at men and women aged 20–25. It was positioned in the 'soft and smooth segment' of the market (*refer to **Exhibit 4***). Kirin Cool's unique selling proposition was 'a taste never before experienced'.

Makita also indicated that *Kirin Fine Pilsner* was ready to be launched. Positioned in the 'rich and smooth' segment, Kirin Fine Pilsner would be targeted at people in their 20s and 30s. Its unique selling proposition was: 'A new standard beer with creamy froth like a velvet touch'. The Corporate Planning Department favoured launching all three products in the next year, reasoning that a full-line strategy would give Kirin complete coverage of the market. Makita was not convinced:

> With so many new products on the market, we run the risk of confusing the consumer. Moreover, the launch of each new product will cost us at least ¥1 billion. For next year, I would personally favour launching 'Malt Dry and *only* Malt Dry'.

Ryosuke Murata, also from Marketing Department, disagreed:

> I don't think that we should launch a new dry beer. We should get away from this segment and prepare for the after-dry era. I am in favour of pushing Kirin Lager more aggressively. After all, it's still our best-selling product, and it has a rich thick taste with a fine aroma.

Makita presented a final proposal concerning *Kirin Fine Draught*, which aimed to reposition Kirin in the draught segment by 'recreating the taste in beer halls'.

Tani also had in front of him some new marketing data collected by the Mitsubishi Research Institute (*refer to Exhibit 6*) as well as some data on dry beer blind tests in which consumers had been asked to compare competitive products according to different attributes (*refer to Exhibit 7*). It was now time to make a decision on Kirin's product strategy and develop a marketing plan for 1989.

EXHIBIT 1

Beer Sales by Japanese Brewers by Segment (1986–88) (in kilolitres)

	Lager	Draught	Dry	All malts	Total*
1986					
Kirin	2,352,900	388,800	0	22,100	2,763,800
Asahi	71,400	436,100	0	2,500	510,000
Sapporo	207,800	783,200	0	33,500	1,024,500
Suntory	0	408,200	0	41,500	449,700
	2,632,100	2,016,300	–	99,600	4,748,000
1987					
Kirin	2,491,800	479,000	0	42,000	3,012,800
Asahi	60,200	441,900	165,000	19,200	686,300
Sapporo	170,400	886,500	0	33,900	1,090,800
Suntory	0	394,800	0	110,000	504,800
	2,722,400	2,202,200	165,000	205,100	5,294,700
1988**					
Kirin	2,001,600	245,500	501,800	37,900	2,786,800
Asahi	12,500	210,800	943,100	14,000	1,180,400
Sapporo	105,800	712,300	275,200	38,700	1,132,000
Suntory	0	234,000	182,000	89,000	505,000
	2,119,900	1,402,600	1,902,100	179,600	5,604,200

*Totals exclude sales of light beer (15,000 kl) and imported foreign beers (32,000 kl).
** Projections for 12 months as of late September 1988.

Source: Kirin Brewery Co., Ltd.

EXHIBIT 2

Comparative Market Shares in the Japanese Beer Industry (1949–87)

Year	Brewer				
	Asahi	Kirin	Sapporo	Suntory	Takara
1949	36.1%	25.3%	38.6%	–	–
1950	33.5	29.5	37.0	–	–
1951	34.5	29.5	36.0	–	–
1952	32.5	33.0	34.5	–	–
1953	33.3	33.2	33.5	–	–
1954	31.5	37.1	31.4	–	–
1955	31.7	36.9	31.4	–	–
1956	31.1	41.7	27.2	–	–
1957	30.7	42.1	26.2	–	1.0%
1958	30.9	39.9	27.5	–	1.7
1959	29.3	42.4	26.5	–	1.8
1960	27.2	44.7	26.0	–	2.1
1961	28.0	41.6	27.8	–	2.6
1962	26.4	45.0	26.4	–	2.2
1963	24.3	46.5	26.3	0.9%	2.0
1964	25.5	46.2	25.2	1.2	1.9
1965	23.2	47.7	25.3	1.9	1.9
1966	22.2	50.8	23.8	1.7	1.5
1967	22.0	49.4	25.0	3.2	0.4
1968	20.2	51.2	24.4	4.2	–
1969	19.0	53.3	23.2	4.5	–
1970	17.3	55.4	23.0	4.3	–
1971	14.9	58.9	22.0	4.2	–
1972	14.1	60.1	21.3	4.5	–
1973	13.6	61.4	20.3	4.7	–
1974	13.1	62.6	19.5	4.8	–
1975	13.5	60.8	20.2	5.5	–
1976	11.8	63.8	18.4	6.0	–
1977	12.1	61.9	19.5	6.5	–
1978	11.6	62.1	19.6	6.7	–
1979	11.1	62.9	19.2	6.8	–
1980	11.0	62.2	19.7	7.1	–
1981	10.3	62.6	20.1	7.0	–
1982	10.0	62.3	19.9	7.8	–
1983	10.1	61.3	20.0	8.6	–
1984	9.9	61.7	19.5	8.9	–
1985	9.6	61.4	19.8	9.2	–
1986	10.4	59.6	20.4	9.4	–
1987	12.9	57.0	20.5	9.6	–

Sources: Figures up to 1981 – estimated by the Brewers Association of Japan. 1982–87 – casewriters' estimates.

EXHIBIT 3

Comparative Marketing Expenditures of the Major Japanese Brewers (1983–87) (in billion yen)†

	Advertising expenses	Promotion expenses	Total marketing expenses	As % of beer sales
Kirin				
1983	10.5	16.0	26.5	2.5
1984	11.4	18.1	29.5	2.7
1985	15.9	21.7	37.6	3.2
1986	13.9	21.4	35.3	2.9
1987	15.9	28.1	44.0	3.5
Asahi				
1983	6.8	6.8	13.6	6.3
1984	7.9	7.5	15.4	7.1
1985	8.9	10.0	18.9	8.0
1986	7.9	10.9	18.8	7.9
1987*	11.7	13.8	25.5	9.8
Sapporo				
1983	7.5	4.0	11.5	3.2
1984	8.6	4.9	13.5	3.7
1985	11.0	5.5	16.5	4.3
1986	12.1	6.0	18.1	4.5
1987*	13.3	7.8	21.1	4.8
Suntory				
1983	25.7	36.6	62.3	7.0*
1984	27.9	39.6	67.5	7.9
1985	26.7	39.8	66.5	8.7
1986	22.8	39.6	62.4	8.1
1987	22.9	46.6	69.5	9.2

* Estimated.

† Expenditures are for all products, including beer. Beer as a percentage of total sales (1983–87) is as follows: Kirin 93%; Asahi: 79%; Sapporo: 94%; Suntory: 28%.

Source: Dentsu Inc.

EXHIBIT 4

Positioning Map for Kirin's Products

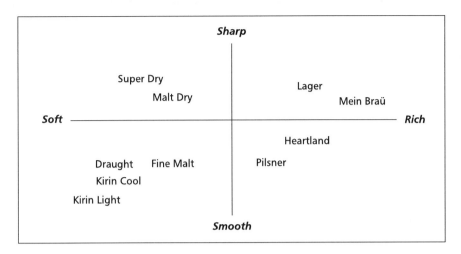

Source: Kirin Brewery Co., Ltd.

EXHIBIT 5

Comparative Performance of Japanese Brewers (1987–88)

	Lager		Draught		Dry		All malts		Total	
	1987	1988*	1987	1988*	1987	1988*	1987	1988*	1987	1988*
1. Comparative market shares by segment										
Kirin	91.5%	94.4%	21.8%	21.5%	0%	26.4%	20.5%	29.6%		
Asahi	2.2	0.6	20.1	14.3	100	49.6	9.4	7.0		
Sapporo	6.3	5.0	40.2	48.3	0	14.5	16.5	19.2		
Suntory	0	0	17.9	15.9	0	9.5	53.6	44.2		
Total	100%	100%	100%	100%	100%	100%	100%	100%		
2. Comparative product mix by brewer										
Kirin	82.7%	69.6%	15.9%	11.0%	0%	17.4%	1.4%	2.1%	100%	100%
Asahi	8.8	1.1	64.4	17.9	24	79.9	2.8	1.2	100	100
Sapporo	15.6	9.3	81.3	62.9	0	24.3	3.1	3.4	100	100
Suntory	0	0	78.2	46.3	0	36.0	21.8	17.6	100	100

* As of September 1988.

Source: Kirin Brewery Co., Ltd., 1988.

EXHIBIT 6

Results from the Mitsubishi Research Institute Concerning Consumer Opinions on Dry Beer in Japan

Survey design
Area: Tokyo
Timing: September 1988
Sample: 504 people (all beer drinkers)

Question 1: What is your favourite type of beer?
Responses by sex

	Men	Women	Total
Lager	15.8%	6.0%	12.1%
Draught	20.9%	20.2%	20.6%
Dry	55.6%	65.6%	59.3%
All malts	4.9%	4.9%	4 9%
Light	1.3%	2.2%	1.6%

Responses by age bracket

	20s	30s	40s	50s
Lager	6.2%	9.2%	17.0%	27.3%
Draught	21.2%	20.9%	20.6%	18.2%
Dry	61.6%	63.8%	54.6%	50.0%
All malts	7.5%	3.7%	4.3%	2.3%
Light	2.7%	1.2%	0.7%	2.3%

Question 2: What made you drink dry beer?'

I saw some commercials on TV	64.0%
I read an article about it	37.7%
I saw it in a store	14.3%
I read some comparative studies	36.2%
It's available at home	34.2%
People around me drink it	36.2%

Question 3: What made you drink . . .

	Asahi Super Dry?	Kirin Dry?	Sapporo Dry?	Suntory Dry
I saw some commercials on TV	63.4%	62.8%	72.0%	76.2%
I read an article about it	38.8%	35.9%	38.0%	33.3%
I saw it in a store	14.6%	12.8%	12.0%	28.6%
I read some comparative studies	34.8%	37.2%	38.0%	42.9%
It's available at home	35.1%	30.8%	32.0%	38.4%
People around me drink it	34.8%	37.2%	38.0%	42.9%

EXHIBIT 6 (continued)

Question 4: Why do you think beer drinking attitudes changed?

Preferences have changed	12.7%
New products have been introduced	68.8%
People make comparisons	18.5%
Newspapers and magazines reported on it	30.2%
Lifestyles have changed	16.0%

Question 5: What were your impressions when you first tasted a dry beer?

It tastes different	28.0%
It has good body	30.8%
It has a sharp taste	38.1%
It has a smooth taste	35.6%
It has more alcohol	20.3%
It tastes like other beers	17.8%
It is trendy	15.1%
It has a good label and a good name	15.3%
Others	2.9%

Question 6: What do you mean by 'beer with good body'?

A sharp beer	22.9%
A thick beer	52.2%
A bitter beer	30.4%
A sweet beer	18.8%
A good feeling in the throat	19.0%
It smells good	17.0%
A stronger beer	14.4%
The real beer	57.5%
Others	2.4%

Question 7: What type of beer do you associate most with this concept of good body?

Lager	14.0%
Draught	17.8%
Dry	28.5%
All malts	20.6%
Light	0.2%
Black	11.7%
Others	1.6%

Question 8: What do you mean by 'a sharp beer'?

A good feeling in the throat	60.1%
A pure taste	38.5%
Bitterness disappears rapidly	51.6%
No bitterness	20.0%
A beer with a higher degree of fermentation	24.3%
A stronger beer	14.6%

(continued)

EXHIBIT 6 (continued)

Question 9: With what kind of beer do you associate most with this concept of sharpness?

Lager	5.5%
Draught	21.9%
Dry	55.1%
All malts	4.7%
Light	3.8%
Black	0.2%
Others	1.6%

Question 10: Do you think that your consumption of dry beer will increase or decrease?

Will decrease	23.2%
Will remain stable	48.7%
Will increase	25.2%

Question 11: Why will your consumption of dry beer decrease?

It is not my taste	44.6%
I don't see any difference from other beers	8.0%
I don't drink it because it is a fad	4.5%
People around me don't drink it	8.9%
It does not taste good	28.6%
I'm getting tired of it	28.6%
That's the way it is	25.0%
Other reasons	10.7%

Question 12: Why will your consumption of dry beer increase?

I like the taste	52.2%
People around me drink it	17.6%
It's trendy	21.3%
I'd like to try other beers	19.1%
It tastes good	63.2%
It's available at home	25.7%
I'm tired of other beers	5.1%
Other reasons	8.1%

Source: Mitsubishi Research Institute, September 1988.

EXHIBIT 7

Blind Tests for Different Beers

Survey design

Area:	Tokyo
Timing:	September 1988
Sample:	450 people

Attributes	Products		
	Kirin Lager	*Asahi Dry*	*Sapporo Draught*
Flavour	100*	99.4	98.8
Bitterness	100*	92.6	94.9
Softness	100*	113.3	113.0
Lightness	100*	116.0	114.5
Richness	100*	88.1	91.7
Carbonization	100*	99.3	97.0

*Index (a higher figure indicates rated better than Kirin; a lower figure indicates rated worse).

Source: Kirin Brewery Co. Ltd.

9. Competing in the Asia-Pacific Region

CASE 9.1A # HONG KONG & SHENZHEN BANK

This case was prepared by Professor Dominique Turpin and Giana Klaas of MSR as a basis for class discussion rather than to illustrate either effective or ineffective handling of a business situation. Names and data have been disguised to protect confidentiality.

On a rainy day in January 1993, Jian Cheng was sitting in her office on the 35th floor of one of the newly built towers facing the bay of Hong Kong. Jian had called a meeting with the management team of the International Trade Division of the Hong Kong & Shenzhen Bank to discuss what steps should be taken to improve the employees' motivation.

A report lying on Jian's desk gave the results of an internal survey, showing that 30% of the bank employees were unclear about their work objectives. Jian felt that if she could reduce this number, the gain for the bank could be substantial. During the last two weeks, Jian had visited several customers, Hong Kong Chinese as well as Western manufacturers who were struggling with similar issues. Several of her clients had turned to total quality programmes. Others had started customer-satisfaction campaigns as a way to enhance employee satisfaction. Jian had been struck by their enthusiasm. In one factory that she had visited recently, Jian had been surprised to see creative posters on the walls emphasizing customer satisfaction and the importance of the customer. After talking to colleagues both inside and outside the bank, Jian had also been surprised to find out that their definition of customer service remained vague. Every employee and manager within the Hong Kong & Shenzhen Bank seemed to have a different definition of what an optimum level of customer service should be. While almost every manager was complaining about the increasing toughness of competition, Jian felt that improving employee satisfaction could help the bank in its search for new sustainable competitive advantages.

The Hong Kong & Shenzhen Bank

The Hong Kong & Shenzhen Bank was a major Chinese commercial bank with headquarters in Hong Kong, and 162 subsidiaries in Hong Kong and other Asian countries. In 1992, the bank had 9,000 employees and had made a profit of US$272 million from a turnover of US$1.9 billion. The bank was organized around five divisions:

- The **Private Banking Division** managed the investment portfolio of wealthy Hong Kong residents and foreign customers.

- The **Business Banking Division** was in charge of loans to business firms.

- The **International Trade Division** took care of all banking operations dealing with foreign exchange, international credit and overseas businesses.

- The **Subsidiaries Division** managed all subsidiaries in charge of savings, loans and credits to the general public.

- The **Logistics Division** managed all the general services of the bank administration.

Jian Cheng

Jian Cheng, 42, had been in banking since graduating in Finance from the Chinese University of Hong Kong in 1973. Jian had joined the Hong Kong & Shenzhen Bank six years earlier and had had various experiences working in the different divisions of the bank in Hong Kong as well as in New York, London and Singapore. Six months previously, she had been transferred from the Hong Kong & Shenzhen Bank in Tokyo (Japan) to her new job in Hong Kong as general manager of the International Trade Division.

The Hong Kong & Shenzhen Bank's International Trade Division

The International Trade Division was divided into four departments (*refer to Exhibit 1*):

- International Trade;

- International Clients;

- Letters of Credit;

- Foreign Currency.

The International Trade Department

This department was in charge of financing exports from Hong Kong as well as providing credit to Hong Kong firms with international activities. The head of this department, Bernard Chang, was responsible for evaluating financial risks, managing customers' files and approving letters of credit. His department was organized by cells. Each of the eight cells was run by a manager and his assistant. Each manager looked personally after the business of his or her assigned clients, ensuring follow-up on all business transactions and interfaces with the Letters of Credit and Foreign Currency departments.

The International Trade Department dealt with about 300 customers. The majority of customers in this department were small and medium-sized companies, engaged in international trade. Most of these firms were financially weak. Because of the risks involved with this type of activity, Jian Cheng kept a close eye on this department. Customers of the International Trade Department were of different cultures and nationalities: Chinese, British, American, etc. The bank made contacts and followed them up mostly by phone. Each manager received an average of 12 calls per day and two or three calls per week from the same customer.

According to Bernard Chang, the definition of good service quality for the customers of his department was speed, friendliness and competence. Customers would visit the bank, ask for information and expect immediate answers to their problems, whether positive or negative. Customers also expected extra services such as obtaining privileged information – for example, locations where goods could be warehoused at a cheaper price. They would also expect to be put in touch with potential business partners.

In order to serve customers promptly, Mr Chang believed that the key success factors for customer service were:

- Smooth communication between the different departments of the Division and the Logistics Division of the bank.

- Flexibility within the Foreign Currency Department. (Indeed, it was common that customers would call the bank for immediate transactions rather than make payments at a fixed date. Customers also often called outside the regular business hours.)

- State-of-the-art computers that could provide customers with instant information about their accounts and help the bank make a quick decision about whether or not to give credit.

- An understanding of the customer's ethnic culture and needs.

The International Clients Department

This department dealt mainly with special credit conditions for private customers overseas. It also dealt with firms and accounts in fiscal paradises (such as Panama, the Cayman Islands, etc.) and credit services for banks with low liquid assets.

This department, headed by Annie Wong, worked closely with the Foreign Currency Department, the Letters of Credit, leasing services and the Accounting Department. Much like the International Trade Department, the International Clients Department employees complained about the many operations they had to handle and the errors that resulted because of understaffing and overwork. Employees in this department worked mainly on the phone and rarely met customers.

The customers of this department were big multinational corporations that typically made 50% or more of their turnover overseas. These customers were more 'sophisticated' than those of the International Trade Department. The International Clients Department had about 50 customers. They tended to be extremely demanding clients who would not hesitate to call the bank to check at what time a fax had been sent. In Annie Wong's view, the key success factors for customer service were speed and precision in information delivery.

The largest customers needed a careful follow-up on all their operations. They wanted better deals (typically lower commissions) and expected the bank to follow their orders blindly. They were also less loyal. As a result, Annie Wong's subordinates felt that these customers were less interesting for the bank. Consequently, the employee turnover in this department had traditionally been higher than in other departments.

The Letters of Credit Department

This department issued letters of credit and managed project financing for all kinds of firms, regardless of their size. The department was organized into two cells: the "Regular Business Cell' and the 'Special Affairs Cell'. The first cell issued letters of credit for export businesses. The second dealt with letters of credit in which foreign manufacturers were involved. This department was managed by Ying-Ming Yeh and Charlie Wang. Their offices were next to each other, one floor above their 16 subordinates. The 'Special Affairs Cell' was organized differently from the 'Regular Business Cell'. In the former, new customers' files would arrive in a box located at the entrance to the office. In the morning, employees in the 'Special Affairs Cell' would pick up a file (either at random or they would take one that looked interesting). Charlie Wang felt that this process could be handled differently so that employees would be more motivated and flexible.

The Foreign Currency Department

This department had two main activities. First, it dealt with currency arbitrations for the bank; and second, it fulfilled customers' orders. The first activity was managed by a team of four young managers, each specializing in a particular currency. One key requirement for doing this job was being fast and using efficient computer systems. Six brokers were responsible for the second activity. These two teams were in touch with customers almost exclusively by phone. Since exchange rates changed by the minute, speed was the key success factor in this business. The employees in this department worked independently and, in Jian's view, lacked team spirit.

The Next Steps

Jian Cheng was managing one of the bank's highest performing divisions. Jian's division was also perceived internally as one of the most customer-oriented divisions. However, Jian believed in the philosophy that 'good can always be made better'. She was wondering how she could increase her staff's motivation while, at the same time, turn the International Trade Division into a customer-driven organization. Should she start with the employees or the customers? Jian was particularly concerned about any potentially negative reaction from the staff. At all costs, she wanted to avoid such comments as: "Here comes another 'great idea' from the boss" and "We have gone through quality service issues before and they didn't work. Why should it work this time?" Jian knew that she could count on the support of Harry Lee, Executive Vice-President of the Bank, but what about her own staff?

A week before, Jian Cheng had attended a board meeting of the bank. The President of the bank, Kenneth Tan, had emphasized his goals for the next three years. He particularly emphasized that he wanted the bank to become the industry leader in customer service. Each subsidiary had been given 'carte blanche' to achieve this objective. The only constraint imposed by Mr Tan was that each subsidiary must focus first on internal quality – namely, improve the motivation of its staff. Harry Lee, the Vice-President to whom Jian Cheng reported, asked Mr Tan to set up a Quality Committee to improve customer service. The team consisted of Peter Lim, manager in charge of training, Chuck Li, a trainer, David Chan, head of personnel, Paul Jiao, assistant manager and Jian Cheng herself. The team had to decide on the following key issues:

- What steps should be taken to improve employees' motivation?

- How could the division become more quality-oriented?

- Should the team work exclusively inside the Division or include members of other divisions?

- Should the team be extended to include other members of the organization?

- When should the quality programme start?

EXHIBIT 1

Organization Chart of the Hong Kong & Shenzhen Bank

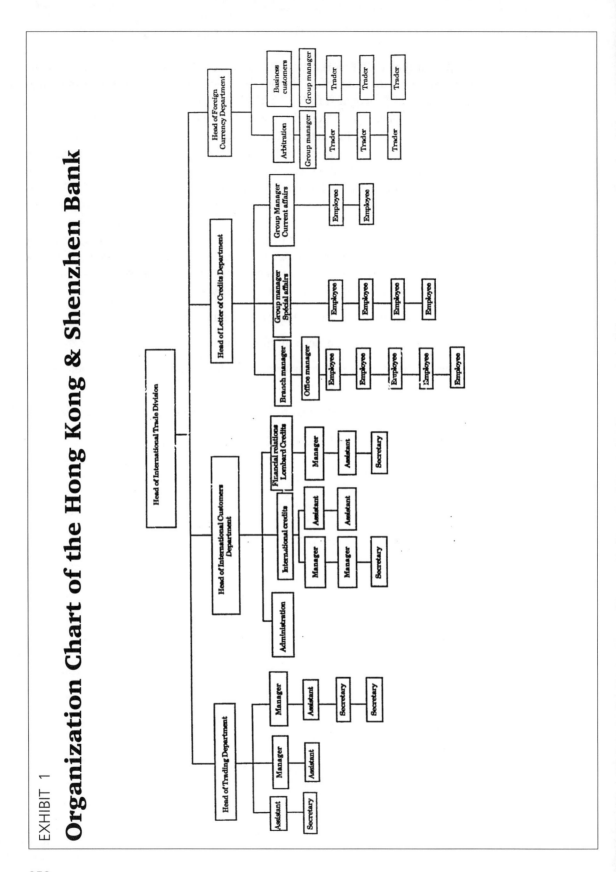

CASE 9.1B HONG KONG & SHENZHEN BANK

This case was prepared by Professor Dominique Turpin of IMD and Giana Klaas of MSR as a basis for class discussion rather than to illustrate either effective or ineffective handling of a business situation. Names and data have been disguised to protect confidentiality.

Following the initiatives taken by Jian Cheng in January 1993, the Hong Kong & Shenzhen Bank decided that the International Trade Division would serve as the test ground for its quality movement. In the meantime, the Quality Committee members met on a monthly basis after work to discuss quality issues, employees' motivation and customer service. After four months of internal debate on how to proceed, very little action had taken place. Jian felt the reason was linked to a lack of experience in quality control management. The committee decided to call in an external consultant, Charlie Yu, for advice on how results could be achieved. Mr Yu was part of MSR, a leading consulting firm specializing in customer service with offices in London, Paris, New York, Tokyo, Singapore and Hong Kong. In November 1993, Charlie Yu made an initial presentation to the members of the bank's quality committee. He suggested that the quality movement start by looking at the customers' needs. It was essential, he stated, to understand the customers' expectations in order to work on the gap between expectations and actual delivery of the bank's services.

Following Mr Yu's presentation, a heated discussion took place. This approach was not what Jian Cheng had had in mind. She was convinced that the quality programme should start by improving the motivation of the employees. Jian Cheng immediately referred to a recent internal survey which clearly indicated that morale among the staff was low.

Employees in the different departments of this division are too independent. There is no team spirit. Look at the conclusions of this survey: 25–30% of our employees are unclear about their work objectives. If we can reduce this amount to 10%, it would be a major achievement. A more highly motivated spirit among the staff will result in better work output and thus greater customer satisfaction.

Mr Yu counter-argued that motivated people would certainly try to do a better job but not necessarily the job customers wanted. Jian was puzzled. Mr Yu persisted in asking the same questions again and again:

- Who are your customers?
- Why are they using the services of your bank?
- How do you differentiate yourself from the competition?

- What's unique about this bank?

- Do you know your customers?

- Do they get consistent service every time they set foot into one of your branches, whether in Hong Kong or Macao?

For Jian, the answers to these questions were so obvious. "Of course, we know our customers! Of course, they get what they want!" Mr Yu was not convinced; he wanted to hear some real facts. Tension between Jian Cheng and Charlie Yu reached a high peak, but Mr Yu would not give up. He continued to elicit more specific arguments from Jian, but then always returned to the same conclusion – that motivated employees would certainly do a better job but would they be able to deliver what the customer really wanted? The meeting ended there. Over the next two weeks, Charlie Yu did not hear from Jian Cheng.

Therefore, Charlie Yu was rather surprised when Jian Cheng called him a few weeks later to announce: "I have thought about what you were saying the other day. Let's give it a try. Let's put the customer at the centre of our concern."

Meeting with the Staff

A week later, Mr Yu was back at the Hong Kong & Shenzhen Bank to make a second presentation on customer service to all the employees of the International Trade Division. In the meantime, Jian Cheng had allocated the equivalent of US$350,000 to a fund called the 'Customer Care Project' – a pioneer project being sponsored by the bank in her division. Since employees at the front desk probably handled less than 30% of the services to the bank's customers, Jian Cheng also invited all the employees working in the back office to attend Mr Yu's presentation. Employees of the Logistics Division had also been invited to join. To Jian's surprise, almost everybody working in this division came to the meeting. Employees in this division were flattered to receive Jian's invitation. As one of them told Jian, staff members felt that it meant that they were considered as not mere 'accessories' but key players in the customer–supplier chain. However, the feedback received informally after Mr Yu's presentation to the staff was rather mixed. Many employees were sceptical about the idea of putting the customer at the centre of the bank's concerns. They needed to be convinced about the benefits that this project could produce. In the last three years, other quality projects had been launched without much success. The comments that Jian Cheng had not wanted to hear were already beginning to spread: "This is just another 'great idea' from the boss ... time will kill it."

Analysing the Market

Having come to an agreement with Jian Cheng and the other members of the Quality Committee, Mr Yu prepared the first steps of the quality programme: an analysis of the bank's customers. He proceeded to take the following steps:

1. Research and analyse customers' expectations regarding the bank's services (quality perceived by the customers).
2. Measure the satisfaction level of the clients of the International Trade Division.
3. Measure staff's sensitivity to customer service.

The aim of the first survey was to generate customers' input on what services were needed (not reflecting specifically on the Hong Kong & Shenzhen Bank's present offering). In-depth interviews with customers were non-directed. Mr Yu scheduled 15 interviews – of about one hour each – to gather qualitative input from customers.

The purpose of the second survey was to measure the satisfaction level of the clients of the International Trade Division – based on a representative sample of customers. This survey was conducted by mailing a questionnaire to every Division customer. A letter signed by Jian Cheng explaining the objective of the survey was included with the questionnaire. A reminder letter was also prepared by Jian Cheng to be sent two weeks later – in order to increase the response rate.

The third survey was intended to measure the staff's sensitivity to customer service and identify the essential components of service quality to the clients. Interviews conducted with the staff focused on the employee's definition of:

- his or her particular job;

- his or her concept of quality;

- customer and client segmentation;

- customers' expectations;

- the essential elements required to ensure customer service;

- what was actually being done to satisfy present customers;

- reasons for errors, and the significance of the delays in recognizing them and doing the job correctly.

The surveys would indicate what services the bank's customers were currently receiving and would contrast them with the customers' expectations, so that steps could be taken to fill the potential gap between the two.

Before launching the surveys, Mr Yu suggested communicating the objective of the project to the staff in a totally transparent manner. Posters explaining the different steps of the project were placed on the walls. The mission statement was visible everywhere: 'Our goal is to achieve the highest customer service level in the industry'. As well, memos were distributed regularly to explain the different steps of the project and their execution.

CASE 9.1C # HONG KONG & SHENZHEN BANK

The following summarizes the findings of the surveys undertaken by the consulting company MSR on behalf of the International Trade Division of the Hong Kong & Shenzhen Bank.

Steps of the International Trade Division Quality Project

This case was prepared by Professor Dominique Turpin of IMD and Giana Klaas of MSR as a basis for class discussion rather than to illustrate either effective or ineffective handling of a business situation. Names and data have been disguised to protect confidentiality.

STEP 1a

Action:
Analysis of quality perceived by the client.
Results:
The clients' expectations,
The division's performance

STEP 1b

Action:
Analysis of the quality conceived by the employees.
Results:
Sensitiveness of the employees towards quality.

STEP 2

Action:
Definition of the level of quality the company wishes to offer targeted clients.
Results:
Chart, standards.

STEP 3

Action:
Implementation of standards in the field, follow-up on the level of quality attained and corrective actions.
Results:
Action plan to improve quality.

STEP 1a: Summary of Clients' Expectations

This survey indicated that customers could be segmented into four categories – each with a different profile:

The 'Negotiators'

'Negotiators' were typically Chinese businessmen. To them, giving their word meant a strong moral obligation. They dealt with other business people throughout the world. To be accepted by the 'Negotiators', the bank had to understand their particular businesses and their needs. These customers expected the bank managers to pay a visit to their firm occasionally and even become part of the 'family'. 'Negotiators' personally took care of most transactions and wanted a smooth operation without last-minute 'surprises'. They were not interested in technical details. They preferred to delegate these functions to their banker – someone they could fully trust.

'Negotiators' expected their banker to:

- trust them and be trustworthy;

- talk their language and understand their business;

- be honest and practise fair play;

- be a stable and unique contact;

- take the initiative;

- be present when needed;

- be flexible;

- be discreet;

- know their job and not waste the client's time.

The 'Entrepreneurs'

'Entrepreneurs' had a strong sense of 'financial opportunism'. They took a position quickly and wanted to be in control in any business situation. They knew the value of every HK dollar. Therefore, they needed constantly updated information about the dollar's performance in order to take decisions. 'Entrepreneurs' also needed flexibility and to have confidence in their suppliers. They considered their banker as a technical partner.

In short, 'Entrepreneurs' expected:

- fast and reliable information in real time;

- an open relationship with the bank;

- audacity;

- quick response time;

- flexibility;

- good prices and conditions.

The 'Managers'

'Managers' loved systems, budgets and plans. They worked for a manufacturing company or the subsidiary of a large corporation. For them, good organization and trouble-free services were essential. They worked with suppliers they could trust. 'Managers' were less sensitive to price, provided that new services helped them increase productivity as well as the company's bottom line. 'Managers' were proud of their company, and so they wanted partners who would ensure that their identity was retained.

What 'Managers' expected from their banker:

- optimal use of resources;
- quick, trouble-free services;
- competence;
- honesty, confidence;
- a single, stable contact at the bank;
- a well-informed team;
- speedy transactions;
- information.

The 'Financiers'

'Financiers' worked in companies of sizable importance. They were well versed in financial management. For them, financial instruments were the critical elements of corporate success. 'Financiers' wished to participate directly in financial markets with or without the support of their bank. They wanted to be able to act fast. 'Financiers' were looking for partners who could take decisions and react very quickly. Simultaneously, they needed enough time to think and put things in perspective. 'Financiers' looked for advisors with a vision of where their markets were going. They strongly believed that banks offered a lot of predigested information with too much focus on the very short term. 'Financiers' needed analysed information. They were also very interested in the latest developments in information technology and data systems.

'Financiers' expected the bank to provide:

- information with added value;
- in real time;
- a good knowledge of international business;
- audacity;
- good and flexible prices;
- permanent mobilization;
- a personal relationship with a team;
- technological innovation and state-of-the-art financial products.

STEP 1a: Division's Performance

Appraisal of the Service Quality of the International Trade Division Departments by its External Customers

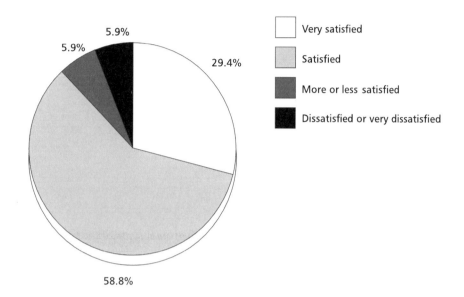

Level of External Clients' Satisfaction with the Service Performed by the International Trade Division Compared with the Competition

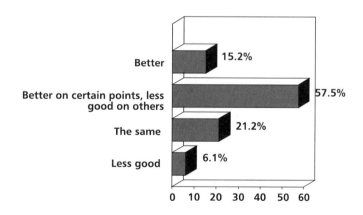

External Clients' Satisfaction Level with the Service Dimensions of the International Division

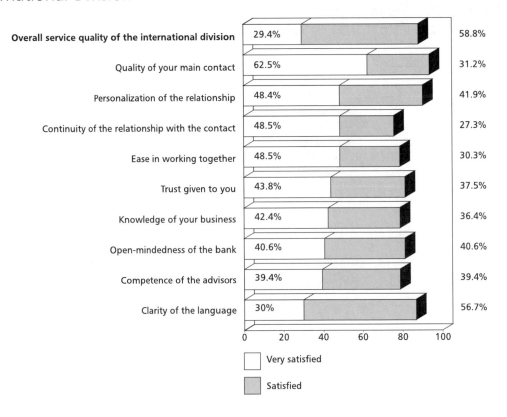

Appraisal of the Service Quality of the International Trade Division Departments by its External Customers

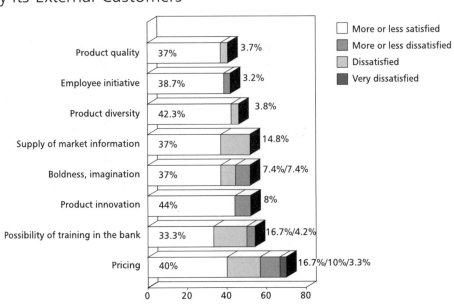

Appraisal of the Service Quality of the Hong Kong & Shenzhen Bank by its External Customers

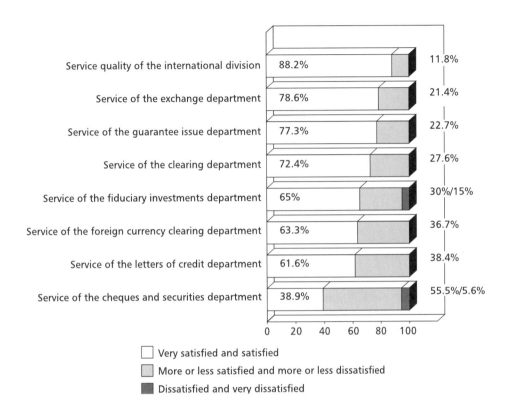

Service quality of the international division — 88.2% / 11.8%
Service of the exchange department — 78.6% / 21.4%
Service of the guarantee issue department — 77.3% / 22.7%
Service of the clearing department — 72.4% / 27.6%
Service of the fiduciary investments department — 65% / 30%/15%
Service of the foreign currency clearing department — 63.3% / 36.7%
Service of the letters of credit department — 61.6% / 38.4%
Service of the cheques and securities department — 38.9% / 55.5%/5.6%

☐ Very satisfied and satisfied
▨ More or less satisfied and more or less dissatisfied
■ Dissatisfied and very dissatisfied

External Clients' Reactions when Dissatisfied

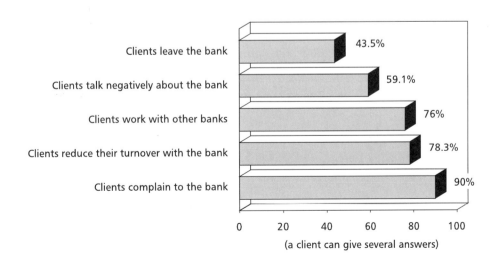

Clients leave the bank — 43.5%
Clients talk negatively about the bank — 59.1%
Clients work with other banks — 76%
Clients reduce their turnover with the bank — 78.3%
Clients complain to the bank — 90%

(a client can give several answers)

STEP 1b: Sensitiveness of the Employees Towards Quality

Summary of the Internal Qualitative Study and Survey

1. Employees see service quality for their clients as part of internal procedures, in order to give greater satisfaction.
   Satisfying the clients takes priority, with each one doing his best, however...

   - Employees confuse 'quality of work' with 'quality of service to clients'.

   - Work well done is perceived as conformity with the internal procedures rather than results for the client.

   - Employees think they understand the clients' needs, but frequently they do not. As well, they are satisfied to merely fulfil the needs expressed by the client, without looking further.

   - Taking initiative is important for service leaders, but most of them stay within the framework they have learned.

   - Employees in the back-office often feel isolated and that they are not participating in serving the client.

2. Employees see quality as accepting differences and working as a team:

   - Employees think that being a service leader means working as a team, while developing individual competences – being autonomous within a team framework.

   - Employees find their work interesting and motivating for the time being.

   - There is a good team spirit within each department but it is non-existent at the International Division level.

   - Everyone looks out for himself or herself and blames the errors on others – the back-office is a convenient excuse for non-quality.

   - At all levels, employees feel a sort of internal segregation (the 'nobles', those in the bank, in the front and back-offices, etc.).

   - Education programmes are perceived as too general and not related to either the service chain or attitudes and service behaviour.

   - The existing management tools are not known and not mastered.

Employees' Satisfaction Survey: Reasons for Satisfaction and Dissatisfaction at Work

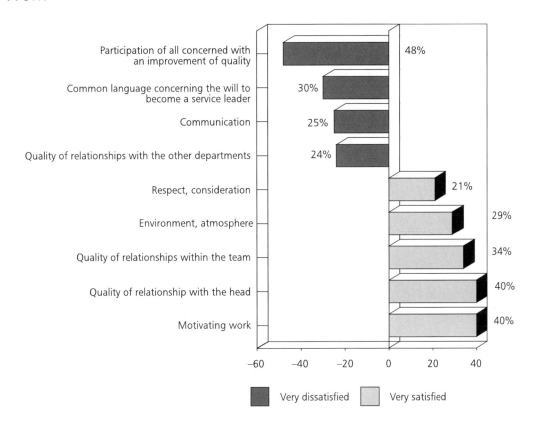

Appraisal of the Service Quality of the International Trade Departments by the Different Members of the Department

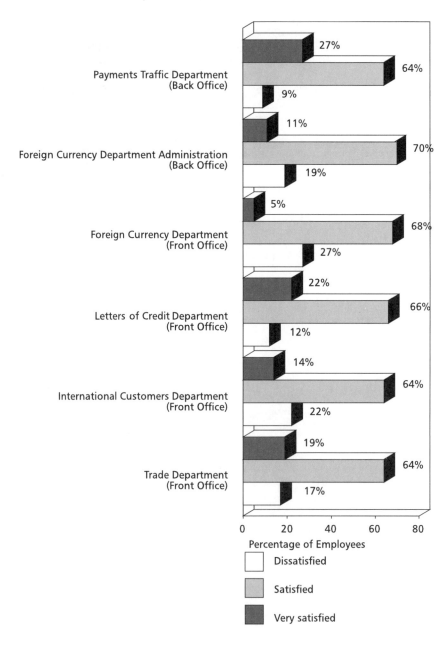

Appraisal of the Service Quality of the International Trade Division Departments by the Trade Department

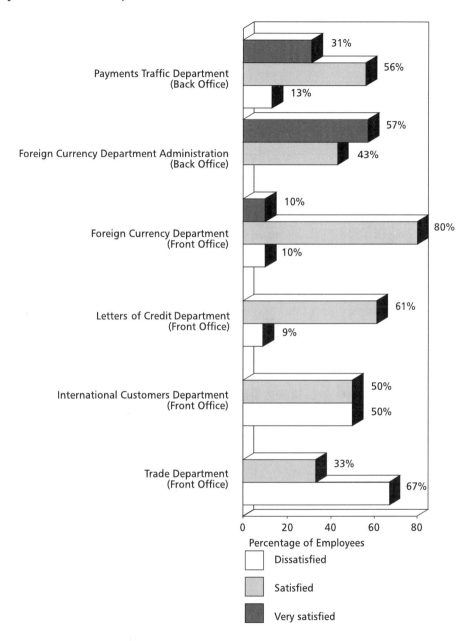

Appraisal of the Service Quality of the International Trade Division Departments by the International Customers Department

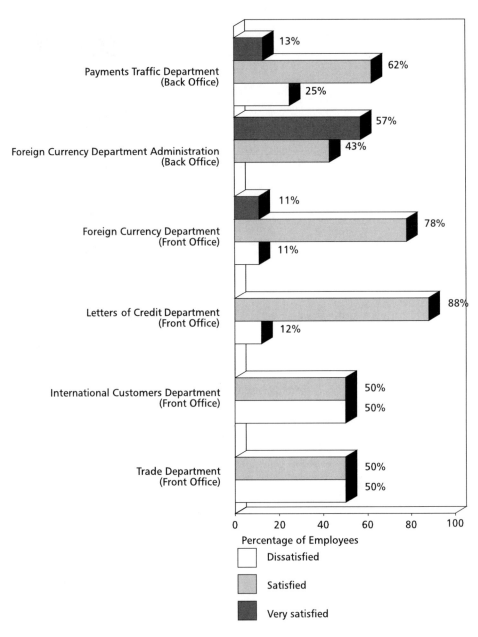

Appraisal of the Service Quality of the International Trade Division Departments by The Letters of Credit Department

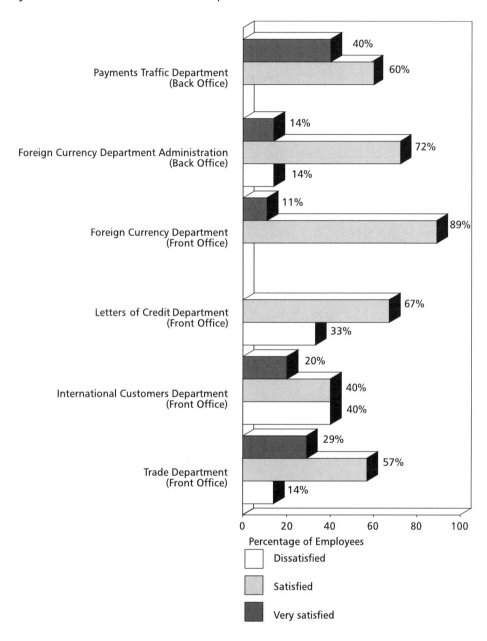

Appraisal of the Service Quality of the International Trade Division Departments by the Foreign Currency Department

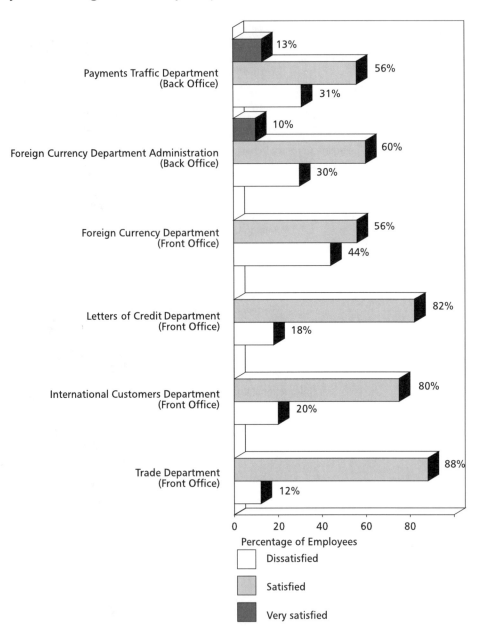

Appraisal of the Service Quality of the International Trade Division Departments by the Foreign Currency Administration Department

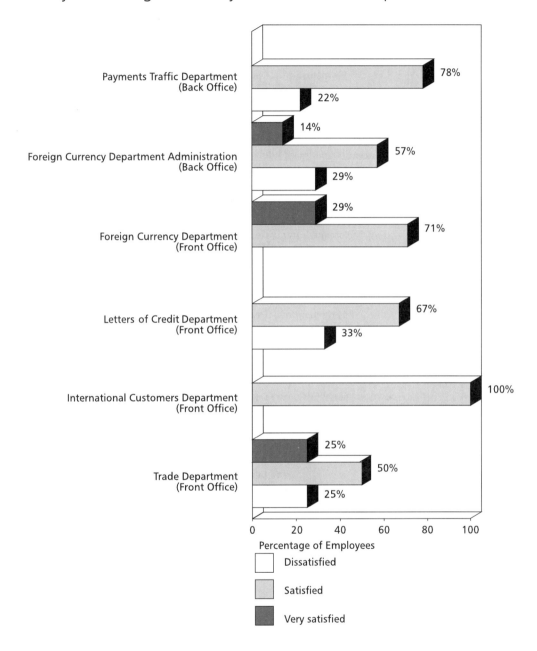

Percentage of Employees

☐ Dissatisfied

☐ Satisfied

■ Very satisfied

Appraisal of the Service Quality of the International Trade Division Departments by the Payments Traffic Department

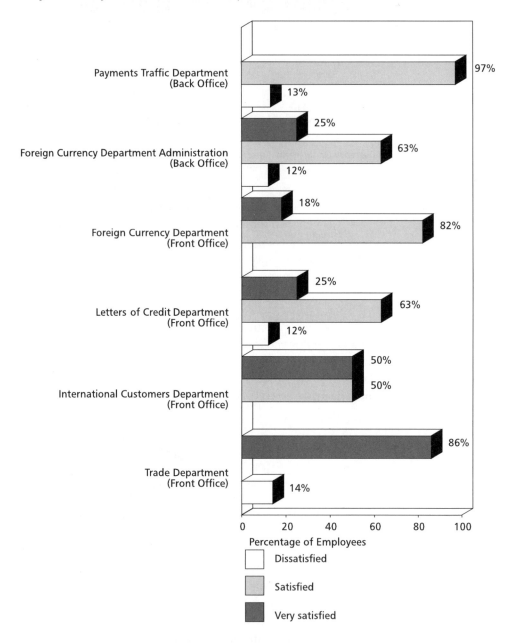

CASE 9.1D # HONG KONG & SHENZHEN BANK

This case was prepared by Professor Dominique Turpin of IMD and Giana Klaas of MSR as a basis for class discussion rather than to illustrate either effective or ineffective handling of a business situation. Names and data have been disguised to protect confidentiality.

In January 1994, Jian Cheng was invited to present the results of the progress made by the International Trade Division to the top management of the Hong Kong & Shenzhen Bank. Jian's presentation of the internal and external surveys generated mixed reactions. Jian explained that the next steps for the International Trade Division were: first, to communicate the results of the survey to all internal staff; second, to establish teams to analyse the survey and provide recommendations along with a calendar for implementation; and third, to establish a charter for customer service as well as working norms. "Oh, that's too technical!" one senior vice president complained. "What you have to do is change the mentalities." Another executive commented: "In five years, we'll have great people but no more customers." A third senior executive made it clear that he thought it had been a mistake to ask an outside consultant to work on this problem. "We have all the expertise inside," he said. "There's no need to have outsiders looking into our problems." Kenneth Tan, the president of the bank, had remained silent during the whole presentation. He had listened to the different arguments around the table without showing any emotion. Finally, Mr Tan spoke up: "I think that we should support Jian's initiative. Other divisions have been working on this same issue, but none of them has set priorities, the way Jian has."

Cheng was also wondering how to proceed with the quality charter. The charter had to be unique and inspiring for the staff. According to Mr Yu, the charter was the expression of the bank's will to offer uncompromising service to customers. The charter had to give direction and define the bank's strategy. It should also help the bank differentiate itself from the competition. In order to see some examples, Mr Yu gave Jian Cheng copies of charters containing quality statements from several leading international firms (*refer to **Appendix 1***). Then, Jian Cheng and her team were ready to meet the challenge of preparing a quality charter that would reflect the bank's values and commitment to its customers. In March 1994, Jian Cheng and the heads of the International Trade Division Departments defined the service strategy or chart of the International Trade Division, based on customers' expectations. They had defined the chart after three workshops. Jian Cheng was happy with the result (*refer to **Appendix 2***). Customers who were consulted about the validity of the chart had provided the team with very positive feedback.

The next step was to translate the strategy or chart into operational terms: the norms. Four groups of employees from the International Trade Division began fixing quality norms. The groups worked once a week, from 6 to 8 p.m. over a period of four weeks. However, after two weeks, the two workshops had made very little progress. The four groups had been unable to reach a consensus. In Jian Cheng's mind, the problem was that the staff did not understand the purpose of the workshops. A member of the team had confessed to Jian Chen that he did not consider the procedure 'real', but rather considered it 'a nice intellectual exercise'. However, Jian Cheng felt that the bank's strategy must be established in a charter and then translated into operational terms. As well, the level of service rendered would have to be measured if it were to be improved. "This is the same technique used in industry to measure the number of defective pieces," Jian Cheng explained.

A whole year had passed since Jian Cheng had decided to improve employees' motivations. Although the groups had lost confidence when the other employees could not see any real results, Jian Cheng remained convinced that improved customer service was the key to success for the bank.

Appendix 1: Examples of Company Charters

British Telecom (UK)
We put our customers first.
We are professionals.
We respect each other.
We work as a team.
We are committed to continuous improvement.

Kao (Japan)
Consumer trust is Kao's most valued asset.
We believe that Kao is unique in that our primary emphasis is neither profit nor competitive positioning. Instead our goal is to increase consumer satisfaction through useful, innovative products that meet real market needs.
A commitment to consumers will continue to guide all our corporate decisions.

Appendix 2: The Hong Kong & Shenzhen Bank's Quality Chart

- We aim to be our customers' favourite banking partner.
- We deal with our customers in their own language.
- We welcome all new business.
- We give our customers a direct answer or propose a satisfactory solution.
- We share our excellent know-how in banking with all our customers.
- We handle customers' orders promptly.
- We provide our customers with an original and viable approach to banking.
- We maintain a relationship of mutual confidence with our customers that is lasting and trouble-free.

CASE 9.1E

HONG KONG & SHENZHEN BANK

This case was prepared by Professor Dominique Turpin of IMD and Giana Klaas of MSR as a basis for class discussion rather than to illustrate either effective or ineffective handling of a business situation. Names and data have been disguised to protect confidentiality.

Mr Yu of MSR suggested that Jian Cheng herself take over the work of the four groups and define the norms, using only the department chiefs. According to the consultant, having conviction and believing in the visible implications were what the project needed to succeed.

It was then decided that Jian Cheng would proceed as Mr Yu proposed. Several norms were defined. It was thus appropriate that she should continue to manage the following workshop on quality norms – with Mr Yu and MSR working behind the scenes.

Six months later, the working groups had produced the quality norms.

For example:

1. Clients are assured that the bank's handling of their business will be faultless.

2. Clients are always offered a service adapted to their individual needs.

3. Clients always feel that the Division is interested in their affairs and are sure that the bank will defend their interests.

4. Clients always deal with a counsellor who is well informed about their business affairs.

5. Clients can always express themselves (and be understood) in one of the world's major commercial languages.

Once the norms were defined, real measures then had to be implemented – namely, to improve the services so that they met the level fixed by the norms. Decisions had to be made about how to put these norms in place and what procedure should be adopted. The staff decided to implement the norms at the rate of one per month: each head of department had to present the norm to the staff, solicit ideas for improving the service, and reach the level of quality fixed by the norms. Then, Jian Cheng and the heads of the International Trade Division Departments met once a month to decide on which ideas to implement. Jian Cheng felt that soliciting ideas from the staff was a huge success – 120 different suggestions were given for the first norm. The collection process was accompanied by a communication campaign that included graphic illustrations of the norm being implemented as well as information about the suggestions received and put into practice. The intent was to demonstrate to the staff that the management was actually using their ideas and rapidly putting them into practice.

For Norm 5, 'Clients can always express themselves (and be understood) in one of the world's major commercial languages', it soon became evident that one barrier to implementation was the staff's lack of fluency in foreign languages. Therefore, lessons were provided which successfully improved language capability, a fact that was noted and appreciated by several clients.

For other issues, inter-departmental or even inter-divisional working groups were set up. For Norm 4, 'Clients always deal with a counsellor who is well informed about their business affairs', follow-up tended to be poor whenever the counsellor was changed. Consequently, a group was set up to find ways to ensure a smooth transition between counsellors.

The last stage was to establish indicators for each norm that measured the quality level and observed the progress being made. It was also necessary to determine the method to be used for collecting and centralizing the data, as well as for communicating it. To address this issue, a preliminary analysis of all the existing data and statistics in-house was conducted. The objective of this task was to avoid unnecessary duplication.

For Norm 1, 'Clients are assured that the bank's handling of their business will be faultless', Jian Cheng felt that it was relatively easy to define indicators and corrective steps – the first indicator chosen was the percentage of badly executed orders. A list of existing customer complaints was prepared. Managers then wrote down a short report each time a client had a problem. Complaints concerning badly handled orders were added to those particular statistics and then were submitted to the Foreign Currency department for correction. This system enabled them to learn, based on the number of customer complaints received after the norms were established, that the majority of the problems concerned the Foreign Currency department. Thus, the Foreign Currency department was ordered to centralize all data in order to intercept and correct errors more easily, and to show them once a month to the division chief.

Jian Cheng felt that it was more difficult to address Norm 2, 'Clients are always offered a service adapted to their individual needs'. After giving it some thought, it was decided to measure this norm by appraising the clients' satisfaction through monthly surveys.

CASE 9.1F # HONG KONG & SHENZHEN BANK

This case was prepared by Professor Dominique Turpin of IMD and Giana Klaas of MSR as a basis for class discussion rather than to illustrate either effective or ineffective handling of a business situation. Names and data have been disguised to protect confidentiality.

In September 1994, Jian Cheng was proud of the results achieved. Profits per client had increased substantially, poor quality had diminished and morale was up! Two years after implementing the programme on quality service, the badly handled orders had decreased by more than half. Clients were regularly congratulating employees for the improvements (listening more, greater attention and stronger efforts to resolve their problems). Team spirit among employees of the International Trade Division was greatly enhanced, and the turnover was lower. After creating the inter-departmental working groups, cooperation among the different departments also improved considerably.

A few months later, Jian Cheng was promoted to a new job at the bank headquarters, and Kenneth Tan, the president, decided to follow up by extending the experience to the other divisions of the group.

However, Jian Cheng was somewhat concerned about the future of the International Trade Division. Would her successor have the interest and the motivation to keep the customer satisfaction momentum going? Would her successor have the same commitment? Was she being overly emotional or committed about her success?

CASE 9.2

THE MATSUSHITA GROUP IN MALAYSIA

This case was prepared by Professor Vijay K. Jolly as a basis for class discussion rather than to illustrate either effective or ineffective handling of a business situation. The author wishes to acknowledge the generous assistance of many officers of the Matsushita Group, particularly Mr Hiroaki Kosaka, Regional Representative of the Group in Malaysia.

Founded in 1918 with a capital of Yen 100 (about $50 at that time), the Matsushita Electric group of companies grew to become one of Japan's largest consumer electronics groups. In 1982, it recorded a consolidated sales turnover of over $14 billion, employed 156,000 people worldwide and sold over 14,000 different products in 130 countries under the brand names *Panasonic*, *Technics*, *Quasar* and *National*. The Matsushita Electric Industrial Co. Ltd. (MEI), the mother company of the group and the first to be founded, ranked as the sixth largest manufacturing company in the country that year in terms of sales and the fourth largest in terms of net profits. Among its worldwide peers, it ranked fourth in terms of sales and second in terms of net income.

"What makes the Matsushita group different from most large companies in Japan," stated Toshihiko Yamashita, President of MEI since 1981, "is the unique management philosophy of its founder, Konosuke Matsushita." Despite its enviable record of profitability, the company insisted on putting service to society before profits. According to the company creed, a business could exist only by using resources – people, real estate, municipal services and so on – from society, therefore the primary goal should be to contribute to society in return for the use of its resources. This belief formed the basis of a unique 250-year mission established in 1932: "Through our industrial activities, we strive to foster progress, to promote the general welfare of society and to devote ourselves to furthering the development of world culture."

Early Internationalization

With the Japanese economy entering into a decade-long depression, Matsushita began exploring foreign opportunities toward the end of the 1920s. Lacking experience, it initially accepted whatever orders Osaka-based trading companies could generate, particularly from the neighbouring markets of China, Taiwan, Korea and Manchuria. By 1932, these orders had become regular and significant enough for the company to set up its own export department, which was later spun off as an independent trading company called Matsushita Electric Trading Co., Ltd. (MET).

The decision to create its own trading company, rather than rely on another large general trading company, stemmed from Matsushita's traditional policy of maintaining close contact with its customers. A well-established trading company – such as Mitsubishi, Mitsui or Marubeni – would probably have enabled Matsushita to expand its exports faster, and in a greater number of countries, but would not have given the kind of 'feel for the marketplace' and 'control over sales' that Matsushita deemed essential for its business. Having set up MET, however, the company soon turned it into more than just an exporter of the Group's products. In 1938, an import division was added, which began by importing raw materials used in manufacturing – such as mica, zinc and lumber. Imports on behalf of unaffiliated companies and products for local distribution were to come later.

By 1940, MET had succeeded in establishing a wide distribution and sales network throughout the Far East. World War II, however, interrupted not only production in Japan but also the nature of Matsushita's foreign activities. From being essentially an exporter of finished products, the company was suddenly asked by the authorities to start building factories in China and various South-East Asian countries. The first factory to be established was in Shanghai to produce batteries for communications equipment in 1940. This was followed by a similar factory in Hankow. During the next years, factories were set up to make a variety of products in Manchuria, Korea, the Philippines and Indonesia. In all, Matsushita had established 39 overseas factories and sales depots by 1945. However, at the end of the war, only 17 remained, and all of them had to be given up.

After equipping its factories and re-establishing its production base in Japan at the end of the war, Matsushita slowly resumed exporting in the early 1950s. MET returned to its old markets in South-East Asia at first and then began exploring further afield. A branch office was established in New York in 1953, which was converted into a subsidiary company, Matsushita Electric Corporation of America, in 1959. In 1962, the first European sales office was established in Hamburg. *Exhibit 1* lists the main sales companies established by the company up to 1970.

Other than its wartime activities, Matsushita's first foreign manufacturing venture was in Thailand in 1961. This was the time when many South-East Asian countries had embarked on an active programme of import substitution industrialization. Matsushita's sole agent in Thailand had succeeded in building up a significant business by then and approached the company to start local production in line with the government's policy. Even though Matsushita had no 'strategy' calling for such an investment, it agreed to set up a joint venture with the agent – initially to manufacture dry batteries.

Following the same reasoning, and always in collaboration with its local agents, Matsushita set up a number of other joint-venture manufacturing companies during the 1960s: Taiwan (1962), Malaysia (1966), Philippines (1967), Australia (1968) and Indonesia (1970). Manufacturing companies were also established in Puerto Rico (1965), Mexico (1965), Tanzania (1966), Costa Rica (1966), Peru (1966), Brazil (1967) and Venezuela (1969). Except for the Tanzanian company, which continued to manufacture batteries only, all of these units gradually added new products to their initial manufacturing operations. *Exhibit 1* provides a list of the main products each one manufactured by 1970.

While these ventures were being established in developing countries, essentially to serve local markets, Matsushita was also approached by a number of European countries seeking investment opportunities. Starting in the mid-1960s, delegations representing states and even cities from Ireland, France (Lyon region), Spain, the UK (Wales) and West Germany (Hamburg) visited Osaka to entice the company by offering incentives of one kind or another. Land at concessional rates, fully prepared industrial estates, tax incentives and even outright grants were offered. The Deputy Director General of Corporate Overseas Management, Takao Mizutani, recalled this period with some bemusement:

> First came the representatives from Wales and Scotland and then some people from the Hamburg area in 1967. They wanted us to create jobs in their region. The next ones were representatives from Ireland and Spain, who were mainly interested in export-oriented projects and offered us very attractive incentives; they really wanted to export, but not receive imports from Japan. But we were not ready for these offers at that time and so we treated everyone politely but made no commitments.

Not only was Matsushita uninterested in a European investment, it was also barred from using its colour TV technology there because of the PAL/SECAM patents which had not been licensed to it. On other products, European tariffs were generally quite low and it made more sense to produce and export from Japan.

MELCOM – Matsushita's First Investment in Malaysia

In 1957, around the time that Matsushita was pursuing the US as an export market, it began exporting to Malaysia. Organizationally, Matsushita Electric Trading Co. (MET) was responsible for prospecting the market and getting manufacturing divisions in Japan to supply products suited to local conditions. Hagemeyer Trading Co. (Malaysia) Ltd., a Dutch trading company with offices in many Asian countries, was appointed sole distributor for Matsushita products – which initially consisted of batteries and radio sets.

When Malaysia achieved independence on 31 August 1957, among the first things the new government, headed by Tuanku Abdul Rahman, did was to formulate a policy for stimulating industrialization based on import substitution. The Pioneer Industries Ordinance, passed in 1958, permitted products which had not been manufactured in the country before to be a 'pioneer industry' status. Companies that began manufacturing such products were given income tax exemptions as well as special import protection on a case-by-case basis.

Having created a favourable investment climate, the government sent out high-level delegations, particularly to the US and Japan, to contact potential foreign investors. In 1962, Prime Minister Tuanku Abdul Rahman went in person to Japan several times, and Matsushita Electric was among the companies he visited. By then, the latter had expanded the scope of its exports to Malaysia beyond just dry batteries to include fans, radios, refrigerators and other home appliances (*refer to Exhibit 2*). Partly in response to the personalized invitation and partly out of fear of losing its small but attractive export business, Matsushita agreed to set up local manufacturing facilities in Malaysia.

When the Matsushita Electric Company (Malaysia) Berhad (MELCOM)[1] was established in September 1965, it was the first company to begin manufacturing electronic products in Malaysia. As such, it was granted pioneer status for all the products it planned to manufacture – black-and-white (b&w) TV receivers, refrigerators, electric fans, radio receivers and radiograms, gas cookers, rice cookers, water kettles, toasters, irons and tape recorders. The only product exempted from this status was dry cell batteries, which were already being produced locally.

Profits earned from the manufacture and sale of pioneer products were exempted from Malaysian income tax for a period of five years, along with dividends paid out of these profits. In addition to these tax concessions, the government introduced an import quota and raised tariffs on the products MELCOM was to manufacture. In the case of b&w TV sets, for example, tariffs on imported sets were raised from 25% to 35% in 1966 or M$180 per set, whichever was higher. Furthermore, of the estimated demand of 33,000 sets in 1967, Matsushita was to assemble 12,000 sets locally. To protect the firm during its pioneer status period, the government established an import quota of 70% of demand over the next 5-year period. Components imported by Matsushita were exempt from duty, too, during this period.

Soon after MELCOM commenced production, a number of other foreign companies set up assembly operations in Malaysia. By 1970, three Japanese firms (Toshiba, Sanyo and Roxy – a Hong Kong-based licensee of Sharp) had begun producing b&w TV sets and radiograms, as had Philips in Holland. Toshiba and Sanyo had, in addition, begun assembling a broad range of home appliances in competition with Matsushita. With domestic supply of these products expanding, imports diminished over time. In b&w TV sets, for example, locally installed capacity grew to 68,000 sets by 1970, with the number of sets actually produced growing from 500 in 1966 to 43,700 in 1970. The number of sets imported fell from 27,000 sets in 1966 to 4,150 in 1970 – implying that some Malaysian consumers were still purchasing sets from abroad and paying the necessary duty.

Responding to Changing Malaysian Priorities

Towards the late 1960s, the Government of Malaysia changed its industrialization strategy, moving away from import substitution. In an effort to sustain economic

---

[1] The initial share capital of M$1,500,000 was held 90% by MEI (Japan) and 10% by Hagemeyer Trading Co. By 1966, the share capital was M$3,000,000, with an entirely new subscription of M$1,500,000 offered to the public in response to governmental policy, bringing MEI and Hagemeyer's ownership down to 45% and 5%, respectively. In 1982, MEI owned 43.1% of the share capital; Hagemeyer owned 4.6%; 32.3% was owned by Malaysian investors and the remaining 20% by non-Malaysian, mainly Singaporean, investors.

growth and provide greater job opportunities in a rather small domestic market, exports of manufactured goods began to be emphasized for the first time. In 1968, the Pioneer Industries Ordinance (1958) was repealed and a more comprehensive Investment Incentives Act (1968) was passed. This Act maintained the notion of Pioneer Industries Status, but added provisions for granting Investment Tax Credits and Export Incentives.

The 1968 Act was passed just a year before major racial riots broke out in Malaysia. These riots and the intense discussion that followed resulted in a new strategy of development, the so-called New Economic Policy (NEP). The two main objectives of this policy, whose implementation was to start with the Second Malaysian Plan (1971–75), were to eradicate poverty among all Malaysians, regardless of race, and restructure Malaysian society to reduce and ultimately eliminate the identification of race with economic function and geographic location. As one government official put it: "until then, if you were Malay, you were automatically identified as a farmer, if Chinese as a businessman, if Indian as a rubber tapper or a professional. The NEP aimed to eliminate this compartmentalization of society."

In view of the objectives of the NEP, the Investment Incentives Act (1968) was amended in 1971 to incorporate additional provisions, the main ones being Labour Utilization Relief (so as to encourage the use of more labour by industries) and Special Incentives to Export Oriented Industries. About this time, an Ordinance allowing for the establishment of free trade zones in Malaysia was also enacted. Special benefits were also given for siting factories in a so-called 'development area,' and for manufacturing so-called 'priority products'. (**Exhibit 3** provides a list of the main incentive schemes under the Investment Incentives (Amendment) Act 1971, in the form in which they were available in 1982.)

With electronic components/equipment declared a priority industry, firms expanding their investments were given longer tax holidays. Those with 50% Malaysian content, employing a certain level of manpower and located in development regions could, in fact, benefit from up to ten years of tax holiday under the new rules, particularly if they also exported a share of their output.

As with the previous industrialization drive, the announcement of the new policies was accompanied by a series of visits around 1970 to foreign company headquarters by Malaysian officials. Once again Matsushita was contacted in Osaka, where the new Prime Minister, Tun Abdul Razak, met with Konosuke Matsushita personally. "Matsushita was quite reluctant to establish export-oriented companies at first," recalled a MIDA[2] official. "In parallel with the Prime Minister's intervention, we had repeated meetings with their top brass, but they were only interested in assembly for the local market."

Part of the reason for this reluctance was the fact that these visits coincided with Matsushita's internal review of its internationalization policy. Whereas it had previously responded to invitations on an *ad hoc* basis, and on the merit of

---

[2] The Malaysian Industrial Development Authority, responsible for coordinating and approving major foreign investment projects in the country.

each individual proposal, the company started to formulate a more 'positive' policy during the early 1970s. Malaysia indeed figured on its list of attractive sites, but there were other countries in South-East Asia making similar demands and offering comparable investment climates (*refer to **Exhibit 4***).

While discussions on an export-oriented project continued, MELCOM decided to initiate some exports on its own, in line with the government's new policy. Using the services of MET, dry cell batteries were exported to Singapore as early as 1968. Following this move, MET allocated a small quota for the Australian market to MELCOM, permitting the latter to regularly export 10% of its battery production. A couple of other export ventures met with less success. An attempt was made to export small single-band radios to the US in 1971, but it proved to be uncompetitive and their production was discontinued a year later. Similarly, a few b&w TV sets were shipped to Mauritius through MET, but only because the order was too small to interest the head office department concerned. These too ceased after a couple of years with a change in demand.

The only product manufactured by MELCOM that turned into a significant export item was electric irons. In 1972, a decision was made at MEI to stop the production of irons in Japan of the kind made by MELCOM and to use Malaysia as a sourcing base. As a result of this decision, MELCOM's exports of electric irons grew rapidly from 1973 onwards with over 85% of production being exported. In support of this venture, a new company (Melcom Industries Sdn. Bhd.) was set up in 1972 for manufacturing cast iron and aluminium parts, and die-cast components for electric irons as well as for the fans and rice cookers being made by MELCOM.[3]

The Truly Export-Oriented Ventures

When Matsushita finally decided to accept the Malaysian invitation for a fresh, export-oriented project, it proposed not one but two ventures. The first concerned the manufacture for export of window-type room air-conditioners. A new company, Matsushita Industrial Corporation Sdn. Bhd. (MAICO), was set up in April 1972 in the Sungei Way Free Trade Zone near Kuala Lumpur as a wholly owned subsidiary of MEI (Japan), reporting directly to the air-conditioner department at the head office.

MEI's own entry into air-conditioner manufacturing in Japan dated back to 1957. By 1970, Matsushita had become Japan's leading producer of both window-type and split-type room air-conditioners, and had also diversified into associated products including drinking water coolers, fan coil units and dehumidifiers. A giant new *National* air-conditioner plant was completed in 1970 at Kusatsu with an annual capacity of 960,000 units/year from which some 20,000 units were being exported annually.

Even though wages represented a small percentage of the total cost of producing air-conditioners, the Malaysian project came at a time when fears

---

[3] Melcom Industries was incorporated as a wholly owned subsidiary of MELCOM.

began to be expressed about Japan's future competitiveness. According to Yoshinori Kobe, MAICO's present Managing Director:

> The more important reason for choosing air-conditioners was the fact that the Malaysian Government was seeking a large-sized investment and that air-conditioners were easier to manufacture locally than, for example, colour TV sets. For the latter, you either need a small assembly unit or, if you want to have a fully integrated plant with tube and component manufacture, a very large one demanding a high level of skill. Also, about this time we had chosen Taiwan as a base for wireless exports and had contemplated setting up colour TV plants elsewhere.

With just 20,000 sets being exported annually from Japan at the time, there was natural scepticism on the part of some within Matsushita regarding the planned capacity of 240,000 sets/year for MAICO. Once the commitment was made, however, no effort was spared in making MAICO a viable unit. In order not to compete with MEI's Kusatsu plant, the latter gradually began specializing in split-type units, for which there was a better market within Japan, while MAICO concentrated on window-type units.

By 1982, MAICO was turning out some 240,000 window-type air-conditioners a year, exporting them through MET to more than 122 countries. As such, it made Malaysia the third largest exporter of air-conditioners after the US and Japan. With the Malaysian Government's new policy of allowing export-oriented companies located in Duty Free Zones to sell up to 20% of their output domestically, MAICO's aim was to build on its already leading 35% share of the domestic market.[4]

The second export-oriented project proposed by Matsushita was somewhat smaller in terms of investment than MAICO, but it was potentially as important in terms of technology and skill transfer. Set up in December 1972, the Matsushita Electronic Component (Malaysia) Sdn. Bhd. (MECON) was incorporated as a joint venture between MEI (Japan) (70%) and Matsushita Electronic Components Co. Ltd. (Japan) (30%), with its plant also located in the Sungei Way Free Trade Zone. When it was established, it was the first overseas manufacturing and export company of Matsushita Electronic Components Co. Ltd. Starting with variable resistors and electrolytic capacitors in 1973, MECON added a line of TV tuners (both mechanical and electronic) in 1977. Gradually, other components were added, raising MECON's turnover to M$55 million in 1982, 95% of which was exported through MET and the remainder sold locally, including to MELCOM. In 1982, MECON ranked as the largest of Matsushita's 17 overseas component manufacturing units. It was also the largest supplier of the three main components being made in Asia, with the exception of Japan and South Korea.

---

[4] Some of this share was accounted for by products, especially split-type, imported directly from Japan. At the time, there were four other companies (two US and two Japanese) assembling air-conditioners for the domestic market. In order to compete with them, MAICO needed to pay a 45% import duty as well as a M$100/set tax, the latter meant to cover duties paid by local assemblers on components. According to MAICO, such duties were actually somewhat less than the M$100 it had to pay.

Following MAICO and MECON, Matsushita established a third primarily export-oriented company in Malaysia in 1979. This company, Matsushita Precision Industrial Co. Ltd. Sdn. Bhd., was located in the Senai Free Trade Zone in Johor, on the southern tip of the Malaysian peninsula. About half the size of MECON, it manufactured a range of electronic components for colour TV sets – such as deflection yokes and flyback transformers – for shipment to a number of countries in the region.

Establishing a Strong Position in the Malaysian Market

Throughout the period during which Matsushita was implementing its export-oriented ventures, the domestic market for its products continued to expand rapidly. With increasing prosperity and the percentage of households with electricity rising from 30% in 1960 to over 70% by 1982, home appliance sales in Malaysia grew by over 10% a year. Being the first to establish local assembly facilities, Matsushita naturally had a head start over competition but, by 1976, had barely retained a 10% average market share for its line of products. Even though a bulk of the remainder was supplied by other companies establishing manufacturing facilities during the late 1960s, a significant amount was also accounted for by imports.[5]

Sensing that its sole distributor relationship with Hagemeyer was part of the reason for its lack-lustre performance in Malaysia, Matsushita decided to assume the sales function itself. In 1976, the relationship with Hagemeyer was terminated[6] and a new sales company established – Matsushita Sales and Service Sdn. Bhd. (MASCO). In line with government policy regarding sales companies, 30% of the shares were offered to Bhumiputra investors, 40% was subscribed to by MELCOM, 15% by MET and the remaining 15% by Hagemeyer. "Even though the latter had treated their work as no more than a job function," stated Kikyo Miyake, Managing Director of MASCO since 1976, "it was Matsushita's philosophy of gratitude that determined our offer of participation to them." By 1982, Hagemeyer's interests were down to 5%, with MET's stake increased to 25%. *Exhibit 5* gives a summary of the ownership structure of the various companies, including MASCO.

Soon after MASCO's establishment, an aggressive campaign to recruit dealers dedicated to selling National products was launched. A scheme, known locally as Kedai National, or National shops, was also launched whereby some dealers were chosen to carry a full range of exclusively National products. The advantages of such a relationship, according to Miyake: "was an effective usage of space, effective stock control, effective after-sales service, improved customer confi-

---

[5] Except for a brief period during the mid- and late-1960s, when specific import quotas were applied, importation of products into Malaysia was freely allowed, with duties and taxes constituting the only form of protection.

[6] Hagemeyer continued to act as agent for JVC and KDK (both Matsushita companies). MASCO took over National brand products only.

dence and various forms of assistance from MASCO." Constituting the latter were things such as training in sales and management by MASCO, bearing 50% of the shop renovation costs by MASCO, assistance in sales and promotion activities, a priority supply of goods as well as a cash bonus for outstanding sales performance.

To support the Kedai National scheme, a number of seminars were held by MASCO throughout Malaysia which were widely written up in local newspapers. Seminars were also held in Japan, and staff that had already been recruited was sent at company expense. At the same time, Miyake went out personally to visit hundreds of dealers nation-wide to convince them of the scheme's benefits. By 1982, some 160 dealers had been appointed as Kedai National dealers, of whom 132 represented main or single shops and the rest branches of a main shop. Starting with barely 4% in 1977, Kedai National dealers accounted for about 70% of MASCO's turnover in 1982, with the remainder coming from the 533 National Authorized Dealers that also handled other manufacturers' products, and from some special products such as batteries and telecommunication equipment that MASCO sold through other channels.

Apart from its dynamic sales and promotion campaigns and the Kedai National programme, MASCO proved to be a successful venture for another reason. It was able to do a better job of matching the proportion of locally made (by MELCOM) products and those imported from Japan. Whereas 83% of its turnover was accounted for by MELCOM products in 1976, this ratio had dropped to 46% by 1982, with the remainder being imports. Thus, a good deal of its stupendous performance since 1976 could be directly attributed to its selling imports, particularly videotape recorders and special products not made in Malaysia. MELCOM's own sales also benefited by MASCO's existence, which considered itself duty-bound to push its sister company's products in Malaysia. In 1982, the average market share of National products had reached 25%, more than twice its size five years earlier (*refer to* **Exhibit 6**).

Transferring More Than Technology

"Japan has traditionally been learning from foreigners," stated Hiroaki Kosaka, Managing Director of MELCOM and Regional Representative of the Matsushita Group in Malaysia. "First, in the 6th century, from China, then from the Portuguese and the Dutch and, more recently, from the Americans. Now we are the ones being asked to teach and we are not really prepared to do this." Yet, in Malaysia, Matsushita contributed generously in the realm of technological and managerial know-how transfer.

Technology Upgrading

At the level of products and manufacturing equipment, the pressure for constant upgrading came from both the nature of Matsushita's activities and the relatively high degree of competition in Malaysia. For MAICO and MECON, the two main export-oriented ventures, the introduction of modern machinery was dictated by increases in Malaysian wage rates, the need to compete with labour-saving manufacturing equipment installed elsewhere, and sometimes for technical and quality reasons. The fact was that labour accounted for only a small fraction of the manufacturing costs for most of the products manufactured in Malaysia. In room air-conditioners, for example, labour represented roughly 9% of manufacturing costs in Malaysia compared with about 10% in Japan, partly explained by the latter's tenfold greater capacity. With rapid technological changes taking place in manufacturing processes, this difference began narrowing down in Japan's favour.

MELCOM, on the other hand, had to contend with the dual pressures of controlling costs while constantly introducing new products and models. Although the domestic market enjoyed some import protection, the level of this protection was seldom high enough to prevent low-cost imports from countries such as Hong Kong and Taiwan, or top-of-the-line products from Japan and elsewhere.

Some of the processes and equipment being introduced at MELCOM in the early 1980s followed Japan with only a short time lag (refer to **Exhibit 7**). "In colour TVs, for example, we are now only 2–3 years behind MEI," claimed Ismail Mohamad, MELCOM's Works Manager, with obvious pride. Also, while a couple of other Japanese companies had succumbed to import competition by shutting down their TV plants in Malaysia, MELCOM refused to follow their example.

The same technological upgrading occurred at MAICO and MECON. MAICO was the first factory of its kind in South-East Asia with a Sound Equipment Proofing System facility for noise level inspection and an Electro Deposition Paint system for high-quality paint coating. In 1982, it became the first factory in Malaysia to be awarded the Japanese Industrial Standard (JIS) mark of approval and also the first to have its product 'Topcool' awarded the JIS mark of approval for a complete appliance manufactured outside Japan. Built as a modern, reasonably automated unit, its local content was around 80%, with 78% being manufactured in-house.

Given the nature of electronic component manufacture, the level of factory automation at MECON was even greater than at MAICO. In terms of equipment, MECON was probably no more than 4–5 years behind Japan and somewhat ahead of Thailand and Taiwan. A new chip-mount machine, for example, had recently been ordered from Japan, where the same machine had been installed for the first time 3 years earlier. As a testimony to MECON's technological level, it had even asked MEI's production engineering department to design a combined joining and coking machine specially for the Malaysian factory.

Despite the constant technological upgrading, the Malaysian companies remained heavily dependent on Osaka because "that is where things originate," according to Ismail Mohamad. To offset some of this dependence, Malaysian engineers had come up with their own design for resistors, while those working at MELCON had an important input in new product designs for the Malaysian market.

Making People First

As with other companies, regardless of origin, Matsushita transferred a lot more than product and manufacturing know-how, or the technical skills required for manning its factories. It attempted, from the beginning, to transfer its own unique management philosophy and basic business principles as well.

"Making people first, and only then products," one of the company's principles, meant giving an enormous amount of attention to training and character development at all the Matsushita companies in Malaysia. As in Japan, all new recruits were put through an orientation programme, followed by a series of apprenticeships and on-the-job training. The latter was imparted both by experienced senior colleagues as well as advisors sent from Japan on assignment. This training within units such as MELCOM was complemented by sending employees to training courses both within Malaysia and to MEI in Japan. Between 1967 and 1982, for example, 207 Malaysians were sent for training to Osaka, some more than once.

The training programmes at Osaka served a number of purposes in addition to skill development. One employee who visited Japan 7 times during his 15 years with MELCOM explained:

> The first time was just to see Japan. I was put in a dormitory and made to sleep on a tatami (floor mat) just to see whether I worked for Matsushita for money. During subsequent trips I was accommodated in relation to my rank. On these visits I learned a lot about quality control, industrial engineering, value engineering, on-time scheduling, etc., but also came to know the Matsushita philosophy and its business principles. I learned why they do things the way they do here.

Transplanting Management Methods and Culture

Right from the beginning, morning assembly meetings were introduced in MELCOM at which all employees recited the company's seven objectives and sang the company song in Malay. Other management practices, such as MEI's suggestion system, Quality Control Circles, Labour–Management Consultation Committees, the Big Sister Programme, the company newspaper, and the practice of giving employees gifts on special occasions and organizing recreational trips were all introduced into MELCOM progressively over the years (*refer to* **Exhibit 8**).[7] Numerous slogans were often seen in Matsushita facilities throughout Japan. One observer who had been familiar with the company for a long time elaborated: "When I visited MELCOM in May 1973, the first thing that drew my attention was placards of the company's annual slogans – such as 'Heart-to-Heart Dialogue'. 'Zero-Defect Campaign', 'Everyone's Participation in Management,' etc."[8]

Unlike technical skills, the transfer of Matsushita's organizational policies and culture was not always easy. Kosaka recalled:

---

[7] Other Japanese companies did not introduce company songs and the recitation of objectives in their Malaysian subsidiaries, even though they were in the country for about the same length of time.

[8] Hideo Ishida, Japanese Management Abroad (mimeograph, undated), pp. 2–3.

When I arrived here in Malaysia in 1983, I found a big difference between Japanese and Malaysian employees in terms of discipline, sense of loyalty and the commitment to Matsushita's objectives. For example, I used to watch one group's morning assembly meeting that normally took place outside my window. People would often come in late; while some would participate actively, others would just stand there with crossed arms and not in a straight line. After noticing this for a time, one day I went out to explain to them why we have these meetings. It is not enough to transfer the know-how of management; one must also transfer the 'know-why'. I explained that these morning assemblies were meant to promote a sense of punctuality and unity among the members. They were to help create communication between managers and workers and among all employees. The five-minute speech that an employee makes when it is his turn would help to establish contact. And, when people talk, others get a better idea of who they are. I said that it was also a form of education since people have to concentrate and study before they get up front to make a speech. As for the recitation of our business principles, I reminded them that they are important and by repeating them just once a day, they would become more conscious of them. After I had explained all this, I saw a noticeable improvement in these assemblies, which is something I am very proud and happy about.

Of all the Japanese companies doing business in Malaysia, Matsushita probably made the greatest effort in transferring management practices developed in Japan. Its success could be attributed to the step-by-step fashion it used to introduce its culture, to the nation's own avowed intention to learn from Japan as part of the 'Look East' policy, and to the supporting policies that accompanied the transfer of organization-specific practices. The latter included the policy of minimizing line-staff and blue/white-collar differences, and a personnel evaluation system that stressed not just job performance but also such aspects as 'positive attitude', 'eagerness to improve' and attendance at quality control circle meetings. Learning from the parent company was also facilitated by the continuous presence of Japanese expatriates, most on short-term advisory assignments (*refer to **Exhibits 9** and **10***). A few key expatriates, furthermore, spent as long as 7–8 years with the Malaysian companies.

Anyone visiting MELCOM in 1982 would have been impressed by the standard blue overalls being worn by every employee – from Kosaka down to the workers on the assembly line. Dining halls and rest rooms were shared by all levels of employees. Parties were attended by everyone, regardless of job status. Also, as one Japanese executive explained: "We can and want to become close to our employees by visiting those who are sick in bed, and by participating in recreational activities. In my view, the 'personal contact' approach works in South-East Asia."

Despite the enormous resources put into educating employees in appropriate skills as well as their attitude to work, the company was conscious that some culturally rooted differences between Japanese and Malaysians would remain. The task of melding the two cultures was a difficult one, made even more so by the presence of three distinct ethnic groups in Malaysia – Malays (54% of the population), Chinese (35%) and Indians (10%) – and by a somewhat large employee turnover. Professor Ishida commented on this situation in 1973:

> In Malaysia, serving tea is generally thought to be an inferior, low-grade job, for which waitresses are employed from outside. But in MELCOM it is the receptionist's job to serve tea to visitors. At one time, the girls got together to protest against doing this task. The Japanese top management explained the importance of service to visitors at length, and eventually the girls agreed to continue serving the tea. Yet, only recently, a Malaysian executive still protested when asked about the health of his wife: "What has my wife's health got to do with this place?"

Notwithstanding these difficulties, Matsushita considered the transfer of its management principles to the Malaysian environment a success. Based on its philosophy of harnessing 'collective wisdom', a suggestion committee was set up in MELCOM in 1976 with 11 subcommittees in various departments and factories, each consisting of 3–4 members. In 1982, some 20,975 suggestions were received, of which 986 were graded as being valuable. In 1977, of 7,329 suggestions, only 182 were similarly graded.[9] The number of suggestions per employee increased from 3.5 to 17.2 between 1978 and 1982.[10]

With MELCOM facing increasing competition and price pressures, group activities in the industrial engineering (IE) area were also introduced in 1980. Eight presentations on improving the engineering aspects of production were made in 1980. By 1982, the number of presentations had grown to 25. Based on the company's philosophy of co-prosperity, presentations were also invited from suppliers and dealers as part of this programme. For 1983, the objective set for the IE group programme was to bring production time down by 10%.

One of the results of the IE group activities was the introduction of quality control circles (QCC) at MELCOM starting in March 1982. Since its inception, 129 QCCs were formed with a total of 950 participating members out of a workforce of 1,200. Like the IE programme, QCCs were organized by a Central Committee with individual subcommittees in each of the departments and factories. As two committee members explained:

> The QC Circle activity opened a new dimension in the approach towards participative management by our members. For the first time, ordinary shopfloor members have been allowed to have a say in what goes on in their immediate workplace. The results of their efforts to overcome problems are regularly presented to their colleagues during the morning assembly, which

---

[9] Anthony Gomez and Mohd. Rashid Yusof, 'Effective Use of Small Group Activities in MELCOM', Paper presented to the *3rd Asia–Oceania Matsushita Personnel Managers' Conference*, Taiwan, June 8–10, 1983.

[10] Based on grading by the Central Suggestion Committee, the best are selected and given prizes. The suggestion winners for 1982, for example, were sent to visit MELCOM's sister company in Thailand in addition to other prizes.

gives a sense of purpose and meaning to the QCC activity. The better presentations are taken for company-wide presentation, thus also adding an element of competition.[11]

The IE and QCC activities served as instruments for implementing the ensuing campaigns at MELCOM – 'Up Quality Down Cost' and 'Defect Reduction Campaign'. Some M$800,000 were saved in defects and M$2.5 million in manufacturing costs. Equally important, perhaps, these small group activities created a dramatic improvement in the climate of industrial relations as well as the communication between and among management and workers at all levels. Staff turnover, too, was considerably reduced.

Organizational Links with Osaka

At the head office level in Osaka, the Matsushita Group was organized into 110 manufacturing departments, of which 40 were within MEI itself and the remainder in controlled subsidiary companies (*refer to* **Exhibit 11** for the list). The desire to maintain a strong entrepreneurial flavour within the company was reflected in the considerable autonomy given to each product department, which generally had its own fully dedicated plants. The heads of each department – with the title of *Jigyo Bucho*, or General Manager – were responsible for their own personnel, product development, marketing, production and sales. Whenever they needed the assistance of a particular central department – such as R&D or production engineering – they had to request it and then pay for its services. They would also have to pay a flat uniform charge, a percentage of sales turnover, for various other services that were provided and for which there was no precedent of separate billing. Other than that, they were even expected to manage their own finances. Each department, in fact, was financially structured like an independent firm, including having a capital account. While their equity was owned by the corporation, each was responsible for managing it in the same manner that an independent firm would follow.

Manufacturing departments were under no obligation to buy products from other departments if they could obtain better prices from outside. The only Group level obligation each department had was to pay 60% of its pre-tax profits to the head office to cover the costs of financial administration, personnel, product group management, R&D and production engineering, as well as providing the head office with the equity base for its internal venture capital fund. The 40% that they kept for themselves, deposited with the 'Matsushita Bank' and which earned interest, could be spent on such things as facility expansion and updating, production engineering, and 'self-renewal', that is, bringing in a new generation of products to replace the older ones. Each

---

[11] Anthony Gomez and Mohd. Rashid Yusof, 'Effective Use of Small Group Activities in MELCOM', Paper presented at the *3rd Asia–Oceania Matsushita Personnel Managers' Conference*, Taiwan, June 8–10, 1983, pp. 10–11.

department was expected to become financially self-sufficient in five years, and there was no provision for using the earnings of more profitable units to subsidize loss-making units. Mature products were expected to regenerate themselves – with help from central departments, if necessary – and were not to die in a pre-ordained fashion. As one executive put it: "We will continue to make radios till there is no demand in the world."

A good example of this system of divisional autonomy at work could be seen in the way JVC operated. Acquired by Matsushita soon after World War II, this company not only did its own product development, often duplicating MEI's, but also sold its products in competition with MEI departments. Although MEI owned 50.1% in 1982, it did not review JVC's strategic plans. Only financial data were sent regularly by JVC to MEI's finance department. Also, while other departments exported through MET, JVC used an independent General Trading Company for its exports.

The company's socialization and training system served as a counterbalance to the centrifugal tendencies that having such an attachment to product division autonomy was bound to create. If a division supplying components to another became uncompetitive, it would be 'aided' to do better before the buying division went outside for supplies. This spirit of familism and mutual aid often seemed to override short-term profit considerations. The fact that managers were frequently transferred from one division to another – including between subsidiary companies – and usually went through similar training programmes under the watchful eye of the Central Personnel Department, made them keep the Group's interest foremost in mind.

To handle its international business, the Matsushita Group traditionally relied on MET, which dealt with each product department directly. The first attempt at central coordination was made in 1958 by setting up an Export Division at the head office. Then, in 1964, with the start of the company's first post-war foreign manufacturing activities, the Export Division was renamed – thereby becoming the International Division (coordinating exports only) – and a new Overseas Operations Division was created to coordinate foreign manufacturing ventures.

More recently, the functions of the International Division were taken over by MET in cooperation with the export departments located within each of the major manufacturing departments. The Overseas Operations Division was also renamed – to Corporate Overseas Management (COM), headed by a Vice President who sat on MEI's Board. Reporting to him were three Deputy Director Generals, one for overseas manufacturing, one for Planning and Project Execution, and another for Marketing and Sales; the latter was simultaneously the Vice President of MET. The COM, consisting of some 90 employees, was departmentalized into five regions (North America, Latin America, Asia and Pacific, Middle East and Africa, and Europe), the head of each being responsible for coordinating the company's activities in his region – assisted by a Planning department and an Administration department.

In keeping with Matsushita's principle of decentralized management, the various companies in Malaysia functioned independently of one another and, except for major investments or problems, independently of Osaka as well. Given Matsushita's management style, however, a constant give-and-take would frequently override decisions resulting from a strict adherence to the financial autonomy of each company. The relationship between MELCOM and MASCO was one clear example. All of MELCOM's product divisions were expected to make a 10% profit margin on sales after the deduction of overhead expenses. Products sold by these divisions, in turn, were expected to result in a 25% margin for MASCO to cover the latter's expenses. Whenever prevailing market conditions did not allow this to happen, a negotiated compromise was reached between MELCOM's marketing department and MASCO, with both watching out for their own interests and doing independent market research to obtain a fair deal. Traditionally, the Managing Director of MELCOM served as the Group's representative in Malaysia, but this role ended with acting as the spokesman vis-à-vis the Malaysian community and government authorities. While MELCOM reported to MEI's top management as a 'mini-Matsushita', the export-oriented companies reported directly to their counterpart manufacturing departments in Japan.

All the companies in Malaysia, however, actually had two permanent links with the head office – one with the ASEAN department within Corporate Overseas Management and the other with the respective manufacturing departments. The latter tended to be more important for export-oriented ventures than for a company such as MELCOM. In addition, regular reports were submitted to a third head office unit, the International Audit Department of the Finance Division. The frequency of reporting to these three units was typically once a month. Individual production units in Malaysia, including those within MELCOM, maintained frequent though irregular contacts with their counterparts in Japan for technical matters. Also, while the Malaysian companies did not 'report' to MET, with the exception of MASCO, there was a built-in system for information exchange on a regular basis.

Superimposed on this web of relationships was the one between Kosaka and the upper levels of management at MEI. Kosaka elaborated:

> I usually visit the head office every two months or so and each time I see Funahashi (Managing Director, Corporate Overseas Management) and Yamashita (President of Matsushita Electric). Although this is not required, my predecessors would do the same. It is a way of keeping them informed of some qualitative features of our business here, something they cannot easily pick up in the numbers they see. Also, like my predecessor, I write a monthly letter to Yamashita, informing him of how things are faring here generally.

When it came to specific projects, the process adopted was similar to the way the head office operated. The initiative for introducing a new product at MELCOM, for example, usually had to come from MELCOM itself in the form of a *kesai* (request for approval) – it would be on a single sheet of paper covering everything from marketability, investment required, profitability envisaged, future business expansion prospects, etc. Kosaka explained:

Previously, of course, all the concerned people were consulted following our tradition of *nemawashi* (root binding); the head office manufacturing department typically was involved in the feasibility study from the beginning anyhow and Corporate Overseas Management informed in advance. When the President goes through the *ringi*-based decision process, most of the people involved have usually seen the proposal or been party to its formulation. The fact that all units, including those in Malaysia, are expected to be self-financing, puts the burden of failure not on the approver but on the initiator.

Issues Facing the Matsushita Group in Malaysia

By 1982, the Malaysian operations of Matsushita were among its largest and most profitable in the region. Also, while most of its competitors in Malaysia began to show an erratic profit performance, MELCOM – as well as the other Matsushita companies – continued to grow in terms of sales, market share and profitability (*refer to Exhibits 12 and 13*). MELCOM was able to pay a 20% dividend to its shareholders regularly for over a decade, while still retaining enough earnings to finance new investments. In recognition of the group's contribution to the local economy, the government awarded Matsushita's founder, Konosuke Matsushita, the Panglima Mangku Negara carrying the title 'Tan Sri' in February 1979, Malaysia's highest civilian award.

Looking ahead into the future, Matsushita was facing some interesting new challenges but remained committed to Malaysia and was determined to succeed. At MELCOM, even though consolidated profits (including those of the Melcom Industries and MELCOM's equity share of MASCO's profits) increased by 27% in 1982 over the previous year to reach M$21.3 million, sales only grew by 3% because of a 43% decline in exports. In the near term, the company was facing keener competition both from locally manufactured products as well as imports. Imports increased for practically all the products made by MELCOM in spite of duties and taxes (*refer to Exhibit 14*). With the recent reduction in some import duties, import competition was expected to be even greater in the future.

Part of the reason for the reduction in import duties was the government's desire to have Malaysian firms produce more of their components in-house or have them sourced locally. "The colour TV industry," said a senior MIDA official on this subject, "is not one we are particularly proud of. There are too many low value-added assemblers, with the cabinet as their sole indigenous component. Naturally, they complain when we lower duties on the import of complete sets." The same official, however, pointed to Matsushita as an exception. Compared with an average parts localization of 15–20% among its competitors, Matsushita was sourcing almost 65% of its parts locally (*refer to Exhibit 15*). At the level of demand, while product diffusion rates in Malaysia were still low compared with advanced, industrialized countries (*refer to Exhibits 16 and 17*), the potential market was relatively small. Demand patterns within Malaysia, furthermore, had become increasingly segmented. While a small number of rich people wanted the latest in design and microprocessor controls in their products, the majority could

EXHIBIT 2

CASE 3.1: **LESTRA DESIGN**

LESTRA SPORT

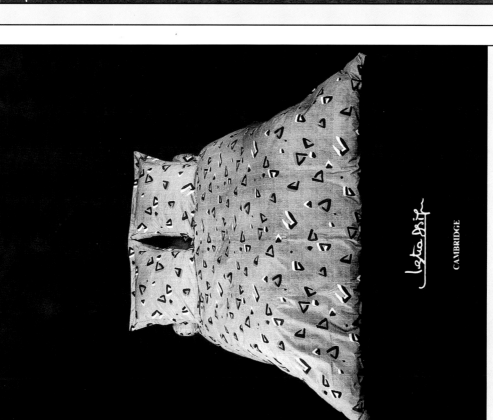

SC/P4 – RAMATUELLE

LF/3P – NEW-LOOK

LF/3P – PEKIN

LF/4P – SPI

SC/P4 – CABOURG

LF/3P – FUN

LF/3P – MAMOUNIA

LF/4P – CASINO

LF/3P – OFF-SHORE

LF/5P – IBIZA

Source: Lestra Sport, company brochure.

CASE 3.1: **LESTRA DESIGN**

EXHIBIT 1

CAMBRIDGE

Source: Lestra Design, company brochure.

CASE 7.1: **HILTI CORPORATION**

EXHIBIT 1: **The HILTI Product Line**

Sources: Top left – *1994 Hilti Corporation Annual Report.* Others – 1996 Hilti Corporation Catalogue, *Kompakt-Katalog Producte und Anwendungen.*

CASE 8.2: **KONICA CORP.**

EXHIBIT 16: **Konishiroku Photo Industry Product Line for Colour Print Film (Film for Amateurs Only)**

CASE 9.4: **CHINA'S XFM PROJECT** EXHIBIT 1: **The XFM**

CASE 11.1: **SINGAPORE AIRLINES** EXHIBIT 3: **Advertisements of Singapore Airlines**

Perhaps a little cognac to accompany your after-dinner chocolate.

Singapore Airlines Raffles Class.

IN THE NOT TOO DISTANT FUTURE,
WE COULD FLY YOU FROM LONDON TO SINGAPORE
IN 50 MINUTES.
WE HOPE YOU PREFER YOUR BEEF RARE.

CASE 11.1: **SINGAPORE AIRLINES** EXHIBIT 4: **Advertisements of Competing Airlines**

only buy relatively cheap, basic models. Given Malaysian wage and productivity levels at the time, import competition was expected to come from both ends. A MIDA official explained what could happen when others moved in: "Since MELCOM cannot do everything at once, it runs the risk of not obtaining permission to manufacture products because they would delay the introduction process."

As for the long term, the main commercial issue facing the Matsushita Group in Malaysia was deciding what to produce for the local market and what to export. The issue was complicated by the fact that 'mini-Matsushitas' had been established in a number of other countries in the region – i.e. Thailand, Indonesia, the Philippines and Taiwan. These countries also wished to increase their exports, and industrialized country markets were not so open as they used to be. Furthermore, starting with a joint venture with Philips in Europe in 1970 to produce dry cell batteries, a number of manufacturing ventures were also being established in industrialized countries (*refer to* **Exhibit 18**).

EXHIBIT 1

Overseas Affiliates of Matsushita Electric Industrial Co., Ltd. Established up to 1970

Name of firm	Country	Date established	MEI ownership ratio	Major lines of business
A. Manufacturing				
National Thai Co., Ltd.	Thailand	1961	48.65	TV, radio, components, other HEA
Matsushita Electric (Taiwan) Co., Ltd.	Taiwan	1962	60	TV, stereo, radio, air-conditioners, other HEA
Matsushita Electric of Puerto Rico, Inc.	Puerto Rico	1965	80	Speakers, record players and sales of imported products
Matsushita Electric Co. (Malaysia) Bhd.	Malaysia	1965	43.1	TV, stereo, DB, components, other HEA
National Centroamericana SA (NAC)	Costa Rica	1966	100	Radio, stereo, speaker boxes, dry cell batteries
National Peruana S.A.	Peru	1966	66.6	TV, radio, stereo, batteries, HEA, etc.
Taimatsu Industrial Co., Ltd.	Taiwan	1966	60	Carbon for dry cell batteries
Matsushita Electric Co. (East Africa) Ltd.	Tanzania	1966	100	Radio, dry cell batteries
National do Brasil Ltda. (NABRAS)	Brazil	1967	75	TV, radio, stereo, batteries & special products
Precision Electronics Corporation	Philippines	1967	40	TV, radio, DB, components, other HEA
Matsushita Electric Co. (Australia) Pty.	Australia	1968	100	TV, speaker boxes
National de Venezuela CA	Venezuela	1969	49	Stereo, CTV, speaker boxes, speakers, car stereos
P.T. National Gobel	Indonesia	1970	55	TV, radio, stereo, components, other HEA
Philips Matsushita Battery Cor. N.V.	Belgium	1970	50	Dry cell batteries
B. Sales only				
Matsushita Electric Corporation of America (MECA)	U.S.A.	1959	100	TV, VTR, radio, other HEA, Panasonic sales distribution
Panasonic Company	U.S.A.	1959		TV, VTR, car radio, electronic components
National Panasonic Vertriebsgesellschaft	F.R.G.	1962	MET:70/MEI:25	TV, VTR, radio, other HEA
Panasonic Hawaii, Inc.	U.S.A.	1964	MECA 100	TV, radio, stereo and HEA
Matsushita Electric of Canada Ltd.	Canada	1966	MECA 100	TV, radio, stereo, HEA and special related products
Matsushita Electric del Peru S.A.	Peru	1966	100	Wireless, HEA, etc.
Matsushita Electric (Costa Rica) S.A.	Costa Rica	1967	100	Wireless, HEA, DB, etc.
Panasonic France S.A.	France	1968	100	Wireless, HEA, etc.
Matsushita Electric de Mexico S.A. de CV	Mexico	1969	100	Wireless, special products, HEA, etc.
National Panasonic (Panama) S.A.	Panama	1970	100	Wireless, HEA, etc.

EXHIBIT 2

Product Transfer to Malaysia

Item	Year of first production in Japan (MEI)	Year of first export to Malaysia	Year of first production in Malaysia
1. Electric irons	1927	1956	1970
2. Dry batteries	1931	1956	1966
3. Radios	1936	1962	1969
4. Electric fans	1950	1962	1966
5. Ceiling fans	1950	1962	1971
6. Clothes washers	1951	1955	1979
7. Refrigerators	1953	1961	1967
8. Black & White TVs	1953	1962	1966
9. Rice cookers	1954	1967	1969
10. Gas cookers	1955	1966	–
11. Air-conditioners	1960	1970	1973
12. Colour TVs	1960	1976	1974
13. Microwave ovens	1962	1978	–
14. Radio cassettes	1967	1970	*
15. Car air-conditioners	1970	1972	–
16. VTRs (VHs)	1976	–	–

*Introduced in 1969 but production ceased following year.
– Not introduced until 1982.

Source: MASCO.

EXHIBIT 3

Malaysia – Incentives for Industrial Development

Malaysia's investment incentives under the Investment Incentives Act 1971 are designed to provide total or partial relief from the payment of income tax (40%) and development tax (5%) to companies manufacturing new products or undertaking expansion and/or diversification. The relief is granted in various forms and investors may select the type of incentives most beneficial to them.

1. Pioneer Status

Companies which intend to produce goods not already manufactured on a commercial scale suitable to the economic requirements of Malaysia, or whose establishment is vital to the public interest can apply for Pioneer Status. Companies which intend to manufacture their products wholly for export can also apply.

Pioneer Status companies are allowed an initial tax relief period of two years beginning on production day. Extensions to tax relief will be granted according to the level of capital investment. Hence the tax holiday period is:

- 2 years for fixed capital expenditure less than $250,000;

- 3 years for fixed capital expenditure not less than $250,000;

- 4 years for fixed capital expenditure not less than $500,000;

- 5 years for fixed capital expenditure more than $1,000,000.

In addition to the above an extension of a further year of the tax relief period is granted for each of the following conditions, thus bringing the total period to a maximum of 8 years:

(a) if the pioneer factory is sited in a development area;

(b) if the product/industry is a priority product of industry;

(c) if the percentage of Malaysian content attained is more than 50%.

Where losses are incurred for the whole of the tax relief period, capital allowances are allowed to be notionally calculated and aggregated as deduction in the post tax relief period. Dividends from pioneer companies are also exempted from tax.

2. Labour Utilization Relief (LUR)

The Labour Utilization Relief provides for exemption of income tax in the same way as in pioneer status except that in this case, the granting of such exemption is based upon the number of full-time paid employees engaged in the project instead of on the amount of capital expenditure incurred.

Under the LUR the tax exemption period and the qualifying requirements are:

Qualifying full-time employment	Tax exemption period
51–100 employees	2 years
101–200 employees	3 years
201–350 employees	4 years
351 employees and above	5 years

EXHIBIT 3 (continued)

In addition, an extension of a further year of the tax relief period is granted for each of the following conditions:

(a) if the factory is sited in a development area;

(b) if the product/industry is a priority product of industry;

(c) if the percentage of Malaysian content is more than 50%.

The above investment incentive is designed to encourage industrial ventures which will generate greater employment opportunities in the country.

3. *Investment Tax Credit*

The Investment Tax Credit can be granted to approved companies not enjoying Pioneer Status. The amount of tax credit given is not less than 25% of the total capital expenditure incurred by the project. It is given for the year of assessment in the basis period in which the expenditure was incurred and for not more than 5 years from the beginning of the basis period in which the project is approved.

The credit will be increased by an additional 5% of the expenditure for each of the items in 2(a)–(c) above.

The benefit amounts to an exemption of income tax on profits equal to the tax credit given. The credit may be carried forward in case of loss or insufficiency of income until fully utilized against subsequent profits.

The incentive is particularly beneficial to projects that have a high investment level and a long gestation period before profits are made.

4. *Increased Capital Allowance*

In order to encourage existing factories to modernize their production techniques and to encourage the setting-up of modernized factories, the Government has also designed a tax incentive called Increased Capital Allowance. In the case of qualifying plant expenditures, initial allowance is 20% while annual allowance is 40%. (*With the adoption of the straight line method for depreciation, total plant expenditure can be written off within 2 years.*) The initial allowance for qualifying expenditure incurred on the construction of a building is 10% with an annual allowance of 3%.

5. *Export Incentives*

Three kinds of Export Incentives can be granted to companies which export their Malaysian manufactured products.

(a) *Export Allowance*

The amount of allowance is 2% of the ex-factory value of all export sales of the year and an additional 20% of the difference between the ex-factory value of export sales of the year in question and the ex-factory value of export sales of the basis period which constitutes the year in which the company was last exporting and any such basis period being not earlier than the basis period for the year of assessment 1973.

(b) *Accelerated Depreciation Allowance*

Resident companies, if they export 20% (by value) of their total production and if they incur qualifying plant expenditure for the purpose of modernizing the company's production techniques or to set up a modernized factory, are entitled to an Accelerated Depreciation Allowance of 40% per annum, in addition to an initial allowance of 20%. (*With the adoption of the straight line method for depreciation, total plant expenditure can be written off within 2 years.*)

(c) *Deduction for Qualifying Expenses for Overseas Promotion*

(continued)

EXHIBIT 3 (continued)

6. *Locational Incentives*

Locational Incentives were introduced to encourage the dispersal of industries away from the existing industrial concentration in the urban areas. A company locating its factory in an area specified by the Government as a Locational Incentive Area may be considered for tax relief depending on the amount of investment, labour employed, Malaysian content and whether it is a priority product. Thus, the maximum tax relief of 10 years is granted for projects employing more than 350 people, with capital expenditure not less than M$1 million and manufacturing a priority product with significant Malaysian content.

EXHIBIT 4

Japan Electronic Industry Development Association's Survey of the Electronics industry in South-East Asia (1969)

1. Summary of Labour Conditions Prevalent in Various South-East Asian Countries

	Japan	Korea Tokyo/Seoul approx. 1,300 km	Taiwan Tokyo/Taipei approx. 2,300 km	Hong Kong Tokyo/Hong Kong approx. 3,200 km	Thailand Tokyo/Bangkok approx. 5,000 km	Malaysia Tokyo/K. Lumpur approx. 6,300 km	Singapore Tokyo/Singapore approx. 6,500 km
Labour matters							
Labour force	Limited availability but overall shortage	Abundant	Abundant. Localized shortage (Taipei & Kaoshiang)	Still available	Abundant	Abundant	Abundant (in case of shortage, import from Malaysia)
Quality	Good	Good	Good	Good	Depending on training (females are good)	Chinese are good, others depending on training	Good
Monthly wages (mainly females)	Yen 18,000–23,000 tends to rise	Yen 6,500–8,000 yearly rising by 20%	Yen 7,000–9,000 tends to rise in Taipei and Kaoshiang	Yen 10,000–15,000 rising 10% annually	Yen 5,000–8,000 established	Yen 11,000–12,000. But away from K. Lumpur Yen 6,000–8,000 only	Yen 9,000–12,000 established
Bonus	Approx. 3 months' pay	Approx. 1–2 months' pay	Approx. 1–2 months' pay	Approx. 1–2 months' pay	Approx. 1–2 months' pay	Approx. 1–2 months' pay	Approx. 1 months' pay

(continued)

EXHIBIT 4 (continued)

	Japan	Korea	Taiwan	Hong Kong	Thailand	Malaysia	Singapore
		Tokyo/Seoul approx. 1,300 km	Tokyo/Taipei approx. 2,300 km	Tokyo/Hong Kong approx. 3,200 km	Tokyo/Bangkok approx. 5,000 km	Tokyo/K. Lumpur approx. 6,300 km	Tokyo/Singapore approx. 6,500 km
Trade unionism	Civil Service banned. Others active	Trade union activities are either banned or remaining at low level. Female workers can work late hours subject to certain conditions in some areas					
Education	Very enthusiastic	Very enthusiastic	Enthusiastic	Average	Somewhat inferior	Average	Very enthusiastic

Source: Report on Survey of Electronics Industry in South-East Asia, 1969 by Japan Electronic Industry Development Association.

Currency rate: 1US$ = 360 Yen.

2. Comparison of Wage Rates for Electronics Industry in the Countries of the South-East Asian Region (Mainly Female Workers) (1969 Figures)

Country	Monthly wage in US$			Comparison with Malaysia, Kaula Lumpur is 100	Comparison with Malaysia, away from K.L. as 100
	Minimum	Maximum	Average		
Japan	50	64	57	184	300
Hong Kong	28	42	35	113	185
Malaysia, Kuala Lumpur	30	33	31	100	163
Singapore	25	33	29	94	153
Taiwan	19	25	22	71	116
Korea	18	22	20	65	105
Malaysia, away from K.L.	17	22	19	61	100
Thailand	14	22	18	58	95

Source: Adapted from Report on Survey of Electronics Industry in South-East Asia, 1969 by Japan Electronic Industry Development Association.

Currency rate: 1US$ = 360 Yen.

EXHIBIT 5

Japanese and Malaysian Organization

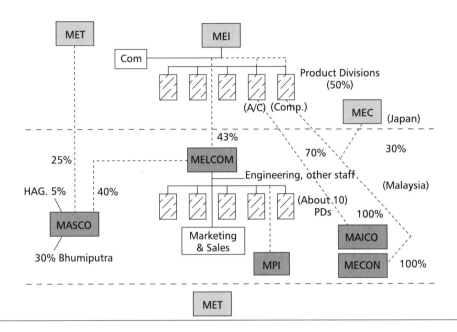

EXHIBIT 6

Market Share Evolution for Selected National Products in Malaysia

	1973	1978	1980	1982
b/w TV	21%	18%	18%	14%
Colour TV	–	9%	14%	22%
Dry battery	23.5%	27%	31%	32%
Fridge	19%	17%	20%	27%

Source: MELCOM.

EXHIBIT 7

Introduction of Production Equipment and Processes at MELCOM

Nature of equipment and/or process	Dates when introduced	
	In Japan (MEI)	In Malaysia (MELCOM)
1. Flow-process conveyor system for parts assembly	1948	1968
2. Printed circuit boards (PCBs)	1955	1968
3. SCS soldering – automatic feeding of PCBs through molten solder bath	1957	1968
4. Lead wire automatic cutting machine	1960	1973
5. Formed leg process requiring no lead wire cutting	1968	1976
6. PANAVISETTOR – automatic screw fastening machine	1971	1978
7. Semi-automatic video-checker (for small-capacity plants)	1975	1979
8. Free-flow conveyor system for parts assembly (can be stopped by individual operators)	1975	1980
9. PANASERT – robotized component insertion machine (the earlier 1958 version, called DYNASERT, was never introduced in Malaysia as human-inserted PCBs found more economical)	1970	1981
10. Fully-automatic video-checker	1970	1984

EXHIBIT 8

Introduction of Management Techniques at MELCOM

Nature of management techniques	Dates when introduced	
	In Japan (MEI)	In Malaysia (MELCOM)
A. *Organization*		
1. Morning and evening assemblies	1932	1968
2. Suggestion system	1920s	1976
3. Big sister and senior companion system	BS: 1961	1969
	SCS: 1963	1973
4. House newsletter	1934	1974
5. Annual policy announcement	1940	1971
6. Quality control circles	1963	1980
7. Total quality control	1955	1982
B. *Production*		
1. Work factor analysis (time and motion study)	1952	not introduced
2. Work standardization	1952	1968
3. Quality assurance department – evaluating products from customer standpoint and proposing changes in specification	1946	1979
4. Industrial engineering committee		1980
5. Rated work factor (RWF) (micro-motion studies)	1970	1983

EXHIBIT 9

Matsushita Electric Company (Malaysia) Berhad Organization Chart (as of 30 April 1973)

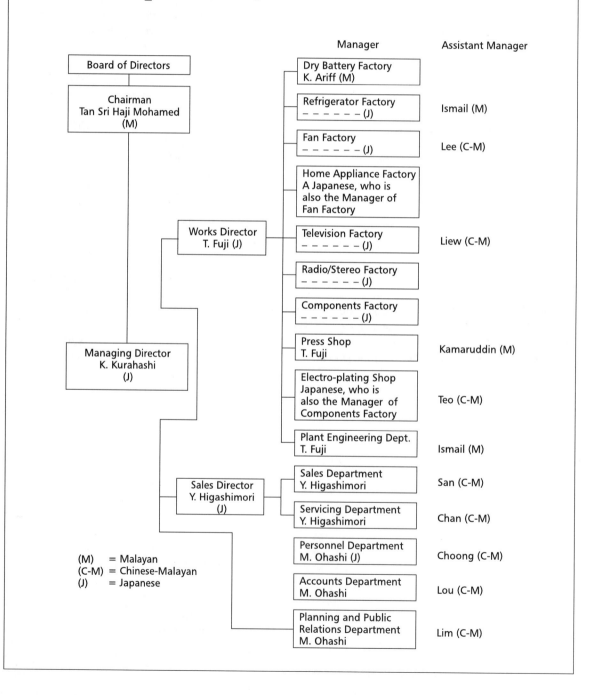

	Manager	Assistant Manager
	Dry Battery Factory K. Ariff (M)	
	Refrigerator Factory – – – – – – (J)	Ismail (M)
	Fan Factory – – – – – – (J)	Lee (C-M)
	Home Appliance Factory A Japanese, who is also the Manager of Fan Factory	
	Television Factory – – – – – – (J)	Liew (C-M)
	Radio/Stereo Factory – – – – – – (J)	
	Components Factory – – – – – – (J)	
	Press Shop T. Fuji	Kamaruddin (M)
	Electro-plating Shop Japanese, who is also the Manager of Components Factory	Teo (C-M)
	Plant Engineering Dept. T. Fuji	Ismail (M)
	Sales Department Y. Higashimori	San (C-M)
	Servicing Department Y. Higashimori	Chan (C-M)
	Personnel Department M. Ohashi (J)	Choong (C-M)
	Accounts Department M. Ohashi	Lou (C-M)
	Planning and Public Relations Department M. Ohashi	Lim (C-M)

Board of Directors

Chairman
Tan Sri Haji Mohamed
(M)

Works Director
T. Fuji (J)

Managing Director
K. Kurahashi
(J)

Sales Director
Y. Higashimori
(J)

(M)   = Malayan
(C-M) = Chinese-Malayan
(J)   = Japanese

EXHIBIT 10

MELCOM Organization Chart, 1983

```
CHAIRMAN
YB Tan Sri
Mohamad Noah

BOARD
OF DIRECTORS

MANAGING
DIRECTOR
Mr Hiroaki Kosaka
```

GENERAL MANAGER
OF ADMINISTRATION

(T. Thara) … Executive Director
(S. Y. Lou)… Admin. Management
Officer

CORPORATE PURCHASE
(ASST. C. C. FAN)

COMPUTER
(S. Y. Lou)

SECRETARY

QUALITY ASSURANCE
CONTROL

PLANNING
(K. K. Lim)

PERSONNEL
(M. Rushid)

IND. RELATIONS
(Anthony Gomez)

ACCOUNTS
(E. S. Fong)

MARKETING
(W. H. San)

SERVICE
(Asst. C. Y. Khoo)

GENERAL
ADMINISTRATION
(Asst. Yahaya Salleh)

IMPORT/EXPORT
(Ismail Mahbut)

GENERAL MANAGER
OF PRODUCTION

(T. Kurozuka) … General Manager
(Ismail Mohd) … Production
Management Officer

PRODUCTION &
QUALITY CONTROL
(E. S. Lim)

PRODUCTION
ENGINEERING
(E. S. Lim)

PLANT
ENGINEERING
(Ismail Mohd)

INDUSTRIAL
DESIGN
(P. S. Lai)

TELEVISION
(K. S. Liew)
(Asst. C. M. Lee)
(Asst. J. Y. Koh)   (S. Kawamura)

AUDIO
(David Hor)   (H. Sawae)

REFRIGERATOR
(L T. Lee)   (A. Kobayashi)
(K. Tanaka)

WASHING MACHINE
(N. Yoshihara)
(Asst. K. L. Low)

DRY BATTERY
(Asst. Mohd. Bassir)   (M. Uesaraie)

FAN/CEILING FAN
(A. W. Tan)

HOME APPLIANCES
(N. Logan)   (M. Akao)

PART SHOP
(Asst. A. Karim)   (H. Yoshida)

ELECTRO-PLATING
(C. L. Teo)

DIE & MOULD   (K. S. Teo)
(T. Shibata)

MELCOM
INDUSTRIES

ADMINISTRATION
(M. Nagaosa)   (Ng Kai Yin)

MANUFACTURING
(H. Hayasaka)   (Lee Beng Hee)

EXHIBIT 11

Consolidated Manufacturing Companies within the Matsushita Electric Group

Matsushita Electric Industrial Co., Ltd.
Full range of electric and electronic home appliances.

Matsushita Electronics Corporation
Cathode-ray tubes, electric lamps, etc.

Matsushita Electronic Components Co., Ltd.
Electronic components such as LSIs, ICs, transistors, diodes, image pick-up tubes, capacitors, resistors, tuners, speakers, etc.

Matsushita Battery Industrial Co., Ltd.
Manganese and alkaline batteries, lead–acid storage batteries, lithium and other cells, solar energy equipment, etc.

Victor Company of Japan, Ltd.
Video equiment such as VTR and related equipment, colour TV and radio cassettes, etc.

Matsushita Seiko Co., Ltd.
Electric fans, air-conditioners and air-cooling equipment.

Matsushita Reiki Co., Ltd.
Refrigerators, compressors and air-conditioners, etc.

Matsushita Communication Industrial Co., Ltd.
Communication, measuring and business equipment.

Matsushita Housing Products Co., Ltd.
Solar energy equipment and electric heater appliances and gas appliances.

Matsushita Kotobuki Electronics Industrial Ltd.
Video equipment and colour TV.

Matsushita Electric Trading Co., Ltd.
Export of all Matsushita's products and components and import of parts, materials and components for manufacturing.

Kyushi Matsushita Electric Co., Ltd.
Power equipments, coils, etc.

Matsushita Industrial Equipment Co., Ltd.
Welding equipment, industrial robot and power distribution equipment.

Teichiku Records Co., Ltd.
Musical tapes and records.

EXHIBIT 12

Earnings Performance of Domestic Electrical Appliances Companies (KLSE)

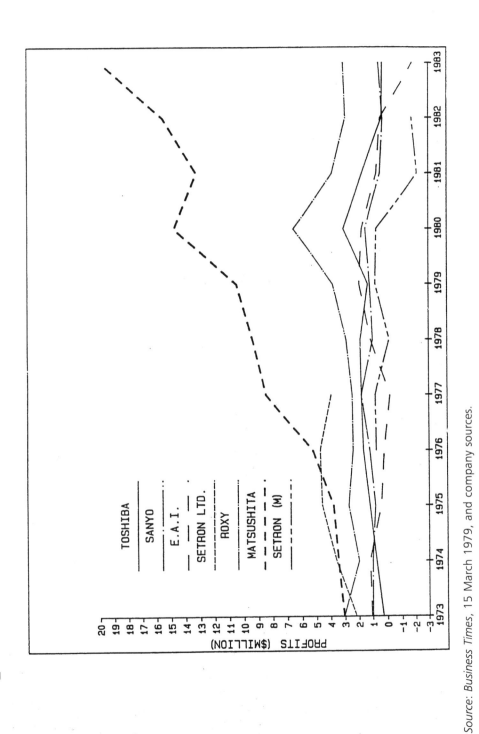

Source: Business Times, 15 March 1979, and company sources.

EXHIBIT 13

Evolution of the Matsushita Group in Malaysia (unit: M$1,000)

		1966	1968	1970	1972	1974	1976	1978	1980	1982
MELCOM[1]:	Sales	298	8,383	15,664	22,365	40,468	51,838	80,063	129,412	147,800
	Export (M$)	–	932	1,856	245	4,618	4,824	6,786	11,561	8,782
	% Sales		11.1	11.8	1.1	11.4	9.3	8.5	8.9	5.9
	Investment (M$)	3,762	4,167	6,032	7,486	11,312	13,506	24,038	40,040	62,367
	Employment	160	222	307	373	634	752	900	1,175	1,212
M.I.[2]:	Sales	–	–	–	–	220	3,519	5,445	8,485	8,205
	Export	–	–	–	–	–	–	–	–	–
	Investment	–	–	–	–	1,650	3,198	4,898	6,006	5,854
	Employment	–	–	–	–	38	75	99	152	131
MAICO[3]:	Sales					38,760	43,859	67,563	106,049	121,947
	Export (M$)					36,307	38,137	54,319	81,646	90,703
	% Sales					93.4	87.0	80.4	77.0	74.4
	Investment					20,674	30,080	38,885	50,882	56,248
	Employment					603	578	759	901	882
MECOM[4]:	Sales	–	–	–	–	3,536	10,424	23,349	41,704	41,137
	Export (M$)	–	–	–	–	3,509	10,386	22,400	40,467	39,021
	% Sales	–	–	–	–	99.2	99.6	95.9	97.0	94.9
	Investment	–	–	–	–	815	1,358	5,205	7,840	10,382
	Employment	–	–	–	–	349	718	995	1,207	1,150
MPI[5]:	Sales	–	–	–	–	–	–	–	13,336	20,901
	Export (M$)	–	–	–	–	–	–	–	13,307	18,031
	% Sales	–	–	–	–	–	–	–	99.8	86.3
	Investment	–	–	–	–	–	–	–	11,252	14,161
	Employment	–	–	–	–	–	–	–	218	420

EXHIBIT 13 (continued)

	1966	1968	1970	1972	1974	1976	1978	1980	1982
MASCO[6]: Sales – total						45,565	94,360	188,896	325,977
Of which imported products						7,562	21,906	74,713	176,495
Investment						907	1,180	5,280	10,515
Employment						241	257	265	328
Total for Group[7]									
Sales (MELCOM, MAICO, MECOM, MPI)	298	8,390	15,664	22,365	82,764	106,121	170,975	290,501	331,785
Exports (M$)	–	932	1,856	245	44,434	53,347	83,505	146,981	156,537
% Sales	0	11.1	11.8	1.1	53.7	50.3	48.8	50.6	47.2
Investment	3,762	4,167	6,032	7,486	34,451	49,049	74,206	121,300	159,527
Employment	160	222	307	373	1,624	2,364	3,010	3,918	4,123

[1] MELCOM – Matsushita Electric Company (Malaysia) Bhd. manufactures a range of home appliances mainly for the local market.

[2] M.I. – Matsushita Industries Sdn. Bhd., a wholly owned subsidiary of MELCOM, manufactures cast-iron and aluminium parts and die-cast components for the assembly of electric irons, fans and rice cookers by MELCOM.

[3] MAICO – Matsushita Industrial Corporation Sdn. Bhd. manufactures window-type room air-conditioners, mainly for export.

[4] MECOM – Matsushita Electronic Components (M) Sdn. Bhd. manufactures electronic components, mainly for export.

[5] MPI – Matsushita Precision Industrial Co. (M) Sdn. Bhd. manufactures electronic components, mainly for export.

[6] MASCO – Matsushita Sales & Service Sdn. Bhd. markets and services Matsushita products in Malaysia.

EXHIBIT 14

Matsushita Group in Malaysia: Production and Import Statistics by Products

Item	1972	1974	1976	1978	1980	1982
1. Dry batteries (1966)						
1.1. Total Malaysian production (million pieces)	57.3	55.3	91.0	107.7	131.0	138.0
1.2. MELCOM's production (million pieces)	18.1	24.5	32.7	33.2	45.2	53.3
1.3. MELCOM's unit price index (1972 = 100)	100	110	119	123	126	152
1.4. Total Malaysian imports (million pieces)	1.1	3.8	5.3	3.8	9.7	15.9
1.5. Total import unit price index (1972 = 100)	100	76	110	117	152	107
1.6. Import duties (per cell) – as of 1.12.83 = 5¢ + 5% surtax	5¢	5¢	5¢	5¢	5¢	5¢
2. Electric fans (1966)						
2.1. Total Malaysian production ('000 pieces)	47.1	74.1	175.7	320.9	386.5	463.8
2.2. MELCOM's production ('000 pieces)	46.3	63.3	62.5	100.1	118.7	154.2
2.3. MELCOM's unit price index (1972 = 100)	100	138	130	158	149	118
2.4. Total Malaysian imports ('000 pieces)	5.5	20.7	26.4	46.4	97.3	86.9
2.5. Total import unit price index (1972 = 100)	100	119	106	123	122	93
2.6. Import duties – as of 1.12.83 = 35% or $23 + 5% surtax	45%	45%	45%	45%	45%	35%
3. Refrigerators (1967)						
3.1. Total Malaysian production ('000 pieces)	29.0	45.9	61.8	88.7	126.7	192.6
3.2. MELCOM's production ('000 pieces)	8.0	11.3	24.2	46.4	53.8	62.5
3.3. MELCOM's unit price index (1972 = 100)	100	137	119	123	147	160
3.4. Total Malaysian imports ('000 pieces)	3.5	11.5	9.3	20.4	18.0	14.4
3.5. Total import unit price index (1972 = 100)	100	107	110	120	148	145
3.6. Import duties – below 12 C.F. as of 1.12.83 = 45% or $360 + 5% surtax	45%	45%	45%	45%	25% (or $250)	45% (or $360)
– above 12 C.F. as of 1.12.83 = 50%					25% (or $250)	45%

EXHIBIT 14 (continued)

Item	1972	1974	1976	1978	1980	1982
4. *Electric rice cookers* (1969)						
4.1. Total Malaysian production ('000 pieces)	28.7	56.7	84.9	108.0	163.4	214.0
4.2. MELCOM's production ('000 pieces)	28.71	46.5	72.9	106.0	150.1	183.8
4.3. MELCOM's unit price index (1972 = 100)	100	126	134	137	149	139
4.4. Total Malaysian imports ('000 pieces)	0.9	24.6	8.5	24.6	23.1	17.6
4.5. Total import unit price index (1972 = 100)	100	127	174	139	157	N.A.
4.6. Import duties – as of 1.12.83 = 50%	25%	25%	25%	25%	55% (or $15)	45% (or $10.5)
5. *Electric irons* (1970)						
5.1. Total Malaysian production ('000 pieces)	24.9	81.6	268.8	401.2	614.4	518.7
5.2. MELCOM's production ('000 pieces)	N.A.	65.7	78.2	99.0	112.5	185.0
5.3. MELCOM's unit price index (1972 = 100)	100	101	94	101	111	125
5.4. Total Malaysian imports ('000 pieces)	15.3	28.5	10.9	23.9	51.2	49.4
5.5. Total import unit price index (1972 = 100)	100	113	145	117	113	128
5.6. Import duties – as of 1.12.83 = 40%	45%	45%	45%	45%	25%	45%
6. *Colour TV* (1974)*						
6.1. Total Malaysian production ('000 pieces)	–	N.A.	N.A.	150.1	157.3	249.0
6.2. MELCOM's production ('000 pieces)		0.07	0.08	3.0	24.0	44.9
6.3. MELCOM's unit price index (1972 = 100)		100	100	117	76	54
6.4. Total Malaysian imports ('000 pieces)				15.9	173.0	182.4
6.5. Total import unit price index (1978 = 100)				100	58	37
6.6. Import duties – 16″ and below** as of 1.12.83 = 30%	N.A.	25%	25%	25%	25%	30%
– above 16″ as of 1.12.83 = 50%	N.A.	35%	35%	35%	35%	40%

*Colour broadcasting commenced in Malaysia in 1978.

**The average duty on components in 1982/83 was around 25%. A duty rebate was given, however, for components not manufactured in Malaysia.

EXHIBIT 15

Matsushita Malaysia: Local Content (1982)

Products	Self-manufacture	Local purchase	Import
Electric iron	70.0%	9.4%	20.6%
Rice cooker	66.1%	6.0%	27.9%
Fan	54.4%	12.3%	33.3%
Dry battery	57.1%	28.3%	14.6%
Refrigerator	37.5%	28.5%	34.0%
CTV	1.0%	50.3%	48.6%

Source: MELCOM.

EXHIBIT 16

Household Ownership of Selected Durables – 1980 (% of households)

Country	Car	Refrigerator	Washing machine	Vacuum cleaner	TV	Radio
Brazil	30	65	17	14	89	97
U.S.A.	92	100	94	89	100	100
Bangladesh	1	–	–	–	–	19
India	1	15	10	5	9	28
Japan	60	99	99	98	98	99
Korea	3	26	21	35	41	80
Malaysia	24	20	15	14	50	38
Philippines	5	42	33	27	29	69
Singapore	29	45	39	38	86	91

Source: Euromonitor, International Marketing Data and Statistics 1983 (Euromonitor Publications Ltd., 1983).

Note: Unlike Exhibit 17, above data include households without electricity. Because of estimation methods used, the Malaysian data presented in Exhibits 16 and 17 are not directly comparable.

EXHIBIT 17

Malaysia: Electronic and Electric Appliance Diffusion Ratios (% Households Owning Electricity)

Item	1972	1974	1976	1978	1980	1982	(Forecast) 1985
1. Electric irons	54.4	63.3	73.5	87.5	89.5	93.3	101.0
2. Electric fans	35.8	42.9	50.0	76.1	93.9	120.0	N.A.
3. b/w TVs	31.8	39.2	47.7	70.7	67.8	63.1	N.A.
4. Refrigerators	20.4	24.2	30.3	35.1	43.3	54.0	86.0
5. Rice cookers	14.4	19.7	27.3	45.9	58.4	77.8	94.0
6. Radio-cassettes	N.A.	N.A.	N.A.	N.A.	32.0	45.0	100.0
7. Stereograms	N.A.	N.A.	N.A.	N.A.	9.0	11.0	10.0
8. Colour TV	N.A.	N.A.	N.A.	N.A.	30.0	46.0	81.0
9. Car air-conditioners (% cars equipped)	N.A.	N.A.	N.A.	N.A.	N.A.	42.0	85.0
10. Microwave ovens	N.A.	N.A.	N.A.	N.A.	0.5	0.5	0.7
11. Video tape recorders	N.A.	N.A.	N.A.	N.A.	3.0	10.0	20.0

Source: MASCO/MELCOM.

EXHIBIT 18

Matsushita Electric Industrial Co., Ltd.: Overseas Affiliates Established Between 1970 and 1984

Name of firm	Country	Date established	MEI ownership ratio	Major lines of business
A. *Manufacturing*				
Matsushita Industrial Canada Ltd.	Canada	1972	100	TV, speaker systems
Matsushita Industrial Corporation Sdn. Bhd.	Malaysia	1972	91	Air-conditioners, air-compressors
Matsushita Electronic Components (Malaysia) Sdn. Bhd.	Malaysia	1972	100	Electronic components
Matsushita Refrigeration Industries (S) Pte. Ltd.	Singapore	1972	100	Compressors for refrigerators
Lakhampal National Ltd.	India	1972	40	Dry cell batteries
Indo National Ltd.	India	1972	40	Dry cell batteries
Melcom Industries Sdn. Bhd.	Malaysia	1973	MELCOM 100	Parts for HEA
National Electric Industrial Co. (Iran) Ltd.	Iran	1973	30	Rice cookers, mixers, blenders
Korea National Electric Co.*	Korea	1973	50	Colour & b/w TV, radio, stereo, amplifiers
Panasonic Espana S.A.	Spain	1973	86.7	Radio, Hi-Fi, vacuum cleaners, etc.
Quasar Company	U.S.A.	1974		
Matsushita Electric de El Salvador S.A.	El Savador	1974	NAC 90	Radio, stereo, speaker boxes
National Componentes Eletronicos do Brasil Ltda (NABRAS)	Brazil	1974	50	Electronic components
Matsushita Electric (U.K.) Ltd.	U.K.	1974	100	TV, Hi-Fi, tuners
Meitek Corporation	U.S.A.	1976	100	Technological R&D for various electronic components
Matsushita Electrica de Guatemala SA	Guatemala	1977	NAC 96	Radio, stereo, speaker boxes
Matsushita Electronics (S) Pte. Ltd.	Singapore	1977	100	Radio, stereo
Matsushita Precision Motor (S) Pte. Ltd.	Singapore	1977	100	Precision motors
Matsushita Electronic Components (S) Pte. Ltd	SIngapore	1977	100	Electronic components
Panasonic de Mexico S.A. de CV	Mexico	1978	100	Radio, stereo, speakers, electronic components

EXHIBIT 18 (continued)

Company	Country	Year	Ownership %	Products
Matsushita Precision Industrial Co. (Malaysia) Sdn. Bhd.	Malaysia	1978	100	Electronic components
Matsushita Denshi (S) Pte. Ltd.	Singapore	1978	100	Transistors
Matsushita Technical Center (S) Pte. Ltd.	Singapore	1978	100	Technical training centre
Matsushita Industrial Company	U.S.A.	1979		TV, video projectors, microwave ovens, fans
Matsushita Industrial de Baja California	Mexico	1979	MECA 100	CTV chassis
A.P. National Co. Ltd.	Thailand	1969	45	Air-conditioners, refrigerators, rice cookers
Tennessee Fan Company	U.S.A.	1980		TV, video projectors, microwave ovens, fans
Matsushita Electronic Components Company	U.S.A.	1980		Electronic components
Baterias Panasonic Aullan S.A. de CV	Mexico	1980	49	Dry cell batteries
Springer National da Amazonia S.A.	Brazil	1981	NABRAS 30	TV, radio, stereo, etc.
Matsushita Electric Institute of Technology (Taipei) Co. Ltd.	Taiwan	1981	100	R&D for system software
Panasonic Industrial Company	U.S.A.	1982		TV, VTR, car radio, electronic components
Matsushita Engineering & Service Company	U.S.A.	1982	71.4	Service for Panasonic and Quasar products
International Fan Manufacturing Co. Ltd.	Hong Hong	1982	50	Ceiling fans
Indo Matsushita Carbon Co. Ltd.	India	1982	40	Carbon for dry cell batteries
M.B. Video G.m.b.H.	F.R.G.	1982	65	VTR
Matsushita Communication Company	U.S.A.	1983		Car telephones
Panasonic Nigeria Ltd.	Nigeria	1983	40	TV
National Electric Cote d'Yvoire	Ivory Coast	1984	60	TV, radio

B. Sales only

Company	Country	Year	Ownership %	Products
Panasonic Svenska AB	Sweden	1972	100	Wireless, BEA, etc.
Panasonic U.K. Ltd.	U.K.	1972	100	Wireless, HEA, etc.
National de El Salvador S.A. de CV	El Salvador	1973	99	Wireless, HEA, DB etc.
'National' Corporacion Venezolana S.A.	Venezuela	1973	50	Wireless, HEA, etc.
Panasonic Belgium N.V.	Belgium	1973	100	Wireless, HEA, etc.

(continued)

EXHIBIT 18 (continued)

Name of firm	Country	Date established	MEI ownership ratio	Major lines of business
National de Guatemala S.A.	Guatemala	1974	99	Wireless, HEA, DB, etc.
Matsushita Electric Trading (Singapore)	Singapore	1974	100	Wireless, HEA, components, special products
Panasonic Battery Sales Europe N.V.	Belgium	1974	100	Dry cell batteries
Panasonic Service Scandinavia AB	Sweden	1975	50	Service and service parts
Panasonic Arberg a.s.	Denmark	1975	72	Wireless, HEA, etc.
National Panasonic (Latin America) S.A.	Panama	1976	92.5	Wireless, HEA, etc.
National Panasonic Ecuador S.A.	Ecuador	1976	99	Wireless, HEA, etc.
Sung Tien Mon Co., Ltd.	Taiwan	1976	7	Special products, components, etc.
Matsushita Sales and Service Sdn. Bhd.	Malaysia	1976 MET	MELCOM 40 25	Wireless, HEA, special products, etc.
Matsushita Electric Trading AG	Switzerland	1976	100	Wireless, HEA, etc.
Panasonic Service Deutschland G.m.b.H.	F.R.G.	1977	NDG 100	Service for NDG products
National Panasonic (Philippines) Inc.	Philippines	1978	30	Wireless, HEA, etc.
National Panasonic (Australia) Pty. Ltd.	Australia	1978	75	Wireless, HEA, special products, etc.
National Panasonic S.A.	Argentina	1980	100	Wireless, HEA, DB, etc.
Panasonic Norge A/S	Norway	1980	100	Audio, wireless, HEA, etc.
Panasonic Italia S.p.A.	Italy	1980	100	Wireless, HEA
AMAC Corporation	U.S.A.	1981	100	Electronic equipment, etc.
Panasonic Deutschland G.m.b.H. (NDG)	F.R.G.	1981.	100	Wireless, HEA, special products, components
MET (Hong Kong) Ltd.	Hong Kong	1982	100	Ceiling fans
Panasonic Wiener G.m.b.H.	Austria	1982	90	Audio, wireless, HEA, etc.
Panasonic Industrial U.K., Ltd.	U.K.	1983	50	Special products

* Discontinued.

NAC = National Centroamericana S.A.
MECA = Matsushita Electric Corporation of America.
NABRAS = National Componentes Eletronicos do Brasil Ltda.
HEA = home electric appliances. DB = dry batteries. Wireless = TV, radio, stereo, etc.

CASE 9.3 MALAYSIAN AIRLINE SYSTEM – FLYING INTO THE FUTURE

This case was prepared by Research Associate Joyce Miller under the supervision of Professor George Taucher as a basis for class discussion rather than to illustrate either effective or ineffective handling of a business situation

With the opening of the new international airport in Sepang in 1997, we see the possibility for Kuala Lumpur to become a gateway to the ASEAN region, which is an integral part of Vision 2020. Air transport has an important role to play in helping Malaysia achieve developed nation status. Accordingly, we would like our national air carrier to transform itself into a major carrier and to do this, MAS has to be cost-effective and efficient.

Long See Wool, Principal Assistant Secretary
Aviation Division, Ministry of Transport, Malaysia

In 1993, there was a sense that Malaysian Airline System (MAS) had reached a crossroad. After years of strong growth in revenues, the airline had posted dismal results, well under half of the RM372 million in pre-tax profits that had been anticipated for 1991–92. At the time of this forecast, MAS had raised RM700 million in the largest rights issue ever placed domestically, enabling the airline to phase out leased and ageing aircraft, and to increase its fleet from 80 aircraft to 101 over a 4-year period (*refer to Exhibit 1*). By the end of 1997, MAS would take delivery of 72 airplanes – costing a total of RM10.6 billion, thus forming one of the youngest fleets in the world.

Over the past year, MAS' overall load factor – a key performance indicator in the airline industry – had dropped from 65.9% to 62.9% (*refer to Exhibit 2*). The sharp drop in passenger and cargo traffic was blamed on intense competition, over-capacity on many international routes, continuing economic recession in industrialized countries, and the threat of terrorism during the Gulf War, a situation that had driven many business travellers to use the telephone, telefax and teleconferencing systems rather than physically attend meetings. With 55% of MAS' revenue denominated in foreign currencies, the appreciation of the Malaysian ringgit (RM) had also negatively affected the company's performance.[1]

---

[1] In 1992, US\$ = RM2.612 = Singapore \$1.6449 = Thai Bhat 25.52 = Indonesian Rupiah 2,062. In 1991, US\$ = RM2.724 = Singapore \$1.6305 = Thai Bhat 25.28 = Indonesian Rupiah 1,992. In 1990, US\$ = RM2.7015 = Singapore \$1.7445 = Thai Bhat 25.29 = Indonesian Rupiah 1,901.

For years, Asian air carriers had consistently ranked among the most profitable airlines in the world (*refer to **Exhibit 3***). But the cornerstone of that position was beginning to erode. As nations developed economically, labour and material costs also increased. For MAS, the next two years would be *critical*. The airline was coming up against rising operating costs at a time when the costs for financing its ambitious expansion programme would reach their peak. At the same time, management had to begin laying down tough strategies in order to capitalize on the opportunities represented by the new international airport being constructed in Sepang, 80 kilometres outside Kuala Lumpur, due to open in 1997.

MAS and National Integration

Until October 1972, the Malaysian and Singapore governments had held equal shares in Malaysia Singapore Airlines (MSA), a small regional airline domiciled in Singapore. Growing differences between the governments regarding the development of the airline had resulted in the creation of Malaysian Airline System (MAS) and Singapore Airlines (SIA). At the time, MAS was given an explicit mandate to develop Malaysia's domestic network and to integrate the 13 states spread across the two land masses separated by the South China Sea (*refer to **Exhibit 4***). Given the poorly developed rail and road links, air transport was seen as vital in drawing the regions closer together and accelerating the socio-economic development of the country. Many governments in developing countries viewed the airline industry as having a direct bearing on the development process, providing foreign exchange, creating employment and fostering technology transfer. Shamin Ahmad, who joined MAS in 1972 and was currently the Director of International Sales, commented:

> With MSA, Singapore was being developed as an aviation hub with all the related technologies, and the Singaporeans were only interested in expanding internationally. The Malaysian government decided that we should have our own objectives and be able to develop ourselves domestically. As well, the government saw the development of aviation as a way to develop Malaysia's manpower and managerial skills. If we had not split apart, today we would probably only be feeding services into Singapore.
>
> Back in 1972, we were not so ambitious. We had to start from scratch. As most MSA employees were Singaporean, they all joined SIA. We took in a lot of people, and we had teething problems for the first two years. We didn't have the expertise or the people to maintain a fully-fledged international operation, so we began by developing domestic routes and operating regional services to Jakarta, Hong Kong, Manila, Singapore and later Bangkok.
>
> In 1974, we began looking at international routes to Taipei, Tokyo, Sydney and London. We couldn't expand rapidly because of traffic rights constraints. It took a long time to negotiate traffic rights. Sandwiched between Singapore and Bangkok, which had a head start on us, it was hard

for the Malaysian Ministry of Transport to interest other governments in exchanging traffic rights. In fact, many airlines had found that they could serve the Malaysian market from Singapore.

The Malaysian government was the airline's controlling shareholder, holding 42% of the stock through the central bank, Bank Negara. Long See Wool, Principal Assistant Secretary in the Aviation Division in the Malaysian Ministry of Transport, remarked:

> The Malaysian government has put significant resources into developing an airport network. We have four international airports, another one in the design stage as part of the Sixth Malaysia Plan, and a number of minor points operating on a hub-and-spoke system so that people from other parts of the country can reach each other. We have several airstrips, which were developed for tourism-related reasons, and we have 13 rural airports. For a small country, we have a substantial, comprehensive, well-developed airport network. In fact, we have too many airports; every state has one.
>
> Initially, MAS was to operate services in Peninsular Malaysia. Then it became important for economic and political reasons to link East and West. The majority of the population in Sarawak and Sabah is not ethnically Malay. Integration was a real issue. We have succeeded in bringing Kuala Lumpur closer to Kuching and Kota Kinabalu in this sense.

Thus, from its inception, MAS had been expected to fulfil a range of political objectives. David Yong, Strategic Planning Manager, noted:

> In 1985, MAS was partially privatized. We needed capital and we had gone to the government for an injection. At the time, both the government and the airline wanted to reduce the burden on national activities and get more private funding. Increasingly, the government has been trying to encourage the private sector to take over certain activities because then there is a better chance of acquiring foreign technology.
>
> The government is still an important stakeholder in our operation and expects MAS to provide certain political and social services for the country. Judging from the pattern of requests and the responses that MAS gets about certain aspects of its operations, there has yet to be any fundamental changes in the government's expectations of us. MAS cannot do things very differently from what has been done before. Sometimes we have to go along with the government's political objectives, which may not correspond to commercial objectives. At the same time, our shareholders want a return on their investment.

Long See Wool commented:

> MAS operates services at three levels: international, domestic and rural. MAS is not strictly a commercial operation. MAS understands that it will have to subsidize domestic routes with revenue derived from the company's international operations. This is in exchange for being given a monopoly

on ground handling. The rural services are definitely a loss. There is a formula by which the airline can apply to the government for a subsidy in each financial year. Domestically, the tariff is controlled by the government and a review is possible every 3–4 years.

After a 10-year freeze on domestic airfares, the government had granted increases of 15–20% – effective in July 1992, to offset rising operational costs and alleviate the airline's projected loss of RM 241 million on its domestic operations for 1991–92. MAS officials maintained that the increase was necessary as the airline was being suffocated by escalating overhead costs, purchases of new aircraft, maintenance of existing planes and fuel costs.

MAS' Domestic Activities

MAS carried over 7 million domestic passengers each year. Domestic routes accounted for 26% of corporate revenues (*refer to* **Exhibit 5**). Tan Kok Khon, Regional Manager for Peninsular Malaysia and Singapore, remarked:

> Peninsular Malaysia and Singapore – MAS' 'home base' – is the heaviest production area domestically. Overall, MAS' sales strategy is to have an equal emphasis on domestic and international routes. We've been seeing good growth, but times are a bit tough right now. Compared to other areas in the region, Malaysia has a strong economic base. We have not yet reached our full potential.

Most of MAS' domestic flights were out-and-back to individual points, although some were multi-sector, calling in at several small towns both inbound and outbound from Kuala Lumpur (*refer to* **Exhibit 6**). Some flights integrated Singapore as an intermediate stop and were considered to be international flights.

Between 1986 and 1991, domestic scheduled passenger traffic in Malaysia had increased steadily at an average annual rate of 17.1%, reaching upwards of 3.8 million passengers. IATA had forecast that domestic traffic would grow by 15% each year between 1991 and 1996, and 8% and 6% during the periods 1996–2001 and 2001–2006 respectively, to exceed 15 million passengers.[2] This growth was linked to an expected surge in tourism to Malaysia, especially to the Penang area, and the strong economic development of various parts of the country, particularly in Johor. The formation of the 'Nusa Tiga Growth Triangle', combining Johor's strategic location for resource-based industries, Singapore's status as a newly industrializing country and the abundance of labour in Batam, Indonesia, was described by one observer as "the most exciting economic concept in South-East Asia."

In the period following IATA's forecast, the growth of domestic traffic in Malaysia actually dropped from 18% to 3.7%. A reduction in timber quotas and less logging had resulted in less traffic in Sabah and Sarawak since July 1992.

---

[2] *Kuala Lumpur Airport Traffic Forecast, 1991–2006*, prepared by the International Air Transport Association in November 1992.

The decline in passenger growth was also seen to reflect a general slowdown in the Malaysian economy, which had been expanding at a rate of more than 8% annually over the past five years.

Recently, the Malaysian government had initiated talks with a group of interested parties, including several state investment bodies, about setting up a second airline to operate mainly on domestic routes. One view was that MAS "was expanding so fast that it had become overstretched." The new airline could be based on Pelangi Air, a small carrier which already operated on some domestic and regional routes. David Yong observed:

> MAS has a voice in these discussions. The scope of a second airline has yet to be decided, as well as the concessions. Such an operation could deprive MAS of opportunities in the future, but we don't really know at the moment.
>
> By definition, our large domestic network cannot be operated on a commercial basis. We can only try to reduce the losses, by decreasing the frequency of flights. Recently, for example, we've cut down the level of daily flights from KL to Kuching from 18 to 15. It is not really possible to decouple the domestic operation from our international routes. These services are scheduled to mesh with domestic arrivals and departures.

The Airline's International Network

In 1993, MAS operated into 53 foreign destinations. The Malaysian government had negotiated air traffic agreements with 63 countries and expected to have signed about 100 air accords by the end of the decade. Long See Wool remarked:

> Air links are the first links between governments. Any economic and cultural cooperation starts with air links. The negotiation of air traffic agreements is part of the government's strategy to enhance bilateral relationships, and the airline is an important part of this strategy. With good air links, we can achieve an increase in trade and investment, which will give us the political and economic strength to play a more prominent role in world affairs.
>
> At present, we are keen to establish South–South links. For instance, we would like to link Kuala Lumpur with Mexico City, Buenos Aires and Johannesburg. For each country, we ask MAS to do a feasibility study. The viability of the service is crucial in the final analysis.

MAS' international operations accounted for almost 74% of total revenues and were set up on a route basis:

- Orient/America;

- Europe/Australia;

- Asia/Africa.

MAS carried close to 5 million passengers on scheduled international flights (*refer to* **Exhibit 7**). More than half of international traffic was recorded to and from the rest of South-East Asia. With 22 flights daily in each direction, Kuala

Lumpur–Singapore was the most important route, accounting for over 40% of MAS' international traffic. IATA had forecast that international traffic would grow at an annual average rate of 10.2% between 1991 and 1996, and 8% and 7.3% during the periods 1996–2001 and 2001–2006, respectively, to exceed 17 million passengers.[3]

MAS in the Cargo Business

In 1991, MAS had carried close to 300,000 tonnes of freight (*refer to* **Exhibit 7**). Cargo traffic in Malaysia was expected to increase to 1,320,000 tonnes by the year 2006. Currently, MAS operated several Boeing 737s as cargo aircraft both domestically and regionally, and would take delivery of a Boeing 747 in 1993 as part of its strategy to tap into the burgeoning air cargo market. The airline had identified five key cities in Asia and Europe, and was keen to launch full-freighter service to Los Angeles, New York, Amsterdam, London and Hong Kong. MAS hoped to increase its capacity to current destinations as well.

Over the past few years, it was felt that significant revenue from air cargo services had been lost to foreign carriers that passed through Subang with substantial payload transported on to Singapore. Recently, MAS' newly established cargo services planning department had launched a major promotional campaign aimed at strengthening the image of Kuala Lumpur as a hub for international operations. Shamin Ahmad elaborated:

> Domestically, the growth of the cargo market depends a lot on the economic development of Malaysia. The government is providing incentives for the development of a special industrial zone near Sepang for manufactured goods, like electronics, that can be shipped by freight. The government is also planning to revise the air cargo tariff later this year. One of the visions behind the development of KLIA is to make Kuala Lumpur a major cargo transshipment area for the Asia-Pacific region.

Construction of a New International Airport

In 1965, the Malaysian government built an international airport in the Klang Valley, 30 kilometres from Kuala Lumpur's city centre. At the time, Subang had the longest runway in the region, and the Prime Minister was subjected to substantial public criticism. The initiative required taking land away from the nearby Rubber Research Institute (RRI) at a time when rubber was the country's main lifeline.

Long See Wool recalled:

> The development around Subang was not controlled in any way. Housing estates were developed, townships were formed and whole industries sprang

---

[3] *Kuala Lumpur Airport Traffic Forecast, 1991–2006,* prepared by the International Air Transport Association in November 1992.

up. In the meantime, Subang was upgraded and a second terminal was added. In 1982, we looked at the alternatives for future expansion and concluded that a second runway would have to be built to go beyond the existing capacity, which meant acquiring more land. With the Royal Malaysian Airforce Base located opposite the existing runway, we had only one other choice. The RRI stalled the runway plan with arguments that Malaysia would lose its competitive edge and the rubber industry would die.

By 1989, Subang was experiencing heavy congestion and problems with ground management, terminal building services and flight scheduling. We looked at the situation again and decided to build more parking apron, as well as add a third terminal, which will be completed in 1994. Again, the RRI objected, but now rubber is not so vital for Malaysia. We are third after Indonesia and Thailand, and our manufacturing sector is also expanding. We know that this is only a temporary solution. By 1997, we anticipate that there will be 16.7 million passengers travelling through Kuala Lumpur each year.

It is clear that we need to construct a new international airport to transform Kuala Lumpur into a gateway to the region. It's not a question of building or not building; it's only a question of when. Subang is inefficient because of the way it has been upgraded in a piecemeal fashion. To expand Subang, we would have to acquire land to replace the RRI's existing plots, and they would lose years of technology. Ultimately, it's hard to quantify the cost. Subang already exceeds international standards on noise pollution and, with further construction, it's possible that the government would have to pay out compensation. KLIA is key in moving growth out of the congested Klang Valley. If we wait, the property will be more difficult and more expensive to obtain. Already, there has been tremendous speculation around Sepang, and much of the land has been bought up by the private sector.

If we want Kuala Lumpur to be a competitive hub in the region, then we can't stay in Subang. Today, we're losing a lot of traffic to Singapore and Bangkok. The development of KLIA will be key to our ability to attract foreign airlines into Kuala Lumpur. KLIA will accelerate our prospects for obtaining reciprocal traffic rights. In this way, MAS can also grow.

KLIA to Open in 1997

In February 1993, the Malaysian government approved the plan submitted by a consortium of consultant firms to construct a new international airport 80 kilometres outside Kuala Lumpur. Costing some RM20 billion, KLIA was the largest project ever undertaken by the government and was expected "to become a central piece of economic infrastructure acting as a catalyst for Malaysia's future growth." Malaysian Transport Minister, Dr Ling, commented:[4]

---

[4] 'Mastering a Grand Take-off', *Business Times*, 9 July 1992.

KLIA is expected to look 'very Malaysian'. Once the passengers land, they'll know it's Malaysia, and not somewhere else. They'll see lots of greenery inside the airport itself, even right next to the runways... On completion, KLIA will be one of the best airports in the region in terms of aesthetics, design, engineering and user-friendliness.

Sited on 100,000 hectares and developed on a modular basis, KLIA would ultimately be able to accommodate 100 million passengers annually. The RM 10 billion first phase of the Sepang facility would consist of:

- two parallel staggered runways;

- a mega-terminal building complex and satellite to serve 25 million passengers and 7,000 peak hour passengers;

- an integrated complex with sheds, bonded warehouses and customs facilities, to accommodate 1 million metric tonnes of cargo.

In addition, a north–south expressway was to be constructed between Kuala Lumpur and KLIA, with a journey time of 40 minutes. As well, a 30-minute express rail link between the two points was to be built. Long See Wool commented:

> We are still debating whether or not we should copy the Singapore/Changi model. While airports traditionally have a 'stadium effect' with inefficient disembarking and long processing lines in customs, Changi provides a roomy 'hotel lobby' atmosphere. Changi has $54\,m^2$ per passenger. They could even close down Terminal 1 and still operate. They are providing luxury, but it has a cost.
>
> The success of Changi is that Singapore is Changi, and Changi is Singapore. Singapore only has aviation and shipping, and they only have Singapore to offer, whereas Malaysia has many destinations. Malaysia has a strong primary sector and good potential for manufacturing. Do we want to take Singapore's approach and divert all our financial and human resources into developing the aviation industry, or do we take the middle-of-the-road approach and provide a sufficient level of service?
>
> The question has been asked: 'If Changi is a good airport, why not use it as a hub for the ASEAN region, in light of the developments globally?'. But it's a question of pride. And we have our own ideas that we want to project.

Financing the KLIA Project

The Malaysian government was funding the core facilities through the creation of a corporate entity. The private sector was expected to contribute upwards of RM1.5 billion in constructing hotels, car parks, cargo operations, airline offices and so on. Long See Wool elaborated:

> The private sector isn't interested in investing in an existing airport. It's only when you're building a new airport and looking at it as a development project

that people become interested. With a new site, we can plan for the longer term, and we can get substantial private sector involvement from businessmen, contractors and investors to spearhead economic growth.

As well, we have the possibility of obtaining foreign funding through soft loans and grants from the British and Japanese governments. The National Employee Pension Fund is cash rich and could provide substantial funding. Some of the land around Subang that is not useful for aviation purposes could be commercialized, and the proceeds could be put towards KLIA. It is doubtful how much MAS could contribute.

When MAS begins operating in Sepang, it will have to invest in infrastructure and buildings, and the company will have to pay landing costs and a higher tariff than at present. We'll be looking for a return on our investment. Today, MAS is being subsidized, paying rates well below the commercial level. There's no turning back. MAS cannot continue to be protected as an infant industry. Monopoly is a bad thing, and it's a growing problem for Malaysia. Companies cannot become efficient in this way. Organizations become complacent. We don't want MAS to continue to use its responsibility for domestic and rural services as an excuse.

Other Regional Airport Projects

Currently, several airports were under construction or expansion to alleviate the increasing airport and airspace congestion in the Asia-Pacific region. Together, Taiwan, Japan, South Korea, Thailand, Malaysia and Hong Kong were investing more than US$30 billion in airport facilities and related infrastructure. As an example, in the spring of 1993, the Thai cabinet approved a plan to build a second international airport in Bangkok at a cost of US$3.2 billion. The Nong Ngu Hao airport would handle 20 million passengers annually by the year 2000, and 55 million passengers by 2020 at the project's completion. Bangkok's existing Don Muang airport – which handled 17 million passengers and was undergoing renovations to accommodate 25 million passengers annually – was expected to reach its full capacity by the turn of the century.

The new airport was part of Thailand's Seventh National Economic and Social Development Plan, which aimed to enhance the country's role as a leading economic, financial, trade and investment hub in South-East Asia. At present, 63 international airlines operated to and through Thailand's four international airports. Although Thailand received fewer tourists in total numbers than the leading Asia destinations – Hong Kong and Singapore – the average length of stay for visitors to Thailand was 7.09 days, twice as long as either of the other two.[5] Akira Kato, IATA's Regional Director for Asia/Pacific, remarked:

The airports in the region under construction or renewal will not be able to compete with Changi within the next five years. They are all having problems

---

[5] 'Sky's the Limit for Asia-Pacific', *Business Times*, 23 November 1992.

acquiring enough land. Also, in some instances, the development of aviation is really not well coordinated. In the case of Malaysia, for example, the country has oil reserves, tin, rubber, timber and huge offshore natural gas supplies; the government's resources and attention are thus spread across a range of priorities. Moreover, different parts of the Malaysian government have different views on airport development. Also, if you do something for one state, you have to give something to all 13 states.

MAS cannot do the same thing as SIA, although it might like to. Singapore is a city state with 2 million people, oriented to transit traffic. MAS has to rely more on the Malaysian market and they have many domestic points. In Kuala Lumpur, flight schedules are not set according to the needs of transit passengers. In Malaysia, each state takes precedence over transit traffic.

Singapore Airlines and Changi Airport

From a fledgling airline in 1972, SIA had grown at a rate substantially ahead of that achieved by its competitors, currently ranking among the world's top 20 airlines. The construction and operation of Changi airport had transformed Singapore into a major tourist destination in South-East Asia and an easy and logical point for onward travel. According to the Civil Aviation Authority of Singapore (CAAS), 40% of passengers travelling through Changi were in transit to destinations beyond Singapore. Few airlines could boast the full realm of SIA's comparative advantages: a superb hub at Singapore, a supportive government, location in a fast-growth region, expanding frequencies and destinations, unutilized route licences in hand, an established successful image, one of the youngest fleets in the world, a good order book attractively priced, a strong balance sheet with no debt and reasonable asset backing.[6] SIA management's single-minded focus on productivity had enabled the company to reap significant gains over its competitors in terms of revenue per employee (*refer to* **Exhibit 8**). Akira Kato remarked:

> Singapore has no natural resources. The development of Changi is intimately linked to the development of Singapore. Changi is an easy-to-transit airport with an excellent timetable and excellent amenities. There are reasonable operating charges for the close to 60 airlines that currently fly into Changi, and SIA benefits the most from this situation. SIA has only one point and a small home market. It relies heavily on 6th freedom traffic. With its management style and small range of aircraft – which translates into savings in crew and maintenance, the company can make changes quickly. However, Singapore is becoming a more expensive city and losing its cost advantage over Bangkok, Jakarta and Kuala Lumpur.
>
> With the new airport development, the Malaysian government is hoping to transform KL into a major regional hub. Like Singapore, Hong Kong has long benefited as a gateway to South-East Asia. By air, Singapore is not

---

[6] James Capel (Investment Analyst), Sydney, Australia, 1989.

naturally in the centre of activities in the region. Actually, Bangkok is the best distribution point geographically. Kuala Lumpur and KLIA would have a medium advantage.

KLIA's Implications for MAS

As the major user of KLIA, MAS would be hit the hardest by increased landing charges and space costs. At the same time, the airline would have to invest about RM 200 million in hangars, cargo buildings, flight kitchens and other support facilities in Sepang. Shamin Ahmad observed:

> KLIA can only be an asset for MAS. What we have at Subang are all of the constraints and none of the opportunities. Currently, many people destined for Malaysia are travelling from Singapore because of the number of flights, the fact that many airlines operate there and Changi is a good airport. With a modern airport, we can provide good passenger movement in a way that is not possible at Subang, which was built on an *ad hoc* basis. In Subang, the minimum connecting time (MCT) for international flights is 1 hour, and 1 hour and 45 minutes for domestic flights. Our aircraft utilization is not very good at the moment. You have to be in the air to make money, and now our planes are spending more time on the ground. In Sepang, our goal is to bring the MCT down to 45 minutes.
>
> The airlines that come in and out of Sepang will take some of our market share on certain routes, but the total traffic level will be higher, so we are not particularly worried. With the service we provide, we are confident that MAS will still benefit. With KLIA, we will be able to retrieve the domestic passengers currently going down to Singapore to travel out and beyond. Moreover, as Malaysia develops, KLIA will be able to draw heavily on our own population base.

David Yong commented:

> The government has a big task ahead. They have to take the lead and show that it is advantageous to fly to Kuala Lumpur. We need to get a critical mass in KLIA. It will not necessarily be easy to increase Sepang's business, because the airlines will compare the options with wherever they are already established in the region. One question that we will have to confront is, are we doing anything more than just transferring our competitors from Singapore to next door?

The Break-up of Ground Handling

There was speculation that when KLIA became operational in 1997, MAS would lose its monopoly over ground service activities. Bashir Ahmad, Director of Corporate Planning, commented:

> If we no longer are able to monopolize ground handling, we'll do things differently. If we have to compete, we'll set these activities up in subsidiaries.

Then, these profit centres won't have to take the burden of our costs. Five cross-functional teams are looking into this at the moment, and they should complete their studies by the end of 1993. We're targeting the implementation for 1995.

Repositioning Subang as a Service Centre in the Region

To cope with the move to Sepang, MAS had proposed using and marketing Subang Airport as a major service centre for international carriers. As part of the current upgrading of Subang, the airline had invested over RM 125 million to construct service hangars, and aircraft engineering and maintenance facilities. As the world's largest operator of Boeing 737s, MAS had developed significant inhouse expertise in maintaining these particular aircraft. MAS had also established a joint venture with a German firm to carry out engine blade maintenance as an early step towards value-added services. Shamin Ahmad elaborated:

> Because of the breadth of our services, we maintain a broad range of aircraft, which translates into high-cost service requirements. The variation drives up the cost. We need an army of engineers licensed to work on all our airplanes – unlike SIA, for instance, which only has 2–3 models of wide-body aircraft for long-haul flights.
>
> We have the capability to do everything from basic checks through to heavy maintenance because we can benefit from the economies of scale. Other airlines, however, are too small. Yet, at the moment, each airline continues to do its own maintenance. But, the current trend is to move towards more cooperation. Airlines are starting to work together to reduce costs and share the work. We're seeing many smaller carriers joining forces to get a stronger positioning.

The Pursuit of Strategic Alliances

MAS was also considering entering into a series of strategic alliances to leverage the development of KLIA and Kuala Lumpur as a major regional hub. Shamin Ahmad explained:

> We can't spread our resources too thin. We need to feed traffic to partners, and we need them to feed traffic into our network. Currently, we are looking at who would be good partners for us. Whoever we choose cannot be a direct competitor from the start. There are not too many candidates left. Many European carriers are in the preliminary stages of forming alliances. Even though they've initiated talks, it's still premature to approach them. We have to see what happens when the dust settles. We're also looking at some US carriers.

Tan Sri Abdul Aziz Abdul Rahman, MAS' former Managing Director and now an aviation consultant, remarked:[7]

> The national carrier, which is neither big nor small, cannot compete without such partnerships…In 10 years, the trend towards globalization of airlines will result in about 10–15 global airlines. The rest will become regional or niche carriers. The big ones will be able to exert their influence to gain market share through marketing strategies, and the combination of domestic and international operations. The smaller airlines cannot afford to do this. They will have to trim their costs to compete with the giants and find partners to form whatever alliances they can with those in Europe and the US…We still do not know what will happen following the EC single market. We are still in the dark about who we should talk to in order to negotiate for rights. The latest we heard was that negotiations would be carried out through a single bloc rather than individual countries. Then again, this is not definite.

Possibilities for Regional Cooperation

Currently, seven regional carriers – MAS, SIA, Garuda, China Airlines, All Nippon, Royal Brunei and Thai Airlines – participated in ABACUS in response to the rise of other large-scale computer reservation systems, like Apollo and Sabre in the US, and Galileo in the UK. Despite the trend towards consolidation and greater globalization within the airline industry generally, observers doubted that there would be any significant merger activity in the ASEAN region. Aziz stated:[7]

> It is a good concept, but it is totally out of the question because of very entrenched vested interests. Why should Singapore Airlines, for example, tie up with Garuda or Malaysia Airlines when it can form alliances with Delta of the US and Swissair? It (a merger of the ASEAN airlines) would not work out. Pooling maintenance resources and cargo movements, however, could be explored.

Recently, MAS, SIA and Cathay Pacific had joined together to launch *Passages*, a frequent flier programme for first and business class. Beginning in September 1993, Swissair and British Airways would participate in the programme as well. Following the North American model, the intention was to also strike agreements with non-airline partners, like hoteliers, credit card companies, car rental agencies, etc. Akira Kato, IATA's Regional Director for Asia Pacific, reflected:

> There are some things being done in a cooperative way, but it's limited. The differences here are bigger than among the Europeans. Much of this stems from the varying stages of economic development. What would give ASEAN

---

[7] Aziz: 'Strategic Alliances, the Buzzword in Aviation Industry', *Business Times*, 1 October 1992.

carriers some economies for regional strength is the selection of a common aircraft engine and the tooling of spare parts.

There needs to be better coordination in the ASEAN region, on scheduling, ticketing, the distribution system, and so on. Cooperation would facilitate more detailed planning, and the airlines could increase their efficiency, and minimize the waste from all the trial and error programmes being launched. The tradition has been that, if you try one programme – for example, wide seats in business class – and it fails, you try another – more leg room. But, the airlines can't keep going down this road. It's hard to measure and evaluate the results.

Taking MAS into the Future

Following a consultant's report in late 1992, MAS implemented a new organizational structure to facilitate its aspirations for expansion and to "support the company's renewed vigour in providing service excellence in fulfilling customer needs." This was the first major reorganization since MAS' formation two decades earlier. As part of the restructuring, the marketing function and domestic operations were given increased emphasis, and a Strategic Planning Department was created. David Yong, who headed the area, remarked:

> We're now in the process of building up our strategic planning capabilities. The challenge has been to delineate a new role, to understand where we could create a new purpose. For now, my group will look at fleet planning and business information. Beyond this, a lot still needs to be defined.
>
> We've never had a very formalized corporate planning process. We had a Planning Division, but the work mostly revolved around the fleet plan, which was about the only formal long-range planning document available within the company. This was used as a guide for manpower planning, investment, and so on. The fleet plan is more of an operational than a strategic document. The last time there was a comprehensive review was in 1988–89. Somehow, the planning mechanism has been too cumbersome. There has been a lot of internal criticism, especially from the Engineering Department. Their main complaint has been the rate of expansion over the past five years. 1988 was a threshold year, when we began to feel greater pressure for profitability. 1989 to 1991 were years of fast growth for us. The rate at which we bought or leased aircraft and brought in ex-patriate pilots was unprecedented. The Engineering Director just couldn't cope. There were not enough engineers to maintain the range of aircraft. This level of growth was not projected in the 1988 fleet plan, yet the growth continued. This has a lot to do with the way the MAS culture expresses itself.

Top Management Holds a Brainstorming Session

In early December 1992, senior management, together with the Board, held a 2-day workshop to determine the company's mission and vision. An integral part of this session involved identifying MAS' strengths and weaknesses, and formulating strategies to alleviate threats and leverage new opportunities. Shamin Ahmad commented:

> Compared to other ASEAN carriers, MAS has lower operating costs. We have excellent inflight service and a good frequency rate of flights out of Kuala Lumpur, serving every major regional point at least once daily. However, our operating costs are increasing, and manpower is the major cost for the airline. The rate of economic development, together with a potential labour shortage, could drive wages up even further. We are looking at ways to mechanize systems that are labour-intensive. It's also possible to outsource. For instance, both Cathay Pacific and SIA are outsourcing revenue accounting to China and Bombay, respectively. As well, we need to make better use of information technology to reach more consistent decisions. Many people have been in the company for 20 years and have everything in their heads. But, a new generation is coming along and they don't operate in this way.
>
> In the short term, the priority is to increase profitability. The airline business is cyclical and tied to the health of the world economy. In a recession, travel is the first area to be cut. We're also facing competition from more destinations. Many countries are promoting tourism to generate foreign exchange. The question is how to position Malaysia as a tourist destination. In the past, MAS had the luxury of being the basic means of transport throughout most of the country. Now, competing forms of domestic transportation have been improved. Many people are using the roads and railway systems.

Tan Kok Khon added:

> Right now, airlines that do a lot of 5th and 6th freedom traffic are looking hard for ways to fill available seats. SIA, for instance, has massive capacity available, so the management is discounting prices heavily and going for the numbers regardless of yield. The company doesn't appear to be making decisions for economic reasons; the intent seems to be more predatory. Do we try to maintain prices and keep what we have, or do we set prices to increase revenues?

David Yong also commented:

> We need to ensure that our costs are under control. A Board Finance Committee was recently set up, and the issue is constantly being monitored. We need to manage our costs so that we can pass through the next two years of the reorganization phase.

Bashir Ahmad offered his view of the current issues facing MAS and the kind of action that would be required:

> Traffic is lower in this financial year, and the challenge is how to cope with the downturn. For many years, our planes and activities were geared to growth. We asked people to work towards targets. Now, we need to change

the way we work. But it takes time to change the mindset; it takes time to comprehend, adjust and act. Now, we also have excess aircraft. We are trying to sell off some planes, but there is too much capacity in the market.

We'll also have to undertake cost reductions, which could mean reducing our work force from the current level of 20,000. We don't have a retrench-ment policy. This is strongly in our culture. At present, our labour costs give us an advantage over European and North American airlines, but the gap is narrowing. We will have to increase our productivity and have less staff doing more work.

EXHIBIT 1

Fleet Expansion Plan (October 1992)

Aircraft type	1992–93	1993–94	1994–95	1995–96**
B747-200	3	*		
B747-400P	3	7	10	11
B747-400C	2	2	2	2
B747-300C	1	1	*	
DC10-30	6	6	4	*
A300B4	4	4	*	
A330	–	–	5	10
B737-200/400/500	37	47	54	59
B737-200F/300F	1	1	2	*
F50	12	12	12	12
DHC-6	6	7	7	7
Total	75	87	96	101

* Phase out.
** Includes options aircraft.

Source: MAS' Corporate Planning Department.

EXHIBIT 2

Selected 5-year Statistics for MAS (for financial years ending 31 March)

	1987–88	1988–89	1989–90	1990–91	1991–92	1992–93
Capacity (million tonne-km)	1,430	1,579	1,994	2,430	3,083	3,316
Load (million tonne-km)	1,101	1,214	1,390	1,675	2,032	2,086
Overall load factor (%)	77	76.9	69.7	68.9	65.9	62.9
Cargo carried (thousand tonne-km)	352,080	376,316	439,763	602,353	740,124	N.A.
Passengers carried (million pax-km)	7,828	8,932	10,514	12,237	14,929	6,054**
Passengers carried (000)	6,138	6,811	7,873	9,382	10,976	11,593
Passenger load factor (%)	75.9	77.7	74.1	70.9	69.2	67.3
Average employee strength	11,249	11,928	14,013	16,149	17,869	19,783
Revenue per employee (RM000)	144	163	171	182	201	N.A.

* These data do not correspond precisely to those in Exhibit 7 as MAS' fiscal year ends on 31 March, and the data submitted to IATA cover the period 1 January–31 December.
** Available passenger capacity (million pax-km) was 23,862.

Source: MAS Annual Reports.

EXHIBIT 3

Selected Financial Data for the Period 1 January – 31 December 1991 (in $US millions, unless otherwise indicated[1])

	MAS	SIA	Thai Airways	Garuda Indonesia	Philippine Airlines	Cathay Pacific
Operating revenues (RM million)	3,584[2]	3,002	1,807	1,319	N.A.	2,684
Operating expenses (RM million)	3,546	2,343	1,863	1,207	N.A.	2,216
Operating result (RM million)	110.8[3]	659	−56	112	N.A.	468
Net result (RM million)	192.5[4]	539	−201	62	N.A.	378
Total staff	17,482	14,219	18,507	11,867	12,830	12,749

[1] In 1991, US$1 = RM2.724 = Singapore Dollar 1.6305 = Thai Bhat 25.28 = Indonesian Ruplah 1,992 = Philippine Pesos 26.65 = Hong Kong $7.8 [Source: MIF International Financial Statistics].
[2] From MAS Annual Report, year ending 31 March 1992.
[3] Profit after tax and extraordinary items.
[4] Profits available, including unappropriated profits brought forward.

Source: IATA, World Air Transport Statistics, data submitted for the period 1 January–31 December 1991, and MAS Annual Report.

EXHIBIT 4

MAS' Corporate Objectives

1. To provide the people of Malaysia with an efficient and profitable air transport system which enhances the standing of the Nation and the policies of its Government.
2. To develop an efficient domestic service within Malaysia which also directly links East and West Malaysia and contributes to the economic and social integration of the country as a whole.
3. To provide simultaneously competitive and profitable international services which support Malaysia's trade, tourist and other activities.
4. To select, train and develop personnel using the most up-to-date and appropriate managerial techniques.
5. To contribute meaningfully to national aspirations and foster an organization which is in harmony with the multi-racial objectives of Malaysia.

EXHIBIT 5

Revenues Derived from MAS' Domestic and International Operations for Years Ending 31 March (in RM million)

Sector	1988–89	1989–90	1989–91	1991–92	1992–93
Domestic	327	398	507	606	749
International	1,127	1,382	1,712	2,150	2,121
Total	1,454	1,780	2,219	2,756	2,870

Source: MAS.

Casewriter's note: Although revenue figures were available for MAS' domestic and international sectors, the Airline did not separate out its costs in such a manner. Correspondingly, MAS did not have staff dedicated to serve just the domestic or international sectors. Thus, it was not possible to obtain the percentage of profits contributed by the domestic and international operations.

EXHIBIT 6

Characteristics and Constraints of MAS' Domestic Operations

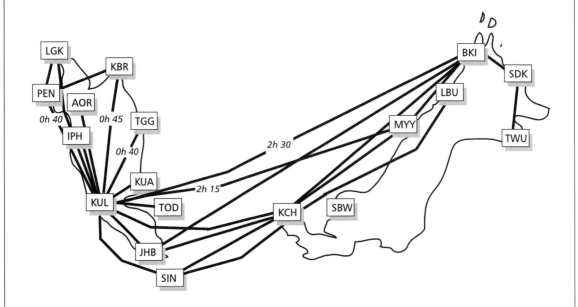

- The majority of the domestic flights in 1992 were straight out-and-back to individual points, but a number of them were also multi-sector, calling in at several small towns both inbound and outbound from Kuala Lumpur. There were a few flights integrating Singapore as an intermediate stop. However, these flights were considered as international.

- The shortest flight is a 20-minute flight linking Kuala Lumpur to Kuantan (KUA). The longest flight is a 2 h 30 min flight linking Kuala Lumpur to Kota Kinabalu (BKI).

- The highest frequencies were recorded between Kuala Lumpur and Penang (PEN) (12 flights in each direction during the 'busy' day), followed by Kuala Lumpur–Johor Babur (JHB) (7 flights) and Kuala Lumpur–Ipoh (IPH) (6 flights).

- The position of Kuala Lumpur, at the centre of the axis Penang–Johor Nahru, two major cities in Peninsular Malaysia, favours the development of either flights transiting through Kuala Lumpur, or domestic connections in Kuala Lumpur. The national airline opted for the second solution. The needs for providing suitable connections led to the development of connecting waves between domestic arrivals and domestic departures.

- In the domestic network, priority is given to the maximization of frequencies, rather than the opening of new direct links, for example, between Sabah, Sarawak and the northern part of Peninsular Malaysia. This strategy will inevitably strengthen the needs for connections and thus contribute to the building-up of peaks at Kuala Lumpur airport.

EXHIBIT 6 (continued)

- Importance is also given to the needs for connections between international and domestic flights. Although there may be cases where additional international direct services will be provided out of regional airports such as Penang, Kota Kinabalu, etc., the majority of international traffic originating or terminating in cities other than Kuala Lumpur will continue to be channelled through Kuala Lumpur's Subang Airport. It means that there will still be a requirement for providing connection possibilities between international arrivals and domestic departures, and vice versa.

- The current lack of aircraft parking positions in Kuala Lumpur airport has forced the national carrier to overnight a large number of aircraft away from base. This situation has led to a massive number of domestic arrivals in the morning (between 8:00 a.m. and 10:00 a.m.) and a concentration of evening departures. Under an unconstrained environment, it is expected that there will be more aircraft overnighting in Kuala Lumpur, thus resulting in a higher proportion of morning departures and late evening arrivals in the future than in 1991.

Source: *Kuala Lumpur Airport Traffic Forecast Study*, prepared by the International Air Transport Association in November 1992.

EXHIBIT 7

Profiles of Selected Asian Airlines – for the Period 1 January–31 December 1991

Scheduled services	MAS			SIA		
	International	Domestic	Total	International	Domestic	Total
Kilometres flown (thousands)	59,788	38,030	97,818	135,280	0	135,280
Aircraft departures (number)	32,684	113,122	145,806	44,904	0	44,904
Hours flown (number)	87,461	88,327	175,788	172,841	0	172,841
Freight tonnes carried (number)	172,063	55,482	227,545	325,558	0	325,558
Passengers carried (number)	4,662,007	7,175,734	11,847,741	7,745,000	0	7,745,000
Passenger-kilometres flown (thousands)	11,283,928	2,941,616	14,225,544	33,461,500	0	33,461,500
Available seat-kilometres (thousands)	16,539,292	3,960,910	20,500,202	45,537,000	0	45,537,000
Passenger load factor (%)	68.20%	74.30%	69.40%	73.50%		73.50%
Tonne-kilometres performed (thousands)						
Passenger (including baggage)	968,829	242,184	1,211,013	3,182,166	0	3,182,166
Freight (including express)	678,474	34,052	712,526	1,853,864	0	1,853,864
Mail	10,423	7,380	17,803	53,261	0	53,261
Total	1,657,726	283,616	1,941,342	5,089,291	0	5,089,291
Available tonne-kilometres (thousands)	2,493,671	416,700	2,910,371	7,245,607	0	7,245,607
Overall load factor (%)	66.50%	68.10%	66.70%	70.20%		70.20%
Fleet	B747 8			B747 31		
	B373 30			A310 15		
	DC10 6					
	A300 4					
	F50 10					
	DHC6 5					
	63					
Total				46		

Note (1). MAS fiscal year ends 31 March; SIA fiscal year ends 31 March.

Source: IATA, World Air Transport Statistics, submitted for the period 1 January–31 December 1991.

EXHIBIT 7 (continued)

Scheduled services	Thai Airways			Garuda Indonesia		
	International	Domestic	Total	International	Domestic	Total
Kilometres flown (thousands)	90,674	16.534	107,208	52,691	34,097	86,788
Aircraft departures (number)	34,190	35,638	69,828	21,174	37,391	58,565
Hours flown (number)	127,770	37,675	165,445	72,352	56,226	128,578
Freight tonnes carried (number)	198,811	17,118	215,929	77,088	47,157	124,845
Passengers carried (number)	4,742,180	2,966,443	7,708,623	2,307,918	3,147,003	5,454,921
Passenger-kilometres flown (thousands)	16,553,838	1,692,584	18,246,422	9,588,893	3,119,031	12,707,924
Available seat-kilometres (thousands)	26,491,236	2,803,026	29,294,262	15,503,936	5,362,020	20,855,956
Passenger load factor (%)	62.50%	60.40%	62.30%	61.80%	58.30%	60.90%
Tonne-kilometres performed (thousands)						
Passenger (including baggage)	1,496,871	152,469	1,649,340	927,335	252,029	1,179,364
Freight (including express)	855,669	10,574	866,243	373,585	50,315	423,900
Mail	44,440	617	45,057	3,918	5,527	9,445
Total	2,396,980	163,660	2,560,640	1,304,838	307,871	1,612,709
Available tonne-kilometres (thousands)	3,762,805	323,330	4,086,135	2,344,157	636,706	2,980,863
Overall load factor (%)	63.70%	50.60%	62.70%	55.70%	48.40%	54.10%
Fleet	B747 13			B747 8		
	B737 6			B737 8		
	DC10 3			DC10 7		
	MD11 2			DC9 11		
	A300 25			A300 14		
	A310 4			F28 7		
	ATR72/42 4					
	BAe 146 6					
Total	63			55		

Note (2). Thai's fiscal year ends 30 September; Garuda's fiscal year ends 31 December.

Source: IATA, World Air Transport Statistics, submitted for the period 1 January–31 December 1991.

(continued)

EXHIBIT 7 (continued)

Scheduled services	Philippine Airlines			Cathay Pacific		
	International	Domestic	Total	International	Domestic	Total
Kilometres flown (thousands)	39,372	20,998	60,370	97,690	7,309	104,999
Aircraft departures (number)	8,776	54,389	63,165	36,828	759	37,587
Hours flown (number)	52,758	56,977	109,735	137,124	10,008	147,132
Freight tonnes carried (number)	45,541	61,741	107,282	308,043	6,101	314,144
Passengers carried (number)	1,833,030	3,605,065	5,438,095	7,167,298	223,438	7,390,736
Passenger-kilometres flown (thousands)	9,306,661	1,721,390	11,028,051	22,277,782	2,154,355	24,432,137
Available seat-kilometres (thousands)	12,963,108	2,441,231	15,404,339	30,507,435	2,677,061	33,184,496
Passenger load factor (%)	71.80%	70.50%	71.60%	73.00%	80.50%	73.60%
Tonne-kilometres performed (thousands)						
Passenger (including baggage)	973,862	132,003	1,105,865	2,125,359	205,039	2,330,398
Freight (including express)	267,377	40,205	307,582	1,398,275	58,804	1,457,079
Mail	18,656	845	19,501	61,386	5,295	66,681
Total	1,259,895	173,053	1,432,948	3,585,020	269,138	3,854,158
Available tonne-kilometres (thousands)	1,917,830	280,371	2,198,201	5,238,635	382,358	5,620,993
Overall load factor (%)	65.70%	61.70%	65.20%	68.40%%	70.40%	68.60%
Fleet	B747 9			B747 27		
	B737 9			L1011 17		
	DC10 2					
	A300 7					
	F50 10					
	BAC111 2					
	Shorts360 7					
Total	46			44		

Note (3). Philippine's fiscal year ends 31 March; Cathay's fiscal year ends 31 December.

Source: IATA, World Air Transport Statistics, submitted for the period 1 January–31 December 1991.

EXHIBIT 8

Selected 5-year Statistics for Singapore Airlines (for financial years ending 31 March)*

	1988–89	1989–90	1990–91	1991–92	1992–93
Overall capacity (million tonne-km)	5,682.7	6,280.3	6,644.3	7,624.4	8,982.3
Passenger capacity (million seat-km)	36,461.6	39,236.4	41,701.2	47,453.3	53,077.6
Overall load carried (million tonne-km)	4,223.3	4,643.5	4,715.0	5,331.2	6,086.3
Overall load factor (%)	74.3	73.9	71.0	69.9	67.8
Cargo carried (million tonne-km)	1,448.6	1,679.4	1,705.7	1,954.8	2,411.5
Passengers carried (million pax-km)	28,785.1	30,737.0	31,332.2	34,893.5	37,860.6
Passengers carried (000)	6,182	6,793	7,065	8,131	8,640
Passenger seat factor (%)	78.9	78.3	75.1	73.5	71.3
Average employee strength	11,485	12,407	13,354	14,113	11,990
Revenue per employee (S$)	371,946	381,293	344,593	355,183	428,240

*These data do not correspond precisely to those in Exhibit 7 as SIA's fiscal year ends on 31 March, and the data submitted to IATA cover the period 1 January–31 December.

Source: SIA Annual Report.

CASE 9.4   CHINA'S XFM PROJECT

This case was prepared by Research Associate Xiaobai Shen, together with Professors Stewart Hamilton, J.B. Kassarjian, Leif Sjöblom and Dominique Turpin as a basis for class discussion rather than to illustrate either effective or ineffective handling of a business situation. It is based on the work of Christian Homsy and Andreas Lusser, IMD MBA participants 1991.

In September 1996, Alex Chang, Senior Vice President of Xia Corporation was on his way from Shanghai to Hong Kong to meet with John Li, President of Xia Corporation. Chang was scheduled to present a marketing strategy for the Chinese introduction of a low-cost motorized bicycle called the 'XFM' (*refer to **Exhibit 1**, in the plate section*). Chang was very excited about the idea of producing low-cost motorized bicycles for the Chinese market. Having put together a 51–49% joint venture with the Fei-Ma Bicycle Company, a bicycle and motorcycle manufacturer in Shanghai (People's Republic of China, or 'P.R.C.'), Chang expected to bring a new concept of transportation to the world's largest bicycle market. On the same flight to Hong Kong was Wang Chung Mei, managing director of the Fei-Ma Bicycle Company and Chang's joint venture partner. The XFM, a 'powered bicycle', was to be produced in Fei-Ma Bicycle's own plant in China from an engine imported from Germany and locally supplied components and labour.

The Fei-Ma Bicycle Company

With local government support, the Fei-Ma Bicycle Corporation had been established in Shanghai in 1979 to assemble bicycle components into complete units. Ten years later, the company was privately owned and producing 140,000 bicycles a year to reach sales of Rmb49 million[1] and profits of Rmb7 million. The Fei-Ma Bicycle Corporation had 49% of the equity in the joint venture concluded with Chang. Both partners were faced with some key decisions regarding the introduction of the XFM, a basic transportation concept 'between a bicycle and a moped' that Chang had borrowed from France. The XFM project had derived its temporary brand name from the joint venture company: Xia/Fei-Ma Corporation.

The Velosolex Concept

In 1994, Alex Chang, a Shanghainese-born entrepreneur living in the United Kingdom, brought back to Asia some interesting information on the 'mythical' French Velosolex. The Velosolex concept had immediately intrigued Wang Chung

---

[1] US$1 = Rmb8.30 (the Rmb was not convertible when these events took place).

Mei, managing director of Fei-Ma Bicycle. He thought it would be a great business idea to introduce a similar model of motorized bicycle into the Chinese market. From then on, Chang and Wang began to collect all available information on the French Velosolex.

The Velosolex (or 'Solex' as the French called it) was a simple, inexpensive and rugged motorized bicycle invented in France in the late 1940s. It had a front engine that you pushed on to the front wheel with a sort of handle while pedalling to get started, and which could easily be raised when you wanted to revert to bicycle mode. Unlike most motorized bicycles which transmitted engine movement through a chain and pinions, the 'Solex' worked through friction. A small rotating wheel under the engine applied power directly to the specially designed and reinforced front-wheel tyre. This transmission concept had the merit of being extremely simple and clean (no oily chain). Users had to pedal to help the engine keep the bicycle going on steep uphill roads.

From the early prototype version in 1941 to the final 5,000 series, numerous improvements had been made on the Velosolex. The 3,800 model, with its distinctive shape and its black colour had been the most successful product of the Velosolex family. With a 49.9 cc, 0.8 horsepower engine that used a mix of gasoline and oil, it ran at 35 km/hour. Later improvements to the engine reduced its fuel consumption to 67 km per litre and enabled it to run on unleaded fuel. Its noise level was below 65 decibels. The Velosolex had a very basic clutch and gas control located on the handle bar. The frame looked like a normal, yet reinforced bicycle. However, it was not made out of ordinary steel tubes, like most bicycles, and included many parts from pressed sheet metal. It did not feature shock absorbers on the front or rear wheels. The front wheel brakes were similar to bicycle brakes. The Velosolex was equipped with a headlight, back and warning lights.

Immediately after its launch in the French market, the Velosolex proved to be a popular mode of transportation, particularly with young urban customers (especially students, young girls and women) who enjoyed its simplicity of use and lack of 'messy/oily' parts. From May 1946 to November 1988, more than five million units were sold in France and Europe, with a peak of 380,000 units delivered in 1964. In spite of a high residual demand and a 'cult' image, the production line was closed in 1988 when the manufacturer of the Velosolex was taken over by Yamaha, Japan's second largest motorcycle producer. Between 1980 and 1995, the Velosolex manufacturing facilities had been successively owned by Velosolex, Renault, MBK, Yamaha and, more recently, by a Hungarian company named Cyclon Berstal, operated by a Mr Gathy-Kiss. In 1995, the company and manufacturing line were under juridical protection in Hungary. With Gathy-Kiss having defaulted on payments to suppliers, production of the Velosolex had stopped, despite hard evidence of strong interest, a backlog of orders, and potential distributors and buyers in developing economies.

When Chang learned that most of the patents on the Velosolex had expired or were on the verge of expiring, he bought manufacturing equipment from the administrative receiver of a bankrupted company in the Czech Republic. This Czech company was making a product similar to the Velosolex and sold to Chang all the manufacturing equipment necessary to make the equivalent of a Velosolex in the P.R.C. for a total landed cost of US$2,500,000.[2] Chang was planning to depreciate the equipment over a period of five years. The core equipment included 350 and 250 ton presses. The rest consisted of a very large number of various 10 to 80 ton presses as well as welding, moulding and state-of-the-art painting equipment. Chang had figured out that the same equipment would be worth four times this amount if purchased new. He had signed a contract to import engines from Germany until Xia/Fei-Ma Corporation was ready to produce engines on its own in the P.R.C. The German manufacturer had agreed to supply Xia/Fei-Ma with a minimum order of 75,000 units (of which 37,500 units would be shipped and payable in the first year). Chang was confident that, with sound management and hard work, there was a huge market for a concept like the XFM, both in China and in a number of emerging Asian economies.

Thanks to his many business connections in Hong Kong, Chang was confident of being able to raise more money when needed. When he met with Wang Chung Mei in 1994, he had no trouble persuading his Shanghainese friend of the huge potential of the XFM concept. For Wang, a key strategic long-term objective was to move the Fei-Ma company from bicycle to motorcycle manufacturing by the year 2005. At the time, less than 1% of the Chinese population could afford a high-priced motorcycle, but they could now develop into potential customers for motorized bicycles and later move up to more expensive Fei-Ma motorcycles. The hope was that XFM customers would build loyalty to the Fei-Ma brand. For Chang, timing for the launch of the XFM could not have been better, as the Chinese economy had been growing in double digits over the past five years. Demand for motorized vehicles was booming. Better transportation was a key priority for the Chinese government. Right now, cities like Beijing and Shanghai had respectively 570 and 350 kilometres of road per million inhabitants. This compared with 1,040 for Singapore, 1,200 for New York and 3,220 for London. Over the next 30 years China intended to build 30,000 km of roads to develop the main urban centres.[3] Road infrastructure in China was expected to grow at 2.5% per annum between 1996 and the year 2000, while economic growth was expected to run at 10% per annum until the beginning of the next century.

The Two-Wheeler Industry in China

The two-wheel vehicle industry in China was divided in four main categories:

1. The motorcycle, defined as a two-wheel vehicle with an engine bigger than 75 cc, gearbox operated with a foot lever, and manual clutch. Motorcycles above 125 cc could be driven from the age of 18 and required a special driver's licence. Sales to date of motorcycles in Shanghai alone totalled 300,000 units, and future sales were estimated to increase at 8,000–10,000 units every month.

---

[2] Landed cost included transportation and import duties.
[3] In 1996, China had one million km of roads, of which 6,000 km were Class 1 or Class 2 (i.e. paved roads, with at least two lanes in each direction).

2. Scooters, derived from the famous Italian Vespa, had engines between 50 and 125 cc, a gearbox operated by a grip on the handle bar, a frame to give water protection and two small-diameter wheels. Sales of scooters in China were estimated at 120,000 units monthly.

3. The moped was defined as a two-wheel vehicle with an engine smaller than 50 cc and a gearbox. This market could be subdivided into two categories: the mopeds as such, and the 'powered bicycles' (like the XFM), with engines applied directly to the wheel. A recent survey by the Shenzhen China Bicycle Company and Standard China Securities had found that 7% of all urban consumers intended to buy a moped within the next eighteen months.

4. Bicycles: China was the largest market for bicycles in the world. Every Chinese household had an average of 1.5 bicycles. The total annual sales of bicycles in China had reached 31.5 million in 1994 and over 19 million in the first half of 1995. The breakdown between sales of motorcycles, scooters and mopeds was difficult to estimate. Some experts estimated the size of the Chinese mopeds market at 2,300,000 units. Chang's confidence in the accuracy of Chinese statistics was limited, given the lack or unreliability of most data available.

The XFM Project

It had taken almost two years for Chang and Wang to convince suppliers, employees at the Fei-Ma Bicycle Company and all the necessary authorities that they ought to manufacture something similar to the Velosolex in the P.R.C. Provisionally, it was named the 'XFM Project', and Chang and Wang wanted everything to be ready for a formal launch in September 1996. The XFM prototypes (all with a 49 cc engine) tested by Xia/Fei-Ma Bicycle Co. had the following technical characteristics:

- 49 cc engine with a starting time of less than 15 seconds (for temperatures between $-7°C$ and $+35°C$): at the moment, the XFM was only available in black.

- Maximum speed: 35 km/hour with a 49 cc engine developing 0.8 HP and using a mix of gasolene and oil. Late improvements could enable it to run on unleaded fuel, and consumption could fall to 1.5 litre per 100 km.

- Noise level produced: better than any moped on the market today (below 65 dB[4]).

- Carbon monoxide exhaust: maximum 4%, hydrocarbons 8,800 ppm.[5]

With so much attention devoted to cars, Wang felt that it was easy to lose sight of more appropriate light urban transport – the humble two-wheeler. Wang

---

[4] dB: decibels.
[5] ppm: parts per million.

believed that, rather than cars, today's Chinese needed more motorized two-wheelers. The latter required fewer resources to produce, were fuel-efficient and, moreover, seemed like natural successors to the bicycle. On top of that, the two-wheelers were affordable, reasonably priced and convenient for traffic conditions and parking.

Among motorized two-wheelers, motorcycles that could compete with cars in speed were very attractive to prosperous urban youngsters. However, they required not only a general driver's licence with stringent requirements, but also a licence to drive in town. It was easy to obtain a licence for rural residents who drove in the countryside, but not for urban youngsters. There were also many restrictions on scooters in cities, since city governments wanted to control heavy traffic, noise and air pollution. In Wang's mind, scooters were less attractive to youngsters because of their lower speed, but more attractive to middle-aged urban dwellers and/or people less concerned with being 'fashionable'. Mopeds or powered bicycles, particularly the powered bicycle, were different from these two. Wang felt that the XFM concept would not scare away ordinary bicycle users; instead, it would be accepted as an evolution of the bicycle, requiring less physical strength by the users. Its customers could be anybody able or willing to ride a bicycle, old or young, man or woman. For the time being, government restrictions on circulation of motorized bicycles in large cities were less severe, although Wang was concerned that legislation on noise and emissions could get tougher as traffic of motorized bicycles increased. One strength of the XFM was that it made less noise than any other domestic model available on the Chinese market.

Shanghai's Potential

Wang had also searched across China for the moped market with the most potential. China was slightly larger in area than the United States, with almost six times the population. In Wang's mind, choosing the right geographic market to launch the XFM was a key strategic decision, and Shanghai seemed the logical choice because of the location of the Xia/Fei-Ma factory. However, Chang and Wang had to think about the next geographic markets to move into. Shanghai was the most important industrial, commercial and economic centre of the country. Although Guangdong province had opened economically since the reforms of the late 1970s, Shanghai remained a huge metropolitan city where people had one of the highest per capita incomes in China (estimated at the equivalent of US$1,200 in 1995).[6]

In 1996, Shanghai had 13.8 million official residents, with over eight million of those living in urban areas. North to south, the city was approximately 120 kilometres long; east to west it was 100 kilometres. As the city had become more and more crowded, downtown Shanghai in particular, many Shanghainese had moved to less crowded suburbs. Consequently, more and more people

---

[6] *Source*: Bank of China.

commuted between their homes and their workplaces. Such a trip, twice a day, could take as long as two hours each way by bus, sometimes even longer because of heavy traffic. As in other large Chinese cities, the infrastructure could not cope with economic development. As a result, major traffic jams in large cities like Shanghai were now common. Because of restrictive road conditions, Shanghai's public transportation system had long been operating at the saturation point. Every public transport user in Shanghai was skilled at getting on to a fully packed bus, finding the best position for enough air and space without irritating other passengers, and eventually getting out of the bus on time. During the cooler seasons, travelling by public transport could be fine, but in the summer, when the temperature could rise as high as 35–39°C, it could be unbearable. Traffic jams were the worst – there was no fresh air on the bus, only the smell of steamy sweat.

According to official statistics, Shanghai had more than 6.5 million bicycles in 1995.[7] A recent survey on public transportation had concluded that 31% of Shanghai residents travelled by bicycle, 24% by public transport and 41% on foot.

With improving living standards, Shanghai residents had begun to seek better transport tools. An average worker in Shanghai was now making between Rmb700 and Rmb1,000 per month and a skilled worker up to Rmb1,500. Wages for skilled workers were increasing faster than the inflation rate. With more and more multinationals operating in the Shanghai area, Wang could see a significant potential market of affluent customers for the XFM. Secretaries working for foreign joint ventures could make over Rmb50,000 a year. From the late 1980s to the early 1990s, motorcycles had become fashionable among well-off youngsters. Since there were government restrictions on the total number of motorcycles permitted in towns, a motorcycle licence plate could cost as much as Rmb18,000 in swap markets. Meanwhile, so-called 'engined bicycles', ordinary bicycles with a little engine mounted on the front or rear wheel, had started to emerge in the market. Because of low-quality and poor after-sales service, most potential consumers were waiting and looking to the further development of this market.

Since Chang and Wang had come up with the XFM concept, they had noticed an emerging market trend toward the rapid development of so-called motorized bicycles. As cars still remained a mere dream for most Shanghai residents – prices were exorbitant and parking and licensing difficulties practically insurmount-able – people had turned their attention to motorized bicycles. "Maybe the market economy very much suits the Chinese culture," Wang thought. "People have learned very fast to seek new opportunities in the market and to get things fast too."

China's Potential

Chang and Wang had big plans for the XFM. Given the size of the Chinese market (*refer to Exhibits 2 to 4*) Wang was meeting with potential partners for licensing

---

[7] Alex Chang regarded all official Chinese information and statistics with suspicion.

the production of the XFM in different parts of China. The provinces along the East Coast accounted for 72% of China's population and 77% of the P.R.C.'s GDP. GDP per capita in cities like Shenzhen was now close to the equivalent of US$2,000, while in Guangzhou, Beijing and Tianjin, it had broken the US$1,000 limit. This compared with a GDP per capita of US$666 in Indonesia (population 220 million) and US$1,800 in Thailand (population 62 million). By the year 2000, it was estimated by foreign observers that almost 250 Chinese cities would have sufficient annual income levels to support consumerism. More than 160 of these cities would have populations exceeding one million. And many would have the absolute spending power that Guangzhou had in 1995[8] (*refer to* **Exhibit 5**). Medium and large inland Chinese cities had an average income per capita of Rmb3,000, while small/medium cities were in the range of Rmb800–1,100.

Chang had also had a number of promising discussions with entrepreneurs in Pakistan and Bangladesh to export or license XFMs to these markets. The prospect of earning foreign exchange for exported XFMs had received favourable comments among Chinese officials in Shanghai and Beijing.

Major Competitors in the Two-Wheeler Industry in China

In 1996, there were already over 100 companies in China producing mopeds and motorized bicycles. Thirty-eight of these manufacturers were in Shanghai, with an estimated annual total turnover of 200,000 units.

Piaggio

Piaggio, an Italian moped manufacturer (Europe's largest motorcycle producer and the third biggest worldwide), had also set up a US$150 million joint venture in Guangdong province to build a plant and set up a distribution network of mopeds in the whole country. Piaggio had first sold imported two-wheelers into China with growing success, and had acquired significant brand awareness. Through a joint venture with a local partner, Piaggio had begun producing mopeds and scooters in 1995. Piaggio's output of mopeds and scooters in China was expected to reach 80,000 units in 1996, with anticipated sales of US$70 million, mainly in the Shanghai area and Guangdong province. With the help of a Hong Kong-based agency, Piaggio had taken its mopeds to the television screen in Shanghai with a sophisticated European style campaign. Piaggio's message was: 'Here is a product which is no longer a luxury but a daily urban necessity; Piaggio provides high quality and reliability. Piaggio mopeds are also fun and fashionable, a natural accessory of the modern, urban lifestyle'. The capacity of the Piaggio plant was estimated to be 300,000 mopeds and motorcycles per year. Neither Chang nor Wang had any estimate of the breakdown between the two product categories. Piaggio's products were positioned between 36 and 200 cc. Its 36 cc and 49 cc sold respectively for Rmb5,180 and Rmb5,980 (*refer to* **Exhibit 6**).

---

[8] GDP per capita in 1995 in Guangzhou was estimated at US$1,320.

Forever Bicycle Company

Another competitor, Forever Bicycle Company, had been one of the first Chinese companies to enter the moped market by adding a small imported engine to the Forever Bicycle frame. Relying on its long-established position in the bicycle industry, Forever Bicycle was a strong competitor with two key products: the Forever-951 (using the Japanese Zenoah's BE30-D engine) and the Forever-958 (with the American G3500 engine). In 1995, sales of these two products had reached 52,000 units per year at an average retail price of Rmb5,200 per unit. Wang had recently heard that Forever Bicycle Company was planning to decrease the price of its model with imported engines because the Chinese government had recently reduced import duties on foreign-made engines from 120 to 80% (effective 1 April 1996).

China Motorcycle Group

The 'Fire Bird', a motorized bicycle made by Jinan China Motorcycle Group (in Shandong Province), had recently become more visible in the major cities of China. Introduced in the middle of 1995 at a retail price of Rmb4,280 for the MS model, 'Fire Bird' sales had reached 12,000 units within two months. 'Fire Bird' used local components, including engines.

Other Competitors

Other players with substantial production were: Philips Zhejiang Motorcycle Ltd. and Thomos Shanghai Motor Ltd., an American joint venture with Shanghai Vacuum Electronics Ltd. Moreover, second-hand Japanese mopeds could be purchased in Shanghai for less than Rmb5,000. Because of their strong brand name and reputation for reliability and longevity, Japanese products were in high demand. Also, the XFM was not perhaps as aesthetically attractive as the Japanese model. Wang was also aware that Shanghai Phoenix Bicycle, the largest bicycle manufacturer in China (and incidentally in the world), was also building motorized bicycles under seven different brands. However, these models had not sold as well as 'Forever' and 'Fire Bird'.

Market Prospects

Most motorized bicycles sold in China were built on Shanghai bicycle frames with a tiny engine and exhaust system (produced mainly by a Japanese company, Komatsu Zenoah). Since Wang felt that cars were and would probably remain out of reach of the average Chinese family for the foreseeable future, he estimated potential sales at 600,000 units per year, although this figure was a very rough estimate and difficult to check.

Other market data (*refer to* **Exhibit 7**) collected by Chang and Wang had led them to conclude that moped sales tended to balloon when annual income rose above US$1,000. This phenomenon had occurred earlier in parts of the affluent Guangdong Province in southern China. Wang estimated that in 1995, Guangdong accounted for 10% of the country's estimated ten million plus privately owned mopeds and motorcycles.[9] In the P.R.C. as a whole, 3.42 million motorcycles and mopeds had been sold in 1995, a 70% increase over the same period of time in 1994, greatly exceeding Beijing's official production plan. In late 1995, the Ministry of the Machine Industry had announced plans to consolidate China's one hundred or so motorcycle producers into ten enterprises, each capable of producing more than half a million motorcycles per annum by the year 2000.

Government Restrictions

Owning a motorcycle in China required a number of licences. Every motorcycle owner had to pass a driving test (which required a long series of lessons). Furthermore, a registered number plate had to be bought to drive in towns. To reduce heavy traffic, serious restrictions existed in main cities like Shanghai, where a registered plate cost Rmb18,000 on average.

Scooters had been under similar government restrictions. A licensed scooter plate, at about Rmb7,000, was worth merely half that for a motorcycle. Their lower speed did not seen to limit their use in urban areas.

In 1993, the Chinese government had issued an ordinance entitled *Technical Specifications for the Two-Wheeled Vehicle Industry – QB 1839-93 Motorized Bicycles*, restricting the production and use of motorized bicycles. The ordinance introduced the following constraints:

- engine starting time should be less than 15 seconds (for temperatures between $-5°C$ and $+30°C$);

- maximum speed should not exceed 24 km/hour;

- fuel efficiency should be at least 67 km/litre;

- noise level at any speed should not exceed 72 dB;

- exhaust should meet the carbon monoxide standards: maximum 4%, hydrocarbons less than 8500 ppm.

The previous year, the Shanghai Municipality had issued its own regulations for motorized bicycles, limiting engine capacity to 36 cc, speed to 34 km/hour, fuel efficiency to 67 km/litre and wheel diameter to 51 cm (suitable for pedalling). Similar regulations also affected Beijing and Guangzhou. Chang was not confident that the technical features of the XFM would be acceptable for the Shanghai authorities. Consequently, the Fei-Ma Bicycle Corporation had obtained an option from its German engine supplier to substitute a more advanced engine for the standard design. The cost of this new engine would be 15% higher than the

---

[9] *Source: Euromonitor.*

regular engine, but it would meet the existing environmental regulations of all major Chinese cities, including Shanghai.

Wang had heard that more government restrictions were on their way in China's largest cities to ensure safety for this growing mode of transportation, to reduce exhaust pollution, and to respond to growing consumer complaints about the quality of products and services. It was expected that regulations on technical features such as speed, engine capacity, noise level, exhaust, fuel consumption and safety were likely to be tightened in the largest three Chinese cities: Shanghai, Beijing and Guangzhou. Wang estimated that smaller cities would not be affected by this type of regulation before the year 2000. These cities included about fifty large coastal cities such as Dalian, Xiamen and Tianjin as well as 95 medium/large inland cities like Jinan, Wuhan, Chengdu and Xian.

Other Potential Markets

Given increasing government regulations and intense competition in the Beijing and Shanghai areas and Guangdong province, Wang was wondering whether it would not make better sense to target Chinese rural areas where plenty of opportunities also existed. He kept remembering Chang's comment that: "China is such a huge country that you do not need to fight where all the competition is concentrated. Take Sichuan province, with a population of roughly 120 million people, it provides you with a market as large as Japan!" Wang felt that rural areas along the coast of the South China Sea were also becoming more affluent and probably offered untapped business opportunities. Saving rates in the coastal regions were over 35% (versus 29% for the rest of China).

Sixty-six million people lived around Shanghai in a radius of 300 kilometres. (Within the same radius of Beijing and Guangzhou, there was a population of 32 million.) Shanghai[10] was surrounded by two large provinces: Jiangsu in the north and Zhejiang in the south. Both provinces had sizeable and homogeneous populations (close to 70 million inhabitants for Jiangsu and over 40 million for Zhejiang – *refer to* **Exhibit 2**). Each counted about 27 sizeable urban centres with concentrated populations. Several cities, like Nanjing, Suzhou and Wuxi (Jiangsu Province) and Hangzhou, Ningbo and Wenzhou (Zhejiang Province), had more than one million inhabitants each. Jiangsu was the most densely populated province in China. It was also the province with the greatest concentration of cities and towns. Zhejiang, which meant 'zig-zag river', was the smallest province on the Chinese mainland. Hangzhou was by far the largest city in the province, with 1,695,000 people.

Hubei Province also offered interesting prospects. The focus of all interior trade for the last 500 years, Wuhan (Hubei's capital) had come to be known as 'the crossroads of the nine provinces'. Linked to Shanghai by the Yangtse River,

---

[10] Shanghai, located in Jiangsu's south-east corner, had been an independent municipality since 1958 and functioned outside the jurisdiction of Jiangsu.

Wuhan had a population of 5.3 million people. Apart from its mountainous western region, Hubei Province was also China's fifth largest grain and soya-bean producer. Although competition for the XFM was limited to a few local players, Fei-Ma bicycles distribution was limited to one department store in Wuhan. Chang had also heard rumours that Piaggio had plans to be more aggressive in this province.

Whatever area Chang decided to target, XFM growth was constrained by three key factors. First, Chinese banks, still owned by the State, were unlikely to provide loans or any form of consumer credit for the acquisition of motorized bicycles. Money supply was just too tight.[11] Second, Fei-Ma's distribution network was very much dependent on its existing network of state-owned department stores (most of Fei-Ma's distributors were located in Shanghai, plus one or two in the main cities of most provinces). Independent bicycle dealers in China were almost unknown and accounted for less than 10% of all two-wheelers sold in China. Although independent dealers were more dynamic, most of them had major credit problems. Very few distributors would offer after-sales service. As Chang explained: "This is not part yet of the Chinese mentality!" After-sales service was traditionally carried by an army of individual 'street entrepreneurs' with very limited capital and equipment who would repair tyres and fix bicycles. The third constraint was logistics. Rail in China was slow and unreliable. Freight for the People's Liberation Army often had priority over commercial goods. Trucks were 'faster' but on average eight times more costly. It typically took about ten days to ship goods by train between Suzhou and Beijing, and eight days by truck. The growth of truck registration was three times the growth of new road infrastructure, which had resulted in major traffic slowdowns. The consequences of delayed transportation were often lost customers. As Wang explained: "Although infrastructure development is a key priority for the Chinese government, traffic will get worse before it gets better."

Potential Customers

Looking more carefully at the huge size of the Chinese market, Wang had identified four potential market groups for motorized bicycles:

1. A former university colleague of Wang who was now working as a high ranking official for the Ministry of Posts and Telecommunications had suggested that something like the XFM concept was well suited for the several millions of postmen China employed around the country to deliver the mail. Indeed, the sturdy construction of the XFM, its low fuel consumption, extreme reliability and ease of service, had allowed the Velosolex to build a unique market position for many years with the French Post Office. For an extra Rmb300, two tailor-made satchels and a carrying case could be attached to

---

[11] The comparative gross domestic savings rate in China was estimated by the Asia Development Bank as 38% of Gross Domestic Product (GDP).

the back of the XFM and make the life of postmen much easier. Purchase in fleets by ministries and public utilities would ensure large-volume, very fast sales for the Xia/Fei-Ma Corporation. Fifteen per cent of the Chinese working population was employed by government agencies and public utilities, so the post office market could be extended to other government-owned fleets.

2. As more and more large cities were becoming more and more crowded, many urban Chinese had to commute from one side of the town to the other to go to work. However, the commuting distance increased as people lived further away from the centre of town, and the percentage of people walking to the office was decreasing. Wang felt that for a large majority of urban Chinese, a two-wheel vehicle was the most convenient transport. On a bicycle, Chinese commuters were rarely stopped by traffic jams, and they could cycle on even the narrowest streets or lanes. Furthermore, they were in better control of their time. In addition, bicycles were affordable for most people. In 1996, the average retail price of a bicycle was around Rmb350. The only problem in the large cities was that the distance from home to workplace was sometimes too far to manage, particularly on rainy, windy and snowy days. With the emergence of many new manufacturers of mopeds or motorized bicycles, Wang wondered whether the commuter market could reasonably continue to be treated as an undifferentiated, i.e. generic, market, and whether the time had not come to segment it further. He wondered whether the XFM would appeal to and attract specific customer groups.

3. The XFM could also be purchased by young farmers in rural areas, as their first motorized vehicle for transportation and pleasure. No restriction regarding emissions or noise existed in rural areas. Owing to its extremely rugged frame and simplicity of use and servicing, the XFM would provide the rural population with a versatile vehicle for transportation. The XFM could enable farmers to reach their far-off fields and transport a few chickens or cabbages to the nearby markets. With 90% of the Chinese population working in rural areas, this category represented the largest potential customer group for the XFM – close to 980 million potential customers. Chang estimated that the selling task for distributors would probably be a tough one since it might be the first transportation purchase for many rural customers. However, Wang felt that their effort would be worthwhile given the potential large orders that distributors could generate, at least in more developed areas with a reasonable network of dirt-roads. Selling to individual farmers or farming communities would probably take some time. Rural areas could be reached through radio and cinema advertising. Wang also felt that word of mouth would also be critical. Financing would also need to be arranged, with a down-payment of 20–30% of the retail price.

4. Chang further believed that the versatility of the XFM concept could make it ideal for rural and urban communication, a purchase by individuals or a group for all purposes including personal transportation. China was now booming with 'Township and Village Collective Enterprises' (TVCEs) being established

in almost every Chinese city and village. TVCEs were collective enterprises made up of 10 to 200 people, engaged in all kinds of semi-private business activities in small, medium and large cities where no legal restriction could challenge the circulation of XFMs. TVCEs had aroused a great deal of interest at Fei-Ma Bicycle Company, since they now made up the most dynamic sector of the Chinese economy. TVCEs were led by the local governments and displayed a very marked 'neo-localist' orientation. TVCEs tended to be relatively small and to be found in those sectors where scale economies were limited and state enterprises did not limit access to customers. TVCEs were engaged in many diverse economic activities such as construction, trade, sericulture, handicraft, etc. According to China's Township Enterprise Association, TVCEs would generate 55% of China's total industrial output by the year 2000. Wang estimated that the TVCEs were a formidable customer base. However, dealerships were often located in or near large cities, making it more difficult to reach TVCEs and sell them XFMs. At a recent fair where the XFM had been demonstrated, Wang had been pleased to meet several heads of TVCEs from Guangdong Province who wanted to place orders for the XFM as a means of transportation for their sales people. Chang felt that some of them might be worth considering as partners should he decide with his present partner to license the fabrication and distribution of the XFM.

Distribution

Wang had already talked to some potential distributors in Shanghai as well as in Jiangsu, Zhejiang and Hubei Provinces. He had convinced a distributor named Yang Xiao to start distributing the Fei-Ma products for a trial period of six months. Yang Xiao distributed a range of motorcycles with an average retail price of Rmb12,000 in two additional stores in central Shanghai and Jiangsu Province. He had a network of seven motorcycle dealers in six major cities in a radius of 100 kilometres around Shanghai, plus one in Wuhan. Yang Xiao was working hard at building a network covering China's major cities.

To target the rural areas, Wang figured out that he would have to convince small local entrepreneurs or TVCEs to turn themselves into distributors. However, with good margins and sufficient volume, Chang thought that distributing the XFM would be a golden opportunity for the 'red entrepreneurs' hungry to apply Deng Xiaoping's famous slogan: To get rich is glorious!

Chang knew that it would be more difficult to reach potential customers in rural than in urban areas. Rural inhabitants could probably be reached through a combination of radio and cinema advertising. Word of mouth was also considered a major form of information for the people in rural areas. The many large villages and small cities were considered important because they were central communities. One suggestion for reaching them was to send a travelling caravan of XFMs out to demonstrate the 'motorized bicycle' firsthand. Potential customers in urban areas, including Shanghai, were more accessible through a combination of newspapers, television and radio advertising.

Communications Budget

Chang and Wang had calculated that, in the first year, they needed a minimum of Rmb2.5 million to run an effective advertising campaign in one large urban area like Greater Shanghai. Other communication costs were estimated as follows:

Demonstrations	Rmb800,000
Lucky Draws	Rmb 65,000
Trade Rebates	Rmb428,000
Cash Incentives	Rmb356,000

However, with limited marketing experience, Wang was wondering whether these numbers would be realistic or not (*refer to **Exhibits 8 to 14** for additional information on Chinese media*). Chang thought that communications costs for the following years would have to be determined.

Potential Markets Outside China

Wang had targeted several markets outside China that offered great potential for a concept like the XFM. India, the second largest market for mopeds in 1995, was estimated at 413,000 units per year and growing at an annual rate of 30% in 1995 as compared with 1994. Pakistan, Indonesia and Vietnam were also large and growing markets. Sales of mopeds in Indonesia (282,000 units per year) and Vietnam (280,000 units per year) were growing at an annual rate of 30%.

Thanks to contacts with Western engineers he had met at Fujian University, Wang felt that Europe could also be a big potential market for the Fei-Ma Bicycle Company, mainly because congested cities and economic difficulties were forcing young students to consider a cheaper alternative to the motorcycle. Wang had gathered different information on average selling prices for mopeds in different countries. Prices for mopeds started at roughly US$750 in China, India and Vietnam for the cheapest model. He had also learned that Shanghai Phoenix Bicycles intended to introduce a cheap moped at a retail price of US$600 for both domestic and export purposes.

Chang, meanwhile, had learned that, in France, mopeds ranged from US$1,000 to 2,000 retail. This price included a 25% mark-up for the retailer and a 18.6% tax. Bicycle customer prices had reached the equivalent of US$660, and scooters started at US$2,200.

Working on the Numbers

Chang had worked out the cost structure of the XFM operation in Shanghai (*refer to **Exhibit 15***). At the time when these costs were calculated, only a few XFMs had come off the assembly line. The plant capacity was constrained by the availability and training of the work force. Chang expected the practical capacity to be 26,000 units for the first year, then gradually move up to 50,000 units the second year and reach 100,000 units during the third year. The physical capacity of the plant (floor space) was enough to produce up to 100,000 units annually.

The cost estimates were the best possible available, but they were probably not going to reflect the unit costs after the plant had gained experience. Chang expected them to improve by as much as 10–20%. The cost of the imported engines would be influenced by possible changes in costs at the plant in Germany and currency fluctuations. After considering his costs and possible changes in them in the future, Chang had to decide on the retail list price to the customer. Because of government regulations, it would be very difficult to change the prices once set, except to reflect inflation.[12] Distributors like Yiang Xiao were expecting a mark-up of at least 25% (based on the ex-factory price) on the XFMs sold to them by Xia/Fei-Ma Corporation.

Next Steps

During the last six months, Xia/Fei-Ma Corporation had conducted numerous technical tests on the prototypes that had been built in the Fei Ma Bicycle facilities. Fifty people (all from Fei-Ma Corporation) were now working full time on the project. Chang and Wang expected the market demand to exceed the capacity, with production reaching 100,000 units in three years. This was without counting possible licensing agreements to produce XFMs in other parts of China. Chang also saw additional opportunities in accessories, not only for the XFM, but also for the driver: mirrors, lights, bags, helmets, gloves, jackets, raincoats, etc. Chang and Wang were now faced with decisions regarding product positioning and market segment choice. Should they stick to the XFM name or find a brand name that could mean something exciting to the customer? They also had to decide on a suggested retail price and a communication strategy for the XFM. Then they would be in a position to design an appropriate advertising and promotional campaign (*refer to Exhibit 7*). Where should they start? Alex knew that his boss John Li was totally committed to the project. As his plane approached the bay of Hong Kong, Chang was hearing the message he had heard again and again from Li: "Everything in this project has to be right. Absolutely everything!"

---

[12] According to the Chinese government, the inflation rate in 1996 was not expected to exceed 10%. The official inflation rate for 1995 had been estimated at 9.6% by the Chinese authorities. Some unofficial sources put inflation rate as high as 25% in China.

EXHIBIT 1

The XFM

See Plate Section

EXHIBIT 2

China's Administrative Structure (1994)

	Cities	Counties	Population
Beijing Municipality	–	8	10,819,000
Tianjin Municipality	–	5	8,785,000
Hebei Province	25	124	61,082,000
Shanxi Province	13	93	28,759,000
Inner Mongolia Autonomous Region	17	71	21,457,000
Liaoning Province	22	36	41,446,000
Jilin Province	22	25	24,659,000
Heilongjiang Province	25	54	35,215,000
Shanghai Municipality	–	9	13,342,000
Jiangsu Province	28	47	67,057,000
Zhejiang Province	26	50	39,460,000
Anhui Province	18	63	56,181,000
Fujian Province	16	54	30,048,000
Jiangxi Province	16	74	37,710,000
Shandong Province	36	74	84,393,000
Henan Province	27	103	85,510,000
Hubei Province	30	49	53,969,000
Hunan Province	26	78	60,660,000
Guangdong Province	20	78	62,829,000
Guangxi Zhuang Autonomous Region	12	76	42,246,000
Hainan Province	3	16	6,557,000
Sichuan Province	24	168	117,218,000
Guizhou Province	9	73	32,392,000
Yunnan Province	11	114	36,963,000
Tibet Autonomous Region (Xizang)	2	76	2,196,000
Shaanxi Province	12	85	32,882,000
Gansu Province	13	67	22,371,000
Qinghai Province	3	37	4,457,000
Ningxia Autonomous Region	4	16	4,655,000
Xinjiang Uygur Autonomous Region	16	71	15,156,000
TOTAL	476	1,894	1,140,474,000

Source: State Statistical Bureau.

EXHIBIT 3

China's Gross Domestic Product by Region

	% Share	Average % real growth 1990–94
Beijing Municipality	2.4	10.4
Tianjin Municipality	1.6	9.2
Hebei Province	4.7	12.7
Shanxi Province	1.9	8.8
Inner Mongolia Autonomous Region	1.5	9.5
Liaoning Province	5.7	8.8
Jilin Province	2.1	9.7
Heilongjiang Province	3.6	6.9
Shanghai Municipality	4.3	10.8
Jiangsu Province	8.9	15.8
Zhejiang Province	5.9	16.4
Anhui Province	3.3	11.8
Fujian Province	3.7	9.6
Jiangxi Province	2.3	11.8
Shandong Province	8.5	14.2
Hubei Province	4.1	10.4
Hunan Province	3.7	9.6
Guangdong Province	9.3	18.3
Guangxi Zhuang Autonomous Region	2.7	14.9
Hainan Province	0.7	19.0
Sichuan Province	6.1	9.8
Guizhou Province	1.1	7.9
Yunnan Province	2.1	9.7
Tibet Autonomous Region (Xizang)	0.1	8.2
Shaanxi Province	1.9	8.8
Gansu Province	1.0	8.8
Qinghai Province	0.3	6.7
Ningxia Autonomous Region	0.3	7.1
Xinjiang Uygur Autonomous Region	1.5	11.6

Source: State Statistical Bureau, China Statistical Yearbook, 1996.

EXHIBIT 4

Population and Per Capita Income in the People's Republic of China, 1960–94

	Inhabitants*	Per capita income (Rmb)**
1960	662,070	183.0
1965	725,380	194.0
1970	829,920	235.0
1975	924,200	273.0
1980	987,050	376.0
1985	1,058,510	668.0
1986	1,075,070	737.0
1987	1,093,000	859.0
1988	1,110,260	1,066.0
1989	1,127,040	1,178.0
1990	1,143,330	1,267.0
1991	1,158,230	1,401.0
1992	1,173,843	1,459.1
1993	1,180,045	1,534.3
1994	1,197,036	1,638.1

* '000 at year ends.
** Rmb billion at current prices.

N.B.: While officials claim that as many as 30 million of China's 720 million employed people are working outside their home provinces, unofficial and international sources put the figure in 1996 at around 130 million – which was about 12% of the population. The *China Daily* estimated that one in three of all agricultural workers had left the land to join manufacturing and service industries, either openly or unofficially. Other estimates indicated that as much as 60% of the population should be considered to be urbanised.

In 1996, it was estimated that rural incomes were 43% below those of urbans. The Chinese Academy of Social Science had estimated that the real ratio of rural to urban incomes might be as low as 25%, if subsidies and other factors were taken into account.

Nine per cent of the Chinese population lived in cities of a million or more inhabitants, and just 1% in the capital Beijing.

The average size of a household in urban districts was 3.66 persons.

Source: Government Statistics /State Statistical Bureau/World Bank, 1996.

EXHIBIT 5

High-potential Consumer Markets in China in the Year 2000 (average income as multiple of US$1,000 threshold level)*

City	Av. income	City	Av. income
Shenzhen	3.9	Harbin	1.2
Shanghai	2.6	Wuhan	1.1
Guangzhou	2.4	Haikou	1.1
Beijing	2.2	Xining	1.1
Tianjin	1.6	Urumqi	1.1
Hangzhou	1.3	Taiyuan	1.0
Nanjing	1.3	Changchun	1.0
Shenyang	1.2	Xiamen	1.0

* Assume 8% income growth per annum, after adjustments for subsidies and savings.

Source: China State Statistical Bureau, McKinsey.

EXHIBIT 6

Comparative Retail Price for Motorized Bicycles in Shanghai

Products	Engine	Engine power	Retail price (Rmb)*
Forever-951	Imported	36 cc	4,980
Forever-958	Imported	49 cc	5,380
Piaggio 36	Local production	36 cc	5,180
Piaggio 49	Local production	49 cc	5,980
Tomos A	Imported	36 cc	4,980
Tomos B	Imported	49 cc	6,280
Fire Bird ES**	Local production	49 cc	5,280
Fire Bird MS***	Local production	36 cc	4,280
Hai Ying 100	Imported	36 cc	5,180
Hai Ying 200	Local production	36 cc	4,180
Second-hand 'Made in Japan' moped		36 cc***	4,000
		49 cc***	4,900

* Retail price includes a 17% Value Added Tax (VAT).
** Electric starter.
*** Manual starter.

EXHIBIT 7

Major Market Research Findings in Hubei and Guangdong Provinces

1. *Research sample and format*

Total number of interviews completed: 840 (420 rural interviews and 420 urban interviews, of which 92 in Wuhan and 106 in Wuhan). Interviews were also equally split between Guangdong and Hubei.

2. *Potential customers*

The most enthusiastic potential customers are farmers, followed by TVCEs and young urbans. In interviews, several farmers indicated that they intended to use the XFM for their own transportation and the transportation of light goods (chickens, vegetables, etc.) to near-by markets. Greater buyer interest was expressed among rural rather than among the urban segments in larger cities. Generally, people in urban areas are more concerned about status than are the rural population. Workers in the urban segment are the most interested customers in the urban segment – they value highly the option to commute with the XFM.

There appears to be more interest in purchasing the XFM among people who own bicycles but not a motorized vehicle, than among those who already own a motorized vehicle (Piaggio Series, Forever-900 Series or 'Fire Bird' Series). The XFM is thought of as 'unusual-looking'. It generates curiosity. The fact that it is only available in black causes the most negative reactions. Noise and pollution was also a concern among potential urban buyers, though less with potential rural buyers. The XFM is considered a rugged-looking motorized bicycle, well-suited for fairly good roads. Rural inhabitants consider it more of a city vehicle, while potential urban buyers consider it better suited to use in non-urban areas. Potential buyers may over-estimate the capabilities of the XFM. Power and capacity are most likely to be over-rated. Many are convinced that it will perform better than it actually does under various loads, and road and climatic conditions.

3. *Perceived value of the XFM*

For potential buyers, the XFM is seen as particularly well-suited not only to rural and urban use but also for recreation and transportation. A group of 22 postmen interviewed in Wuhan perceived the XFM as an improved means of transportation. Heads of TVCEs also showed interest in buying XFMs in large numbers. According to the sample, XFM should have the following characteristics: strength and durability; economical to operate and fuel efficient; powerful enough to climb hills; good brakes; readily available spare parts; and price competitive. Brand is significant for urbans but far less so among potential rural buyers. For young urbans design is important, but is not a *deciding* factor for the XFM in any of the customer segments considered.

4. *Price considerations*

Price only becomes important when prospective buyers are convinced that the XFM offers the features and qualities they value (see item 6). Young urbans and TVCEs estimate a slightly lower retail price than rurals. The people who estimated a low purchase price generally have less interest in buying it. Average estimated retail prices were: young urbans, Rmb5,500; TVCEs, Rmb5,200; and rurals, Rmb5,800.

For most buyers, financing was considered important. 30% of the retail price was the suggested mean down-payment, in order to be competitive in the market. Suggested monthly instalments should be no more than 5%.

5. *Name for the XFM*

XFM does not appear to be a good name. In the light of the XFM's capabilities, all segments suggested a new name. Names of animals and insects were proposed. Using Chinese ideograms seems important. The fact that

(continued)

EXHIBIT 7 (continued)

Fei-Ma Bicycles is the manufacturer of the XFM had a positive effect on possible buyers. The German engine is also seen as a plus and gives the XFM a competitive advantage over similar models with locally produced engines. Still, around 30% customers interviewed were disappointed to know that the engine is not 'Made in China'.

6. Competitive environment

For urbans and semi-urbans, the dominant competitors to the XFM are Japanese mopeds and Piaggio. Both are perceived as more durable and more stylish.

7. Distributing the XFM

Distribution of the XFM in rural areas will require a special effort. Few buyers from these regions appear to be at ease with urban dealers. It seems likely that a significant portion of the possible XFM market will be lost if special sales approaches are not undertaken to attract possible buyers in the interior of the provinces. Many of these possible customers say they need the XFM but also appear to be unfamiliar with city business practices. The thrust of the sales effort should therefore be made beyond the walls of the dealer showroom. The XFM should be taken to the backwoods buyer; additionally, other buyers should be encouraged to go to the urban dealerships.

     To reach potential buyers, new outlets, new sales efforts, new finance and service schemes in the interior should be considered, particularly those that address the special needs of users who cannot or prefer not to go to sales-service centres in the major cities.

EXHIBIT 8

Television Households 1990–95

	1990	1992	1995
Television households ('000)	85,000	98,400	112,000
% of all households	30.7%	35.4%	42.3%

Source: Industry sources.

EXHIBIT 9

Commercial Television Availability (1994–95)

Channel	Year	Daily hours	Ad minutes/week	Household penetration
Guangdong TV	1959	18	730	90%
Beijing TV	1979	18	410	90
Shanghai TV	1958	15	460	90
CCTV	1958	19	640	90

Source: Industry sources.

EXHIBIT 10

Radio Statistics (1990–94)

	1990	1992	1994
Radio households (million)	213	220	242
% of all households	76.9	79.2	83.4

Source: Industry sources.

EXHIBIT 11

Press Statistics (1990–95)

	1990	1995
Total magazine titles	5,751	6,347
Circulation (millions)	1,790	2,260
Total newspaper titles	773	871
Circulation (millions)	16,050	18,540

Source: State Statistical Bureau.

EXHIBIT 12

Main Publications

	Circulation ('000)
Newspapers (national)	
People's Daily	4,500
Reference News	4,000
China TV News	2,800
Workers' Daily	1,730
China Youth News	1,420
Magazines (monthly)	
Family	2,100
Family Doctor	1,700
Young Generation	1,200
Democracy & Law	1,200
Modern Family	1,100

Source: Industry sources.

EXHIBIT 13

Cinema Statistics (1995)

Number of cinemas	4,500
Total attendance (millions)	16,878
Gross receipts (Rmb million)	1,950
Admission per capita	14.9

Source: #UNESCO/Euromonitor/China Market.

Advertising rates per cinema show in 1996 were between Rmb50 and Rmb70 (agency commission inclusive). There are approximately 4 shows per day. (*Source*: Euromonitor, B&B.)

EXHIBIT 14

Examples of Media Rates (1996)

TV Rate

Market	TV stations	Time slot	Station rate (Rmb) 30-sec. (JV)
Beijing	Channel 6 (M-T)	1800–1820	14,000
	Channel 6 (M-T)	1820–1930	28,600
	Channel 6 (M-T)	1930–2035	31,000
	Cable TV (M-T)	2000–2130	10,800
	Cable TV (M-T)	2000–2130	11,500
Shanghai	Channel 8	1900–1920	32,000
	Channel 8	1920–1930	28,000
	Oriental TV	1930–2030	28,000
	Oriental TV	after 2030	22,800
	Cable TV (M-T)	2020–2115	16,000
	Cable TV (M-T)	after 2115	13,200
Guangzhou	GZ Cable TV – TVB	1800–2300	7,200
	GZ Cable TV – ATV	1800–2300	4,300
	GD Cable TV – TVB	1755–2140	6,800
	GD Cable TV – ATV	1755–2140	3,900

Press Rate

Market	Press titles	Size (H × W) cm	Cost to client (Rmb)
Beijing	Beijing Wanbao (full-page b/w)	34 × 22	165,887
	Beijing Wanbao ($\frac{1}{2}$ page b/w)	17 × 22	82,943
	Beijing Wanbao (banner b/w)	7 × 22	33,177
Shanghai	Xinmin Wanbao (full-page b/w)	34 × 22	149,086
	Xinmin Wanbao ($\frac{1}{2}$ page b/w)	17 × 22	74,543
	Xinmin Wanbao (banner b/w)	7 × 22	46,589
Guangzhou	Yangcheng Wanbao (full-page b/w)	34 × 22	257,173
	Beijing Wanbao ($\frac{1}{2}$ page b/w)	17 × 22	123,443
	Beijing Wanbao (banner b/w)	7 × 22	37,407

Source: DMB&B Hong Kong & China.

N.B.: There were no major restrictions on advertising in China. The market in 1996 was still relatively small (about 1% of GDP) but growing at an exponential rate. Advertising was only restricted by the lack of truly national newspapers or magazines. It should be noted that only 10% of the population lived in cities of more than a million inhabitants. Direct mail was becoming very popular among small factories and TVCEs in China. In 1995, direct mail was reported to have accounted for 17% of all mail delivered in China. (*Source*: Euromonitor, B&B.)

EXHIBIT 15

XFM Manufacturing Cost Structure in China: Alex Chang's Assumptions

1. Second-hand plant purchased in Europe with a landed cost in China of US$2.5 million (or Rmb20,750,000), to be depreciated over five years.

2. Plant capable of producing (single shift) 30,000 units per annum with 60 employees and 50,000 units per year with 100 people.

3. Six thousand square metre factory at Rmb3.5/day/square metre. Three year lease signed. Subletting not possible. Physical space to produce 100,000 units per annum.

4. Production employees:
   - One-third at Rmb700 per month;
   - Half at Rmb1,000 per month;
   - One-sixth at Rmb1,500 per month (supervisors).

5. Start-up costs (factory): Rmb500,000.

6. Administration/support: five employees at Rmb1,000 average per month.

7. Variable costs (per unit):
   - Frame   Rmb   800
   - Engine   Rmb 1,750*
   - Wheels and tyres   Rmb   350
   - Other components   Rmb   300
   - Labour (at maximum capacity)   Rmb   24

8. Licence fee (royalty): 2.5% on the ex-factory price of the XFM for the use of valid patents.

9. Suggested distributors' mark-up on ex-factory price (including expected profit for the manufacturer): 25% (to be decided).

10. Value Added Tax (VAT) at 17% is applied to the dealer price to the end user. (Example: ex-factory price = 80; dealer's mark-up at 25% = 20; total is 100; add now VAT at 17%, total retail price to end-user = 117.)

*Total landed cost including import duty was 346 German Marks (DEM) – Exchange rate: DEM1 = Rmb5.05. The second-hand plant from the Czech Republic included all that was necessary to produce the engine in the P.R.C. The cost structure to produce a XFM engine locally was: variable costs (primarily parts): Rmb900; licensee: Rmb300 (DEM60). In addition, about 60 skilled workers would be necessary to produce 30,000 engines per annum.

FOODWORLD SUPERMARKETS IN INDIA

This case was prepared by Research Associate David Wylie under the supervision of Professor Nirmalya Kumar as a basis for class discussion rather than to illustrate either effective or ineffective handling of a business situation.

Madras, India

August, 1996

In May, we opened our first FoodWorld Supermarket in Madras. We were convinced that such a modern concept would work in India, but the early results have exceeded our expectations. We will be opening two more this month and have plans for over 100 within the next ten years. It is a terrific opportunity!

I am confident overall, but unsettled about a number of issues. After all, this will be India's first national chain of supermarkets. Most people still shop at all the small mom and pop stores which almost completely dominate Indian food retailing. Do we have the formula right? Should we adjust the merchandise mix or the marketing plan? Is the store really large enough to generate excitement, and if not, will suitable real estate be available? Will we be prepared to manage such a large chain and adapt to the different market conditions in different parts of India? Will our people be qualified to manage and operate all these stores?

I would like to think that we have all of this resolved. You see, we have no direct experience in food retailing and no significant modern retailing expertise exists in India. We are inventing things as we go along. Things have to be different here, we can't just copy what is done in other parts of the world.

Pradipta K. Mohapatra
President, Retail Group, RPG Enterprises

RPG Enterprises and the Spencers Acquisition

RPG Enterprises (RPG) was the fourth largest conglomerate (called business house in India) in India, with sales of over 45 billion rupees (US$1.3 billion) in 1995. RPG business interests spanned a variety of industries including tyres,

---

power/transmission, agribusiness, telecommunications, financial services and, with the acquisition of Spencers & Co. in 1989, retailing. It boasted partnerships with a number of international companies, including 16 of the Fortune 500 companies.

Spencers & Co. had been founded in 1865 as a small store in Madras offering imported specialty items to the large British expatriate and military population. By 1897, it had grown to be the largest store in India, a 65,000 square foot enclosed collection of specialty stores. In 1981, this facility was destroyed by fire. Spencers had been at its peak in 1940, when it had 50 stores in virtually all major cities throughout India. Still it offered only imports, and had virtually no Indian customers. When India gained independence from Britain in 1947, Spencers' executives didn't believe that the demand for imports would erode. It plummeted, however, and in the early 1970s, the deteriorating chain was sold to an entrepreneur who continued to offer food, clothing, cosmetics and other high priced specialty items to the expatriate community.

Spencers' fortunes continued to slide. By 1989, it was only a shell of its former self. Only nine stores remained in operation in several of the larger cities in India, including a 20,000 square foot store in Madras and a 10,000 square foot store in Bangalore which were the largest stores of any kind in each city (*refer to Exhibit 1*). The other stores only had 2,000 to 3,000 square feet, but had excellent central locations. Spencers' profits were fleeting and it was offered for sale.

RPG purchased Spencers that year, and established it as a separate division with Pradipta K. Mohapatra, a seasoned RPG executive, at its helm. The decision to acquire this retail company was largely justified by its undervalued real estate portfolio, a distribution infrastructure (which in fact was non-existent), and a profitable travel agency specializing in the distribution of airline tickets.

A number of Spencers' stand-alone divisions were obvious losers and were quickly destined for closure: furniture manufacturing, restaurants, manufacturing of air conditioners and other small electrical appliances, pharmaceutical production and repair shops. The travel agency was clearly a winner and was kept. RPG executives were, however, initially undecided about whether to close down the retail operations altogether.

The 'Spencers' brand name was well known throughout India as synonymous with quality, but unfortunately also with high prices. Indeed, there was a popular expression in India: 'You don't have to pay the Spencers price'. In addition, RPG had no experience in retailing. They couldn't rely on existing expertise within Spencers, since its employees were poorly qualified at every level and grossly underpaid, even by Indian standards. The general manager of the large Madras store, for example, was only paid the equivalent of about $70 per month. It appeared that it would be most prudent and profitable to close down the stores and simply rent the space.

Yet Spencers' nine stores still remained the largest department store or supermarket type of chain in India, and it seemed wasteful simply to throw away whatever potential there might be for improvement. The decision was ultimately made to refit one store to test its potential. If the experiment failed, they would close the retail operations.

The store in Bangalore, therefore, was modernized in 1991, retaining its profile as a department store offering hardware, food, kitchen appliances and clothing. When it reopened, sales exploded to four times the previous levels and the store broke even in the first month.

FoodWorld

The following year, interest in retailing among RPG executives derived from the initial success of Spencers' experiment was undermined when a large international consulting firm was retained to assist with the strategic growth planning for RPG. Retailing had been flagged as one of the target industries to consider as part of the RPG engine for growth, along with telecommunications and financial services. It was apparent that an emerging middle class in India might provide a catalyst for bringing modern retailing to India, where retailing had remained virtually unchanged for generations. The consultants, however, stopped short of recommending what kind of retailing to enter, suggesting instead that RPG executives themselves should explore those formats which might be the best match for RPG and mesh with the future growth of India. Several broad objectives were drafted:

- Become a pioneer in an organized, large-scale, world standard retailing operation in India.

- Become the largest retail chain in India.

- Be willing to make substantial investments to establish a national presence.

Fine-tuning the Spencers' format appeared to be the most obvious next step in preparation for expansion, especially since Spencers' executives were unfamiliar with alternative formats.

After a careful study of retailing formats in relation to the opportunities in India, RPG executives then narrowed their choice to clothing or supermarkets, wanting to choose the least risky option. While clothing had high growth prospects and margins, it would require, they surmised, expertise in design, branding and managing independent manufacturers. In addition, a potential threat appeared to loom from current and future competition, making it more difficult to achieve a meaningful scale of operations. Supermarkets, however, offered the same growth prospects and a more moderate investment. While initial margins and entry levels for other pioneering companies might be low, the option of starting a chain of supermarkets seemed to offer the most potential.

A consumer study was then commissioned to assess consumer attitudes towards current retail options and to measure responses in particular to proposed new formats. Nine focus groups were formed in two major cities and 2,110 households were interviewed in depth in six cities. The results were summarized as follows:

- Consumers regarded shopping as a chore, although few consumers were familiar with any alternatives to traditional store formats.

- Convenience was important since daily shopping and sensitivity to food freshness remained an integral part of shopping habits. Few families had cars in which to carry large quantities of purchases.

- There was a growing dissatisfaction with the range of products available. Traditional stores did not have the space to carry a selection of different brands of any item. Increasing television penetration among the Indian population and brand advertising were whetting consumer appetites for choice as international branded goods were now available for the first time in many categories.

- Quality was important, but there was a reluctance to pay a price premium.

- Added services such as home delivery and credit were desirable, but were seldom actually used.

- Trust in the retailer, especially with regard to quality of food and replacement of defective goods, was important.

- Self-service was seen as a distinct advantage. An exploding number of new brands were being introduced and promoted (often by international consumer goods manufacturers), generating demand for hands-on comparison shopping.

Given the results of this survey, it was decided to focus efforts on developing a suitable format for a national supermarket chain. Executives realized, however, that they would have to face the challenge of a steep learning curve. They would need a partner well versed in food retailing technology because of the importance of using technology to achieve suitable operating efficiencies and low cost logistics. Without any experience in modern food retailing, they were reluctant to proceed without such a partner. For almost a year, they travelled abroad searching for a partner, finally negotiating an agreement with Dairy Farm, a Hong Kong-based retail giant with a great deal of experience in multinational operations, a focus on Asia, and familiarity with the operation of both supermarkets and drug stores. Most importantly, they felt there was a positive chemistry with Dairy Farm executives who demonstrated the patience to invest in the long-term opportunity presented in India.

The supermarket visualized would have about 4,500 square feet of selling space, a self-service format in an air-conditioned and pleasant ambience. It would have extensive assortments of groceries, personal care and cleaning products, kitchenware and tableware. No meat would be offered, but a fresh produce stand would be leased to an independent vendor. It would also incorporate fast food and bakery sections. Executives realized that they would need to deliver outstanding service with an empowered and well-trained staff. They would have to achieve dominance in tightly focused geographical areas. Finally, they would have to achieve suitable margins by developing a scale to negotiate better prices from suppliers and by achieving the efficiencies of regional distribution centres for at least 15 to 20 stores.

India

India is the second most populous country in the world with a population approaching a billion people. It is also one of the densest with over 724 people per square mile. In contrast, the United States, France and Switzerland have densities of 26, 265 and 434 people per square mile respectively. India's geographic diversity is only exceeded by the diversity of its people. From the towering Himalayas of the North to the densely populated alluvial plains in the middle to the plateaus of the South, more than 1,500 languages are spoken. Although Hindi and English are the official languages, 14 other languages are recognized by the constitution. The population is overwhelmingly Hindu, but there are significant numbers of Muslims (more than 10% of the population), Christians, Buddhists, Sikhs, Jains and Parsis.

Rural India, comprising 80% of the population, is largely supported by primitive agriculture. Most of its hundreds of millions live below the poverty level. Urban India, however, is heavily industrialized, although vast numbers of people lived in slum conditions, many of them rural refugees. The population is growing at 2% per annum while becoming increasingly urban (see Table 1). The inflation adjusted gross domestic product of India has been growing at an average of 5.1% over the previous ten years.

While a stereotype of mal-nourished masses dominates the perception of many Western visitors, the economic diversity of the Indian population is much more complex. While reliable statistics are often unavailable, around 40 million Indians live in relative luxury, enjoying annual household incomes of over 90,000 rupees, or about US$2,500. The buying power of the rupee, however, is considerable and such an income results in a very comfortable upper-class life style. Another 150 million people live in households with incomes exceeding 30,000 rupees (US$850). This newly emerging middle class is growing at over 5% per year and can afford many of the staples of a middle-class existence, including televisions, refrigerators and motorcycles or mopeds. Automobiles, however, are generally only within reach of the top 1% of the population.

Growth of this middle class is, however, a relatively new phenomenon. Since India gained independence in 1947, the economy has been centrally planned by a large government bureaucracy which controls investment, production and

Table 1 *Population distribution*

Population (millions)	Number of towns
More than 10	3
5–10	4
1–5	4
0.5–1.0	26
0.1–0.5	178
Less than 0.1	3,543
Villages	570,000

competition without regard for market forces. A severe financial crisis in 1991, however, forced a liberalization of economic restrictions. This cleared the way for widespread entrepreneurialism, foreign investment, imports without restrictive tariffs and unleashed market opportunities. Multinational companies like Coca-Cola rushed in to unleash their brands on the Indian marketplace. Indeed, the number of national brands available had exploded in the previous ten years. The number of tea brands, for example, had grown from 31 to 148 and washing powders from 26 to 61. Since 1991, this foreign investment in India had created so much demand for office space and professional managers that Bombay had the most expensive real estate in the world. Managers' salaries had often grown ten-fold within four years while inflation had fallen from over 16% in 1991 to under 7% in 1995.

Food Retailing in India

Retailing in urban India still remained about the same as it had for several generations. While several larger stores and specialty shops in each major city catered to the less-price-sensitive appetites of the most wealthy segments of the population with wide selections of imported goods, virtually all other retailers were small independent, owner-managed shops. Most had no employees other than family members who might assist with cleaning or deliveries. As almost every store sold products at the MRP (the maximum allowed retail price printed by the manufacturers on every item and enforced by the government), very little price competition existed between formats, and since the cost of goods was very similar for all of the stores, gross margins were determined mostly by the mix of products offered (see Table 2).

Table 2 *Typical gross margins by product category*

Product category	Gross margin
Staples	3%
Other food products	15%
Furniture	25%
General merchandise and hardware	18%

Table 3 *Number of retail outlets in India*

Grocery stores	1,575,000
General merchandise stores	531,000
Convenience stores/tobacconists	276,000
Chemists	212,000
Confectioners	141,000
Supermarkets	30
Other retail	805,000

The one main exception to this rule were the 400,000 fair-price shops, a government sponsored distribution system which sold medium-quality staple products (mostly rice, wheat, cooking oil and sugar) at prices generally lower than market. 78% of these outlets were in rural areas, constituting an essential element of the government's safety net for the poor. In urban areas, these shops accounted for only 5% of total retail food sales.

The number of stores outside the fair-price shops was huge. Estimates varied, but one 1993 survey by Euromonitor suggested that there were over 3.54 million retail outlets in India (see Table 3). This did not, however, include the vast number of vendors and street markets who did not generally report to the government and were not counted in the census. Unofficial estimates indicated that there might be as many as five to eight million such retailers in the informal economy.

Grocery Stores

Dry groceries were usually purchased by the housewife from small neighbourhood grocery stores with an average size of about 250 square feet. Her loyalty was strong, based on convenience and added services such as credit and free home delivery. These grocers sold primarily unbranded staples which were individually weighed and packed. Staples such as rice would frequently be purchased on a monthly basis, coinciding with monthly pay days. Typically, these retailers would also carry a small range of branded cleaning and personal care products. These were often offered in 'sachets', or single use packages. Space constraints often limited the selection to no more than one or two brands. Such stores lined the more heavily travelled streets, often simply counters which opened on to the sidewalk behind which the owner/manager would take orders.

The gross margins of these small grocers ranged between only about 7 and 10% of sales, but operating costs were similarly low. Property costs only represented 1 or 2% of sales, while labour costs were generally provided by the store owner and his family, working fifteen hours a day, seven days a week. Profits before tax, therefore, ranged from 4 to 6% of sales. Since most sales were not formally logged, virtually none of these small grocers paid any income tax. Working capital requirements represented only about two weeks of sales.

General Merchants

General merchandise stores (400–600 square feet) were somewhat larger than the small grocery stores and stocked a wider range of cleaning and personal care products, as well as snack foods and confectionery. Groceries were generally prepackaged, but unbranded, and service was still from behind the counter. Services such as home delivery and credit were also available.

Gross margins were several percentage points higher than in the small grocery stores, mainly due to the product mix being skewed towards higher margin items. Since operating costs were somewhat higher as well however, profits remained about the same.

Convenience Stores

These outlets were found on virtually every street corner and ranged in size from kiosks of 50–60 square feet to larger shops of 100–150 square feet. Usually run by a single owner from behind a counter, they offered such items as cigarettes, soft drinks or betel leaf (a popular chewing snack containing tobacco and spices wrapped in a betel leaf). Some might also offer a very restricted range of household cleaning and personal-care products as well as biscuits, confectionery and some over-the-counter medicines.

Convenience stores were generally open every day of the week for eighteen hours a day. Their prices were equivalent to other stores, and gross margins were a similar 7–10% of sales. Operating costs, however, were so low that profits were often 5–7%.

Vendors

Along every sidewalk in the cities were vendors who operated small booths or carts, or simply laid out their products on the ground. They would usually offer only a single product such as fresh coconut milk, bananas, or a very limited selection of clothing, household items, or fruit and vegetables.

Supermarkets

Supermarkets were a more recent phenomenon in India. By 1996, only a handful had appeared in the major cities. These 3,000 to 5,000 square foot self-service stores stocked a wide range (by Indian standards) of groceries, snacks, processed foods, confectionery, cleaning and personal care products, and cosmetics. They generally stayed open from 9:30 a.m. to 7:30 p.m., six days a week. They stocked most national brands as well as a number of regional and specialty brands, and also their own brands of pre-packaged dry groceries. Many had small bakery sections, and some were experimenting with fresh produce and dairy products. Frozen foods were often stocked as well, although only a very limited selection was generally available in India. Most consumers were in the habit of buying fresh products daily from local stores and vendors. In addition, freezer space was expensive and limited in both stores and homes.

A typical supermarket carried about 6,000 SKUs (stock-keeping units). Most, however, had no item-based inventory control, still using a cash register at the point of sale and tracking sales only on a category or departmental basis. Supermarket margins were typically in the range of 14–16%. These higher margins were largely due to the ability to get somewhat better prices from suppliers on bulk purchases, and the ability to generate income from selling advertising space and special in-store promotions to manufacturers.

The cost structure of a supermarket was typically 3% for property and 3.5% for labour. Air conditioning and lighting increased utilities to 3.5%, interest costs were 1.5%, leaving 3–5% of sales as profits before tax.

There were virtually no multi-unit supermarket chains. One German company, Nanz, in partnership with Marsh supermarkets of the United States and Escorts, an Indian engineering firm, had set up a six-store chain in and near the Indian capital city of Delhi. However, this chain specialized in imported and other higher priced foods for the most well-to-do segment of the population. Most supermarkets, like their smaller counterparts, were owner managed.

Most of the supermarkets tried to cater to that portion of the population which sought a wider selection, could afford and had storage space for and the means of transport for a larger shopping basket, and were not scared off by the typical perception that large, brightly lit and air-conditioned supermarkets must be more expensive.

Distribution of Consumer Goods

Consumer goods were distributed through a multi-level distribution system. Hindustan Lever (HL), a subsidiary of Unilever, had the most extensive distribution system in India. Its structure, however, was typical of those used by other consumer packaged goods companies.

Forty-seven exclusive HL carrying and forwarding agents (CFAs) transported merchandise from the factory or warehouse to 3,500 redistribution 'stockists' or distributors. While the CFAs did not take title to the product, they received a 2–$2\frac{1}{2}$% margin, invoiced the stockists and received payment on behalf of the manufacturer.

The stockists had exclusive geographical territories and a sales force which called on both wholesalers and directly on larger retailers and retailers in urban areas. They offered credit to their customers and received margins in the range of 3–9%.

The wholesalers provided the final link to those rural and smaller retailers who could not purchase directly from the stockists. Sales to these retailers were cash only. Wholesalers carried a full range of products including brands competing directly with HL. Wholesalers received 2–3% margins out of that received by the stockists and distributed about 40% of the total volume of merchandise handled by the stockists. The remaining 60% of merchandise was sold directly to retailers by stockists.

The network was completed by whatever means was required to reach remote villages, including vans, motorized rickshaws, bicycles, bullock carts and, in some areas, boats. It was estimated that through this network, HL reached only about 64% of all villages and a total of about three million retailers. HL had a 400-person sales force to oversee this distribution network. Each salesperson made about 40 calls a day on distribution channel members.

Gross margins for retailers ranged from 5% to 15% while the total cost of the distribution network represented between 10% and 25% of the final retail price. This cost was considerably lower than distribution costs in most Western countries.

Consumer Buying Behaviour

The Wealthy

Those within the more wealthy segment of the population with household incomes greater than 90,000 rupees per year (US$2,500) relied almost entirely on domestic help for their shopping. They would buy staples, vegetables and fresh foods from a number of loyal local small grocers and vendors, and other products from a variety of general merchants. This segment was concentrated in urban areas and comprised only about 4% of the population.

The Poor

The poorer segments of the Indian population tended to buy basic staples with the first part of their paycheques which typically were distributed on the first of each month. For most food stores, over 40% of total sales came within the first few days of each month. During the month, poor customers would buy whatever fresh foods and consumer goods they could afford daily, often filling in at the end of the month with some additional staples purchased on credit. Many consumer products such as soap, toothpaste, or over-the counter drugs or cosmetics were bought only in single-use packages (sachets). Indeed, many of the smaller stores were festooned with linked packets of such items. Twenty-five per cent of the population lived below the poverty level while another 56% enjoyed only modest household incomes below 30,000 rupees (US$850) per year.

The Middle Class

The middle class comprised those who enjoyed household incomes between 30,000 rupees (US$850) and 90,000 rupees (US$2,500) per year (about 15% of the population). This segment was divided in its purchasing habits. Many families on the upper end often would emulate the wealthy and use part-time domestic help to do their shopping, often necessitated by a growing pattern of households with two working parents. Many families at the lower end of the middle class,

Table 4 *Shopping patterns*

Outlet type	Percentage who named outlet as most frequently used
Big grocery store	30
Supermarket	16
Small grocery store	11
General merchant	11
Wholesale dealer	8
Others/No fixed shop	24

Table 5 *Monthly household expenditures*

Food category	Rupees per month	Percentage of total purchases
Cereals and breads	779	43.2
Oils and oilseeds	244	13.6
Sugar	191	10.6
Meat, eggs and fish	189	10.5
Pulses (lentils)	106	5.9
Coffee, tea and spices	104	5.8
Tobacco	104	5.8
Beverages (including alcohol)	83	4.6
Total (Rs/month)	1,800	100.0

however, would continue to do their own shopping, especially if they had recently emerged from the ranks of the poor and remained extremely cost conscious, frequenting their favourite local shops. They were, however, concerned about quality, often leaving a list with a trusted shopkeeper to pick out and deliver the best-quality products. Almost always (92% in one survey), it was the wife who did all the shopping for a household.

In a survey conducted by Spencers, upper-middle-class consumers frequented the outlets shown in Table 4 for their food needs.

The typical middle-class household spent 1,800 rupees per month for those categories of foods which FoodWorld anticipated offering (see Table 5). This did not include milk or fresh vegetables.

The Decision to Start FoodWorld

P.K. Mohapatra and his staff ultimately made the decision "to offer the Indian housewife the freedom to choose from a wide range of products at a convenient location in a clean, bright and functional ambience without a price penalty." It was determined that households with incomes over 4,000 rupees per month would represent the target customers. Choosing locations, sourcing the right merchandise, developing a promotional plan, designing, building and fixturing the stores, and attracting the best people to staff the stores and corporate office still, of course, remained a challenge.

The name FoodWorld was chosen after extensive research and deliberation because it reflected the breadth of the offering and because it translated well into every major regional language in India. Government regulations also necessitated posting the name in the local language at every location.

Based on their now expanded experience, Spencers' executives developed a pro forma financial plan for the FoodWorld concept (*refer to **Exhibits 2 to 4***).

Human Resources

Hiring suitably trained people to manage and staff each store offered perhaps the most formidable obstacle to implementing the FoodWorld concept.

Because most retail stores were owner operated and retailing as a career was considered to be at the bottom end of the social scale, graduates of prestigious universities did not want to work in retailing. Therefore, few qualified candidates for management positions could be found. Some could perhaps be attracted from other service industries to run one or two stores, but not enough to accommodate the planned growth. Recruiting and retaining professionally trained managers was and would continue to be a major challenge facing the firm.

Attracting and training enough front-line staff members would also be a challenge, since FoodWorld would need a cast of thousands to implement the full expansion plan. Spencers therefore created a school for retailing, the National Institute of Retailing (NIR). The curriculum consisted of such courses as store maintenance, working the cash register, serving the customer, and self-grooming and presentation. Students for the NIR were recruited from rural high schools, particularly those who had chosen vocational paths and did not plan on or could not afford any further education. They were accepted for either a three-month certificate course or a six-month work/study programme based on their aptitude to learn, their self-confidence and their energy, rather than on any particular skills that they might have acquired.

Given the wage levels and social status associated with a front-line retail position, albeit at a modern supermarket, most of the candidates came from the lower end of the socio-economic strata of Indian society. Consequently, attending NIR represented a tremendous opportunity for them and generated a high level of enthusiasm. However, because India was a highly stratified society, these employees perceived themselves, as did the customers, as being considerably lower in social status then their customers. A delicate balance was required to overcome this cultural bias. Instilling the confidence to smile, make eye contact and help customers while not being perceived as cheeky would be a challenge.

Expansion Plan

There were a number of arguments in favour of an expansion plan based on achieving saturation in several cities first, rather than starting with seeding FoodWorlds across the country. Certainly, the former model allowed for distribution efficiencies and simplicity in dealing with suppliers and manufacturers on a regional basis. In addition, each state in the country had its own regulations and tax policies, which made it cumbersome to do business in more than one state. Manufacturers, for example, usually kept title to products as they moved into regional warehouses owned by 'stockists', the first level in the national distribution chain, in order to avoid paying rather stiff tax penalties on goods moving across state lines. Often, each metropolitan area had its own language or dialect and particular food preferences. While major differences appeared between neighbourhoods, for example, when moving from a strictly vegetarian Hindu neighbourhood to a Muslim neighbourhood, even more substantive differences existed between regions of India.

The areas surrounding Delhi (the capital) and Bombay (the centre of commerce) were ruled out immediately because of the high cost of real estate. Indeed, Bombay's prices for commercial real estate exceeded those of Hong Kong, Tokyo, or New York, and Delhi did not lag far behind. It made most sense to concentrate around those areas where Spencers had a strong remaining presence and where real estate prices and availability were within reason. Madras and Bangalore were therefore chosen to become the first epicentres for FoodWorld based on the size of the target population (*refer to **Exhibit 5***). Each neighbourhood within the city was further broken down to reveal target neighbourhoods where there were over 4,000 households within a two kilometre radius of the store with incomes of over 4,000 rupees per month (US$114). On average, there were about five people per household. It was estimated that a store would have to attract 2,000 households for most of their shopping needs in order to break even. In Madras, seven neighbourhoods were chosen. Real estate availability then dictated the ultimate choice of sites.

Ramaswamy Road

The first store was opened on 9 May 1996 on Ramaswamy Road in a predominantly upper-middle-income residential area of Madras where over 8,000 target households were within a two kilometre radius. The street was heavily trafficked, but less cluttered with small shops than many of the other larger streets in the area. Still, the store's brightly lit and colourful facade stood in stark contrast to its surroundings. Some thought it might even be seen as imposing or threatening, suggesting the higher prices often associated with more modern environments.

Dedicated parking was unavailable, but most customers were expected to live within walking distance of the store. Several spaces were available, however, on the street in front. The store stood back from the street, providing a small courtyard in which a snack-food and a fresh-fruit vendor leased space.

While Mohapatra and his colleagues had wanted a store with between 3,000 and 6,000 square feet of selling space, they found that such large areas were virtually impossible to find in Madras. They had therefore settled on this 2,400 square foot store. With no space for any back room or storage area, a 600 square foot apartment on the third floor had also been rented for an office and employee lunchroom, and some storage had been created above the display racks in the store and at the side of the courtyard in front. It was clear that adapting the store design and layout to each available location was going to be a continuing challenge as FoodWorld expanded in different locations and cities.

Inside the store, the aisles were arranged with clear signage and easily accessible arrays of choices of staples, processed foods, health and beauty aids, and dairy products. The decision had been made to offer a selection of all national brands and a more limited selection of the more popular regional and local brands. Since tastes varied so much by city and even by neighbourhood within a city, it was important to have just the right products in stock. In order to assure a complete offering, one of each item from competing stores had been purchased and a list compiled and shown to a sample of prospective customers, who added or deleted items that they considered necessary or irrelevant. A final list of 3,500 SKUs was thus created.

The ends of each aisle were rented to manufacturers as promotional displays. Revenue from the seven available end-aisles averaged about 4,000 rupees per month, or about 190 rupees per square foot.

It would have been too labour-intensive to offer rice, lentils and other basic commodities in bulk, so a FoodWorld private label was created for pre-packaged amounts of these items. It was expected that up to 25% of total sales would be 'FoodWorld' products, lending both customer convenience and image to the store offering.

Every item in the store was marked individually with both a price and a bar code which could be scanned at any of the four cash registers. Believing that item-by-item inventory control would be critical to the success of a chain of markets, FoodWorld had invested in state-of-the-art cash registers and bar code scanners. Since there was no established norm for bar coding in India, however, Spencers' staff itself had designed and implemented a complete bar coding system.

Obtaining shopping carts was also a problem, but they were considered necessary to maximize the amount customers would buy on each visit. Imported carts were far too costly an investment, and no company in India manufactured such unusual items. Raghu Pillai, chief executive of FoodWorld, had therefore designed and worked closely with a local metal fabrication shop to develop a cart of their own. While several small problems remained and required fine-tuning before the carts could go into production, by late August the first were scheduled to arrive in the stores.

Display racks had presented a similar challenge. Imported racks were too costly, and the desired high racks were not available in India, so that all of the racks for the new store had to be custom designed and manufactured.

Since customers were used to paying the MRP (maximum retail price) established by manufacturers and enforced by the government for all foodstuffs and packaged goods, FoodWorld prices were set at the MRP.

There was one deviation from this policy. FoodWorld offered something which had never been tried in India, as far as anyone knew. Certain items in the store were offered at prices below normal (5–10%), and labelled as special values within the store. Four thousand 'Value Shopping Guides' (fliers announcing these special bargains along with a series of weekly contests) were delivered by local youngsters directly to each household that fell within the target demographics and were within a 2-kilometre radius of the store. The cost for this flier and its distribution was 0.75 rupee per flier (US$0.02), net of the contribution by manufacturers which essentially covered production costs. Another 4,000 monthly fliers were mailed to target households at an average cost of 5.5 rupees. Customers seemed to respond enthusiastically to these promotional programmes.

Each store had one store manager to whom three supervisors reported. Reporting to the supervisors were ten full-time customer service representatives (CSRs) and eight part-time CSRs who were attending the work study programme at the NIR. They were all well paid by local standards, ranging from front-line CSRs, who were paid 2,000 rupees per month (US$57), to the manager, who was paid 10,000 rupees per month (US$285). A bonus programme representing between 10 and 20% of total compensation was based on store sales, results of a monthly customer satisfaction survey and a management service audit. Total payroll per store was 72,000 rupees per store per month.

At the corporate level, general managers of human resources, operations and merchandising reported to Raghu Pillai, the chief executive of the retail group. He in turn reported to Pradipta Mohapatra, president of the retail group. A total of 17 professionals as well as an administrative staff supported these executives. It was projected that a total of 110 people would be required in the corporate offices by the time 50 stores were in operation. Corporate overhead was projected to be 1,416,000 rupees per month.

Early Returns

During the first three weeks of operation, 36,000 customers visited the new store. Sales volume and gross margins by the end of the month exceeded pro forma estimates (*refer to* **Exhibit 6**). Some manufacturers and suppliers were showing a willingness to be creative and innovative, even to the point of discussing the implications of a changed relationship derived from dealing with a large chain of stores.

Bolstered by this response, Spencers' executives were eager to proceed with the continuing roll-out of the FoodWorld stores. The basic offering, they realized, was strong, as was the broad product offering. Sales and margins were beyond expectations. The results from one store, however, were not enough to validate their initial assumptions and conclusions. Another two stores in Madras were already in the pipeline for August openings, and plans were in place for a fourth. A similar roll-out scheduled for late autumn and early winter in Bangalore would provide a much more meaningful picture and give more direction in determining what adjustments they would have to make to the formula.

EXHIBIT 1

Map Of India

EXHIBIT 2

Operating Assumptions

	Monthly sales per square foot and gross margins (sales expressed in rupees per square foot)	
Period	Stores opening in years 1 and 2	Stores opening in years 3 and onwards
Year 1 QI	500	750
Year 1 QII	750	900
Year 1 QIII & IV	900	900
Year 2 QI & II	900	900
Year 3	10% increase	10% increase
Year 4	10% increase	10% increase
Year 5 and onwards	5% increase	5% increase
Gross margins – store	12%	12%
Gross margins	Year 1	2%	
Back room*	Years 2–5	Growing to 6%	

*Back room margins comprised merchandising efficiencies, including volume and cash payment discounts, and revenues from suppliers and manufacturers for promotions and displays.

Operating and opening costs

Rent	Rs25 per square foot Assumed to grow at 5% above inflation
Salaries	Staffing at 22 full-time equivalents for 7 days of weekly operation Salary cost at Rs72,000 per store per month Assumed to grow at 5% above inflation per year
Packing	Rs1 for every Rs250 of sales (shopping bags, etc.)
Taxes	1% on 50% of sales (for Bangalore stores only)
Bank charges	2% on credit card sales 20% of sales assumed to be on credit cards
Depreciation	Computers – five years Others – seven years
Advertising	Mailings – Rs25,000 per month Semi-weekly fliers – covered by supplier funding
Property	40% owned (purchased at Rs3,500 per sq. ft.) 60% leased (Rs25 per month per sq. ft.) Growth at 5% above inflation

(continued)

EXHIBIT 2 (continued)

Store fittings	Computers	Rs800,000
	Shelving	800,000
	Air conditioning	950,000
	Electrical	300,000
	Furniture	200,000
	Generator	250,000
	Chillers & freezers	250,000
	Construction, signs, bakery	450,000
	TOTAL	Rs4,000,000

Rent advance   15 months

Working capital   25% of sales

Paid-up stock (inventory less accounts payable)   Year 1 – 4 weeks
                                                         Year 2 – 3 weeks
                                                         Year 3 – 2 weeks
                                                         Year 4 – 2 weeks
                                                         Year 5 – 1 week
                        (Primarily from improved credit terms and efficiency)

Inventories   2.5 weeks at store, 3.5 weeks at warehouse

Inventory turnover   8 times

EXHIBIT 3

FoodWorld Stand-Alone Store Model Pro Forma (4,000 square feet)

(× 100,000 rupees)	Year 1		Year 2		Year 3		Year 4		Year 5	
	Rs	%	Rs	%	Rs	%	Rs	%	Rs	%
Sales	366.0	100.0%	453.6	100.0%	499.0	100.0%	548.9	100.0%	576.3	100.0%
Sales per sq. ft. (Rs/month)	762.5		945.0		1,039.5		1,143.5		1,200.6	
Gross margin	43.9	12.0%	54.4	12.0%	59.9	12.0%	65.9	12.0%	69.2	12.0%
Store operating expenses										
Salaries	8.6	2.4%	9.7	2.1%	10.2	2.0%	10.7	1.9%	11.2	1.9%
Rent	12.0	3.3%	12.6	2.8%	13.2	2.6%	13.8	2.5%	14.4	2.5%
Utilities	3.0	0.8%	3.0	0.7%	3.0	0.6%	3.0	0.5%	3.0	0.5%
Packing	1.5	0.4%	1.8	0.4%	2.0	0.4%	2.2	0.4%	2.3	0.4%
Taxes	1.8	0.5%	2.3	0.5%	2.5	0.5%	2.7	0.5%	2.8	0.5%
Bank charges	1.5	0.4%	1.8	0.4%	2.0	0.4%	2.2	0.4%	2.3	0.4%
Advertising	6.0	1.6%	3.0	0.7%	3.0	0.6%	3.0	0.5%	3.0	0.5%
Other	3.5	1.0%	4.5	1.0%	4.5	0.9%	4.5	0.8%	4.5	0.8%
SUBTOTAL	37.9	10.3%	38.6	8.5%	40.3	8.1%	42.0	7.7%	43.5	7.6%
Lease	8.5	2.3%	8.5	1.9%	8.5	1.7%	8.5	1.5%	8.5	1.5%
WC interest	2.8	0.8%	3.5	0.8%	3.8	0.8%	4.2	0.8%	4.4	0.8%
SUBTOTAL	11.3	3.1%	11.9	2.6%	12.3	2.5%	12.6	2.3%	12.9	2.2%
Depreciation	2.3	0.6%	2.3	0.5%	2.3	0.5%	2.3	0.4%	2.3	0.4%
Profit	−7.5	−2.0%	1.7	0.4%	5.1	1.0%	8.9	1.6%	10.5	1.8%

EXHIBIT 4

Supermarket Project Pro Forma – Five Year

(× 100,000 rupees)	Year 1 Rs	%	Year 2 Rs	%	Year 3 Rs	%	Year 4 Rs	%	Year 5 Rs	%
Number of stores	8		20		30		40		50	
Square feet per store	4,000		4,000		4,000		4,000		4,000	
Sales	2,557	100.0%	6,585	100.0%	12,259	100.0%	17,494	100.0%	23,243	100.0%
Sales per sq. ft. (Rs/month)	799.1		823.1		1,021.6		1,093.4		1,200.6	
Gross margin	307.0	12.0%	790.0	12.0%	1,471.0	12.0%	2,099.0	12.0%	2,789.0	12.0%
Store operating expenses										
Salaries	55.0	2.2%	150.0	2.3%	269.0	2.2%	389.0	2.2%	521.0	2.2%
Rent	51.0	2.0%	129.0	2.0%	218.0	1.8%	310.0	1.8%	410.0	1.8%
Utilities	23.0	0.9%	47.0	0.7%	80.0	0.7%	110.0	0.6%	140.0	0.6%
Packing	11.0	0.4%	26.0	0.4%	49.0	0.4%	70.0	0.4%	93.0	0.4%
Taxes	25.0	1.0%	33.0	0.5%	61.0	0.5%	87.0	0.5%	116.0	0.5%
Bank charges	13.0	0.5%	26.0	0.4%	49.0	0.4%	70.0	0.4%	93.0	0.4%
Other	31.0	1.2%	71.0	1.1%	119.0	1.0%	163.0	0.9%	207.0	0.9%
SUBTOTAL	209.0	8.2%	482.0	7.3%	845.0	6.9%	1,199.0	6.9%	1,580.0	6.8%
Store contribution	98.0	3.8%	308.0	4.7%	626.0	5.1%	900.0	5.1%	1,209.0	5.2%
Other income	55.0	2.2%	198.0	3.0%	490.0	4.0%	875.0	5.0%	1,395.0	6.0%
Central cost										
Corporate	110.0	4.3%	141.0	2.1%	151.0	1.2%	160.0	0.9%	170.0	0.7%
Advertising	17.0	0.7%	96.0	1.5%	120.0	1.0%	150.0	0.9%	180.0	0.8%
Warehousing	79.0	3.1%	109.0	1.7%	184.0	1.5%	175.0	1.0%	232.0	1.0%
SUBTOTAL	206.0	8.1%	346.0	5.3%	455.0	3.7%	485.0	2.8%	582.0	2.5%
PBDIT	–53.0	–2.1%	160.0	2.4%	661.0	5.4%	1,290.0	7.4%	2,022.0	8.7%
Finance cost										
Lease rent	55.0	2.2%	106.0	1.6%	212.0	1.7%	296.0	1.7%	381.0	1.6%
W.C. interest	42.0	1.6%	50.0	0.8%	62.0	0.5%	89.0	0.5%	59.0	0.3%
Debt	0.0	0.0%	21.0	0.3%	0.0	0.0%	0.0	0.0%	0.0	0.0%
Depreciation	7.0	0.3%	47.0	0.7%	70.0	0.6%	93.0	0.5%	116.0	0.5%
Contingency	50.0	2.0%	75.0	1.1%	100.0	0.8%	100.0	0.6%	0.0	0.0%
Profit before tax	–207.0	–8.1%	–139.0	–2.1%	217.0	1.8%	712.0	4.1%	1,466.0	6.3%

EXHIBIT 5

Populations and Income Levels of Households in Key Cities within the FoodWorld Market Area

Town	Population	Households* with monthly incomes of			
		Rs5,500 and above	Rs3,000 to 5,500	Rs1,500 to 3,000	Total
Madras	5,600,000	75,000	100,000	150,000	325,000
Hyderabad	4,300,000	30,000	50,000	70,000	150,000
Bangalore	4,100,000	45,000	65,000	90,000	200,000
Cochin	1,100,000	20,000	30,000	50,000	100,000
Coimbatore	1,200,000	20,000	30,000	50,000	100,000
Madurai	1,100,000	20,000	25,000	45,000	90,000
Trichy	700,000	15,000	20,000	35,000	70,000
Salem	600,000	10,000	20,000	30,000	60,000
Warrangal	500,000	2,000	5,000	13,000	20,000
Vizag	1,100,000	20,000	15,000	25,000	60,000
Vijayawada	800,000	10,000	20,000	30,000	60,000
Gunter	500,000	2,000	5,000	13,000	20,000
Mysore	600,000	10,000	15,000	20,000	45,000
Hubli/Dharwar	600,000	10,000	15,000	20,000	45,000
Trivandrum	800,000	10,000	20,000	25,000	55,000
Calicut	800,000	10,000	15,000	20,000	45,000
TOTAL		309,000	450,000	691,000	1,450,000

*There were approximately five people per household, on average, in Indian cities.

EXHIBIT 6

Results from the First Two Months (9 May to 30 June 1996)

Sales	Rs3,931,000
Average sales per day	Rs85,000
Number of customers	68,820
Number of transactions (average per day)	
Cash	475
Credit card	23
Average transaction value	
Cash	Rs148
Credit card	Rs652
Sales volume (average per day)	
Number of units	3,968
Number of SKUs	992
Average sale per unit	Rs21.54

Category sales:

	Sales (in rupees)	Percentage of total	Gross margin (%)
Staples	1,134,000	28.85	13.18
Processed foods	807,000	20.53	12.00
Beverages	450,000	11.45	8.86
Cleaning aids	359,000	9.13	9.86
Health & beauty	658,000	16.74	12.10
General merchandise	90,000	2.29	22.41
Perishables	433,000	11.07	11.09
TOTAL	3,931,000	100.00	12.03

FoodWorld Brand Sales:

	Sales	Percentage of total
FoodWorld brand	740,000	19.00
Other brands	3,191,000	81.00

Note: The prevailing exchange rate was approximately 35 rupees per US dollar.

PART THREE

Asian Businesses in Global Competition

Introduction

Today, the so-called 'West' is no longer the only power able to conquer the world with its advanced technologies and superior products. Asian businesses have been gradually expanding across the rest of the world. Japanese companies have been at the forefront, and the Newly Industrialized Countries are catching up. This part includes ten cases that look at how Japanese companies compete in the global economy.

In many respects, such as science and technology, European and North American countries are still in the leading position. But in terms of business management, Japanese firms seem to be performing particularly well. In their strong performance, one could say that Asian companies, particularly companies from Japan and the NICs, have obtained strengths from their Western counterparts through technology transfer, acquisition, business alliances and partnership, etc. They have gradually been able to bypass the stages that the Western companies went through step by step in developing technology and management skills from scratch, and have benefited from being late-comers.

Despite this, for Asian businesses, to be successful in globalizing their business has never been easy. Companies have had different experiences from those in the West in expanding their business across the world, from a less mature market to a more mature market, from a less-developed economy to a more-developed economy, from a less-industrialized society to a more-industrialized society, etc. From the outset, Asian businesses are facing strong rivals *and* a Western business environment that they are not familiar with.

In terms of the state of technology development, in comparison with Europe and North America, Asia still has a long way to catch up. So it is crucial to use management instruments effectively to gain access to advanced technology, to transfer technological competence or utilize technology through alliances and partnerships with companies that possess these advanced technologies.

The experiences many Asian companies have been through are particularly valuable for late-comers. Effectively using management methods is the key to success, in particular in analysing companies' strengths and weaknesses, identifying their own position in the international market, then determining the best strategies in order to compete with their counterparts in the West and eventually, keeping up the position achieved or even creating new challenges for the rest of the world.

10. From Internal Management Excellence to International Business Competencies

We have seen that many Japanese companies have been successful in global competition. Their successes are always associated with a clear vision of business objectives and particularly a high quality of internal management. Japanese management style has even influenced the Western business world. The management in Matsushita was regarded as a model of management for many Japanese companies.

Matsushita Electric Industrial Co. explores the key elements that led to the success of Matsushita both in its domestic market and overseas. Furthermore, the case analyses its strengths and weaknesses in relation to the proposed acquisition of a US-based entertainment company. It examines issues regarding the company's vision, philosophy, the nature of strategy formation, inter-relationship of different core competencies, and organizational structure and configuration. The culture of Matsushita started in Japan and has built into the world's largest consumer electronics company.

Kao in Singapore places the student in the position of a country manager for a Japanese multinational. A decision has to be made regarding strategies for future goals and profits. In the process, conflicts between local managers and head office need to be resolved.

11. Competing in the World Market with Information Technology

As we all know, in whatever business, manufacturing or service, better communication between product suppliers, distributors, retailers and customers is crucial. Using information technology can help communication between them, and therefore enhance companies' business competitiveness. Compared with Western firms, Asian companies are relatively new in the world market. In particular, they have little experience of running businesses in the West. Using information technology is the one way for them to overcome their disadvantages in operating in an unfamiliar market. However, the application of information technology involves many aspects of companies' everyday agendas. Management needs to have a clear vision about what the information technology would bring to the company, to make a strategic plan about using information technology and then to adapt the system effectively to the business.

Singapore Airlines – Using Technology for Service Excellence describes how Singapore Airlines made its way into the top ten world airlines, with an international reputation for the service, comfort and luxury it provided both on board the aircraft and in its airport facilities. Facing intensifying competition from US and Asian carriers, Singapore Airlines used technology-based services to maintain its customer-oriented image. The key topic of this case is product differentiation in a very competitive industry where the core product is virtually a commodity. It leads students through market and customer analysis to identify SIA's position in the market and its major strengths and weaknesses, and therefore to determine SIA's marketing strategy and the role that information technology plays in SIA's success.

Sony Manufacturing Company UK (Bridgend Colour Television Operations) – Appropriate Use of Information and Technology in Manufacturing reviews a successful Japanese business in Europe, Sony Manufacturing Company UK. This provides an example of using a range of approaches: 'total quality control', 'flexible manufacturing systems' and 'effective information management strategies'. It focuses on the appropriate use of information and technology in manufacturing, highlighting the connection between information management and manufacturing, the basic principles of information management and process improvements, and the relationship between the supplier, distributor and sales downstream.

Sony Barcelona – Achieving World-Class Product and Market Quality Through Strategic Information Management exemplifies the Japanese company, Sony's operation in Europe. Sony Barcelona, in particular, creates an international challenge for world-class manufacturing excellence. It focuses on issues of strategic information management at three levels: improving quality through better information on its TV

sets by monitoring units sold to Sony personnel and by putting a design engineer in local Sony sales centres; developing an IS/IT system and strategy; and implementing the corporate supply-chain information management system (STREAM).

12. Finding Complementary Competencies – Managing Business in Europe through Alliances and Partnerships

Canon, a Japanese company, has developed its business in the European market through alliances and partnership. The advantages of joint ventures are gaining complementary competencies from partners. But, joint ventures can also be a joint source of problems.

Three cases are presented: *Canon in the European Copier Market, Olivetti in the European Copier Market* and *The European Copier Industry*. The first two together provide background information on these two companies: Canon, a Japanese company, and Olivetti, an Italian company – their history, product evolution, culture and management approaches, as well as the business of each in Europe (strengths and weaknesses). On this basis, their embarkation into the strategic alliance is analysed, in terms of the state of technology, market trends, distribution systems, office automation, impact of EU regulation and potential competitors. The third case provides background information on the European Photocopier Industry that should help the participants gain a better understanding of potential business opportunities for both Canon and Olivetti. The case 'The Olivetti–Canon Alliance: The 1995 Situation' (not included in this book) gives some recent information on the development of the Canon–Olivetti alliance.

13. Competing in COMECON[1] Countries

The former COMECON states in Eastern Europe and the former Soviet Union are increasingly becoming the focus of Asian companies, for many reasons. In particular, the standards of product quality demanded by this market are easier to meet than in the West. Asian companies are in a better position to produce at a price that matches the living standards of the majority of people. In addition, a less-organized market in Eastern Europe may be less frightening for Asian Companies, which come from a more or less similar background. Japan was the leader in investing in Eastern Europe among Asian companies and has been followed by many others.

Sony in Poland describes how the Japanese company saw a significant business opportunity in COMECON countries after it made a successful entry into the Polish market with its consumer electronics goods. In addition, the company was reviewing its

policy about how to best serve the burgeoning market in the COMECON countries in general. The case highlights implications of the political and socio-economic changes in Eastern and Central Europe for doing business in these countries, particularly in Poland. It invites students to consider a variety of distribution channels that would best match the rapidly growing market demand in Poland, and therefore decide upon the degree to which any approach can be generalized into a model for Sony's operation in other COMECON countries.

14. Shifting from National to Regional Organization Structures

Matsushita Electric Industrial Ltd. Europe – Sales and Marketing, 1994 describes how one of the world's largest electronics firms has managed its European sales and marketing activities as a set of autonomous country organizations. In the 1990s, with increasing competitive pressures and customers who are themselves operating regionally, Matsushita must re-examine the organization of its sales and marketing in Europe. Some factors that shape recommendations include customer needs, cost duplication, logistics, competitive positioning and the careers of managers.

[1] The Council of Mutual Economic Assistance was formed in 1949 by the Soviet Union. At that time, COMECON included the USSR, Bulgaria, Czechoslovakia, East Germany, Hungary, Poland and Romania.

10. From Internal Management Excellence to International Business Competencies

CASE 10.1 **MATSUSHITA ELECTRIC INDUSTRIAL CO.**

This case was prepared by Research Associate David Hover under the supervision of Professors Dominique Turpin and Per Jenster as a basis for class discussion rather than to illustrate either effective or ineffective handling of a business situation.

In December 1990, Matsushita Electric Industrial Company, Ltd. (MEI), the largest consumer electronics manufacturer in the world, offered $6 billion for the purchase of MCA Corporation, one of the US's leading producers of entertainment. Not only was it the largest acquisition ever proposed by MEI (and the largest purchase of a US company by a Japanese company to date), but it was also a bold manoeuvre for a company that had almost become synonymous with predictability and conservatism. MEI's reputation belied its impressive performance: *Fortune* magazine ranked MEI the 12th largest company in the world by sales in 1989.

The movies, records, television programmes and other products of entertainment companies like MCA were the 'software' that made MEI's video recorders, stereo equipment and televisions (its 'hardware') valued products. The idea of 'hardware' manufacturers also trafficking in 'software' was not new. In 1987, Sony Corporation, MEI's arch rival, spent $3.4 billion to buy Columbia Entertainment. Now, paying almost twice as much, MEI too was seeking to find synergies between 'hardware' and 'software'". The purchase renewed criticism that MEI was just a copycat of whatever new developments its competitors made. If that were true, however, the record also showed that when it followed the lead of other companies, MEI usually finished first. According to many, the key to its success was the powerful company culture developed by MEI's legendary entrepreneurial founder, Konosuke Matsushita.

Company History

Although Konosuke Matsushita would one day head the world's largest consumer electronics company, he had decidedly humble beginnings. He was born in 1894, in a small town near Osaka, Japan. At the time, his father was a land-owning farmer of comfortable means. Unfortunately, Matsushita senior was also a speculator on the local rice exchange and, when K. Matsushita was four, lost his land, house and almost all the family's possessions during a downturn in the market. Within a few years of the family's financial disaster, three of the elder Matsushita children died, leaving K. Matsushita as the only boy in the traditionally male-dominated Japanese family. At the age of nine, after he had completed the compulsory four years of education, K. Matsushita was apprenticed. Despite his poor health, his family's continuing economic plight had made the decision necessary.

Watching electric trains being installed in Osaka where he was working as an apprentice in a bicycle shop, K. Matsushita became fascinated with the potential of electricity. Shortly afterwards, at the age of 15, he took a job with the Osaka Electric Light Company as a technician intent on learning everything he could about this new energy source. To supplement his on-the-job training, K. Matsushita also briefly returned to school. Hampered by his poor primary education, however, he was unable to complete more than a year at the technical school. He made up for what he was unable to achieve at school by an unrelenting effort to excel at his job.

Driven perhaps by the expectations of his then deceased father, K. Matsushita was quickly promoted. His promotions, however, failed to give him personal happiness. He quickly found that the reduced workload in his new positions left him with too much idle time. The idleness sapped the energy and drive of such a young and ambitious individual.

Dispirited, K. Matsushita's health, never very good, deteriorated. His one consolation was the thought of developing an innovative light socket he had designed. His employer, the Osaka Light Company, rejected his idea, but he remained convinced that, with proper modifications, his idea would be successful. Determined to make his idea work, he resigned on 15 June 1917 and started his own company. He recalled later in his autobiography that his decision to start his own company achieved "the dream my father had cherished for me." With his wife and brother-in-law, he began manufacturing his light sockets in the two-room $13\,m^2$ house in which he lived.[1] His initial capital was the equivalent of five months' wages.

The effort failed. The company's small size, lack of reputation and the novelty of its product conspired to prevent sales from materializing. However, in the process of developing the socket, K. Matsushita had accumulated some knowledge about manufacturing insulators. When an order appeared for insulator plates, K. Matsushita did not allow pride to interfere with his ambitions. Temporarily abandoning the work on light sockets, he focused his efforts on fulfilling the new order.

As a result, the company was reborn in 1918. With the influx of capital from the sale of insulator plates, the company was able to improve its marketing efforts on sockets, and gradually a customer base was established. In time, other products were added; a battery-powered flashlight and a bicycle lamp, both of which replaced traditional candlelight with electric light, sold remarkably well. These and other early products helped the fledgling company build a reputation for developing and marketing high-quality innovative products.

---

[1] The house where he first started his business was made into a museum dedicated to the history of MEI. A replica of his house was also put on display at the MEI Taining Centre in Hirakata, Osaka.

Organization

The company grew quickly and achieved impressive results, continuously guided by K. Matsushita's steadfast commitment to doing his best. One of his most significant innovations was organizing the company around product divisions. In 1933, three divisions were established, each dedicated to a specific product range: (1) radios, (2) light fixtures and batteries, and (3) wiring implements, synthetic resins and heating appliances. Each of the divisions was an autonomous corporate entity, responsible for production, sales, product development and accounting.

K. Matsushita believed that the divisional structure would help maintain the competitive spirit necessary for a successful company. Not only would each product group be able to track its achievements against other units, but corporate management would be able to ascertain quickly which product areas were being the most successful and which needed action. With the smaller business units, managers were kept closer to the scene of action. Changes to product lines could be made faster and new sales efforts could be rapidly developed as market conditions warranted. Also, as independent organizations, the divisions were ideal training grounds for future managers. Keeping alive the entrepreneurial spirit that helped him build the company initially would ensure its continued success. Furthermore, he was fully aware that, as the company grew, he would not be able to manage everything himself nor would it be advantageous if he could.

The divisional structure had been maintained at MEI and by 1989, there were 19 major subsidiaries, many of which had evolved because of specific products. Competition in new product development and profitability was fierce between the divisions, just as K. Matsushita originally had hoped it would be. Although he had not been the only one to develop the concept (Alfred Sloan at General Motors and others in the US had instituted the same concept in the late 1920s), K. Matsushita's work was indicative of the creative energy he brought to his company.

After World War II

At the end of World War II, the US-led Occupation Forces dissolved the Japanese 'zaibatsu', which were accused of having supported the Japanese expansionist policies that had led to the outbreak of the war. 'Zaibatsu' literally meant 'financial clique' and was used to describe the old industrial and banking groups of interlinked companies which had dominated the pre-war Japanese economy. The Occupation authorities targeted MEI as a suspected 'zaibatsu' and ordered the company to stop production. Although MEI had manufactured military equipment during the war and operated through a number of companies (a result of its divisional organization), the company was not considered a 'zaibatsu' by most Japanese. The determined efforts of K. Matsushita and his employees convinced the Occupation authorities not to break up the company and it was allowed to resume production.

Once the restrictions on MEI were lifted in 1950, K. Matsushita began working hard at rebuilding the company to its former stature. In 1951, he made a trip to the US and Europe to learn more about Western management practice and to explore international opportunities. After visiting Philips Gloeilampenfabreiken N.V., a company which MEI had done some business with in Japan prior to World War II, K. Matsushita decided a link with the company would be mutually advantageous. The negotiations were difficult but an agreement was reached to form a joint venture to produce various types of bulbs in Japan, using management know-how supplied by MEI and Philips' technology. The link was very successful, and both companies agreed to extend the venture for a number of years. K. Matsushita noted its success was partially based on the mutual contributions of the two parties: as long as both sides were able to contribute, the link worked.

Retirement of K. Matsushita

In 1961, as the company continued its rapid growth, K. Matsushita retired as president and appointed his son-in-law, Masaharu Matsushita (Masaharu had adopted his wife's family name, as was customary when there were no male heirs), as his successor. K. Matsushita remained as Chairman, however, and continued to exercise control over many of the company's activities. In 1973, at the age of 79, K. Matsushita retired as Chairman, assuming the title of executive adviser. His influence was still considerable despite his old age. He demonstrated this in 1977 when he promoted Toshihiko Yamashita, a young (58) executive, past many of his seniors to the presidency. The promotion was considered very unusual in Japanese business circles where seniority was considered the prerequisite for advancement.

The Business of Matsushita Electric Industrial

MEI's business was divided into seven broad product categories: videos, communications and industrial equipment, home appliances, electronic components, audio equipment, batteries and kitchen-related products, and other (*refer to Exhibits 1, 2 and 3* to see some statements and balance sheets). Within the product categories were also six areas of strategic focus which had been established in the late 1980s: semiconductors, information/communications, new audiovisual equipment (notably HDTV and liquid crystal displays (LCDs)), factory automation (FA), automotive electronics, and housing and building products. Each area received special attention and was expected to be the source of new product lines. The first three were considered especially important for the company's mid- to long-term future. Besides the areas of strategic focus, management was very interested in developing integrated systems based on coordination between the R&D, production and sales activities.

Video Equipment

Video equipment was the company's largest product category. In 1990, sales were ¥1,598 billion (27% of the total). Although 1990 results were up 2% from the previous year, they were still well below the ¥1,947 billion level reached in

1985. The slow growth in 1990 stemmed from a reduced demand for VCR equipment overseas due, in part, to the appreciation of the yen, and to an actual decline in domestic sales. The introduction of new specialized amateur and professional models helped MEI in the growing video camcorder equipment market. High-performance and compact models had also performed especially well. Among the latest product developments were a modular VHS-C (small format, akin to Sony's 8 mm video cameras) offered through JVC; and a soon-to-be-released single hand-held Super (a high-resolution VHS system) VHS-C camcorder with a fuzzy logic image stabilizer.[2]

Colour televisions sold well in both international and domestic markets, largely under the Panasonic and Quasar brand names.[3] MEI maintained its market leadership in the fast-growing and high-margin, large-screen, high-quality units. Increased screen size, and enhanced sound and picture quality, were key strategies for the TV area. Satellite broadcast tuners, antennas and related equipment continued to sell well as increased programming options became more widely available. The company was also developing numerous types of LCD TVs, including sets for use on airlines. High-definition TV, included in the audiovisual strategic area, was successfully marketed for special applications in anticipation of further market developments. Much of MEI's work in the latter area was done in conjunction with NHK, the Japanese Broadcasting Corporation.

Communication and Industrial Equipment

Sales of communication and industrial equipment reached ¥1,375 billion in 1990, 23% of total sales. This amount was up 24% from the previous year, making it the fastest growing product area at MEI. The growth was partly due to MEI's increased emphasis in this area as the consumer electronics segments slowed.

Two of MEI's strategic areas were centred in this group: information/communications and factory automation (FA). Although MEI had entered the information/communications market at a late stage, its concerted marketing efforts showed results both in Japan and overseas. Major products in the category included facsimile machines, word processors (a Japanese character model had been exceptionally received in the market), personal computers, copiers, CRT displays, telephones, PBX, CATV, instruments, industrial robots, welding machines, air-conditioning equipment, compressors and vending machines.

In 1988, MEI paid $50 million for 52% of a small workstation manufacturer, Solbourne Computer, Inc., based in Colorado, USA. Solbourne's engineering workstations were similar to the products of such large US companies as Sun and Apollo (later purchased by Hewlett-Packard). The workstations also complemented MEI's factory automation efforts, its line of 32-bit PCs and its business workstations. The company had briefly entered the mainframe market in the early 1960s, but had subsequently withdrawn.

---

[2] The VHS system had been invented by JVC, the Victor Company of Japan. JVC was 50.1% owned by MEI.

[3] Other well-known brand names owned by MEI included National and Technics.

Industrial equipment sales were also strong. MEI was the world leader in the area of parts-inserting machines and precision chip mounters. One of its leading customers for these machines was Sony. Other parts of the group also performed well, notably mobile telephones, pagers, cordless phones, power distribution equipment and vending machines.

Home Appliances

In 1990, sales of home appliances reached ¥802 billion (13% of total sales), up marginally (3%) from the previous year. Home appliances was one of the oldest product groups at MEI; the company produced its first iron in 1927. In the late 1980s, MEI concentrated on developing high value-added appliances, incorporating leading-edge technologies and superior design through a campaign known as HALS (High Amenity Life System). The group's latest products included washing machines and dryers incorporating fuzzy logic. With the aid of a microprocessor, the machines gauged how dirty (or wet) the clothes were and adjusted the wash (or dry) cycle accordingly. Other significant developments included cordless irons, pressurized microwaves and induction heating rice cookers.

Sales of combined air-conditioning/heating units were strong after MEI introduced new compressor technology which increased the customers' convenience. Changes in domestic lifestyles benefited refrigerator sales because the market demanded more large-capacity units. Overseas production was also an important area for future developments, given the low penetration MEI had so far achieved.

Electronic Components

Sales of electronic components totalled ¥781 billion in 1990, 13% of total sales. The 7% increase from the previous year was the result of strong overseas and domestic sales, especially for industrial applications. Products in this category included integrated circuits, discrete devices, CCDs (MEI was the market leader in these image-sensing devices for video cameras), CRTs, image pick-up tubes, tuners, capacitors, resistors, speakers, magnetic recording heads, motors and electric lamps. The group also manufactured various types of semiconductors such as RAMs, ROMs, ASICs (application specific integrated circuits) and microprocessors for internal MEI customers and external markets.

Industrial components (office automation and automotive products) accounted for roughly 50% of total group sales. Overseas sales had also grown substantially as local production expanded in South-East Asia, Europe and the US. Rising demand for TVs had helped sales of the company's 'standard-setting' large-screen colour picture tubes.

Audio Equipment

Sales of audio equipment were ¥561 billion, 9% of 1990 total sales and up 9% from 1989. The increased sales were due to favourable market conditions in both

Japan and overseas. MEI sharply expanded its market share in 1990, as new high-quality multifunctional CD radio cassette players, portable CD players and portable headphone stereos were introduced.

MEI also developed a new technology with Nippon Telephone and Telegraph which greatly improved the quality of analogue-to-digital conversions. Other products included electronic musical instruments, speakers, tape recorder, stereo hi-fi equipments and car audio products.

In 1991, MEI again joined with Philips to develop the DCC (digital compact cassette). It was anticipated that the DCC would revolutionize the audio world in the same way that the compact disk had a decade before.

Batteries and Kitchen-related Products

Sales in the batteries and kitchen-related product category improved 10% to ¥312 billion in 1990 (5% of total sales). This category included dry batteries, storage batteries, solar batteries, solar energy equipment, gas hot water supply systems, gas cooking appliances, kitchen sinks and fixtures.

The market for batteries was undergoing a fundamental change in character as more and more products required lightweight small-sized high-performance batteries. MEI had begun manufacturing batteries in the 1930s and had a major market presence in the world. MEI batteries led in the areas of nickel–cadmium (used in portable electronic products such as cordless phones), lithium batteries for cameras, and alkaline manganese for audio equipment.

Lifestyle-enhancing products, part of the HALS programme, benefited from the considerable amount of new construction and renovation talking place in Japanese homes.

Other

Just under 10% of MEI's sales came from a wide range of miscellaneous products – bicycles (reminiscent of K. Matsushita's early apprenticeship), cameras, pre-recorded tapes and disks, water purifiers, and imported products including cabin cruisers, forest products, medical equipment and non-ferrous metals. Sales in this product area had increased 8% from the previous year. MEI was the largest importer of products (for resale and use as components) into Japan.

Distribution and Marketing

MEI's distribution system was acknowledged as one of the company's real successes. One executive noted: "Sony is known for new products, Hitachi for industrial machines, and Matsushita (MEI) for marketing and distribution." All sales were handled by the central corporate offices and fell into four areas: (1) domestic consumer, (2) industrial (components and subsystems), (3) over-seas, and (4) commercial, industrial and government. The product divisions were allowed to sell directly to wholesalers and important or large individual customers, but only under strict guidelines established by the corporate offices.

Captured retail outlets were a favoured distribution pattern for most of the large Japanese consumer electronics companies but, for MEI, captured retail outlets were the centre point of the company's strategy. In Japan, MEI sold 60% of its total domestic sales through 25,000 'National' shops (where sales of MEI products exceeded 80% of sales) and 'National' stores (MEI products sales were greater than 50%).[4] The average percentage of sales through captured outlets in the Japanese consumer electronics industry was 40%. MEI, with the largest network of its kind, expended considerable effort to maintain the effectiveness of this channel. Reflecting K. Matsushita's concern for 'cross-prosperity', sales managers were regularly asked about the profitability of their customers. Only after it was assured that their customers were making money were managers asked about their results.

MEI did not participate in the ownership of the retail outlets. Instead, MEI provided management assistance, and shared advertising promotional campaigns and long-term contracts to ensure the achievement of continued sales.[5] MEI had a strong history of close relations with its retailers dating back to K. Matsushita's efforts to sell his first bicycle lamp in 1927. To demonstrate the dramatic improvement incorporated into his new product, he donated more than 1,000 lamps to stores on the condition that the owner would leave the lamp on until the batteries died, about 20 hours longer than the best results from previously available lamps. The technique was a success as the greater efficiency of the Matsushita company product was easily visible.

MEI also had close ties with its exclusive wholesalers, frequently formalized by an equity position of at least 20%. The wholesalers and retailers both benefited from the presence of about 100 sales offices distributed throughout Japan. The sales offices provided management training and consultation as well as retail and showroom support.

Captured retail outlets had come under significant pressure in the 1980s because of a proliferation of large discount chains. Increasingly, captured retail stores had found their margins squeezed. ME management was clearly concerned about this erosion of the company's primary market interface and was making a concerted effort to improve the competitiveness of the stores. The improvements included rationalizing marginal outlets and encouraging remaining retailers to upgrade their lifestyle counselling and other community services. By adding value through improved service at the time of the sale, captured stores would be able to compete against the discount stores which could not and would not provide advanced customer services.

MEI had also initiated an integrated information network connecting retailers, sales companies and manufacturing divisions. Pana Van, as the

---

[4] For comparison, Sony had approximately 4,000 captured retail outlets the same year.

[5] MEI spent ¥24 billion in 1986 on advertising, which was slightly more than Sony (¥22 billion). The advertising-to-sales ratios of the two companies, however, differed dramatically (0.8 for MEI versus 2.2 for Sony).

system was called, provided on-line information on orders, marketing and inventory levels, increasing delivery efficiency, improving product availability and increasing knowledge of customer needs.

Non-consumer items were sold through two dedicated sales divisions: one handling corporate and government sales, and the other dealing with both domestic and overseas sales to manufacturers. Product divisions were allowed to sell directly to wholesalers.

Production and Manufacturing

Production was another area in which MEI had developed a reputation for quality and effectiveness. As with all functional areas at MEI, production had its own policies as a guideline. Managers tended to avoid any particular manufacturing systems. Instead, most believed it was essential to give careful attention to every aspect of production, i.e. initial hiring (Matsushita's goal was not to necessarily hire the 'best' workers, but to make them into the 'best' teams), quality design, excellent machinery and a complete understanding of the materials used to make the components. It was the combination of all these areas that made high-quality products.

One aspect of MEI's manufacturing which set the company apart from its competitors was that the company manufactured most of its own production machines. Because MEI built the machines itself, many believed it was better able to service and utilize them. The workers usually knew their machines intimately and, when there was a problem, were able to correct it immediately or have the engineers design the necessary modifications. About 20% of Matsushita's overall production was in machinery.

Research and Development

MEI's R&D was concentrated in four primary research centres focused on specific areas: information and communications, audiovisual, semiconductors and living systems. MEI was also proud of having two laboratories dedicated to basic and applications technologies: the Central Research Laboratory, and the Device Process Technology Laboratory. Major product innovations from MEI included a 64-bit RISC-type microprocessor, anamorphic aspherical lenses for use in digital photocopiers and camcorders, and a quasi-continued-wave oscillation blue laser source for possible application in small compact optical disks.

MEI also operated R&D labs in North America (4 in the US), Europe (West Germany) and Asia (Taiwan), staffed by local technicians and scientists. Ostensibly, these labs were to serve the needs of the local markets and to provide for technology transfer.

MEI spent ¥345.7 billion in the fiscal year 1990 on R&D, almost twice the ¥174.2 billion spent in 1983. (*Refer to **Exhibits 2 and 3** for information on R&D expenditures and capital spending.)

Management Style and Philosophy

MEI's corporate culture, built by K. Matsushita himself, was very strong. Company employees liked to think that, without the corporate culture, MEI would be just another electronics company. Konosuke Matsushita had firmly believed that hard work led to prosperity, and he had worked hard throughout his life to make his company a success. In his many writings, he proselytized on topics ranging from society to education, to management, to civilization and others. The values he held dear were typically those honoured in traditional Japanese society – responsibility, perseverance; gratitude and understanding (*refer to* **Exhibit 4**).

What set K. Matsushita apart from so many of his contemporaries, and won their respect, was that he took his beliefs seriously. He believed that the welfare of the company depended on management and labour working together. In 1920, two years after the company was established, K. Matsushita founded an association for all employees including himself. At the end of World War II, K. Matsushita had readily accepted the formation of a labour union at the company. Despite their demands for better conditions, when K. Matsushita was removed from office by the Occupation authorities, delegates from the union appealed on his behalf, citing his dedication to his work force and the quality of the company.

K. Matsushita wanted his company to be more than just a business endeavour. In 1932, he opened the company's first annual founding day, commemorating the founding of the company 15 years before, by declaring the company mission:

> Only after there is a limitless supply of material goods, as well as spiritual peace of mind, will man achieve true happiness. I believe that here is the manufacturer's true mission. I would like you all to keep in mind that the true mission of Matsushita Electric is to produce an inexhaustible supply of goods, thus creating peace and prosperity throughout the land.

K. Matsushita developed his ideas further and set out a 250-year plan to achieve the corporate mission of developing an ideal world, a remarkable goal for the small company it was at the time. The corporate mission was read at every annual meeting. Ever eager to enlist the support of his employees, K. Matsushita actively cultivated their involvement.

When the mission statement was first presented, employee representatives offered a response which read:

> We, the employees of MEI, are all pleased to be present at this ceremony.... While being the recipients of your kind and cordial guidance... we fear our accomplishments have been inadequate and poor. We take to heart your words and pledge to devote ourselves wholeheartedly to the performance of our role in the realization of the MEI mission.

The employee response was also read at the annual meetings.

The importance of the relationship between the company and the employees had also been demonstrated more recently. MEI endeavoured to continually hire new managers, regardless of short-term economic cycles; people were considered an investment in the future. Contrary to most corporations, MEI would continue to hire university graduates at a relatively consistent level in both good and bad times.

The mission statement was also the basis for the Company Creed and Pledge which, in turn, led to the company guidelines for behaviour (*refer to Exhibits 4 and 5*). The guidelines provided a code of ethics which the employees could refer to at any time. K. Matsushita believed that the employees would take these guidelines to heart and, in so doing, would become both better employees and better people.

Frequently, at the morning meetings held throughout the MEI company, employees were encouraged to present their thoughts on what these guidelines meant to them. The morning meetings were also an opportunity for birthday announcements of employees and other events within the company. Although expensive in terms of foregone work time, these morning meetings were considered fundamental to the company culture.

International Responsibilities

The 1990 Annual Report stated: "MEI is dedicated to becoming a truly international corporate citizen that contributes to the well-being of every community in which it operates." The company was also dedicated to increasing the role of local managers in its foreign subsidiaries. This project was still in its infancy in the early 1990s. Unlike Sony, MEI had initially used Japanese managers to run the company's first overseas operations (Taiwan and Thailand). As MEI's international operations were further expanded, there were a number of Japanese executives with international experience available to head up the new operations. Sony was not able to draw on a core of managers with experience overseas and drew from local sources to find managers, partially explaining the company's more international character. It was not until 1990 that MEI appointed an American as president of its 36-year-old US subsidiary, the company's largest outside Japan.

In Europe, however, as of 1991, all MEI country managers were Japanese. Akio Tanii, appointed as MEI's president in 1989, was open to using local managers to cope with the growing internationalization of the Japanese economy and MA operations. Such a move, however, would have major implications for such a traditional company, and many observers considered it one of the company's great challenges for the 1990s.

MEI operate overseas through 117 companies located in 38 countries. The company's local operations were expected to be an antenna which would perceive the needs of local markets and communities.

In fiscal year 1989, MA launched its 'Action Plan for International Cooperation' in order to further the company's global manufacturing and operations presence. MEI took the issue seriously; K. Matsushita himself had expressed his intent to spread wealth throughout the world. This plan also included technology transfer. Results showed persistence in the effort: 36% ($5.3 billion) of overseas sales were provided by local production in 1989, an increase of 21% over the previous year. The goal was 50% by fiscal year 1994. Additionally, MEI planned to increase imports of both parts and finished goods from ¥270 million in 1990 to ¥420 million in 1994, to meet domestic Japanese demand.

Future Prospects

When Konosuke Matsushita died on 27 April 1989 at the age of 94, his mark had been firmly stamped on the MEI corporate culture and identity. Before his death, K. Matsushita wrote extensively about his thoughts on how business (and life) should be conducted. Besides his writings, K. Matsushita's legacy survived in the many policies he designed within the company, and in the many executives he nurtured and encouraged during his many years of service. Some MEI managers, reacting to recent corporate activities, have recently emphasized that K. Matsushita was never wholly comfortable with a big company. His primary concern, they claim, was that MEI be a good company. These managers and others wondered if K. Matsushita would have approved of the MCA acquisition.

EXHIBIT 1

Matsushita Electric Industrial Co.
Consolidated Statements of Income
Years ended 31 March 1990–88

Income	Yen (millions)			US dollars (thousands)
	1990	1989	1988	1990
Net sales	¥6,002,786	¥5,504,250	¥5,067,188	$37,753,371
Cost of sales	4,009,590	3,670,885	3,343,520	25,217,547
Gross profit	1,993,196	1,833,365	1,723,668	12,535,824
Selling, general and administrative expenses	1,540,475	1,416,176	1,363,800	9,688,522
Operating profit	452,721	417,189	359,868	2,847,302
Other income (deductions)				
Interest and dividend income	213,242	177,857	151,707	1,341,145
Interest expense	(109,202)	(88,932)	(81,937)	(686,805)
Other, net	14,969	23,333	23,592	94,144
	119,009	112,258	93,362	748,484
Income before income taxes	571,730	529,447	453,230	3,595,786
Provision for income taxes				
Current	309,664	309,938	297,105	1,947,572
Deferred	(8,717)	(23,023)	(45,679)	(54,824)
	300,947	286,915	251,426	1,892,748
Income before equity in earnings of associated companies and minority interests	270,783	242,532	201,804	1,703,038
Equity in earnings of associated companies	11,272	11,650	8,810	70,893
Minority interests	46,494	40,720	45,991	292,415
Net income	¥235,561	¥213,462	¥164,623	$1,481,516
Net income per share of common stock	¥ 108.34	¥ 99.94	¥ 80.34	$ 0.68

EXHIBIT 2

Matsushita Electric Industrial Co.
Consolidated Balance Sheets
31 March 1990, 1989

Assets

Assets	Yen (millions)		US dollars (thousands)
	1990	1989	1990
Current assets			
Cash and cash equivalents	¥2,010,848	¥1,440,144	$12,646,843
Short-term investments, at cost, which approximates market	335,406	211,968	2,109,472
Trade receivables			
Notes	120,873	113,259	760,207
Accounts	1,015,719	696,098	6,388,170
Allowance for doubtful receivables	(24,251)	(22,179)	(152,522)
Net trade receivables	1,112,341	787,178	6,995,855
Inventories	846,005	796,509	5,320,786
Other current assets	308,364	295,356	1,939,396
Total current assets	4,612,964	3,531,155	29,012,352
Non-current receivables	344,261	280,782	2,165,164
Investments and advances	1,647,575	1,516,985	10,362,107
Property, plant and equipment			
Land	163,481	145,218	1,028,182
Buildings	605,201	541,915	3,806,296
Machinery and equipment	1,769,704	1,532,743	11,130,214
Construction in progress	56,530	55,912	355,535
	2,594,916	2,275,788	16,320,227
Less accumulated depreciation	1,637,274	1,451,576	10,297,321
Net property, plant and equipment	957,642	824,212	6,022,906
Other assets	288,769	248,754	1,816,157
	¥7,851,211	¥6,401,888	$49,378,686

EXHIBIT 3

Matsushita Electric Industrial Co.
Consolidated Balance Sheets
31 March 1990, 1989

Liabilities and Stockholders' Equity

Liabilities and stockholders' equity	Yen (millions)		US dollars (thousands)
	1990	1989	1990
Current liabilities			
Short-term bank loans, including current portion of long-term debt	¥1,045,848	¥829,671	$6,577,660
Trade payables			
Notes	72,839	76,041	458,107
Accounts	439,358	315,484	2,763,258
Total trade payables	512,197	391,525	3,221,365
Accrued income taxes	168,281	167,388	1,058,371
Accrued payroll	144,087	124,161	906,208
Other accrued expenses	372,599	301,136	2,343,390
Deposits and advances from customers	117,344	108,430	738,013
Employees' deposits	125,504	120,906	789,333
Other current liabilities	116,638	100,810	733,572
Total current liabilities	2,602,498	2,144,027	16,367,912
Long-term debt	1,197,082	621,903	7,528,818
Retirement and severance benefits	269,070	247,081	1,692,264
Minority interests	581,658	522,361	3,658,227
Stockholders' equity			
Common stock of ¥50 ($0.31) par value Authorized – 5,000,000,000 shares Issued – 2,080,234,037 shares (1,955,629,195 shares in 1989)	184,940	164,251	1,163,145
Capital surplus	541,786	486,554	3,407,459
Legal reserve	52,181	47,917	328,182
Retained earnings	2,487,093	2,283,310	15,642,094
Cumulative translation adjustments	(65,097)	(115,516)	(409,415)
Total stockholders' equity	3,200,903	2,866,516	20,131,465
Commitments and contingent liabilities	¥7,851,211	¥6,401,888	$49,378,686

EXHIBIT 4

Guiding Principles of Konosuke Matsushita

1. *Service to the public*
We shall fulfil our responsibilities to the public by providing high-quality goods and services at reasonable prices, thereby contributing to the well-being and happiness of people throughout the world.

2. *Fairness and honesty*
We shall be fair and honest in all our business dealings and personal conduct, always making balanced judgements free of preconceptions.

3. *Teamwork for the common cause*
We shall pool our abilities and strength of resolution to accomplish our shared objectives, in mutual trust and full recognition of individual autonomy.

4. *Untiring effort for improvement*
We shall strive constantly for improvement of our corporate and personal performances, even in the worst of adversity, to fulfil our mission to realize lasting peace and prosperity.

5. *Courtesy and humility*
We shall always be cordial and modest and respect the rights and needs of others, to help enrich our environment and maintain social order.

6. *Accord with natural laws*
We shall abide by the laws of nature and adjust our thought and behaviour to the ever-changing conditions around us, to bring about gradual but steady progress and successes in our endeavours.

7. *Gratitude for blessings*
We shall forever be grateful for all the blessings and kindness we have received, so that we may live in peace, joy and strength and overcome any obstacles we encounter in the pursuit of true happiness.

EXHIBIT 5

Company Creed
In full awareness of our responsibilities as a manufacturer we will devote ourselves to the progress and development of society and the well-being of people, thereby contributing to the growth of human civilization.

Pledge
We pledge to work together, in the spirit of mutual trust and through selfless devotion to our jobs, for the continuous improvement of corporate and personal performances.

CASE 10.2 **KAO IN SINGAPORE**

This case was prepared by Professor Joseph D'Cruz as a basis for class discussion rather than to illustrate either effective or ineffective handling of a business situation.

As he sat at his desk on the evening of 16 April 1980, Toshio Takayama pondered uneasily over what he should do about Kao Singapore Private Limited, where he was the newly appointed director and representative of the Japanese parent, Kao Corporation. Kao was the leading soap and toiletries manufacturer in Japan. (*Refer to **Exhibit 1*** for data on Kao and its position in the Japanese economy.)

In September 1974, after Kao and its former agent in Singapore decided to terminate their business arrangements, Kao Singapore had been set up to take over the distribution of Kao products in Singapore. At that time, Kao's sales in Singapore were only about S$2.4 million a year.[1] By 1979, sales had grown to S$4.5 million; however, the Singapore operation had never made money. Already by 1976, cumulative loss was exceeding equity. Nevertheless, the Japan head office continued to hope that Singapore could be made into a model international operation. Hence Kao Singapore was sustained through repeated injections of equity in 1977 and 1978. In addition, bank loans fully guaranteed by the parent were arranged to overcome cash flow difficulties. (*Refer to **Exhibit 2*** for financial data on Kao Singapore.)

Before Takayama was assigned to the Singapore Company, he had had an interview with his mentor, Kozaburo Sagawa, who was then Senior Managing Director of Kao Japan and Chairman of Kao Singapore. Sagawa had stressed:

> The Singapore market, though small, is ideal to be a model international operation. The market is competitive, complex but manageable. we want to learn from this compact international operation and use the experience to develop our other larger international markets.
>
> However, the current performance of our operation in Kao Singapore is far behind our expectations. We want to experiment, to lead and be profitable in this market. We want to turn Singapore into a model Kao international market which our other markets can emulate.

Takayama found that Kao's product lines were usually concentrated in the high-quality and relatively high-priced end of the market, while the Singapore market in general tended to be dominated by a wide range of lower-quality and lower-priced products. Knowing Kao's tradition of positioning its products as market leaders, Takayama was reluctant to adopt a low-price strategy in Singapore to achieve brand leadership. On the other hand, Takayama wondered how Kao could become market leader in Singapore.

---

[1] In 1980, 1S$ (Singapore dollar) = US$0.4670 and ¥105.54.

A proposal to launch Biore facial cleanser in Singapore lay on his desk. The proposal had been prepared by Chia Hock Hwa, the most senior local manager in Kao Singapore. Chia was pressing for an immediate decision on Biore. However, Takayama knew that the officials at the Tokyo head office would be firmly opposed.

Kao Corporation in Japan

Founded in 1890, Kao Corporation[2] had developed into Japan's leading cleaning products company for the household sector. Its first product, Kao toilet soap,[3] gave the Company its direction, which it continued to follow thereafter. Early efforts were focused on fats and oils (tallow and coconut oil), the basic raw materials of the soap industry. Thus Kao's interest in organic chemistry began. Progressively, Kao began to emphasize research in surface and polymer sciences because of the role surface tension played in soap chemistry and the detergent industry. More recently, the Corporation was engaged in research on skin physiology and other aspects of biological science, as part of an attempt to understand how the Company's products worked on the human body. (*Refer to Exhibit 3* for details on R&D at Kao.)

In Kao, senior managers went about the Company's business activities with an almost religious sense of dedication. This was reflected in the Corporation's slogan, 'A Clean Nation Prospers'. It was generally accepted that it was the duty of every Kao employee to 'strive hard to create products that will truly benefit people in their everyday lives'.

Fulfilling this mission required more than emphasizing research and development (R&D). Early in its development, Kao made the strategic decision to develop and produce in-house, wherever possible, the essential ingredients that would affect the quality of its products. The Corporation was not satisfied with merely mixing purchased raw materials to formulate finished products. Instead, it established laboratories to work on developing new materials which could be subsequently manufactured in the Corporation's own plants as the raw materials for its fished products.

This strategy of vertical integration was later extended into the marketing system. Many toiletries and cosmetics manufacturers in Japan tended to rely heavily on the country's multi-stage wholesaling system to place their products in retail outlets. Kao, however, worked through a network of wholesalers who distributed Kao products exclusively. In many ways, these wholesalers operated like Kao branches. In fact, Kao salesmen frequently worked from the wholesalers' premises. They would take orders for the wholesaler in addition to performing

---

[2] The company changed from its former name, Kao Soap Company, Ltd., to Kao Corporation in July 1982.

[3] This was a high-quality soap which, when launched in Japan, was the only soap that could claim 'so high in quality that it can be used to cleanse your face'. In fact, in Japanese the word 'Kao' means 'face'.

their regular jobs, which included promoting new products, doing administrative work with the trade (such as merchandising and handling complaints), and collecting information about competitors' activities. The close working relationship between Kao salesmen and the wholesalers often strengthened the bonds between Kao's sales managers and the owners/managers of the wholesalers. These exclusive Kao wholesalers were acutely aware of the advantages of distributing Kao products. They benefited not only from Kao's having wide product lines that were extremely popular with consumers, but also from the philosophy, style and management system at Kao. Thus, they were very eager to cooperate with Kao. Unlike other wholesalers, they were totally dedicated to that one company.

When Kao introduced its integrated Marketing Intelligence System (MIS) – designed to track sales by product, region and market segment, the wholesalers cooperated enthusiastically. They installed Kao's data terminals in their offices and even allowed Kao's salesmen to enter their own orders. The MIS was used both to monitor sales and market trends, and as a tool for market research. Kao market researchers frequently visited retailers along with the wholesalers' salesmen to gather information directly from the trade. Kao was known to operate one of the most sophisticated trade intelligence systems in Japan.

Supplementing its trade intelligence, Kao developed an equally sophisticated system of consumer intelligence. An integral part of this system was a 24-hour 'hot line' which consumers were encouraged to use if they had a complaint or any question about using Kao products. An on-line computer system assisted the hotline staff in answering queries. This system also recorded pertinent data from every call. Analysis of these data and other computerized data on market research served as the basis for monitoring consumer interests and identifying new product opportunities.

Managing Corporate R&D at Kao

Kao's managers firmly believed that R&D was an important element in the Corporation's strategy. Kao operated 12 laboratories employing about 1,700 people (roughly a quarter of the total employees), who worked in many different areas of science and technology (refer to **Exhibit 3**). The Corporation had developed a number of organizational devices and management processes in its R&D activities.

An example of the unique R&D operating style was the monthly R&D conference, usually attended by all members of top management and key R&D staff. These informal meetings were conducted like university seminars. Researchers reported on studies in progress and presented the results of their projects. The theoretical and practical implications of the research findings were openly discussed by the participants. During these meetings, researchers received prompt feedback on their projects from other researchers. They also benefited from the advice and encouragement that members of top management offered on the commercial implications of their work.

All R&D meetings at Kao were 'open door', i.e. any interested employee could attend. It was a strictly observed rule, however, that visitors never spoke unless asked for their opinion. It was not unusual to find employees from sales and marketing at R&D meetings. Occasionally, these employees even brought along outside visitors – suppliers, customers or academics. Visitors were often struck by the open and informal nature of these meetings. Kao's managers felt that this informality encouraged individual creativity, a vital ingredient to maintain the quality and momentum of the Company's R&D.

This practice gave Kao's R&D efforts tremendous flexibility and enabled the Corporation to undertake large-scale interdisciplinary projects. Furthermore, the projects were usually undertaken in spacious, open office research laboratories where scientists and engineers from various disciplines worked together daily in close physical contact with each other. Kao's top management considered this type of environment essential for its R&D activities as it facilitated integrated technological development.

The process of R&D was commonly referred to as 'sowing seeds for improved products to better satisfy consumer needs'. R&D was highly integrated with the Corporation's various other components, especially marketing. The Corporation's key technologies were continuously being applied in primary chemicals for new product development.

In developing and introducing new products, Kao closely observed a basic set of principles to ensure that the products would truly meet consumer needs:

1. Is the new product truly useful to consumers and society?

2. Is Kao's basic technology being fully utilized?

3. Is its performance superior to that of similar products made by competitors, both in terms of quality and cost?

4. Has the product recorded significant acceptance in consumer tests?

5. Has the marketing communication plan been effectively formulated, so that accurate information on the product's value is received by every participant in the distribution channel (from the Corporation to the consumer)?

Management would have to be fully satisfied with the responses to these questions before deciding to launch any products. Kao usually avoided the standard test marketing programmes favoured by its competitors before launching a new product. Instead, when basic requirements were fulfilled, Kao's products were often launched on a nationwide basis, mobilizing the entire sales force and wholesaling network to achieve rapid distribution. National advertising would then quickly follow.

Development of Biore in Japan

The development of Biore, a non-soap facial cleanser, followed the typical strict but simple process of Kao's R&D. Its impetus came from analysing data received by Kao's consumer hot line. These data showed that using soap to wash after removing facial cosmetics, the conventional method used by Japanese women, was not really effective. Consumers were asking Kao for a product that would give a cleaner wash. Laboratory tests confirmed that soap was not efficient for cleaning thoroughly after removing make-up. This was because the facial pores were often clogged with cosmetic pigments after using cleansing cream and paper tissues to remove make-up. Leaving pigments in the pores harmed the skin's natural mechanisms. Kao researchers concluded that a water-soluble product, gentle yet effective in cleansing delicate facial skin, was needed.

This challenge was solved by MAP, a neutral non-soap-based chemical developed by Kao's organic chemists. Biore was formulated with MAP and blended with a subtle flowery perfume specially developed by Kao's fragrance researchers to complement the product's image as a gentle facial cleanser. It was decided to package the product in a plastic tube to emphasize its quality image. Recommended prices for consumers were ¥300 for the 60 g size and ¥550 for the 120 g size, substantially higher than an equivalent amount of soap.

Kao considered two factors when developing its positioning strategy for Biore. One element was cleansing ability. Competitive products were cleansing creams, and facial and toilet soaps, mostly sold by cosmetic companies as part of a line of branded cosmetics.

The second element was the prevention of pimples. Since this was one of Biore's claims, it had to compete with the drug products positioned for treating pimples and acne. The major product in this category was Clearasil, an anti-acne cream marketed by Nippon–Vicks K.K., the Japanese subsidiary of Richardson–Vicks, a US-based multinational. Clearasil was marketed as a registered drug. Under Japanese law, registered drugs could be sold only through pharmacies. Hence, though Nippon–Vicks had extensive distribution of Clearasil at drug counters in retail outlets, its overall retail coverage was poor. Despite Clearasil's heavy advertising, its market share was small, as sales were limited to registered druggists only, where it held a dominant position.

Kao decided to avoid the constraints that applied to a registered drug product. Biore was positioned as a skin cleanser that also helped to prevent skin problems rather than as a product just to prevent or treat acne and pimples. Advertising focused on the benefits of a clean face, emphasizing the importance of thoroughly cleaning the face after the superficial removal of make-up (*refer to Exhibit 4*). This approach contrasted sharply with Clearasil's hard-selling commercials that focused on pimple treatment. Biore's advertising also deliberately aimed to downplay the product's treatment role.

Because Biore was not registered as a drug, Japanese law allowed Biore to have a significantly broader retail coverage than Clearasil. Biore was sold widely by conventional toiletries' retailers as well as at self-service toiletry counters in pharmacies.

The product was an instant success and a new category of facial cleansing creamy was created.

Kao's International Operations

Kao's first ventures outside Japan had been to search for raw materials. Coconut oil was an important raw material for many of the Company's products such as soaps, shampoos and detergents. As it was important to have a reliable source of high-quality coconut oil, a major subsidiary was set up in the Philippines to produce coconut alcohols and their derivatives. Later, other subsidiaries were established in Spain, Mexico and Indonesia to produce fatty acids, fatty amines and other raw materials. These chemical subsidiaries also benefited from Kao's R&D efforts in Japan. For example, Kao developed a species of more productive coconut plant which matured more quickly and produced fruits at a lower height. In Japan, Kao also conducted extensive R&D in natural fats and oils, using the results in its overseas operations.

Other subsidiaries were established in Taiwan, Thailand, Hong Kong, Malaysia, Indonesia, the Philippines and Singapore to produce and sell consumer products in overseas markets. While initial efforts in these countries were mainly to facilitate exports from Japan, Kao also emphasized the principle that subsidiaries' activities 'contribute toward improving people's lives in the host countries'. In every case, Kao tried to maintain close control of raw materials and the manufacturing process to ensure a consistently high-quality product.

In 1980, Kao began to expand marketing operations to developed countries. Overseas branches were established in the US and Germany, and plans were being made to set up branches in other countries. Progress was deliberately slow, partly because Kao's philosophy was to investigate the local consumer habits before introducing any fundamental product in a developed country. For example, when introducing a shampoo, the structure and physiology of the people's hair would be carefully studied so that Kao's product formulations could be modified accordingly.

As the Senior Managing Director, Kozaburo Sagawa was responsible for the major policy and strategy issues in Kao's international operations. At the same time, he was head of the Household Products Division to which the international counterpart reported.

Sagawa was a dynamic individual with a strong personality. Though some members of top management tended to be conservative in thought and action, Sagawa appeared to enjoy being different. He was known to use strong language and was reputed to have a fiery temper. However, he was generally respected for his creativity and ability to adopt a difficult course of action for the Company's long-term benefit. For example, he received credit for the strong performance made by an unorthodox but successful joint venture business between Kao and Beiersdorf AG, a major German company. Sagawa had always been critical of Kao's foreign operations. Therefore, when international business was added to his portfolio, there was much speculation among Kao's managers as to how he would improve things.

Takayama's Appointment to Singapore

Sagawa was widely recognized as Takayama's mentor in the Company. Takayama had joined Kao in April 1967 after graduating from Tohoku University. His first assignment had been in the Personnel Department where Sagawa was Director. Although Sagawa was a chemist by training and had been Tokyo Plant Manager for six years, he had a keen interest in general management and particularly in strategic marketing. With his persuasive personality and strong interests in human relations, Sagawa had succeeded in creating a very dynamic personnel department.

Takayama, then a new employee, respected Sagawa not only because of his seniority but also for his dynamism. Sagawa often challenged, with great conviction, the wisdom of continuing traditional practices. Sagawa's revolutionary ideas occasionally caused friction intra-departmentally as well as within his own department. However, his fine achievement record continued to earn strong support from most of his colleagues, particularly in top management. He aired his views openly and critically. He was hard on his staff, always demanding their best efforts in the shortest time possible. However, Sagawa had always been disposed kindly to Takayama, perhaps because Takayama was then only a trainee, but perhaps also because his open and straightforward behaviour was similar to Sagawa's. Takayama himself felt that it was his persistence and old-fashioned patience that appealed to Sagawa.

In May 1968, Sagawa was appointed to the main board of the Corporation. Three years later, he was promoted to the head of marketing operations. In June 1974, Takayama was transferred to the Chemical Division. He worked for another three years in the Chemical Division, responsible for the accounting and financial functions of two subsidiaries within the Division. In September 1976, Sagawa requested Takayama's transfer to the Marketing Division. Takayama was made directly responsible for a line of French perfumed soaps and fragrance products for which Kao then acted as the sole agent in Japan. For reasons not clear to anyone, Takayama reported directly to Sagawa. That was unusual, for Takayama's new role was of no particular significance, and his position in the management hierarchy was in fact considerably lower than the others reporting directly to Sagawa.

One day in February 1980, Sagawa called Takayama into his office. He explained that Kao's Singapore subsidiary was having difficult problems. For the past four years, sales had been growing but, despite financial support from the head office, the business did not appear to be viable. He showed Takayama the following summary:

Kao's Operations in Singapore (unit: S$000)

	1976	1977	1978	1979
Sales	2,517	1,967	2,642	4,497
Contribution of margin	908	692	973	1,922
(% of sales)	(36%)	(35%)	(37%)	(43%)
Overhead	1,206	890	1,163	1,965
Operating loss	298	198	190	43
(% of sales)	(12%)	(10%)	(7%)	(1%)
Kao's subsidy in overhead	–	471	778	963
'Actual' loss	298	669	968	1,006
(% of sales)	(12%)	(34%)	(37%)	(22%)
'Actual' breakeven sales level	3,350	3,889	5,246	6,809
(% of actual sales)	(133%)	(198%)	(199%)	(151%)

Sagawa provided Takayama with more details:

Like Hong Kong, where we have been relatively successful, Singapore is a free and competitive international market. Because of Singapore's strategic position in the region, I want Kao to be successful there too. This can be done by applying correct marketing strategy and an appropriate management style.

You may be too young (Takayama was then 35) to take charge of an overseas company. However, I have to send someone to replace the current manager and I want you to go there. I don't want to hear anything from you about accepting this job, but do ask your wife if she will go with you to Singapore. That's all.

After seeing Sagawa, Takayama knew that his transfer to Singapore had been already decided. Sagawa was right. Not only was he young, he had never been outside Japan, let alone working in isolation in an overseas subsidiary. Though he was nervous, he felt he had to do what Sagawa instructed. Outwardly he appeared confident. Inside, he knew this confidence was only because he felt that he had Sagawa's support. He was amused that Sagawa had said he should consult his wife. She knew Sagawa well as she had previously been a secretary for a Senior Managing Director in Kao. When Takayama mentioned the transfer to his wife, she calmly replied, "Is there a choice? If Sagawa-san says so, we have to go. Let's pack!" Next morning, Takayama sent a message to Sagawa, "My wife says 'yes'."

Three weeks later, he was in Singapore tasting his first overseas posting as a Director of Kao Singapore. In the months that followed, as he struggled to understand the various problems confronting the subsidiary, he often wondered how such a short simple meeting with Sagawa could have resulted in this dramatic change in his career and way of life.

When Takayama first arrived in Singapore, he knew that he faced a difficult situation. The outgoing Japanese Director, Nagase, had reported regularly that sales were improving and that the operational activities were going well. However, the Company was continuing to lose money, which was attributed to the high operational expenses. Although Nagase was eager to return to Japan and rejoin his family, he did spend a few days with Takayama to explain the Singapore crisis thoroughly. After Nagase's excellent briefing, Takayama felt that he understood the situation well, but he continued to feel uneasy, since the reasons for these problems remained vague and confusing.

Before arriving in Singapore, Takayama had decided that, since this was his first working experience abroad, he should spend most of the first year observing and learning about the Singapore operations, its market and culture. When he had previously done business with the French in Japan, he had found it difficult to understand foreigners. He remembered the cultural differences between the French and the Japanese. Therefore, he assumed that the Singaporean way of thinking might also differ from the Japanese. Until he understood the local people, he felt that he should avoid speculating or imposing his ideas about what needed to be done. After meeting with Nagase, he felt even more strongly that his 'observe first, do later' strategy was appropriate. With this in mind, he set about getting to know his local staff. He took an immediate liking to Chia Hock Hwa, a local manager. Board meetings with him were often 'conducted' in the local 'pubs'.

Sagawa had told Takayama that he would be in Singapore around four years. However, given the Singapore situation, Takayama estimated that it would need at least six or seven years to achieve something worthwhile during his term of stay. It would take one year to understand, the next two years to plan and experiment, and the last three years to set up a strategic plan. Takayama explained:

> I feel I should wait until the second or third year after I understand the local situation before trying out my ideas. At Kao, top management tends to say, 'hurry up' or 'do it now', but this Singapore situation reminds me of the old Japanese proverb, 'haste makes waste'.
>
> However, I am aware of my responsibility at Kao Singapore. Although I prefer to be an observer for at least the first year, I am prepared to accept the full responsibility from my first day in charge if things don't go well.

The Crisis of Kao Singapore

Kao's products had been sold in Singapore as early as 1965. At that time, Kao had appointed a sole distributor in Singapore – Boustead Trading Sob. Bhd., then a major British-owned trading house with significant operations in Singapore and Malaysia as well as in several other South-East Asian countries. Boustead had a strong network and considerable experience distributing consumer goods in these countries. In fact, when Boustead took on the Kao line, it was already representing P&G (Proctor & Gamble, a major competitor of Kao) besides other well-known brands such as Gillette, Ovaltine, Kellogg's and Del Monte. However, under Boustead, growth of Kao's sales in Singapore was slow. In 1975, Kao and Boustead agreed to terminate their Singapore trading arrangement. This was partly because Boustead was increasingly being pressured by P&G to decide between the two competing companies. Boustead chose P&G as it had a much larger volume of business than Kao. Despite this decision, Kao and Boustead parted on friendly terms; in fact, the two companies continued their shampoo joint venture operation in Malaysia which had started in 1972.

Instead of appointing another agent, Kao decided to set up its own operations in Singapore. Chia Hock Hwa was hired to run the operation. Chia had previously worked for Boustead, where he was responsible for sales of Kao, P&G and Gillette products in Singapore. Chia found Kao's corporate philosophy attractive and was interested in building the new business. He felt confident that with hard work and financial support from Japan, the Singapore operation could be made highly successful.

At the start, overall responsibility for the Singapore office was given to a Kao manager, a Japanese named Akimi Suzuki, who had been the director of a newly established Kao joint venture in Indonesia. To ease communication and accommodate his family, he had been technically based in Singapore, returning there once a month. For the rest of the time, he travelled throughout Indonesia.

When Kao's Singapore office commenced business, its major products were laundry detergents and a few shampoo items. Since detergents were bulky, transportation from Japan was expensive. To overcome this problem, Kao had made an arrangement with UIC (United Industrial Corporation), a local competitor in Singapore, to manufacture the Kao detergents for the Singapore market. Kao supplied or specified the raw materials and packaging, set quality standards and conducted regular quality checks. Despite difficulties in implementing this arrangement, Kao felt that it could be made to work well. This system enabled Kao to obtain detergents in Singapore at a lower cost than importing them from Japan. Another advantage was that Kao did not have to make investments in production facilities. Chia tried hard to convince the head office that Kao's detergent was not an appropriate product for the Singapore market even with this arrangement. He explained repeatedly that the Singapore market differed from the Japanese. In Japan, consumers had been using home washing machines for many years. They were quality conscious and willing to pay higher prices for better products. In Singapore, on the other hand, the market was acutely price conscious. Machines in the home were still relatively uncommon and laundry was mainly washed by hand. Thus the market potential for high-priced, high-quality detergents was limited. Despite vigorous marketing efforts, sales of detergent products in Singapore remained small.

In a final attempt to increase the detergent business, Kao decided to launch a product at the lower end of the market. Sales increased somewhat, but the costs of selling grew even more rapidly.

At the same time, other non-detergent product lines were gradually being added, mainly hair care products imported from Japan. Sales of these new products grew significantly. Kao Singapore consciously limited itself to those household and basic toiletry products that were well-established in Japan. To expand this business, Chia was constantly looking to Japan for new non-detergent products. In late 1976, Kao was persuaded to provide some funds to help advertise some of the new products. Though sales of these products responded well to advertising, Kao's head office was really more interested in promoting detergent products. Instructions were often being sent to Singapore to push detergent products more aggressively.

As Kao's Singapore business grew, Japan felt that Singapore required a stronger senior management team than the prevailing arrangement. Accordingly, Teruyuki Nagase was sent from Japan in 1978 to be the full-time Japanese director. Nagase was new to overseas operations and was persuaded to operate the Singapore subsidiary along the lines of the parent company in Japan. He emphasized detergents the same way as in Japan, obtaining more funds from Japan to advertise Kao's detergent products. Chia managed to persuade Nagase to maintain the level of funds previously allocated for hair care products. Total sales then began growing significantly; profitability increases, however, came mainly from sales of hair care products. Sales of detergent products also climbed, but the expenses for detergent sales grew at an even faster rate. As a result, Kao Singapore continued to incur losses.

With the newly available funds from Japan for advertising and promotion, Chia regained his confidence and optimism about Kao's future in the market. However, he said:

> We have got to be willing to do things differently. We are emphasizing the wrong products here. We must be sensitive to the environmental factors and move from a selling company to a marketing company. We must have a range of products that will give us steady growth based on both sales and profits.

Chia made no effort to hide his dissatisfaction with the detergent product line. He repeatedly complained about its low-price positioning. On the other hand, he admitted that the Singapore market was price sensitive, and any attempt to move the Kao product line upscale was unlikely to be successful. Until laundry washing habits changed, high-quality detergents would not have a chance, he reasoned. At the same time, Kao had no opportunity to become a low-cost producer in Singapore, because its detergents were being manufactured by UIC, the only viable local detergent manufacturer. Thus, Kao's costs would always be higher than UIC's, which had its own brand in the market. Chia was firmly convinced that detergents could not provide the base for a successful Kao business in Singapore.

When Takayama came to Singapore, Chia explained to him:

> We will never make it with detergents. If we want to lead and be profitable here, we have to think of something else or forget the whole thing.

When Takayama reported this opinion to the head office, he received a sharp negative reaction:

> Our company has been built on soaps and detergents.[4] That is the base of our business in Japan, and that should also be the base of our business in Singapore. It is not wise to change a corporate strategy that has been so successful. Instead, you must convince your people in Singapore to think correctly about the importance of detergents. Don't you understand your role in Singapore?

Biore for Singapore

On one of his frequent visits to the head office in Tokyo, Chia learned about the Biore development project at one of the open door meetings. Chia was fascinated by the Biore idea. He was convinced that he had found the product that could turn Kao Singapore around and give it a new direction. However, Biore had become a controversial product at Kao. In a company that had been built on soap, many were sceptical of a non-soap cleanser like Biore. Kao's longtime employees said:

---

[4] At that time, about one-third of Kao's total sales in Japan were in detergent products.

All these years, we have been telling our customers that they should use our high-quality soap to clean their faces. Now, with Biore, we need to say soap is bad for the face. That's ridiculous. It is also extremely difficult to convince women to clean their faces with a chemical product in a tube.

Chia obtained a sample of Biore. When he tried it in his hotel room in Tokyo, he was amazed by its cleansing action. He was deeply impressed and convinced that Biore's unique properties would give Kao Singapore a real chance to develop and lead a new market.

The more he studied the Biore proposition, the more he liked it. The Singapore market for cleansers was underdeveloped. There was only one major product sold as a facial cleanser – Dearland. It was manufactured in Taiwan and imported into Singapore by a local company. On his return, Chia bought a tube of Dearland. When he tried it, he was pleased to find that Biore clearly seemed to be a superior product.

Chia particularly liked the Biore idea because he felt that the product was capable of satisfying a need, and was effective and unique. He also realized that the product could be sold at a price high enough to sustain advertising. He said:

> With the higher margin, Biore is capable of making a significant contribution to fixed operating costs. This could turn the Company into a profitable operation within a short period of time. In fact, Biore could also help project the Company from a completely sales-oriented organization into a more strategy-directed consumer marketing company.

During his years working with Gillette and P&G, Chia had learned various aggressive marketing tools that he was eager to use but could not because the margins in the detergent business were so low. He felt Biore would give him this opportunity.

The Dilemma

Takayama stared at the proposal from Chia on his desk; it strongly recommended that Biore be launched in Singapore right away.

Although he knew that Chia was right, Takayama remembered his decision to act only as an observer during the first year. He was also familiar with the attitude of the managers at the head office in Japan. Facial cleansers were still new in Japan, and Biore was a new product category just created by Kao. The parent company had been built over the years on toilet soaps (launched in 1879), shampoos (1930s), detergents (1950s), laundry additives (1960s) and sanitary products (1975). Biore facial cleanser marked a challenging entry into the high value-added cosmetics business. That was not an easy entry in Japan, where the established competitors in cosmetics were strong and well-entrenched. Kao's managers felt that there was still much more to be learned about the facial cleanser business. Many regarded Biore as an experiment which could easily fail. The Biore product team, of course, was enthusiastic about their new product's prospects, sure that they had a winner. But they admitted that there were many uncertainties.

Takayama was at a loss about how to respond. He told Chia:

> We are not sure whether this new product will succeed or fail in Japan. If we fail in Singapore and they fail in Japan, we will be reprimanded for being impatient and not waiting for Japan's results to be known. If we succeed and they fail, we will have to withdraw the product from the market anyway, since it will be discontinued and no longer available. Introducing this product will work only if we all succeed, a situation that is uncertain at this point. The head office has instructed us to wait another two to three years. Furthermore, to launch this product now, we would need more advertising money from the head office. Even if we proceeded without their blessing, we would still have the problem of funds.

An integral part of Chia's proposal was his recommendation that Singapore should get out of the detergent business to free up the sales team for the Biore business. This recommendation was even more disturbing, and Takayama knew that the response from the head office would be strong and sharp. Chia stubbornly upheld his stand. He told Takayama:

> Kao should get out of the detergent business in Singapore. We've not yet made and will never make a profit in detergents. Actually, we are only helping to build UIC's business. The opportunities for us here are in hair care and cosmetic products, not detergents.

Takayama could see the merits of Chia's proposal and was particularly impressed by Chia's calculations:

> If only 10% of our sales in Singapore come from Biore, we will become profitable. For the same result, we would have to increase detergent sales six times.

Takayama also felt that this strategy might be the only way to fulfil Sagawa's goals to make the Singapore operation profitable and to start establishing Kao brands in leadership positions. On the other hand, he was afraid to take the risks that most of his colleagues in Japan were advising him to avoid. He knew that they were counting on him to proceed with building up the detergents business. Furthermore, he did not know the market well enough to be able to evaluate Biore's prospects in Singapore. Would Biore really do as well as Chia claimed?

As he pondered these questions, Takayama felt very alone and suddenly realized how much he missed his network of contacts at Kao. Takayama was well known and liked at Kao where so many different jobs had brought him into contact with a large number of people. After office hours, he had often met casually with his colleagues in bars and small restaurants. When something troubled him seriously, he would usually talk it over informally with several people. He had found that such dialogues would help him understand the various aspects of his problem and usually the appropriate solution would emerge.

In Singapore, Takayama was the only Japanese manager on the spot. He was alone with no opportunity to talk things over with his peers and superiors. It was then he realized why Sagawa had insisted that he take his wife to Singapore. Though she knew little about business matters, her support and confidence in him were comforting and he could talk to her in the traditional way.

Even so, Takayama's confidence in himself was becoming increasingly shaken. Having to decide about Biore was the major cause of his depression. He looked again at Chia's proposal for Biore. How should he respond to Chia? Should he stay with his original strategy merely to observe during the first year? Should he call Sagawa to ask his advice? Or was this the opportunity he should seize to make a personal impact in the Company?

He noticed that his ashtray was filled to the brim and that he had run out of cigarettes. The time had come to act. He looked around the empty room and murmured to himself: "I will decide this by myself!"

When Takayama officially presented the plan for launching Biore in Singapore to his seniors in Tokyo, he was severely criticized:

> You were sent to Singapore to teach the locals how to implement our corporate strategy. Instead, it appears that you have been convinced by them!

Takayama decided not to start by defending the Biore plan; first he reaffirmed Singapore's commitment to detergent products as Tokyo had prescribed. He reassured his senior colleagues in Tokyo repeatedly that he had no intention of abandoning the detergent business in Singapore. He promised that he would continue to try hard to build up that business. Then he sought their understanding and support for Biore. As he had planned his presentation, he had asked himself many times: "How else can I accomplish what I feel is best? After all, what is my role supposed to be?"

EXHIBIT 1

Growth of Japanese Economy/Total Advertising Expenditure and Growth of Kao Japan/Advertising Expenditures

| Year | Japan | | | | Kao Corporation | | | | | Rank in ad. expenditure |
| | Nominal GNP | | Ad. expenditure | | Net sales | | Ad. expenditure | | | |
	¥ (billion)	Growth rate	¥ (billion)	Growth rate	¥ (million)	Growth rate	¥ (million)	Growth rate	% of sales	
1965	33,602	13.3%	334	−4.3%	32,813	17.0%	2,894	19.3%	8.8	Unknown
1966	39,509	17.6%	383	14.7%	39,230	19.6%	3,982	37.6%	10.2	Unknown
1967	46,239	17.0%	459	19.9%	43,691	11.4%	5,264	32.2%	12.0	Unknown
1968	54,761	18.4%	532	15.8%	45,435	4.0%	5,688	8.1%	12.5	7
1969	64,920	18.6%	633	18.9%	50,179	10.4%	6,223	9.4%	12.4	8
1970	75,152	15.8%	756	19.5%	57,708	15.0%	7,169	15.2%	12.4	9
1971	82,806	10.2%	787	4.1%	66,131	14.6%	8,920	24.4%	13.5	5
1972	96,539	16.6%	878	11.6%	83,785	26.7%	12,419	39.2%	14.8	2
1973	116,679	20.9%	1,077	22.6%	116,189	38.7%	14,791	19.1%	12.7	2
1974	138,156	18.4%	1,170	8.6%	142,057	22.3%	12,804	−13.4%	9.0	4
1975	152,209	10.2%	1,238	5.8%	146,917	3.4%	13,910	8.6%	9.5	2
1976	171,153	12.4%	1,457	17.7%	161,056	9.6%	17,742	27.5%	11.0	2
1977	190,035	11.0%	1,643	12.8%	186,753	16.0%	17,858	0.7%	9.6	2
1978	208,781	9.9%	1,846	12.4%	214,246	14.7%	20,431	14.4%	9.5	2
1979	225,453	8.0%	2,113	14.5%	245,698	14.7%	21,243	4.0%	8.6	2
1980	245,163	8.7%	2,278	7.8%	252,438	2.7%	22,052	3.8%	8.7	2
1981	259,669	5.9%	2,466	8.2%	280,628	11.2%	26,612	20.7%	9.5	3
1982	272,383	4.9%	2,627	6.5%	305,551	8.9%	27,963	5.1%	9.2	2
1983	284,058	4.3%	2,782	5.9%	330,612	8.2%	28,361	1.4%	8.6	3
1984	303,020	6.7%	2,915	4.8%	369,812	11.9%	30,718	8.3%	8.3	1
1985	320,775	5.9%	2,983	2.3%	405,709	9.7%	32,026	4.3%	7.9	1
1986	334,026	4.1%	3,052	2.3%	441,172	8.7%	35,430	10.6%	8.0	1

Sources: GNP – *National Economic Accounting Annual Report by the Japanese Government, Economic Planning Agency.*
Total Japanese advertising expenditures – *Advertising Yearbook of Dentsu Incorporated,* Dentsu Japan Marketing, Tokyo, Japan.
Kao figures – Company records.

EXHIBIT 1 (continued)

Kao Corporation: Balance Sheet, Profit and Loss Account (unit: ¥ million)

	Mar 1976	Mar 1977	Mar 1978	Mar 1979	Mar 1980	Mar 1981
Current assets	36,605	39,415	54,379	62,998	74,042	74,384
Fixed assets	40,154	40,944	46,687	67,193	108,407	97,866
(Tangible assets	31,540	31,714	36,732	50,213	84,281	70,609)
(Investments,others	8,614	9,230	9,955	16,980	24,126	27,257)
Total	76,759	80,359	101,066	130,191	182,449	172,250
Current liabilities	40,752	41,784	53,777	65,882	78,093	69,953
Long-term liabilities	12,897	7,667	13,271	25,216	56,330	48,845
Shareholders' equity	23,110	30,908	34,018	39,093	48,026	53,452
(Common stock	3,632	4,400	5,397	6,165	7,479	7,749)
(Legal reserves	4,261	9,229	9,377	11,538	16,790	19,731)
(Retained earnings	15,217	17,279	19,244	21,390	23,757	25,972)
Total	76,759	80,359	101,066	130,191	182,449	172,250

	Apr '75– Mar '76	Apr '76– Mar '77	Apr '77– Mar '78	Apr '78– Mar '79	Apr '79– Mar '80	Apr '80– Mar '81
Net sales	146,917	161,056	186,753	214,246	245,698	252,438
Ordinary profit	4,422	6,127	7,377	9,797	8,835	8,880
Income before tax	4,243	5,988	7,089	9,269	8,149	9,233
Income after tax	2,059	2,749	2,930	3,304	3,619	3,885

EXHIBIT 2

Kao (Singapore) Private Limited

Sales Amount by Product Category (unit: S$000)

	Sep '75– Dec '75	Jan '76– Dec '76	Jan '77– Dec '77	Jan '78– Dec '78	Jan '79– Dec '79	Jan '80– Dec '80
Toilet soap	–	29	14	28	106	310
Shampoo and other hair care	211	359	431	945	1,878	2,980
Laundry detergent	818	2,082	1,248	1,249	1,664	1,717
Other detergents	5	14	249	389	805	769
Others	6	33	25	31	44	60
Total	1,040	2,517	1,967	2,642	4,497	5,836

Sales Contribution by Product Category (unit: %)

	Sep '75– Dec '75	Jan '76– Dec '76	Jan '77– Dec '77	Jan '78– Dec '78	Jan '79– Dec '79	Jan '80– Dec '80
Toilet soap	–	1	1	1	2	5
Shampoo and other hair care	20	14	22	36	42	51
Laundry detergent	79	83	63	47	37	30
Other detergents	0.5	0.5	13	15	18	13
Others	0.5	1.5	1	1	1	1
Total	100	100	100	100	100	100

EXHIBIT 2 (continued)

Balance Sheet (unit: S$000)

	Dec 1975	Dec 1976	Dec 1977	Dec 1978	Dec 1979	Dec 1980
Current assets	553	110	412	686	1,547	2,010
Cash	359	1	3	5	4	27
Trade debtors	123	43	141	298	873	994
Inventories	60	41	235	300	511	527
Others	11	25	33	83	159	462
Fixed assets	62	140	129	153	197	405
Motor vehicles	57	129	115	130	164	370
Others	5	11	14	23	33	35
Total	615	250	541	839	1,744	2,415
Current liabilities	547	516	774	924	1,821	2,345
Trade creditors	372	183	401	461	1,110	1,305
Bank overdraft	–	213	272	314	398	480
Others	175	120	101	149	313	560
Shareholders' equity	68	(266)	(233)	(85)	(77)	70
Share capital	100	100	300	600	600	600
Revenue reserve	(32)	(366)	(533)	(685)	(677)	(530)
Total	615	250	541	839	1,744	2,415

(continued)

EXHIBIT 2 (continued)

Profit and Loss Account (unit: S$000)

	Sep '75–Dec '75	Jan '76–Dec '76	Jan '77–Dec '77	Jan '78–Dec '78	Jan '79–Dec '79	Jan '80–Dec '80
Net sales	1,040	2,517	1,967	2,642	4,497	5,836
Cost of sales	842	1,609	1,275	1,669	2,575	2,934
Gross profit	198	908	692	973	1,922	2,902
Admin., selling exps.	83	432	619	848	1,121	1,609
Marketing expenses	151	774	271	315	844	1,121
Operating profit/(loss)	(36)	(298)	(198)	(190)	(43)	172
Non-operating profit/(loss)	(1)	(33)	33	43	41	(25)
Profit/(loss) before taxation	(37)	(331)	(165)	(147)	(2)	147
Taxation	–	–	–	–	–	–
Profit/(loss) after taxation	(37)	(331)	(165)	(147)	(2)	147
Depreciation charged for the year	3	30	38	48	65	123
Kao Japan's Subsidy*	–	–	471	778	963	901

* For marketing activities not included in the above profit and loss account.

EXHIBIT 3

R&D at Kao Corporation

Kao had 12 R&D laboratories with more than 1,700 researchers.

Laboratories	R&D activities
(1) Wakayama First Laboratory	• Fat and oil chemistry • Organic chemistry • Polymer science • Manufacturing processes
(2) Wakayama Second Laboratory	• Specialty chemicals • Lubricant additives • Foundry chemicals
(3) Tochigi First Laboratory	• Biological science • Skin physiology • Organic chemistry
(4) Tochigi Second Laboratory	• Household products
(5) Tochigi Third Laboratory	• Hygiene products • Technology of developing composite materials
(6) Tokyo First Laboratory	• Hair care products • Colour science • Fragrances and flavours
(7) Tokyo Second Laboratory	• Skin care products • Cosmetics
(8) Kashima Laboratory	• Fat and oil chemistry • Edible oils and foods • Fermentation and enzymes
(9) Recording and Imaging Science Laboratories	• Applied physics • Information and electronic industries related products
(10) Knowledge & Intelligence Science Institute	• Computer science • Information science
(11) Production Technology Institute	• Production technology systems
(12) Kao Institute for Fundamental Research	• Fundamental research in cooperation with domestic and foreign universities and research institutes

EXHIBIT 4

New Product Launch Plan for Biore Facial Cleansing Foam in Japan (Extract)

1. *Market situation*
(a) Products currently used for facial cleansing are cleansing cream, facial soap and toilet soap.
    The market shares of these products are 44%, 31% and 25%, respectively. It is projected that the share of cleansing cream will grow considerably because of some changes observed in the facial cleansing habits of consumers.

(b) The usage rate of cleansing differs among age groups:

Age group (year)	15–19	20–24	25–34	35–44	45–54	55–59
Usage rate	56%	70%	54%	48%	34%	28%

Heavy users are the young 20s followed by high teens, and older 20s or young 30s.

(c) What are product benefits that consumers expect to get from cleansing cream?

	15–24 years	25–39 years
• Gentle on skin/Less skin irritation by use	21%	34%
• No tight feeling/Feel moisturized after use	22%	23%
• Helps to prevent pimples	11%	2%

Though a good cleansing ability is the common expectation, there are differences between age groups. That is, high teens and young 20s expect gentleness on the skin and pimple prevention as well, while the other age groups show higher expectation on gentleness even on delicate skin.

(d) The market size of cleansing cream has been reported as follows:

1978	*1979*	*1980*
¥12 billlion	¥13 biillion	¥14 biillion

The total market size of cleansing cream and facial soap is estimated to be approximately ¥25 billion in 1980.

2. *Biore facial cleansing foam*
(a) Biore performs differently compared with other existing facial cleansing products.
    It is gentle even on delicate skin. It does not leave a 'tight' feeling but leaves the moisturized feeling even if it is repeatedly used in a day. It is also effective in the prevention of pimples.

(b) Biore's main ingredient is MAP (Mono-Alkyl Phosphate) which was developed by Kao's R&D.
    MAP is neutral and non-alkaline. It is totally different from soap. It is not harmful to the skin but is as gentle as water. MAP's cleansing ability is as good as that of soap. While cleansing by soap washes away the NMF (natural moisturizing factor) of the skin, MAP washes off dirt but retains the NMF of the skin. This is why cleansing by soap leaves a 'tight' feeling on the skin but MAP does not.
    Together with an antiseptic agent and an antiphlogistic agent, MAP also works effectively to prevent pimples.

EXHIBIT 4 (continued)

3. *Biore marketing objectives*

(a) To emphasize the gentleness of the product on the skin, together with the reduced chance of skin troubles or irritation, even with the frequent use of the product.

(b) To create and encourage a new cleaner and gentler washing habit.

(c) To achieve a good product distribution in the market and to secure a dominant position against existing competitors' products.
   Note: Almost all of existing competitors' products are packed in a tube or a jar, and all are soap-based.

4. *Biore marketing activities*

(a) To launch the product in March 1980.

(b) Media advertisement

   • To start in April mainly using TV and magazines;

   • To target females in the 20s who are heavy users of cleansing cream and high teens who are concerned with pimple prevention;

   • To promote brand awareness, explain product characteristics and encourage a new facial cleansing habit.

(c) Product distribution

   • To achieve high product distribution, especially at self-service outlets and pharmacies;

   • Targeted distribution ratios are 85% and above at self-service outlets, 60% and above at pharmacies, and 50% and above at other types of outlet.

(d) Product sampling

   • To carry out a sampling programme to the targeted user group, and encourage trial usage of the product.

11. Competing in the World Market with Information Technology

CASE 11.1 # SINGAPORE AIRLINES – USING TECHNOLOGY FOR SERVICE EXCELLENCE

This case was prepared by Professors Sandra Vandermerwe and Christopher H. Lovelock as a basis for class discussion rather than to illustrate either effective or ineffective handling of a business situation. This case has won a 1994 European Case of the Year prize, awarded by ECCH (European Case Clearing House, Cranfield,UK)

As Robert Ang left the marketing executives' meeting and walked through the open air gallery back to his office in Airline House, he remembered what J. Y. Pillay, Singapore Airlines' Chairman, had said four years earlier at the company's 40th anniversary celebrations in 1987. "At 40 the symptoms of middle age begin and that's when complacency sets in," he had warned. Ang thought to himself: "and now that we are 44, this risk is even greater if we don't do something to hold on to our customer-oriented image." The discussion at the meeting on this fine May morning had centred on the role of technology in achieving this goal.

Ang paused to watch a Boeing 747-400 coming in to land. Dubbed the 'Megatop' because of its extended upper deck, the aircraft was the most recent addition to the company's ultra-modern fleet. Singapore Airlines' blue, white and yellow colours shone brightly in the steamy mid-day heat.

As Ang entered the office complex that housed his marketing systems team, he imagined the passengers starting to disembark after a 12- to 13-hour non-stop trip from Europe. What sort of flight had they had? Had the long journey gone well, reinforcing Singapore Airlines' reputation as one of the world's best airlines? The cabin crew would now be saying goodbye, and the passengers would soon be welcomed into the spacious elegance of Terminal 2 at Changi Airport, one of the largest and most modern in the world.

Ang knew that the company's achievements were already considerable; it had become one of the world's 10 biggest international airlines. But now, on the threshold of a new decade, the question was: could Singapore Airlines continue to attract increasing numbers of international customers?

"We are leaders in service, in comfort and luxury. Our customers tell us they fall in love when they fly with us. Where do we go from here?" were some of the remarks voiced at the meeting. For Robert Ang, there was only one logical answer: they had to satisfy the needs of contemporary travellers, which meant being able to bring the sophisticated technology found in people's homes and offices into the air. "Very little attention has been given to adapting technology strategically for our business," he had declared to his colleagues that morning. "For instance, home audio systems are fantastic. But in the air, they're terrible.

We have to close this technology gap and provide modern customers with interesting and useful technology-based services."

Ang's views had been received with interest. His boss, the director of marketing planning, had closed the meeting by asking him to come up with some specific suggestions. "But," he had cautioned, "don't suggest anything that might conflict with the romance and superb personal service we're rightly famous for!"

Background

"How did it all begin?" was a question that people encountering Singapore Airlines for the first time often asked. Many were surprised that a small island republic, measuring only 38 km long by 22 km wide (16 × 24 miles), and with a population of 2.7 million, could have one of the world's largest and most profitable airlines. Even more remarkable were the accolades bestowed by air travel organizations. In 1990, *Air Transport World* magazine named SIA 'airline of the year'; *Conde Nast's Traveler* termed it the 'world's best airline'; and *Business Traveler International* called SIA the 'best international airline'.

Republic of Singapore

Just north of the equator, with a command of the straits between Malaysia and Indonesia, Singapore was ideally located for both shipping and airline routes. Being at the intersection of East and West, it saw itself at the heart of trade and business between the two.

In the 26 years since its independence in 1965, the nation had made what most observers considered to be astonishing economic progress. Per capita national income had reached US$10,450, representing 37% that of Switzerland, which Singaporean planners often cited as their economic model. It boasted not only one of the world's largest and most modern port facilities, but an airport, opened in 1981 and expanded in 1990, of equal calibre. Other accomplishments included a state-of-the-art telecommunications system, well-engineered highways, and the new Mass Rapid Transit rail system. Heavy investments in education and a strong work ethic had created a well-trained and motivated work force. By 1991, Singapore was one of the world's largest shipbuilding and ship-repairing centres, the third largest oil refining and distribution complex, and had also become an important banking and financial centre.

Singapore had made a particular effort to attract high-technology firms, and many international companies had set up offices and plants on the island. Government planners saw technology as a driving force in the economy. As advances in telecommunications proceeded, and Singapore Telecom continued to push towards a fully digitalized system, planners spoke about creating an 'intelligent island'.

History of Singapore Airlines

Who would have believed that a country only one-quarter the size of Rhode Island, the smallest state in the US, would produce one of the most profitable airlines in the world? The story of Singapore Airlines officially started on 1 May 1947, when the first scheduled flight of Malaysian Airlines from Singapore landed in Penang. When both Malaysia and Singapore became independent in the mid-1960s, the name of the carrier was changed to Malaysia–Singapore Airlines. However it soon became obvious that the two nations had different priorities. Malaysia's main interest was having a flag carrier that would provide domestic and regional routes. But, being a small island, Singapore did not need domestic services; instead, its goal was to have long-distance international routes. It was agreed that the assets should be divided and two separate airlines created.

Singapore Airlines first flew under its own colours in October 1972. When it was announced that Malaysia and Singapore had agreed to establish two separate flag carriers, optimism was tempered by uncertainty and disbelief. Could an airline from such a small country compete in the international big league? Nevertheless, the 1970s seemed to be a good time for an airline to take off and succeed. Not only did the remarkable passenger growth of the 1960s – when traffic was doubling every five years – promise to continue, but ever increasing numbers of people worldwide were travelling to more places. In addition, exciting new high-performance jets were being introduced.

Although Singapore Airlines (SIA) was state owned, the government's role in policy making and day-to-day management was minimal; senior executives were told not to expect any subsidy or preferential treatment. What the government did do, however, was to offer foreign carriers the opportunity to operate out of Singapore, under the condition that SIA would receive similar rights, even if they were not exercised immediately. The new airline pushed relentlessly for growth and innovation. Three months before operations began, it signed a contract with Boeing for the delivery of two B747-200s, with an option on two more. It was the first airline in South-East Asia to order jumbo jets.

Singapore Airlines also concentrated on marketing: the airline's name and its logo – a stylized yellow bird – decorating the aircraft's dark blue tail fins soon became well-known on the routes it operated. The goal was to create a distinctly different airline that would be international but retain its Asian personality. Most importantly, top management insisted that it emphasize service to passengers who, they constantly reminded staff, were the unique reason for the airline's existence. In a world where one carrier resembled another, they realized that the cabin crew was the prime link between the passenger and the airline. The idea was to use the island's only real resource – the natural hospitality of its people – as a competitive advantage. In this way, it seemed certain that Singapore's national carrier would be remembered – and remembered favourably.

Research had shown that, when all other things were equal, passengers responded most to the appeal of high-quality in-flight services. SIA was the first airline to put 'snoozers' (fully reclining seats) in its aircraft. Since the company did not belong to IATA (International Air Transport Association), SIA's management went against the rules by serving free drinks, offering free movie headsets and other extras. The intent was to firmly establish an image of SIA in customers' minds as *the* airline for fine service.

The 'Singapore Girl' – the personification of charm and friendliness – became a reality after painstaking recruiting, training and retraining. The best-looking and most helpful young women were selected as stewardesses. They were given a maximum of three contract terms of five years each, above average wages and high status in the company. Better staff were given the possibility of promotion to senior jobs within SIA after the 15-year period. An extensive and distinctive advertising campaign promoted these stewardesses dressed in multi-coloured, ankle-length dresses made from beautiful batik fabric designed by the Paris couturier, Balmain. Male flight attendants were more conventionally dressed in light blue blazers and black trousers.

These sarong–sebaya-clad women became the symbol of the airline's mission to deliver high-quality personalized service. Research showed that they had the most lasting impact on passengers. Travellers reported that their distinctive uniform and charm were, in reality, all that the advertising had promised, and that in-flight service was better than anything they had experienced in a long time.

Top management was equally concerned with services on the ground. In 1973 a subsidiary company, Singapore Airport Terminal Services (SATS), was formed to perform ground handling, catering and related tasks. Later, it started offering its services on a contract basis to other carriers that had operations in Singapore. In 1985, SATS was restructured into a holding company with four subsidiaries –SATS Passenger Services, SATS Catering, SATS Cargo and SATS Apron Services.

Singapore Airlines survived the two oil shocks of the 1970s and continued to grow, creating headlines with such innovations as supersonic Concorde service between London and Singapore, operated jointly with British Airways, featuring BA colours on one side of the aircraft and SIA colours on the other. It also expanded its route structure. Huge aircraft orders, including what was then the largest in civil aviation history, were made. Thanks to strong profits, the airline was able to invest in new equipment without incurring significant debt. These enormous purchases were not all incremental additions to the fleet, for the company resold used aircraft after only a few years. Because they had been so well maintained, the 'old' aircraft found ready buyers at good prices in the second-hand market.

The Situation in 1991

As one industry observer remarked: "1990 was a year that most airlines would sooner forget!" Battered by recession, a high rise in oil prices, high interest rates on heavy debt loads, and the tensions arising from the Iraqi invasion of Kuwait, most major airlines suffered heavy financial losses. The outbreak of hostilities in the Gulf intensified problems; fear of terrorist attacks sharply reduced passenger loads on most international routes. But, at a time when many other airlines were retrenching, Singapore Airlines actually increased its advertising budget.

SIA's consolidated financial results for the fiscal year ending 31 March 1991 showed only a slight decline in revenues, from S$5.09 billion to S$4.95 billion.[1] The number of passengers carried climbed from 6.8 million to 7.1 million, even though the load factor dropped from 78.3% to 75.1% as a result of a jump in fleet size. In 1990, SIA had the highest operating profit of any airline in the world: US$775 million. Apart from its marketing appeal, Singapore Airlines had another point in its favour – the higher margins obtained on airline services in Asia. The Asian carriers did not compete on price among themselves. They preferred non-price forms of competition such as better service, more destinations, more frequent schedules and newer fleets. With the entry of US players into the region, however, price became a more important feature.

The airline's fleet of 29 Boeing 747s and 14 Airbus 310s was the youngest fleet of all international carriers, with an average aircraft age of 4.75 years, compared with an industry average of around 10 years. The company had 36 new aircraft on order (of which 28 were the new B747-400s) and another 34 on option. Management was convinced that newer planes were not only more attractive to passengers and helped staff provide better service, but also offered other advantages such as greater reliability and lower fuel consumption. *Exhibit 1* compares Singapore Airlines' performance measures with those of other major international airlines.

By 1991 Singapore Airlines was among the ten biggest airlines in the world, as measured in terms of international tonne-kilometres of load carried. Its network linked 63 cities in 37 countries, and soon it would fulfil a long-held ambition to serve the East coast of the United States with a transatlantic service from Frankfurt to New York. Singapore Changi Airport had become one of the world's largest and busiest terminals.

Government holdings had been reduced through stock sales to 54% of the company's assets. The airline had joined in a trilateral alliance with Swissair and the US carrier, Delta Airlines, to cooperate on customer servicing, interchangeable tour packages, through check-in, joint baggage handling, sharing of airport lounges and joint promotions. It had also become a member of IATA in order to give the airline a voice in key industry forums, and greater access to their technical expertise and accredited sales agents. However, SIA did not want to participate in deliberations on tariff coordination where fare issues were discussed.

Despite the airline's achievements, there were some disquieting signs on the horizon. Competition was intensifying and service quality improving among a number of both Western and Asian airlines, including Hong Kong-based Cathay Pacific, Japan Airlines, a new strongly financed Taiwanese start-up called Eva Air, Thai International and Malaysia Airlines. The latter two both featured stewardesses in eye-catching uniforms based on traditional costumes.

---

[1] At the end of March 1991, the exchange rate for the Singapore dollar was:
SwissF1.25 = S$1.00; US$1.00 = S$1.70; £1.00 = S$3.10.

With rising living standards in Singapore came higher expectations among its more than 13,000 employees, of whom some 4,200 were cabin crew. The company was finding it increasingly difficult to attract younger people, motivate existing employees and maintain its policy of employing the best staff for customer contact roles.

Maintaining the Customer Service Philosophy

Recognizing that the most exciting years were now over, top management continued to stress the importance of SIA's customer philosophy and service culture. The underlying principle that the customer came first was carried through at all levels of the organization. How customers were handled at each point of contact was considered of paramount importance. Company policy stated that if a trade-off had to be made, it should be made in favour of the customer. For example, contrary to the practice at other airlines, no customer was allowed to be downgraded for a Singapore Airlines senior executive who wanted a special seat.

Ground had recently been broken for a new US$50 million training centre, designed to drill all employees in the fine art of serving customers. As reported in the *Straits Times*, Singapore's leading newspaper, everyone – from the floor sweeper to the deputy managing director – would receive this training. The underlying philosophy was to enable staff to place themselves in the customer's position. A lot of the training time was thus experientially based. Key people were sent on special missions to see what other airlines were doing and how customers were handled. Special delay simulation games groomed staff on ways to cope with delay situations, one of the major complaints received from passengers.

One principle remained constant: staff had to be as flexible as possible in their dealings with customers, even if it took more time and effort. Management constantly reiterated that customers could not be told what to do simply because it suited the company. Some passengers wanted to eat as soon as they boarded, others preferred to wait. Customers could not be pigeonholed; they often changed their minds. They might come on board intending to sleep and then decide to watch a movie after all. On long hauls, flexibility was especially important. Most passengers had individual habits that corresponded to their travel agendas, which could include sleeping at the beginning and working later, or vice versa.

Staff had learned that customers were happier when given a choice. Offering more meal variations automatically reduced the number of unhappy people. Menus, typically changed by other airlines no more than four times a year, were altered every week on SIA's high-frequency flights. Information technology enabled the chefs to fine-tune menus and immediately withdraw any dishes that were poorly received. Although there were marginal costs associated with such tactics, management firmly believed that these efforts distinguished Singapore Airlines from its competitors. Staff were instructed to find other ways to save money. For instance, the chefs prepared meals only from ingredients in season. Crew members were briefed by the kitchen on how to prepare and serve anything new.

Complaints were encouraged as they provided insight about problems. Once they were received, something could be done to rectify the situation; all complaints were tracked down and followed up. Travellers were invited to submit these complaints in writing. While some customers – typically Americans, Germans and Australians – readily complied, others were less willing to do so in writing. These customers were specifically questioned in follow-up surveys.

A Service Productivity Index (SPI) was computed each quarter in order to assess service quality standards. Multilingual in-flight surveys were used to itemize customers' impressions on key issues; then this information was compiled along with data on punctuality, baggage mishandled/recovered per 1000 passengers, and the ratio of complaints to compliments addressed to management.

As soon as a complaint relating directly to a specific in-flight experience was received, crew members could be temporarily taken out of the system and given training. Cabin crew members were released from their flight schedules three or four times a year to meet with training experts. Senior cabin crew members met every Monday morning for feedback and exchange sessions with service support personnel. One 'ritual' practised was to address the crew from the control centre just before take-off about topical issues, special promotions and other issues relevant to services.

At the airport in Singapore, staff were encouraged to do everything possible to deal with legitimate customer problems. One story – now part of company folklore – was about a supervisor who found a tailor at midnight and paid a deposit from his own funds to have a suit made for a customer whose luggage had been lost so that the customer could attend an important meeting at noon the next day.

Customer Profile and the Product Line

The product line was divided into three classes of travel – First, Raffles (business) and Economy. First Class accounted for 5% of passengers, Raffles Class for 10% and Economy Class for 85%. About one million of the seven million seats sold annually were to Singaporeans. Revenues from non-Singaporeans were proportionately higher since they tended to fly longer distances. Of the airline's passengers, 75% were from outside the country and 25% were from home base.

Flights varied in length – from less than one hour to over 13 hours for non-stop flights to Europe. Flights under four hours were all non-smoking, reflecting Singapore's strong national commitment to curtailing tobacco use. *Exhibit 2* gives the airline's daily flights by number of hours and amount of overnight travel.

On average, the load factor was somewhat higher in Economy Class (close to 80%) than in Raffles or First. Passengers who flew Raffles Class on a daytime flight might travel First Class on an overnight flight for the extra comfort.

Top management believed that the business passenger market held the future for the airline – both in numbers and yield. At the marketing executive meeting Robert Ang had just attended, everyone had concurred that technology was the key to improving service to this segment of the market. The expectations of these particular customers, the executives knew, were constantly rising and their needs had changed greatly since the previous decade. Research revealed that business travellers:

- preferred to eat small amounts and less often;

- wanted more nutrition in their diet;

- tended to be impatient and resented having to wait;

- wanted to have the facilities found in airport lounges – such as showers and fax machines – also available in the sky;

- disliked wasting time on board and wanted to be occupied throughout the flight.

At the start of the meeting, Robert Ang had pointed out that the only way for the company to genuinely cater to travellers' increasingly sophisticated needs was to use technology more strategically for enhancing the quality of service. It was not enough to simply pick easily replicated innovations on an *ad hoc* basis. He had declared:

> Just going out and looking for technology-based solutions will give the market the impression that we are gimmicky and arbitrary in our approach. If we want to protect our competitive position, we've got to find ways to move faster than our competitors and create an enduring advantage for the company. There will be a million problems but, once we agree on the principle of 'technology in the sky' as a competitive tool, we can solve the technical hassles. We have to use technology in the future as we used people in the past to serve customers. If we can match our high-tech services with our soft services, we will be irresistible to customers and will be distinguished from the rest.

Several technological innovations were already planned for introduction later that year. One was the installation of small TV screens at each First and Business Class seat, offering passengers video entertainment. Since other airlines were also doing this, ensuring variety would be pivotal. Another was satellite-linked air-to-ground telephone service which, unlike previously, allowed passengers to make calls even when the aircraft was above the ocean. Although these innovations were important, Ang felt it was not enough. He knew that there would be innumerable possibilities for adding value to the customers' total flying experience – but only if the know-how and technology could be applied correctly.

Almost 80,000 travellers were registered in the Priority Passenger Service (PPS) programme. To become a member, a passenger had to fly at least 60,000 km (37,500 miles) a year in First or Raffles Class. Benefits included extra baggage allowance, automatic flight reconfirmation, priority wait listing, a complimentary magazine subscription, and discounts on car rentals, hotels and shopping. Information about each PPS member, such as seat and meal preferences, was stored in a computer and could be automatically implemented when reservations were made. Ang considered this kind of service to be only the beginning; there was no end to what information technology could do to improve customer service. There was also no reason to confine the system to only 80,000 people simply because the company's technology capacity was limited.

Advertising Campaigns

Around 2% of Singapore Airlines' gross income was devoted to advertising and promotion. All expenditures were carefully controlled by the head office, and strategic advertising decisions were all centralized. Tactical advertising that focused on specific routes, schedules or promotions were handled locally, but were strictly monitored in Singapore to guarantee consistency.

The 'Singapore Girl' theme had remained a key element in the company's advertising strategy since day one. Initially, the aim of this strategy was to impart a feeling of romance and luxury service, and so it was dominated by images of sarong-clad women against exotically romantic backdrops. The modern fleet campaign which followed featured aircraft exteriors or interiors with just a small cameo inset of a stewardess at one side.

The purpose of the fleet modernization campaign was to give another strong message to the market: that Singapore Airlines was a leader in aircraft technology. The object was to show that the 'steel' did not overpower the 'silk'. The photographs gave the advertising a deliberately dream-like quality, a theme carried through in the 1990 Raffles campaign – SIA's first attempt to aim specifically at business class travellers. *Refer to* **Exhibit 3**, *in the plate section*, for examples of recent SIA advertising *and to* **Exhibit 4**, *also in the plate section*, for advertising by Malaysia Airlines and Thai International.

Research revealed that two out of every three Europeans, Americans and Australians preferred the romantic ads to the technical ones. These passengers were spellbound by the beauty of the stewardesses and impressed by their competence and caring. Japanese and other Asian clients, on the other hand, seemed to prefer the high-tech ads which denoted modernity, reliability and new experiences. The Singapore Girl did not seem so exotic, unusual or appealing to this group.

Sales and Distribution System

Like most fleets, Singapore Airlines depended heavily on independent agents to sell its services. In 1973, the airline initiated its own computer reservation and check-in system, KRISCOM. By 1991 this had been replaced by ABACUS, a computer reservation system which provided travel agents with an extended array of services including airline and hotel reservations, ground arrangements and regional travel news. Originally created by Singapore Airlines and two other Asian carriers, ABACUS was now owned and operated by SIA and nine other carriers, including three US firms. More than 100 carriers, 80 hotel chains and many other travel services had signed up with ABACUS to distribute their services through the system.

When reservations were made on Singapore Airlines by travel agents, the recorded preferences of Priority Passenger Service (PPS) travellers would automatically be retrieved from the computer. A wide variety of special meal options, reflecting travellers' many different health and religious needs, were offered. Special meal requests were forwarded to the catering department which received a print-out of all such requests for each flight. The special meal request was linked to the seat allocated to the passenger. *Exhibit 5* shows a simplified flowchart of the linkages between the different databases and the departure control system.

Technology and On-the-Ground Services

The Ground Services Department was responsible for the ground handling of passengers, baggage, cargo and mail at all 63 airports in the Singapore Airlines' network. At Changi, SATS were in charge, but at other airports the airline had to rely on subcontractors. Even though some Singapore Airlines' employees were allocated to these stations, most staff members were host country nationals and frequently had a different way of thinking.

Since what people really wanted most was to get in and out of airports as quickly and easily as possible, Ang believed that interventions with staff should be kept to a minimum. Specific problems had to be dealt with and overcome:

> It's easier to control the quality of service in the air than on the ground. Key decisions are made at the head office and implemented on board. Airports, on the other hand, are difficult to control. Technology is the key. The airports themselves are too crowded, with too few gates, too few counters and long lines. While in-flight service staff typically *give* customers something – free headsets, free newspapers, free drinks, free meals, free movies – ground service staff *take* – tickets, excess baggage fees, or they say you can't have the seat you want. Thirty per cent of all complaints relate to seat assignments, another 20% to aircraft delays. How these delays are handled has a big impact on customer opinion. Passengers become really unhappy when staff can't provide information, find them seats on alternative airlines, or obtain hotel rooms when they are delayed overnight. Lost baggage also accounts for about 20% of total complaints. With better technology and information, not only can we give the same kind of service on the ground as in the air, but we can minimize our risk by providing everyone around the world with a system we know works.

An Outstanding Service On-the-Ground Programme (OSG) had been started for all passengers and complemented the lounges, equipped with every possible luxury and convenience, instituted earlier for First and Business Class travellers. When Terminal 2 opened at Changi, a new Departure Control System (DCS90) was phased in. A key component was an improved simplified format for the screens used at check-in. It had become increasingly difficult to recruit and retain staff for check-in positions, and the complex software led to delays for passengers.

A new user-friendly program, with menu-driven, on-screen commands was introduced, which simplified both the task and the training.

The benefits for passengers included a simplified and speedier check-in process, with boarding passes and baggage tags being automatically encoded and printed at the check-in. The boarding pass included seat allocation and gate information, and confirmed special requests such as vegetarian meals. At the boarding gate, passengers would simply slip their boarding passes through a reader at the gate and the DCS90 software would verify check-in details against boarding passengers. An important security benefit was the automatic matching up of checked baggage with passengers going on board (refer to *Exhibit 5*).

A Telecar system was introduced to take baggage from one terminal to another within three minutes. It was then manually sorted and handled. If an urgent flight connection had to be made, this fact was communicated to the staff in advance so that baggage could be taken by trolley to the awaiting aircraft. Unlike the situation at most other airports, the Skytrain not only took passengers to and from terminals, but staff directed and accompanied passengers to flights with short connecting times, thus minimizing confusion and delays.

Technology and In-Flight Services

By realizing such innovations as video screens at each seat and better air-to-ground telecommunications, Ang wanted to transform the cabin into an 'office and leisure centre in the sky' which would enhance entertainment as well as business services. Surely almost anything could be possible in the future thanks to technology. But, what did customers value? What was feasible? What would distinguish Singapore Airlines from the competition? What were the real issues? At the meeting, he had told the others:

> We have to be able to provide passengers with as much distraction – be it entertainment or professional – as possible during their flight. It's just the opposite from the situation on the ground. Customers must be able to do whatever they need to do throughout their time with us. And, the choice must be theirs, not ours. They shouldn't have to encounter any problems in dealing with our staff and should, in fact, be encouraged to interact with them as much as possible, since we're very good at that. If technology is used properly and creatively, we can personalize our services still more and make people feel that we really care. For instance, hand-held computers can tell on-board crews everything they need to know about each customer so that services can be customized.

After the meeting, Ang's boss, the director of marketing planning, commented on the suggestions Ang had made. Although the ideas were interesting, he said, there should be nothing to disturb other passengers, reduce valuable seating space, or adversely affect the company's high level of personal service. Ang, who had anticipated this reaction, responded by saying that the location of the technology on board would be the determining factor. He could think of several options: centring the technology at each passenger's seat; demarcating work and leisure centres at a given spot inside the aircraft; or, alternatively, using crew members to handle the bulk of passenger requests, for instance sending faxes.

Ang Sets to Work

Back in his office, with a good feeling about the meeting that morning, Robert Ang thought about the three pillars which provided the quality experience that the company insisted on for its customers: first, modern aircraft (where it was already well ahead); second, on-the-ground services (where much remained to be done, despite the accomplishments at Changi Airport). In particular, technology had to be developed so that the company's worldwide network of sales and air staff, agents and subcontractors could function in unison.

The third pillar was in-flight services. What technology-based services should be developed to improve the customers' experience in the air? Could an 'office in the air' actually work? To what extent could more comfort and entertainment be provided, and how could the first and business class facilities be differentiated from those in economy? Most importantly, how could all these ideas be consolidated and effected so that Singapore Airlines would be the technological leader in civil aviation?

Ang knew that the *how* questions needed a lot of thought before a formal presentation could be made to his boss. But, it was even more crucial to find a cohesive concept that would be appreciated and bought company-wide. Perhaps it would be best to set out the various customer activities in a framework. He began to sketch out a rough flowchart showing the sequence of a typical journey. Before long, he had segmented the chart into three sections: pre-flight activities, in-flight activities and post-flight activities (*refer to* **Exhibit 6**). He began to fill in his ideas for using technology at each key point.

When he finally stopped for a coffee break, the sun had already begun to touch the horizon, creating a pale pink haze in the tropical sky. As he rose and stretched, he heard the soft hum of a plane above. "Must be the flight leaving for Frankfurt," he said aloud.

EXHIBIT 1

Key Performance Measures 1990

Rank	1990 Scheduled passengers carried (international) Numbers (in thousands)	Rank	1990 Scheduled passenger-kilometres performed (international) Numbers (in millions)	Rank	1990 Operating profits of the top ten of these airlines US dollars (millions)
1. British Airways	19,684	1. British Airways	62,834	1. Singapore Airlines	774
2. Lufthansa	13,326	2. Japan Airlines	42,690	2. Cathay Pacific	468
3. Air France	12,417	3. Lufthansa	38,744	3. Japan Airlines	464
4. Pan American	10,096	4. Pan American	38,241	4. British Airways	345
5. Japan Airlines	8,354	5. United	35,334	5. SAS	264
6. American Airlines	8,343	6. Singapore Airlines	31,544	6. American Airlines	67.9
7. SAS	8,335	7. Air France	29,023	7. Lufthansa	0
8. Cathay Pacific	7,378	8. Qantas	27,687	8. KLM	(19.3)
9. Alitalia	7,105	9. KLM	26,382	9. Alitalia	(75.7)
10. Singapore airlines	7,093	10. American Airlines	24,086	10. Air France	(286)

EXHIBIT 2

Details on Duration of Flights

Duration of Flights

	up to 3 hrs	4–8 hrs	9 hrs+
flights	60 %	18 %	22 %
revenues	25 %	25 %	50 %
*mainly during day / mainly during night	all	60 % / 40 %	25 % / 75 %

* Depending on whether it goes through midnight at the originating point.

EXHIBIT 3

Advertisements of Singapore Airlines

and

EXHIBIT 4

Advertisements of Competing Airlines

See Plate Section

EXHIBIT 5

Flowchart of Databases

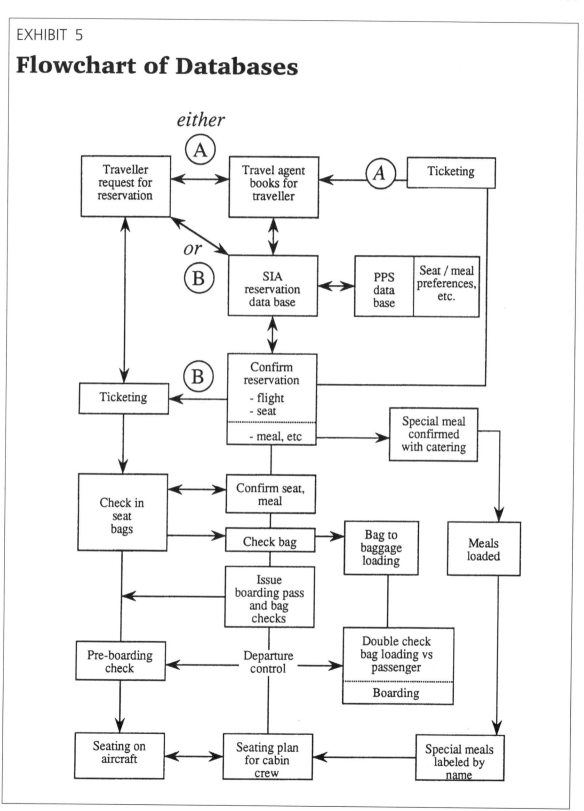

EXHIBIT 6

Customer Experience Pre-Flight

Activities

Potential Technological Innovations to Enhance Experience

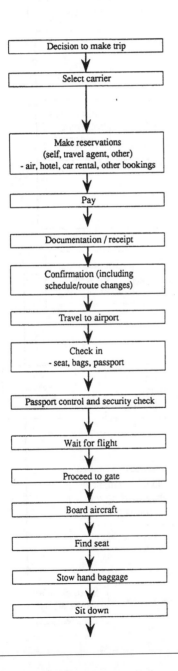

Decision to make trip

Select carrier

Make reservations
(self, travel agent, other)
- air, hotel, car rental, other bookings

Pay

Documentation / receipt

Confirmation (including schedule/route changes)

Travel to airport

Check in
- seat, bags, passport

Passport control and security check

Wait for flight

Proceed to gate

Board aircraft

Find seat

Stow hand baggage

Sit down

EXHIBIT 6 (continued)

Customer Experience In-Flight

Activities

**Potential Technological
Innovations to Enhance
Experience**

```
┌─────────────────────────────┐
│       Fasten seat belt       │
└─────────────────────────────┘
              │
              ▼
┌─────────────────────────────┐
│ Safety demonstration and other│
│   mandatory announcements    │
└─────────────────────────────┘
              │
              ▼
┌─────────────────────────────┐
│   Basic inflight amenities   │
│   - Audio/video system       │
│   - Seats                    │
│   - Overnight kits           │
│   - Pillows, blankets        │
│   - Toilets                  │
└─────────────────────────────┘
              │
              ▼
┌─────────────────────────────┐
│  Informational announcements │
└─────────────────────────────┘
              │
              ▼
┌─────────────────────────────┐
│  Inflight diversions         │
│                              │
│  - Newspapers, magazines     │
│                              │
│  - News updates              │
│                              │
│  - Games for kids / adults   │
│                              │
│  - Food / beverages          │
│                              │
│  - Movies                    │
│                              │
│  - Audio channels entertainment│
│                              │
│  - Audio/video for business  │
│    and other purposes        │
│                              │
│  - Medical help              │
│                              │
│  - Assistance with work      │
│                              │
│  - Physical exercise         │
└─────────────────────────────┘
              │
              ▼
┌─────────────────────────────┐
│          Shopping            │
└─────────────────────────────┘
              │
              ▼
┌─────────────────────────────┐
│ Pre arrival connection / transfer│
│          activities          │
└─────────────────────────────┘
              │
              ▼
```

(continued)

EXHIBIT 6 (continued)

Customer Experience Post-Arrival

Activities

Potential Technological Innovations to Enhance Experience

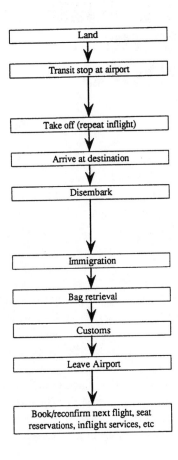

CASE 11.2

SONY MANUFACTURING COMPANY UK (BRIDGEND COLOUR TELEVISION OPERATION) – APPROPRIATE USE OF INFORMATION AND TECHNOLOGY IN MANUFACTURING

This case was prepared by Research Associate Cathy B. Huycke, under the supervision of Professor Michael D. Oliff of IMD and Professor Donald A. Marchand of the School of Information Studies, Syracuse University, NY, USA, as a basis for class discussion rather than to illustrate either effective or ineffective handling of a business situation. It was developed within the research scope of Manufacturing 2000, a development project conducted with global manufacturing enterprises.

On 10 July 1991 Richard Jones, Deputy Director of Engineering at Sony Bridgend, was preparing for a meeting with Michael Rigby, the newly appointed Managing Director at the UK Bridgend facility. Rigby had taken over recently from Tony Abbott who had been assigned to set up a new CTV plant in Pittsburgh, Pennsylvania, USA. In 1990, Bridgend manufactured 1.15 million televisions and was Sony's largest European TV manufacturer.

Over the past ten years, Bridgend had made phenomenal progress internally in terms of quality and process improvements that had resulted in compound annual sales growth of 21% (37% over the last six years). Effective information management strategies were instrumental in realizing these achievements. The future challenge was now external to the plant. Bridgend needed to extend its expertise in information management to Sony's other facilities, and to distributors, retailers and customers downstream.

"In the past, we've been a small fish in a medium-sized pond but as Bridgend gets bigger, Sony Corporate looks at us differently. We must be more responsible from a corporate perspective. We are at a turning point now. It's difficult to say which way it will go over the next few years," commented Jones.

Consumer Electronics Industry

In 1991, the worldwide consumer electronics industry was valued at $66 billion, and was forecast to reach $70 billion by 1994. Geographically, 1990 sales were concentrated in three regions: Europe 33%, the US 29% and Japan 22%.

Typically, analysts segmented the industry into three categories: video equipment, audio equipment and accessories. The video segment included television sets and accounted for approximately 30% of industry sales. Video-cassette recorders (VCRs) represented roughly 25% of industry sales. Audio, which made up approximately 40% of industry turnover, included a complete range of Hi-Fi equipment such as stereos, compact disk players, tape players and car radios. Accessories included products such as microphones, headphones, blank audio and video media. See Appendix 1 for the competitive pressures of the consumer electronics industry.

The Sony Corporation – Background and Beginnings

The Sony Corporation was one of the best-known names in consumer electronics. Established shortly after World War II, Sony had introduced a stream of revolutionary products, including the transistor radio, the Trinitron television, the Betamax VCR and the Walkman portable cassette player.

Sony was founded in 1946 by Akio Morita, a former naval lieutenant and Masaru Ibuka, a defence contractor. Starting with only $500 in borrowed capital, the Sony Corporation quickly grew to become one of the best-known names in consumer electronics. In part, Sony's early success stemmed from transistor technology which it licensed from Western Electric and which formed the basis of a stream of innovative products. In 1990, Sony was the second largest consumer electronics manufacturer, with ¥102 billion ($654 million) of profit on ¥2,879 billion ($18.3 billion) sales. The company employed 95,600 people. *See Exhibits 1 and 2* for highlights of Sony's financial performance and European activities, and Appendix 2 for descriptions of Sony Corporation and Sony Europa.

Sony Manufacturing Company UK (Bridgend)

Located in Bridgend, Wales, Sony Manufacturing Company UK was established in 1974. Bridgend was the largest integrated (i.e. producing cathode ray tubes as well as the final product) TV manufacturing complex in the region. The site consisted of two plants, one produced cathode ray tubes (CRTs) and the other, larger plant produced colour TV sets (CTVs).

Sony Bridgend reported to the European TV business division which in turn reported to the TV business group in Tokyo. Bridgend also reported to Sony Europa. *See Exhibit 3* for the organization chart.

At Bridgend, global localization meant more than promoting local talent – it also meant localizing research and development, design and supply. In 1984, a local R&D facility was set up which, within three years, was run completely by local staff, using Japanese engineers on assignment only. Since 1988, all TV designs had originated in Europe. Moreover, unique parts were supplied locally, roughly within 50 kilometres of the Bridgend facility. Common parts, however, were supplied all over the world.

The message Bridgend conveyed to its workers was that Sony's competitive advantage was not necessarily technological. As one manager commented:

> It's a very competitive market and the technologies are not very different. Buying decisions are not based on technology, but on picture quality, styling, reliability, value for money and relative quality. For employees, that translates into the elimination of defects and complaints, everyday incremental improvements, and not allowing success to make them complacent but reaching for ever higher goals so that Bridgend will be the best. It also requires that everyone undertake their role and responsibility seriously. It demands participation from everyone.

Sony Bridgend's corporate mission was to 'become an excellent company on a world basis'. To achieve this goal, Bridgend focused on three critical areas: quality, suppliers and product design.

Quality

Quality was critical for success in the consumer electronics industry. But in 1984, over 50% of Bridgend's products had defects. The 50% defect rate was attributed equally to incoming component quality and internal plant 'problems'. Re-work was built into the plant's production process, with many systems and procedures to catch the defects.

To enhance quality, in 1986 Bridgend established an improvement programme that eventually led to a *zero-defect* campaign embodying total quality control. Bridgend started at the front end of the operation and ensured that no defective products left the factory. The staff worked back from final assembly to total process, bringing in the cathode ray tubes and PCB manufacturing. Finally, faults were measured under statistical process controls using frequency charts because defects had become so rare. By 1990, a 70-fold fault reduction had been achieved. *See Exhibit 4* for defect reduction performance data.

Suppliers

Bridgend later extended this programme to its suppliers. In 1986, defects on incoming components were causing 50% of all product failures within the plant. Management admitted: "We can't survive on the long term in the UK without a strong base of component suppliers. We need an infrastructure of excellent component manufacturers." In 1986, Bridgend began a *Suppliers' Zero Defects* campaign where each supplier was benchmarked and informed of its relative performance. This close cooperation enabled Bridgend in 1989 to operate a 'no incoming component inspection' policy. The results of this programme were excellent: in 1991 defects on incoming components were reduced to 0.6% (as shown in *Exhibit 5*). In 1991, Bridgend worked with 140 suppliers – 30 of them key ones – versus 250 suppliers in 1984.

To improve the quality of the suppliers to the Bridgend plant, various techniques were used depending on:

- the size and resources of the supplier;

- the type of component supplied (cost, size, etc.);

- the physical location of the supplier.

In all cases, the supplier had to remember that he was part of a chain of operations. The success of the whole chain depended on each individual contribution to maintain the strength of that chain.

Information and knowledge flow were very important to Bridgend's suppliers. Hence, in 1988 the plant introduced an electronic data interchange (EDI) system called 'Tradanet', which sent orders and invoices digitally. Initially, this was an isolated system but, in 1991, it was integrated into Bridgend's plant-wide information systems.

A fundamental requirement of any supplier to Sony Bridgend was that the supplier's top management was 100% committed to quality improvements. "If we are convinced of this fact, then we will stay with the supplier," explained Jones. "This is regardless of the starting point. If a supplier makes incremental improvements, then eventually he will achieve excellence," he added.

The results of Sony's total quality approach included dramatic improvements in manufacturing cost savings, minimizing of materials loss and scrapped goods, as well as significant reductions in the cost of quality. Moreover, these achievements enabled Bridgend to receive the British Quality Award in 1988, followed by 'Britain's Best Factory' Award and the National Training Award presented in 1989.

Product Design

Bridgend also focused on product design with an emphasis on component standardization. Bridgend exported 75% of its output to the rest of Western Europe which, until 1984, required numerous variances in production; the plant needed four versions of the chassis to manufacture its 80 different television models. In 1986, Sony designed a Eurochassis (the base of the television to which the printed circuit boards (PCBs) and other components were fitted) which was largely common to all its products. Productivity increased significantly so that, by 1991, some 200 models were manufactured with only two different types of chassis. Since 1986, products have been designed for *manufacturability*, with standardization starting at the beginning and running as far along the production line as possible.

As a batch producer of high volumes, Bridgend had made significant investments in information technology and automated production to build its flexible manufacturing system. Component manufacture was almost entirely automated. In television assembly, the manual parts of PCB production lines were divided into cells operated by teams of workers, each pulling in work from its predecessor. Only a few hours of component inventory sat in a small central area. Small automated guided vehicles were sent out in teams to pick up the required materials when required.

The results of Bridgend's *Manufacturing Excellence* programme were impressive: its sales volume from 1985 to 1991 increased 37%, compounded annually. *See Exhibit 6* for highlights of Bridgend's production quantities.

The Evolution and Role of the Information Services Department (ISD)

The goal of ISD was to *encourage, develop and support* the use of information technology. ISD encouraged the use of IT with users: "We don't actually push projects, we let the users come and push us. We then help the users develop the systems which they need. Once the end product has been designed, we provide active support," explained Peter Clark, ISD Manager.

Clark went on to describe the three elements of ISD's role:

- To establish integrated business systems that gave a competitive edge to the operation of the Bridgend plant – or any sister company that could utilize Bridgend's methods.

- To utilize the best available tools that made effective use of computer hardware (mainframe, workstation or PC) yet offered enhanced functionality and improvements in development time. *See Exhibit 7* for a description of Bridgend's information system strategy.

- To prepare an environment where *everyone* was capable of utilizing information systems – so that they became as easy to use as the telephone.

In response to the rapid growth of the business, in 1988 the ISD department was split into four main groups: Material, Financial, Process and Services. Each group was then better able to support the actual business needs of the company.

The basic sections of the material control system were organized into a series of process focused projects (as indicated in *Exhibit 7*). These sections extended from the *sales order taking* (SIPS) through *planning* (AMOS I and III), *material ordering* (PADICS – Bill of Materials) and *control* (AMOS II) to the *customer dispatch* (SIPS).

The system was the result of 17 years of information systems evolution (as shown in *Exhibit 8*). One of the key success factors was that all the major systems design work was carried out in-house with high-quality, experienced ISD staff. This meant that ISD staff became knowledgeable about the *whole* factory operation and, if mistakes occurred in any of the system designs, then additional care was used to prevent the same mistake from occurring again on subsequent systems. Staff movements between departments also took place on a routine basis, which aided knowledge transfer. In this way, the evolving material control system was increasingly being fine-tuned to satisfy present and future demands.

See Exhibit 9 for a description of the responsibilities of the Process, Financial and Services Groups.

According to one senior manager, the most important element of the system development was that "the actual users controlled the process. ISD made sure that it operated and gave the users the right output; they made sure that they put the right input into it."

Information Management's Role in Achieving Manufacturing Excellence

Information management was critical to Bridgend's drive to pursue customer satisfaction through manufacturing excellence, therefore information as a key resource was taken seriously. *Manufacturing excellence* adhered to five principles in order to achieve its strategic objectives to pursue costs, flexibility and quality:

(1) **Design for manufacturing** – *information* was seen as a critical design resource in a plant that had 100–125 model changes each year.

As described by Jones, linking information flow with design was critical:

> We run with about 200 models per year, but we introduce about 120–150 new ones per year. There may only be minor differences such as changing the cabinet colour, or dramatic changes for a radically different product. Controlling information flow is therefore crucial.

One of the important features of Bridgend's information system was its flexibility, which enabled Bridgend to make frequent production plan changes:

> We are constantly changing our production plans; it's essential in order to keep track of the AMOS system. With the complexity of the printed circuit boards, a human being cannot accommodate changes. You cannot imagine the changes in detail you have to do to change a German to a French TV – physically you cannot do it.

(2) **Reduce lead times** – *information* resources were perceived as critical to streamline material flow and assembly.

At Bridgend, there was an overall corporate mandate to continually reduce lead time. According to Abbott, the rationale was "no one can forecast accurate market sales, therefore anything the manufacturing side can do to deliver on a shorter lead time is beneficial."

In 1991, Bridgend's lead time from start of process to product shipment was 5–6 days. Although the company was twice as fast as its nearest competitor, management's goal was to have a two-day lead time. The industry standard was anywhere from 10 to 14 days for a fully integrated process. Abbott believed that in order to achieve a two-day lead time: "it's more important that the decision-making process be locked into what's actually happening rather than into a model. The model is probably never up-to-date."

(3) **Continuous improvement** – *information* was used as a way of visualizing change in operational terms. The use of posted charts throughout the site was a successful way of implementing performance measurement and worker/team productivity.

Bridgend believed in the effectiveness of the visual display of data at the point of action. The philosophy around the plant was *visual* rather than high tech or complex. The walls of the plant were covered with charts, each filled in by the workers themselves, in different colours to denote different shifts and so encourage competition. Some followed the status of quality or the training progress of individual shift members, while others charted daily production levels.

As described by Abbott:

We've purposely stopped any automation of measurement of what's happening day to day. So when you walk around the factory, you will notice a very strong emphasis on the visual display of data. Rather than a computer terminal, the line supervisors report by hand – it's not documented. This emphasized frontline employee/operator involvement and responsibility. If all production figures were written down, they would be passed to someone else who would feed them into the computer. No one would look at it until the end of the week when a nice management report told you that you didn't make anything.

Rigby described how Sony monitored production line quality:

You can monitor production line quality in a thousand different ways. A computer buff can tell you how many you're making per second, etc. You can also display a digit of light over the production line so there is a counter coming up telling you how many you've made. But, the reality at the end of the day is – what do you really want out of that information? You want the person on the line, the supervisor, the manager to know that they're gaining or losing their hourly rate. So what we do is write it on a big board on the wall every hour. Every day, we put up a sheet that has the hourly target and the accumulation. We write down the actual and the variance every hour. So when anybody walks through the plant they can see where that line is exactly at any point in time. We know the person on the line knows the variance and that's all that is required. We don't use computers to automate reporting.

(4) *Communicate at all levels and to everyone* – sharing of *information* which was necessary for performance and improvement was constantly pursued. Sony managers scheduled regular meetings at each level of the plant. These meetings were the cornerstone of the information sharing and performance improvement approach.

Bridgend's communication systems were structured to focus on product output. Output was the key aspect of information communicated each week. Jones described the nature of his meetings:

Every morning we have a 5 to 10-minute meeting with approximately 60–70% of the engineering staff so that everyone knows what yesterday's quality and quantity was and what the problems were in those individual areas. Those five minutes are valuable because everyone knows the impact. We haven't got all these statistics flying around. It's a common sense approach – one which everyone understands.

(5) *Creating value – information* was used only to create and add value, and where this was not possible, eliminate information and preferably the problem.

Bridgend constantly re-evaluated its use of information and eliminated it if possible. Abbott described the procedure Bridgend went through with the accounts area:

> We asked what are the key performance indicators for Bridgend. Two years ago, I went to Tokyo and I took a load of paper, listed all the reports we sent from the UK, just on our finances. We said to them: "This is all the information Bridgend puts out every month, who uses it? Are we serious about it?" So we did an organization review of what information we used, what was necessary and what was not. We eliminated a lot of unnecessary reporting.

Ongoing change and growth prohibited managers from analysing endless amounts of data. As Rigby explained:

> I think we are fortunate in that the growth we've seen over the past four years has caused constant reorganization, reappraisal of where we are. That has caused enormous change – this has gone on continuously. From the manufacturing side, we are so busy trying to achieve today's result that we have to keep very focused on what we need to do today. Therefore, people don't have a lot of time to bury their heads in meaningless data.

Eliminate, simplify then automate was an established practice at Bridgend. According to Jones:

> IS and production automation should both follow the same philosophies. In production automation, we want to eliminate the process. We don't want to automate something we don't need to do. So we've gone through the elimination phase. Once we've done that, we simplify the necessary processes manually. Once we're satisfied it's working properly in its simplified manual form, then we automate it. That's when we succeed. If we tried to jump straight into automation, it would cost us a lot of money and it may not bring us anything.

This philosophy towards information management was also supported by other managers. As Abbott explained:

> The information system was designed to make the operation more effective. This was its primary function. Improving accuracy was also critical. We deliberately followed some routes in search of accuracy – to go from a manual process and make it as automatic as possible. But, like anything, we tried to simplify it first then make it automatic. Therefore we get the benefits of speed and accuracy.

Bridgend also stopped IS projects if they were no longer appropriate. For example, Bridgend removed a $3 million automated WIP warehouse and some automatic counting systems – the rationale being that management wanted to eliminate inventory. A warehouse only made it easy to accumulate work-in-process inventory and speed material fast enough to render counting unnecessary. Bridgend also removed a high-tech plant-wide communication system. Management realized that this communication system did not enhance people's awareness of how the plant was operating. Instead, they found that workers were much more aware of the plant's performance when daily production levels of the plant were charted on walls in the plant cafeteria.

Key Issues to Resolve

Improvements in information management were driven by the following strategies:

- eliminate the step or work process and therefore eliminate the information involved;

- simplify the work process and information uses involved;

- automate the essential and necessary and not the 'nice to have';

- constantly re-evaluate and improve what you have done – you can always do it better.

But, according to some managers, these goals were not enough. Bridgend's information management strategies needed to go *beyond* the plant to truly maximize overall company performance.

Coordinating Manufacturing with Marketing, Sales and Distribution

Jones realized that information could be used to better coordinate the manufacturing function with marketing, sales and distribution.

Marketing and Product Design

Previously, information flow between the marketing functions of the sales companies, and the design and manufacturing facilities, had been done on a rather formal basis with new model communication held once per year. In order to be responsive to the market needs, the knowledge transfer had been considerably improved over recent years. Two key areas of concern included:

- Marketing staff must be more technically aware of the manufacturing operation. This would enable them to offer wider model variations to Bridgend's customers without increasing the complexity of the production operation.

- Production and design staff required greater awareness of the long-term marketing strategy so that future model design and production facility design achieved harmony. Items such as features, styling, price strategy, etc. needed to be thoroughly understood by the design and manufacturing decision makers.

Sales Companies

There was not a good fit between the advance order forecasting and the actual orders that the sales companies placed. Jones described the order taking process:

> During the first three days of the month, firm orders automatically come into the mainframe computer from all of Bridgend's 12 sales companies. The lead time on their orders is four months. The third day we close off the books, then we analyse the orders and send the sales companies their order status. For the fifth, sixth and seventh month, they send in their feelings. But what happens is that, within the 4-month period, there are a lot of telexes passed to and from the Planning Department changing their orders. That means a lot of manual intervention which leads to errors.

The order lead time for Bridgend was four months, although Bridgend was capable of running with a 1-month rule. But as described by one senior manager:

> We operate a 4-month sales order because of the constraints of STREAM.[1] The STREAM system puts a constraint on us by saying that we must fix our orders at four months, and that any changes during the four months cannot be made through the computer system. But, actually, our local planning and process technology are systems capable of operating under the 1-month rule.

Distribution

Improvements in the distribution of the final product were regarded as one of the key improvement opportunities for the future. The quantity and variety of products had increased which had highlighted the weaknesses in this area. Future actions being considered included:

- restructuring the distribution outlets to enable direct shipment from the manufacturing plant to large dealers;

- analysing the operation of the distribution system to simplify the process;

- establishing an extremely fast, simple and clear method of accurately identifying stock levels at each stage of the distribution chain – speed of information and product flow were regarded as vital.

As an initial exercise to achieve the above and to construct better knowledge flow between manufacturing and distribution, Sony Bridgend had embarked on a policy of inviting key dealers and distributors to the manufacturing plant for open discussion to take place. In addition, specific investigations of product and information flow were taking place by the manufacturing group to ensure that the most suitable product/packaging/documentation, etc. were being supplied.

---

[1] STREAM was a pipline management project started at corporate headquarters in 1987.

Retail Outlets

The company used various types of retail outlets throughout Europe. The individual sales companies were responsible for deciding their own policy under the umbrella of Sony Europa. The key activities which needed to be resolved were:

- ensuring that the communication between the distributor and retail outlet was fast and accurate;

- understanding comprehensively what the retailer needs to have from the design and manufacturing operations in order for a sale to be completed.

It was often said that the most difficult distance travelled for any product was the one metre from the retailer's hands to the customer's hands. The whole organization needed to appreciate this fact.

Consumer

End consumers had constantly changing requirements for the product that they wished to purchase. The communication and understanding of what their needs were and what technically was practical formed a constant source of concern. Issues being addressed were:

- To ensure that design staff had background knowledge of the target customers. This needed to be well researched and accurate. Several routes needed to be taken to ensure that no false trails were followed. Items such as lifestyles, living standards, age profile, etc. were considered.

- The clear understanding of pre-purchase, actual purchase and post-purchase requirements by the customer was essential.

- The strengthening of brand loyalty always needed to be addressed.

The Introduction of Europa STREAM and its Impact on Bridgend's Autonomy

Started in Tokyo in 1987, STREAM (*Supply Timely REquired Amount Merchandise*) was a pipeline management project which enabled both goods and information to flow smoothly through sales, planning, procurement, manufacturing and logistics. Information technology integrated the pipeline. STREAM's targets were to decrease lead time, minimize inventory and avoid lost sales.

In 1991, Sony Corporate was pleased with STREAM's success in Japan's domestic operations. The next step, however, was to become *global* and to integrate the STREAM system into the rest of the Sony Group.

One of the effects of this globalization policy in Europe was that, in early 1991, Bridgend had to consider what effect the corporate STREAM project would have. The key objectives of STREAM were:

- to improve communication between the sales companies and the manufacturing groups;

- total reduction of inventory levels;

- reduction of lead time between order placing and delivery without any loss of sales.

Fortunately, Bridgend's internal situation was already well advanced compared with some other Sony manufacturing operations, since AMOS had already been well established. The concepts of STREAM fit well into the continuous improvement activity which had been such a part of Bridgend's history. Here was an opportunity now to improve the IS operations – external to the factory operations.

Conclusion

Sony Bridgend had been successful at developing a highly advanced integration of the manufacturing processes; however, the difficulty Jones faced was how to utilize IT in other dimensions while still preserving the base of value that the company had achieved already. Perhaps it was sub-optimizing if IT only benefited the plant and the rest of the value chain was ignored. Jones needed to consider the risks if corporate decided to navigate itself into other directions away from what Bridgend had been building incrementally over the last 15 years. Jones had to consider whether Bridgend was going to be positioned as a leading manufacturing site which would guide the rest of the integration and coordination processes. Otherwise, would the company find itself out of step with these activities in Europe?

How should Bridgend use its experience to influence the definition of the strategic direction and the criteria related to it, to influence the relationship between manufacturing, sales distribution and customers?

Appendix 1: Consumer Electronics Industry – Competitive Pressures

To remain competitive in the consumer electronics industry, three elements were deemed essential: manufacturers needed to produce their own semiconductor chips; they required the know-how for making computers and telecommunications equipment as well as consumer products; and they needed strong and cooperative management that linked the technical, production and marketing departments. Industry experts believed that new entertainment products would be more a 'computer-in-disguise' than a record player, tape recorder or television.

The consumer electronics industry was highly competitive. Matsushita, by far the world's largest consumer electronics company, had 1990 sales estimated at over $45 billion. Typically, Matsushita let others pioneer new products and then used its superb manufacturing skills to come out with cheaper models a year or so later.

The cost of staying competitive in consumer electronics was expected to become prohibitive for many firms. Companies that wanted to keep up with the leaders would have to spend at least 7% of their net sales on research and development. Sony and Matsushita had consistently invested almost 8% annually.

Appendix 2: Sony Corporation and Sony Europa

Sony Corporation

At Sony, management prided itself on its policy of 'local globalization'. According to Akio Morita, the policy recognized that Sony was a global corporation and had to act in a global manner, but also that the company's markets were local and, in attacking them, Sony had to adapt to local conditions. For example, each of the company's main markets – the US, Europe and Asia – had its own network of factories. Of its 500 overseas subsidiaries, 475 were run by foreigners. Aside from the long-term strategy, R&D and corporate principles handed down from Tokyo, regional managements made all their own investment and product decisions.

Sony Europa

Established in 1960, Sony's European Operations started with the foundation of Sony Overseas S.A. in Baar, Switzerland. Since the early 1960s, sales, service, manufacturing and support activities have spread out throughout Europe. (*See Exhibit 2* for a summary of Sony's European Activities.)

Representing approximately 28% of Sony's 1991 worldwide turnover, Sony Europa played an important role in Sony's global business activities. Sony group's 1991 net sales in Europe reached DM12,228 million ($7,366 million), an increase of 42% over the previous period.

EXHIBIT 1

Summary of Sony Corp. Financial Performance

	1991	1990	1989	1988	1987*
Net sales by product group (% of total)					
Video equipment	25.1	25.8	26.7	29.0	30.9
Audio equipment	24.4	25.1	26.2	30.8	31.2
Television	15.3	15.5	15.9	20.3	21.2
Other products	15.5	14.6	15.3	17.4	16.7
Music entertainment	13.1	15.8	15.9	2.5	0.0
Film entertainment	7.1	3.2	0.0	0.0	0.0
Net sales by area					
Japan	26.3	30.2	34.1	34.6	34.8
United States	29.2	29.8	27.3	27.9	27.0
Europe	28.1	24.8	23.2	22.6	24.0
Other areas	16.4	15.2	15.4	14.9	14.2
Total sales (¥ billion)	3,617	2,880	2,415	1,555	609
Operating income (¥ billion)	297	295	160	61	19
Net income (¥ billion)	116.9	102.8	72.5	37.2	13.3
Share equity (¥ billion)	1,476	1,430	912	646	604
R&D exp. (% of sales)	5.7	5.7	6.6	8.3	8.4
Capital investments (¥ billion)	412	324	216	134	58

* Five-month fiscal period ended 31 March 1987.

Source: Annual Reports.

EXHIBIT 2

Highlights of Sony's European Activities

Headquarters & Support Companies

1960 Sony Overseas S.A., Baar, Switzerland – financial services
1971 Sony Logistics Europe B.V., Vianen, Netherlands
1973 Sony Service Centre (Europe) N.V., founded in Antwerp, now Londerzeel, Belgium
1986 Sony Europa GmbH in Cologne, Germany – management headquarters
1986 SBC R&D Centre in Basingstoke, United Kingdom
1987 Stuttgart Technology Centre in Fellbach, Germany

Sales & Service Companies

1968 Sony UK Ltd. in Staines, United Kingdom
1970 Sony Deutschland GmbH in Cologne, Germany
1973 Sony France S.A. in Paris, France
1973 Sony Espana S.A. in Barcelona, Spain
1973 Sony Italia S.p.A. in Milan, Italy
1974 Sony Danmark a/s in Copenhagen, Denmark, now Sony Scandinavia a/s
1977 Sony Belgium N.V. in Brussels, Belgium
1979 Sony Nederland B.V., first established as joint venture with Brandsteder Electronics B.V. in Badhoevedorp, Netherlands
1979 Swiss sales branch, renamed Sony Schweiz AG in 1986, in Schlieren, Switzerland
1979 Sony GmbH, in Vienna, Austria
1986 Sony Portugal Lda., in Lisbon, Portugal
1986 Sony International Sales Division Europe (ISDE) in Frankfurt, Germany, for Eastern Europe and USSR

Business Group Organizations

1978 Sony Broadcast & Communications Ltd. (SBC) in Basingstoke, United Kingdom
1986 Magnetic Products Group Europe (SMPE) in Cologne, Germany
1986 Components Marketing Group Europe (CMGE) in Cologne, Germany
1987 TV Group Europe (TVE) in Fellbach, Germany, now Staines, United Kingdom
1987 Microsystems Europe (SMSE) in Cologne, Germany
1989 Semiconductor Sales (SSE) in Basingstoke, United Kingdom
1989 Production Technology Europe (PTE) in Fellbach, Germany
1990 Consumer Video Europe (CVE), in Badhoevedorp, Netherlands

Manufacturing Facilities

1974 Sony UK Manufacturing Company, Bridgend, Wales – colour televisions, CRTs
1975 Sony-Wega Produktions GmbH in Fellbach, Germany – colour televisions, robots
1980 Bayonne plant in France – audio-cassettes
1982 Barcelona plant in Spain – colour televisions, video tape recorders, audio products
1984 Dax-Pontonx plant in France – video cassettes and coating
1986 Alsace plant in Ribeauvillé, France – CD-players, car audio, video camcorders and tape recorders
1987 DADC GmbH in Anif, Austria – compact disks and laser disks
1989 Sony Italia S.p.A. in Rovereto, Italy – audio-cassettes
1990 Bayonne, France – key components

EXHIBIT 3

Organization of Sony Manufacturing Company (UK) in Europe

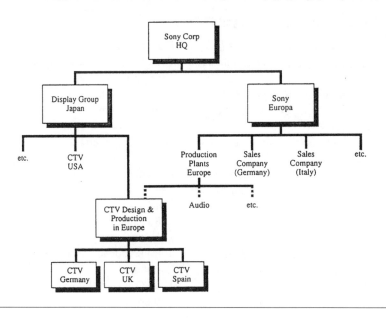

EXHIBIT 4

Sony Bridgend's Defect Reduction Performance

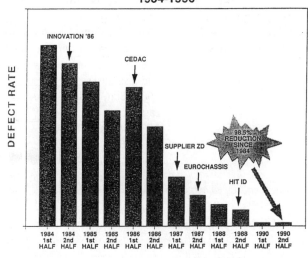

MAIN LINE DEFECT RATE
1984-1990

EXHIBIT 5

Defect Reduction Performance on Suppliers' Components

% of all products rejected for: component supplier quality problems (failure in any process)

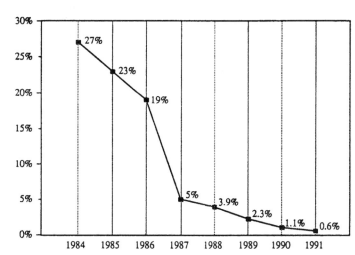

EXHIBIT 6

Sony Bridgend's Production Quantities (1975–90)

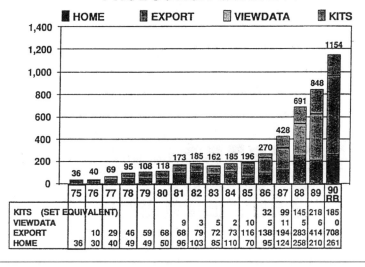

BRIDGEND CTV PLANT
PRODUCTION QUANTITY

	75	76	77	78	79	80	81	82	83	84	85	86	87	88	89	90 RB
KITS (SET EQUIVALENT)												32	99	145	218	185
VIEWDATA							9	3	5	2	10	5	11	5	6	0
EXPORT		10	29	46	59	68	68	79	72	73	116	138	194	283	414	708
HOME	36	30	40	49	49	50	96	103	85	110	70	95	124	258	210	261

EXHIBIT 7

Sony Bridgend's Information System Strategy

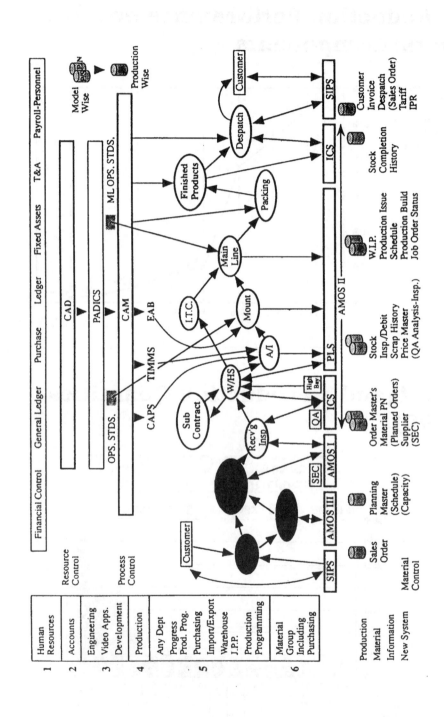

List of Acronyms

A/I: Production Area – Auto Insert
CAD: Computer Aided Design
EAB: Engineering Assisted Boards
ICS: Inventory Control System
IPR: Import Process and Relay

ITC: Tube Docking
ML OPS.STDS: Main Line Operating Standards
OPS.STDS: Operating Standards
PLS: Picking List
PN: Parts

QA: Quality
SEC: Spare Parts Component Supplier
SIPS: Sales Information Process System
T&A: Time and Attendance
TIMMS: NC Program Sequencer

EXHIBIT 8

Sony Bridgend's Evolution of the Information System for Manufacturing

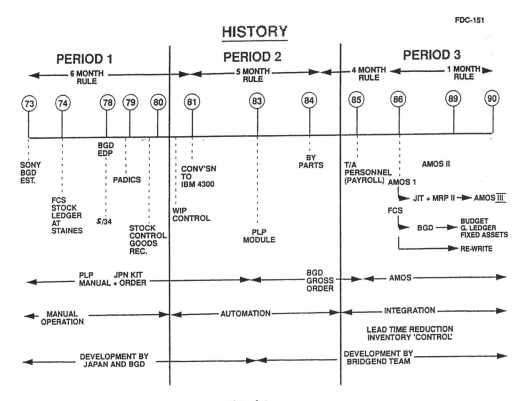

List of Acronyms
FCS: Financial Control System
JPN: Japan
PLP: Picking List
T/A: Time and Attendance

EXHIBIT 9

Description of ISD's Process, Financial and Services Groups Supporting Activities

ISD Process Group, supporting

Computer Aided Design
Speeds up drawing creation by 35%; speeds up drawing changes 35 times; interaction of data to other systems

Computer Aided Engineering
Information to engineers, information to non-engineers; automate repetitive jobs, checking and calculations; heart of all CAE systems (integration) is PADICS

Computer Aided Manufacturing
Production quality systems; real-time feedback of information

Office Automation
Off-the-shelf products; word processing; spreadsheets; graphical presentation; network to integrate all systems; electronic fax, telex and mail; mainframe gateway; framework, Harvard, multimate, lotus, token ring network

Financial Group, supporting

Accounts Department
General ledger & accounts payable; fixed assets; cost of sales integration; time and attendance; budgets; ETFA (European Free Trade Association qualification rules – to ship product with lower import duty); model costing

Human Resources Department
WP; dBase system; McDonnell Douglas system; currently producing requirements for HRMS to be integrated with time and attendance

Purchasing Department
Model costing; EFTA; purchase ordering (non-production)

Services, supporting

Help desk: mainframe services: PC services: hardware and software contract; consumables; communications; mail, telex and fax; photocopiers

Source: Sony Bridgend.

IMD
INTERNATIONAL

CASE 11.3 | # SONY BARCELONA – ACHIEVING WORLD-CLASS PRODUCT AND MARKET QUALITY THROUGH STRATEGIC INFORMATION MANAGEMENT

This case was prepared by Research Associate Kimberly A. Bechler under the supervision of Professor Donald A. Marchand, as a basis for class discussion rather than to illustrate either effective or ineffective handling of a business situation. It was developed within the research scope of Manufacturing 2000, a research and development project conducted with global manufacturing enterprises.

Fernando Gil, Deputy Plant Manager of Sony's Spanish TV manufacturing plant, slipped his Sony smock on over his shirt and tie. Wearing this uniform made the entire staff feel part of the Barcelona plant team. "After all, we're all working towards the same goal," he thought to himself.

Mr Gil knew that the plant's goal of achieving world-class manufacturing quality would require very reliable and accurate customer and market information, where speed-to-market was critical. Therefore, in May 1993 Fernando Gil and his senior management team had launched a campaign to gather data on the plant's colour television product quality by monitoring the units sold to personnel in the company stores.

However, this programme only addressed one of his information needs: customer information on after-sales quality. How could timely, reliable and accurate sales order information be ensured, especially while lead times were being drastically reduced?

Buttoning his smock, Mr. Gil wondered how the plant would be able to achieve its goal within the next few years.

The Consumer Electronics Industry

In 1993, the global consumer electronics industry was valued at $62 billion, having experienced a continuous decline since 1991 ($66 billion), with Sony, Matsushita and Philips controlling 50–60% of the world market for many kinds of products. Geographically, sales were concentrated in three regions: Europe

33%, the US 29% and Japan 22%. Typically, analysts segmented the industry into three categories: video equipment, audio equipment and accessories. The video segment, including television sets, video-cassette recorders and camcorders, accounted for approximately 50% of industry sales; video-cassette recorders (VCRs) alone represented roughly 25% of industry sales. Audio, which made up approximately 40% of industry turnover, included a complete range of Hi-Fi equipment such as stereos, compact disk players, tape players and car radios. Accessories included products such as microphones, headphones, blank audio and video media.

The 1990s had proved slow for the industry. Demand for the industry's mainstay products – televisions, VCRs and video cameras (camcorders) – had peaked and was in decline (*refer to Exhibit 1*). Consumers, once dazzled by the vast array of audio-visual gear, had become overwhelmed; there were too many models, too many gadgets and they wanted a smaller, high-quality selection. Industry experts believed that the global consumer electronics industry had reached maturity, as exemplified by one of the world leaders, Matsushita Electric Industrial Company, which had shifted to a policy of 'Zero Growth Management'. Since 1991, Matsushita had been focusing on 'building up a corporate structure which will maintain profitability even with zero sales growth'. Coupled with the maturity of the industry had been the global economic recession. In June 1993, the US was still experiencing slow growth, high unemployment, weak consumer demand and inadequate business investment; the Japanese were embarking on a major overhaul of their economy and business practices, in addition to dealing with a rising yen; and the anticipated political and economic union of Europe had not yet been achieved. Europe was struggling with major political upheavals, slow economic growth, massive immigration and rising unemployment; from 10% in the previous year, the EC was expecting unemployment to hit 11.5% in 1993, compared with 7% in the US and 2.5% in Japan.

Television

By the end of 1992, there were 725 million TV households worldwide. In the 1990s, the fastest growth in TV sales had been in Asia, Central and South America, and Africa (*refer to Exhibit 2*).

Colour TVs typically had a life span of about eight years. Continued product development was the only way manufacturers could shorten the replacement cycle and increase the market size. They had hoped that the most recent development in TV – the widescreen, 16:9 aspect format,[1] high-definition television (HDTV) – would boost TV receiver sales, but its high price and limited programming had kept sales low. In addition, the US had decided to develop a digital HDTV system. Rather than providing a new product, HDTV would

---

[1] The TV's aspect format was defined as the ratio of the screen's width to its height (conventional televisions had an aspect ratio of 4:3).

significantly spur a range of 'building block' technologies such as microelectronics and would become an integral part of a vast telecommunications network encompassing television, computers and hybrid computing-entertainment products known as multimedia.

The Sony Group

Akio Morita and Masaru Ibuka, Sony's founders, had brought Sony a long way from its early days in a bombed-out Tokyo department store in 1946 and their first consumer products – the electric seat warmer and Japan's first electric rice cooker – which were commercial failures. By the 1990s, Sony's product portfolio ranged from semiconductors, batteries and recording tapes, to video and audio gear for both consumers and professionals, computers, communications equipment and factory robots. Sony was focusing on personal entertainment, personal information and personal communications – all part of the future of digital technology. (See the Appendix for a description of Sony's corporate strategy and structure.)

Lagging Sales

Faced with the decline in the consumer electronics industry, Sony had reduced the number of television sets in its product line, dropping the 27″ and 31″ models in October 1992. With its consumer electronics business lagging, Sony was relying on entertainment to drive its growth, using 'entertainment software' to stimulate sales in electronics hardware. Related to this strategy of cross-marketing and product tie-ins, Sony's 300-page product magazine, *Sony Style*, was launched in the spring of 1993 in the US: for $4.95, consumers could learn about over 600 products produced by the firm.

For the fiscal year ending 31 March 1993, Sony had a net income of ¥36.3 billion ($313 million)[2] – a decrease of almost 70% from the previous year – on net sales of ¥3.993 trillion ($34.4 billion). Geographically, 30.4% of sales were made in the US, 26% in Europe, 25.8% in Japan and 17.8% elsewhere, with 5.83% of these sales being spent on R&D. Employees numbered 126,000 worldwide, of which roughly 50% worked outside Japan (*refer to* **Exhibit 3**).

Sony and Multimedia

With its solid grounding in consumer electronics, video equipment and entertainment, Sony was naturally one of the most enthusiastic promoters of the 'new order' – multimedia. Sony saw the digital future as 'computing plus entertainment'. Sony was selling the latest gadgets as well as the software they used. In 1990, Sony introduced the Data Discman, a hand-held electronic book player that allowed users to quickly search and retrieve a vast amount of

---

[2] Approximate current exchange rate as of 31 March 1993, ¥116 = US$1 (according to *Sony Annual Report 1993*).

information in the form of text, graphics or sound. Then, in 1992, Sony introduced the Mini Disc (providing digital sound, this 2.5″ platter had the capacity of a standard 5″ compact disk) and the Multimedia CD-ROM (MMCD) Player. Weighing less than 2 lb and about the size of a portable audio-CD player, the MMCD included a CD-ROM drive, black and white LCD display (and connectivity to a colour TV or computer monitor), speaker and miniature keyboard. The MMCD played standard audio compact disks, CD-ROM and photo CD disks. CD-ROM-based video games, the first digital spin-offs from Sony's entertainment group, were also being introduced. Sony had not been as successful in computers and telecommunications, and would therefore be seeking partnerships in these areas.

Sony España SA

Sony's Spanish subsidiary, Sony España SA, employed around 1,300 people – with 50% of its employees located at the TV plant in Viladecavalls and 50% working in marketing and sales. For the 1992 fiscal year, consolidated sales were Pta84.6 billion ($735,174,000) and net profits before taxes were Pta866 million ($7,525,540).[3]

Sony España was founded in 1967 under the name of Kosmos Electrica SA as an initiative of the people of Catalonia (the north-east region of Spain). Kosmos Electrica's management had wanted to produce a high-quality product. After visiting several companies, Kosmos Electrica had contacted Sony to pursue licensing activities. In 1973, Sony became a majority shareholder and the name was changed to Hispano Sony SA. Then, in 1983, Sony purchased 100% of the company, which then became Sony España SA.

In August 1983, production started in Parets, Spain. This 8,500 m^2 plant (with production spanning over two floors) was located on a 20,000 m^2 site and had an annual production of 350,000 colour televisions. In August 1991, the plant was closed and production was moved to Viladecavalls, where a new 42,000 m^2 plant (with production laid out on one floor) was built on a 200,000 m^2 site (with room for expansion). The new plant's capacity was over 1.2 million sets. Then, in April 1992, Sony invested over Pta4 billion in a new logistics centre, located close to the plant, to serve southern Europe.

Sony Barcelona TV Manufacturing Plant

A New Set of Walls

The opening of the new plant in Viladecavalls provided Sony Barcelona with the opportunity to change. Mr Gil commented:

> This new plant gave us a lot of opportunities to 'break through' with a new management style and a new way of doing things. If you are explaining a

---

[3] Market exchange rate as of 31 March 1993, Pta100 = US$0.869.

new history within old walls, it does not work. You need new walls. The larger-sized plant also allowed the workers to 'see' new opportunities. In addition, the size of the company grew very rapidly, helping to accelerate the change process. If you have a stable plant that is always producing the same things, it is much more difficult to react, to motivate people to prepare their jobs in a different way. This was a positive thing for us during this period of time, not only for management but in terms of real needs.

Sony Barcelona's challenge, internally defined as the 'Barcelona Strategic Role', was to be the most advanced and profitable plant in the world. The plant was working towards this goal by treating the 'human being' as a core element of the plant and its operations, by promoting job rotation and job enrichment, and by maintaining an 'urgency' of action policy. Mr Gil elaborated:

> I always say that we can buy the technology. We can buy the materials (if we have the money). We can buy many things, but it is the *people* in the company that make the difference to a company. To have a young, efficient management team with the possibility of promotion, vibrating with the company, and just fighting for the company is the most important thing for me.
>
> The new plant has also helped to reinforce the culture of urgent, continuous improvement. Workers can see what is happening to the other electronic manufacturers. Then they see the empty space in the plant and they understand our need for more products. These examples make it easy to explain that, even if we have a good position in the market today, we have to work for tomorrow. We need passion *now*.

The Plant Organization

Sony Barcelona was organized into four divisions:

- *Manufacturing*: production, engineering, design, maintenance and quality assurance.

- *Logistics*: planning, procurement, material and warehouse control.

- *Personnel*: recruiting and human resource activities.

- *Control and accounting*: accounting, finance and information systems.

Almost all of Sony Barcelona's communication was with the TV business group in Europe, TV Group Europe (TVE). Issues regarding logistics, quality, marketing, engineering and product allocation were all handled by TVE. "There is daily contact between the three TV plants in Europe and TV Group Europe, and there is a monthly meeting with the three plants, especially for new product and market information. It's a good cooperation," stated Mr Gil. Sony Barcelona's interaction with Sony Europa was primarily for the development of human resources plans and common policies as well as for a common understanding of Sony's strategic direction.

Sony Barcelona's TV sales information was reported to the TVE marketing group, while Sony España's total company sales information was reported directly to Sony Europa. Sony España provided guidelines to ensure the development of common policies at the sales company and the plant in order to maintain 'harmony'. TV Group Europe, together with the Barcelona plant management, was the engine driving the plant.

The Catalonian Work Ethic

In the 1990s, there were four different languages in Spain – Spanish (Castilian), Basque, Catalan and Galician – which reflected the main regional cultures: Spanish was the official common language. The northern part of Spain had the longest industrial experience, with the first industry in Spain starting in Catalonia, while the central and southern parts were more agricultural and service-oriented.

Catalonians typically were hard workers, trying to save money and plan for the future. They also had strong negotiating skills, perhaps because of their heritage of Eastern and Mediterranean trading activity. This ability to maintain a continuous negotiation process was highly valued at Sony. "It means that our way of thinking closely resembles that of the Japanese," commented Mr Gil.

The Marriage of Two Cultures

Over 182 Japanese companies were located in Spain, 64% in the Catalonia area. The Sony Group had always tried to emphasize its 'internationalism' rather than its Japanese origins. Mr Gil stated:

> We are working for the same company and getting the information from Japan, trying to standardize or harmonize with the other plants or even Japan. I think that we are taking the merit of each idea, of each area. If something is good from Tijuana, we can import from Tijuana, why not? Why do we have to develop or rediscover the wheel again? Let's just try to improve the situation. Sony was a Japanese company because its top management was Japanese, but it was also a local company with a mutual acceptance of local characteristics, following the 'global/local' concept which formed the basis of Mr Morita's philosophy. Sony Barcelona's culture remained well balanced with 12 young Japanese engineers and 750 local staff.

Harmonizing

Because of the high level of innovation required to constantly launch products providing new possibilities, the Sony Group had cultivated the development of a strong and powerful engineering capability. Therefore, central to Sony Barcelona's management approach was the notion of harmonizing, balancing the various functions, activities and people – i.e. considering the total business. Managing the proper balance was a continuous process.

Sony Barcelona had started to update all the 'indirect' or non-production areas to fulfil the company's real needs and to move some people into different departments so as to increase synergy and reduce the individual fiefdoms within the company. Every job was considered necessary, with an emphasis on readapting them to meet the daily necessities.

The plant promoted the idea that production was the core of the business and that all activities should support more efficient production. Mr Gil remarked:

'Indirect' or non-production staff must work for 'direct' or production people. Finally, the main task of plant management is to manage all that the company is putting in our hands – materials, people and machinery – in the best way. We have to use all these activities and resources as efficiently as possible in order to benefit the company as well as ourselves. It is necessary to open our minds a little bit, not only to view things from the technical point of view, but also from the business and management point of view – to have a broader view of the business.

Production

The plant began by producing audio and, eventually, also video products (both the Beta and VHS video-cassette recorder models). Colour television production started in 1985. In 1991, audio and VCR activities were discontinued and Sony Barcelona focused on television, producing its one millionth set. The plant produced colour televisions (since October 1992, TV models included 46″ large-screen rear projectors) and components for other plants (tuners and IF – intermediate frequency – blocks). By June 1993, the cumulative goal of two million colour televisions had been reached.

For fiscal year 1993, Sony Barcelona's colour television production was 750,000 sets (compared with the previous year's production of 482,000). This growth had been mainly achieved through exports: 70–80% of its colour television production was exported, supplying almost the entire market in southern Europe – Italy (27%) and France (26–27%) were its two largest customers. Sony Barcelona's mid-term plan was to grow continuously until 1996 and to attain a production capacity of 1.2 million colour televisions. For fiscal year 1993, sales were forecast at Pta35–50 billion ($304–435 million).

The manufacturing facility was laid out across one large room, except for the two warehouses – a north warehouse for incoming components, and a south warehouse for receiving bulky parts (such as the rear cover) and for packing and shipment, as well as for finished goods inventory (about 1 day's worth). There remained 9,000 m^2 for future expansion. With the material flow from north to south, the colour TV production process started with auto-insertion, hand-mount of hand components, soldering and then final adjustment. The televisions were then transferred via a monorail aerial system to the two main lines. Sony Barcelona's main line (200 metres long) was the longest one found in Sony European TV manufacturing facilities. Sony Barcelona had a colour television production capacity of 1,500 stereo and 2,200 mono models per 8-hour shift.

Production of 46″ large-screen rear projectors was kept low (an average of 10–11 sets per 8-hour shift) until the market could be better defined. From the product point of view, Sony's rear projector televisions could be characterized as both a consumer and a non-consumer good, with a high-quality picture and sound, and with superior brightness compared with competitors' models. Rear projectors were aged for 24 hours and production capacity was 50 sets in 8 hours.

Recycling was a priority. Sony Barcelona had a compacting machine to break down cardboard and paper. Styrene was sent to the Sony Bridgend/Pencoed plant for reuse in packing or sold to construction companies for use as insulating material, reinforcing the recycling policy of Sony's top management.

Market Quality

Working towards their goal of world-class manufacturing excellence, management at the Sony Barcelona plant had examined how they could satisfy their need for more reliable and accurate customer and product performance information. Plant management had then decided to start its own campaign to get closer to the market.

Appropriate and Reliable Information

After-sales information was a mixture of technical and commercial data, making it difficult to control service activity done during warranty periods. In addition, with two departments (sales and after-sales) between manufacturing and the marketplace, it took a long time for manufacturing to 'see' just what was happening in the market. Recognizing the need for shorter feedback cycles, the Barcelona management team had developed new information systems.

Two Approaches

There were two different views on how to deal with product problems. Service/repair centres were more concerned with servicing or *fixing* problems and satisfying customers directly, whereas the plant was more interested in removing or *solving* the problem and eliminating it as a service issue. According to Mr Gil: "We don't want to repair. We want to grasp problems and solve the problems with the information collected."

The priority of service centres (many of which were subcontractors) was to repair products. Service centres were technically oriented and 'reporting' was a secondary consideration. Mr Gil explained:

> Four or five years ago, we found a resoldered bracket in one component. But no one had said anything because it was very easy just to resolder this point. It turned out to be a material stress not detected in the plant's reliability tests. It was occurring in sets from the third year on and for us to simulate more than three years takes a long time. We had to determine how to discover these kinds of things in a long communication channel, including the factory quality department, salesmen, after-sales group, subcontracted workshop centres, service centres, etc. The only way is to have direct information from

all groups by working with and visiting all of them. In other words, *going to the information* rather than waiting for the information to come to us. It seemed that the only way for the plant to be able to really solve product problems was to find another channel to get more reliable information on an ongoing basis.

Moving Closer to the Customer

Sony Barcelona had taken an intermediate step toward '*going to the information*' by monitoring sets sold to staff to complement its monitoring of external data. It was easier to monitor cost and technical information from these 'staff customers' than from primary customers. Starting with sales made in April 1993 (beginning of the 1993 fiscal year) in Sony Barcelona's staff shops (located in the Barcelona sales office and in the manufacturing plant), Sony would collect information on product usage and related problems for 1,500–2,000 sets a year. The Barcelona management team believed that it would be necessary to collect one to two years' worth of data to have statistically meaningful and reliable information for justifying product engineering changes.

Purchasers would receive a letter explaining the project's purpose and would be asked to contact the quality assurance department directly with any problems. The official warranty was for one year, but the plant was offering service for two years in order to see not only the defects, but the *timing* of these defects. Was it at the very beginning of the warranty period or in the beginning of the second year (at the end of the normal warranty period)? Purchasers would have a specific telephone number to call. The Quality Assurance department would then monitor and record the data. Visits to the user's home would be made to see if problems were related to the installation of the TV set or antenna problems, or whether malfunctions were due to users not using the thick user manual and therefore just switching on the TV set. "We don't want to repair. We want to grasp *all the information* and find out what is really happening by visiting the customer at home, not just receive parts. We want information on how to improve!" Mr Gil remarked.

Another approach being considered was to send a market quality engineer to the Barcelona sales and service centre to learn about 'problems' and 'defective equipment'. In this way the engineer would act as a filter; because he knew what to look for, he could translate what he had learned from the 'commercial' language into an 'industrial' language for product design.

Quality Assurance: Inspection after Production versus Continuous Improvement

The Sony Barcelona TV plant was among Sony's top plants. In 1992, Sony Barcelona received the Gold Award for quality improvement from the TVE Group. For the past year, the plant had achieved a defect ratio of under 1% (the average was around 0.85%). Mr Gil commented:

Inside TVE, in terms of in-warranty cost, Barcelona's performance is outstanding. Maybe our TV sets are not as sophisticated as those produced by Sony Bridgend/Pencoed or Sony-Wega, but in relative terms – in warranty costs per set – producing in Barcelona is lower than producing a set in the other two plants.

Like the other TV plants, Sony Barcelona had ensured quality by sampling batches after production. There was a wide tolerance when the sample size was very small, which was a problem with the sampling system. With the number of models produced daily constantly increasing, the batch sizes were smaller so that this sampling method no longer made sense. The plant had moved from the production of a batch size of 3,000 two years earlier, where 50 sets were picked for sampling, to batch sizes of 50–100 sets with a sample size of only 3. The Barcelona management team believed that the only way to ensure high quality with these small sample sizes was to have a system that *assured the process*. It was necessary to have some complementary items as a rolling test for reliability – some daily sets for inspection, for example, that were not only visual but with measurements, to ensure that everything was within specification.

Therefore, in 1991, Sony Barcelona introduced a new quality assurance concept into its TV production. The production process was 'controlled' by acting within the system – checking procedures, the labour content of each work block (the line was split up into work blocks), and keeping certain content and controls inside each block; it also meant that no production was transferred to the next block if there were a mistake. "By assuring the process, you can assure the final product," Mr Gil explained. Sony Barcelona was the pioneer in the TV Group to introduce this approach. In 1993, the TV Group was pushing to implement this new system in all plants.

Every block measured its own production and quality activities. These '100% quality assurance systems' meant that quality was measured both on the line and at the end of the production process – TV sets were played non-stop for 300 hours to uncover and identify issues of reliability rather than waiting for market complaints.

The Role of Information and Sony Barcelona's IS Strategy

Information Sharing at the Barcelona Plant

Every Friday, Sony Barcelona had a management meeting to share official information (corporate communications, the previous week's production figures, quality and expected problems) and to discuss current issues. This information was then passed on to the production workers on Monday morning; before starting activity, each line leader met with his or her team (20–25 operators) to explain the important items as company 'top-down' information. "Monday is a good time to do this because it is starting a new period. With instruction, it makes the group into a kind of football team which gets really motivated – 'we have to win'," Mr Gil explained.

In addition, the plant posted information on productivity, quality and absenteeism on a weekly and monthly basis. Plant management was striving to find the optimum point for necessary information – not an excessive or deficient amount. However, defining this 'optimum' point was a definite challenge as it varied according to each person's point of view.

Sony Barcelona's IS Strategy

Sony Barcelona had chosen to follow the corporate and European approaches to software and systems. The plant tailored corporate software programs and packages to its needs, adding value locally. Plant management was implementing a 'downsizing' scheme to escape from heavy systems with high cost/benefit ratios. Therefore, big projects were being used for corporate purposes and information systems on the PC network for interdepartmental activities.

Information systems costs were increasing, the plant's ES/9000 environment inhibited it from moving to a lower-cost platform, and the plant could not yet commit to distributed client/server systems – Sony Barcelona's future direction for IS was unclear (*refer to* **Exhibits 4 and 5**). The Barcelona plant had adopted a 'wait and see' attitude – until Sony Corporate and, more importantly, Sony's Information Systems Planning Europe Group (ISPE) had decided what direction to take. STREAM (Sony's 'pipeline' management project) and other corporate projects were tying Sony Barcelona and the other TV plants closer together, creating an even greater dependency on what ISPE did in terms of technology direction related to the plant. The importance of what ISPE did was expected to grow within the corporation as a result of the pan-European integration being driven by projects like STREAM. Recently, several mid-range task force teams had been created in order to simplify and harmonize the whole Sony business in Europe. Harmonization would have an impact on information systems in three ways: the technology (to get it faster), the operation (to run it more cheaply) and the application systems (to make them better). What would be the appropriate direction for ISPE to take relative to the plants? Sony Barcelona did not have the flexibility to make choices without considering the compatibility of software and the connectivity of hardware with what ISPE was building and making available in the way of information and databases.

Barcelona plant management was also talking with technicians to get their point of view on what the future direction should be. Plant management was re-thinking the role that information played in its business and how it could harmonize information systems within Europe for hardware and software. The target was to have the same information system for the same business function in Europe.

Mr Gil also emphasized the need for compatibility among the three TV plants: "If every plant independently develops its own systems, growth for the company overall will be handicapped. It will not be easy to communicate purchase orders and inventory control, and it would be a very expensive solution." Sony Barcelona's Japanese engineers trained staff in CAD/CAM (Computer Assisted Design and Computer Assisted Manufacturing) and other related technologies.

These 'corporate' technologies facilitated the timely exchange of information on a database between Sony Barcelona, Sony Bridgend/Pencoed, Sony-Wega and Osaki TVE (TVE's central information office).

In designing information systems, key issues that Sony Barcelona had to determine were:

- What could be done to improve the work process?

- How could the use of technology be matched to the needs of that process and the needs of the people?

- How well would they function with that technology?

Sony Barcelona strived to harmonize the interaction between people, information, work processes and technology. One criterion for automation was the consideration of the human being as a critical part of the company. Everyone participated – 'bottom-up' involvement with 'top-down' initiatives and a focus on continuous improvement. In addition, the principle of concurrent design was applied – major users and systems technicians designed the information systems together.

Sony Barcelona's IS Group

The IS Group consisted of 12 people, with roughly half of them working on the development of new software packages and new applications, or 'local' interfaces for corporate software packages. The other 50% worked in production and operations. Mr Gil commented:

> For me, the IS Group's most important mission is to organize the company, not to automate. We must first simplify, find the best organization to work with this kind of system. Then later, when we have a clear department vision, we can automate. For me, the biggest problem is to determine the channels that will enable us to simplify and avoid duplication.

Plant management was striving for focused use of information. What information was really necessary and how could it be kept simple so as to develop a common understanding of jobs and processes? This 'information focus' proved especially challenging with the non-production staff, whose priority was not to simplify or eliminate but rather to make even more information available. However, more was not necessarily better.

In addition to focusing on improving its own operations, plant management also had to remain flexible so that it could respond to corporate projects.

Impact of STREAM and Local Response

STREAM (Supply Timely REquired Amount Merchandise) covered the chain of activities from the purchasing of parts to the final delivery to the dealer, and would have an impact on operations in the TV, Audio and Video business divisions. STREAM was perceived as necessary to achieve European integration and to standardize common corporate packages for moving towards a 'real-time' company (e.g. to simplify processes between sales companies and the TV plants with compatible and 'real-time' information systems, by providing timely information on purchase orders, inventories and country markets). STREAM would also provide the Sony Barcelona plant with the opportunity to add 'local added value'.

STREAM was affecting the TVE business group through lead time and inventory reduction programmes; for the three TV manufacturing plants, the ultimate goal was a lead time of 1 week.

Reducing Lead Time
Sales Companies and Production

Sony Barcelona had gone from a 5-month rule to a 4-month rule and currently had a 3-month rule for lead time; this meant that every month sales companies placed orders for the finished goods that they wanted in the third month. The 3-month rule provided the sales companies with the opportunity to give three 'feelings' regarding their sales forecasts for the third month – the second and third 'feelings' could then be adjusted according to actual sales.

However, the plant was trying to reduce lead times even further. In a first step, Sony Barcelona's goal was to move from three months to two by October 1993 (for the plant, a 2-month lead time was actually 4 weeks, as delivery of finished goods was started in the beginning of the second month). The 2-month lead-time rule would mean that, in the current month, sales companies would place firm orders for the next month. Therefore, starting in October 1993, sales orders would have to be fixed week by week using *weekly revisions*.

Then, as a second step, Sony Barcelona was aiming to decrease lead times from 2 months to 1 week by the end of 1994. (Japan was already operating under a 1-week lead-time policy.) With the constantly decreasing lead times, sales forecasts would be increasingly driving the 'production system' and the need for accurate and reliable sales forecasts would be crucial. Mr J. M. Pallarés, Sony Barcelona's General Manager of Logistics, commented:

> To achieve this 1-week lead time, we must consider the standardization and homogenization of our models. Now, we have at least two different chassis and there are still unique parts. Another problem is the difference between the sales company's 'feeling' and actual sales, sometimes it is a big change. Therefore, it is not just a matter for the factories, but also for the sales companies. They have to change their mindset. Another point is related to the information systems used. A 1-week operation means that we have little time to prepare the weekly planning. Now, we use two to five days to prepare monthly planning but, in the future, we will only have one day to prepare a 1-week programme. It will become critical for IS to support this compressed ordering, planning and procurement cycle. The other thing that is important is having a good forecast for our vendors so that they can

have the parts prepared for that 5-day lead-time operation. They have to work with a focus, to have enough parts in stock so that they can deliver when we need them.

Suppliers

Sony Barcelona was increasing its use of local suppliers to reduce lead times, and decreasing its purchases from Japan and Singapore. Roughly 90% of the plant's purchases were of European origin. Currently, lead time (excluding parts from Japan and Singapore) was 10 days from Europe. The next target was 5 days from official purchase order to plant reception. Shortening lead times was also pursued by using Electronic Data Interchange (EDI) instead of telefax communications. "We use EDI with the main vendors in Europe and now we have a total of 13 using the system – with the idea being to expand every month. With these short lead times, EDI is the only way to ensure that there are no failures in the system. Using a fax or telephone to confirm orders is a very risky operation," Mr Gil explained. The EDI approach required equipment and software compatibility, linking Sony Barcelona and suppliers ever closer together.

Management realized that the information systems at the plant played a critical role in enabling the achievement of these shortened lead times: "Our philosophy is that, without good support from our information systems, achievement of these lead times is not possible," Mr Pallarés stated.

Inventory Reduction

STREAM in Japan and STREAM in Europe were very different. In Japan, the business division was responsible for the stocks of the sales companies; the business division acted as the 'middle man' between the sales company and the plant. However, in Europe, the plant was responsible for the stocks, enabling the plant to respond faster to sharp fluctuations in demand. Sony Barcelona's plan was to reduce its 14-day parts inventory to 10 days by the end of 1993, and its 2- to 3-day finished goods inventory on limited products down to one day.

Local Response

Sony Barcelona believed that it was important to add 'local value' to the STREAM project rather than just implementing a 'standard' package. "We want to introduce some advantage or easier operation that is our 'added value' and that is our contribution to the Sony Corporation," Mr Gil commented. The plant was therefore working through TVE to influence Sony Europa on the project.

Usually, when Japan made a project proposal, the sites being affected would suggest modifications. This cooperative approach was currently happening with a new final assembly schedule package (FAS) that Sony was trying to implement. All three European TV plants had requested changes in order to make the operation easier. The FAS package had first been introduced in Japan and Malaysia, but needed to be adapted to suit the local situation in Europe, where there were different lead times and products had important technical differences. Sony Barcelona was acting as a pilot plant and the changes, modifications and improvements were being applied right in the plant.

The Future

The STREAM project was considered necessary for European integration. STREAM's reduced lead-time schedules would make the sales companies the 'drivers' of plant production, and being able to ensure reliable and accurate information would be critical for the Barcelona plant. Sony Barcelona had started its own campaign to move closer to the customer, with pilot projects – such as the FAS package – being developed at the manufacturing plant. However, the future direction of Barcelona's information systems depended on the development of new technologies and the direction that Sony's ISPE Group would take.

Sony Barcelona's management team was in the process of determining the necessary 'next steps', particularly in the area of innovation (manufacturing, quality, design, etc.), to achieve its goal of world-class manufacturing excellence within the next few years.

Appendix: Sony Corporation

During its 47-year history, Sony had popularized the pocket-size transistor radio, the battery-powered TV set, the video-cassette recorder (VCR), the camcorder and the compact disk player. The Walkman portable cassette player was considered the most famous Sony gadget. Sony's Emmy Award-winning Trinitron televisions (first sold in 1968) continued to set the standard for video monitor picture quality. Even Sony's most celebrated setback in the marketplace – the Betamax video-cassette recorder – remained a profitable business despite the overwhelming success of the competing VHS format.

Industry analysts considered Sony's engineers to be among the most prolific and innovative in the world – turning out new products at a rate of 1000 a year – an average of four every business day; 80% of these were improved versions of earlier devices, with new features, better performance and often lower prices. The other 200 were aimed at creating entirely new markets. One of Sony's latest developments was the installation of the Jumbotron, the largest display system in Europe, for the Seville Universal Exposition in April 1992.

The Sony Global Organization

Since 1946, Sony had oriented itself to be an international enterprise which, although based in Japan, would do business all over the world. As early as 1958, Tokyo Tsushin Kogyo K.K. (Tokyo Telecommunications Engineering Corporation, or TTK), the Japanese corporate name, was changed to 'one that would be pronounced the same all over the world': Sony, from *sonus* – the Latin word for 'sound'.

Sony recognized that, even as a global enterprise, its markets were local markets and, in attacking them, Sony had to adapt to local conditions. Support and promotion of Sony's policy of 'global localization' was demonstrated by its 'localization' of functions, management practices, handling of management recruitment and promotion, and the transfer of technology. Product planning to engineering and design, production, marketing, service and finance were conducted locally by local people, and Sony had a network of factories spanning its main markets – the United States, Europe and Asia. Of Sony's more than 600 overseas subsidiaries, 75% were run by 'foreigners.' These non-Japanese managers understood the local customers' needs better.

In 1970, Sony was the first Japanese corporation to have its shares listed on the New York Stock Exchange. By the 1990s, Sony's shares were listed on major stock exchanges all over the world. The worldwide Sony Group, whose headquarters were in Tokyo, Japan, was organized along two business segments: Electronics and Entertainment. Sony's operations were further divided into six product groups (with fiscal year 1993 sales): video equipment ($7,141 million), audio equipment ($8,000 million), televisions ($5,463 million), other products ($6,653 million), music entertainment ($3,849 million) and filmed entertainment ($3,315 million). A total of 23 business groups had the responsibility for planning, engineering, producing, assuring quality and strategic marketing for their respective product lines.

The organizational units closest to the market were Sony's national sales and service companies. In Western Europe, there were sales and service companies in every country. In 1991, an accredited office in Moscow was opened to serve as a bridgehead to Russia and the CIS. In 1992, operations started up for Sony Polska, a wholly owned sales and service subsidiary in Warsaw, and for Sony Turkey in Istanbul. The business groups and sales and service companies shared common management and functional headquarters, engineering centres and support companies (*refer to* **Exhibit 6**).

Sony Europa GmbH

Sony's activities in Europe were led by Sony Europa GmbH, with Group net sales of DM14.4 billion ($8.9 billion[4]) for the fiscal year ending 31 March 1993. The headquarters were in Cologne, Germany. Sony Europa's 18,000 employees accounted for 25% of Sony's worldwide net sales. European operations were organized into five business sectors/groups: consumer products (TV, video and audio), professional products, computers and peripherals, recording media and entertainment (music and pictures). Sony's TV organization in Europe included three TV manufacturing plants (Sony Bridgend/Pencoed, Wales; Sony-Wega, Germany; and Sony Barcelona, Spain), and the TV Group Europe headquarters, in Staines, England.

---

[4] Market exchange rate as of 31 March 1993: 1DM = $0.62.

More than 40% of Sony's products sold in Europe by its 21 sales and service organizations were produced in 15 European manufacturing facilities, 10 for electronics hardware and 5 for entertainment software. Sony's European technological centres, operating in a flexible network of research and engineering activities, helped to maintain and develop technological know-how in Europe.

EXHIBIT 1

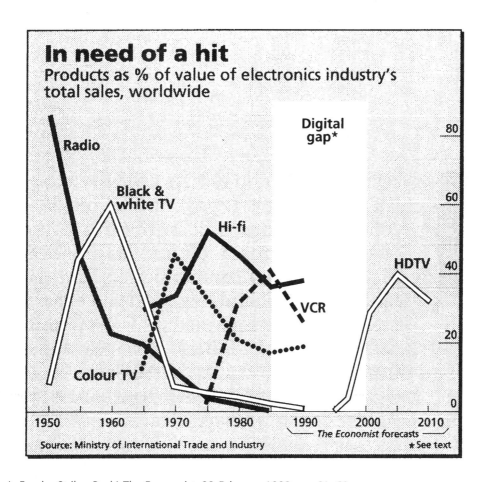

In need of a hit
Products as % of value of electronics industry's total sales, worldwide

'America's Empire Strikes Back' *The Economist*, 22 February 1992, pp. 61–62.

EXHIBIT 2

World Regional Shares of TV Homes 1970–2000 (%)

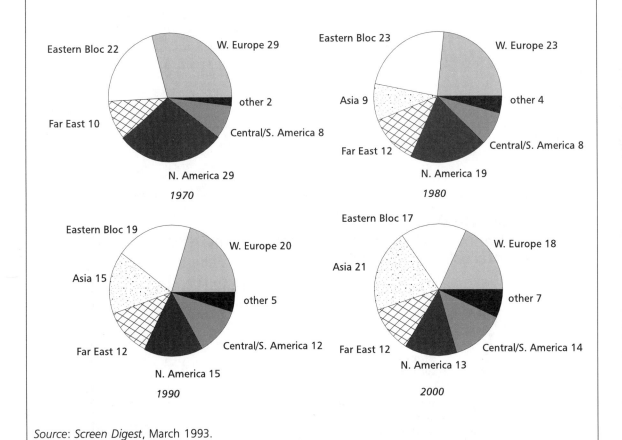

Source: *Screen Digest*, March 1993.

EXHIBIT 3

Summary of Sony Corp. Financial Performance*

	1993	1992	1991	1990	1989	1988**	1987***
Net sales by product group (% of total)							
Video equipment	20.8	22.8	24.6	25.2	26.0	29.0	30.9
Audio equipment	23.2	24.1	23.9	24.5	25.5	30.8	31.2
Television	15.9	15.1	14.9	15.1	15.5	20.3	21.2
Other products	19.3	18.2	16.7	16.6	17.6	17.4	16.7
Music entertainment	11.2	11.4	12.9	15.5	15.4	2.5	0.0
Filmed entertainment	9.6	8.4	7.0	3.1	0.0	0.0	0.0
Net sales by area							
Japan	25.8	26.9	27.7	31.7	35.7	34.6	34.8
United States	30.4	28.5	28.6	29.1	26.6	27.9	27.0
Europe	26.0	27.5	27.5	24.3	22.6	22.6	24.0
Other areas	17.8	17.1	16.2	14.9	15.1	14.9	14.2
Total sales (¥ billion)	3,993	3,929	3,696	2,948	2,204	1,555	609
Operating income (¥ billion)	126	179.5	302	297.5	162.6	61	19
Net income (¥ billion)	36	120	116.9	102.8	72.0	37.2	13.3
Stockholder's equity (¥ billion)	1,428	1,537	1,476	1,430	912	646	604
R&D expenditure (% of sales)	5.8	6.1	5.6	5.6	6.4	8.3	8.4
Capital investments (¥ billion)	251	453	411.6	323.7	215.6	134	58

*Fiscal year includes period from 1 April to 31 March. Data from Sony, *Annual Report*, 31 March 1993.
**Data from Sony, *Annual Report*, 31 March 1992.
***Five month fiscal period ended 31 March 1987. Data from Sony, *Annual Report*, 31 March 1991.

Source: *Annual Reports*.

EXHIBIT 4

Sony Barcelona IS Hardware Configuration

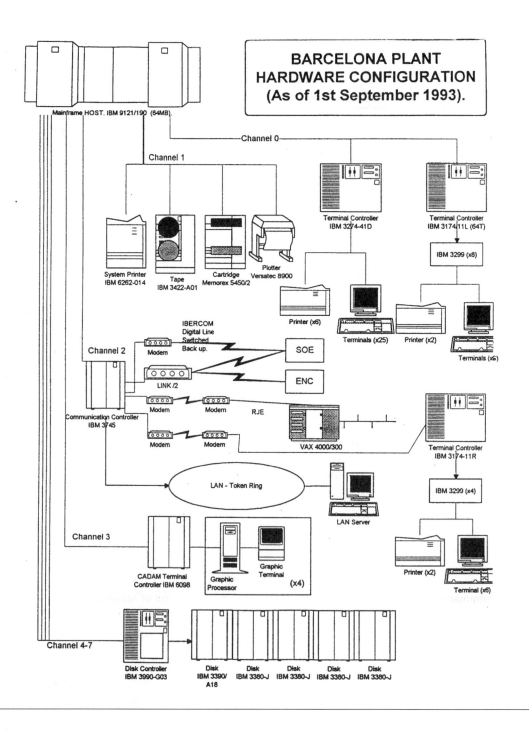

BARCELONA PLANT HARDWARE CONFIGURATION (As of 1st September 1993).

EXHIBIT 5

Sony Barcelona Application Relationship Chart

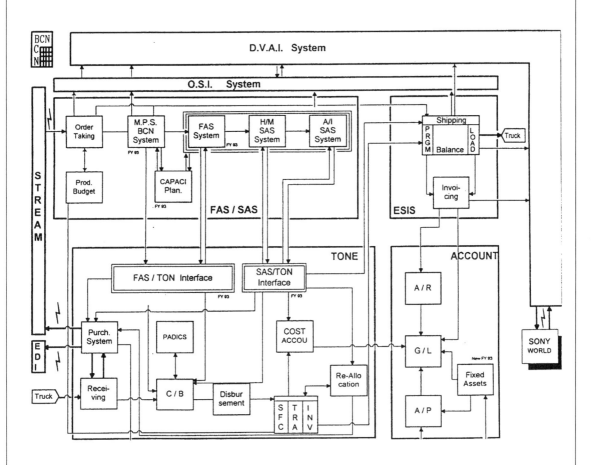

Key

A/I SAS	Auto-Insertion Sub-Assembly Schedule	H/M SAS	Hand-Mount Sub-Assembly Schedule
A/P	Accounts Payable	INV	Inventory Control System
A/R	Accounts Receivable	MPS	Master Production Schedule
C/B	Code-Bill of Materials	OSI	Order Status Information
DVAI	Document Vanning & Accounting Information	PADICS	Parts & Drawing Information Control System (Bill of Materials)
EDI	Electronic Data Interchange	SFC	Shop-Floor Control
ESIS	Export Shipping & Invoicing System	STREAM	Supply Timely REquired Amount Merchandise
FAS	Final Assembly Schedule	TONE	Task Order Number Environment
G/L	General Ledger	TRA	Transferring Requirement Analysis

EXHIBIT 6

Business Groups and Sales and Service Companies

Headquarters and Support Functions

Sony Europa GmbH, Cologne, Germany – Management Headquarters

Sony Brussels, European Affairs, Belgium

Sony Overseas S.A., Baar, Switzerland – Financial Services

Sony Financial Services (Europe), London, UK

Sony Europa B.V., Badhoevedorp (Amsterdam), Netherlands – Operations Centre

Sony Service Centre (Europe) N.V., Londerzeel (Brussels), Belgium

Sony Logistics Europe B.V., Vianen, Netherlands

Sony European Computer Services, Düsseldorf, Germany

Basingstoke Technology Centre, Basingstoke, UK

Stuttgart Technology Centre, Fellbach, Germany

Sony Telecom N.V., Brussels, Belgium

Business Group and Manufacturing Organizations

Consumer Products
TV Europe, Staines, UK

Sony Manufacturing Company UK, Pencoed (TV) and Bridgend (CRT), UK

Barcelona Plant, Viladecavallis, Spain

Sony-Wega Produktions GmbH, Fellbach, Germany

Consumer Video Europe, Badhoevedorp, Netherlands

Audio Sector Europe, Badhoevedorp, Netherlands

Audio/Video Manufacturing Europe, Alsace Plant, Ribeauvillé, France

Professional Products (PPE)
Headquarters, Staines, UK

Sony Broadcast International, Basingstoke, UK

Sony Business & Industrial Products, Badhoevedorp, Netherlands

Sony Medical & Printing Products, Cologne, Germany

Computers, Peripheral Products & Components (CPCE)
Headquarters, Cologne, Germany

Sony Semiconductors Europe, Basingstoke, UK

Electronic Devices Europe, Bayonne, France

Recording Media (RME)
Headquarters, Bayonne, France, and Cologne, Germany

Coating and Video Tape Plant, Pontonx/Dax, France

Audio Tape Plant, Bayonne, France

Audio Tape Plant, Rovereto, Italy

Entertainment Software
Sony Music Entertainment Europe, London, UK

Sony Classical GmbH, Hamburg, Germany

Sony Music European Operations Group, Manufacturing Headquarters, Anif, Austria

Columbia TriStar Films, European Coordination Office, London, UK

Sales & Service Companies

Sony Austria GmbH, Vienna, Austria

Sony Belgium N.V., Brussels, Belgium

Sony Praha, Prague, Czech Republic

Sony Danmark, Taastrup (Copenhagen), Denmark

Sony Finland, Espoo (Helsinki), Finland

Sony France S.A., Paris, France

Sony Deutschland GmbH, Cologne, Germany

Sony Hellas S.A., Psychiko (Athens), Greece

Sony Ireland, Tallaght (Dublin), Ireland

Sony Italia S.p.A., Cinisello (Milan), Italy

Sony Nederland B.V., Badhoevedorp (Amsterdam), Netherlands

Sony Nordic a/s, Taastrup (Copenhagen), Denmark

Sony Norge, Oslo, Norway

Sony Poland sPzoo, Warsaw, Poland

Sony Portugal Lda., Lisbon, Portugal

Sony Moscow, Moscow, Russia

Sony Espana S.A., Barcelona, Spain

Sony Sverige, Spanga (Stockholm), Sweden

Sony Schweiz AG, Schlieren (Zurich), Switzerland

Sony Turkey, Caglayan (Istanbul), Turkey

Sony United Kingdom Limited, Staines (London), UK

12. Finding Complementary Competencies – Managing Business in Europe through Alliances and Partnership

CASE 12.1

CANON IN THE EUROPEAN COPIER MARKET

This case was prepared by Research Associate Joyce Miller, under the supervision of Professors George Taucher and Dominique Turpin as a basis for class discussion rather than to illustrate either effective or ineffective handling of a business situation. We are grateful for the assistance of Professor Gene Gregory in the preparation of this case study.

From its humble beginnings in a small workshop in Tokyo's Roppongi district, Canon Inc. had become, by 1986, one of the world's leading manufacturers of cameras, business machines and precision optical equipment. In the following year, Canon would celebrate its 50th anniversary, and President Ryuzaburo Kaku planned to use the occasion both to review the company's past achievements and to plan carefully for the future. Mr Kaku's aim was to make Canon into a premier global corporation:

> Well before the yen entered the steepest arc of its upward curve, Canon had seen the necessity of moving manufacturing into its markets, of putting production close to the place of consumption. The new phase of 'internationalization' was initially prompted by the trade imbalance (and trade friction) between Japan and the chief countries where Canon sells... Canon has advanced quite briskly towards becoming truly global – and the intention is to take the global process further by establishing R&D centres in its markets as its national companies develop into free-standing businesses within the global corporation.
>
> The imperatives of global rationalization – especially in copier operations – require Canon ownership and finely-tuned management of R&D, production and marketing. As with all strategic alliances, the fine line between compelling necessity and expediency is not always readily apparent.

In the mid-1980s, Olivetti, a long-time player in the office equipment market with particular strength in Italy, was looking for a way to bolster its presence in the European copier market. Canon, at the time, was eager to expand its market share in Italy and to strengthen its European manufacturing base.

Canon Inc.

A young company by Japanese standards, Canon traced its history back to November 1933 when a small group of camera enthusiasts led by Goro Yoshida founded the Precision Optical Research Instruments Laboratory in Roppongi, then a suburb of Tokyo, to conduct research into quality compact cameras. Two years later, the Hansa Canon, Japan's first 35 mm focal plane shutter camera, remarkably resembling the German-made Leica, was introduced in Tokyo. In 1937, Precision Optical Industry Co., Ltd. was established to manufacture the Hansa Canon, with Saburo Uchida as its first Executive Managing Director. When Mr Uchida was drafted for service in the army in the late 1930s, Dr Takeshi Mitarai, a practising physician who had invested in the new company and become its auditor, took over the company's management and became its president in September 1942.

During the war, Precision Optical was forced to abandon 35 mm camera production to become a supplier to the Japanese military. In this capacity, the company developed an indirect X-ray camera for mass-screening to detect tuberculosis infection. In 1944, the company diversified into binocular production with the acquisition of Yamato Kogaku Seisakusho. After rapid reconversion to camera production, with the war's end, the company changed its name to Canon Camera Co., Ltd. in 1947. Over the next two decades, the company grew into the world's leading camera manufacturer.

Canon's international operations began modestly in 1951 with the appointment of Hong Kong-based Jardine Matheson as its sole worldwide agent. Responding to the growing US market for quality cameras, Canon established its first overseas branch office in New York in 1955, and two years later formed Canon Europa in Geneva as an exclusive distributor in Europe.

Vertical Integration and Product Diversification

Early in the decade, Canon began the dual processes of vertical integration and product diversification that accounted for much of its strength in the domestic and world markets. Subsidiaries were established to produce micrometers and metal parts, and a supplier of precision components was acquired. Then, in 1956, the first major expansion of the product line was made with the addition of personal ciné-cameras.

An overly ambitious diversification strategy led to Canon's first and, thus far, only major product failure. Introduced in 1958, the Synchroreader, designed to record voice messages on paper for educational use, proved to be technologically far ahead of its time. Within a year after its introduction, the product had to be withdrawn from the market, leaving the company with a division staffed with electronic engineers who could not be dismissed simply because management had made a serious strategic error in product planning and marketing.

Determined to transform adversity into advantage, Canon harnessed the skills of these people to make a major move into business machines with microfilm equipment for banking use in 1959 and, in a major new departure, with the development of the Canola 130 electronic calculator introduced to the market in May 1964. Success in the calculator market set the stage for venturing into the copier market in 1968, with a 'New Process' plain paper system that challenged and eventually broke the tight hold of Xerox.

Competitive Pressures Intensify

In 1974, Canon found itself in serious trouble. Malfunctioning calculators, with faulty light emitting diode displays, had to be recalled in large numbers, a mishap that could not have come at a more inauspicious time. Ferocious competition, led by Casio and Sharp, had driven prices to the ground, forcing many calculator makers to withdraw from the market. Those that remained were operating at the margin, with little or no profit. At the same time, the growth of camera sales slowed as markets became increasingly saturated. Exports of camera and other products decreased under the pressure of a higher yen, and production costs were rising as a result of higher petroleum prices. In the first half of 1975, Canon was forced to suspend dividends for the first time in its history, an experience still regarded in the company with some horror almost 20 years later. The combination of forces battering the company exposed the company's structural and managerial weaknesses. Ryuzaburo Kaku, then in charge of Finance, recalled:

> Canon's technical strength – demonstrated in a stream of pioneering that began with Japan's first 35 mm precision cameras – had not been backed by a coherent management strategy. Marketing was weak. Competitors were copying [our] products before [we] could fully exploit [our] sales potential. Canon was like a ship that constantly changed course and got nowhere... Components were being manufactured in too many scattered locations... As in many old Japanese companies, our people were so afraid of making mistakes that they did nothing. We've had to teach them not to fear being creative – or even failing.

Introduction of the Premier Company Plan

Takeo Maeda, the new president who had assumed office just before the gale of misfortune swept over the company, responded with a 6-year premier company plan. Launched in 1976, the plan called for a restructuring and internationalization of the company, and the introduction of new efficient production systems, to avoid the pressures of yen appreciation, protectionism and energy shortages in the future. The objectives of the plan were clear and ambitious. Canon was to become a leading corporation in Japan within three years, and a world leader in the subsequent three years. The new plan began by reducing operations, curtailing costs, and undertaking efforts to strengthen camera, calculator and copier sales. An operating profit rate of 15%, with no debt, became the principal tenets of financial management. Sales were targeted to increase 15% annually – considered to be a reasonable growth rate – with the goal of substantially increasing market share in all product lines. All this was to be achieved through more rapid and higher quality product development, improved production and total marketing management.

A new matrix organization linked the three major product divisions – camera, business machines and optical products – with functional committees for new product development, production and marketing. The Canon Development System (CDS) was established to improve the efficiency of R&D, shortening the time to market for new products. The task of the Canon Production System (CPS) was to resolve quality problems, eliminate waste and activate employees within the new rationalized organizational structure. The objective of the Canon Marketing System (CMS) was to relate the company's products and services to customer satisfaction in all of Canon's worldwide markets. Pushing responsibility down the line, the three product divisions were to operate as autonomous vertical profit centres. Division chiefs were appointed and delegated the authority to act fairly independently.

The new plan was only just put into action when Mr Maeda suddenly passed away. Mr Kaku, who as Managing Director had been largely responsible for shaping the new direction of the company, was elevated to the presidency and charged with the task of completing the reforms underway.

The Canon Way

From the outset, Canon had been endowed with a strong corporate sense of purpose. Self-motivation, self-awareness and self-management were the three pillars on which the company had been created. Mr Kaku continued to give these philosophical principles primary importance, adapting and embellishing the company purposes for the task ahead (*refer to* **Exhibit 1**). In his words:

> When I took over, Canon was 'sluggish' and full of bureaucratic attitudes which drained the organization of its ability to respond to changes in the operating environment...
>
> [My basic philosophy was] to build a company which further upholds human rights and dignity, while striving to develop better technology and products through innovation.

A decade later, in 1985, Canon was well on the way to becoming a premier company by world standards. Significant increases in investment and R&D had resulted in a spate of new products, many of them 'firsts' in the marketplace. Canon's product line ranged from 35 mm and video cameras to copiers, electronic typewriters, laser printers, facsimile machines and microlithographic equipment for producing semiconductors and medical equipment. At this time, Canon's manufacturing and marketing organization spanned over 100 countries and employed 34,100 people (*refer to* **Exhibit 2**). In 1985, profits rose to ¥37 billion on net sales of close to ¥956 billion. Business machines accounted for 71% of sales, with cameras and optical equipment generating 21% and 8%, respectively.

The Response to *Endaka*

But new problems were on the horizon. Unlike most other Japanese companies, Canon relied heavily on overseas markets for the bulk of its business, with North America and Europe each accounting for 30% of sales. Although the process of globalizing manufacturing was well underway, a high percentage of overseas sales were still generated by exports, making Canon particularly vulnerable to *endaka* (yen appreciation), which followed the Plaza Accords in 1986.[1]

Canon's response to the rising yen was guided by past experience. R&D expenditures were increased, cost reduction efforts were broadened and intensified, and capital outlays for overseas production facilities were boosted. After posting record profits for the previous ten years, Canon's income dropped 70% in 1986 to ¥10.7 million, threatening a cut in dividends. Shinji Tatewaki, who had just returned to Canon's copier division in Tokyo after heading up the company's Chicago sales office for several years, recalled:

> The US government devalued the dollar and, within the space of virtually a day, the yen was worth significantly more against other currencies. In 1984, the yen was strong at ¥251 to one US dollar. Then the level dropped down to ¥150. Production costs increased dramatically, and there was no way that we could recover the loss. We had to reconstruct our entire operations. We launched a large-scale cost reduction activity and a campaign to avoid waste. In Canon Tokyo, people soon began pinning '¥150 badges' on their shirts. We were all focused on what we had to do to live in a ¥150 world.

Because of the strength of the yen, Canon products made in Japan had become more expensive overseas. Further expansion of overseas production was essential. In addition, as a *Forbes* reporter commented:[2]

> Canon's strongest defence against a rising yen is innovation. With innovative products, price is less important than in commodity-type products...
>
> This means heavy spending on research and development, of course. Canon's R&D amounts to some 11% of parent company sales, one of the highest ratios among Japanese companies outside the chemical and pharmaceutical industries.

Given the increasing trade friction in the US and European markets, Canon had further cause to reposition itself to maintain future growth. Three-quarters of the company's sales were in office equipment, including both stand-alone machines, such as copiers, and the systems that would combine them in the 'office-of-the-future'. It was in this sector that globalization became increasingly imperative.

Canon's Copier Business

Canon first entered the copier market in 1965 with a coated paper copier, based on technology licensed from RCA. Realizing the limitations of this technology, Canon formed a team of engineers led by Dr Keizo Yamaji, to develop a copier drum with an insulating layer that would be suitable for plain paper copying using a more photosensitive chemical than the one then used in xerography. This

---

[1] In 1985, the lowest rate was US$1 = ¥263.65; the highest rate was US$1 = ¥199.80. In 1986, the lowest rate was US$1 = Y203.30; the highest rate was US$1 = ¥152.55 in Tokyo.
[2] From Fuji to Everest, *Forbes*, 2 May 1988.

new design prolonged the drum's life and reduced the risk of discharging toxic chemicals. Introduced in Japan in April 1968, Canon's 'New Process' (NP) plain paper copying system was completely free of Xerox patents. Hiroshi Tanaka, who was part of this effort, commented:[3]

> Engineers working on the plain paper copying project thoroughly investigated the patents held by Xerox. In the process, we learned how not to violate patents and how to obtain patents to protect our own technology. The NP technology was completely free of Xerox's airtight patent network.

In 1972, the company launched a second generation 'liquid dry' NP system, which used plain paper and liquid toner and turned out dry copies. This new technology reduced machine breakdowns by eliminating the complex heat-fusing mechanism and simplifying the developing and cleaning process. These machines had lower production costs, were more compact and more reliable than anything available at the time, and they matched Xerox on copy quality. Canon subsequently licensed out this technology to 20 manufacturers in Japan and three in the United States.

NP copiers were manufactured at the Toride factory on the outskirts of Tokyo, which had been set up a decade earlier to make synchroreaders and, later, cameras. Toride used a flexible manufacturing system that could accommodate differences in models and electrical specifications. The four assembly lines could handle any NP model after a 2-day changeover. Each line had the capacity to turn out between 3,000 and 8,000 units monthly. About 2,000 parts were required to produce the range of NP copiers.

Initially, copiers were sold in Japan through Canon Business Machines Sales Inc., set up in 1968 to market calculators. In 1971, this subsidiary was merged with Canon Camera Sales Inc. to form Canon Sales Inc., whose shares were listed on the first Tokyo Stock Exchange a decade later. Beginning with 200 people dedicated to the sale and service of copiers, the new company sold Canon copiers outright and offered customers a Total Guarantee System.

In the early 1970s, Canon established a dealer network throughout Japan. Dealers received extensive training and, within a few years, had completely taken over the task of servicing copiers. Canon did not begin selling its NP systems in the US until 1972, when a dealer sales network was established. However, these copiers were being distributed in Europe through Canon's marketing unit in The Netherlands as early as 1972, although sales were modest.

The Personal Copier Breakthrough

Canon's copier strategy was formed largely by its camera strategy: 'a camera for everyone' was translated into 'a copier for everyone'.

Canon's copier line initially was aimed at small and medium-scale users, a market that had been largely ignored by Xerox, The Xerox strategy focused on

---

[3] Harvard Business School case study, *Canon Inc., Worldwide Copier Strategy*, 1983, page 2.

large users in government, business and universities. Following Canon's strategy, Dr Keizo Yamaji who had become the General Manager of Canon's Reprographic Products Division, wanted to open up an entirely new market for the PPC. Dr Yamaji had market data showing that there were over 4 million offices in Japan with fewer than five employees which were not being addressed by the conventional copier business. The lowest-priced unit available was ¥500,000, about US$2,300, which was too expensive for a small business. As well, professional service engineers needed to come in regularly to maintain these machines. Again, this cost-limited their use to larger offices. The 'dream' was to come up with a compact, maintenance-free copier that would cost about $1,000 and could be sold to small offices, for home use or as a personal desk-side copier. This idea was totally different from the Xerox system which, until this point, had dominated the world copier business.

Introduced in late 1982, Canon's personal copier (PC) represented a revolution in reprographic technology. The PC used a replaceable cartridge that eliminated the need to maintain the machine regularly. After making 2,000 copies, the user simply replaced the cartridge, which contained a photoreceptive drum, toner assembly, cleaner and charging device. Cartridges were available with four toner colours.

In time, copier manufacturers around the world began purchasing Canon's personal copier on an OEM basis. For example, Olivetti began importing Canon personal copiers in late 1984. Increasingly, large firms operating internationally were completing their product line by buying certain models from other producers.

Canon in Europe

In 1957, Canon Europa was established in Geneva as Canon's sole distributor for Europe. Over the following decade, a network of national distributors was developed to market, distribute and service Canon cameras and calculators. To better manage the increasing volume of European business, especially in EC countries, the European headquarters functions were transferred to Canon Amsterdam NV in 1968, leaving Canon Geneva as a finance company.

With the introduction of the Premier Company Plan and the Canon Marketing System, the first task was to reorganize the complex system of multiple national distributorships that had evolved over the first two post-war decades. Given the rapid diversification of product lines and the increasing importance of global rationalization of marketing, total control over the marketing and distribution system became imperative to respond to customer needs. In 1975, Canon gradually began the process of replacing distributors with integrated Canon marketing subsidiaries in each country. Over the following years, Canon Europa NV was established, with 19 subsidiaries, including Canon Amsterdam NV, to manage the intricate European organization. A senior manager in Canon described the process:

> In some countries, we had to start from scratch; in others, we already had relationships with distributors. In France, for instance, Canon's camera

importer wanted to get into the copier business, and we quickly had the 200 people in this organization selling copiers directly. In the UK, we were using Marubeni, a *sogo shosha* or general trading house, which then sold products through several companies. This arrangement lasted only 2–3 years. Then we had to build something up ourselves. We put cameras and copiers together and distributed through dealers. In Germany, Canon's camera distributor was not so interested in selling copiers. Eventually, we were able to put together an arrangement, but it was strictly a sales and marketing venture. In Italy, our camera importer was also not interested in copiers. Cash recovery was a real problem. For copiers, Canon couldn't expect to get payment for up to ten months after the sale. In the camera business, payment was available within 30 days. We had a good business in Italy with calculators, but it was clear that we needed more sophisticated salespeople to market copiers.

In many cases, Canon ended up buying out the distributors because of their limited financial strength and cashflow problems. This put a major strain on Canon's own financial resources.

Over the next several years, Canon's marketing capabilities in Europe grew substantially. Over time, the various national subsidiaries that were established began to operate more independently and purchase products directly from Japan.

Canon Begins Producing Copiers in Europe

In 1972, Canon acquired the assets of ECE GmbH, a small German R&D house specializing in advanced electrostatic technology in Giessen, near Frankfurt. ECE had contributed significantly to perfecting Canon's 'liquid dry' copy technology, and Canon had been helping the firm financially since 1969. By mid-1973, the ECE facility had been converted into a factory with the capacity to turn out 1,500 low-volume PPCs monthly, to be sold throughout Europe as well as in some Middle East and African markets.[4]

ECE's original management team had remained in place after the acquisition, and Canon Giessen was staffed almost entirely by Germans. Tsukasa Kuge, one of the few dispatched from Tokyo, arrived in 1973 and remained in the operation until 1975, returning for an additional five months in 1977. Mr Kuge recalled:

By acquiring a well-organized high-technology company with considerable experience and know-how in copier development, we were able to start up a new production unit rather quickly. Much of the time usually spent on the details of technology and transferring know-how was saved, which reduced the drain on managerial and technical resources in Tokyo. After a time, R&D activity was to be dedicated entirely to the development of Canon's product,

---

[4] InfoSource's classification scheme was generally used as a way to segment the market, as follows: Category 1 – less than 20 copies per minute (cpm); Category 2 – 20–39 cpm; Category 3 – 40–59 cpm; Category 4 – 60–89 cpm; Category 5 – 90+ cpm. The Personal Copier category was subsequently added for copiers generating fewer than 10 cpm.

and the R&D activities both in Giessen and in Tokyo had to be performed in conformity with each other, so I was sent over.

In the early 1970s, the copier market was not so segmented as it is today. We began making what we felt would sell the best, and we planned to move up in quality. In the beginning, more than 30 people were doing research and development, and they were creating many ideas that were also implemented back in Japan. Over time, Giessen's R&D capability was made smaller as production became more important.

After two years in operation, a team of 130 people were manufacturing 500 NP machines (20 cpm) each month under a rigid quality control programme. Production was scheduled to increase at a level of 20–35% annually. Giessen's assembly process was similar to Toride's, but on a much smaller scale. In 1975, the production capacity at Giessen was doubled, and new lines were added to produce copier drums and toner.

A Second Plant in Europe

In August 1983, Canon responded to an invitation from the French government to establish a personal copier factory in Liffre, in Bretagne (Brittany). At this time, Canon was also looking at the feasibility of establishing a PPC assembly plant in Virginia, USA.

By the end of 1984, the Liffre plant was turning out about 3,000 copiers per month, and lines were subsequently added to produce electronic typewriters and facsimile transceivers.

Canon's European Presence in 1986

By 1986, Canon had become a leading player in the European market, placing more than 200,000 units out of an estimated total market of 897,780 (*refer to* **Exhibit 3**). Canon's aim was to become the world's leading PPC manufacturer. To achieve this, the company's goal was to obtain at least a 30% unit share in the three major copier markets: Japan, Europe and the US (*refer to* **Exhibits 4 and 5**).

Canon offered the full range of copiers, from its innovative personal copier to its NP-8000 series (up to 70 cpm), which competed head-on with Xerox and Kodak machines. In the near future, Canon planned to introduce a digital colour copier that many believed would not only transform the office environment, but also revolutionize the whole industry. It was rumoured that newly emerging domestic competitors were also developing colour copiers based on a different product concept.

Currently, Canon had sales subsidiaries in virtually every European country (*refer to* **Exhibit 6**), as well as independent business machine distributors that dealt with a network of retailers. Many of Canon's European distributors sold only Canon products. In the camera business, they relied mostly on the retailers. In calculators, they used another channel. Business equipment needed more support, and it was becoming apparent that more sales channels were needed to sell copiers. At the same time, Canon's machines were becoming more expensive because of the 15.8% duty that the European Commission had placed on most copiers imported from Japan. This temporary rate was set in 1986, but there was an expectation that the rate would be officially set at 20% in 1987.

At the low end, Canon was also finding that its copiers were not competitive enough. Other Japanese copier manufacturers were very price conscious. Moreover, customers were getting more sophisticated. In the past, they would accept lower copy quality, but increasingly they wanted superior reproduction from easy-to-use machines with low maintenance requirements, and customers were becoming more concerned about environmental factors. Canon needed to get a new product in this category, or come up with a new technology.

Canon's Giessen facility was one of the largest and most integrated copier plants in Europe, employing 400 people and turning out 4,000 PPCs each month. Giessen manufactured NP systems in Category 2 and Category 3, together with components like photosensitive drums, the heart of the plain paper copier. About 80 suppliers were contracted locally to provide services and parts, including moulded casings, lids, platen glass, print boards, paper supply cassettes, fixing rollers, solenoids, DC controllers, halogen lamps and low-voltage electric sources. Likewise, Canon's Bretagne operation employed about 430 people and used numerous local suppliers. Little R&D was being earned out of either of these operations, aside from modifying designs sent from Tokyo to meet local manufacturing and local market needs. In principle, the R&D laboratories that Canon set up abroad were linked with R&D in Japan and part of the global rationalization of Canon's R&D effort. These laboratories were intended to serve Canon's global operation, not local production. Currently the General Manager of Canon's 145-person Peripheral Development division in Tokyo, Tsukasa Kuge, had also been directly involved and was familiar with Canon's European operations. Kuge remarked:

> The idea was for Giessen to concentrate on mid-range copiers. We had personal copiers being produced in Liffre and Category 1, 4 and 5 in Toride. We had significantly fewer people working in R&D in Giessen than in the beginning. Over time, production became much more important, and it was more effective to do the R&D in Japan.
>
> In developing products, Canon follows a policy of *mochi wa mochi-ya*. The idea is to have the proper development in the proper place. *Mochi* is the sticky rice cake that is traditionally cooked for New Year's celebrations. The raw material is popular and the cooking process is simple. Anyone can make rice cakes, but *mochi*-making is a hard and time-consuming task. The job of making rice cakes should belong to the most skilful rice cake maker: namely, *mochi-ya*.
>
> Ultimately, Canon needs to have a greater R&D capability in Europe if we are to become an insider. We could develop this capability with some incremental investment based on Giessen's original potential or, alternatively, we could set up a new, greenfield site in Germany or Switzerland, for instance. As well, we need to further investigate options for locally produced parts.

Mr Kaku commented:

> When we first began production in Europe...there were no compelling economic reasons to transfer this original technology. But it is our established policy, in keeping with our basic corporate purposes, to participate to the fullest in the development of the societies which we serve through our products.

A Possibility for Cooperation

In late 1986, Elserino Piol, Executive Vice President Strategies and Development in the Olivetti Group, travelled to Tokyo to discuss with senior Canon management about joining forces in the copier business. Olivetti had a firm hold on 85% of the copier market in Italy – which represented about 5% of the total market in Europe – and Olivetti was looking for a way to double its share. Canon had had some difficulty serving the southern part of Europe, and it was possible to conclude that combining the sales effort with Olivetti could expand the total sales for both companies. However, it was also possible that such an alliance would lead to conflicts between the two sales forces.

Currently, Canon had the highest number of installed copiers in all of Europe. However, the market was still relatively undeveloped. There was a huge potential for growth with the coming developments in digital technology and colour copying, and the further integration of the copier into the office environment. At this point, the question for Canon was whether it made sense to enter a venture with a company that was ostensibly a competitor in the copier business. Olivetti was a leading player in the office products market with a long history in the business, and this was an area that Canon wanted to enter more strongly in the future. For both partners, such a venture would be a way to learn the way of thinking, history, technology and philosophy of the other.

In the past, Japanese manufacturers had tended to manufacture products in Japan and then export them to Europe and North America. Early on, Canon realized that this tendency could not continue. Canon's philosophy was to produce products in the market where they were used. In fact, Canon was the first Japanese company to set up a factory for copiers in Europe, which was done to have some insurance for the future. Over the years, Canon had set up many ventures, but they had always been built up from ground zero. The transfer of technology was much easier this way, and it was more secure. This would be the only major joint venture for Canon in copiers that involved manufacturing and R&D, and it would be only the second joint venture that Canon had entered into outside Japan. The first one, Lotte Canon, was established in 1985.

Canon's technology was ahead of Olivetti's, so its patents, know-how and projects would probably be put into the joint venture. Canon had just started production of a new Category 1 copier in Toride. In looking at Olivetti's R&D and manufacturing capability and its sales channels, there was also the possibility of transferring this production into such an operation. The question of Olivetti's relationships with other OEM suppliers would still have to be resolved. Furthermore, Olivetti's suppliers had quite different standards from those of Canon on quality, and significant improvements would probably have to be sought on the product cost side. More than 20 years earlier, Canon had launched programmes to study the potential of its suppliers. Although studies could be expensive, the result often saved time and costs in terms of quality assurance. As well, Canon came to understand the level of quality support it needed to provide to its suppliers. As a result, Canon's suppliers had become involved in developing Canon machines, and they operated on a just-in-time basis. This collaboration was natural and ongoing. Moreover, through this arrangement, Canon had gathered a lot of cost data and continually looked for ways to improve. Typically, Canon's inventory level in Japan was less than five days. In Giessen it was seven days, although work was ongoing to bring this level down further.

In Tokyo, Canon had a very different system from the one used by Olivetti and most other European and North American manufacturers. Canon used a mass production system, and the underlying driver was how to improve production volume within a certain timeframe. This was based on minutes and seconds, and the idea was to look continually for ways to shorten the work cycle. Canon used conveyor belts, and most people in the copier area worked on a 20–30 second cycle. In contrast, in Olivetti, one person typically worked 25–30 minutes at a station and assembled a lot of parts. The whole unit was manually pushed on a cart to the next station, and there was usually some waiting time for the next step.

There were also differences in the development system. Traditionally, Canon's R&D people concentrated on perfecting the design. There were no major modifications once the drawing was completed and moved into production. Canon looked continually for ways to improve the quality in each step, to make cost reductions and to develop products faster. In Canon, the objective was for production costs to be reduced every year, which could be achieved by changing the design to use cheaper parts, negotiating with suppliers for price discounts, changing the production process in the factory to work more effectively, and so on. This was the kind of thinking that Canon would need to transfer into a joint venture.

Canon had never entered into this kind of alliance before. The challenge for both parties would be how to adapt and how to implement changes. The key would be how to structure such a venture, how to keep the good parts of each partner's culture and build on a common basis. Canon had always had a philosophy of co-existence.

EXHIBIT 1

The Canon Way

Our Corporate Philosophy

- To be a global corporation providing kyosei (living and working together for the common good) in all countries where we operate.

Our mission	Our objectives	Our business development goals	Our values
• To make a positive contribution through continued growth and reinvestment in the world's communities.	• To be a responsible global citizen. • To have unique and quality products. • To build an ideal company for continuing prosperity.	• To combine our traditional hardware strength with software systems development. • To create information systems and networks which integrate hardware, software and services. • To operate on a global scale.	• Respect cultural differences. • Encourage self-motivation, self-awareness and self-management. • Respect dignity, value initiative and recognise merit. • Work together in harmony. • Sustain our physical and emotinal health.

EXHIBIT 2

The Canon Organization

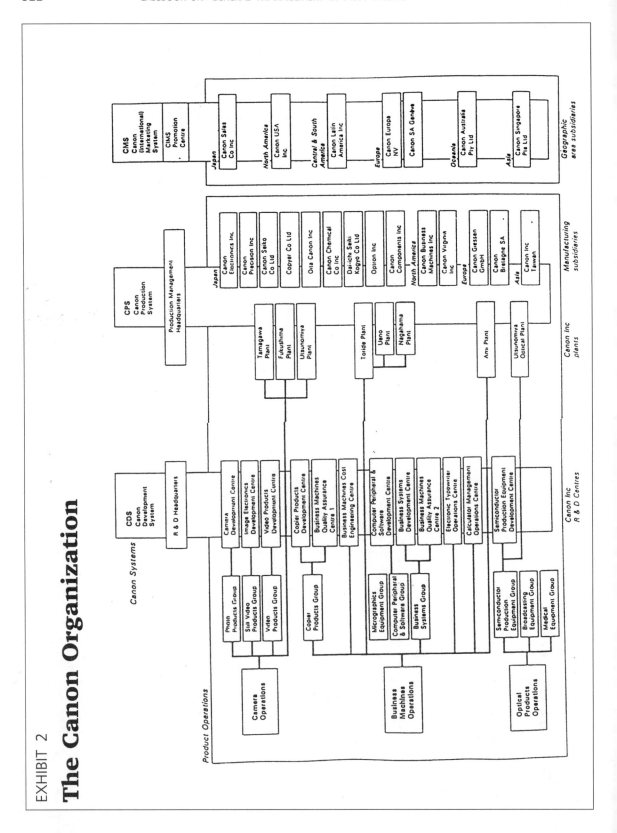

EXHIBIT 3

Canon Brand: Sales, Quantity and Market Share in Europe (1984–86)

	1984	1985	1986 (estimated)
Personal copiers	82,640 81.7%	111,350 65.2%	110,050 52.8%
Category 1 (up to 19 cpm)	57,880 15.0%	49,110 12.6%	54,020 13.0%
Category 2 (20–39 cpm)	30,370 16.2%	28,500 15.2%	31,410 14.6%
Category 3 (40–59 cpm)	11,960 19.9%	10,050 19.1%	7,330 14.2%
Category 4 (60–89 cpm)	0 0	0 0	640 8.5%
TOTAL	182,850 24.7%	199,010 24.7%	203,450 22.7%

Source: InfoSource S.A.

EXHIBIT 4

Estimated PPC Placements in Japan, in 1985 and 1986, by Brand (in thousands of units)

	Placements	
Company	1985	1986
Canon	125	138
Fuji Xerox	97	111
Konishiroku	35	35
Matsushita	6	7
Minolta	34	33
Mita	28	27
Ricoh	168	162
Sharp	33	38
Toshiba	32	36
TOTAL	558	587

Source: Dataquest Incorporated.

EXHIBIT 5

Estimated PPC Placements in the US in 1986, by Brand (in thousands of units)

	Personal copiers	Segment 1	Segment 2	Segment 3	Segment 4	Segment 5	Segment 6	TOTAL
Adler-Royal	–	16.0	3.2	–	0.4	–	–	19.6
Canon	165.0	52.0	48.3	4.5	13.5	1.4	–	284.7
A.B. Dick	–	3.2	0.8	0.5	0.3	–	–	4.8
Gestetner	–	8.1	2.5	0.3	0.4	–	–	11.3
Harris/3M	–	34.0	13.5	5.2	–	–	–	52.7
Kodak	–	–	–	–	7.2	3.4	1.1	11.7
Konica	–	26.0	7.5	4.1	5.0	0.1	–	42.7
Minolta	5.4	26.1	25.8	1.7	0.6	–	–	59.6
Mita	–	53.0	20.4	–	4.5	–	–	77.9
Monroe	–	11.5	5.0	–	0.6	–	–	17.1
Océ	–	–	–	–	2.6	–	–	2.6
Panasonic	–	19.2	12.1	0.8	–	–	–	32.1
Pitney Bowes	–	7.4	11.8	1.8	2.0	–	–	23.0
Ricoh	5.0	26.0	7.9	3.6	4.0	–	–	46.5
Sanyo	3.6	3.1	–	0.9	–	–	–	7.6
Savin	–	17.6	2.0	12.1	5.4	–	–	37.1
Sharp	28.0	64.3	8.2	10.1	10.0	–	–	120.6
Toshiba	43.2	13.0	7.0	–	–	–	63.2	126.4
Xerox	–	59.0	18.0	26.3	9.1	0.8	9.2	122.4
Others	7.0	4.9	2.4	–	–	0.6	–	14.9

This segmentation is based on the following criteria:

Segment	Speed (copies per minute)	Typical monthly volume range
PC	under 20	N/A
1	0–20	0–10,000
2	21–30	5,000–20,000
3	31–45	5,000–30,000
4	40–75	10,000–75,000
5	70–90	25,000–125,000
6	91+	100,000+

Source: Dataquest Incorporated.

EXHIBIT 6

Canon's European Distribution Capabilities (number of employees as of December 1985)

Country	Canon subsidiaries	Canon affiliated companies
France*	1,868	–
UK	1,071	–
Germany	812	–
Spain	–	387
The Netherlands	384	–
Finland	380	–
Sweden	332	–
Austria	193	–
Italy	187	–
Belgium	105	–
Switzerland	51	–
Luxembourg	9	–
TOTAL	5,392	387
	COMBINED TOTAL	5,779

* Canon Bretagne is included in the French subsidiaries.

Source: Canon Handbook.

IMD
INTERNATIONAL

CASE 12.2 # OLIVETTI IN THE EUROPEAN COPIER MARKET

This case was prepared by Research Associate Joyce Miller, under the supervision of Professors George Taucher and Dominique Turpin as a basis for class discussion rather than to illustrate either effective or ineffective handling of a business situation.

In late 1986, Elserino Piol, Executive Vice President Strategies and Development in the Olivetti Group, one of the world's foremost information technology companies and the second largest indigenous personal computer manufacturer in Europe, was concerned about the company's photocopier business. Their Agliè plant located near Olivetti's headquarters in Ivrea was producing about 20,000 units annually, most of which were sold in Italy. This operation was expected to be an important component for Olivetti in creating the 'integrated office', where several pieces of stand-alone equipment would be linked up in a multi-functional, automated system.

But the window of opportunity was closing. With the fast pace of development in the telecommunications technology that provided the networks and links between formerly disparate pieces, several new contenders were poised to enter the office-of-the-future market. A few months earlier, Mr Piol had travelled to Tokyo to meet with senior management in Canon Inc., a major Japanese copier manufacturer, to sound out the possibilities for cooperation. At this point in time, Mr Piol wondered whether it might make sense to form a basic technology alliance with a leader in the copier field.

Ing. C. Olivetti & Co., SpA.

Ing. C. Olivetti & Co., SpA. was the parent company of the Olivetti Group, whose product line included distributed data processing and office automation equipment, typewriters, calculators, cash registers and photocopiers (*refer to* **Exhibit 1**).

In 1986, the Olivetti Group obtained a net income of L565.5 billion on sales of L7,317 billion, up 12.3% from the previous year.[1] At this time, Olivetti had manufacturing activities in 27 plants in seven countries.

Founded in 1908 and headquartered in the foothills of the Italian Alps, just over the border from Switzerland, Olivetti was known for many years as the family-owned company that turned out elegantly designed typewriters. By the mid-1960s, Olivetti was the sixth largest industrial organization in Italy, and 80%

[1] In 1986, US$1 = L1490.

of its revenues from the sale of manual and electronic typewriters, calculators, accounting machines and office furniture were generated outside Italy.

In the following decade, as a result of its ambitious growth strategy, Olivetti became seriously undercapitalized, and it appeared that the company would either go bankrupt or fall into the hands of the Italian government. In April 1978, a dynamic leader from outside the family was brought in to turn the company around. Carlo de Benedetti, an Italian industrialist who had previously spent several months as Managing Director of Fiat, took over as Vice Chairman and CEO. De Benedetti invested over $17 million of his own personal fortune in the company (and thereby became the majority shareholder) and launched a programme to revitalize Olivetti.

Olivetti Becomes a Strong Force in Office Automation[2]

By the mid-1980s, De Benedetti had established Olivetti as the strongest European competitor to IBM in office automation by upgrading the company's electronic typewriters, and introducing a line of microcomputers and mini-computers. An industry analyst commented:

> De Benedetti immediately slapped a 10% price increase on products, laid off 20,000 workers, and gave priority to developing the company's pioneering electronic typewriter. He subsequently replaced Olivetti's mechanical models with a new line of electronic machines, and he did this in record time. He accelerated the development process and beat IBM to the market by several months. In the processs, de Benedetti incurred debts of over $1 billion to pay for retooling Olivetti's plants and boosting the output of electronic-based equipment. In three years, R&D costs – which had been less than $30 million when de Benedetti took over – soared to more than $100 million.

To support these outlays, de Benedetti undertook a series of venture capital moves in the US, spending $60 million to assume interests in 22 small high-tech companies, a strategy that de Benedetti hoped would give Olivetti early access to new developments and keep the company abreast of emerging trends. During the 1970s, Olivetti had often been too late into the market with new products, which had weakened its position in the office equipment market. De Benedetti believed that tracking progress in the US market would provide insights to enhance Olivetti's position in Europe and ensure that the company anticipated customer demands. As well, de Benedetti searched relentlessly for ways to improve performance, cut costs and reduce debt while maintaining Olivetti's forward momentum towards the integrated office market. New accounting systems were introduced, control was tightened, low-profit products were discontinued and plants were closed or revamped. Competition in office automation from IBM,

---

[2] Parts of this section are paraphrased from IMD Case GM 352, Building Alliances (B): Ing. C. Olivetti, & Co. SpA.

DEC and Xerox was the greatest threat to a small contender like Olivetti. These giants had significant financial resources and had spent heavily on R&D in the early 1980s. De Benedetti was also concerned about emerging competitors in the office automation field, namely the Japanese. De Benedetti was convinced that Olivetti needed a more global thrust.

Increasingly, computer-based office information systems were replacing conventional office machines, although the typewriter was still the core of Olivetti's business. In 1982, de Benedetti launched Olivetti's first personal computer – the M20, which generated sales of $56 million worldwide within one year. According to a senior marketing executive:

> We put our personal computer lab in Cupertino, California, in order to be right there in Silicon Valley, where you literally breathe the state of the art.

At this time, Apple Computer, the market leader, had total sales of $850 million and IBM obtained revenues of $630 million in this sector. Olivetti subsequently launched the M24, an IBM-compatible desktop PC, which laid the foundation for Olivetti to become the second largest personal computer manufacturer in Europe. An Olivetti salesman remarked:

> The M24 was the most successful PC we ever had. When PCs came out in the US, there were only a few outlets able to sell them. This led to the birth of PC dealers, and each manufacturer had to create this infrastructure.
>
> In Europe, Olivetti helped shape this market because we had an established network of dealers, or *concessionaires,* who were selling our typewriters and other office products. In some countries, like Spain, we'd had these dealers in place since before World War I. No one in the US had a network like ours, or was this far along. These were exclusive outlets, and most got on the bandwagon to sell PCs as well. We also had a tier of independent dealers. We couldn't manufacture enough M24s to keep up with the demand.

A Strategic Alliance with AT&T

In December 1983, Olivetti entered into an agreement with American Telephone & Telegraph Co. (AT&T), which had dominated the American telecommunications industry for years. The AT&T monopoly was deregulated in early 1983, and the company launched its first digital private branch exchange (PBX) system soon afterward. Such a system enabled an office to become its own in-house phone company. PBX systems could be connected to other digital equipment such as terminals, PCs and even large mainframe computers. Voice and data were transmitted over a single telephone line, which combined to make the PBX the "hub of the automated office-of-the-future and the target of every equipment manufacturer wishing to stay in the race."

AT&T spent $260 million to acquire a 25% stake in Olivetti. The 1983 agreement was described as an industrial, commercial and financial alliance in the office automation field, and it granted Olivetti exclusive European distribution rights for all AT&T office automation products. AT&T received reciprocal distribution rights for Olivetti products in the US market. The idea was that the Olivetti dealers would sell AT&T's private automatic branch exchanges in Europe in addition to their existing line of office products. By July 1984, one out of every three microcomputers moving off the assembly line in Olivetti's modern Scarmagno plant, near the company's headquarters in Ivrea, carried the AT&T logo and went into a box marked for shipment to the US. The PC6300 and PC6300 Plus, both supplied by Olivetti, were AT&T's most successful personal computers on the market. An Olivetti executive commented:

> By mid-1986, the bloom was coming off the alliance. We were just too different. We were each part of the other's product line, but we each continued to manufacture products in competition when we should have been sourcing them from the partner. This was only one of the things that put stress on the relationship. It was also becoming clear that AT&T was rethinking its computer strategy and planned to emphasize its local area networks and data communications equipment in order to go after the larger network business – between office locations or between big computers in different places.
>
> 1984 to 1986 were very successful years for us, and the alliance with AT&T certainly helped Olivetti build its reputation in Europe and the US. No one had any trouble making their budgets. Around this time, people began thinking that maybe the copier was an interesting product to get serious about.

Olivetti's Copier Business

Olivetti entered the copier business in 1962 through a licensing agreement with Old Town Corporation, a US firm based in New York. By the mid-1960s, Olivetti had come up with its own design for a low-end machine that used a liquid toner, an approach employed by many copier manufacturers at the time. Olivetti had arrangements to buy both the toner and the specially coated zinc-oxide paper that served as a photoconductive surface as well as the final copy. The company had some commercial success with this machine, primarily with vendors in Italy, France and Spain. Giovanni Ravera, who joined Olivetti around this time, recounted:

> Initially, we concentrated on developing our processes. It wasn't long before we realized that the electrofax technology we were using was becoming obsolete, and we began developing plain paper copiers (PPCs). Everyone was doing this. In 1968, a design group was formed in New Jersey, and much of their effort was focused on a high-speed, high copy volume machine invented by one of the American technicians.
>
> There was some commercial development but not a lot of success. These machines were sold through Olivetti's sales organization for general office products. It was difficult for this group to sell these more sophisticated high-end products, these rather delicate machines. At the time, Xerox was building

a specially dedicated sales and service organization, which eventually became its key success factor in the industry, and we had no equivalent effort.

Olivetti began active development work on manufacturing PPCs following the US Federal Trade Commission's 1975 decree that required Xerox to offer unrestricted licensing of all of its copier patents and related know-how. Throughout the development phase, Olivetti purchased low-volume copiers (under 20 copies per minute, or cpm) from Sharp Corporation on an original equipment manufacturer (OEM) basis. These units were sold under the Olivetti label with some minor customization. Olivetti's intention was to replace these machines with its own production of low-end copiers at a later stage. Beginning in 1978, Olivetti produced and marketed a mid-volume copier.

Expanding OEM Relationships

In 1976, Olivetti began buying in high-end machines on an OEM basis from Sharp as well. This relationship lasted for close to seven years, at which time Olivetti renewed the arrangement with Konishiroku Photo Industry (now called Konica), another Japanese copier manufacturer. Typically, OEMs were companies that produced their own copiers and/or manufactured products in the office electronics or reprographics sectors. OEM machines generally had a different design and different technical specifications from those sold under the manufacturer's own badge.

Olivetti, like many of its competitors, completed its product line by purchasing machines on an OEM basis. This was seen as a way to protect the existing customer base against competition from other suppliers able to offer the full range of models. The argument was made that these OEM sales were subsidiary to and aimed at facilitating the placement of the company's own-manufactured machines. In general, Olivetti resold these machines at a higher price than the level at which they were offered in the European Community by the original suppliers.

Olivetti Introduces its Own Low-End Machine

In 1981, Olivetti began producing low-volume copiers (10–20 cpm) in a newly refurbished plant in Agliè, 25 km north-west of Torino. At this time, Olivetti was one of the few companies in Europe still designing and manufacturing copiers. Kodak and Xerox each had a significant market position in Europe, but the designs came primarily from Japan and the US, respectively. UK-based Gestetner was also in the market, and Océ, a Dutch firm, was manufacturing mid-volume machines in Europe for the European market. Both of these companies imported OEM machines to fill out their product lines. In the mid-1970s, Océ had carried out basic research aimed at developing a low-volume model to replace OEM imports. However, the project was later abandoned when the company saw that it could not earn an adequate return while such low market prices prevailed.

In the early 1980s, Olivetti was able to reduce its reliance on OEM imports to one model with technical features between those of its own low- and mid-volume products. However, Olivetti's dependence on Japanese imports subsequently increased, as the company was unable to develop a successor product to its mid-volume machine. Market prices were depressed at the time of the investment decision. An economic evaluation of the project showed a negative return, and production was never begun. In late 1985, Olivetti concluded an arrangement to import personal copiers from Canon Inc., the inventor of this technology and the only producer of these machines worldwide. Mauro Achiluzzi, in Olivetti's Office Products Marketing area, elaborated:

> We wanted to sell Canon's personal copier in Italy under the Olivetti badge. Canon had a good product, and we had a good commercial network that we needed to feed with products. We're strong in Italy and have a presence in Spain, France, The Netherlands and the UK, as well as some activity in Scandinavia. Initially, Canon Tokyo wasn't prepared to do OEM business with what was theoretically a competitor, but eventually we convinced Canon Europe to go ahead. The arrangement didn't create too much turbulence in the marketplace. Canon was selling in its own channel and we were selling these products in ours, and there wasn't too much competition between the sales organizations.

Olivetti's Sales and Marketing Organization

In 1986, the Company was set up in four independent business units: office products, personal computers, systems and software. Olivetti had 33 marketing subsidiaries that operated in conjunction with a dealer organization to cover more than 100 countries (*refer to* **Exhibit 2** for more details on Olivetti's coverage in Europe). Mr Achiluzzi explained:

> Each of our marketing subsidiaries has a specific geographic responsibility, and within these organizations we have division managers responsible for each of the product lines. Annual budgets or targets – in terms of quantity, product mix, cost, bottom line – are prepared and submitted to Ivrea, and this is the commitment of the subsidiary to the headquarters. A local stock is kept to feed customer orders locally.
>
> We have a strong franchise in Italy, with 1,250 dealers. Close to half of them are exclusive. We have *concessionaires* in Spain as well but fewer than in Italy. Olivetti gives these more exclusive dealers a territory that is not covered by our existing branches, and they give us a commitment about what they will sell, within a limited category of products.

Most observers concluded that Olivetti's marketing and distribution organization was the key factor in its success, particularly in Italy. A salesman in Olivetti Nederland, one of Olivetti's smaller European subsidiaries, remarked:

> Beginning in the mid-1980s, there was an opening up of new technology. Quality was coming out as a buzzword, and people were prepared to make

the necessary investments. Everyone was trying to come out with quality products, from cars to copiers.

In the early years, we burned our fingers on coated paper technology where we used a ball of ink and created copies from that. We've always been in the office equipment business, and at a certain stage, the copier became an indispensable part of this. We had to get into this business. Olivetti had carefully built its image as a total office supplier. We were even making office furniture.

Historically, we haven't done very well because we were so bloody awful at copiers. There was a general reluctance in many of the sales arms to handle copiers. This was not the best job to have. We had no specific know-how and we didn't have the best copier. This was not our core business. We were in typewriters – office products – and more recently, in computers. At the moment, we're producing copiers at a limited level, and most of these go into Italy where we have a strong dealer network. In the marketplace, Olivetti is not really perceived as having a decent product range. We have tended to follow with me-too products rather than come in with something highly innovative. The reason we didn't do very well in copiers was also a result of the management focus at the time. In the mid-1980s, we had made a substantial investment in the M24, and we needed to understand the technology and the software, as well as whether or not we had to work with partners or could do it alone. We were also thinking about how to build up the sales channel to support this activity. The PC business was a big money generator per unit, for the organization and for the individual salesman.

In late 1986, Olivetti held a 5% share of the PPC market in Western Europe, with most of those sales being made in the southern European countries: 85% in Italy, 10% in France and 3.5% in Spain (*refer to Exhibit 3*). Filippo Demonte, the head of Olivetti's Office Products business, commented:

The Office Products group is an industrial division handling calculators, cash registers, typewriters, printers, copiers and hard disk drives. Historically, Olivetti has held a strong position in many of these sectors, but it is becoming clear that the hard disk drive and copier operations will not be able to survive on their own. The market that Olivetti has access to is too small, and we can't finance the necessary R&D efforts to sustain these activities. In the copier division, in particular, the production volume doesn't justify the overhead required to produce these relatively high-tech products. Copiers are a key part of Olivetti's overall strategy; otherwise, we could continue simply on an OEM basis. We need to look for an opportunity to transform this liability into an asset.

The Copier Operation in Agliè

In 1955, Olivetti had acquired the land and buildings of what had formerly been a large-scale textile operation in the small town of Agliè, near Olivetti's head-quarters in Ivrea. Olivetti transformed this property into a factory to assemble typewriters initially, and beginning in 1970, low-end copiers. Over the years, Olivetti had built up a network of local suppliers for fine mechanical parts (metal, plate and plastic) to faciliate its production of office machines in numerous factories located around Ivrea. These firms also supplied other Italian companies, like IBM and Honeywell–Bull.

From the beginning, the Agliè operation benefited from the existing supplier infrastructure. This operation was expected to become a key component for Olivetti in creating the 'automated office'. One of Olivetti's major strategic objectives was the integration of different technologies to develop the office-of–the-future. Mr Demonte elaborated recently:

On its own, the copier is a self-standing machine; a huge black and white instant camera. The copier becomes interesting in the automated office – the application of information technology to the office – when there is not only a power cord connected to a wall outlet, but there is also a second cord connected to an office computer; in effect, when the copier becomes a computer peripheral. For the copier to be a true peripheral, it must be possible to cut in between the object page to be copied and to thus separate the image-generation function from the image-reproduction function. Digital technology makes this possible, for the most part. The digital copier is the building block for integrating the copier into the automated office. In principle, the digital copier is made from a scanner and a laser beam printer. Once you have this, it's not necessary to have the scanner unit and printer unit in the same electrophotographic box.

At present, there is competition among several technologies to enable the copier to become a computer peripheral. A decade ago, everybody was using a thermal transfer approach, which required a special ribbon where the ink was melted by the printer heads. Today, the ink-jet technology used in bubble jet printers is a much better approach, offering a standard of reproduction that was once thought impossible to achieve. Many companies, including Olivetti, are working to further develop ink-jet technology. Currently, Canon is using a lightweight printer head to spray ink through nozzles that are one-third the diameter of a human hair. The biggest obstacle to increasing the speed is finding a way to dry the ink fast enough. There is no solution yet, but many are working on it.

Olivetti's ink-jet area is expected to develop into a growing and profitable business over the next decade. Until this point, we've developed a technology that is similar to Hewlett-Packard's technology to make bubble jet printers, and we've gained a strong position with our dry-inkjet non-impact printing calculator. Our bubble jet printers are very sophisticated electromechanical printers, and we're now the largest producer of printers in Europe. For Olivetti, this was a natural transition from the typewriter. We have a research lab of 70 people in Ivrea working on ink-jet physics, chemistry and application, and in addition, we have about 60 people in an R&D group in Yverdon, Switzerland, looking at how this technology could be implemented in new products.

Olivetti had put together a group of close to 70 engineers in Agliè who were involved in designing low-end copiers. These machines were fully developed by this group, and there was ongoing R&D concentrated on photoconductors and toners.

By late 1986, the Agliè operation was turning out about 20,000 units annually. However, several assembly line problems were occurring, and the source of these difficulties could often be traced back to external parts. The high reject rate was resulting in additional costs for Olivetti as well as its suppliers. Mr Demonte remarked:

> We're losing money in the copier business. But, closing up the operation entirely would certainly lead to additional expenses. We have a large infrastructure built up to support this business. We have a strong market position in Italy, and we can't just pull out of that. There would also be a question of what to do with the dealer channel and after-sales service organization. It isn't part of Olivetti's culture to just switch off something like this. Moreover, there are strong employment laws in Italy.
>
> We have tried several times to enter a partnership in the copier business. Sometimes, the companies we contacted wanted to buy our operation out-right. At one point, we approached one of our Japanese OEM suppliers, but they didn't want to be in a joint venture with an industrial operation. We always asked for R&D, management and production to be put into such a venture, and the Japanese counter-proposal was always to have the management and R&D in the venture and then subcontract out the production to a Japanese company. They were concerned about the quality of the end product as well as the level of production know-how.

Exploring the Possibilities for Cooperation

In late 1986, Elserino Piol, Executive Vice President, Strategies and Development, travelled to Tokyo and approached senior Canon management with the idea of cooperating in some way in the copier business. Mr Piol was intrigued by Canon's replaceable cartridge technology, which was introduced in 1982 in the world's first personal copiers, and he believed that great potential benefits for both parties could be derived if the two companies could work together. Mr Piol elaborated:

> I strongly felt that we could mutually benefit from this kind of cooperation. In our initial meetings, I found Canon's top management to be quite open and willing to talk about cooperating with a foreign company. Before going to Tokyo, I had also initiated discussions with another large copier manu-facturer that was not Japanese but had a large European presence. Olivetti needs a partner to share R&D with, one whom we could acquire technology from and would give us access to an additional market in the copier business.
>
> Olivetti was one of the first firms with a strategy to acquire technology not strictly by in-house development but also through joint ventures,

alliances, venture capital companies, and so on. At present, we have close to 200 joint ventures in operation. Olivetti has a lot of experience with this kind of arrangement.

In 1986, Canon was the dominant player in Europe, placing an average of 17,000 units each month, which represented a 22.7% share of the European copier market. For years, Canon had used an OEM strategy in Europe, while all other sales were handled by its Amsterdam-based regional headquarters, Canon Europe. This arrangement had enabled Canon to concentrate on cementing its position in the highly competitive domestic market. Over time, the larger of Canon's European sales subsidiaries that were subsequently put in place began to operate more independently. As of late 1986, Canon had only a small position in southern Europe and believed that it would be expensive and time-consuming to develop its own distribution channels there.

Filippo Demonte, who as head of the Office Products Group was directly responsible for Olivetti's copier business, remarked:

> For whatever arrangement we might enter into, it is important that Olivetti be the majority shareholder. Any venture has to be 100% under Olivetti management so that we can guarantee to the government and to the company that we would not be selling Italian technology to a foreign company. In these things, it is important not only to show but also to *be*. Moreover, succeeding in Italy is more likely if you are a successful Italian company than if you are a successful foreign company; the same principle that exists everywhere. It is important to the policy makers, the opinion makers, the unions and other national bodies. Having majority ownership would also ensure that we could participate in Italian government, inter-government programmes and Europe-wide programmes.

Mr Piol believed that much could be learned from being in a partnership with a company like Canon, particularly with regard to production process, supplier relationships and basic copier technology. He explained:

> If we were to put together some kind of joint venture with Canon – and I'm not sure just what that would look like in terms of ownership, structure, and the kind of assets and staff each partner would put into it – there could be some significant benefits on both sides.
>
> This could be an opportunity for Canon to strengthen its presence in Europe, and we could learn about Japanese techniques. The Japanese have more exacting goals for quality and better control over development time. Right now, we're working with an inventory level of 45 days, and in Canon, it's five. We've used value engineering techniques many times in the past to improve this level, but not with the same success as the Japanese. They apply these techniques in a strict and methodical way, with a determination not to stop until good results – results which may seem impossible to obtain – are achieved. On the other side, it's hard to know how strongly Canon would ask us to adopt the Japanese way.

In the early stages of such a venture, I imagine that we would manufacture an Olivetti machine, which would be received by the Canon and Olivetti sales organizations, as well as their dealers in Europe. Over time, we would license the basic technology from Canon Japan and refine it for European needs. Perhaps we would also buy the photographic drums and mirror mechanisms from Canon factories in Japan and/or France, and Canon would presumably make a profit on these sales. One of the essential negotiating issues would be to determine the kind of R&D that would be done in Agliè and its scale, as well as whether we could eventually compete with other Canon design centres.

Mr Demonte added:

It would be interesting to have Canon as a partner because then we would have a parent that is both a shareholder and a customer. When we're speaking with the shareholder, we'll be talking about profit and loss, net equity, and so on. When we're speaking with the customer, we'll be talking about the level of logistical and quality improvement. As well, we'll be trying to anticipate what the customer wants, which should help us with the product design specifications and in the production level we attain.

On the one hand, we would be an Olivetti company. On the other side, we would become part of Canon's copier machine division and part of the Canon family of copiers. One of the inherent challenges with any venture where two partners are involved is to manage the identity question. There will always be some people on both sides who will have difficulty making the distinction. Big companies are not made in such a way as to understand that they don't own a whole organization.

EXHIBIT 1

Olivetti Group Revenue Breakdown, by Market Sector in 1986 and 1985 (in percentages)

	1986	1985
Distributed data processing and office automation		
Electronic professional typewriters, videotyping systems	14.0	13.2
Personal computers	28.5	29.5
Minicomputers and terminals	28.0	32.2
Printers	7.0	7.2
Telecommunications equipment	2.8	2.7
TOTAL	80.3	84.8
Office products		
Portable and office manual and electric typewriters	8.2	5.9
Calculators, cash registers	6.7	5.7
Copiers	3.6	2.3
Office furniture	1.2	1.3
TOTAL	19.7	15.2
GRAND TOTAL	100.0	100.0

Source: Annual Report.

EXHIBIT 2

Olivetti's 1986 Sales Network in Western Europe, the 'Domestic Market'

Country	Branches	Dealers
Italy	150	1250
Germany	30	610
France	45	500
Spain	35	275
UK	25	380
Other	15	685

Source 'Olivetti's Worldwide Copier Strategy', presentation delivered at *Dataquest's Copying and Duplicating Industry European Conference*, 24–26 June 1987.

EXHIBIT 3

Olivetti Brand: Sales, Quantity and Market Share in Europe (1984–86)

	1984	1985	1986 (estimated)
Personal	2,830	10,620	14,600
copiers	2.8%	6.2%	7.0%
Category 1	16,880	16,920	16,220
(up to 19 cpm)	4.4%	4.4%	3.9%
Category 2	4,830	4,350	4,370
(20–39 cpm)	2.6%	2.3%	2.0%
Category 3	2,010	0	0
(40–59 cpm)	3.3%	0	0
TOTAL	23,720	21,270	20,590
Own production	3.7%	3.4%	3.0%
GRAND TOTAL	26,550	31,890	35,190
	3.6%	4.0%	3.9%

Source: InfoSource S.A.

CASE 12.3 # THE EUROPEAN COPIER INDUSTRY

This case was prepared by Research Associate Joyce Miller, under the supervision of Professors George Taucher and Dominique Turpin, as a basis for class discussion rather than to illustrate either effective or ineffective handling of a business situation.

1970 was a balmy year for the West's traditional producers of office equipment. Makers of typewriters, accounting machines, tabulating devices and adding machines from the United States and Europe dominated world markets . . . With their mere 6.8% market share, Japanese companies were no more than a niggling inconvenience on the horizon. In those days, if you wanted an office typewriter, the chances were that you would buy an IBM; and if it was a photocopier you were after, it would almost certainly have been a Xerox. However, the industry was about to undergo two periods of fundamental change. Within a decade, the low-cost electronic calculator would sweep away the electromechanical adding machine, and small photo-copiers would find their way into almost every office. Traditional suppliers of office equipment would not be the ones to take most advantage of the opportunities afforded by this first wave of change during the 1970s. Rather, it was to be a handful of more or less unknown manufacturers of cameras, sewing machines and consumer durables who would best grasp the significance and take advantage of the new openings. All of them were Japanese.

Phillip Oppenheim[1]

Reprographic Technology

Reprography, the replication of text or graphic material through the use of light, heat, chemicals or electrostatic charges, traced its origins back to the 1880s, with the commercial introduction of the stencil duplicator by A.B. Dick and Gestetner, a British firm. The duplicator was based on the concept of transferring an original to an intermediate 'master' or plate that was then inked and used to reproduce the image. Although this was a relatively inexpensive process, it could be rather messy. More sophisticated offset duplicators became available in the early 1940s, which produced good quality copies at high speed. In offset

---

[1] *Japan Without Blinders: Coming to Terms with Japan's Economic Success*, page 235. Copyright © 1991, 1992 by Phillip Oppenheim. Reprinted with the permission of the Author's agent, Harvey Klinger, Inc., New York.

Copyright © 1993 by IMD – International Institute for Management Development, Lausanne, Switzerland. Not to be used or reproduced without written permission directly from IMD.

duplicating, an oil-based image covered with a mixture of ink and water was 'offset' or transferred on to a rubber blanket, and the reverse image was then printed on to paper.

A Revolutionary Invention

In 1937, Chester Carlson, a US physicist, invented xerography – from the Greek meaning 'dry writing' – as a convenient way to copy his patent drawings and specifications. Xerography subsequently became the technological foundation for most modern office photocopiers. Xerography rested on the principle of using a photoconductive substance whose electrical resistance decreased when exposed to light. When the document was scanned by an optical system, the photo-conducter – a rotating drum coated with positively charged selenium or cadmium sulphide – allowed an electrostatic charge to leak away in proportion to the exposure. The image was made visible by dusting the plate with a magnetically charged ink powder, or toner, which adhered only to the image portions and could then be transferred to a sheet of plain paper. A final heat treatment fused the powder into the paper to create a permanent picture. Alternatively, a zinc oxide-coated paper could be used in place of the selenium plate whereby the powder deposit fused directly on to the paper surface.

Carlson patented his plain paper xerographic process in 1940 and spent the next several years trying unsuccessfully to garner interest in developing and marketing his invention. At least 20 companies turned him down, including A.B. Dick, General Electric, IBM, Kodak and RCA. Carlson's efforts finally bore fruit in 1947 when the Haloid Company based in Rochester, New York, obtained the commercial rights to xerography.

The Development of the Copier Market

After investing upwards of $12 million, Hall introduced its Model 914 in 1959, so named because of its ability to generate $9 \times 14''$-sized copies on plain paper. Phillip Oppenheim recalled:[2]

> Dubbed by *Fortune* magazine as 'the most successful product ever marketed in America', it changed the business world. It also changed Haloid. Once a struggling manufacturer of photographic paper and copiers turning over $31.7 million a year, Haloid grew to be a multi-billion dollar giant called Xerox Corporation. At that time, the main competition in copying, besides carbon paper and photographic and diazo copiers, was the Kodak Verifax and 3M's Thermofax. Both were slow, messy little boxes requiring special paper,

---

[2] *Japan Without Blinders: Coming to Terms with Japan's Economic Success*, page 260. Copyright © 1991, 1992 by Phillip Oppenheim. Reprinted with the permission of the Author's agent, Harvey Klinger, Inc., New York.

but they only cost $350. The 914, in contrast, was simple, clean and used ordinary paper. But it was also the size of a desk and cost several thousand dollars. So [Xerox] came up with a superb marketing ploy: [it] rented out the machines for $95 a month with 2,000 free copies and charged a few cents for each additional copy, and amazingly, allowed a 15-day cancellation clause. It is doubtful that any corporation had ever made an offer so favourable to the customer. At a stroke, all the objections to unproven new technology and high costs were eliminated. Although the machines sometimes did catch fire and had to be equipped with a small internal fire extinguisher... [they] were a hit.

The 914 produced seven copies per minute (cpm), which was significantly faster than anything else available at the time. With the patents for the basic xerographic process and related products and know-how, Xerox dominated the copier industry for much of the following two decades. Internally, Xerox viewed the reprographics market as four segments: low-volume convenience copying, the mid-volume market, the high end and duplicating. Top management made a decision not to produce machines aimed at the low end and, instead, directed R&D activities towards developing high-speed copiers and duplicators to tap the corporate reproduction market.

Xerox's dry-toner plain paper copiers (PPCs) were fairly complex machines and required considerable maintenance. The company built up a specially dedicated sales and service organization, and technicians called on customers regularly to maintain copiers and replenish supplies, including paper. Within a short period of time, the name Xerox became synonymous with copying. Although some other companies had developed copiers that used alternative technologies, like coated paper, their typically low-end offerings captured only a small sector of the market.

In an effort to quickly establish an international network and lacking the funds to achieve this on its own, Xerox formed a 50/50 joint venture with the Rank Organization in Britain. Rank Xerox subsequently formed a 50/50 joint venture with Fuji Photo Film, a leading Japanese manufacturer of photographic film. Fuji Xerox obtained exclusive rights to xerographic patents in Japan, and manufactured and sold PPCs throughout the region. Until this time, diazo copiers had dominated the office reproduction market in Japan. Originally developed in the 1930s, the diazo used special copy paper together with an ammonia vapour or alkaline solution to produce copies. Although these machines were awkward to operate and produced poor-quality copies, they had been quite successful because the large number of Japanese and Chinese characters used in everyday language made typewriters difficult to use and made copiers essential even in small offices.

In 1970, Canon Inc. introduced its low-end 'New Process' (NP) copiers, the first plain paper alternative to xerography. These machines were developed in-house and were completely free of Xerox patents. Ricoh and Konishiroku Photo Industry (now called Konica), Fuji Photo's major rivals in film production, soon followed with their own technologies. Canon pioneered a second generation system in 1972 that used liquid instead of dry toner and later licensed this technology to Saxon, Ricoh and Copyer. Liquid-toner copiers were smaller and less expensive to manufacture than dry-toner units. These machines were also more reliable and required fewer service calls. An industry analyst noted:

> The liquid-toner machines were a cheap alternative to Xerox copiers, but they were cumbersome to use. In addition, the image quality was not as high as with dry-toner copiers, although without regular service, the copy quality of dry-toner copiers deteriorated faster than that of liquid-toner copiers. The important thing here is that these machines represented the first real threat to Xerox's stranglehold over the industry. Canon's NP sparked a proliferation of competitive developments. Several companies in the optics field – Minolta, Sharp, Mita and Toshiba, to name just a few – got into the copier business. Their expertise in silver-based film technology was a good fit. For cost reasons, the Japanese became important players. By the mid-1970s, upwards of thirty companies were jockeying for position in the Japanese market, and the North American and European copier markets were undergoing significant changes as well.

The Market Opens Up

In 1973, the US Federal Trade Commission launched an investigation into Xerox's activities, alleging that the firm controlled 95% of the PPC industry, and that its pricing, leasing and patent-licensing practices violated the Sherman Antitrust Act. As a result, Xerox was required to license 1,700 of its patents to other companies beginning in 1975. At this point, Japanese manufacturers that had entered the market with liquid-toner copiers switched to Xerox's dry-toner process, and tended to concentrate on developing PPC models at the low-volume end of the market. Some European makers followed the same course, while others began developing higher-end models, relying on Japanese manufactured low-end machines to fill out their product range. IBM and Eastman Kodak both introduced machines aimed at the medium- and high-end segments of the market, squarely in Xerox's territory.

By the end of 1975, there were 20 PPC manufacturers operating worldwide, including reprographics companies such as A.B. Dick, Addressograph, Multigraph, Copyer, 3M, Mita and Ricoh; paper companies such as Dennison, Nashua and Saxon; office equipment companies like IBM, Litton, Pitney Bowes and SCM; photographic equipment companies such as Canon, Kodak, Konishiroku and Minolta; and electronics companies such as Sharp and Toshiba.

Segmentation

In general, copiers were categorized by copy volume – usually measured in copies per month. Copy volume was a function of speed measured in copies per minute. InfoSource, a Swiss market research firm, had developed a classification scheme based on purchase price and the copier's technical characteristics, which was generally used as the industry standard *(refer to **Exhibit 1**)*. Increasingly, copiers came equipped with special features, such as enlargement and reduction, colour capabilities, duplexing, the ability to handle varying paper sizes, and so on. As well, a range of optional accessories could be purchased to enhance the unit's efficiency and usability, like automatic document feeders, collators, sorters and staplers.

Copiers could also be distinguished by the quality of the copies they produced, which was assessed according to the sharpness of the image, background whiteness and copy uniformity. Consumable supplies, like paper and toner, used in conjunction with the copiers, could influence the quality of the output as well. Paper had to be selected based on moisture content, tendency to curl and surface characteristics, which affected the paper feeding and finish. Many PPC manufacturers produced their own toners with slightly modified chemical compositions, which discouraged the entry of third-party vendors. As well, PPC manufacturers encouraged customers to use the paper they supplied. With the exception of a few companies that had their origins as paper manufacturers, PPC makers tended to purchase paper and resell it, which yielded reasonably sound margins.

Given the number of moving parts that had to be cleaned and replaced, PPCs required regular maintenance. The major replacement part in a copier was its photoreceptive drum. Service accounted for the bulk of a copier's total operating cost, which averaged 1.5–2.5 cents per copy for mid- to high-volume machines.

Distribution Channels

Copiers could be obtained directly from the manufacturer or were available through dealers. In general, high-volume machines were rented from the PPC manufacturer because of their high cost and ongoing service needs, whereas low-volume units were usually purchased outright, either from a manufacturer or dealer. Specialized dealers offered customers assistance throughout the buying process, together with extensive post-purchase service. Business machine dealers that carried a range of office products – including typewriters, calculators, personal computers and copiers – provided a more limited level of knowledge and service. Increasingly, stationery and office supply dealers were carrying low-end copiers as an extension of their existing business, but they tended to provide little or no service. Although many dealers were exclusive, there was a growing trend towards carrying multiple brands. Margins ranged from 30 to 50%, and PPC manufacturers frequently provided dealers with attractive financing programmes as well as sales and service training.

The Evolution of the European Copier Market

From 1976 onwards, the PPC market in Europe expanded dramatically. The demand for office equipment was on the increase fuelled by the integration of the personal computer into the office environment. With the Xerox monopoly broken, many new competitors had entered the market. Over 100 different copiers were introduced by the end of the decade, either under own-brand or OEM labels. Almost all were Japanese. It was estimated that machine placements increased five-fold by 1981, and Japanese exports to Europe increased six-fold. Initially, Japanese PPC manufacturers sold copiers on an OEM basis. By 1986, however, most had established sales and service organizations on the continent. Throughout this period, several companies in the European Community with good production facilities, distribution networks and well-known brand names – such as Agfa, Olympia and Gestetner – either left the market entirely or ceased manufacturing to focus on marketing copiers made in Japan under their own badge. A Japanese manager elaborated:

> Initially, some European producers were using coated paper technology and consequently had not committed sufficient resources to developing more compact, lower-cost models incorporating PPC technology. The companies that withdrew from the industry in the late 1970s and early 1980s were the victims largely of their own incorrect investment decisions. For example, both Océ and Olivetti hesitated before making the transition to plain paper methods at a late stage and chose to minimize their competitive disadvantage by taking the OEM route while belatedly preparing to manufacture their own PPC products.
>
> Recently, the industry has begun to change along another dimension. We are finding that we can no longer calculate the profitability of PPCs in isolation from the related products. The sale of a PPC generates considerable income in the sale of consumables. As a result, there has been a trend, particularly in Japan, towards selling copiers at a loss or with minimal profit, and making the return on the sale of toner and paper.

Over the past several years, the price levels for copiers in Europe had slowly deteriorated. This coincided with a massive increase in the share held by PPCs of Japanese origin, particularly in the low- and mid-volume sectors of the market. Between 1980 and 1981, Japanese market share in terms of placements rose from 73% to 81%. By the end of 1985, Japanese producers held an 85% share of the European copier market.[3] By 1986, Japanese suppliers were making around 2.2 million of the 3 million or so PPCs that were being sold worldwide.

Aside from the fall in prices, the 1981–84 period was characterized by frequent model changes by the Japanese manufacturers and the addition of technical features such as reduction and enlargement capabilities, zoom and coloured toners to basic models.

Canon's Revolutionary Personal Copier

Introduced by Canon in 1982, the personal copier represented a revolution in an otherwise maturing and crowded industry. This development helped expand the

---

[3] These figures include machines imported by European PPC manufacturers from Japanese exporters, which constituted around 5% of total Japanese imports into the European Community in the 1981–85 period.

market for small copiers and simultaneously increased competition at the low end. Moreover, the personal copier created a new segment in the market. Conceived two years earlier, the idea was to produce a typewriter-sized, service-free unit costing less than $1,000 for people who were not currently using a copier. The personal copier also invoked a change in the existing distribution patterns. Rather than using conventional dealers and specialty retailers, these copiers could be handled through mass merchandisers and department stores.

By 1986, close to 900,000 copiers were being sold each year in Europe, generating $10 billion in revenues. Placements ranged from about 170,000 units each in Germany and France to fewer than 10,000 units in Austria and Portugal (*refer to* **Exhibit 2**). One analyst estimated that Canon and Rank Xerox had similar positions in most European countries, while other companies tended to be strong in only certain countries. Olivetti, for example, had its most solid position in Italy, Spain and France (*refer to* **Exhibits 3** *and* **4**).

Largely driven by replacement demand over the past few years, the copier market had been growing at close to 16% annually, although the growth rate did vary across the individual segments (*refer to* **Exhibit 5**). The introduction of colour copiers based on digital technology, which enabled the reproduction of subtle tones, was expected to rejuvenate the entire market. Where analogue copiers read the original copy through a lens and used a drum to transmit the text to paper, the new generation of digital copiers being developed would use a laser beam to scan and store images as digitalized information. Canon was the first manufacturer to see the marketing potential of offering coloured-toner cartridges, allowing customers to make red, green and blue copies. Although there had been little need in the past for such equipment, the growing use of colour personal computer displays and laser printers in the office environment was expected to ignite the demand for colour copiers.

Copiers and the Integrated Office

The typewriter was one of the first pieces of office equipment to be affected by digital technology. In place of activating a bar when the key was depressed, an electronic digital instruction was sent by wire to the typehead, which only then mechanically hit the paper through a ribbon. Digital technology was being used across an increasing range of equipment, from compact disk audio machines to copiers. In fact, people were talking about an 'office-of-the-future' where several pieces of stand-alone equipment would be linked up in a multi-functional automated system (*refer to* **Exhibit 6**). However, these ideas were not all that well formed, and the extent to which copiers could be integrated into such a system was unclear. An executive in a major European copier manufacturer elaborated:

> In the 1970s, there would have been little technological or manufacturing overlap between a producer of a typewriter and a Hi-Fi system, for instance. By the mid-1980s, all that had changed. With the rapid advances in semiconductor technology, it was becoming increasingly possible to use personal

computers to link up or even displace several separate, usually electromechanical pieces of equipment. People are even beginning to talk about integrating a copier, a printer, a facsimile and a personal computer into one unit.

A copier is used to scan a document. In the old days, people used a photoreceptive light sensitive mechanism to replicate an image. A fax is also a scanner. It translates an image into a digital picture and transmits this data by way of electrical impulses through a telephone line. These technologies can be combined and hooked up to a PC. The physical principles are there to integrate all of these units. What will drive this is the willingness of people to use this equipment in an integrated way. At the moment, people tend to see a copier, a printer and a PC as stand-alone equipment. In the 'office-of-the-future', they will be integrated.

In 1986, 78% of the manufacturing capacity for copiers was located in Japan, 19% was in Europe and the remaining 3% was in the US. However, European capacity was expected to virtually triple its present level by 1989 in response to efforts by the European Commission to compel the Japanese to do more manufacturing in Europe.

The European Commission Takes Action

As early as 1984, EC investigators had called on the home offices of Brother, Canon, Matsushita, Sharp and Silver Seiko, to comb through their books looking for evidence that electronic typewriters were being dumped – sold at lower prices in Europe than in Japan. At this time, these five companies commanded 40% of the European market for electronic typewriters, which was worth about $350 million. According to one Japanese executive:

> We had little choice but to cooperate. If we didn't, the Commission would make a decision based on the information that was available to them – like from our European competitors.

In June 1985, duties of up to 35% were slapped on electric typewriters imported into the European Community. Because of its heavy local procurement activities, Brother had escaped the penalties. For the most part, the affected companies responded by dramatically boosting their production of typewriters in Europe. An EC Trade Commissioner explained:

> We were convinced that many of the new plants that were quickly put into operation were illegitimate ploys to evade the duties. They were 'screwdriver plants' that did little more than cobble together products from imported parts. They weren't really there to add value. This was purely a way around the anti-dumping duties. Our investigations revealed that, in some cases, over 80% of the parts being used originated in Japan.

Since the EC's adoption of anti-dumping legislation in 1984, numerous proceedings had been initiated to investigate foreign-owned plants in Europe that turned out mobile phones, microwave ovens, video recorders, dot-matrix printers, compact-disk players, memory chips, and so on. The objective was to determine whether the interests of Community consumers in having low-cost goods was more important that the interest of Community industry in being protected from unfair competition.

In the spring of 1985, a group of European PPC manufacturers – including Develop, Océ, Olivetti, Rank Xerox and Tetras – banded together to lobby the European Commission regarding the activities of Japanese copier manufacturers within the Community. Their collective output accounted for a major proportion of the Community production of copiers. In July, the Committee of European Copier Manufacturers (CECOM) lodged a complaint with the Commission which resulted in the initiation of an anti-dumping investigation. There were 17 Japanese exporters and 28 importers into the Community that were cited (*refer to Exhibit 7*). The investigation covered the period from January to July 1985.

On the one hand, the European manufacturers claimed that PPCs imported from Japan were being sold into the Community at exorbitantly low prices, and the downward pressure on prices had progressively decreased the profitability of Community producers. As a result, the introduction of new models had been delayed or abandoned altogether, and European producers had been forced to scale down their R&D expenditures on PPCs to a level substantially below that of their Japanese competitors, which threatened the future of the domestic industry. Furthermore, CECOM members asserted that, as their share of the market deteriorated, they were no longer able to obtain the economies of scale arising from the higher production volumes that the Japanese obtained. One company attributed the loss of one-third of its potential profits to this situation.

On the other hand, the Japanese manufacturers argued that the Europeans had fallen behind in the development of PPCs and that the Japanese were helping them by supplying PPCs on an OEM basis. Moreover, the Japanese contended that CECOM members were not just temporarily importing to protect their existing customer base and maintain their share of the market, they were instead acting solely to maximize their profits by sourcing from the cheapest supplier.

The Commission Levies Anti-Dumping Duties

In late August 1986, provisional anti-dumping duties were imposed on all models of plain paper copiers imported into the Community from Japan, aside from those machines classified in Dataquest segments 5 and 6. A 15.8% duty was applied to machines when they entered the Community frontier, with the exception of products manufactured and exported by three companies that warranted special duty rates: Copyer (7.2%), Mita (13.7%) and Toshiba (15.3%). After these duties were applied, most Japanese PPC manufacturers and their OEMs raised or stabilized prices. Average increases in the various market segments ranged from 3% to 10%. In its preliminary findings, the Commission stated:

> The allegations made by the OEMs that the high share of Japanese exports is caused by their superiority in terms of range, quality, reliability and rate of innovation over those of the European producers and that, consequently, the

technological gap is unbridgeable, are not supported by sufficient evidence. The likelihood of this occurring, however, will increase if European producers are unable, by virtue of the low or negative profit margins on existing products, to devote sufficient resources to R&D for developing new products.

The photocopier industry forms a key part of the office equipment industry as a whole, and the retention of the technology employed will be crucial for the development of future reprographic products. From the side of the Community producers, the elimination of injury due to dumping is important to their survival as manufacturers and their ability to compete with Japanese exports both within the Community and worldwide.

The imposition of an anti-dumping duty is required to ensure the continued existence of Community PPC producers with the consequent benefits to the Community of employment, technological expertise and local source of supply. Without the imposition of these measures, the number of competitors in the market will be reduced with potentially detrimental results to Community consumers in terms of price and supply.

The provisional duties applied for a period of four months. During this time, the Commission was carrying out an investigation covering the reference period January 1981 to July 1985 to determine whether definitive measures, which had a 5-year duration, should be instituted. An industry observer commented:

Ultimately, the Commission is hoping to force Japanese companies to integrate into the European economy in the way that American companies – such as DuPont, Ford and IBM – did in the 1950s and 1960s. The EC is clearly intent on getting the kind of foreign manufacturing investment that creates jobs, transfers technology and forces Japanese companies to pay costs comparable to their European rivals. Many Japanese managers acknowledge that a deeper integration into Europe is inevitable. They recognize the need to get closer to the market, to defuse trade friction and to reduce yen-dominated parts, inventories, and shipping and financing costs.

But, even the seemingly simple task of buying more local components rattles many Japanese managers. Their biggest worry is whether they can maintain their standards for quality and at least match the efficiency of their factories in Japan. Brother, for instance, has had to add extra quality-control procedures in its European operation to compensate for the lower quality of parts purchased locally. Its rejection rate for parts in Europe is up to five times higher than the minuscule 0.1% that is typical in Japan.

Successfully transferring Japan's renowned manufacturing prowess to Europe's fragmented, heavily unionized and politically treacherous markets will require wrenching changes both in how companies function and in how their managers think ... Europe doesn't enjoy some of Japan's advantages: a tightly disciplined labour force, low social welfare charges and tight control over suppliers.

In the past few years, several Japanese copier makers had established production operations in Europe. For instance, in 1983, Canon had set up a factory in Liffre, France, to produce personal copiers, electronic typewriters and facsimile transceivers. More than a decade earlier, Canon had acquired a small, insolvent electrophotographic company in Giessen, Germany, which was subsequently transformed into a plant producing most of the NP range of copiers sold by Canon's subsidiaries and distributors in the European Community. Konica, Ricoh, Minolta, Toshiba, Matsushita and Sharp had also already established production facilities in Europe, or had indicated that they would be doing so in the near future. At present, many of these manufacturers were speculating that the European Commission might pass a tough new law aimed at crippling these operations by requiring them to use at least 40% non-Japanese components. In anticipation of such an action, several companies were scrambling to buy more local parts.

EXHIBIT 1

PPC Characteristics by Market Segment

Market segment	Speed (copies per minute, or cpm)
Personal copier	up to 10
Category 1	non-PC copiers generating <20
Category 2	20–39
Category 3	40–59
Category 4*	60+

*As the technology evolved, this category was subsequently broken down further into Category 4 copiers that generated 60–89 cpm and Category 5 copiers that generated 90+ cpm.

Source: InfoSource S.A.

Notes

Copiers in Categories 1 and 2 were often called 'convenience copiers', while those in Categories 3 and 4 were called 'copiers/duplicators'.

A broad range of buyers was interested in convenience copying. At one end of the spectrum, there were small businesses, which made fewer than 5,000 copies monthly, with run lengths of less than five copies per original. Financial considerations were the most important criteria for these buyers, and copy quality was relatively fewer important because most copies were used internally. At the upper end of the convenience copying market, medium-sized offices (with fewer than 35 employees) had monthly volume needs of up to 25,000 copies. Larger offices were also beginning to use convenience copiers as satellite units in combination with a high-speed copier/duplicator.

High-volume copiers were generally purchased by large reproduction departments, which required high-speed, highly reliable machines that produced high-quality copies. These copiers were usually purchased directly from manufacturers, who were increasingly providing assistance in configuring entire reproduction systems.

Essentially, the market for low-volume traditional duplicating consisted basically of small institutions, like schools and churches, that had low copy volume needs and limited budgets. Commercial print shops and in-house reproduction departments in major companies purchased high-volume duplicating equipment. Their most important criteria were copy speed, quality, cost and reliability.

EXHIBIT 2

Estimated PPC Placements in Europe in 1986, by Country

Country	Personal copiers			Category 1			Category 2			Category 3			Category 4			TOTAL		
	Units	Market share	Rank	Units	Market share	Rank	Units	Market share	Rank	Units	Market share	Rank	Units	Market share	Rank	Units	Market share	Rank
Austria	4,920	2.4%	12	7,600	1.8%	12	4,770	2.2%	11	1,060	2.0%	13	270	3.6%	10	18,620	2.1%	12
Belgium	5,720	2.7%	11	11,560	2.8%	9	7,280	3.4%	9	1,470	2.8%	10	310	4.1%	8	26,340	2.9%	9
Denmark	7,000	3.4%	9	9,490	2.3%	11	4,560	2.1%	12	1,490	2.9%	9	200	2.7%	12	22,740	2.5%	11
Finland	4,740	2.3%	13	6,630	1.6%	13	3,470	1.6%	13	1,110	2.1%	12	70	0.9%	13	16,020	1.8%	13
France	37,600	18.0%	2	74,350	17.9%	2	44,920	20.9%	1	12,080	23.3%	1	1,420	18.9%	2	170,370	19.0%	2
Germany	44,750	21.5%	1	78,600	18.9%	1	43,000	20.0%	2	8,530	16.5%	3	1,020	13.5%	3	175,900	19.6%	1
Ireland	460	0.2%	15	2,200	0.5%	15	880	0.4%	15	210	0.4%	15	10	0.1%	15	3,760	0.4%	15
Italy	29,500	14.1%	3	72,650	17.5%	3	27,300	12.7%	3	5,050	9.8%	4	770	10.2%	4	135,270	15.1%	4
Netherlands	9,700	4.7%	6	14,220	3.4%	8	7,630	3.5%	8	2,190	4.2%	7	540	7.2%	5	34,280	3.8%	8
Norway	6,550	3.1%	10	10,950	2.6%	10	5,090	2.4%	10	1,440	2.8%	11	320	4.2%	7	24,350	2.7%	10
Portugal	1,260	0.6%	14	5,330	1.3%	14	2,350	1.1%	14	590	1.1%	14	60	0.8%	14	9,590	1.1%	14
Spain	8,100	3.9%	8	26,130	6.3%	5	9,390	4.4%	5	3,640	7.0%	5	280	3.7%	9	47,540	5.3%	5
Sweden	8,200	3.9%	7	15,600	3.8%	7	9,820	4.1%	6	2,200	4.2%	6	420	5.6%	6	35,240	3.9%	7
Switzerland	10,830	5.2%	5	16,030	3.9%	6	7,990	3.7%	7	1,840	3.6%	8	230	3.1%	11	36,920	4.1%	6
UK	29,250	14.0%	4	63,600	15.3%	4	37,500	17.4%	3	8,880	17.1%	2	1,610	21.4%	1	140,840	15.7%	3
TOTALS	208,580	100%		414,940	100%		214,950	100%		51,780	100%		7,530	100%		897,780	100%	
Category %	23.2%			46.2%			23.9%			5.8%			0.8%			100%		

See notes to Exhibit 3.

Source: InfoSource S.A.

EXHIBIT 3

Estimated PPC Placements in Europe in 1986, by Manufacturer

Manufacturer	Personal copiers			Category 1			Category 2			Category 3			Category 4			TOTAL		
	Units	Market share	Rank	Units	Market share	Rank	Units	Market share	Rank	Units	Market share	Rank	Units	Market share	Rank	Units	Market share	Rank
Canon	129,650	62.2%	1	54,020	13.0%	1	31,410	14.6%	1	11,780	22.8%	2	640	8.5%	2	227,500	25.3%	1
Copyer				12,160	2.9%	10	6,690	3.1%	10	1,880	3.6%	8				20,730	2.3%	10
Konishiroku (Konica)				32,190	7.8%	6	16,270	7.6%	7	4,140	8.0%	5				52,600	5.9%	7
Matsushita (Panasonic)				15,850	3.8%	9	7,270	3.4%	9	760	1.5%	10				23,880	2.7%	9
Minolta	24,520	11.8%	3	24,140	5.8%	7	29,790	13.9%	3	1,880	3.6%	7				80,330	8.9%	6
Mita				86,650	20.9%	1	28,460	13.2%	5	3,120	6.0%	6				118,140	13.2%	2
Ricoh	35,910	17.2%	2	41,340	10.0%	5	32,660	15.2%	1	4,830	9.3%	4	110	1.5%	4	114,850	12.8%	3
Sharp	17,100	8.2%	4	23,100	5.6%	8	8,090	3.8%	8	1,640	3.2%	9	390	5.2%	3	50,320	5.6%	8
Toshiba				64,430	15.5%	2	23,640	11.0%	6	5,180	10.0%	3				93,250	10.4%	4
Xerox				42,900	10.3%	4	29,780	13.9%	4	13,040	25.2%	1	2,540	33.7%	1	88,260	9.8%	5
Others	1,400	0.7%		18,250	4.4%		890	0.4%		3,530	6.8%		3,850	51.1%		27,290	3.1%	
TOTALS	208,580	100%		414,940	100%		214,950	100%		51,780	100%		7,530	100%		897,780	100%	
Category %	23.2%			46.2%			23.9%			5.8%			0.8%			100%		

Placement estimates are based on end-user transactions during the calendar year. Equipment sold to intermediate links in the distribution chain is considered 'in the pipeline' and is not reflected. Estimates measure initial installations via sale, lease or rental of new equipment.

Vendor is defined as a local market *importer or manufacturer* of equipment, whether multinational subsidiary or independent distributor.

Brand is the label under which the equipment is distributed. In the larger markets where most multinationals have sales subsidiaries, vendor and brand are generally the same.

Manufacturer denotes the original equipment manufacturer.

Vendors, brands or manufacturers having less than 3% total market share are generally consolidated in the 'Others' classification. Exceptions to the 3% minimum are made for players essentially predominant in the upper segments only. In a limited number of cases, as a result of the 3% minimum criterion, the sum total of the individual markets for a given vendor, brand or manufacturer will be less than the consolidated European total estimate for the same vendor, brand or manufacturer.

Source: InfoSource S.A.

EXHIBIT 4

Estimated PPC Placements in Europe in 1986, by Brand

Brand	Personal copiers			Category 1			Category 2			Category 3			Category 4			TOTAL		
	Units	Market share	Rank	Units	Market share	Rank	Units	Market share	Rank	Units	Market share	Rank	Units	Market share	Rank	Units	Market share	Rank
Agfa	5,210	2.5%	7	9,160	2.2%	14	8,270	3.8%	9	4,520	8.7%	3				27,160	3.0%	12
Canon	110,050	52.8%	1	54,020	13.0%	1	31,410	14.6%	1	7,330	14.2%	2	640	8.5%	2	203,450	22.7%	1
Gestetner				15,040	3.6%	13	5,040	2.3%	12	1,030	2.0%	11				21,110	2.4%	13
Harris/3M				22,510	5.4%	8	7,360	3.4%	11	2,150	4.2%	7				32,020	3.6%	11
Konica/U-Bix				26,390	6.4%	5	11,900	5.5%	7	4,140	8.0%	4				42,430	4.7%	8
Minolta	18,410	8.8%	3	24,040	5.8%	6	27,180	12.6%	3	1,880	3.6%	9				71,510	8.0%	3
Mita				32,380	7.8%	4	8,410	3.9%	8	980	1.9%	12				41,770	4.7%	9
Nashua	14,200	6.8%	6	16,360	3.9%	11	14,930	6.9%	5	2,590	5.0%	6	210	2.8%	4	48,290	5.4%	7
Olivetti	14,600	7.0%	5	16,220	3.9%	12	4,370	2.0%	13							35,190	3.9%	10
Ricoh	19,050	9.1%	2	19,160	4.6%	9	13,810	6.4%	6	1,980	3.8%	8	90	1.2%	5	54,090	6.0%	5
Sharp	17,100	8.2%	4	23,100	5.6%	7	8,090	3.8%	10	1,640	3.2%	10	390	5.2%	3	50,320	5.6%	6
Toshiba				41,920	10.1%	3	16,280	7.6%	4	3,030	5.9%	5				61,230	6.8%	4
Triumph-Adler				16,420	4.0%	10	4,040	1.9%	14	150	0.3%	13				20,610	2.3%	14
Xerox				42,900	10.3%	2	29,780	13.9%	2	13,040	25.2%	1	2,540	33.7%	1	88,260	9.8%	2
Others	9,960	4.8%		55,320	13.3%		24,080	11.2%		7,320	14.1%		3,660	48.6%		100,340	11.2%	
TOTALS	208,580	100%		414,940	100%		214,950	100%		51,780	100%		7,530	100%		897,780	100%	
Category %	23.2%			46.2%			23.9%			5.8%			0.8%			100%		

See notes to Exhibit 3.

Source: InfoSource S.A.

EXHIBIT 5

Growth of Western European PPC Market (in thousands of units)

Segment	1981	1986	Estimated 1991	Compounded annual growth rates	
				1981–86	Estimated 1986–91
PC	0	203.7	445.0	N/A	16.9%
1	319.4	441.1	490.0	6.7%	2.1%
2	86.8	182.1	188.0	16.0%	0.7%
3	30.5	65.3	86.0	16.4%	5.7%
4	10.0	44.5	74.0	34.8%	10.7%
5	1.8	4.5	0.8	20.1%	(29.2%)
6	2.6	2.4	0.6	(1.6%)	(24.2%)
TOTAL	451.1	943.6*	1,284.4	15.9%	6.4%

This segmentation is based on the following criteria:

Segment	Speed (copies per minute)	Typical monthly volume range
PC	under 20	N/A
1	0–20	0–10,000
2	21–30	5,000–20,000
3	31–45	5,000–30,000
4	40–75	10,000–75,000
5	70–90	25,000–125,000
6	91+	100,000+

*Casewriter's note: The slight inconsistency between this number and the level that is indicated on Exhibits 3 and 4 (i.e. 897,780) is explained by the fact that different market research firms calculated these numbers.

Source: Dataquest Incorporated.

EXHIBIT 6

Equipment in the 'Office-of-the-Future'

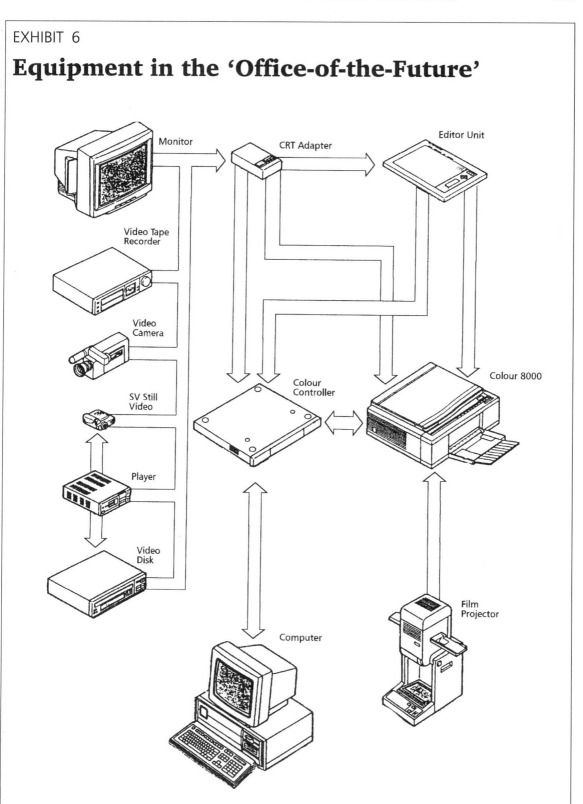

EXHIBIT 7

Companies Cited in the Notice of Initiation Regarding Imposing Anti-Dumping Duties on Plain Paper Copiers in Europe

European Community Producers
Develop, Dr. Eisbein GmbH., Germany*
Océ Nederland B.V., The Netherlands
Ing. C. Olivetti & Co., SpA., Italy
Rank Xerox Ltd., United Kingdom and The Netherlands
Tetras SA, France

Japanese exporters
Canon Inc., Tokyo**
Copyer Co., Ltd., Tokyo
Fuji Xerox Co., Ltd., Tokyo
Konishiroku Photo Industry Co., Tokyo**
Kyocera Corporation, Tokyo
Matsushita Electric Industrial, Osaka
Minolta Camera Co., Ltd., Osaka**
Mita Industrial Co., Ltd., Osaka
Ricoh Company Ltd., Tokyo**
Sanyo Electric Co., Ltd., Osaka
Sharp Corporation, Osaka
Toshiba Corporation, Tokyo

Importers in the Community
Canon (France) SA, France
Canon Copylux GmbH., Germany
Canon (UK) Ltd., United Kingdom
Minolta (France) SA, France
Minolta Germany GmbH., Germany
Minolta (UK) Ltd., United Kingdom
Mita Copystar Ltd., United Kingdom
Mita Italia SpA., Italy
Panasonic Deutschland GmbH., Germany
Ricoh Deutschland GmbH., Germany
Ricoh Netherlands BV, The Netherlands
Ricoh UK Ltd., United Kingdom
Sanyo Büro Electronic Europa
    Vertriebs GmbH., Germany
Sharp Electronics Europe GmbH., Germany
Sharp UK Ltd., United Kingdom
Toshiba Europa GmbH., Germany
U-Bix (France) SA, France
U-Bix International GmbH., Germany
U-Bix (UK) Ltd., United Kingdom
Yashica Kyocera GmbH., Germany
Agfa-Gevaert NV, Belgium
Fratelli Milani SrL., Italy
Gestetner Holdings Ltd., United Kingdom
Kalle GmbH., United Kingdom
Lion Office Ltd., United Kingdom
Nashua (UK) Ltd., United Kingdom
Nashua GmbH., Germany
Regma Systèmes SA, France

*Develop, a German producer of copiers, was effectively taken over in May 1986 by Minolta, a Japanese exporter, and subsequently withdrew its support for the complaint.
** At this time, these Japanese companies had manufacturing plants in operation in Europe. Canon had operations in Giessen, Germany (1973) and Liffre, France (1983); Konishiroku had a plant in Lunenburg, Germany (March 1986); Minolta/Develop had a joint operation beginning in June 1986; and Ricoh had set up a plant in Telford, UK (May 1986).

Note: Representations were also made to the Commission by Canon that the Community industry should be defined to include not just the complainants but also Canon Giessen and Canon Bretagne, producers of copiers in the community but which did not support the complaint. The Commission subsequently determined that since the complainants formed a major proportion of the industry, irrespective of whether Canon's subsidiaries were included or not, it was sufficient in the proceeding to assess whether injury had been caused to this major proportion of the industry.

Source: *Official Journal of the European Communities*, Commission Regulation (EEC) No. 2640/86 of 21 August 1986, imposing a provisional anti-dumping duty on imports of plain paper photocopiers originating in Japan.

13. Competing in COMECON Countries

CASE 13.1 **SONY IN POLAND**

This case was prepared by Research Associate Robert C. Howard, under the direction of Professor Robert S. Collins, as a basis for class discussion rather than to illustrate either effective or ineffective handling of a business situation. The support of Sony Europa GmbH executives in the development of this material is gratefully acknowledged. This case has won the 1992 European Case Writing Competition prize, awarded by EFMD (European Foundation for Management Development, Brussels, Belgium). It has also won a 1994 European Case of the Year prize, awarded by ECCH (European Case Clearing House, Cranfield, UK).

In June 1991, Jack Schmuckli, Chairman European Operations at Sony Europa GmbH in Germany, recalled the evening of 9 November 1989, when the Berlin wall was opened:

Suddenly, one of the most potent symbols of Europe's political and economic division was breached. As I watched television and saw the crowds streaming from East into West Berlin, it was evident that we were confronted with a significant business opportunity and needed to rethink our strategy regarding the COMECON countries.[1] Imagine, a region comprising some 400 million consumers, 20% more than Western Europe, was at last opening up. In 1989, the COMECON markets accounted for roughly 1% of our DM7.7 billion in sales for all of Europe. This region, which we once considered low priority and best served by intermediaries, was at last joining the world of free markets. Sales of consumer electronics in these markets, estimated to be worth nearly $40 billion by the turn of the century, had to be looked at in a new perspective. How was Sony to enter this world and serve these countries?

I immediately called Kazuo Matsuzaki, General Manager of Sony's European Operations Office, and urged him to accelerate Sony's development in Eastern Europe. At the time, he reminded me that we were in the midst of a major expansion with Mitte, an Austrian trading company that acted as the distributor of our products to Poland, Hungary and Czechoslovakia, through those countries' foreign trade organizations (FTOs). He was quick to point out, however, that with the collapse of the wall, Mitte's value as a distributor became questionable. For that matter, we had to reconsider our trading arrangements throughout the region, and ask whether they would hold up or whether we should begin to build national subsidiaries immediately. Our initial focus concentrated on Poland which accounted for almost 35% of our 1989 East European sales. Moreover, Poland, with over 40 million inhabitants, was the first country in the former East bloc to attain a non-Communist government and to implement market reforms.

---

[1] The Council of Mutual Economic Assistance (CMEA or COMECON) was formed in 1949 by the Soviet Union and the then Communist states in Eastern and Central Europe to divert trade away from Western nations and achieve a greater degree of self-sufficiency among Communist nations. At that time, COMECON included the USSR, Bulgaria, Czechoslovaka, East Germany, Hungary, Poland and Romania.

For Sony, the most important of these reforms was the move toward a free market, enabling the country's retailing entrepreneurs to begin legitimate operations. A part of this move was currency convertibility. Prior to 1989, only those citizens who had worked abroad or with relatives in foreign countries were allowed to possess hard currency, Thus, for companies such as Sony, retail distribution was limited to hard currency outlets and sales were restricted to tourists and the few Poles with access to hard currency. In mid-1989, the government had relaxed its currency restrictions, making it legal for all Poles to possess hard currency. Sony's 1988 sales of DM7.9 million subsequently climbed to DM25 million for 1989.[2] On 1 January 1990, in a first step towards having a convertible currency,[3] Poland devalued the zloty by nearly 60%. Even though the devaluation made Western goods more expensive for those paying in zlotys, by the end of the year, Sony's sales had reached DM33.5 million.

Despite increased supply, demand for consumer electronics exceeded the official supply available through Photex, the FTO used by Mitte in Poland. To meet this demand, Polish entrepreneurs, or private dealers, began selling Sony products on the gray market,[4] independently of Photex. Matthew Lang, Assistant Manager in Sony's Corporate Strategy Department, felt that the mere existence of a gray market implied something was wrong with the current channel arrangement. "Was Sony supplying enough product to the market? Were its products priced too high? Were existing channels ineffective?" he asked.

In devising a future strategy for Poland, Matsuzaki and Lang had two major objectives: increasing sales through legitimate sales channels; and establishing an authorized sales and service network in an intermediate step towards a national company. Because a national subsidiary implied terminating agreements with Mitte and Photex, some managers were reluctant to invest any more time and energy into upgrading the existing Mitte–Photex distribution channel, and wanted to establish a Sony-owned network as soon as possible. In part, the desire to establish a fully owned distribution network stemmed from Sony's 30+ years of experience in Western Europe. On more than one occasion, local distributors had become so powerful that they were able to influence the distribution policy to a greater extent than Sony preferred. Not surprisingly, deciding when and how to alter distribution agreements was of paramount concern to Sony management. In Poland, where Photex, a representative of the 'old' system, already accounted for nearly 100% of Sony's sales, some managers believed that it was in the

---

[2] In 1989, $1 = DM1.88; in 1990. $1 = DM1.62.

[3] Convertibility referred to the right of an enterprise to obtain foreign exchange to pay for imports, with no restrictions from a government or central bank. Under 'internal convertibility', on the other hand, any legal import could be paid for by bringing zlotys to a bank with the invoice for import. Thereafter, the bank paid the invoice in foreign exchange, converted at the official rate.

[4] The gray market, also known as 'parallel imports', referred to trade in legal goods and services that took place outside the channels normally controlled by distributors or company-owned sales subsidiaries.

company's best interest to build a 'counterbalance' to Photex's market presence by developing business with Poland's emerging private dealers.

By contrast, some other managers believed it was too soon for Sony to invest independently in Poland, and that extricating itself from Mitte and Photex could not be accomplished quickly, owing to Photex's dominant position. Moreover, this same group of managers cited Photex's extensive retail chain in Poland as another reason to stick with, or modify, the existing distribution agreement. Ideally, Matsuzaki and Lang sought a solution that would satisfy Poland's demand for consumer electronics and preserve the company's goodwill with each stakeholder. As the two resumed their discussions, they were keenly aware that any decisions and actions in Poland would be viewed as an indication of how, or how not, Sony might approach other markets in Eastern Europe and the USSR.

Sony in Europe

One of Sony's stated objectives was to achieve share leadership in all major product categories in each national market. To achieve its goal, the company nurtured each market segment with strong competitive products and an excellent sales and service network.

Sony had begun marketing its products in Europe during the 1960s through Sony Overseas SA (SOSA), a subsidiary based in Switzerland. From the 1960s on, SOSA expanded the company's sales and service activities throughout Europe by appointing national distributors. By 1970, these distributor organizations were taken over or changed to Sony's own subsidiaries so that, by 1990, Sony had 10 national organizations in Europe, plus two regional organizations – Sony Scandinavia and Sony Europe International (SEI); the latter served Eastern Europe and the USSR. Each organization reported to the European headquarters and normally consisted of three main marketing divisions: Consumer Products, Professional Products and Magnetic Products.

In this evolution, SOSA typically identified a country distributor which, at a later date, might become a joint venture partner. Some years after that, these same entities might become wholly owned Sony subsidiaries. Sony devoted significant energy to managing the relationships with its distributors, especially during the transition period to joint venture partner and/or wholly owned subsidiary. Matsuzaki emphasized that how and when Sony made these transitions was key and represented a part of the company's corporate ethic. He added: "Sony's image works both for and against us. If we cut links to a distributor abruptly, we may find it difficult to recruit distributors in other parts of the world thereafter. With long-standing distributorships, Sony typically does not simply terminate agreements, but offers phase-out periods with generous compensation."

In planning the company's approach to Eastern Europe, and Poland in particular, Matsuzaki and Lang had to keep these points in mind. At the same time, however, the two also had to consider the challenge of managing distributor relationships in Europe. As an example, Lang cited Nissan's problems in the UK. When Nissan had first entered the UK market, it had sold its cars through Nissan UK, an independent privately owned distributor. In 1990, executives from Nissan and Nissan UK began arguing over the pricing policy for the Nissan Primera. According to Octav Botnar, Chairman and Managing Director of Nissan UK, Nissan's pricing was unfair to British consumers because UK-built Nissan cars sold more cheaply in Germany, The Netherlands and Belgium where the distributors were owned by Nissan Motor Company itself. Eventually, the relationship between Botnar and Nissan management became so strained that Nissan chose to establish a wholly owned distributorship with a view to disenfranchising Botnar. Throughout the process, both parties became involved in highly publicised legal proceedings. At Sony, management was loath to become involved in such disputes.

Sales and Service in Europe

Within Sony Corporation, management was proud of its after-sales service. According to Lang, Sony's products had one of the lowest failure rates in the industry but, nonetheless, service was considered an integral part of the marketing mix and the company's 'customer satisfaction' philosophy. He added that the key elements for providing service were reliability and speed, and that together the two maintained Sony's image and brand reputation. Therefore, training for Sony personnel, from the telephone operator at a service centre through to the service technician, emphasized a customer orientation.

Apart from training, each national sales organization decided the best way to handle service in its particular market. As a result, no standard Sony service concept existed Europe-wide. Generally speaking, though, Sony sold its products through authorized dealers who, typically, also sold competing brands. Sony service, on the other hand, fell into one of three categories: fully-owned service departments, authorized service stations or a combination of both.

Fully-Owned Service Departments

As noted, Sony established sales and service organizations in Europe from 1968 on. Initially, national subsidiaries identified and authorized dealers to sell, but not repair, Sony products. Customers faced with a repair problem in these markets could return the product to the dealer who, in turn, sent the product to the service department at the country subsidiary. A customer could, of course, take the product directly to the service department himself.

Authorized Service Stations

With the growth of sales in larger markets, some subsidiaries authorized dealers to service, as well as to sell, Sony products. Typically, an authorized service station repaired Sony as well as other brands of consumer electronics. Customers seeking repair in these markets could take their products to an authorized Sony service station.

Mixed Service Organizations

More recently, some markets had established mixed service organizations. In these markets, a customer could go to a fully owned service department directly, or to a dealer who sold, but did not repair, Sony products. Alternatively, a customer could go to an independent authorized dealer who sold as well as repaired Sony and other brands of consumer electronics.

In addition to repairing locally purchased products, Sony's West European subsidiaries were obliged to service Sony products purchased in other markets. Aside from these service options, customers in any market could take a chance with an unauthorized service station. Those willing to do so ran the risk of having non-Sony components installed in their products or, worse, untrained personnel damaging their products. It was this very scenario which Matsuzaki and Lang wanted to avoid in Poland, lest Sony's brand image be damaged. Nonetheless, the two remained uncertain whether to adopt a fully-owned service department, authorized service stations or a mixed service organization in Poland.

Eastern Europe

In the near future, Sony management believed that the opening of Eastern Europe would be one of the most important events to influence their business. Indeed, with most of the consumer electronics markets in the developed world at or near saturation, Sony's competitors had already begun to focus on Eastern Europe's emerging markets. According to one market research firm,[5] the market for consumer electronics in Eastern Europe was forecast to reach $38 billion by the year 2000 based on the 50% penetration of electronic consumer goods achieved in Western countries.

In addition to the companies active in Poland (described later in this case study) other companies in Eastern Europe included Philips, the large Netherlands electronic and electrical goods company. In mid-1990, Philips announced plans to establish offices in Poland, Czechoslovakia and Hungary, in order to identify opportunities for cooperation and to serve as the nucleus for future sales organizations in those countries. In Czechoslovakia, with 1991 sales of its consumer electronic products expected to reach Sch150 million,[6] the company announced plans for a network of 75 retail shops. In the USSR, Philips had established a sales and service organization, and had announced joint manufacturing plans for video-cassette recorders (VCRs).

Additional companies building an East European presence included Nokia Consumer Electronics, Europe's third largest consumer electronics manufacturer. Specifically, Nokia announced plans to supply and assemble kits, in former East Germany, for distribution throughout Eastern Europe. Following the reunification of East and West Germany, Grundig, the German consumer electronics firm

---

[5] BIS Mackintosh Lid in *Electronic-World-News*, 23 July 1990, page 6.

[6] In Czechoslovakia, the Koruna or Crown was devalued several times in 1990 and 1991. For this reason, sales forecasts were often denominated in hard currencies. In 1990, $1 = Austrian Sch 11.4.

based in Fuerth, concentrated its East European sales efforts on the former DDR. In mid-1991, a Grundig spokesman said the company had targeted a turnover in excess of DM100 million in the former East Germany. To achieve its goal, the company established a marketing outlet in Boehlitz-Ehrenberg, in what was previously East Germany, to supply retail dealers with its consumer goods.

Other companies involved in manufacturing deals were Akai with video-cassette recorders in Bulgaria, Samsung with colour television in Hungary, and Thomson with colour television and VCRs in Hungary and the USSR. Regardless of the company, each of these joint venture activities was building a local manufacturing presence in Eastern Europe. For the management of Sony, who saw Eastern Europe as a natural extension of their presence in Western Europe, success in Poland played a key role in securing its place in an increasingly volatile global battle.

Doing Business in Poland

In 1991, Poland celebrated the 200th anniversary of a constitution proclaimed on 3 May 1791 by Stanislaus Augustus, King of Poland. During those 200 years, Poland had been subjected to a number of wars and territorial revisions that had positioned the country substantially west of its traditional boundaries. Because of these geographical changes, significant Polish minorities still lived in Lithuania, Byelorussia and the Ukraine. For example, in Lithuania, roughly 8% of the population in the Vilnius area was Polish. Likewise, in Byelorussia, approximately 12% of the population was of Polish extraction. One analyst commented that, because of this distribution of minorities, there was a certain 'artificiality' to Poland's borders. Moreover, Polish, Lithuanian, Byelorussian, Ukrainian and Russian belonged to the same sub-group of languages, and thus shared many common words and expressions. In brief, because of its historical, economic and cultural place in Europe, Poland was seen by many as a springboard for future investment into the neighbouring republics of the USSR. *See **Exhibit I** for maps depicting the changes in Poland's borders from the 18th century to World War II.

Excluding the USSR, Poland was the single biggest market in Eastern Europe, with a population of 37.9 million. With a growth rate of 5.7% between 1980 and 1988, Poland had one of the fastest growing populations on the continent, most of which was concentrated in urban communities. And, unlike other countries in Central and Eastern Europe, such as Czechoslovakia or Yugoslavia with their many ethnic groups, Poland had a more homogeneous population, a factor many analysts believed would contribute to future political as well as economic stability. Indeed, in 1990, the Polish government's statistical office estimated that the output of private industry grew by 50% and accounted for 18% of national income, up from 11% in 1989. Moreover, the number of people employed in private enterprise grew by more than 500,000 in 1989, bringing the total to between 1.8 and 2 million people.[7]

---

[7] *The Economist*, 26 January 1991.

One journalist, commenting on Polish behaviour, went so far as to say that no other group in Eastern Europe rivalled the Poles for being the most business minded, and that Polish merchants were favoured for their bold and widespread commercial activities.[8] Typically, he added, merchants bought low-priced commodities in Poland and earned a substantial gain in foreign currency by selling these commodities in the West. Profits were easily doubled by using the gain to purchase Western merchandise for resale back in Poland. Normally, these goods were sold through private enterprises, instead of Poland's FTOs.

For Sony, product demand was driven by the company's outstanding brand image and by the unexpected volume of zlotys and dollars circulating in Poland. To clarify, a survey in five European countries rated Sony number three after IBM and Mercedes Benz in terms of popularity, dynamism and corporate image.[9] In another survey, Sony was considered number one in Poland and the USSR in 'image power'.[10] With respect to currency, one spokeswoman commented that Poles had been saving their money for years and were a lot more Western in their thinking than others in the former Eastern bloc. Then, too, hard currency remittances to Poles from relatives living abroad were estimated at over $3 billion in 1990.

Despite the growth of private industry, other factors – such as the lack of effective communications – hindered business conduct in Poland. According to one businessman, Poland had one of the worst telecommunications infrastructures in Central and Eastern Europe. With only seven phones per 100 people, it was extremely difficult to perform tasks taken for granted in the West. Fax machines, mobile phones, data transmission and other advanced services were equally, if not more, scarce than telephones. Yet another burden was the lack of local managers with experience in accounting, finance and other Western business practices. In summary, the poor infrastructure and shortage of managerial talent in Poland could prolong the country's transition from a centrally planned to a market economy.

Foreign Trade Organizations

As of mid-1991, most foreign trade in Poland was still carried out by specialized foreign trade organizations (FTOs) with monopoly positions. Typically, an FTO acted as the main authority for foreign trade transactions, dealing with any one product or related group of products. FTOs were responsible for all commercial activity with foreign partners in that product area, including negotiating and signing contracts, preparing and implementing cooperation agreements, conducting market research, organizing sales and purchases, advertising, and participating in international trade fairs. After-sales service, however, was strictly limited to products purchased within the country and from a particular FTO.

---

[8] *Living in Europe*, 18 May 1990.
[9] *Le Point*, June 1990.
[10] Landor Associates.

Of the 86 FTOs in Poland, Photex[11] and Baltona were the two largest that specialized in consumer electronics. With roughly 350 outlets throughout Poland, Baltona was the second largest of the two consumer electronics FTOs and sourced its products primarily from Hitachi and other smaller less well-known Japanese companies.

From 1990 onwards, there was increasing talk of privatization of state-owned enterprises in Poland. Retailing was at the forefront of the government's privatization programme, and, according to one ministry official, roughly 90% of the 120,000 state stores were expected to be transferred to private owners by 1996. It was hoped that the largest of these, including Photex and Baltona, would be privatized before the end of 1991. In an interview on the eventual privatization of Photex, Managing Director Marian Zacharski proposed allocating 49% of Photex's shares to Western companies, 20% to employees and the rest to domestic investors. Despite this insight about Photex's possible future owners, Photex was still 100% state owned as of mid-1991.

Competition in Poland (*refer to Exhibit 2*)

Matsushita Electric Industrial Co., Ltd

With 1990 sales of nearly $38 billion, Matsushita was by far the world's largest consumer electronics company. Within the industry, Matsushita was considered to be less innovative than its competitors although it was renowned for its manufacturing skills. With the help of 25,000 company-owned shops in Japan, Matsushita usually flooded the domestic market and crushed the competition before repeating the exercise in overseas markets. In contrast to Sony, whose goods tended to appeal to more affluent consumers, Matsushita's products were geared for the mass market, for families of modest means with little technical interest.[12]

Additional brands owned by Matsushita included Panasonic, Quasar, Technics and National. Also, JVC was 51% owned by Matsushita. The Panasonic brand was distributed exclusively by the Mitsubishi Trading Company (MTC) in Poland. MTC worked through Photex; however, Panasonic was unofficially reputed to be looking for private dealers, independent of MTC.

To reinforce Panasonic's brand awareness in Poland, second to Sony in 1990, Panasonic began a massive promotion campaign using posters on buses and trams. In this way, the company hoped to strengthen its image position and, at the same time, maintain its 2:1 lead, in unit terms, against Sony. To service Panasonic's products, the MTC had established two service stations in Poland and planned to open 10 more in the near future. Although the service network was fully owned by MTC, Panasonic provided technical assistance. As part of their ongoing cooperation, Panasonic and Mitsubishi announced plans in early 1991 to form a joint manufacturing venture in Poland. They had not disclosed, however, what products would be made.

---

[11] See later in this case study for additional information on Photex.
[12] 'A Survey of Electronics', *The Economist*, pages 10–11.

Hitachi

Hitachi had conducted its business in Poland for nine years through International Trade & Investment (ITI), a trading company founded by two Poles, which sold Hitachi products through Baltona. In contrast to Sony or Matsushita, however, which had approached private dealers directly, Hitachi had allowed ITI to manage such contacts in Poland. Then, so as not to miss out on the growing opportunity with entrepreneurs, in the spring of 1991, ITI started offering Hitachi products to the private dealers, supported by an office building that ITI was constructing for Hitachi in Warsaw. According to one industry participant, ITI's competitive advantage in consumer electronics was in having the best service network in Poland.

Philips

One analyst commented that, with the exception of Philips, which sold its products through Brabok, a private dealer with only two shops, non-Japanese brands were not nearly as popular in Poland as Japanese products. He added that Philips had jointly produced video-cassette recorders in Poland since 1986 and, more recently, had concluded a deal with a local company, Pratork, to assemble televisions in Poland bearing the Philips brand name.

Others

Aside from Sony, Matsushita's Panasonic brand and, to a lesser extent, Hitachi, Sanyo and Sharp were the only other significant Japanese brands sold in Poland. Although Sanyo and Sharp were sold through Photex, both had also been offered to private dealers, independently of Photex.

Distribution and Service of Consumer Electronics in Poland

As noted, the political and economic changes in Poland since 1989 had given birth to a significant gray market in consumer electronics. Sony management, eager to preserve and expand its share of the Polish market, felt an arrangement was needed to balance the interests of Mitte, Photex and Poland's private dealers, to shift distribution away from the gray channels.

Mitte

Mitte was an affiliate of an Austrian holding company based in Vienna and, from the 1960s on, played an important role in supplying Sony products to the Polish as well as the Hungarian and Czechoslovakian markets, through the monopolies of the countries' state-owned foreign trade organizations. One part of the holding company, Mitte Technische GmbH, looked exclusively after Sony and had established representative offices in Warsaw, Prague and Budapest, as well as service stations in Budapest and Warsaw.

As noted, prior to the collapse of the Berlin wall, Sony considered Eastern Europe to be a minor part of its business, best handled by an intermediary – namely, Mitte. One manager pointed out, however, that Mitte was not a typical distributor. That is, unlike other Sony distributors, with operations in the country they served, Mitte was based in Austria. As a result, once the wall fell, Mitte offered little to Sony as a joint venture partner or acquisition candidate. On the other hand, some executives believed Mitte's role was still valuable. In particular, this group of executives emphasized that Mitte carried the risk of non-payment from Photex, not an insignificant point given the volume of Sony's sales and the pace of change in Poland.

Photex

Photex, based in Warsaw, was Poland's largest and best run retail operation with approximately 1,010 outlets across the country. In 1990, Photex reported sales of $936 million, up 68% over 1989 with profits averaging 7–9% of sales when expressed in Western accounting terms. According to Marian Zacharski, Managing Director of Photex, sales in 1991 were forecast to reach nearly $2 billion. Traditionally, Photex had been known for luxury goods but, with Poland's move toward a market economy, it added thousands of items to its product offering – including toys, clothing, drugs and foodstuffs. At the same time, Zacharski expanded Western-style displays and self-service. In addition, contrary to Polish shopping customs of the past, customers were no longer required to stand in separate lines for each purchase category. One Photex customer commented: "In my local store, if I want bread, beer, meat and candy, I must queue four times. Photex is undoubtedly worth the extra money."

Like Photex customers, Photex employees were highly motivated. On 31 December 1990, Photex employees stayed after hours to convert pricing to the Polish zloty so the stores could open on time on 2 January 1991. By contrast, Baltona was closed on 2 January to re-price. To maintain and improve its position in Poland, Photex spent $30 million on a fully computerized accounting and inventory control system.

In Poland, all after-sales service requests for Sony products sold through Photex were handled by Mitte's Warsaw-based service organization, Mittropol, which received all spare parts and training from Mitte Technische GmbH in Vienna. Despite the proliferation of goods sold at Photex, the retail chain was slow in building its service network. Specifically, customers seeking after-sales service for consumer electronics in Poland had to go to Photex's one service station in Warsaw. Alternatively, customers could deposit their products at one of eight Photex outlets in Poland. Once a week, all products in need of repair were sent to the central service station in Warsaw. For Sony products bought outside Poland, or for products bought inside Poland but outside the Photex chain, Polish customers had no alternative but to take their chances with an unauthorized service station.

After visiting Mittropol, Lang commented that the Photex staff members were familiar with technology on traditional products such as stereos, but were not well qualified to service products such as compact disk players or camcorders, based on more sophisticated digital and optical technologies. In a move to upgrade the repair skills of Photex's staff and, at the same time, minimize any damage unauthorized service stations might do to Sony products and the company's image, he and Matsuzaki proposed organizing a training programme in Warsaw. Although seen as a first step, both knew full well that the training initiative would eventually have to be followed by a more comprehensive service organization.

Poland's Retailing Entrepreneurs

Matsuzaki described those in control of the gray market as typical entrepreneurs – dynamic individuals quick to identify and capitalize on an opportunity. He went on to say that one group of three university colleagues owned their own trading company, Digital, based in Gdansk. It had a staff of over 300. The group was clever and hard working, and had franchised businesses across Poland. Moreover, the group was well versed in Western business methods and approaches, using Western-style advertising to sell imported personal computers and satellite antennas, as well as Sony products (purchased from Sony Deutschland GmbH). For all these products, Digital paid hard currency and resold in zlotys.

By comparison, a newspaper journalist described an individual who sold Polish commodities in Germany, then used the DM proceeds to buy video-cassette recorders for resale in Poland. After purchasing 20 VCRs, the individual would re-enter Poland at an obscure border crossing where a small bribe to the border guards secured his passage with the goods, at a customs fee below the goods' true value. Under this system, the private dealer earned a profit of roughly $1,000 per month – approximately 15 times the monthly salary of an average worker in Poland.

Lastly, Matsuzaki mentioned a Polish company called Selko, whose owner bought personal computers in Berlin and resold them in Poland, the Ukraine and Lithuania. According to Matsuzaki, this entrepreneur had become so successful that he had purchased a near bankrupt bookshop in Warsaw, transformed it into a profitable business, and was planning to convert the same building into a personal computer outlet. To top it all off, this same individual, unable to source sufficient product from Sony Deutschland, obtained container loads of Sony products from Singapore, shipped directly to his warehouse in Poland. Like other entrepreneurs, Selko paid for its purchases in hard currency, which it resold for zlotys in Poland.

Unauthorized Service Stations

Aside from selling products on the gray market, several entrepreneurs in Poland had started service stations for consumer electronics. On one visit to Warsaw, a

Sony representative identified five unauthorized Sony service stations in the telephone directory. Although each station claimed they could repair Sony products, none had in fact received training nor did they use Sony parts. For Sony, the possibility of faulty product repair by unauthorized stations posed a serious threat to its brand image.

Sony Europe International

Within the Sony European operations, Sony Europe International (SEI) was responsible for trading with Poland. Strictly speaking, Photex placed its orders through Mitte which, in turn, passed the orders on to SEI. Once received, SEI instructed its warehouse in The Netherlands to ship the products directly to Photex's main office in Warsaw, where they were then distributed to Photex's 1,010 outlets across the country for sale to the Polish consumer. Payment occurred in two steps: first, Photex converted zlotys into hard currency; then it paid Mitte, which in turn paid SEI.

As Poland moved toward a market economy, SEI proceeded to establish contact with 15 private dealers in Poland. Normally, these dealers contacted the SEI sales manager with product requests. Unlike its arrangement with Mitte, however, SEI would not ship from its warehouse to these dealers until it was paid in full, in hard currency. *See Exhibit 3* for a summary of the flow of orders, products and capital between Poland and the Sony organization.

Options

To establish a direct presence in Poland meant renegotiating Sony's distribution agreement with Mitte. Based on past experience, any renegotiation would prove lengthy and, according to one manager, could cost up to DM10 million. All the same, some managers favoured making the transition from distributor to local subsidiary sooner rather than later, based on experiences in both North America and Europe. As Matsuzaki and Lang continued their discussions, they concentrated on four options, all focused on Poland. In a larger context, however, the two were also aware that their decision, and the results that followed, would be scrutinized as an indication of how, or how not, to approach Sony's other markets in Central and Eastern Europe.

Continue Present Arrangements

Until the end of 1992, Sony was obliged to honour its exclusive agreement with Mitte as the distributor to all state-owned organizations in Poland. Sony was permitted, however, under the terms of the agreement, to develop its own network with private companies. Thus, Sony could wait until its agreement with Mitte expired at the end of 1992 and, simultaneously, allow the parallel imports to continue.

On the plus side, Lang mentioned that maintaining the *status quo* was the easiest option as it obviated any immediate renegotiation and/or compensation to Mitte. Also, under the present agreement, Mitte would continue to bear the risk of Photex's non-payment. On the other hand, taking a *laissez-faire* stance would increase Sony's reliance on Mitte to expand the sales and service network in Poland, and thus did little to enhance Sony's control over sales and marketing policy.

Allowing the parallel imports to continue did not mean taking no action. On the contrary, if Sony chose to continue its arrangement with Mitte, it was also intent on furthering its cooperation with some of Poland's private dealers in preparation for the post-1992 era. By waiting until its agreement with Mitte expired, Sony would have 18 months to select some of Poland's entrepreneurs, and develop them as local sales and service representatives. Because many of these entrepeneurs had already demonstrated their ability to market Sony's products, via the gray market, Matsuzaki believed that with the proper incentives, these same individuals could be persuaded to join a future Sony Poland organization. In so doing, Sony might be able to unify its parallel markets in Poland and, at the same time, nurture a pool of talent for an eventual Polish subsidiary.

Supply Directly with Photex

As one alternative to maintaining the *status quo*, Sony could terminate its agreement with Mitte and deal directly with Photex, an idea proposed by Marian Zacharski. As Poland's largest retailer, Photex clearly had an established sales network and possessed formidable buying power. With one-third of Photex's nearly $1 billion 1990 sales attributed to consumer electronics, direct cooperation entailed serious consideration. Specifically, direct cooperation with Photex would allow Sony to exercise more control over the sales and marketing of its products. As an example, Lang mentioned that Photex, with Mitte acting as an intermediary, was unwilling to cut its margins by lowering prices, a factor which may have contributed to the gray market. Photex's intransigence, he added, was in part due to Mitte, which lacked the clout of a Sony or other manufacturer, to persuade Photex to reduce prices. Some managers believed that, in a direct relationship, Photex would be more cooperative.

On the other hand, direct cooperation with Photex implied that Sony would have to renegotiate its agreement with Mitte. Aside from any settlement costs, direct cooperation with Photex meant that Sony would also be fully exposed to the non-payment risk now borne by Mitte. Then, too, with the growth of private dealers in Poland, there was no guarantee that Photex could maintain or increase its impressive $1 billion in sales revenue. Furthermore, Matsuzaki pointed out, cutting the supply line to Poland's FTOs via Mitte might jeopardize Sony's access to the Hungarian and Czechoslovakian markets, one-quarter and one-third the size of the Polish market, respectively.

While keeping the above in mind, Sony management was also keeping a close eye on privatization in Poland. If Photex were privatized before the end of 1992, Sony would be free to supply Photex directly and cut Mitte out of the picture, without violating its agreement. Short of negating any settlement costs with Mitte, the advantages of a privatized Photex were the same as with the existing state-owned FTO.

Supply Directly to Private Dealers from SEI

In a third option, Sony could sever its current channels, through Mitte and Photex, and supply Poland's private dealers directly, via SEI. As advantages, dealing with Poland's private dealers would enable Sony to control its sales and service network directly. As disadvantages, however, Sony would have to carry the risk of non-payment and disentangle itself from Mitte, with the aforementioned cost problem and distribution risks to Hungary and Czechoslovakia. Furthermore, there was no guarantee that private dealers could maintain the country's current sales volume. Finally, despite the existence to date of private dealers in Poland, Sony management was uncertain about the total number of such private dealers or their capacity to perform after-sales service.

Establish Sony Poland

As a fourth option, the management of Sony could initiate its ultimate, longer-term objective and establish a Sony Poland subsidiary. Aside from providing immediate control over its sales and service network, a local subsidiary would also be able to closely monitor any risk of non-payment. Most importantly, a Polish subsidiary could well enhance Sony's local image and would coincide with the company's philosophy of global localization.

To implement this option, Sony would have to renegotiate its agreement with Mitte with the same disadvantages cited above. Moreover, Matsuzaki and Lang did not believe a Sony Poland could support itself below a sales volume of DM150 million per year. Below that level, a subsidiary would be certain to incur losses for an indefinite period. Then, too, although the management of Sony believed they could select a few future employees from among Poland's private dealers, the same possibility did not apply to someone capable of heading up a subsidiary. In Matsuzaki's opinion, the managing director of a Sony Poland would, in addition to speaking Polish, need to speak English to communicate, within Sony, and be comfortable with Lithuanian, Byelorussian and Ukranian to cultivate the neighbouring markets in the USSR.

EXHIBIT 1

Poland – Historical Maps

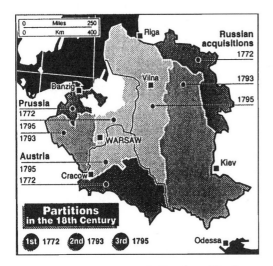

● Poland divided between Austria, Prussia and Russia

● Poland as divided by the Molotov-Ribbentrop Pact

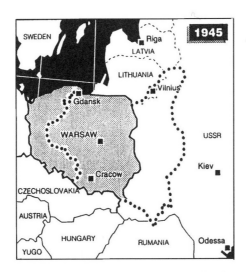

● Post-war Poland shifted westward on both borders

Source: *Financial Times*, 3 May 1991.

EXHIBIT 2

Competition Operations in Poland

Manufacturer	Manufacturing	Marketing & Sales	Channel	Service
Hitachi		ITI – Offices in Warsaw	Baltona + entrepreneurs	ITI – 'Best Service in Poland'
Panasonic	Planned joint venture with MTC	Mitsubishi Trading Company	Photex + entrepreneurs	MTC – two service centres + ten planned, owned by MTC with technical assistance from Panasonic
Philips	VCR and TV assembly joint ventures	Offices in Warsaw – precursor to sales organization	Brabok	
Sanyo/Sharp			Photex	
Sony		Mitte	Photex + entrepreneurs	Photex – one service centre in Warsaw by Mittropol

EXHIBIT 3

Order, Product and Capital Flow for Sony Products Sold in Poland

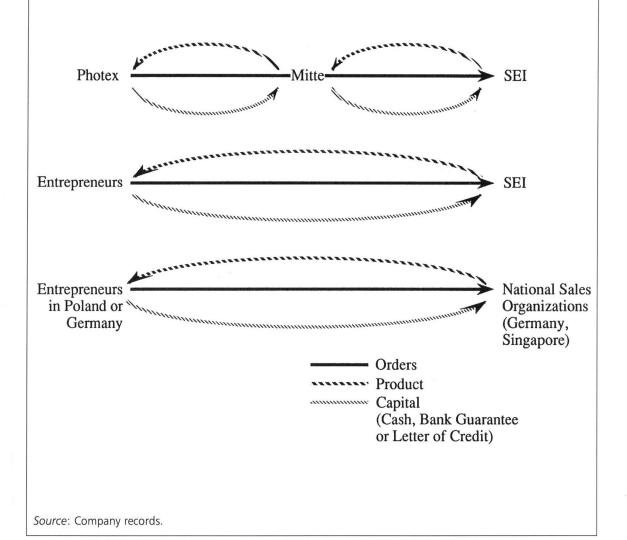

Source: Company records.

14. Shifting from National to Regional Organization Structures

CASE 14.1

MATSUSHITA ELECTRIC INDUSTRIAL LTD. EUROPE – SALES AND MARKETING, 1994

This case was written by Professor Philip M. Rosenzweig as a basis for class discussion rather than to illustrate either effective or ineffective handling of an administrative situation.

Matsushita Electrical Industrial Co. Ltd. (MEI) was one of the leading electronics firms in the world, well-known for its Panasonic, National, Technics and Quasar brands. It was a leader in many industry segments, including video equipment (such as televisions, video-cassette recorders and camcorders); audio equipment (radios, tape recorders and compact disk players); home appliances (refrigerators, air conditioners and home laundry equipment); communication and industrial products (facsimile equipment, personal computers and copying machines); as well as electronic components, batteries and assorted other products. (A breakdown of sales by major product segment is shown in *Exhibit 1*.) While Matsushita was at the forefront of new product technology, it was best known for excellence in manufacturing, rather than for its product innovation or marketing flair.

Matsushita had grown rapidly and prospered in the 1980s, and reached sales of more than ¥7 trillion, or almost $60 billion, by 1990. In the early 1990s, however, a combination of factors led to a dip in revenues and profits. By 1994, revenues stood at ¥6.6 trillion, down 12% from its 1992 level. (A summary of recent financial performance is provided in *Exhibit 2*.)

In response to this shift in fortunes, Matsushita embarked on a three-year Revitalization Plan aimed at restoring profitability and boosting sales. As one part of the Revitalization Plan, key managers were rethinking MEI's approach to European sales and marketing. Matsushita had traditionally conducted sales and marketing in Europe through a series of autonomous country organizations, known as Sales Companies. Now, under a new programme called Vision 35, a team had been assigned to recommend better ways to manage these efforts.

Matsushita Electrical Industrial: An Overview

Matsushita Electric Industrial Ltd. was founded in 1918 by Konosuke Matsushita, then a 23-year old inspector with the Osaka Electric Light Company. In its early years, MEI manufactured battery-powered lamps, electric irons and small radios. As the company grew it expanded into other electrical products. In the years following World War II, MEI was a leading company in the rapidly growing industry of consumer electronics, first producing black and white televisions, then transistor radios, tape recorders, home stereo units and colour televisions. By the 1960s, MEI was also active in home appliances such as dishwashers, ovens, dryers and kitchen disposal units.

The company's growth was guided by the vision and business philosophy of its founder. In 1932, Konosuke Matsushita articulated a corporate mission statement, or *Meichi*, which emphasized the objective of "helping society to achieve happiness by providing an abundance of material goods." Over the next five years, the company's philosophy was codified into Seven Principles:

1. Contribution to Society

2. Fairness and Honesty

3. Cooperation and Team Spirit

4. Untiring Effort for Improvement

5. Courtesy and Humility

6. Adaptability

7. Gratitude.

Matsushita's philosophy was translated into a set of Basic Business Principles, which included an emphasis on profitability as the measure of contribution to society, a respect for competition as the stimulus of improvement, and a belief in autonomous business units. Matsushita's belief in autonomy was reflected in its multi-divisional organizational structure, with each division operating as a separate business unit, responsible for the full range of activities from product design to manufacturing, and fully accountable for its results.

Over the years, the Basic Business Principles remained an integral part of the company, and provided a common set of values for behaviour and decision making. One manager noted that the Principles were broad enough to serve as effective guidelines, yet also allowed differences in interpretation. He added: "The principles do not change, although interpretations and implementation naturally evolve to fit changing circumstances."

Matsushita's International Expansion

During its early years MEI operated exclusively in Japan. International expansion had always been an important element in Matsushita's long-term vision, and as the company grew following World War II, it began exporting consumer electronics products such as radios and tape recorders. Revenues from exports were soon an important part of the company's business, and MEI, like other Japanese firms in the same industry such as Sony Corporation, set up sales offices abroad. Matsushita's first overseas sales office, the Matsushita Electric Corporation of America (MECA), was established in 1959 in New York.

In the following years, MEI continued to expand internationally, and soon established Sales Companies in Europe. In 1962, MEI opened its first Sales Company in Europe, Panasonic Deutschland GmbH, in Hamburg, Germany. Over the next two decades, additional European Sales Companies were set up in France (1968), the United Kingdom (1972), Sweden (1972), Belgium (1973), Italy (1980), Denmark (1980), Norway (1980), Spain (1981), Austria (1982) and Ireland (1985). In several other countries, MEI relied on distributors and sales agents. (*See Exhibits 3A and 3B* for the list of sales companies and sales agents.)

MEI also set up numerous factories overseas. Like many other Japanese electronics firms, MEI in the 1970s found it important to set up manufacturing operations in local markets. At the outset this was due to fears of protectionism, but as the yen strengthened in the 1980s, it became economical to locate production in other countries. In Europe, MEI first established manufacturing plants in Belgium (1970), Spain (1973) and the UK (1974). Over the next decades MEI added several more plants, and by 1993 had 19 manufacturing companies in Europe (*refer to Exhibit 4*). From an organizational standpoint, these factories reported directly to their respective business units in Japan, and were entirely separate from the growing network of Sales Companies.

As Matsushita became an increasingly global company, it articulated a set of principles regarding the conduct of its overseas operations (*refer to Exhibit 5*). It stressed that operations should be welcomed by the host country, and that they should be internationally competitive, profitable and able to generate sufficient capital for their own expansion. Matsushita also emphasized the need for training and development of local personnel, referred to as 'localization' of management.

MEI grew rapidly in the 1980s, with annual sales rising from ¥2,916 billion ($13.7 billion) in 1980 to ¥5,291 billion ($24.9 billion) in 1985. Sales climbed in the late 1980s despite the sharp appreciation of the yen, and reached ¥6,003 billion ($37.7) in 1990. Profitability remained healthy and consistent: in 1990, pre-tax profit was 9.5%, and net income stood at 3.9%.

Although MEI operated globally, with sales companies and manufacturing facilities spread across the world, it retained a strong base in Japan. More than half of its revenues were generated in Japan; the rest was spread across the world. Of its 1993 work force of 252,000 employees, 157,000 (62%) were based in Japan, while 95,000 (38%) were overseas. All of its board members and senior executives, and virtually all top managers in the company, were Japanese nationals.

Matsushita's European Sales Companies

As Matsushita created Sales Companies in Europe, it gave the Managing Directors (MDs) of those companies full responsibility for sales and marketing. One manager suggested that each Sales Company was like a castle, with its Managing Director the 'king'. Whether the country was large, like Germany or the United Kingdom, or whether it was small, like Austria or Denmark, each 'castle' was self-sufficient, and performed the full range of activities from purchasing products from Japan, to marketing and sales, technical support, logistics and warehousing, and supply of spare parts.

Sales Companies worked directly with factories in Japan to develop variations for their local markets, usually related to voltage or broadcast specifications in each country. Occasionally a Sales Company also asked for products to be developed to meet local tastes in design and styling, but in general Matsushita products were similar in appearance and design across Europe.

Each Sales Company ordered its products directly from the factories in Japan, Singapore or Europe. Because Sales Companies varied in size and order volume, they received different prices from the factories. Products were shipped directly from Japan to each Sales Company, which had its own warehouses and spare parts centre. By 1994, there were 22 separate warehouses in Europe, plus a spare parts centre in each country.

Marketing was also handled locally, resulting in a variety of marketing campaigns for the same product. Matsushita's leading consumer electronics brand, Panasonic, was perceived differently across Europe. One manager lamented that "a wide variety of messages are being transmitted in all parts of Europe, and this is working adversely to weaken the influence of the messages and confuse our customers." Sales promotions and merchandising, too, were handled by each Sales Company, with each one deciding whether to use cash rebates, interest-free financing or some other approach. By 1994, Matsushita's European Sales Companies had offered more than 100 different types of cash discount schemes and more than 300 different sales promotion programmes.

Each Sales Company had its own administrative support structure, with its own Finance Department, Human Resource Department and Information System Department. There were, by one estimate, 170 employees in the various European Sales Companies involved in finance alone. The work forces of the Sales Companies comprised local nationals with some Japanese expatriates, usually in management roles. There was little or no movement of managers among the European Sales Companies. Human resource policies were tailored to each country and, as a result, performance evaluation, salary administration and benefits differed among countries.

Creation of Panasonic Europe (Headquarters) Ltd.

By 1988, MEI had 11 Sales Companies in Europe, managed from Matsushita's head office in Osaka. With its European presence growing, Matsushita decided to create a parallel overview office in Europe, and established Panasonic Europe (Headquarters) Ltd. (or PEHQ) near London. In large part, PEHQ was formed to help prepare for the single European market, due in 1992. As one manager recalled, PEHQ was intended to coordinate the several Sales Companies, but not to manage them as an integrated whole. One example of coordination was the establishment of an intra-European invoicing system that handled the movement of products from European factories to European Sales Companies, and also foreign exchange risk management. PEHQ also acted as a point of collection of information from Sales Companies, forwarding that information to Japan but not performing much analysis. It also housed a team of internal auditors who worked with many of the Sales Companies.

In the years following the creation of PEHQ, Sales Companies continued to operate in a largely autonomous manner. Unlike in the United States, where a single country operation had been created first, the tradition in Europe had been one of local autonomy. Bringing about greater integration was therefore a difficult matter. "The role of the European headquarters was never really clarified," explained one manager. "The role was basically one of providing support for the sales companies." In addition to PEHQ, a variety of other support activities, such as training, export promotion and legal affairs, were distributed throughout Europe (*refer to **Exhibit 6***).

Following the fall of communism in 1989, Matsushita planned to set up Sales Companies in Central and Eastern Europe. The first one was opened in Poland in 1993, with additional Sales Companies planned for Hungary and the Czech Republic.

Matsushita Electrical Industrial Ltd. in the 1990s

In the 1990s, Matsushita's performance began to level off. A few reasons explained the shift in fortune. First, the consumer electronics industry as a whole was reaching maturity. Many of the products that had fuelled the industry's rapid growth – such as colour TVs, VCRs and CD players – were now widely owned. New products, such as camcorders, were not reaching the same level of acceptance. Second, the combination of economies of scale and growing competition among global firms led to intense pressure on prices and margins. The prices of consumer electronics products fell year after year, squeezing profit margins.

As a result, MEI's revenues fell from ¥7,450 billion in 1992 to ¥7,055 billion in 1993, a drop of 5%. The next year revenues fell an additional 6%, to ¥6,623 billion in 1994. The decline in net income was even more serious, from ¥133 billion in 1992 to ¥24 billion in 1994. Deeply concerned by its faltering performance, Matsushita announced in 1994 a three-year Revitalization Plan. Under this Plan, the company vowed to restore cost competitiveness, to work aggressively to shift from mature segments to segments of higher growth, and to emphasize new product innovation.

Rethinking European Sales and Marketing

The renewed emphasis on cost reduction and effective marketing stimulated new thinking about MEI's approach to sales and marketing. In particular, a few new developments forced a reconsideration of the autonomous Sales Companies.

Mature Market, Falling Margins

In Europe, the sales volume of TVs, VCRs and other key products was roughly flat after 1990, but a continuing erosion in price per unit drove down margins.

As margins shrank and profits fell, Matsushita felt a special imperative to cut costs. Since the European structure of autonomous Sales Companies involved substantial overlap, there might be some benefits from consolidation.

Cross-national Customers

A second important development was the increasingly multinational nature of MEI's European customers. Many key customers were now operating on a regional basis, and were increasingly looking to MEI for a single approach to pricing, sales terms and technical support.

Some of these customers were end-users with multinational operations. Such firms would approach MEI with a single European bid, and expected a single unified reply. In one such instance, a bid from a major industrial firm called for a great amount of communication among autonomous Sales Companies, and ended up taking more than a year to coordinate internally. Although MEI eventually won the contract, the lesson was a sobering one.

Other customers were dealers, and it was here that the advent of regional integration was most dramatic. A large share of MEI's sales went to retail chains, buying groups and hypermarkets which were themselves operating in more than one country. For example, the retail chain Dixon's had expanded from its UK base and now operated retail outlets in The Netherlands. FNAC had expanded from France into Belgium, Germany and Spain. The buying group Expert operated in 12 European countries, from Finland to Spain. These and several other dealers did not have to place a separate order for product in each country, but could consolidate their orders and place them in the country which offered the lowest price, then ship the product to other countries for sale.

MEI's Sales Companies, which offered different trade prices and repayment plans, found themselves played off against each other. As an example, because Panasonic Austria ordered a lower volume from Japan than Panasonic Germany, it was charged a higher price by the factory. Dealers with retail outlets in both Austria and Germany now tended to place a single large order with Panasonic Germany at the more attractive price, then ship inventory from Germany to retail outlets in Austria. This practice, sometimes referred to as the 'gray market' but officially known as 'parallel imports', was entirely legal within the laws of the European Union, and MEI could no nothing to prevent it. The result for small Sales Companies such as Panasonic Austria: many final sales of MEI products on Austrian soil were recorded as sales for Panasonic Germany, not Panasonic Austria. Yet when consumers had problems with their products, they naturally contacted Panasonic Austria for service and support.

Vision 35

The combination of a more intense business climate and the emergence of cross-border customers led some executives at MEI to reconsider the country-by-country approach to sales and marketing. Taking the lead was Seinosuke Kuraku,

Managing Director of PEHQ, whose vantage point gave him a clear overview of Matsushita's European activities.

In October 1994, Mr Kuraku announced a new initiative called Vision 35, so named because it was to be implemented in 1997, the 35th anniversary of MEI's first European Sales Company. Mr Kuraku stated:

> We have to change the ways in which we do business in Europe and cannot simply continue on the same path.... Europe is changing rapidly, with a large growth in cross-border dealers and increasing requests for central purchasing by large retail groups.

Mr. Kuraku concluded that it had become "necessary for us to establish a Panasonic identity throughout Europe and further promote our marketing function to open the way for better sales achievements." Toward this end, he appointed a six-person Vision 35 team, consisting of four Japanese nationals and two Europeans, one from Germany and one from the United Kingdom. In January 1995, they met for the first time to consider specific actions.

EXHIBIT 1

Revenues by Major Product Segment

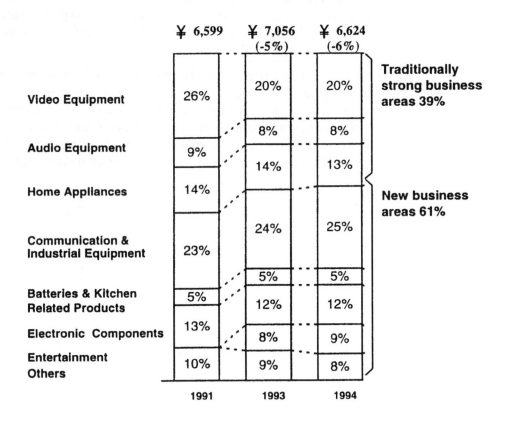

Note: In billion yen.

EXHIBIT 2

Financial Performance, 1992–94

	(Millions of yen, except per share information)		
	1994	1993	1992
For the year			
Net sales	¥6,623,586	¥7,055,868	¥7,449,933
Operating profit	173,606	235,830	383,272
Income before income taxes	128,223	162,207	356,920
Net income (loss)	24,493	37,295	133,904
Capital investment	¥266,097	¥309,097	¥543,223
Depreciation	317,283	355,535	342,852
R&D expenditures	381,747	401,817	418,071
At year-end			
Long-term debt	¥1,260,387	¥1,201,228	¥1,227,642
Total assets	8,192,632	8,754,979	9,149,243
Stockholders' equity	3,288,945	3,406,303	3,473,496
Number of shares issued at year-end (thousands)	2,095,679	2,094,946	2,094,946
Stockholders	217,539	222,436	220,317
Employees	254,059	252,075	242,246
Overseas employees	98,639	94,779	92,238
Per share data (yen)			
Per share of common stock			
Net income (loss)	¥11.67	¥17.66	¥61.13
Cash dividends	12.50	12.50	12.50
Stockholders' equity	1,569.39	1,625.96	1,658.04
Per American Depositary Share, each representing			
10 shares of common stock			
Net income (loss)	¥117	¥117	¥611
Cash dividends	125	125	125
Stockholders' equity	15,694	16,260	16,580
Ratios (%)			
Operating profit/sales	2.6%	3.3%	5.1%
Income before income taxes/sales	1.9	2.3	4.8
Net income (loss)/sales	0.4	0.5	1.8
Stockholders' equity/total assets	40.1	38.9	38.0

Source: Matsushita Electric 1996 Company Annual Report.

EXHIBIT 3A

Sales Companies in Europe

Country	Company	Employees	Initials	Year
1. UK	Panasonic UK Ltd	(650)	PUK	1972
2. Germany	Panasonic Deutschland GmbH	(900)	PDG	1962
3. France	Panasonic France SA	(250)	PFS	1968
4. Italy	Panasonic Italia SpA	(200)	PIT	1980
5. Spain	Panasonic Sales Spain SA	(250)	PSS	1991
6. Sweden	Panasonic Svenska AB	(130)	PSA	1972
7. Denmark	Panasonic Denmark A/S	(50)	PAD	1980
8. Norway	Panasonic Norge A/S	(50)	PNA	1980
9. Belgium	Panasonic Belgium NV	(100)	PBN	1973
10. Belgium	Panasonic Battery Sales Europe NV	(15)	PBSE	1974
11. Austria	Panasonic Austria GmbH	(90)	PAG	1982
12. Ireland	Panasonic Ireland Ltd	(25)	PIR	1985

Note: Employee numbers are case-writer estimates.

Source: Matsushita Electric Company document, 1996.

EXHIBIT 3B

Sales Agents in Europe

Sales agent	Country	Initials	Notes
1. Kaukomarkkinat Oy	Finland	KAUKO	Sales of both living & systems products
2. Haagtechno bv	Netherlands	HATO	Sales of both living & systems products
3. John Lay Electronics AG	Switzerland	JLE	Sales of both living & systems products
4. Intertech SA	Greece	INTERTECH	Sales of systems products
5. Viane SA	Greece	VIANE	Sales of living products
6. Uniclima Grissin-Pappas	Greece	UNICLIMA	Sales of air-conditioning equipment
7. Sonicel	Portugal	SONICEL	Sales of living products
8. Papelaco	Portugal	PAPELACO	Sales of systems products

Source: Matsushita Electric Company document, 1996.

EXHIBIT 4

Manufacturing Companies in Europe, 1993

Country	Company name	Initials	Year founded	Production items
1. Germany	MB Video GmbH	MBV	1982	VTRs, CD players, mini Hi-Fi
2. Germany	Matsushita Video Manufacturing GmbH	MVM	1986	VTR mechanisms
3. Germany	Matsushita Electronic Components (Europe) GmbH	ECOM	1984	VTR tuners, RF converters, remote controls, etc.
4. Germany	Matsushita Communication Deutschland GmbH	MCD	1985	Car audio, CCTV cameras
5. Germany	Matsushita Business Machine (Europe) GmbH	MBM	1986	Plain paper copiers
6. Germany	Matsushita Electronics (Europe) GmbH	EMEC	1995	Cathode ray tubes
7. Germany	Siemens Matsushita Components GmbH & Co	S+M	1989	Passive components
8. UK	Matsushita Electric (UK) Ltd	MELUK	1974	Colour TVs, microwave ovens
9. UK	Kyushu Matsushita Electric (UK) Ltd	KMEUK	1986	Electronic typewriters, printers, PBX telephone equipment
10. UK	Matsushita Communication Industrial (UK) Ltd	MCUK	1988	Mobile telephones
11. UK	Matsushita Electronic Components (UK) Ltd	UKCOM	1988	MWO transformers, etc.
12. UK	Matsushita Graphic Communication Systems (UK) Ltd	MGUK	1989	Facsimiles
13. UK	Matsushita Electronic Magnetron Corporation (UK) Ltd	MMUK	1989	Magnetrons
14. UK	Matsushita Industrial Equipment Co (UK) Ltd	MIECOUK	1992	Flyback transformers
15. France	Panasonic France SA	PFS	1987	VTRs
16. Belgium	Philips Matsushita Battery Corporation NV	PMBC	1970	Dry cell batteries
17. Spain	Panasonic Espana SA	PAES	1973	Vacuum cleaners, Hi-Fi
18. Ireland	Ireland Kotobuki Electronics Industries Ltd	IKEI	1992	3.5-inch Hard disk drives
19. Poland	Philips Matsushita Battery Poland SA	PMBP	1993	Dry cell batteries

Source: Matsushita Electric Company document, 1996.

EXHIBIT 5

Overseas Operations

Objectives: 'To contribute to the society of our host countries'
1. To conduct operations welcomed by host countries.
2. To operate within principles of host governments, while fostering understanding of our company's beliefs.
3. To promote transfer of technology.
4. To manufacture competitive products.
5. To establish profitable operations.
6. To develop local employees' abilities.

Source: Matsushita Electric Company document, 1996.

EXHIBIT 6

Group Support Offices in Europe

Country		Company name	Employees	Year founded	Function
1. UK	(PE)	Panasonic Europe (Headquarters) Ltd	(40)	1988	European Headquarters
1. UK	(PE)	Panasonic Euro-Settlement Centre	(4)	1979	Settlement between manufacturing and sales
1. UK	(PE)	Production Support Centre	(2)	1989	QC, materials, etc.
1. UK	(PE)	Panasonic Training Centre Europe	(2)	1989	Training and seminars
2. UK	(PIF)	Panasonic International Finance (UK) plc	(7)	1986	Finance
3. UK	(OWL)	Office Workstations Ltd	(20)	1984	R&D
4. Germany	(PEL)	Panasonic European Laboratories	(20)	1991	R&D (new AV technology)
5. Germany	(EPC)	Export Promotion Centre	(4)	1973	Export promotion to Japan
6. Belgium	(BLO)	Brussels Liaison Office	(4)	1983	Legal and EC affairs

Note: Employees are case-writer estimates.

Source: Matsushita Electric Company document, 1996.

INDEX